Mail and Internet Surveys

Mail and Internet Surveys

The Tailored Design Method

Second Edition

2007 Update with New Internet, Visual, and Mixed-Mode Guide

Don A. Dillman

BICENTENNIAL 1807 WILEY 2007 BICENTENNIAL

John Wiley & Sons, Inc.

This book is printed on acid-free paper. ♾

Published by John Wiley & Sons, Inc., Hoboken, New Jersey.
Published simultaneously in Canada.

For general information on our other products and services or for technical support, please contact our Customer Care Department within the United States at (800) 762-2974, outside the United States at (317) 572-3993 or fax (317) 572-4002.

Wiley also publishes its books in a variety of electronic formats. Some content that appears in print may not be available in electronic books. For more information about Wiley products, visit our web site at www.wiley.com.

ISBN-13: 978-0-470-03856-7

ISBN-10: 0-470-03856-X

Printed in the United States of America.

10 9 8 7 6 5 4 3 2 1

With thanks to

Joye Jolly Dillman
from Pleasantville, Iowa

faculty colleague, friend, and spouse

Contents

Preface to the 2007 Update

METHODS FOR conducting sample surveys are changing with unprecedented speed. Since the publication of this book in 2000, our ability to conduct reliable telephone surveys has declined because of lower response rates and the trend toward abandoning household telephones in favor of cellular connections. Although our ability to conduct web surveys has increased dramatically, their use remains limited by inadequate coverage of the general population. Caught between these trends surveyors are increasingly drawn toward the conduct of mixed-mode surveys, which collect data from some respondents by one mode and use a different mode to reach other respondents, in order to preserve data quality. However, the design of mixed-mode surveys is itself being affected by new knowledge on the likelihood that different visual layouts for questions produce different answers from respondents.

This update to the second edition adds a new Appendix that traces the interconnections among these recent developments in survey methodology. It summarizes new ideas and research, particularly in the area of visual design and layout, which are changing the way that surveys must be done.

DON A. DILLMAN

June 4, 2006

Preface to the Second Edition

The elapse of 22 years between the first and second editions of this book was not an attempt to set a record. Nor was it planned.

Development of the first edition, *Mail and Telephone Surveys: The Total Design Method,* or the TDM book, as I have often heard it described, was an attempt by a young assistant professor to solve the immediate problem of how to collect meaningful survey data inexpensively. It was begun at a time when neither mail nor telephones were used much for serious surveys.

In the flatlands of Iowa, where roads run true north and south and east and west, sampling was easy and personal interviews the norm, and my graduate education at Iowa State University did not prepare me for the mountains of Washington state. Here, most of the state's population was located on the other side of the Cascade Mountains, nearly 300 miles away from the rolling wheat fields and winding roads that surrounded the small university town of Pullman, Washington. Consequently, collecting data by means of personal interviews was not possible with the small amount of support that seemed within my reach. Initially, as I worked to convince staff to manually type names at the top of letters preprinted on departmental stationery and watched interviewers get sore fingers from dialing the noisy rotary phones, I had little idea of the increased importance that mail, and telephone methods in particular, would soon achieve in the nation's survey system. That would come later.

Ink on the first edition of this book was barely dry before people began asking me questions for which I had few answers. Are you sure those methods will work for diaries? Sending a certified letter to people asking what television program they watched sometime the month before doesn't make sense. Will these procedures work with business surveys? Could I do better if I combined mail and telephone? Will these ideas work for federal government surveys? Why didn't you include financial incentives? And, what about the other sources of error about which so little is mentioned, such as coverage and measurement?

Each of these questions provided grist for experimentation and other research. Although I was only vaguely aware of it at the time, the process of converting to a tailored design approach for self-administered surveys, from the one-size-fits-all approach of the Total Design Method, had begun. Tailored Design refers to the development of survey designs that use common procedures grounded in a social exchange perspective on why people do or do not respond to surveys, similar to the TDM. However, it goes further to describe the additional shaping of procedures and techniques for particular surveys based on a more precise consideration of costs, rewards, and trust associated with specific populations, sponsorship, and/or content. Specific designs are influenced by major changes in the technological options now becoming available for conducting self-administered surveys.

It became apparent in the early 1990s that the benefits of computerization, which had steadily accrued to telephone interviewing since its development in the early 1970s, were poised on at least three fronts to finally benefit the design and delivery of self-administered questionnaires. Yet, another new agenda for research was the result. First, the many formatting alternatives (ranging from font changes to the use of icons and colors) that word processing and printing software presented for designing mail questionnaires made it necessary to understand the specifics of how visual design can influence survey response. Second, the development of self-administered electronic modes of surveying, from e-mail and web to interactive voice response (IVR), made it necessary to research how surveys by these modes should be designed for greater effectiveness. And third, the emergence of optical character recognition and imaging technologies raised the likelihood that the labor-intensive data entry process for turning individual answers into data sets could be automated. That made it necessary to consider how the visual design and layout of questionnaires could best facilitate optical processing.

My goal in this book is to articulate principles for tailoring the design of self-administered questionnaires to population, content, and sponsorship in ways that will reduce survey error from coverage, sampling, measurement, and nonresponse. It is also my purpose to take into account the massive technological changes that are giving efficiency to and expanding the possibilities for the use of self-administered questionnaires to collect survey data in a variety of situations, and to provide further possibilities for tailoring survey designs appropriately.

The decision to omit discussion of telephone interviewing, to which fully half of the first edition was devoted, was a practical one. Whereas only a few dozen published articles about telephone interviewing existed in 1978, there are now thousands. The complexities of conducting telephone interviews expanded even more rapidly than those associated with doing self-administered surveys, and it is no longer possible to adequately discuss detailed procedures for doing both telephone and mail (or self-administered) surveys in the same book.

The elapse of 22 years between the first and second editions does not diminish the excitement I feel about the methods described in this book. Research continues to be done and new ideas put forth as surveyors try to develop designs with greater effectiveness. Just as I had the feeling of being in the midst of a great change in the use of survey methods in 1978, that feeling exists today, as well. Once again we are experiencing a survey revolution, the consequences of which are yet to be clearly known.

DON A. DILLMAN

Pullman, Washington

Acknowledgments

ONE RESULT of publishing the first edition of this book was the opportunity to look at thousands of other people's surveys, spending from a few minutes to many months contemplating means of improvement. Thanks to all of you who have given me that opportunity. Appreciation is also expressed to more than 150 graduate students who have often redesigned my redesigns of questionnaires in the graduate survey practicums I have taught, and encouraged me to rethink ways of doing them. I also wish to thank a number of specific individuals who have influenced the tailored design procedures described in this book.

Roberta Sangster and Todd Rockwood, two of the many extraordinary graduate students I have had the opportunity to work with, and John Tarnai, long-time collaborator and director of the Washington State University Social and Economic Sciences Research Center, helped me work through the difficulties of conducting mixed-mode surveys and other innovations.

The Department of Rural Sociology has provided research support for my work continuously since 1969. In recent years, that support has included participation in a regional research committee, "W-183: Rural and Agricultural Surveys." This group of scientists from agricultural experiment stations of land grant universities throughout the United States continues to influence my thinking about the need to develop better survey methods and has taught me the value of replicating one another's experiments. I am especially indebted to Tommy Brown, John Carlson, Ed Carpenter, Virginia Lesser, Fred Lorenz, Bob Mason, John Saltiel, and Fern Willits.

Gary Machlis and Dana Dolsen introduced me to the problem of how to improve response in personal delivery situations, and helped me to understand the nuances of that special challenge. Lesli Jo Scott and Sonia Hussa provided assistance, and Pat Carraher and Barbara Petura provided the sponsorship needed for researching the difficulties of delivering surveys through publications. Ed Schillmoeller and Bob Patchen introduced me to some of the problems of doing diary surveys. Jon Krosnick, Michael Curtin, and Dean Narcisco helped me to understand the potential of conducting election prediction surveys by mail, as modeled so effectively by the *Columbus Dispatch.*

Working under the Intergovernmental Personal Act as Senior Survey Methodologist in the Office of the Director at the U.S. Bureau of the Census from 1991 to 1995 introduced me to the challenges of doing government self-administered surveys, and particularly the U.S. Decennial Census. I am grateful to the staff of the Census Bureau, whose collective patience was surely tested by getting me to understand why and how government surveys were different. I cannot possibly name everyone whose knowledge benefited me during what I remember as an incredibly stimulating time, as we moved from one research challenge to the next. However, included among the people from this superbly professional organization whom I wish to thank are: Barbara Bryant and Bob Groves (who convinced me that I should go there), Nancy Bates, Pat Berman, Sandy Chambers, Cynthia Clark, Jon Clark, Mary Ann Cochran, Terry DeMaio, Bob Fay, Ed Gore, Debbie Griffin, Carolyn Hay, Jane Ingold, Charlie Jones, Therese Leslie, Betsy Martin, Carol Miller, Susan Miskura, Al Paez, Harry Scarr, Mike Sinclair, Phyllis Simard, Bill Starr, John Thompson, Jim Treat, Kirsten West, and Henry Woltman.

One benefit of the Census experience was to begin work on new concepts of visual design that were not a part of the Total Design Method. This research was a collaborative effort with Cleo Redline (aka Jenkins). Two papers we produced provided the concepts and motivation for taking a much different conceptual approach to the challenge of questionnaire design. Her influence on the ideas expressed in Chapter 4 is substantial. I am especially grateful for the opportunity to work with her, and the Census Bureau's willingness to support continued research on the new and provocative ideas that have come from this collaboration.

I also wish to thank several individuals at the Census Bureau who helped me begin to think about the challenges of doing business surveys, in particular Bud Pautler and Nash Monsour. I also appreciate the opportunities for attempting to redesign business surveys provided by Lynda Carlson, Antoinette Martin, and many other staff of the Energy Information Administration.

The Gallup Organization, where I have had the good fortune to serve as a senior scientist since 1995, encouraged me to learn about the challenges of doing Internet and interactive voice response surveys, and provided the opportunity to try, at a production level, many ideas on visual design of paper questionnaires. I am especially grateful to Gale Muller and Bev Conroy for their support of my work there, Scot Caldwell for teaching me about new methods of converting questionnaires to data without keypunching, and Mary Gansmer, who put many abstract ideas into questionnaire designs.

Bob Tortora, at the Gallup Organization, insisted that I contemplate the problems of doing Internet surveys and contributed to the development of an initial set of design principles. Dennis Bowker, another extraordinary graduate student, has taught me many of the technical aspects of creating web surveys and contributed greatly to the development of the chapter on this topic. I am also appreciative of the help David Schaeffer provided in working through the challenges of e-mail surveys. Kent Miller of the SESRC is co-author of a paper on optical scanning and imaging of questionnaires, part of which is included in Chapter 12, and has contributed continually to my thinking about how to implement mail surveys.

There are a number of other individuals and experiences that affected the rewriting of this book in less specific but very influential ways. They include faculty and staff at the University of Michigan's Survey Research Institute, where teaching since 1988 has given me a nearly annual exposure to new ideas, as did three visits to the Center for Survey Methods Research (ZUMA) in Mannhein, Germany, to work with Hans-Jurgen Hippler. I am also grateful to Edith de Leeuw and Joop Hox from the Netherlands, who visited Pullman at the time writing on this book was beginning, and who, on an excursion into the mountains of Northern Idaho, helped convince me that this book was about Tailored Design. Thanks also to Anton Nederhoff, who was one of the first to teach me about applying the TDM outside the United States, and to Lars Lyberg and staff at Statistics Sweden for their help in doing that as well.

Washington State University provided a professional leave in 1997 to 1998 that allowed me to begin the writing of this second edition. I appreciate the willingness of the Department of Rural Sociology, the Social and Economic Sciences Research Center, and the Department of Sociology to make that leave possible. I also wish to thank the U.S. Bureau of the Census and the Gallup Organization for supporting several visits to their organizations that helped greatly with the writing.

Finally, the staff of the SESRC, who remain, collectively, one of the most challenging groups I have faced when discussing new survey ideas, have influenced significantly my thinking on many aspects of surveying. In addition to the staff mentioned, I want to thank others with whom I have had the pleasure of working for many years on a variety of different projects, including: Thom Allen, Rodney Baxter, Sandy Johnson, Rita Koontz, Danna Moore, Julie Nielson, Jolyn Persons, Renee Petrie, Dretha Phillips, Zoltan Porga, and Dan Vakoch. This local environment for working and thinking daily about surveys is a constant reminder that doing a survey is a team effort for which each person performs an essential role, and that doing surveys can be fun!

Two important members of that team, Tammy Small and Lisa Carley-Baxter, have carried much of the burden of helping to move the book from draft to final pages. I both appreciate and marvel at their professional skills and dedication to quality work.

All of the people mentioned have been my teachers in pursuit of better quality survey design, and for that I am grateful.

Research that led to development of the TDM started within weeks of arriving at Washington State University in 1969, and continues today. The person who knows best what it took to produce both the TDM and the Tailored

Design editions of this book came with me to Pullman and it is to her this book is dedicated. Thanks, Joye, for 35 years of always being there. Thanks also to our children, Andrew and Melody, who learned about the connection between stamps, questionnaires, cover letters, and printouts at about the same early ages that their parents had learned about the connections between tractors, balers, alfalfa, and cows. The TDM has been part of our family life and travels ever since.

Part One

ELEMENTS OF THE TAILORED DESIGN METHOD

CHAPTER 1

Introduction to Tailored Design

IN THE late 1970s, a well-done mail survey was likely to exhibit a series of four carefully timed mailings, laboriously personalized by typing individual names and addresses atop preprinted letters. In combination with other meticulous details, including real signatures and a replacement questionnaire sent by certified mail, this procedure, the Total Design Method (TDM), demonstrated the ability to achieve high response rates (Dillman, 1978). Two decades later, self-administered surveys are recognizable as much for the ways they differ as for their common features. For example:

- In a national test of possible procedures for the Year 2000 Census, a four-contact sequence of prenotice letter, questionnaire, reminder postcard, and replacement questionnaire was sent. Personalization was impossible for such a large mailing, but the outgoing envelope contained these words: "U.S. *Census Form Enclosed;* Your Response is Required by Law." The mailings were sent by first class mail to "residents," and not named individuals, at each address, and a response rate of 78% was achieved (Dillman, Clark, and Treat, 1994).
- In surveys of visitors to national parks, researchers used a several step sequence, ending with a request for the address to which a thank-you postcard could be sent. This procedure resulted in average mail-back response rates of 75% in 21 parks compared to 38% in 11 other parks, where questionnaires were simply handed to the respondent with a request that they be completed and returned (Dillman, Dolsen, and Machlis, 1995).
- In a survey of people who had turned in out-of-state driver's licenses to obtain a Washington state license, researchers used a four-contact sequence of individually signed letters and included a $2 bill as an incentive. A response rate of 65% was obtained from this population, which

was younger (and therefore a more difficult one from which to obtain responses) than most general public samples, with an increase of nearly 20 percentage points as a result of the incentive (Miller, 1996).

- In a survey of university faculty, an electronic mail survey which used no paper or stamps, but did use individually addressed e-mails and a prenotice with three replacement questionnaires, achieved a 58% response rate. This response rate was the same as that obtained by a four-contact paper mail strategy (Schaefer and Dillman, 1998).

These surveys had much in common. Each was designed according to the principles of social exchange theory regarding why people do or do not respond to surveys. Each used multiple contacts and respondent-friendly questionnaires. Communications were carefully constructed so as to emphasize the survey's usefulness and the importance of a response from each person in the sample. All four surveys obtained reasonably high response rates.

On the other hand, the surveys differed from each other in important ways. The Census correspondence was not personalized, in contrast to the other surveys, and was sent to household addresses instead of to named individuals. The announcement on the envelope that response was mandatory added about 10% to the response rate on top of the contribution made by other factors (Dillman, Singer, Clark, and Treat, 1996). The national park survey was delivered personally, providing an opportunity to engage the sampled person in a carefully structured conversation that utilized a foot-in-the-door principle designed to improve response. The general public survey of new state residents used a token financial incentive which seemed especially effective in improving response among younger people. Finally, the electronic mail survey of faculty did not use stationery or return envelopes, essential trappings of the typical mail survey. In sum, mechanically applying one set of survey procedures in lock-step to all survey situations, as was recommended by the original TDM, is not the best way of assuring high quality responses as we begin the twenty-first century.

However, these four surveys do share a commonality, which I call Tailored Design. It is the development of survey procedures that create respondent trust and perceptions of increased rewards and reduced costs for being a respondent, that take into account features of the survey situation, and that have as their goal the overall reduction of survey error. The main features of the Tailored Design perspective are outlined in this chapter.

When the first edition of this book was published in 1978, the mail survey method was considered undesirable—a procedure to be avoided if at all possible because of poor response rates and a host of other deficiencies. In that book, I described the Total Design Method (TDM) as a new system of interconnected procedures for conducting high-quality mail surveys with a greatly improved potential for obtaining acceptable response rates. The TDM was based upon considerations of social exchange, that is, how to increase perceived rewards for responding, decrease perceived costs, and promote trust in beneficial outcomes from the survey. Details were provided for all aspects of designing and implementing mail surveys, from how to order and position questions in the questionnaire to how to fold and address each mailing. The TDM emphasized four carefully timed mailings, the last of which was sent by certified mail. All contacts were personalized, questions were ordered in a way that would increase the questionnaire's salience for respondents, and photo reduction was used to make the questionnaire appear easier to complete. Repeated tests of this one-size-fits-all approach showed that response rates of 70% could be produced consistently for general public populations, and higher rates were feasible for more specialized populations whose education was not particularly low (Dillman, 1978). In the 20 years since its development, the TDM has been used for thousands of surveys. When used in its entirety, the method has consistently produced higher response rates than are traditionally expected from mail surveys (Dillman, 1991).

Much has changed since the TDM was first developed. Most obvious are the kinds of technologies used by researchers who conduct surveys. In 1978, personal computers were relatively unknown. Instead, the most commonplace survey technologies consisted of typewriters and printing machines. Since no one was merging electronic files, personalizing letters entailed a laborious process of typing individual names at the beginning of preprinted letters. We kept track of respondents by hand-tabulating lists of who had returned questionnaires and who had not.

Along with technology, our understanding of why it is important to take full advantage of social exchange principles in survey research has come a long way since 1978. Even though the TDM represented an advance over what was then acceptable survey practice, it soon became clear that the method's emphasis on using the same protocol for all situations was a serious shortcoming. Some surveys required personal delivery of questionnaires, others entailed completion of diaries that had to be filled out on certain days of certain weeks, and still others called for surveying the same individuals in the same businesses year after year. The need to adapt the original method was made even more obvious by massive government surveys in which the use of personalized letters and envelopes was impossible, but for which it was feasible to use other response inducements.

Also, since the TDM was first developed, researchers have realized that mixed-mode surveys, in which some respondents are surveyed by interview and others complete mail questionnaires, can help overcome the difficulties of obtaining adequate response rates using a single method, either face-to-face, telephone, or mail (Dillman and Tarnai, 1988). The need to combine survey modes to achieve high response rates, however, has highlighted the unsettling problem that people's answers to any particular question vary depending on the survey mode (Schwarz, Strack, Hippler, and Bishop, 1991; Dillman, Sangster, Tarnai, and Rockwood, 1996).

Finally, since 1978, the scientific base of survey methodology has expanded dramatically. This revision of the TDM is also a response to a rapid expansion in our scientific knowledge of how to conduct surveys. In the 1970s, research was just beginning on how and why people sometimes provide different answers to the same questions on mail versus interview surveys, and how question order can influence response (e.g., Schuman and Presser, 1981). The layout and design of self-administered questionnaires was something of an art form based on unsystematic observations of response behavior. Scientifically-based principles of layout and design had not yet been specified, nor had cognitive methods for testing questionnaires been developed and formalized as a pretest methodology (Forsyth and Lessler, 1991).

Another significant change incorporated into this book is the recognition that the fundamental nature of self-administered questionnaires is undergoing substantial change. Traditional postal service mail is only one way of sending and retrieving self-administered questionnaires. Electronic mail, the World Wide Web, and interactive voice response to taped telephone messages make possible the delivery and retrieval of questionnaires electronically. Improved computer technology and people's familiarity with computers are also having a great influence on how questionnaires can be completed and returned. Increasingly, people are being asked to enter answers to self-administered questionnaires by keying numbers on telephones or entering answers directly into computers in classrooms or in their homes. Also, optical scanning and imaging of self-administered questionnaires is increasingly feasible, without having a deleterious effect on response behavior. The variety of possibilities for constructing, delivering, retrieving, and processing self-administered questionnaires raises new challenges for survey design that are discussed here. In addition, these modes for conducting surveys exist in a more competitive environment where other respondent mail also seeks attention and response.

This book is a response to all these changes that have transpired since 1978: new technologies, theoretical advancements, mixed-mode considerations, a better understanding of specific survey requirements, and an improved base of social science knowledge. It describes a new method which I call Tailored Design. Tailored Design responds, in particular, to the tremendous design and implementation possibilities now offered by powerful computer and desktop publishing capabilities. Like the original TDM, it is established on a standard set of principles and procedures generally applicable to all surveys

(Part I of this book), but these base elements are shaped further for particular populations, sponsorship, and content (Part II).

THE SOCIETAL TREND TOWARD SELF-ADMINISTRATION

Though exact numbers are difficult to pinpoint, there is little doubt that the number of surveys conducted by self-administration, and mail in particular, exceeds the number of interview surveys conducted each year. In 1981, an assessment by the United States Office of Management and Budget, which must approve all surveys sponsored by the federal government, revealed that 69% were conducted solely by mail, and another 11% were conducted partly by mail (U.S. Office of Management and Budget, 1984). The reasons for this preference undoubtedly involved lower cost and the fact that organizations could conduct such surveys themselves, whereas most interview surveys, whether by telephone or face-to-face, needed to be contracted to professional organizations.

Nonetheless, there can be little doubt that the dominant method for conducting large-scale, nationally prominent, general public surveys was face-to-face interviewing prior to the 1970s, and since then telephone methods. The speed and efficiency of telephone surveys was demonstrated dramatically and with much visibility by overnight surveys during the Watergate hearings in 1974. The fact that the telephone was a fixture in virtually all businesses and most U.S. homes contributed to its becoming the standard survey method for the United States in the 1980s and 1990s. The telephone also was the first survey method to benefit fully from computerized survey methods, especially computer-assisted telephone interviewing (CATI) software which eliminated keypunching. Automatic call-scheduling, dialing of random digit telephone numbers, and data compilation also contributed to the efficiency of the telephone method (Dillman, 1999).

Self-administered questionnaires are now poised to benefit enormously from information age technologies. While U.S. Postal Service delivery and retrieval of paper questionnaires remains essential for some surveys, the possibilities for electronic delivery are increasing rapidly. In addition, the elimination of laborious keypunching is within sight, the result of developments in optical scanning and imaging that result in no loss of data quality (Dillman and Miller, 1998).

A significant cultural change is also occurring which suggests a future of greater prominence for mail and other self-administered surveys (Dillman, 1999). Many activities that once required people to interact with another person are now being shifted to a self-administration mode. Using ATMs to obtain banking information and money instead of going to a bank teller is one example. Others include using touch-tone input to stop and restart newspaper delivery, renew library books, and register for college classes. Home diagnostic kits for all sorts of medical information from blood sugar levels to pregnancy, ordering airline tickets, purchasing gasoline in service stations, and serving as one's own secretary are further examples.

Computer skills are now required for the performance of most skilled work. A lack of effective keyboard skills and the inability to compose and deliver prose quickly significantly limit an individual's ability to succeed in life. This renewed emphasis on reading and writing, requisite skills for responding to most self-administered surveys, follows a period in U.S. society in which verbal skills and the reliance on the telephone as a substitute for traditional letter writing became dominant.

Concern exists that the random digit telephone interview paradigm which has guided most general public surveys during the last decade, and the telephone itself, may have become less effective interview methods. In the mid-20th century, the telephone was a household instrument that controlled behavior. A ringing telephone could not be tolerated by most people. In addition, a norm of politeness prevailed for dealing with callers, in much the same way as it was expected for in-person contacts. There were no answering machines and not to answer the telephone meant missing a call that could have been important. As the telephone became a major method of marketing products and substantial increases in unwanted calls occurred, people increasingly became less tolerant of such intrusions. The prevalence of unlisted numbers began to increase and now includes a majority of phones in many large cities, and 30% nationally (Survey Sampling, personal communication, August 19, 1999). Also on the increase is a call-blocking device that will accept calls only from identified numbers. In addition, answering machines are increasingly relied on to take calls, and active call monitoring is used to select which calls to answer. Many businesses have eliminated receptionists and instead calls are guided through appropriately keyed numbers to personal telephones, where an answering machine becomes the most likely response. Thus, it is becoming more difficult than in the past to complete telephone surveys. A ringing telephone no longer elicits an automatic answer from anyone who hears it. The telephone has evolved from being a controller of human behavior that demanded a response to becoming controlled, so that individuals decide who can reach them and when.

New methods of self-administering surveys are also gaining rapid acceptance. E-mail, web, and touch-tone data entry (or interactive voice response) methods have become feasible, and their use is growing rapidly.

For all of these reasons, the use of self-administered questionnaires will become more important both individually and as a component of mixed-mode data collection systems as we enter the twenty-first century. My aim in this book is to provide principles and procedures for successfully conducting surveys at this time when our reliance on self-administered surveys seems destined to increase.

THE ELEMENTS OF TAILORED DESIGN

The original TDM consisted of two parts. The first was to identify each aspect of the survey process that seemed likely to affect either the quality or quantity of response and to shape each one in such a way that the best possible responses could be obtained. It was guided by a theoretical view, social exchange, about why people respond to questionnaires. The second part was to organize the survey efforts so that the design intentions were carried out in complete detail. It was guided by an administrative plan that assured coordination of all of the parts. Attention to these two aspects of design are retained in Tailored Design, but with a somewhat broader consideration of the causes of survey error and the determinants of response behavior.

Reducing Survey Error

Sample surveys are typically conducted to estimate the distribution of characteristics in a population. For example, a researcher might want to determine in a sample survey of the general public what proportion own their home, have attended college, or favor one political candidate over another. Random sampling allows such characteristics to be estimated with precision, with larger sample sizes achieving ever larger degrees of precision. For example, whereas a random sample of only 100 members of the U.S. general public yields estimates that are ± 10% of the true percent, a sample of 2,200 yields estimates that are ± only 2%, for which we can be 95% confident. The extent to which the precision of sample survey estimates is limited by the number of persons (or other units) surveyed is described by the term *sampling error.* Formally, sampling error is the result of attempting to survey only some, and not all, of the units in the survey population.

This ability to estimate with considerable precision the percentage of a population that has a particular attribute by obtaining data from only a small fraction of the total population is what distinguishes surveys from all other research methods. Neither focus groups, small group experiments, content analysis, nor historical analysis have this capability. However, sampling error is only one of four sources of error which form the cornerstones for conducting a quality survey (Groves, 1989; Salant and Dillman, 1994).

A second source of error which must be minimized in order to conduct a good survey is *coverage error.* Coverage error occurs when the list from which the sample is drawn does not include all elements of the population, thus making it impossible to give all elements of the population an equal or known chance of being included in the sample survey. An example would be the omission of people without telephones from a telephone survey. A third source of error, *measurement error,* occurs when a respondent's answer to a survey question is inaccurate, imprecise, or cannot be compared in any useful way to other respondents' answers. Measurement error results from poor question wording and questionnaire construction. A challenge for all survey methods, it is of particular concern in self-administered surveys, in which direct feedback from respondents about poor questions is less available than in interview surveys. The fourth source of error, *nonresponse error,* occurs when a significant number of people in the survey sample do not respond to the questionnaire *and* have different characteristics from those who do respond, when these characteristics are important to the study.

Surveys can fail to achieve their objectives for any or all of these reasons. For example, I was once asked to assist with a regional survey which had as one of its goals the estimation of unemployment rates. The sponsors proposed to interview only a few hundred of the nearly 100,000 residents, a procedure that would have resulted in being able to estimate unemployment within about five percentage points at best, rather than the desired 1 to 2%. In the same discussion the use of telephone interview methods was suggested, which meant that people without telephones, those probably more likely to be unemployed, would be excluded from any chance of inclusion in the sample. Had this suggestion been followed, significant coverage error would have occurred. One of the draft survey questions gave the options of employed versus unemployed but did not allow for retired, homemaker, or full-time student, thus raising the likelihood of members of these groups being interpreted as unemployed. Measurement error would have been the result. Finally, it was hoped that the survey would be conducted in only two nights of calling, thus raising the likelihood of a low response rate and the possibility that those who did respond would differ from those who did not, i.e., nonresponse error. Figure 1.1 summarizes and provides additional examples of the failure to achieve acceptable error levels in various types of surveys. Efforts to conduct any survey must begin with an understanding of the threat to precision and accuracy that stems simultaneously from these four cornerstones of survey research.

The overall perspective that guides this book is that efforts must be made to reduce all four sources of survey error to acceptable levels; none can be ignored. However, the greatest attention here is accorded to nonresponse and measurement error. Principles for random sampling are generally similar for all types of surveys, and differences for self-administered surveys do not warrant extensive treatment. Coverage error issues are not a problem for many mail surveys, but are prohibitive for others. For example, address lists are often complete for many populations of interest, for example, school teachers, driver's license holders, and organization members. But for groups such as the general public, adequate lists are generally unavailable, and sometimes nothing can be done to solve this problem.

However, a great deal can usually be done to address measurement and nonresponse issues through careful design of questions, questionnaires, and implementation methods. Behavioral theories of design have now been developed for each of these topics. These theories are used in this book to develop the step-by-step methods that are detailed in the chapters that follow.

Figure 1.1 Four sources of survey error and their consequences.

Sampling Error: The result of surveying only some, and not all, (randomly selected) elements of the survey population.	☞	**For example:** A large restaurant chain surveyed thousands of customers to make compensation decisions for individual franchise managers but only received 20–30 responses per franchise, far too few to get acceptable estimates of satisfaction for each franchise.
Coverage Error: The result of not allowing all members of the survey population to have an equal or known chance of being sampled for participation in the survey.	☞	**For example:** A university-sponsored mail survey of the general public in Las Vegas used telephone directories to sample households. But, because more than 60% of Las Vegas households are not listed in directories, most members of the general public did not have a chance of being selected for participation in the survey.
Measurement Error: The result of poor question wording or questions being presented in such a way that inaccurate or uninterpretable answers are obtained.	☞	**For example:** A government agency survey of small business owners asked how business activity had changed during the past year using these answer choices: 1) increased a lot; 2) increased somewhat; 3) increased a little; or 4) decreased. Besides not making it clear what was meant by business activity (sales? product lines? profitability?), the vague answer categories were biased towards "increase." The answers could not be clearly interpreted.
Nonresponse Error: The result of people who respond to a survey being different from sampled individuals who did not respond, in a way relevant to the study.	☞	**For example:** A random sample statewide survey of school superintendents which was designed to estimate the amount and types of previous experience obtained prior to becoming a superintendent, received responses from 80% of superintendents who became superintendents before they were 40 years old, compared to only 20% of superintendents who assumed their position when over 50, and who were, therefore, deemed likely to have additional experience before assuming their current position.

Theoretical Foundation: Why and How People Respond to Self-Administered Surveys

Wrong Questions and Misplaced Emphases

Nearly 30 years of trying to help individuals design surveys has led me to develop an early sense of apprehension that a proposed survey is not going to be well designed. This concern is based upon the kinds of questions asked by the would-be surveyor. For example:

- What color paper should I use to get the best response?
- Would it help to put three small-denomination stamps on the outgoing envelope?
- How much will a pretty questionnaire cover help response rates?
- How small a font can I use to make the questionnaire shorter in order to improve response?

Each of these questions has a legitimate answer. Paper color does not usually affect response rates, nor does the presence of stamps on the outgoing envelope. Cover pages need to convey certain information about the survey, and it is more important to think about content than something subjective like "prettiness." Finally, there is no evidence that using a smaller font to decrease the number of questionnaire pages will improve response.

However, instead of answering each query, I am likely to respond with my own questions: Who are you surveying and what's the topic? What is your overall implementation plan—how many contacts do you plan to make? Will the mailings be personalized? What interval will you use between contacts? How long is the questionnaire? Then, more to the point of the person's queries, why do you want to use colored paper? Do you plan to use stamps on the return envelope or a business reply? What do you mean by a pretty cover, and what will it look like? Is the questionnaire being printed as a booklet?

My intent with such responses is twofold. First, all of the original queries listed above concern factors likely to have relatively little influence on how people respond to a survey. Second, my advice to those individuals who ask the same question has often been quite different once I knew more details of the proposed study. For example, knowing that a questionnaire being sent to employed professionals was going to be printed as a booklet influenced my opinion on reducing the font size from 12 to 10. Few professionals were likely to have great difficulty with a font reduction of this magnitude and it was clear that reduction of the font size would remove four pages (one sheet of paper) by eliminating several inches of type. In contrast, my advice for a survey of retired people would have been to increase the font size to 14, thereby increasing the number of pages, but also making it easier for respondents to read.

In another instance, questions about a plan to use small-denomination stamps revealed that business reply envelopes were planned for the return envelope. My recommendation was to switch the stamps to the return envelope and throw away the business reply envelopes. Although there is no evidence from past research that response rates are improved by the presence of stamps on the outgoing envelope, their influence on return envelopes is well documented (e.g., Armstrong and Luske, 1987; Dillman, 1991). In another instance, I supported their use on the outgoing envelope; the stamps were already available and their use certainly would not hurt response rates.

An inquiry on the proposed use of color revealed that the questionnaire was being printed in color and the sponsor had the ability to produce lightly colored background fields with answer spaces left white, a method of printing that seemed likely to decrease item nonresponse. In this case I encouraged the use of color. In another instance, bright green paper seemed consistent with membership in the environmental organization that was to be surveyed, but the lack of contrast with black print would diminish readability, thus making that color an unwise choice.

In short, a survey involves many decisions which need to fit together and support one another in a way that encourages most people to respond and minimizes inaccurate or inadequate answers. Social exchange theory, to be discussed shortly, provides a basis for making compatible design decisions. It uses knowledge about the causes of human behavior to identify and understand why people do or do not respond to surveys. Human behavior is enormously complex and can seldom be explained by a single cause. However, considerable evidence suggests that certain stimuli are more likely than others to achieve a desired response.

Our challenge is to utilize theory to guide how we organize these multiple stimuli—from paper choice to the content of each communication element that constitutes the survey request—in a way that is most likely to produce the accurate completion and return of a self-administered questionnaire. Designing a quality survey begins with two fundamental assumptions: (1) responding to a self-administered questionnaire involves not only cognition, but also motivation (Jenkins and Dillman, 1995, 1997), and (2) multiple attempts are essential to achieving satisfactory response rates to self-administered surveys regardless of whether administered by e-mail, the web, or postal delivery (Scott, 1961; Heberlein and Baumgartner, 1978; Dillman, 1991).

The first assumption recognizes that people must understand clearly what is wanted of them if they are to respond. However, there is more to getting a response than the four-step cognition model described by Tourangeau and Rasinski (1988), which includes comprehension, retrieval, deciding, and reporting. People must be *motivated* to go through the process associated with understanding and answering each question and returning the questionnaire to the survey sponsor. The conscious consideration of the motivational qualities of questionnaires and mail-out materials distinguishes the challenge of achieving response to questionnaires that are self-administered from those conducted through interviews. In the latter case, design efforts are inevitably aimed at the interviewer who, in a narrow window of opportunity, must use appropriate words, often delivered extemporaneously, to convince the respondent to continue the interview.

The second assumption is a statement of the most dominant finding from research on how to improve response to self-administered surveys: multiple attempts to contact potential respondents are essential, just as they are for personal and telephone interview surveys. From a design standpoint, this means there are several opportunities to encourage a cognitive understanding of what is being requested. We also have several opportunities to motivate recipients of a questionnaire to respond to the survey request, and to do so accurately. Thus, we must design contacts not only as individual entities, but also as components of an implementation system that precede and/or follow other communications. In this regard, I have found social exchange theory a helpful guide for organizing and presenting a sequence of mutually supportive requests to questionnaire recipients.

Survey Response As Social Exchange

Social exchange is a theory of human behavior used to explain the development and continuation of human interaction. The theory asserts that actions of individuals are motivated by the return these actions are expected to bring, and in fact usually do bring, from others (Blau, 1964; Gallegos, 1974; Dillman, 1978; Goyder, 1987). Three elements are critical for predicting a particular action: rewards, costs, and trust. Simply stated, *rewards* are what one expects to gain from a particular activity, *costs* are what one gives up or spends to obtain the rewards, and *trust* is the expectation that in the long run the rewards of doing something will outweigh the costs. The theory of social exchange implies three questions about the design of a questionnaire and the implementation process: How can we increase rewards for responding? How can perceived costs be reduced? How can trust be established so that the ultimate rewards will outweigh the costs of responding?

The ideas I am introducing here should *not* be equated with economic exchange. Social exchange is different from the more familiar economic exchange, in which money serves as a precise measure of the worth of one's actions. First, social exchange is a broader concept. Future obligations are created that are diffuse and unspecified. The nature of the return cannot be bargained over as in economic exchange, but must be left to the discretion of the one who owes it. The range of goods, services, and experiences exchanged is also quite broad. It is assumed that people engage in an activity because of the rewards they hope to reap, that all activities they perform incur certain costs, and that people attempt to keep their costs below the rewards they expect to receive. Fundamentally, then, whether a given behavior occurs is a function of the ratio between the perceived costs of doing that activity and the rewards one expects the other party to provide, either directly or indirectly.

The difference between social and economic exchange is illustrated by results from research on cash payments to respondents. Much research has shown that "token" incentives given with the request to complete a questionnaire, a form of social exchange, consistently improve response rates (James and Bolstein, 1990, 1992; Church, 1993). However, a promise to pay people for completing a questionnaire by sending them a payment afterwards (economic exchange) does not. For example, James and Bolstein (1992), in a survey of small construction companies (often one- or two-person operations), found that response rates received from questionnaire mailings that included one to five dollars produced higher response rates (64–71%) than the promise of $50 (57%), or nothing at all (52%). Similarly, Johnson and McLaughlin (1990), in a large national survey of people who registered to take the Graduate Masters Exam for admission to business school, found that response rates were 10% higher when a five dollar check was included with the request than when a ten dollar check was promised after the questionnaire was returned. Most importantly, the response rate for the ten dollar check was within one percent of the response rate when no incentive at all was used. Social exchange is a subtle but more powerful method for influencing response behavior when the rewards that can be offered to each respondent are relatively small, as is typically the case for self-administered surveys.

Rewards, Costs, and Trust

There are many specific ways that one can attempt to affect the reward, cost, and trust matrix. In addition to traditional elements of social exchange noted by Blau (1964), Homans (1961), and Thibaut and Kelley (1959), I include more recent ideas about influence in a social context from Cialdini (1984). The discussion that follows extends in more detail an argument presented in the first edition of this book (Dillman, 1978). It is based partly on research findings. It is also based on theoretical arguments that are difficult to evaluate experimentally, and as a result have not yet been well tested. These ideas constitute the basis for elements of Tailored Design that are explicated in the ensuing chapters.

Ways Of Providing Rewards

Show positive regard. Thibaut and Kelley (1959) have noted that being regarded positively by another person has reward value to many people. Consider a cover letter that begins abruptly: "You have been selected in our national sample of accounting organizations. Please respond to the enclosed questionnaire within two weeks." Such a letter shows little respect for the individual who receives it. In contrast, giving respondents reasons that a survey is being done, providing a toll-free number to call with questions, and personally addressing correspondence are small, but not inconsequential, ways of showing positive regard to questionnaire recipients.

Say thank you. Blau (1964) argues that a time-consuming service of great material benefit could be appropriately repaid in a social exchange context by mere verbal appreciation. Phrases such as "we appreciate very much your help" or "many thanks in advance" can be added to correspondence. Perhaps for this reason, a follow-up postcard designed as a thank you for the prompt return of "the important questionnaire we sent to you recently" has been found in some surveys to produce a response burst nearly equal to that which followed the original mail-out a week or so earlier (Dillman, Christenson, Carpenter, and Brooks, 1974).

Ask for advice. Both Blau (1964) and Homans (1961) have pointed out that the feeling of being asked for help, advice, or assistance provides a sense of reward to people. People often get a sense of accomplishment from knowing they have helped someone else solve a problem. Explaining to someone that, "I am writing to you because the only way we can find out whether the service we provide is really meeting the needs of people like yourself is to ask you," is a way to provide this kind of reward. In essence, asking people for their advice subordinates the sponsor to the questionnaire recipient, rather than vice versa, which, as explained later, would incur cost to the respondent.

Support group values. Most people identify with certain groups, which may be as broad as a citizen of the country, or narrowly focused, such as a dues paying member of the Freemont Booster's Association. Depending upon the survey population, sponsorship, and topic, one can often appeal to values shared widely by those who are surveyed. Blau (1964) noted that supporting a person's values can instill a sense of reward in individuals. This principle underlies efforts to appeal to respondents on the basis of a study's "social usefulness" (Slocum, Empey, and Swanson, 1956; Dillman, 1978).

Give tangible rewards. As already noted, research has convincingly shown that token financial incentives of only a dollar or two, enclosed with the request to complete a questionnaire, significantly boost incentives, and inevitably outperform promises to send a larger payment after a completed questionnaire is received (e.g., James and Bolstein, 1992). Material incentives sent with a request, such as ball point pens, have also been found effective, although to a very modest extent (Church, personal communication, April 12, 1993). The providing of a tangible incentive, even a token one, is effective because it evokes a sense of reciprocal obligation which can be easily discharged by returning the complete questionnaire.

Make the questionnaire interesting. Blau (1964) noted that it is possible to obtain desired actions from people when the action is experienced as a net gain rather than a net cost. Similarly, Cialdini (1984) argued that "liking" to do something is a powerful determinant of behavior. Thus, it is not surprising that Heberlein and Baumgartner (1978) showed that questionnaires on topics of high salience to recipients are more likely to be returned than those on topics of low salience. Questionnaires can be made more interesting to respondents by improving layout and design, ordering questions so the more interesting ones are placed at the beginning, and making questions easy to understand and answer. The fact that some people enjoy answering questionnaires regardless of content may explain why some response, even if only a few percentage points, can be obtained with almost any questionnaire.

Give social validation. Knowing that other people like themselves have completed a similar action can strongly influence people's willingness to comply with a request (Cialdini, 1984; Groves, Cialdini and Couper, 1992). In other words, some people are socially validated by seeing themselves as similar to most others in a group. Therefore, in later attempts to encourage response, telling people that many others have already responded encourages them to act in a similar way.

Inform respondents that opportunities to respond are scarce. Telling people that there are relatively few opportunities to respond and that they may not have an opportunity to respond unless they do so quickly can influence people to act (Groves et al., 1992). On the surface this argument may seem not to fit with requesting everyone in a specified sample to return a questionnaire. However, the idea of using deadline dates for returning a questionnaire or completing an interview is consistent with this argument. This technique has been used effectively in telephone surveys of businesses when, after 20 or more unsuccessful attempts, "gatekeepers" were informed that all calling had to be completed by the end of the week (Petrie, Moore, and Dillman, 1998).

Ways Of Reducing Social Costs

In some cases, efforts to reduce the costs incurred by respondents represent the flip side of increasing rewards, for example, making a questionnaire more interesting by making it easier to fill out. However, in other cases these two goals are distinctively different. Strategies to reduce social costs include the following:

Avoid subordinating language. Consider these contrasting statements which might be used in communications with questionnaire recipients: "For us to help solve the school problems in your community it is necessary for you to complete this questionnaire," versus "Would you please do me a favor?" The former implies the respondent is dependent upon the letter writer, whereas the latter suggests that the writer is dependent upon the respondent. Blau (1964) argued persuasively that people prefer not to be subordinated to others, and will often make great efforts to avoid that. Not responding is an easy way of avoiding a sense of being subordinated.

Avoid embarrassment. A friend who saw herself as a conscientious respondent to nearly all surveys once described to me why one questionnaire had ended up in the wastebasket. The first question asked about whether the United States should attempt to develop breeder nuclear reactors, which were then being discussed in the media. "I know I should understand these things and read about them, but you know I just don't follow this enough to know," she said. The respondent was clearly embarrassed about her lack of knowledge on the issue.

Thibaut and Kelley (1959) pointed out that costs to an individual are high when great physical or mental effort is required, and when embarrassment or anxiety accompany the action. Complex questions and directions that confuse respondents produce feelings of inadequacy or anxiety that people wish to avoid. Questionnaires often get discarded when the respondent peruses the questionnaire but can't figure out where to start, or what the first question means. The lack of response from people who do not read well or who are not used to expressing themselves in writing may be due to this type of social cost.

Avoid inconvenience. A frequent finding of response rate research is that *not* including an envelope lowers response rates (e.g., Armstrong and Luske, 1987). The likely reason is that it takes additional effort to locate and address an envelope. Including a return envelope with a real stamp(s) on it also improves response rates over a business reply envelope. A likely reason is that people keep stamped envelopes available, whereas a business reply envelope is sometimes inadvertently thrown away. The continued presence of a return envelope contributes to the convenience of responding.

Make questionnaires appear short and easy. Questionnaires that appear shorter and easy to fill out lessen the perceived costs of responding. Such appearances can be reinforced by indicating in the cover letter that responding should only take a few minutes. Research has shown that longer questionnaires achieve slightly lower response rates (Heberlein and Baumgartner, 1978), but does not confirm that putting the same number of questions into more pages decreases response rates (Leslie, 1997). Other research has shown that respondent-friendly questionnaires, with carefully organized questions in easy-to-answer formats, can improve response rates (Dillman, Sinclair, and Clark, 1993).

Minimize requests to obtain personal information. Many survey questions ask for information that some people do not want to reveal to others; for example, their annual income, past sexual behavior, method of disciplining children, or use of drugs. Sometimes asking such questions is the main objective of the survey. So while it is desirable from a response standpoint to minimize intrusive questions, doing so would defeat the purpose of the study. In these cases, specific wording can "soften" such questions. Further, explanations can be offered for why the questions are important and how the information will be kept confidential or even anonymous.

Keep requests similar to other requests to which a person has already responded. People who have committed themselves to a position are more likely to comply with requests to do something consistent with that position (Cialdini,

1984). The implication of this finding is that people feel uncomfortable when they do something inconsistent with their past behavior. It may help explain why in panel surveys, once people have responded to the first request, it is much easier to get them to respond to subsequent requests (Otto, Call, and Spenner, 1976). It also may explain the finding by Nederhof (1982) that the people who are most likely to respond to a survey request are people who typically respond to other survey requests.

People's inclination to behave consistently suggests that arguments can sometimes be offered that point out how responding to a particular survey is consistent with something the questionnaire recipient has already done. For example, a survey of organization members noted, "We really appreciate your support through the recent payment of dues, and, we want to be responsive to your expectations. Completing the enclosed questionnaire will give us guidance on how best to respond to those concerns."

The preference for consistency may explain the effectiveness of the "foot-in-the-door" technique, that is, getting people to perform a large task by first getting them to perform a small task. This procedure was used successfully in a survey of national park visitors, whereby instead of simply handing people a questionnaire with the request to complete it, visitors were asked to briefly pull their car to the side of the road and answer three short questions before being requested to complete the questionnaire at the end of their visit (Dillman, Dolsen, and Machlis, 1995).

Ways Of Establishing Trust

In an economic exchange involving small purchases, payment is typically made when the goods are received. In essence, the complete exchange takes place at a specific point in time and is compressed into a few, rather routine seconds. It is precisely on this issue that social exchange differs most significantly from its economic counterpart. Under conditions of social exchange, there is no way to assure that what the survey sponsor has promised as a benefit of the study, for example, "This survey will help our company do a better job of serving its customers," will actually happen. Several steps can be taken to increase the questionnaire recipient's trust that the survey sponsor will do what is promised. Trust is critical to forming the belief that in the long run the benefits of completing the questionnaire will outweigh the costs of doing so.

Provide a token of appreciation in advance. Although one or two dollars included with the questionnaire may have little direct reward value for respondents, it seems to have a greater value in creating trust. By providing the small token of appreciation in advance, the researcher shows trust in respondents who can, of course, pocket the money and not return their questionnaire. The symbolic gesture of trust probably explains why it is much more effective in improving response than larger post-payments. Further, explaining that the money is a "small token of appreciation" is also consistent with expressing trust. In contrast, saying it is a "payment for your time" is more likely to be subordinating and insulting. Finally, including uncancelled stamps on an envelope, which respondents could choose to use for something besides returning the questionnaire, also contributes to the formation of trust (albeit to a smaller degree than a financial incentive).

Sponsorship by legitimate authority. It has been shown that people are more likely to comply with a request if it comes from an authoritative source, that is, one whom the larger culture defines as legitimated to make such requests and expect compliance (Cialdini, 1984). It is therefore not surprising that Heberlein and Baumgartner (1978) found that government-sponsored surveys achieved higher response rates than those sponsored by marketing research firms. Most surveys, regardless of sponsorship, are voluntary, but some, for example the decennial census survey and many government-sponsored business surveys, are not. Research has shown that informing questionnaire recipients that a survey is mandatory improves response for surveys of both businesses (Tulp, Hoy, Kusch, and Cole, 1991) and individuals (Dillman, Singer, Clark, and Treat, 1996).

I once observed the survey letters and envelopes for a federal government survey being printed with a Midwestern city as the return address so that return mail would go to a processing office rather than to its headquarters in Washington, D.C. The likely effect was that people might not think it was a legitimate government survey. More recently research has shown that government questionnaires sent in packaging designed to reflect a private sector marketing orientation, with bright and colorful envelopes and icons, led many people to believe the mailing was not likely to be from government (Dillman, Jenkins, Martin, and DeMaio, 1996). A follow-up field test with the same forms produced significantly lower (from 5–10%) response rates in a national test (Leslie, 1997).

Make the task appear important. Many surveys try to appeal to people on the basis that something important will ultimately happen as a result of the survey. Form letters produced on copy machines, questionnaires that are sloppily constructed or contain questions that are difficult to understand, and a lack of follow-up mailings targeted to nonrespondents suggest that a questionnaire is relatively unimportant. Trust that something useful will happen as a result of a study can be engendered by making each contact look important. Printing personalized cover letters on letterhead stationary and designing the questionnaire in a way that makes sense to the respondent have a significant role in establishing trust.

Invoke other exchange relationships. One of the first mail surveys I conducted from my university came back complete with this note appended, "I was going to throw this thing away, but my spouse reminded me that our daughter had gotten her education from your university so I guess I owe it to you." The nature of social exchange is that people sometimes do things for other people because they feel they want to repay a favor to someone else. Thus, a letter from a respected sponsor on letterhead stationery may help encourage a survey response.

Linking Social Exchange Elements

Utilization of the social exchange perspective requires that efforts be made to explicitly link the elements of social exchange to form a systematic approach to achieving high quality survey responses. There are several challenges involved in making such linkages.

First, it is important to recognize that a specific design feature may involve more than one of the three major elements (i.e., costs, rewards, trust). For example, inclusion of a token financial incentive such as two dollars with the questionnaire seems on the surface a reward, but because it is sent ahead of time it also promotes trust—the study sponsor has given something to the potential respondent that the respondent can keep, thus creating a sense of reciprocal obligation.

Similarly, if a survey is required by law and the respondent is simply informed, "You are required by law to respond to this survey," then clearly the respondent is being subordinated to the study sponsor. However, by accompanying such directives with a statement explaining why response is required, or even attributing the mandatory requirement to a third party (when appropriate), one can subtly change the reward/cost balance. For example, "Because this survey is the only way the government has of knowing the amounts of natural gas being consumed each month, Congress has passed a law requiring all utilities to respond to it." This statement accurately attributes the mandatory requirement to the source and combines it with an argument of importance.

Second, just as costs and rewards are associated with the decision to respond, they can also be associated with *not* responding. For example, people sometimes respond to questionnaires because they are concerned that not responding will lead to another reminder, which they wish to avoid. On the other hand, there may be an undesirable backlash effect from an offensive request, such as "We are doing this survey of taxpayers to help people like yourself do a better job of completing your taxes on time." Such a statement might be interpreted as a personal criticism, so that the recipient feels a sense of reward from simply tearing up the questionnaire and throwing it away. Thus, it is important to evaluate a proposed implementation strategy with regard to the sense of reward one might get from *not* responding to the survey request.

Third, repetition of appeals diminishes their effectiveness. It was once proposed to me that costs for a replacement questionnaire mailing being used in a large national survey could be greatly decreased by printing extra copies of the original letter and envelopes and simply stamping "second notice" on the outside of the envelope. Not only would this be likely to anger some respondents, so that it would be harder for them to see any rewards to responding, but an opportunity to invoke new arguments for response would have to be forgone. Research has found that even repeating the inclusion of a token financial incentive with a replacement mailing does not increase response over that which can be obtained with a reminder that does not include the repeated incentive (Tortora, Dillman, and Bolstein, 1992).

Fourth, there is some evidence to suggest that pushing certain concepts to an extreme results in effects that are the opposite of the intended ones. For example, making a questionnaire very short as a means of reducing costs of responding may backfire. In general, longer questionnaires achieve lower response rates. However, limiting a questionnaire to only a couple of questions may also have the effect of making it seem less useful or important, and as a result not improve response. Similarly, it has been shown that putting too much emphasis on confidentiality by providing long detailed explanations can backfire by raising concerns about whether a questionnaire is, in fact, confidential at all (Singer, Von Thurn, and Miller, 1995).

Fifth, it is important to recognize that later appeals are aimed at a somewhat different audience than first appeals. Those who respond early to a survey will be deleted from the contact list and therefore not receive reminders. The appeals that worked for these respondents did not work for the nonrespondents. This fact makes a strong argument for changing the look, feel, and content of later contacts. It is at this stage, for example, that one might usefully consider invoking arguments such as the "social validation" concept proposed by Cialdini (1984). That is, "We have already received questionnaires from most people in this national sample, but are writing to those who have not yet responded because. . . ."

Sixth, people differ in what they perceive as rewards and costs. It has long been observed that some people enjoy filling out questionnaires, whereas others do not. Some worry about confidentiality and others do not. Some find the topic of a particular questionnaire interesting, whereas others from the same population do not. Therefore, it is logical to aim different appeals at early and late responders and towards different survey populations.

Seventh, whether an action evokes a sense of cost, reward, or trust is related to how it links with other implementation actions and not just to how it appears when viewed in isolation. For example, considerable research has shown that preletters can significantly improve response to mail surveys (e.g., Dillman, Clark, and Sinclair, 1995). Thus, it came as a surprise to the sponsors when the pretest for a national survey revealed absolutely no improvement from the use of a prior notification letter. However, an examination of the details quickly revealed why. The letter was very long, emphasized that response was not mandatory, and informed the respondents how they could get information about the study. Further, two long paragraphs of the preletter described all of the potential negative aspects (costs) of responding, without the respondent being able to find out what questions were being asked. Yet the questionnaire itself concerned routine aspects of the respondent's health and asked for relatively little information that most people were likely to object to providing. Finally, the preletter was also sent a full month prior to the questionnaire itself being sent. Thus, not only had a preletter been unpleasant by being long and emphasizing potential costs of responding without allowing the respondent to know what was being requested, but it was so far ahead of the questionnaire that by the time the questionnaire arrived, the preletter was likely to be forgotten. How a survey gets implemented, that is, when and how contacts are made, is also an important aspect of what potential respondents see as the costs and benefits of responding to a survey, and whether they think anything useful will come of it. Elements of implementation plans can be seen by respondents both as individual elements and as a part of a larger whole, each of which forms impressions of costs, rewards, and trust.

Communicating Exchange Concepts through Visual Layout and Design

Although questionnaire designers have long been aware of the difficulty of designing easy-to-answer questionnaires, the proposed principles of design have been based more on subjective impressions than on scientific evidence of how people see and process information (Wright and Barnard, 1975; Sless, 1994). The introduction of computers, word processing equipment, and laser printers has provided nearly every questionnaire designer with the ability to vary fonts, insert graphical symbols, change margins, and switch the size and brightness of type. Such changes can be made with less effort than the typist of traditional questionnaires expended in making a carriage return. The designers of web questionnaires have even more possibilities, being able to add color, photographs, sound, and animation. The indiscriminate use of these new possibilities has resulted in producing questionnaires that are often more, rather than less, difficult to read and answer.

It is therefore not surprising that it has become necessary to apply concepts of graphic design and layout (e.g., Wallschlaeger and Busic-Snyder, 1992) to the construction of self-administered questionnaires. These concepts, to be described in Chapter 3, include using such ideas as figure/ground, top-down and bottom-up processing, pattern recognition, brightness, contrast, size, location, and simplicity, and are expressed through organizing principles such as the Law of Pragnanz and Law of Proximity (Jenkins and Dillman, 1997).

Typically, most respondents see a questionnaire only once. The problem each respondent faces might be compared to that of a driver on a new highway. Finding one's way to a particular destination may not be difficult if rules for driving and road signs are the same, such as white dotted lines to divide lanes, solid yellow stripes for no passing, white on green for identification of exits and blue signs for services. Although such standards exist across states and some countries for highways, they do not exist for questionnaires.

Considerable research has been done on how people look at and read material placed in front of them (Jenkins and Dillman, 1997). For example, people tend to start reading near, but not at, the upper left corner of a page. However, brightness (including color) and larger stimuli (bigger letters, blocks of color, or graphical symbols) may pull one's vision towards a particular element of the page, thus distracting them from a natural starting point. People's attention is also guided by symbols with particular cultural meanings. Thus, an arrow may guide a person across the page more effectively than words.

Questionnaires are written in two languages. One language consists of words. The other consists of graphical symbols. These two languages of meaningful information can be placed on a page so they work in concert, stimulating a person to receive information in the same way one would receive it in an interview. They can also be in conflict, actually pulling people in two different directions so that some people proceed through a questionnaire in one way and some people in another. Therefore, two aspects of a questionnaire must be developed and placed in concert with one another:

- *Information organization:* the prescribed order in which we want people to process the words and other symbols used to convey the questions and all needed instructions to respondents.
- *Navigational guides:* the graphical symbols and layout used to visually direct people along a prescribed navigational path for completing the questionnaire.

Accomplishing the first of these tasks requires ordering questions in the sequence they should be answered. It also requires placing any instructions or interpretative information at the precise location that information is needed, and therefore likely to be used. Accomplishing the second task involves manipulation of brightness, shape, size, and location of all the information so that respondents are visually directed to process words in the desired order. Details of this perspective are provided in Chapter 3.

Tailoring to the Situation

A major limitation of the original TDM was its one-size-fits-all approach to survey design. This approach, though seemingly appropriate to the times and the technology, did not allow social exchange considerations to be used to their fullest potential. For example, what constitutes a cost or reward also depends upon the survey content. Most surveys making several contacts within a period of seven to 10 days would produce considerable irritation. However, suppose that an individual has been asked to keep a diary of the television programs they watch for a specific week in the month. The following five contacts in 10-day sequence may not seem unusual to respondents: an introductory letter, followed quickly by a questionnaire, and then a postcard to tell them their "diary week is about to begin," a midweek call to see if they are having any difficulties, and another postcard indicating that their diary week is about over. This is similar to a sequence used for many national television viewing and other diary surveys. Receiving these contacts only a day or two apart probably makes sense to respondents because they have been asked to record their behavior each day for a specific week. Whereas sending a token financial incentive might seem like a good will gesture for an individual person survey, it could produce a quite different reaction if sent to a respondent for a business who envisions an ethical problem should she pocket even a tiny amount of money for responding to a business questionnaire. In this case, the token incentive seems likely to produce a sense of cost rather than reward to the recipient.

Some populations can only be given questionnaires if they are handed to them in person: for example, visitors to museums or parks. In other cases the pressure for quick results, as with election surveys, may leave only a narrow window in which data can be collected. In still other situations, some members of a population may be inaccessible by a single method of administration, so that mixed-mode surveys must be done whereby some respondents respond to a mail survey while others are interviewed by telephone.

The shift to Tailored Design attempts to shape elements of design and implementation in ways that take into account critical differences in survey populations, sponsorship, and content. It then builds on those differences in order to shape the most effective method for achieving a response.

In addition, it is easier to obtain responses from some survey populations than others. For example, in a large meta-analysis of response rates to previous surveys, Heberlein and Baumgartner (1978) showed that whereas school, army, or employee populations are more likely to respond to surveys, general public populations are less likely to respond to the same level of survey effort. Similarly, government sponsorship of surveys is likely to improve response, whereas market research sponsorship is correlated with lower response. It is more difficult for some people, particularly those with less education, to respond to a self-administered survey, and therefore the potential costs, such as the amount of effort required and the risk of embarrassment, are likely to be greater than for others. Whereas government organizations can often appeal to legitimate authority as a basis for responding and avoid the use of financial incentives, market research organizations generally have no such authority that can be used in their appeals for response, and may send sizable incentives as an alternative.

For a variety of reasons, some surveys are also more demanding of respondents than are others. In some cases the difficulty stems from the number of questions, and in others from the content of the questions. In the same meta-analysis noted above, Heberlein and Baumgartner (1978) showed that the salience of a survey, which they defined as topics dealing with important (to the respondent) behavior or current interests, is a significant determinant of response rates. Although interest-getting questions can be added and questions ordered and displayed in ways that make them appear more interesting, practices I advocate, there are limits to how much content can be modified in order to improve salience.

Survey content also interacts with survey sponsorship and population to influence how people are likely to view a particular survey and what response-inducing methods will work best. It is one thing for the U.S. Bureau of the Census to ask people to answer questions about personal income in the decennial census, but quite another for a market research company to ask the same questions on behalf of a sponsor whose name they are not willing to divulge. Similarly, appealing to employees of electric power plants to complete government surveys every month is a very different task, requiring different methods, than a one-time survey of members of a professional engineering association. Government-sponsored surveys can also make different appeals than can private corporations that are seeking feedback from customers.

SUMMARY OF TAILORED DESIGN

In sum, responding to a questionnaire is viewed as social exchange. People are seen as more likely to complete and return self-administered questionnaires if they trust that the rewards of doing so will, in the long run, outweigh the costs they expect to incur. This perspective is summarized in Figure 1.2. Many attributes of the questionnaire and implementation process that I have identified above incur potential costs and benefits, as well as giving trust messages. I also recognize that what constitutes a message of trust (or reward or cost) for some members of a survey population may not do so for others. Furthermore, the survey situation and sponsor may also convey different message through the study details. This, then, is the basis of Tailored Design—attempting to identify and utilize knowledge of sponsorship, the survey population, and the nature of the survey situation in an effort to maximize quality, and quantity of response.

The change in perspective from using one basic method for all survey situations in the original TDM to the tailoring of arguments to account for survey sponsorship, population, and content is the most distinguishing feature of Tailored Design. It is for this reason that the book is divided into two parts,

Figure 1.2 Schematic overview of the Tailored Design perspective.

A. **Tailored Design** is the development of survey procedures that create respondent trust and perceptions of increased rewards and reduced costs for being a respondent, which take into account features of the survey situation and have as their goal the overall reduction of survey error.

B. **Social exchange and respondent behavior:** Actions are motivated by the return these actions are expected to bring and in fact, usually do bring, from others. The likelihood of responding to the request to complete a self-administered questionnaire, and doing so accurately, is greater when the respondent *trusts* that the expected fix *rewards* of responding will outweigh the anticipated *costs*.

C. **Many aspects of questionnaire and implementation process can be shaped to create trust and influence the respondent's expectations for rewards and costs.**

To Establish Trust...

- Provide token of appreciation in advance
- Sponsorship by legitimate authority
- Make the task appear important
- Invoke other exchange relationships

To Increase Rewards...

- Show positive regard
- Say thank you
- Ask for advice
- Support group values
- Give tangible rewards
- Make the questionnaire interesting
- Give social validation
- Communicate scarcity of response opportunities

To Reduce Social Costs...

- Avoid subordinating language
- Avoid embarrassment
- Avoid inconvenience
- Make questionnaire short and easy
- Minimize requests to obtair personal information
- Emphasize similarity to other requests

D. **Exchange concepts** must be communicated visually (rather than verbally) through the use of visual design principles for the development of questionnaire and implementation materials.

E. **Knowledge** of survey population, sponsorship, and survey content must be considered in order to develop the most effective means for increasing rewards, reducing costs, and establishing trust.

F. **Successful Tailored Design seeks to reduce survey errors from coverage, sampling, measurement, and nonresponse.**

elements of theory and design that tend to cut across most survey situations in Part I, and the tailoring to different survey situations, such as population, content, and method of self-administration, in Part II.

SETTING EXPECTATIONS FOR YOUR SURVEY

The first edition of this book listed 48 mail surveys that had used the original Total Design Method, either mostly or entirely (Dillman, 1978). These surveys obtained response rates ranging from 58 to 92%, with an average of 74%. Those which were judged to completely use the TDM obtained response rates of 77% versus 71% for those that omitted certain components.

At the time the TDM for mail surveys was written, application of a companion TDM procedure for telephone surveys typically produced higher response rates, with 31 surveys averaging response rates of 91% (compared to 77% for mail). For both telephone and mail, response rates for general public populations were about 10% lower than for more specialized populations on which the methods were tested.

In the ensuing 20 years, response expectations for interview surveys have changed. As noted earlier, it is increasingly difficult to achieve high response rates for most nongovernmental telephone surveys, and impossible without greatly increasing the number of attempts—from the four to eight typically used at that time to perhaps 20 attempts today. Hox and de Leeuw (1994), in an analysis of changes in response rates over time, show that response rates have decreased for interview surveys; they are slightly higher for mail surveys than in the past.

My own impression of response rate changes for mail surveys is, first, that Tailored Design response rates similar to those obtained with the original TDM can be achieved, but that doing so generally requires using somewhat more intensive procedures, including token financial incentives and five contacts, one of which is done with special procedures such as telephone or priority (or courier) mail, as will be discussed in Chapter 4. Just as surveying by telephone methods now requires more intensive methods than in the past, including refusal conversion and many more contact attempts, the ability of mail to achieve response has benefited from additional efforts, such as the concerted use of token financial incentives. The response potential for other self-administered methods, particularly electronic ones, remains to be seen, but appears promising.

One of the challenges now being faced in survey design stems from conflicting pressures related to response rate and respondent burden. Some survey sponsors and oversight agencies, such as the U.S. Office of Management and Budget, require that very high response rates be achieved. At the same time, many institutional review boards have legitimate concerns about the manner in which individuals are contacted, the number of contacts made, and other survey procedures. One response to these requirements and concerns is to limit the use of multiple contacts and other procedures that questionnaire recipients or institutions may find objectionable. Thus, many surveys, including some of my own, are designed in a way that will inevitably produce lower response rates than might otherwise be obtained. The positive side is that surveyors now have an incentive to better understand issues related to costs, rewards, and trust as viewed by respondents to achieve the highest possible response rates from all segments of survey populations, while keeping the respondent burden as low as possible.

What you can expect for your own survey depends in part on the extent to which you follow the detailed procedures outlined in Part I of this book. It will also depend upon the constraints and possibilities associated with the particular survey population, the content of the survey, and survey sponsorship, as I will discuss for the tailored survey designs in Part II. Suffice it to say here that conducting self-administered surveys of any type is no longer an excuse for low response or poor measurement. In fact, in many situations, we expect their performance to exceed that which can be obtained by other survey modes.

SUMMARY

Tailored Design is a set of procedures for conducting successful self-administered surveys that produce both high quality information and high response rates. As defined earlier, it is the development of survey procedures that create respondent trust and perceptions of increased rewards and reduced costs for being a respondent, that take into account features of the survey situation, and that have as their goal the overall reduction of survey error. Its distinguishing feature is that rather than relying on one basic procedure for all survey situations, it builds effective social exchange through knowledge of the population to be surveyed, respondent burden, and sponsorship. Its goal is to reduce overall survey error, with particular emphasis on nonresponse and measurement.

The most important concept underlying Tailored Design has to do with applying social exchange ideas to understanding why respondents do or do not respond to questionnaires. Attributes of the questionnaire and implementation process, as identified in this chapter, result in both benefits and costs and also convey a message of trust. People are more likely to complete and return self-administered questionnaires if they trust that the rewards of doing so outweigh the costs they expect to incur. Further, what constitutes a message of trust (or reward or cost) to some members of the survey population may not do so for others.

Tailored Design is based on results from numerous experiments that either confirmed or failed to support the importance of certain elements of its predecessor, the Total Design Method, for certain types of surveys, as well as on new insights about how respondents read and respond to the visual aspects of questionnaire layouts and designs. It is also a result of lessons from hundreds of attempts to shape TDM procedures to improve survey quality.

Self-administered surveys are now ready to benefit from computer advancements through e-mail, posting on the World Wide Web, touch-tone data entry, and optical imaging of paper surveys. The advances of computerization that have so dramatically benefitted telephone interviewing in the 1980s and 1990s are now poised to benefit self-administered surveys as well. These applications were only vaguely imaginable when the typewriter/printing press procedures for the TDM were under development for the first edition of this book.

The two-part organization of this book reflects these developments and the need to tailor survey procedures. Part I describes the common procedures essential to all mail and most other types of self-administered surveys. Chapter 2 begins the discussion of measurement and presents 19 principles for writing questions. Although many principles are similar to those in use at the time of the first edition, others have been added to reflect the advancements that have occurred in our understanding of how people process and respond to various elements of questions.

Chapter 3 focuses on questionnaire construction. It includes traditional concerns about how to order questions and build easy-to-answer questionnaires. Most of the chapter is devoted to discussing principles that stem from advances in our understanding of how people decide what to read, the order in which they read it, and how these decisions can be influenced by visual layout and design. In Chapter 4, the focus changes to reducing nonresponse error, as procedures for implementation are discussed in detail. Part I concludes with Chapter 5, a brief discussion of coverage and sampling issues.

Part II begins with a discussion in Chapter 6 of mixed-mode surveys. Few issues have become so important to the design of modern surveys as researchers having more options (new electronic modes plus traditional telephone and mail) to link together in an effort to increase response and lower costs. The idea of unimode construction—writing questions that provide a comparable stimulus across all modes—is critical to the success of mixed-mode surveys.

Chapter 7 describes how the methods in Part I need to be tailored for delivery by means other than traditional mail. Personal delivery, group administration, and the possibility of distribution in periodicals are each considered here. Chapter 8 then reports ways of tailoring to time constraints when responses have to be obtained in a quick and timely manner. The focus of this chapter is on diaries, certain customer satisfaction surveys, and election prediction surveys.

Sponsorship by the government, the focus of Chapter 9, places special constraints on the conducting of self-administered surveys. Such sponsorship makes it difficult to use some response-inducing techniques (e.g., financial incentives), but also makes it possible to use others (e.g., legitimate authority). This chapter relies heavily on my experiences of designing and conducting numerous experiments aimed at improving the response to certain government surveys.

Chapter 10 reports a number of possibilities for conducting surveys in which the respondent reports for an organization and not himself. Large numbers of surveys of businesses and other organizations are conducted each year, posing challenges that require tailored solutions quite different than those discussed in other chapters.

Chapter 11 introduces the brave new world of conducting electronic surveys that simultaneously provides the greatest potential for future self-administration and the most difficult challenges. Tailoring procedures to the Internet and self-administration by telephone are both discussed in this chapter, providing much evidence that the nature of surveying is undergoing tremendous change.

Chapter 12 reports a specific but critical advance in the application of computer technologies to self-administered surveys. This is the advance from simple optical scanning of marks on questionnaires to imaging the entire questionnaire so that large quantities of questionnaires can be processed quickly but with great accuracy. A brief conclusion ponders the future of self-administration and its importance in the information age.

CHAPTER 2

Writing Questions

The goal of writing a survey question for self-administration is to develop a query that every potential respondent will interpret in the same way, be able to respond to accurately, and be willing to answer. However, in practice, producing good questions is often difficult.

A methodologist friend once described the question-writing task as similar to driving in freeway traffic while drinking a cup of hot coffee and answering an emergency call on his cell phone. Many things are competing for attention, and failure to heed any of them can spell disaster. It is the need to consider many competing things at once that makes it difficult to write questions for self-administered surveys. But unlike freeway driving while tending to coffee and telephone calls, which is not advisable, many things need to be considered when writing questions. Moreover, there is no alternative to understanding and dealing with each of the competing concerns that is addressed in this chapter.

Consider, for example, responses to the question, "How many hours per day do you typically study?" asked in a mail survey of university students (Rockwood, Sangster, and Dillman, 1997). As shown in Figure 2.1, different response categories, a high set and a low set, were used. Five of the six categories in the low set cover the same range of hours (less than 2½ per day) as that covered by only one of the six categories in the high set (Figure 2.1). Use of the low set resulted in 23% of the respondents reporting that they studied more than 2½ hours per day, compared with 69% when the high set was used. Clearly, the answers to this question were influenced by more than the words used to describe each response category.

Two other samples of students were interviewed by telephone for this experiment, with half being presented with each set of categories. Among those presented with the lower set of categories, 42% (compared to 23% by mail) reported studying more than 2½ hours per day. Thus, the choice of surveying by mail versus telephone also influenced people's answers. These results could

Figure 2.1 Low and high sets of categories used to ask students how many hours they 1) studied and 2) watched television each day, and the results (Rockwood, Sangster, and Dillman, 1997).

Version A (low) Categories	*Version B (high) Categories*
Less than .5 hour per day .5–1 hour 1–1.5 hours 1–2 hours 2–2.5 hours per day	Less than 2.5 hours
More than 2.5 hours	2.5–3 hours 3–3.5 hours 3.5–4 hours 4–4.5 hours More than 4.5 hours

	Version A (low)		Version B (high)	
Reported Hours/Day	Mail	Telephone	Mail	Telephone
Studying:				
2.5 hours or more	23%	42%	69%	70%
Less than 2.5 hours	77%	58%	31%	30%
Watching Television:				
2.5 hours or more	17%	17%	32%	31%
Less than 2.5 hours	83%	83%	68%	69%

have placed the surveyor in the unenviable position of reporting to the study sponsor that as few as 23% or as many as 70% of the students at this university were studying more than 2½ hours per day, depending upon which version of the questionnaire and survey method she wanted to believe. Unfortunately, the measurement challenge did not end here.

Another, nearly identical question included in these experimental surveys asked about how many hours each day students watched television. For this question the alternative sets of categories had similar effects on responses; 17% reported watching television 2½ hours or more per day in response to the low set, compared with about 32% when the high set was used. However, in contrast to the question about studying, whether the survey was done by mail or telephone made absolutely no difference in how many people selected each answer category.

Why did these results for the alternative sets of categories and the two questions differ so dramatically? Which answers should be trusted? In addition, how can you ever be sure that whatever questions are asked in surveys obtain answers that provide the best possible estimates of the distribution of the characteristic of interest in the population? These issues and more are the topics of this chapter. In the course of this discussion, I will return to the likely reasons that these questions produced such divergent answers. The purpose of this chapter is to provide principles, as well as specific tools, to help you write questions for self-administered surveys in ways that will produce answers you can trust.

CRITERIA FOR ASSESSING EACH SURVEY QUESTION

Survey questions fail in their purpose for many reasons, ranging from use of the wrong words or an inappropriate structure to simply not being answerable. In addition, a question that will work fine in one survey may not be satisfactory for another. Attempting to help hundreds of people, ranging from first-time surveyors to experienced methodologists, with their surveys leads me to conclude that too often sponsors have not figured out what they want to know from respondents, except in a general sort of way: "I want to know why people have such negative attitudes about. . . ." Other sponsors know fairly precisely the questions they want to ask, and still it is very difficult to progress from a list of draft questions to a set of *good* survey questions. Some questions are easy to write and ask, while others require draft after draft and much testing. Once a working draft of proposed survey questions and response choices (if any) has been prepared, ask each of the following eight inquiries about each of the proposed survey questions. Answers to these questions will help diagnose problems and guide you towards the structural and wording decisions that are appropriate for your study.

Question 1: Does the question require an answer?

A survey question is more than a general inquiry. It is the surveyor's tool for gaining responses from subjects in a survey sample that will make it possible to determine the distribution of a characteristic (an attitude, belief, behavior, or attribute of each respondent) in the survey population. In order for an inquiry to constitute a survey question, it must require an answer from each person to whom the question is asked. Neither of the following questions meet that criterion.

If you fixed dinner at home last night, did you eat meat as part of that meal?

❑ Yes
❑ No

When you go out to eat, which type of food do you most prefer?

- ❑ American
- ❑ Italian
- ❑ Chinese
- ❑ Other

A respondent who ate out the previous night could not answer the first question. A respondent who never eats out could not answer the second one. Use of the introductory words "if" or "when," invites some respondents not to provide an answer. Inasmuch as not all respondents are required to provide an answer to the above question, we cannot distinguish nonresponse from those to whom the question does not apply. Even if a "does not apply" box were provided, the wording of the first question implies that no response is needed from those who ate out the previous night. In addition, for us to be able to estimate the distribution of a characteristic in the sample and (through it) the population, respondents must be given the opportunity to answer every question they are asked.

Question 2: To what extent do survey recipients already have an accurate, ready-made answer for the question they are being asked to report?

Some survey questions are easier to get accurate responses for than are others. For example, virtually everyone knows their age. People are frequently asked how old they are (birthdays are special events in the lives of most people) and age is a number that people are expected to know. People are also able to report age accurately in response to many ways of asking the question, as shown in Figure 2.2. Assuming a willingness to report age, it does not make a lot of difference how the question gets asked. From the standpoint of expected precision of the answer, the question with three broad categories will, of course, obtain a less precise answer. However, from the perspective of whether the age question will be answered accurately, the choice of question structure makes little difference.

However, consider the other question shown in Figure 2.2, concerning whether tall people are more likely to be elected president. Most people do not have a ready-made answer that they can immediately report. Some might wonder what is meant by "more likely" in the stem of the question. Others might wonder what the difference is between "somewhat" and "strongly" in the answer choices. To answer, they not only have to give definition to the question and answer choices, but they may also try to recall the height of current and past presidents and the relative heights of their opponents. Some might spend a long time and think about a lot of presidents, while others think

Figure 2.2 Examples of questions to which respondents already have a ready-made answer (which produce accurate answers) versus one that asks about an informed opinion that produces inconsistent answers.

Respondent's age; the exact wording makes relatively little difference to response accuracy:

33. How old are you?

________Age

33. What is your current age?

________Years

33. When were you born?

________Year born

33. What is your date of birth?

___Day ___Month _____Year

33. Which of the following age category describes you:

- ☐ 35 or younger
- ☐ 36–65
- ☐ 66 or older

Respondent's opinion on issue for which wording changes produce substantial inconsistencies in response choice:

"Tall people are more likely to be elected President of the United States."

Do you strongly agree, somewhat agree, somewhat disagree, or strongly disagree with this statement?

(or) Do you very strongly agree, strongly agree, agree, disagree, strongly disagree, or very strongly disagree?

(or) On a scale of 1 to 7, where 1 means entirely agree and 7 means entirely disagree, use a number to indicate how strongly you agree or disagree.

only about the current president's height in relation to the opponent in the last election until a satisfactory answer is reached. Still others may not think about any specific presidents or candidates at all.

In contrast to the near automatic answer for a question about age, when people respond to broad opinion questions they must comprehend the question and answer choices and contemplate what each of them means. They must recall information about the topic, make a judgment about the information they retrieve from memory, and then report a response, a process that has been described in detail by Tourangeau (1992). Each of these stages is influenced by different contextual considerations and processes. People do not have ready-made responses to opinion and belief questions to nearly the same degree that they possess answers to questions about their educational level, the kind of car they drive, or whether they own their home. The vaguer the question, the vaguer the categories (e.g., using only numbers, as in a 1–7 scale), and the more remote these items are from people's experiences, the more likely a question is to produce inconsistent responses if we ask the same person to answer this question at different times.

Sometimes it is necessary to spend a lot of time drafting, writing, and testing alternative wordings of questions, and even then we can obtain only an approximate answer. In other instances, writing questions becomes a very easy task, requiring little time and effort.

Thus, a critical step towards writing good questions is to understand the extent to which respondents have an accurate, ready-made answer, and whether creating an answer demands considerable thought that is subject to myriad influences, including the context in which the question is asked. If people do not have a ready-made answer to a question, getting an accurate answer becomes more difficult.

Question 3: Can people accurately recall and report past behaviors?

Whereas abstract beliefs and attitudes are hard to measure, it would seem on the surface that people should be able to report past behaviors. However, that is not always the case.

Asking how many hours a person watched television on the first Sunday of the previous month is an example of a behavior that is hard to remember. Respondents are unlikely to be able to recall something so precise from that long ago. To solve this problem, surveyors often ask how many hours per day a person "usually" watches television, an example of which was provided at the beginning of this chapter. To answer, the respondent must recall what she "usually" does and estimate. Recalling the frequency of these routine or mundane behaviors is subject to considerable potential error, as evidenced by the effect of the category choices offered as part of the survey question (Rockwood et al., 1997). Asking people to reconstruct how much time they have spent studying or watching television in the last four hours, on the other hand, is less subject to unintentional error.

Frequently, people who write surveys want respondents to provide far more detail about past behaviors than can be recalled. Thus, determining whether people are able to recall information needed for answering each proposed survey question is important. Keeping recall simple and related to recent events helps to produce high quality survey data.

Question 4: Is the respondent willing to reveal the requested information?

The fact that respondents know an answer does not mean they are willing to provide it. Many respondents are reluctant to reveal certain information about themselves, for example, their income. Others may be unwilling to answer questions about previous drug use, or having shoplifted when they were teenagers.

Considerable evidence suggests that people are more likely to give honest answers to self-administered than to interview questionnaires (e.g., de Leeuw, 1992; Fowler, Roman, and Di, 1998; Aquilino, 1994). For example, when asked the question, "How often have you driven a car after drinking alcoholic beverages?" only 52% responded "never" to the self-administered questionnaire versus 63% for the comparable telephone survey (Dillman and Tarnai, 1991).

Although self-administered questionnaires are often selected because of respondents' greater honesty with their answers, there is little doubt that social desirability is somewhat of a problem for this method as well. A recent article suggests that young people responding to computers may provide more truthful answers than with self-administered questionnaires (Turner, Ku, and Rogers, 1998).

Question 5: Will the respondent feel motivated to answer each question?

Motivation to respond distinguishes self-administered from interview surveys dramatically, and in a way that counts. Designers of interview surveys often write questions independent of any motivational considerations, leaving it to the interviewer to encourage, cajole, or otherwise persuade respondents to carefully select and report complete answers. Unless consideration is given to how people react to questions in self-administered questionnaires, instructions may be ignored and incomplete answers given. Also, the question may be skipped or, even worse, the questionnaire not returned.

For example, questionnaires are sometimes constructed in a way that requires respondents to consult a separate instruction booklet to understand unclear questions. Questions are sometimes presented in matrices with row and column headings that must be connected in order to understand the question. Further, it may be impossible for the respondent to understand the question without consulting a separate instruction booklet to determine what is meant by each row and column heading. Thus, three widely separated items of information have to be connected by the respondent in order to figure out an appropriate answer. Another kind of question with adverse motivational qualities is one that asks people to rank a large number of items from top to bottom, such as a list of 20 "priorities for economic development."

Motivation can be encouraged in many ways, ranging from incentives and follow-up reminders to respondent-friendly questionnaire design. In some instances, the questions themselves are the source of a motivational problem and no matter how much one does with other aspects of survey design, wording remains a major impediment to accomplishing the survey objectives. Sometimes, modifying questions (e.g., stating them more clearly) or changing a ranking question to a rating question (e.g., asking the importance of each of the 20 economic priorities on a scale) will improve the likelihood of getting an answer.

Question 6: Is the respondent's understanding of response categories likely to be influenced by more than words?

Responses to the questions about studying and watching television presented at the beginning of this chapter were clearly influenced by more than words alone. Some respondents appeared to see a set of categories that were viewed as running from low to high. Choice of the highest category may have seemed appropriate to respondents who saw themselves as in the "top" group of TV watchers or studiers. Respondents faced with a situation in which they don't have an obvious answer may respond to these questions partly in terms of where they see themselves in relationship to other students, for example, "I study more than most, so I should choose one of the top categories." It is important to recognize that category ranges and visual layout (as discussed in the next chapter) also provide important clues used to select the appropriate answer. Words are only part of the question stimulus.

Attitudinal and belief questions typically rely on vague quantifiers, such as strongly favor to strongly oppose, high priority to low priority, agree to disagree, or even vaguer ones that rely on numbers such as –3 to +3, 1–7, or 1–10. Such numerical scales require respondents to give a certain amount of definition to any category they choose to use. The vaguer the question and answer categories, the greater the potential for measurement error.

Question 7: Is survey information being collected by more than one mode?

Increasingly, more than one survey mode is used to collect information for a single survey. This means that data collected by each mode needs to be comparable with that collected by another. An illustration is the fact that 42% of the telephone respondents versus only 23% of the mail respondents chose more than 2½ hours in response to the hours of study question posed at the beginning of this chapter (Figure 2.1).

It appears from the available research that several different kinds of mode differences may occur between self-administered and interview surveys (Dillman, Sangster, Tarnai, and Rockwood, 1996), and that the introduction of electronic survey technologies such as Interactive Voice Response, as discussed in Chapter 11, introduces even more challenges (Srinivasan and Hanway, 1999). However, several remedial actions, ranging from restructuring questions to changing question wording, can be done to minimize mode effects. For this reason, Chapter 6 is devoted entirely to the special challenges of mixed-mode surveys.

Question 8: Is changing a question acceptable to the survey sponsor?

Questions with recognized defects cannot always be changed. Sometimes a particular question has been used in another survey, and the main objective is to replicate the previous survey or make the new data comparable in some other way. Examples are government surveys that have asked the same question repeatedly in order to produce time-series data, sometimes for decades. In other instances the surveyor may be willing to accept a lower response rate or higher item nonresponse in an effort to get the more precise answers only some respondents are able to provide. This is a tendency of some economic surveys, when offering broad income categories is considered an unacceptable alternative to requesting exact income. Often sponsors want information about which respondents have virtually no knowledge and for which formulating a meaningful answer is difficult. Political considerations may also dictate the selection of question and answer categories. Thus, it is important to ask sponsors whether questions that appear troublesome are subject to change and if so, how much.

Writing questions is a difficult challenge precisely because so many factors simultaneously influence whether a proposed question obtains accurate answers. The eight questions listed here constitute the mental checklist I attempt to apply when, inevitably, surveyors asking for help thrust a draft in front of me and ask, "What do you think?" The search for tools and principles for writing questions is a means of overcoming each of these potential problems. This is the topic to which I now turn.

WHICH QUESTION STRUCTURE IS MOST APPROPRIATE?

Fundamentally, there are only three different ways a survey question can be structured. One way is to pose a query as an open-ended question, an item for which no answer choices are provided. The others provide answer choices which can, in turn, be structured as closed-ended in either of two ways—as ordered or unordered response categories. Shifting from one structure to another is the most fundamental tool available for responding to the kinds of problems suggested above.

Open-Ended Questions

An inability to get adequate answers to open-ended questions is often identified as a chief disadvantage of self-administered surveys. After all, there is no interviewer to respond to an unclear answer with a probe, such as, "Could you provide a little more detail so that I'm sure I understand what you mean?" However, the issue of whether questions that don't offer answer categories are acceptable for mail surveys is somewhat more complicated. Consider, for example, this open-ended question:

A. Why did you purchase a new automobile?

____________________________________ Reason for purchase

Answers to Question A are likely to be inadequate. This question will not elicit self-administered answers that are as complete as those offered in interview surveys when supported by interviewer probes. People don't necessarily have a ready-made answer to such a question in the way they do for such things as age, and the answers are prone to considerable unintentional error. Although the above question format could be improved somewhat by providing more space, perhaps 2–3 lines to visually suggest that a longer answer is desired, answers are not likely to be as complete as one would like. The fundamental problem with questions of this nature is that the answer depends upon the extent to which respondents are willing to think hard about the question and write a complete answer. In such cases a surveyor would be well advised to list possible reasons for buying a car and turn the question from open-ended to closed-ended.

When we have proposed that kind of solution, two counter arguments are often extended. One is that surveyors do not know what the possible reasons might be, so they cannot list them. Second, the question is viewed as "exploratory," that is, an attempt to get some idea of what reasons might exist, which in a future survey could be built into closed-ended formats. Thus, despite the shortcomings of this type of open-ended question, it is sometimes appropriate to use in self-administered surveys.

Question B is quite different from Question A.

B. What kind (make and model) of automobile do you currently drive?

_________________ Make _________________ Model of car

Most people can provide the make (e.g., Ford) and, to a lesser extent, the model (e.g., Taurus) of the car they drive. To list all possible makes and models would require an enormous amount of space and require that respondents search the list carefully to find their car. This type of open-ended question works quite well in self-administered surveys. I find it helpful when asking such questions to provide blank spaces followed by the units for reporting (here, make and model) rather than simply printing an unlabeled space.

At the beginning of this chapter, I noted the biasing effects that result from offering response categories for mundane characteristics such as hours of study or watching television. Asking these questions in an open-ended form with a blank space followed by units, for example, "________Hours/Day," is a better way to obtain accurate answers.

Frequently, when designing self-administered surveys we have been asked to elicit the respondent's occupation, as in Question C below.

C. What is your current occupation?

________________________________ Occupation

This question produces unacceptably vague answers. For example, a "building engineer" might be someone with a college degree in engineering or one who performs custodial services. When faced with the need to obtain occupational information in self-administered surveys, one solution is to break the question into multiple parts, as shown here:

What is your current occupation?

________________________________ Current occupation

What kind of work do you do?

________________________________ Kind of work

What is the name of your employer?

________________________________ Name of employer

Other specific queries, such as the amount of education one normally needs to perform this job, might be added to assure sufficient information for deriving an occupational code. In essence, this format builds in the kinds of probes that an interviewer might ask to get adequate information for understanding a respondent's occupation.

In sum, open-ended questions are frequently very useful in self-administered surveys, but their usefulness depends upon the nature of the questions as well as the way in which they are structured. Sometimes that means changing to an open-ended format, while in other instances it means avoiding it.

Closed-Ended Questions

Consider these two questions:

A. To what extent do you favor or oppose expanding the number of franchises operated by this company?

- ❑ Strongly favor
- ❑ Somewhat favor
- ❑ Neither favor or oppose
- ❑ Somewhat oppose
- ❑ Strongly oppose

B. Which one of the following do you think should be our company's highest priority?

- ❑ Opening more franchises
- ❑ Improving remuneration for current employees
- ❑ Expanding our product line
- ❑ Improving skills of existing employees through training

The first of these two questions provides respondents with a response scale and the answering task is to determine where one best fits on that scale. Thus, it consists of carefully ordered categories. The second question presents categories in no particular order, and respondents are asked to pick the one that best describes their opinion.

The mental effort needed for answering each of these questions is quite different. Whereas the first question requires envisioning a scale and figuring out where on that scale one fits, the other requires comparing each discrete category with the others, a task that usually is more difficult. Typically, questions with ordered categories consist of two basic concepts, with one presented in the stem of the question (expansion of franchises) and another in the answer choices (favor versus oppose). Questions with unordered categories may consist of many different concepts which must be evaluated in relation to each of the others. In addition to the question stem concept (top priority) the answer categories reveal four distinctly different concepts (alternative business goals) for consideration. Typically, closed-ended questions with unordered categories are more difficult for respondents to answer because of the amount of information that must be processed and about which decisions must be made. However, each type can be enormously useful in a self-administered questionnaire. They also provide quite different writing challenges.

Closed-Ended Questions with Ordered Response Categories

This type of question is most useful when one has a well-defined concept for which an evaluative response is wanted, unencumbered by thoughts of alternative or competing ideas. The list of scalar concepts that might be used to evaluate a concept or idea seems almost endless. Here are a few possibilities:

- Strongly agree to strongly disagree
- Very favorable to very unfavorable
- Excellent to poor
- Extremely satisfied to extremely dissatisfied
- High priority goal to low priority goal
- A complete success to a complete failure
- A scale of 1–7 (or 1–10 or 1–100) where 1 means lowest possible quality and 7 (or 10 or 100) means highest possible quality
- A scale of –3 to +3 where –3 means completely lacks this characteristic and +3 means completely exhibits this characteristic

These answer choices are frequently referred to as "vague quantifiers," a moniker that tells a lot about their measurement characteristics. Generally, these types of scales request answers the respondent may not have ready-made, and which are therefore subject to considerable measurement error. However, when a surveyor wants to obtain separate respondent evaluations of many different concepts (e.g., 20 possible areas for spending agency funds) and compare preferences across areas, there may be no alternative to this approach.

Using closed-ended, ordered categories of this nature involves making many decisions. One such decision is how many choices should be offered. A second decision is whether to label each choice and, if so, what to call it. The nature of these decisions and factors associated with making a decision can be illustrated by the experiences of two researchers who became dissatisfied with a community satisfaction measure then in common use (Andrews and Withey, 1976). The traditional four-choice scale shown below was quite common, but because most people tended to be "very satisfied," the clustering of answers into a single cell limited the analyses they could perform. The researchers extended the scale from four to seven answer categories, and relabeled them as shown in alternative B.

A. *Traditional Measure of Community Satisfaction*
How satisfied are you with your community?

❑ Very satisfied
❑ Somewhat satisfied
❑ A little satisfied
❑ Not at all satisfied

B. *Proposed Measure of Community Satisfaction*
How satisfied are you with the community where you live?

❑ Delighted
❑ Mostly satisfied

- ❑ Slightly satisfied
- ❑ Neither satisfied nor dissatisfied
- ❑ Slightly dissatisfied
- ❑ Mostly dissatisfied
- ❑ Terrible

The researchers were successful in dividing people's answers across more categories and accomplished their analytic objective, but they also produced a scale that has not been used much in the ensuing years. I suspect the reason for the lack of use is that the scale labels strike most potential users as a little strange. At first glance the scale appears to convey two distinct concepts, degree of satisfaction plus the delighted-terrible extremes, an inconsistency that one should try to avoid. Moreover, the combination seemed to be unclear to respondents. The intended use of responses may also make a difference with regard to the suitability of these items. If one plans to present results to community officials for discussions on community goals, there is some risk that the terms delighted and terrible might not be taken seriously in that discussion.

In order to appreciate another potential difficulty with this scale, I suggest that you pick up the telephone and ask a friend to allow you to interview him or her. Read the above questions out loud and then assess how easy it is for the scale to be read and comprehended, and whether you think the question is likely to be taken seriously. The movement towards telephone interviewing in the last few decades has encouraged people to use somewhat fewer categories and simplify their presentation to respondents for easier comprehension. Similarly, as discussed in Chapter 6, the need for unimode construction has led me to keep my scales simpler as opposed to more complex.

Simplicity has also been achieved by stripping scales of labels completely and asking people to place themselves on one to seven or other length scales. Most people can use such scales by telephone as well as in self-administered questionnaires. The disadvantage of doing so stems from removing a sense of meaning which a label gives to each point on a scale. One surveyor who frequently conducted policy surveys said he was comfortable going to a city council meeting to report, for example, that 30% of residents were somewhat satisfied with police protection and another 20% were completely satisfied, but did not feel at ease reporting that people were on average 3.1 on a four-point scale. The more abstract the concept and scale presented to respondents, the greater the potential for any given answer to have a less concrete meaning than when a word label is attached.

Closed-Ended Questions with Unordered Response Categories

Some questions that use unordered or nonscalar response categories, such as, "Do you rent or own your home?" are quite simple. However, choosing from among several or many categories is quite complex, as suggested by these two examples:

A. Show which of these six groups you feel should have the most and least influence in deciding whether the proposed community bypass should be built by putting a "1" in the box for most influence, "2" for second most influence, and so on until you have ranked all six choices:

- ❑ Local chamber of commerce
- ❑ State highway department
- ❑ The city council
- ❑ The mayor
- ❑ The voters
- ❑ Local businesses

B. If the highway bypass is to be built on one of these routes, which would you most prefer?

- ❑ A north route that starts west of the city at Exit 21 (Johnson Road) off Highway 30, crosses Division at North 59th Street, and reconnects to Highway 30 three miles east of the city at River Road.
- ❑ A modified north route that starts further west of the city at Exit 19, crosses Division at 70th Street, and reconnects to Highway 30 three miles east of the city at River Road.
- ❑ A south route that begins west of the city at Exit 19, crosses Division at South 24th Street, and reconnects to Highway 30 east of the city at River Road.

Responding to either of these questions requires considerable effort. The first question requires comparing six groups, then five, then four, and so forth to complete the ranking. The second question requires absorbing considerable detail, identifying differences between the choices, and then selecting the most preferred route. In both cases, providing answers requires considerably more effort to comprehend and decide how to answer than is usually the case for closed-ended questions with ordered categories. Yet these are precisely the types of question structures that can sometimes provide the most useful information to survey sponsors.

One of the challenges of writing questions of this nature is to keep the demand on respondents from getting out of hand. Each answer choice adds another concept which must be compared with other choices. Trying to provide detailed information on alternatives, as in the second example above, increases the likelihood of some small detail on a proposal being overlooked (e.g., the exact location of South 24th Street). On paper, a question that lists 15 items to be ranked from top to bottom may not look much more difficult than one which has only six items to be ranked, but the respondent demand is obviously far greater. If all 15 options need to be presented, then the question might be simplified by asking for a ranking of only the top three.

Partially Closed-Ended Questions with Unordered Response Categories

Sometimes a surveyor gets caught between feeling a need to list many categories, despite the difficulty, versus not allowing respondents to give their preferred answer.

Consider, for example, this question about college sports.

Which of the following is your favorite college men's sport?

- ❑ Football
- ❑ Basketball
- ❑ Track and field
- ❑ Baseball
- ❑ Other (Please specify: ________________________________)

Limiting choices to the first four alternatives means that some people will not be able to give the answer they want to provide. Trying to list all of the alternatives means a potential quagmire of making sure to list a huge array of minor sports, such as lacrosse, rugby, bowling, or rowing. Writing a partially open-ended question is a possible solution, but not one that lends itself well to the construction of variables for analysis. It is likely that fewer people will mention other choices if they are not listed. However, the open-ended responses might be analyzed separately to see which other sport is mentioned most often. The difficulty comes when one tries to make statements such as, "Respondents to this survey are 10 times as likely to say football is their favorite sport as they are to say bowling." Such statements cannot be defended because the stimulus of a bowling category was not offered to respondents. Another possible revision may be to change the wording of the question in a way that limits its scope only to the offered categories:

Of the four college men's sports listed below, which one do you most like?

- ❑ Football
- ❑ Basketball
- ❑ Track and field
- ❑ Baseball

In this case, the absence of the "other" category does not force people to give an answer which they think will be misinterpreted with respect to their favorite college sport.

Why is a working knowledge of different question structures important?

Survey sponsors often get locked into a type of question structure, making it much more difficult for them to accomplish their survey objectives. In some instances, they ask only open-ended questions because of concern about forcing people to choose from among alternatives. In other cases, I have been given a confusing mixture of good ideas in formats that intermingled ordered and unordered categories. For example, I was once asked to help a university committee that was preparing a questionnaire to evaluate a dean's performance. All of the questions they proposed were structured as closed-ended questions with unordered response categories, similar to the one shown in Figure 2.3.

The first question sought information about both leadership and innovation skills but seemed destined to produce results that were difficult to inter-

Figure 2.3 Restructuring a question to provide interpretable answers.

An uninterpretable confirmation of closed-ended ordered and unordered categories:

6. Which of these five statements best describes this dean:

- ☐ Innovative but lacking leadership qualities
- ☐ About the same on innovation and leadership qualities
- ☐ Stronger on leadership than innovation
- ☐ A born leader
- ☐ A real innovator

Revision—Ordered categories for each concept:

6. To what extent has the dean demonstrated strong leadership qualities?

- ☐ All of the time
- ☐ Most of the time
- ☐ Some of the time
- ☐ Seldom
- ☐ Never

7. To what extent has the dean demonstrated an ability to innovate?

- ☐ All of the time
- ☐ Most of the time
- ☐ Some of the time
- ☐ Seldom
- ☐ Never

Revision—Unordered categories that achieve head-to-head comparison of concepts:

6. Which one of the following do you feel best describes the dean?

- ☐ A strong leader
- ☐ A strong innovator
- ☐ Both a strong leader and innovator
- ☐ Neither a strong leader nor innovator

---

pret. The proposed solution was to break the question apart using both the ordered and unordered question structures, as shown in the first revision in Figure 2.3. Doing so allowed the committee to accomplish its stated objectives of finding out how faculty viewed the dean separately with regard to leadership and innovation skills, and also on which attribute she scored best.

An examination of questions posed about election candidates also illustrates how a knowledge of different kinds of question structures can help get information of greatest use to survey sponsors (Figure 2.4). When one thinks

Figure 2.4 Voting preference questions posed in four structural formats, appropriate to need.

Completely open-ended:

3. **Who would you most like to see elected President of the United States in the next election?**

   ______________________ Name of person I'd most like to see elected President of the United States

Closed-ended with scalar categories:

3. **For each of the following candidates, please tell how qualified you feel he or she is for becoming president:**

   Emma Cain:
   - ☐ Very well qualified
   - ☐ Fairly well qualified
   - ☐ Somewhat qualified
   - ☐ Somewhat unqualified
   - ☐ Not well qualified
   - ☐ Not at all qualified

   Etc.

Closed-ended with unordered categories:

3. **If the election for President were being held today, for which one of these candidates are you most likely to vote?**

   - ☐ Martha Holmes
   - ☐ David Badger
   - ☐ Harold Gurwell
   - ☐ John Williby

Partially closed-ended question:

3. **If the election for President of the United States were being held today, for whom are you most likely to vote?**

   - ☐ Laurel F. Lugar, Democrat
   - ☐ Charles Young, Republican
   - ☐ Other (Write in name of other choice) ______________________

of election surveys, it is usually expected that head-to-head questions, as represented by the third example listed here, will be used. However, when candidates have not yet declared, and the question of much interest is who has public visibility and exists in people's minds as a potential candidate, then a completely open-ended question may be the best type to ask. If one is thinking about "dimensions" of the candidate, perhaps as a campaign manager devising beneficial advertisements, knowing how one's candidate is perceived and how that differs from perceptions of other candidates would be enormously useful. The scalar question for asking how well qualified each candidate is to be president will provide a sense of "distance" between candidates rather than a comparison of who would be best and worst. The head-to-head comparison, or closed-ended unordered structure, would be of obvious use during an election campaign, providing feedback that is typically used to design campaign strategies. The partially open-ended question is of use when write-in candidates are involved in the race. Thus, each type of question has much usefulness for determining voting preferences.

Changing question structures in this way enables us to formulate appropriate questions for achieving survey objectives. Each type of question structure performs a role that no other type can achieve as well, making an understanding of question structure a fundamental tool for drafting acceptable survey questions.

PRINCIPLES FOR WRITING SURVEY QUESTIONS: THE COMBINING OF WORDS AND STRUCTURE

Words are the building blocks for all question structures, but deciding which words to use and in what order is far from simple. The wrong choice of words can create any number of problems, from excessive vagueness to too much precision, from being misunderstood to not being understood at all, and from being too objectionable to being uninteresting and irrelevant. No one would deny that it is important to find the right choice of words. However, making the right choice in any given situation and knowing when you have achieved it are issues on which agreement is far less likely.

Perhaps no one has summarized the dilemma of writing questions as elegantly as Stanley Payne (1951) nearly 50 years ago in *The Art of Asking Questions.* In one chapter he presents 41 versions of a single question before finding one that he considers acceptable for a survey. Even this question is cautiously labeled "passable," and the reader is admonished that pretesting might shoot this 41st version full of holes. The concluding chapter of the book summarizes Payne's rules for wording questions, with the subtitle of the chapter, "A Concise Check List of 100 Considerations," describing the surveyor's dilemma.

The rules, admonitions, and principles for how to word questions, enumerated in various books and articles, present a mind-boggling array of generally good but often conflicting and confusing directions about how to do it.

There is no shortage of simple admonitions on what to do and what not to do. For example:

- Use simple words
- Do not be vague
- Keep it short
- Be specific
- Do not talk down to respondents
- Avoid bias
- Avoid objectionable questions
- Do not be too specific
- Avoid hypothetical questions

The problem is that these "how to do it" rules often get in one another's way. "Use simple words" is usually good advice, but frequently interferes with advice to "keep it short." It is interesting, for example, to note that Payne's 41st version of the question mentioned previously expanded from only eight words to 28 as difficult words were changed to simple ones. Using simple words also increases the risk of talking down to the respondents rather than communicating with them at the same level. The well-founded advice not to be vague often produces questions that are too specific. The advice to keep questions from being too direct and therefore objectional sometimes results in not heeding the advice to avoid hypothetical questions. In addition, although biased wording is certainly to be avoided, it is precisely such questions that may be required for building many kinds of attitude scales.

The reason that seemingly good advice, taken literally, may turn out to be bad advice is that questions are not written in the abstract. Writing questions for a particular questionnaire means constructing them for a particular population, a particular purpose, and placement next to another particular question. Words that are too difficult for use with some populations may be perfectly acceptable for others. A question that is fairly vague may satisfy the exploratory objectives of one survey, but not the analytic ones of another. A question that makes little sense by itself may be quite clear when asked after the ones that precede it in the questionnaire. A list of admonitions, no matter how well intended, cannot be considered absolute. With these cautions in mind, the remainder of this chapter is devoted to principles I have found useful in making the wording and structural changes necessary for turning an initial draft of respondent queries into acceptable survey questions.

Principle 2.1: Choose simple over specialized words.

We begin by trying to find synonyms that are likely to be understood by more people, and substituting the first word for the second.

tired . . . . .exhausted
honest . . . . .candid
most important . . . . . . .top priority
free time . . . . .leisure
work . . . . .employment
brave . . . . .courageous
correct . . . . .rectify

When a word exceeds six or seven letters, chances are that a shorter and more easily understood word can be substituted, although it should not automatically be assumed that all shorter words are acceptable. For example, it would not be advisable to substitute "deter" for "discourage."

Next, we focus on words that can be simplified only by using combinations of shorter words:

people who live here . . . . .occupants of this household
your answers . . . . .your responses to this questionnaire
what you do after school . . . . .post-school extracurricular activities
job concerns . . . . .work-related employment issues
area of the county . . . . .subnational region

In addition, we search for specialized words or abbreviations that are commonplace for the survey sponsor, but require some translation for survey respondents. Such terms are especially prevalent in government surveys. For example:

Oil inventory questionnaire . . . . . .Form 822
Bureau of Labor Statistics . . . . .BLS

Sometimes it is unnecessary to find substitutes for what appear to be difficult words. Virtually all occupational groups share a particular vocabulary that is not understood by outsiders. The use of such a vocabulary facilitates efficient communication, and the use of simpler words would only confuse matters. In a survey of city planners it seems quite reasonable to talk about "annexation" instead of "an addition." Similarly, in a survey of physicians it seems reasonable to talk about "pharmaceutical companies" instead of "companies that sell medicines." To do otherwise may even suggest a lack of knowledge and understanding of the topic of the survey.

However, the fact remains that people who write questionnaires are far more likely to overestimate than underestimate the knowledge and vocabulary of respondents. Thus, when in doubt, it is prudent to use the simpler of the available alternatives. A thesaurus is an indispensable tool for finding synonyms that might be used. In addition, there is no substitute for asking someone with less education than the survey designer to go through a questionnaire and identify words that are confusing. Pretesting with actual respondents is also very important, because it helps the surveyor identify the commonly shared vocabulary of the study population.

Principle 2.2: Choose as few words as possible to pose the question.

At first glance this goal may seem to contradict the frequent necessity of using several words as a substitute for a single, more complex word. That is the reason I place this goal second, rather than first. Initially, we must be sure that any words we choose are understood by virtually all respondents. Having done that, we attempt to keep questions short. Consider the following example tested for a U.S. Census questionnaire:

> How many people were living or staying at this residence on Saturday, March 3rd, 2000? To make sure each person in the United States is counted only once, it is very important to:
>
> > **Include** everyone who lives here whether related to you or not, and anyone staying temporarily who has no permanent place to live;
> > **But not include** anyone away at college, away in the Armed Forces, in a nursing home, hospice, mental hospital, correctional facility, or other institution.

A cognitive test of this question resulted in one respondent appearing somewhat embarrassed. He then said, "I don't have any idea how many people live in the United States." As a result of this and other interviews, the well-intentioned second sentence that explained the importance of the inclusion/exclusion definition was removed (Dillman and Allen, 1995).

The problem with long questions stems from the fact that when people read questions they attempt to be efficient, thus giving uneven attention to each word. Important words get missed and unimportant ones sometimes receive undue emphasis, especially when the questionnaire language is a second language for some of the respondents.

Figure 2.5 shows a question in which the answer categories are given in the stem of the question and listed separately below. Such redundancy across many questions is a particularly strong indicator to respondents that it is okay to skip words, and may result in the rest of the sentence also being unevenly read. Redundancy can be eliminated easily by not including the answer choices as part of the question stem. However, the problematic version would be appropriate in an interview questionnaire when only the question stem would be read to each respondent.

Figure 2.5 Encouraging even-reading through reduction of redundancy while maintaining a complete sentence format.

Problem:

17. Do you strongly favor, somewhat favor, somewhat oppose, strongly oppose, or have no opinion on whether advertisers should be required to have advertising aimed at children approved by a national board?

- ☐ Strongly favor
- ☐ Somewhat favor
- ☐ Somewhat oppose
- ☐ Strongly oppose
- ☐ No opinion

A revision:

17. Which of the following best describes the extent to which you favor or oppose requiring advertisers to have advertising aimed at children approved by a national review board?

- ☐ Strongly favor
- ☐ Somewhat favor
- ☐ Somewhat oppose
- ☐ Strongly oppose
- ☐ No opinion

PRINCIPLE 2.3: USE COMPLETE SENTENCES TO ASK QUESTIONS.

It is tempting to meet the goal of minimizing words by using incomplete sentences for surveys. It is true that few people will misunderstand, "Your name," or even "Age." However, the series of questions in Figure 2.6 once caused many respondents to provide erroneous answers to the second and third questions. Nearly 20% of the respondents listed the number of years they had lived in the city or town and the county. In addition, several other respondents listed "U.S." for *county,* a word which is only one letter different from *country.* Writing each question as a complete sentence would have helped solve both problems. In addition, county is changed to Idaho County in order to minimize the possibility of listing the United States as the respondent's county of residence.

Government-sponsored business surveys are some of the most frequent violators of this principle, a topic discussed in more detail in Chapter 10.

PRINCIPLE 2.4: AVOID VAGUE QUANTIFIERS WHEN MORE PRECISE ESTIMATES CAN BE OBTAINED.

The ease of using the same categories for many different kinds of questions has led to a tendency to use vague quantifiers when more precise an-

Figure 2.6 Ask questions as complete sentences.

Problem:

30. Number of years lived in Idaho

______________Years

31. Your city or town

______________City or Town

32. Your county

______________County

A revision:

30. How many years have you lived in Idaho?

______________Years

31. In what city or town do you live?

______________City or Town

32. In what Idaho county do you live?

______________Idaho County

swers can easily be obtained. Consider, for example, the question about attendance at religious services in Figure 2.7. Although it is likely that an answer to this question can easily be provided, enormous variation may exist in what respondents mean by their answers. In some religions, "regularly" implies once a week, whereas in others it may imply several times daily.

Also, the standard for regular attendance within religions may vary among respondents. For example, among adherents to a Christian religion, one person may think of regularly as implying at least once or twice a week, whereas another member of the same religion may think that annual attendance at holiday services, such as Christmas and Easter, implies regular attendance. Changing answer categories to numerical amounts, as shown in the revision, eliminates the possibility of widely varied interpretations for regular or occasional attendance.

Figure 2.7 Avoid vague quantifiers when more precise estimates can be obtained.

Problem:

26. How often did you attend religious services during the past year?

- ☐ Never
- ☐ Rarely
- ☐ Occasionally
- ☐ Regularly

A revision:

26. How often did you attend religious services during the past year?

- ☐ Not at all
- ☐ A few times
- ☐ About once a month
- ☐ Two to three times a month
- ☐ About once a week
- ☐ More than once a week

PRINCIPLE 2.5: AVOID SPECIFICITY THAT EXCEEDS THE RESPONDENT'S POTENTIAL FOR HAVING AN ACCURATE, READY-MADE ANSWER.

Nearly as troublesome as too much vagueness is the request for too much specificity. Figure 2.8 asks respondents to list the number of books they have read for leisure during the past year. Most people will have a reasonable idea of how many books they have read, but cannot list a precise number for such a long period of time. As a result, some people may simply make a reasonable guess. It is also likely that the open-ended question will elicit a high-item nonresponse because the respondent is not able to offer a precise answer. One solution to this problem is to provide answer categories, as shown in the first revision.

However, because people sometimes respond to the position of the categories as well as the category labels, great care should be taken to determine whether categories are needed and which ones are appropriate. As discussed at the beginning of this chapter, widely varied estimates of the number of hours students reported studying were obtained by varying the size of categories. Thus, people who think they read more than most people might pick the top categories regardless of the labels. Selecting categories on the basis of a pretest and other known characteristics of a population may help the surveyor make the middle categories correspond to the average numbers of books read by the survey population. This example illustrates one of the significant problems associated with simply taking question and answer choices from a survey of one population and using them for another.

Figure 2.8 Avoid specificity that exceeds respondent's potential for having an accurate ready-made answer.

Problem:

12. About how many books have you read for leisure during the past year?

_________ Number of books

A revision:

12. About how many books have you read for leisure during the past year?

- ☐ None
- ☐ 1-2
- ☐ 3-5
- ☐ 6-10
- ☐ 11 or more

Another revision with more appropriate categories for a population of heavy readers:

12. About how many books have you read for leisure during the past year?

- ☐ less than 10
- ☐ 11-25
- ☐ 26-50
- ☐ 51-75
- ☐ 76 or more

PRINCIPLE 2.6: USE EQUAL NUMBERS OF POSITIVE AND NEGATIVE CATEGORIES FOR SCALAR QUESTIONS.

The fact that respondents draw information from the number of categories as well as from labels means that the midpoint for number of categories can easily be interpreted as the neutral point. Figure 2.9 shows an example drawn from a customer satisfaction survey in which three positive (satisfied) categories were used but only one negative (dissatisfied) category was used. Thus, the visual midpoint on the scale became "somewhat satisfied."

When a recommendation was made to change this format, it was met with objections from the survey sponsor. She pointed out that far more people who responded were satisfied than dissatisfied. Further, she felt that the most important goal of the survey was to obtain significant gradations of satisfaction, a situation similar to that which prompted development of the delighted—terrible scale discussed earlier in this chapter. The solution in this case was simply to add additional categories in a second revision, which then

Figure 2.9 Use equal numbers of positive and negative categories for scalar questions.

Problem:

25. How satisfied were you with the service you received when you bought your air conditioner?

- ☐ Completely satisfied
- ☐ Mostly satisfied
- ☐ Somewhat satisfied
- ☐ Neither satisfied nor dissatisfied
- ☐ Dissatisfied

A revision:

25. How satisfied were you with the service you received when you bought your air conditioner?

- ☐ Completely satisfied
- ☐ Somewhat satisfied
- ☐ Neither satisfied nor dissatisfied
- ☐ Somewhat dissatisfied
- ☐ Completely dissatisfied

Another revision to maintain gradations of satisfaction:

25. How satisfied were you with the service you received when you bought your air conditioner?

- ☐ Completely satisfied
- ☐ Mostly satisfied
- ☐ Somewhat satisfied
- ☐ Neither satisfied nor dissatisfied
- ☐ Somewhat dissatisfied
- ☐ Mostly dissatisfied
- ☐ Completely dissatisfied

allowed the three levels of satisfaction to be distinguished from one another while the scale remained balanced.

PRINCIPLE 2.7: DISTINGUISH UNDECIDED FROM NEUTRAL BY PLACEMENT AT THE END OF THE SCALE.

Sometimes attitudinal questions are posed without giving the option of a neutral opinion or no opinion at all. In other cases, researchers prefer to al-

Figure 2.10 Distinguish undecided from neutral by placing this category at end of scale.

Problem:

8. To what extent do you agree or disagree with this statement: "Living in rural places is better for a person's emotional health."

- ☐ Strongly agree
- ☐ Somewhat agree
- ☐ Undecided
- ☐ Somewhat disagree
- ☐ Strongly disagree

A revision that distinguishes meaning of undecided from neutral:

8. To what extent do you agree or disagree with this statement: "Living in rural places is better for a person's emotional health."

- ☐ Strongly agree
- ☐ Somewhat agree
- ☐ Somewhat disagree
- ☐ Strongly disagree
- ☐ Undecided

Another revision to allow both neutral and no opinion responses:

8. To what extent do you agree or disagree with this statement: "Living in rural places is better for a person's emotional health."

- ☐ Strongly agree
- ☐ Somewhat agree
- ☐ Neither agree nor disagree
- ☐ Somewhat disagree
- ☐ Strongly disagree
- ☐ No opinion

---

low for no opinion in order to distinguish true opinion holders from those who are being "forced" to choose on a topic to which they have given little or no thought.

If an "undecided" category is offered to respondents, it makes a great deal of difference where that category is placed. An experiment by Willits and Janota (1996) compared the first and second alternatives shown in Figure 2.10 for presenting an undecided choice to respondents. When undecided was placed in the middle, respondents were consistently more likely (across 13 items) to use that category. On average, the percentage of respondents using it more than doubled, from 5 to 13%. When the answer was placed in the last position (first revision), respondents were more likely to select one of the directional opinion categories. Thus, it appeared that when placed in this end position, "undecided" responses were being separated from neutral opinions. This revision appears to pick up some of the desirable features of both of the other scales, providing less of an invitation to avoid a directional response while still providing an opportunity for people who have no opinion to say so.

Another alternative is provided by the second revision, offered in Figure 2.10. It allows respondents to report being neutral on the issue, but also allows for having no opinion at all. The middle and final categories are carefully worded; "Neither agree nor disagree" and "No opinion" are used to make the meaning of choices as clear as possible.

PRINCIPLE 2.8: AVOID BIAS FROM UNEQUAL COMPARISONS.

Closed-ended questions with unordered categories may become unbalanced, albeit for somewhat different reasons than in the case of scalar questions as discussed under Principle 2.6. In these questions, the topic of the question appears in the answer choice. Consider the wording of the question in Figure 2.11, designed to find out whom respondents think is most responsible for outbreaks of violence in schools. The terms "irresponsible" places a value connotation on the first category that is not present in the other choices. Although it is unclear whether unbalancing questions in this way leads to more or less frequent selection of such categories (Schuman and Presser, 1981), the credibility of responses to such questions is inevitably open to question.

The difficulty of revising such questions is that true balance may be extremely difficult to achieve. The first revision uses less emotionally charged words, "The way children are raised by parents," but results in a category with many more words than the school and television choices. The last two categories could be made more specific by mentioning school discipline policies and violent television programs, but it is unclear without extensive pretesting whether that would improve or detract from the balance. The challenge of achieving balance on such closed-ended questions often leads to reducing choices to simple nouns (parents, schools, television), a solution that also increases the vagueness of the categories. One might, for example, wonder what aspect of television is being referenced: its use in schools, how much television students watch, or the content of the programming. Still another revision that might be considered is to completely restructure the question, converting to a closed-ended ordered question with a detailed concept presented in the stem of the question, as shown in the final revision offered in Figure 2.11.

Figure 2.11 Avoid bias from unequal comparisons.

Problem:

19. Which one of the following do you feel is most responsible for recent outbreaks of violence in America's schools?

- ☐ Irresponsible parents
- ☐ School policies
- ☐ Television programs

A revision:

19. Which one of the following do you feel is most responsible for recent outbreaks of violence in America's schools?

- ☐ The way children are raised by parents
- ☐ School policies
- ☐ Television programs

Another revision (simplest form):

19. Which one of the following do you feel is most responsible for recent outbreaks of violence in America's schools?

- ☐ Parents
- ☐ Schools
- ☐ Television

Still another revision (retaining more complex descriptions):

19. To what extent do you feel that the way children are raised by parents is responsible for recent outbreaks of violence in America's schools?

- ☐ Completely responsible
- ☐ Mostly responsible
- ☐ Somewhat responsible
- ☐ Not at all responsible

And so forth for the remaining concepts.

PRINCIPLE 2.9: STATE BOTH SIDES OF ATTITUDE SCALES IN THE QUESTION STEMS.

It is tempting to reduce the number of words in questions by mentioning only one side of an attitude scale when posing a question. For example, the question in Figure 2.12 asks the extent to which people agree with a statement, leaving out any mention of disagreement. Structured in this way, the question may encourage people to think of a scale ranging from "not at all" to "strongly

Figure 2.12 State both sides of attitude scales in question stems.

Problem:

14. To what extent do you agree with this statement: "It's easier for people to find work in this community than it was about one year ago."

- ☐ Strongly agree
- ☐ Somewhat agree
- ☐ Somewhat disagree
- ☐ Strongly disagree

A revision:

14. To what extent do you agree or disagree with this statement: "It's easier for people to find work in this community than it was about one year ago."

- ☐ Strongly agree
- ☐ Somewhat agree
- ☐ Somewhat disagree
- ☐ Strongly disagree

Another revision, to avoid acquiescence:

14. Do you feel it is easier, the same, or more difficult for people to find work in this community than it was about one year ago?

- ☐ Easier
- ☐ The same
- ☐ More difficult

---

agree." Substituting "agree or disagree" conveys to the respondent that the scale has a greater range. It also lets the respondent know that disagreement is an acceptable answer. Mentioning both sides of a scale is even more important when the terminology of a scale changes from one end to another, as it would for a scale that goes from "strongly favor" to "strongly oppose."

However, one of the shortcomings of agree/disagree is that there is a cultural tendency in many societies for people to agree rather than disagree, or to acquiesce in their responses. Consequently, the second revision, which maintains the use of closed-ended ordered categories but changes to an "easier, the same, more difficult" format, would seem to be a better solution.

PRINCIPLE 2.10: ELIMINATE CHECK-ALL-THAT-APPLY QUESTION FORMATS TO REDUCE PRIMACY EFFECTS.

In an effort to reduce respondent burden, queries containing unordered response categories are sometimes structured as "check-all-that-apply" items,

Figure 2.13 Eliminate the use of check-all-that-apply question formats.

Problem:

27. Which of the following characteristics would you like to see your child develop as he/she grows up? Please check all that apply.

- ☐ An interest in sports
- ☐ An interest in music
- ☐ An appreciation of art
- ☐ An interest in science
- ☐ An interest in business

A revision:

27. Is each of the following characteristics one that you would like for your child to develop as he/she grows up?

An interest in sports	Like	Not like
An interest in music	Like	Not like

Etc.

Another revision:

27. To what extent would you like or not like for your child to develop each of these characteristics as he/she grows up?

An interest in sports	Very Great Extent	To Some Extent	A Small Extent	Not At All
An interest in music	Very Great Extent	To Some Extent	A Small Extent	Not At All

Etc.

Still another revision:

27. Which of these qualities would you most like for your child to develop when he/she grows up? Put a 1 in the box for most like, 2 in box for second most like, and go on until you have ranked all five qualities.

An interest in sports .... ☐

An interest in music .... ☐

Etc.

as shown in Figure 2.13. Questions of this nature do not meet our criterion of being a survey question; that is, requiring a response to each stimulus. It has been observed that respondents tend to "satisfice" in answering many types of survey questions (Krosnick, Narayan, and Smith, 1996). This type of question is no exception, as respondents begin checking answers and go down the list until they feel they have provided a satisfactory answer. Although certain respondents will read and consider each answer, others will not. As respondents proceed down the list they may feel that "enough" has been done. Thus, the items listed first are more likely to be checked.

In recent years, considerable research has emerged suggesting that respondents to self-administered surveys are more likely to exhibit a primacy effect; that is, a tendency to select from among the first answers presented. Interview respondents are more likely to exhibit a recency effect; that is, a tendency to select from among the last answers mentioned (Krosnick and Alwin, 1987; Schuman and Presser, 1981). Data to support this hypothesis are inconsistent. In particular, an examination of 84 separate mail and telephone experiments conducted by nine investigators showed no systematic effects in either direction (Dillman et al., 1995). Recency effects were nearly as likely to occur in mail surveys as telephone, and vice versa.

The original argument for the existence of primacy effects was based on the presentation of a list of items given to respondents in an interview survey; respondents were more likely to pick answers from items early in the list. I suspect that primacy effects, to the extent that they occur, are most likely to happen when self-administered respondents exercise a satisficing behavior and stop reading the list, as they seem invited to do in "check-all-that-apply" items. Consequently, our first revision shown in Figure 2.13 simply provides a like/not like choice for each item. Two other revisions are also shown, both of which, in addition to requiring an answer for each item, increase the amount of information obtained from each respondent. The second revision uses a rating scale for each item, and the third revision uses a ranking question. Although the latter option is workable for five items, it is less acceptable as the number of items increases. Any of the three revisions is much preferred over the original format.

PRINCIPLE 2.11: DEVELOP RESPONSE CATEGORIES THAT ARE MUTUALLY EXCLUSIVE.

The image that often comes to mind when one discusses the lack of mutually exclusive categories is that a clerical error has been made, as in age categories like these: 35 or less, 35–50, 50–65, and 65 and over. Although the overlap is minor, it can be very annoying to people who happen to fall on the line.

In some instances we have seen deliberate, though minor, overlap created when attempting to ease the task of the respondent. For example, income categories of less than $15,000, $15,000 to $19,999, $20,000 to $29,999, $30,000 to $39,999, and greater have sometimes been changed so that the latter categories read $15,000 to $20,000, $20,000 to $30,000, etc. The latter categories are much easier for interviewers to read than the former ones, and make virtually no difference in the ability of respondents to choose an appropriate category. The sensitivity of reporting income is such that the gain from ease of reading (especially for interviews) probably outweighs the mutual exclusivity concern about the few people whose incomes happen to fall exactly on the dividing line.

Our main concern with mutual exclusivity is when it is used for response categories of survey questions, where there is considerable likelihood that its presence will go unnoticed. Figure 2.14 shows a question in which respondents have been asked to choose one answer to the question of how they learned about a disaster, but choices combine sources as well as location. The revision simply breaks the question into two parts, one about source and the other about location.

Mutual exclusivity provides yet another reason for avoiding check-all-that-apply question formats. If people can check more than one category in the example used in Figure 2.15, it might be reasoned that mutual exclusivity is not a problem. However, Israel and Taylor (1990) have reported experimental results that provide further evidence that check-all-that-apply questions create difficulties for surveys. The check-all-that-apply question about forages fed to cattle in winter months (Figure 2.15) was asked in a survey of Florida beef producers. The answer categories for this question were presented in different orders with quite different results.

Switching the "native range" to fourth on the list decreased the proportion

Figure 2.14 Develop response categories which are mutually exclusive.

Problem:

7. From which one of these sources did you first learn about the tornado in Derby?

- ☐ Radio
- ☐ Television
- ☐ Someone at work
- ☐ While at home
- ☐ While traveling to work

A revision:

7. From which one of these sources did you first hear about the tornado in Derby?

- ☐ Radio
- ☐ Television
- ☐ Another person

8. Where were you when you first heard about it?

- ☐ At work
- ☐ At home
- ☐ Traveling to work
- ☐ Somewhere else

Figure 2.15 Results from check-all-that-apply question that stems from the lack of mutual exclusivity (Israel and Taylor, 1990).

Question: Which of the following forages are used during the winter months to feed your cattle? (Check all that apply.)

First Order ▼	Category ▼	Percent Selected ▼	Second Order ▼	Percent Selected ▼
1	Native range	70%	(4)	30%
2	Deferred grazing (save pasture for fall and winter)	37	(2)	48
3	Hay	84	(5)	79
4	Silage	1	(1)	2
5	Winter pasture	29	(3)	36
6	Other	14	(6)	15

checking that answer from 70% to only 30%, more than a 40% drop. Winter pasture and deferred grazing, which were moved to the third and second positions respectively, both experienced increases. The likely reason for this change is that "native range" is such a broad category that when listed in the first position, respondents who would otherwise have chosen winter pasture or deferred grazing picked it and then mentally subtracted that from the answers they would have otherwise given. Silage, on the other hand, which was switched from fourth to first position, obtained the same proportion of answers both times. This type of livestock feed is distinctively different from any of the other pasture choices.

Another question in this survey that was sponsored by the Agricultural Extension Service asked respondents to check information sources on a list to indicate where they obtained information about beef production and management (Israel and Taylor, 1990). In response, 59% checked "extension agent" when it was presented first on the list versus only 41% when it was mentioned in third position behind "other cattlemen" and "fertilizer and other salesmen." We suspect that the social desirability of indicating Extension (the survey sponsor) as a source of information encouraged this response. It is also possible that the extension agent may have presented information at a meeting attended by other cattlemen and salesmen. The work by Israel and Taylor (1990) underscores the importance of being alert to mutual exclusivity concerns.

PRINCIPLE 2.12: USE COGNITIVE DESIGN TECHNIQUES TO IMPROVE RECALL.

One of the difficulties with many self-administered surveys is that respondents answer questions quite rapidly, spending as little time as possible deciding what answer to choose. Although it is sometimes suggested that an advantage of self-administered questionnaires is that respondents can take their time in completing them and therefore give more thoughtful answers, we know of no evidence to support that as being the typical response behavior (Dillman and Tarnai, 1991).

In addition, Jobe and Mingay (1989) have reported for interview surveys that recall accuracy on visits to health providers can be improved from 41% to 53% by asking about details of the visit. For example, people can be asked who the health care provider was and how they got to the office. Respondents who are asked to recall such visits over a specified period of time, such as the last six months, can also be asked to reconstruct a calendar of important events in their life (e.g., vacations, weddings, etc.) over this period of time before asking about visits to their doctor.

Figure 2.16 shows a quick recall format and cognitively-designed alternative for reporting seat belt use in a survey conducted shortly after a law was passed in Washington state requiring seat belt use, when it was reasoned that people might forget to wear seat belts when starting on a trip in their vehicle, but buckle-up along the way (Dillman and Tarnai, 1991). Use of this cognitively-designed format produced significantly different responses than did the quick recall format; moving people away from a generalized response about the proportion of time the respondent typically wore a seat belt was therefore thought to improve the accuracy of responses.

Although I believe that a cognitive recall sequence of questions has much potential for improving the accuracy of people's responses to survey questions, its use for all questions would result in increased length of questionnaires, not to mention the greater tediousness of responding. Thus, I tend to reserve its use for the most important survey questions—those for which the most accurate estimates of behavior must be made.

Principle 2.13: Provide appropriate time referents.

Respondents are frequently asked to report whether or how often they have engaged in a particular behavior during a recent period of months or years. There are several distinct problems associated with the use of time referents in surveys. First, memory tends to fade and people usually do not categorize information by precise month or year periods. Even if they try very hard to remember, estimating behaviors over a period of the last three years (as suggested by the first example in Figure 2.17) may be impossible. Some people may end up not being able to make a meaningful distinction. One solution, which may or may not be acceptable for some studies, is to shorten the time period and use a cognitive recall set of questions prior to asking for an answer.

Another type of problem is when something is too regular and mundane in life, such as studying, watching television, or eating away from home, as

Figure 2.16 Use cognitive design techniques to improve respondent recall.

Problem:

10. Next, we would like to ask about the most recent time you drove or rode anywhere in an automobile or other vehicle such as a pickup or van. During this most recent ride, would you say that your seatbelt was fastened...

- ☐ All the time; that is, every minute the car was moving
- ☐ Almost all the time
- ☐ Most of the time
- ☐ About half the time
- ☐ Less than half the time
- ☐ Not at all during the time the vehicle was moving

(Question repeated for second and third most recent rides)

A revision:

10. Next, we would like to ask you to please think about the last three times you drove or rode in a car or vehicle such as a pickup or van.

First, when was the last time you drove or rode in a motor vehicle?

- ☐ Today
- ☐ Yesterday
- ☐ Sometime before that

11. Could you tell us generally where this most recent trip began and where it ended?

12. About how long was this trip?

- ☐ Less than a mile
- ☐ One to five miles
- ☐ Longer

13. During this trip were you the...

- ☐ Driver
- ☐ A front seat passenger
- ☐ A back seat passenger
- ☐ Other

14. During this trip, would you say your seatbelt was fastened...

- ☐ All the time; that is, every minute the car was moving
- ☐ Almost all the time
- ☐ Most of the time
- ☐ About half the time
- ☐ Less than half the time
- ☐ Not at all during the time the vehicle was moving

(Repeat entire sequence for second and third most recent trips)

asked about in the second set of questions. A potential solution in these situations is to switch from asking people for a count to asking for a general estimate of how many times they eat a meal away from home in an average week. Faced with this problem, we have sometimes observed questionnaires in which intervals such as "the last three days" are used. This choice is usually unacceptable inasmuch as some activities, such as eating away from home,

Figure 2.17 Provide appropriate time referents.

Problem:

4. How many times in the last three years have you gone to see a doctor or other health care practitioner?

___________ Number of visits in last three years

A revision with shorter time referent:

4. How many times in the last six months have you gone to see a doctor or other health care practitioner?

___________ Number of visits in last six months

Problem:

11. How many times in last six months have you eaten away from home?

___________ Number of times in last six months

A revision that uses an estimation strategy:

11. On average, how many times per week do you eat a meal away from home?

___________ Average number of times per week

Problem:

22. How many times have you played golf so far this year?

___________ Number of times played this year

Revision to take into account different return dates for questionnaires:

22. During the last calendar year, 1998, about how many times did you play golf?

___________ Number of times played in 1998

---

may differ greatly by day of week, so that different responses may be obtained depending upon whether one completes a questionnaire on a Monday, following a weekend, or a Thursday, following three weekdays.

The latter problem has some similarity to the final problem question presented in Figure 2.17, in which respondents are asked how many times they have played golf this year. The problem with this question in a mail survey is that responses are likely to be higher later in the year. The revision for this question asks the number of times played in the previous year. We chose a recall for the previous year rather than a general estimation strategy because people who play golf often keep track of the number of times they have played, or play with sufficient regularity (every Thursday afternoon from June through August) that they can provide fairly accurate estimates of times played in the previous year. The phrase, "your best estimate is fine" is sometimes added in order to limit item nonresponse. Another possibility is to prelist categories, as shown earlier in Figure 2.8.

PRINCIPLE 2.14: BE SURE EACH QUESTION IS TECHNICALLY ACCURATE.

Few features of a questionnaire reflect as negatively on a surveyor's credibility as a technical error visible to certain respondents or a survey sponsor. Such errors range from the misspelling of a political candidate's name to providing an incorrect name for an organization asked about in a survey question. Such errors are very easy to make and few can claim never to have made them.

Some errors are more subtle, such as the one in Figure 2.18, where police are identified as being responsible for catching and fining traffic violators. They only do the former; the judicial system, and not the police, is responsible for determining and administering fines. Sometimes as attitude and opinion questions are drafted and redrafted, technical issues such as this one creep into surveys where they have only a minor role, but nonetheless bring into question the surveyor's competence.

I mention this concern as a separate issue because most surveyors, at some time in their careers, design surveys on topics about which they know little.

Figure 2.18 Besure that each question is technically accurate.

Problem:

31. Another activity of the police department is the catching and fining of traffic violators. Should this activity receive greater, about the same, or less emphasis than at present?

☐ Greater
☐ The same
☐ Less

A revision:

31. Another activity of the police department is the catching of traffic violators. Should this activity receive greater, about the same, or less emphasis than at present?

☐ Greater
☐ The same
☐ Less

Checking questionnaires for technical accuracy becomes a very important aspect of pretesting, which I discuss in the next chapter.

PRINCIPLE 2.15: CHOOSE QUESTION WORDINGS THAT ALLOW ESSENTIAL COMPARISONS TO BE MADE WITH PREVIOUSLY COLLECTED DATA.

Comparison of survey results with previously collected data often represents a major survey objective. Sometimes the comparison is being done with a previous survey of the same population in order to measure change. Another likely comparison is with U.S. Census data for the same geographical area. Figure 2.19 illustrates the dilemma one may face in deciding whether to replicate the wording of previous surveys. This question asks whether people rent or own their homes, and is much like the structure we have seen used in hundreds of surveys. The revision is far wordier, specifies type of home to some degree (house, apartment, or mobile home), and is shown here exactly as used in the 2000 U.S. Census.

This example also illustrates one of the difficulties with many questions asked in national surveys. The wording is determined through a long process involving input from many stake-holders. As a result, the wording may be somewhat more cumbersome than many surveyors feel is needed for their particular survey. Similar issues exist with respect to the racial and Spanish/Hispanic/Latino questions to be asked in the 2000 Census, which will

Figure 2.19 Choose question wording that allows essential comparisons to be made with previously collected data.

Problem:

13. Do you own or rent the home in which you live?

☐ Own
☐ Rent

A revision:

13. Is this house, apartment, or mobile home:

☐ Owned by you or someone in this household with a mortgage or loan?

☐ Owned by you or someone in this household free and clear (without a mortgage or loan)?

☐ Rented for cash rent?

☐ Occupied without payment of cash rent?

provide comparison information for much of the next decade. The race question provides 14 categories and allows for multiple selections. The ethnicity question provides four Spanish/Hispanic/Latino categories plus an "other" category. For policy surveys in which it is crucial to be able to demonstrate similarity or differences from Census data, use of the same questions may be desirable. For other surveys, a different question structure may be quite acceptable, or even more desirable.

PRINCIPLE 2.16: AVOID ASKING RESPONDENTS TO SAY YES IN ORDER TO MEAN NO.

It seems obvious that questions should not include double negatives, thus requiring a respondent to say yes to mean no, as for this question, "Should the city manager not be directly responsible to the mayor?" Yet, such questions are commonly asked in surveys. One of the reasons such questions are so prevalent in surveys is because voters are often asked in elections to vote for measures where a yes vote would result in something not being done, as illustrated by the tax approval question in Figure 2.20. Surveyors are often re-

Figure 2.20 Avoid asking respondents to say yes in order to mean no.

Problem:

5. **Do you favor or oppose not allowing the state to raise taxes without approval of 60% of the voters?**

☐ Favor
☐ Oppose

A revision:

5. **Do you favor or oppose requiring 60% approval by voters in order to raise state taxes?**

☐ Favor requiring 60% approval
☐ Oppose requiring 60% approval

Another revision (for specific policy situation):

5. **In the September election you will be asked to vote on this referendum: "No state tax can be raised without approval by 60% of those voting in a statewide election." If the election were held today, would you vote for or against approval?**

☐ For
☐ Against

luctant to pose the question differently than it would be expressed on the ballot. However, because people tend to read questions quickly, it is likely that some people will miss the word "not." In addition, the mental connection of favoring a "not" is difficult for most people.

Two different solutions for this problem might be considered. The first revision simply asks whether people favor or oppose requiring 60% approval by voters in order to raise state taxes. To help clarify what favor and oppose means for purposes of the question, the answer categories specify what favor or oppose means. This wording would seem appropriate during discussion of an issue before it has reached the ballot measure stage. A second revision, indicating that a vote will be taken, specifies the measure exactly as it will appear on the ballot and asks whether respondents are for or against approval of the measure. The switch of categories from favor–oppose to for–against is also an attempt to bring the language of the question more in line with the voting situation.

Principle 2.17: Avoid double-barreled questions.

A somewhat similar problem occurs with questions that contain two components which require one answer, but about which a respondent may feel differently. At first glance the question in Figure 2.21 appears to be simply another case of asking respondents to say yes in order to mean no. However, this question about whether people want a swimming pool to be built with lap lanes, but without a winter enclosure, is really asking two separate questions with no opportunity to respond to each part. This question was justified by its proponents because that seemed to be the policy issue facing voters—whether to approve a larger pool with lap lanes that would be too expensive to enclose or a smaller one that could be enclosed for winter use.

The first revision is a conventional one that allows people to respond to each of the issues and is effective in eliminating the inability of people who wanted both lap lanes and a winter enclosure to express their true opinion.

The second revision seemed more preferable in this case. By writing the question with a closed-ended unordered structure, and placing more wording into the answer choices, five clear alternatives could be presented to respondents. However, if the objective of this survey were to find out whether people would vote for or against the first proposal, then the third revision offered in Figure 2.21 might be the best question structure.

Principle 2.18: Soften the impact of potentially objectionable questions.

One of the most worrisome aspects of conducting self-administered surveys is that people can skip questions they object to answering, or decide not to answer any more questions. The sources of objections differ, as do the solutions.

Figure 2.21 Avoid double-barreled questions.

Problem:

16. Should the city build a new swimming pool that includes lanes for swimming laps that is not enclosed for winter use?

☐ Yes
☐ No

A revision:

16. Should the city build a new swimming pool that includes lanes for swimming laps?

☐ Yes
☐ No

17. Should the city build a new swimming pool that is enclosed for winter use?

☐ Yes
☐ No

Another revision:

16. It has been proposed that the city build a new swimming pool that could include or not include lanes for swimming laps and being enclosed for winter use. Which one of the following do you most prefer?

☐ I prefer that no pool be built.
☐ I prefer a pool with lanes for swimming laps and winter enclosure.
☐ I prefer a pool without lanes for swimming laps or winter enclosure
☐ I prefer a pool with lanes for swimming laps that is not enclosed for winter use.
☐ I prefer a pool enclosed for winter use without lanes for swimming laps.

Still another revision (for specific policy situation):

16. It has been proposed that the city build a new swimming pool that includes lanes for swimming laps, but will not be enclosed for winter use. If the election were held today, would you vote for or against this proposal?

☐ For
☐ Against

Perhaps the one question most likely to elicit negative reactions from respondents is the request for income. The open-ended format presented first in Figure 2.22 is the format most likely to be left unanswered. Not only does it require respondents to record something they are likely to consider no one else's business, but for some people the question is difficult to answer. That is the case for people who do not know their exact income on a yearly basis, and this format provides an easy justification for skipping. Switching from the open-ended format to broad categories, as shown in the revision in Figure 2.22, will reduce item nonresponse. For some studies these categories may be

Figure 2.22 Procedures for softening the impact of potentially objectional questions.

Problem:

38. What was this person's total income from all sources in 1999?

______________ Total income for 1999

A revision:

38. Which of the following broad categories best describes this person's total income from all sources in 1999?

- ☐ $10,000 or less
- ☐ $10,001 to $20,000
- ☐ $20,001 to $35,000
- ☐ $35,001 to $50,000
- ☐ $50,001 to $100,000
- ☐ $100,001 or more

Problem:

26. Have you ever shoplifted something from a store?

- ☐ Yes
- ☐ No

A revision:

26. Have you ever taken anything from a store without paying for it?

- ☐ Yes
- ☐ No

(Continued)

too broad, and anything less than an exact number may be considered unacceptable. The U.S. Decennial Census, for example, asks not only for exact total income, but also asks for exact amounts from eight potential sources of income. Nonetheless, the use of categories helps greatly in overcoming the difficulties of obtaining income.

The second question in Figure 2.22 presents a different problem. Here the respondent is being asked whether she has performed an illegal behavior, such as shoplifting. Sometimes questions of this nature can be softened by changing the wording, as also shown in the revision in Figure 2.22. Another

Figure 2.22 (Continued)

Another revision:

26. The questions which follow are being asked to help us understand things that have happened to people over the years, and how their lives have been affected. We really appreciate your help and that of the thousands of others who have been asked to complete this national survey.

Have you ever hit someone with your fist?

- ☐ Yes
- ☐ No

27. Have you ever taken anything from a store without paying for it?

- ☐ Yes
- ☐ No

Problem:

30. "Most religions are a parasite on society." Do you agree or disagree?

- ☐ Agree
- ☐ Disagree

A revision:

30. Here are many different opinions on religions we have heard from others. Please tell us whether you agree or disagree with each of them.

"Most religions try to help members as well as nonmembers."

- ☐ Agree
- ☐ Disagree

31. "Most religions are a parasite on society."

- ☐ Agree
- ☐ Disagree

---

possibility shown here is to embed the question in a series of items that starts with a reason for answering, then lists other, less objectionable behaviors before asking about the illegal one.

Some questions elicit objections because of the context in which they are presented. The questionnaire is in many respects a conversation between the surveyor and the respondent, and questions that seem particularly nosy, abrupt, harshly asked, or unclear may motivate people to discontinue the conversation. An example shown in the third question in Figure 2.22 is the abrupt statement, "Most religions are a parasite on society. Do you agree or disagree?" Presented in this form, the statement appears to be the opinion of the surveyor. The revision embeds the statement in a brief context and uses a buffer item, as was done for the revision of the shoplifting question. I consider it important to examine the flow of written items, even reading them out loud to contemplate whether an introductory explanation or change in context will make questions seem less objectionable to respondents.

Principle 2.19: Avoid asking respondents to make unnecessary calculations.

When respondents are asked to report percentages, they are required to make an implicit calculation. Some will take the time to come up with the specific numbers and do the appropriate mathematical calculation, but others will simply make an estimate. To improve accuracy it is usually desirable to ask for the numerical information and reduce the burden on respondents by not asking them to do the calculations. An example is the question about percentage of nights spent away from home for business reasons, as shown in Figure 2.23. Separation into questions about total number of nights away from home, followed by one about number away on business, solves the problem by leaving the calculations to the survey analyst.

An exception to this principle is when the respondent is unlikely to know the base numbers, but might be able to make a reasonable estimate directly. For example, a worker in a large corporation might be able to offer an opinion of what proportion of men usually wear neckties to work every day. Having to determine first the number of employees and then the number who

Figure 2.23 Avoid asking respondents to make unnecessary calculations.

Problem:

17. What percent of the nights spent away from home on trips during 1998 were for business reasons?

____________ Percent of nights away from home spent on business trips

A revision:

17. How many nights did you spend away from home on trips of any kind during 1998?

____________ Number of nights away from home in 1998

18. How many of these nights away from home were because of business trips?

____________ Number of nights away from home in 1998 on business trips.

wear neck ties would be unnecessarily laborious, and an invitation to item-nonresponse.

CONCLUSION

In this chapter a formidable gauntlet of concerns has been presented that must be addressed by the would-be writer of questions for self-administered surveys. Eight criteria have been posed for assessing potential survey questions. Three fundamentally different ways of structuring questions were presented, with advice on when one or another might be most appropriate. Finally, 19 principles for reconciling question wording with the assessment criteria and structures were described and illustrated.

Blind adherence to these criteria and principles is hardly a guarantee of success in writing questions. We have noted that principles sometimes come into conflict, and different survey situations exhibit different needs. Reconciling the issues discussed in this chapter with one's survey situation has sometimes been described as the art of asking survey questions (e.g., Payne, 1951). The information discussed here provides fundamental tools for successfully accomplishing this reconciliation.

However, the outcome of the question writing process must be viewed as incomplete. The complete stimulus presented by any question in a self-administered survey also depends upon the order in which questions are seen and answered, and whether all of the words are read by each respondent. In contrast to interview surveys, there is no guarantee that respondents will read each question in the manner intended by the questionnaire writer. However, careful design and layout of questionnaires, the topic to which I turn next, can greatly increase that likelihood.

CHAPTER 3

Constructing the Questionnaire

SELF-ADMINISTERED QUESTIONNAIRES can be constructed in ways that make them easy to understand and answer. However, they are sometimes designed with features that result in questions being misread and items, or even pages, being skipped altogether. Often these problems have little to do with question wording, as discussed in Chapter 2. Instead, they are the result of unfortunate decisions about questionnaire format, question order, and the appearance of individual pages. Examples encountered through many years of providing consultation to study sponsors include:

- In a university faculty-sponsored survey, the questions were listed in the order they were developed. Respondents were therefore required to switch back and forth to answer questions on similar topics at different places in the questionnaire.
- A several-part income question was placed on page one of a questionnaire for a study about the purchase of health care services. The sponsor considered it the most important question in the survey, and was concerned that including this question on the last page, as I recommended (to reduce perceived costs), would result in its being skipped.
- For a nationwide survey of the general public, a proposed questionnaire was printed on one sheet of paper and folded first to form six pages, and once again so that it would fit into a half-size envelope. Observation of people who tried to fill out the questionnaire revealed that some of them unknowingly skipped pages and others made refolding mistakes so that the return address on the refolded questionnaire did not show through the window of the return envelope.
- In a well-funded survey of electric utilities a variety of graphical forms were intermingled, including font changes, shaded and unshaded backgrounds, boxes that isolated certain text, and combinations of bold,

italicized and underlined words within individual sentences. This visual variation made it difficult for respondents to comprehend and respond to each question, the opposite of the writer's reason for using these graphical variations.

- For a study of environmental attitudes and behavior, the type font was reduced to 9 points, the size shown here, in order to get the questions to fit onto two pages. In addition, background questions on occupation and religion were inserted without explanation on page one, between two sets of opinion questions, because it was the only space left where they would fit.

Transforming a list of questions into a questionnaire involves much more than the manipulation of words. It requires that decisions be made about paper size and binding. It also necessitates determining which questions will encourage the recipient to start responding and keep going to the end. In addition, layout choices must be made that involve spacing, size, and brightness considerations. The graphical aspects of layout and design represent critical decisions that constitute a large portion of the discussion in this chapter. Although my focus here is mainly on paper self-administered questionnaires, this chapter lays the foundation for a discussion of the visual aspects of web survey design in Chapter 11.

CRITERIA FOR DESIGN

Individual design decisions made separately from other questionnaire considerations often have negative results for other parts of the survey process. A friend was enticed by a printer to purchase a brightly colored paper that was on sale for the same price as basic white. However, the lack of contrast with the black print made the words difficult to read. A graphical designer encouraged the writer of a questionnaire on historical aspects of housing to use a stylized font that reminded one of colonial America, and it, too, made reading difficult. Repeatedly, I have been told of well-intentioned printers who responded to a request for a booklet questionnaire with, "I can save you a lot of money if you let me duplex regular size sheets of paper (8½″ × 11″, page printed front and back) and put a staple in the upper left corner instead of using a booklet binding with two staples in the spine." In other cases, the first pages of questionnaires have been expanded in order to include a letter to the respondent (as a way of saving insertion and printing costs), a lengthy list of instructions on how to answer individual questions, and a glossary. As a consequence of these additions, the first question on one government questionnaire I reviewed did not appear until page four!

It is important to think of questionnaire design as an attempt to achieve two objectives. One objective is to reduce nonresponse. It has been shown that respondent-friendly questionnaire design can improve response rates, but only to modest degrees (Dillman, Sinclair, and Clark, 1993). Implementation procedures, the topic of the next chapter, are far more powerful as inducers of high response. Nonetheless, small improvements in response can be achieved. More importantly, some research has shown that making a questionnaire respondent-friendly is most likely to improve response among people who are least likely to respond to surveys, and thus help reduce nonresponse error. For example, in a test of the U.S. Decennial Census questionnaires, response was improved by only 2.9 percentage points in areas of the United States with high response to the previous Census versus 7.5 percentage points in areas with low response in 1990 (Dillman, Sinclair, and Clark, 1993). Specific design features such as the choice of the first question can also contribute significantly to the reduction of nonresponse error, by getting people to whom the survey questions do not apply to return their uncompleted questionnaires.

The reduction or avoidance of measurement error is the second objective of good questionnaire design. Poor questionnaire layout can cause questions to be overlooked or bias the offered responses. A respondent-friendly questionnaire is attractive and encourages people to read words in the same order as other respondents read them. People are guided by graphical layout features from the cover page through the last question. A well designed layout prevents items or answer categories from being missed because of their location on the page.

Design features, which are intended to motivate people to respond, focus on all three of the social exchange elements discussed in Chapter 1. Design features are used to improve rewards by making the questionnaire appear interesting and important. Costs are reduced by making the questionnaire easy to manipulate and easy to complete. Trust is encouraged through attention to detail that makes the questionnaire look and seem important. All of the issues addressed in this chapter, from the size and shape of the questionnaire to cognitive pretesting, are important to achieving the best possible questionnaire.

It has been suggested that one advantage of self-administered questionnaires is that people can fill them out at their own speed, taking time to comprehend each question and provide a thoughtful answer. Based upon many cognitive interview studies I have conducted (e.g., Dillman, Carley-Baxter, and Jackson, 1999), and analyses of mode comparison experiments (e.g., Dillman and Tarnai, 1991), I am convinced that many respondents do not read the entire content of questionnaires in a thoughtful way. Respondents take clues from the layout about what must be read and what can safely be ignored, and some respondents skip many words, with the frequent result that questions get misinterpreted. Our best opportunity for achieving clear responses to questions is to keep both the wording and visual appearance of questions simple. The design concepts and principles that follow are based upon this belief.

Discussion of these concepts is divided into four sections. The first section concerns the physical format of the questionnaire and explains why the booklet format is preferred. It is followed by criteria for deciding how questions should be ordered in the section. The third section, and the longest one in this chapter, introduces knowledge about how people see and process information on printed pages; from this information we can derive principles for deciding on the layout and design of individual questionnaires. The fourth section focuses on only two pages of the questionnaire, the front and back covers. This chapter concludes with a discussion of pretesting, the aim of which is to see whether the goals discussed in the first four sections have been accomplished.

ALTERNATIVE QUESTIONNAIRE FORMATS AND WHY A BOOKLET IS PREFERRED

The negative consequences of certain questionnaire formats are great enough for us to reject them as possibilities. Unacceptable formats include:

- Printing on both sides of sheets of paper with a staple to hold the pages together.
- Printing of pages in a landscape (horizontal) rather than portrait (vertical) orientation.
- Unusual folds; for example, a large single-sheet of paper that unfolds like an accordion or in some other way, as does a typical road map.
- Unusual shapes; for example, square or diamond-shaped pages.

The difficulty with these formats is that each of them is unconventional and respondents must figure out how to handle or comprehend each set of materials at the same time they are attempting to answer the questions. The vertical book or booklet, with pages taller than they are wide, is a standard reading format for most western cultures. In focus groups and cognitive interviews, I have observed people struggling with other formats, sometimes turning pages incorrectly or missing them altogether, much as some people struggle to fold maps regardless of how many times they have done it before (Dillman, Reynolds, and Rockwood, 1991; Dillman and Allen, 1995). Conversely, booklet formats are handled more or less automatically and usually without error. People are familiar with starting on page one and then turning to page two, which appears as the left of two facing pages, and so forth. Additionally, the ease of setting up and printing booklets results in my strong preference for this format. A horizontal orientation or landscape printing is also unconventional and usually results in longer lines of prose, another undesirable feature. Long lines of prose are more likely to be read unevenly, with the result that important words get skipped.

In the first edition of this book I recommended a slight photo reduction (79%) of typed 8½″ × 11″ pages to fit in a 6½″ × 8¼″ space. The questionnaire was printed on 12¼″ × 8¼″ sheets of paper folded in the middle and stapled (when more than one sheet was used). My goal was to make the response task look easier to accomplish, in social exchange terms, and to make the booklets fit into monarch (slightly smaller than business stationery) envelopes. This allowed us to mail a 12-page (three sheets of folded paper) questionnaire for one first-class postage stamp.

These recommendations are now outmoded. Computers allow the manipulation of font and line sizes. The proliferation of printing capabilities has had an opposite effect on page sizes. There are significant cost savings associated with using standard sizes of paper. Consequently, although the size recommendation made in 1978 still works fine, it is now less practical. More importantly, I am aware of no experimental evidence that the smaller booklets have a significant influence on response rates. In fact, there may be a packaging appearance advantage to larger-sized mailouts (as discussed in Chapter 4).

Three basic formats are considered acceptable for use with multi-page questionnaires. The first format is a booklet, similar to that recommended in the first edition of this book. Conventional legal size (8½″ × 14″) paper is used. When folded as a booklet and stapled along the spine, an 8½″ × 7″ questionnaire is formed. Nearly all copy centers stock legal size paper so that printing is widely accessible at competitive rates. These booklets can be folded lengthwise to fit into a regular size (4⅛″ × 9½″) business stationery envelope. These questionnaires are normally printed with one column of questions per page, as shown in Figure 3.1.

A second format consists of full-sized pages, also printed as a booklet. The questionnaire is printed on 11″ × 17″ paper so that when folded, individual pages are of conventional 8½″ × 11″ dimensions. If this size of paper is used, it is desirable to divide each page into columns so that the span of type being read does not extend entirely across the page, except for items in a series (see Figure 3.2). For most questionnaires of this size, a two-column format allows more questions per page and may contribute to more accurate comprehension of each question. Observations of people reading material that spans an entire page, especially when less than 12- point type is used, suggest that words are more likely to be skipped.

A third format is to print pages on one side only and staple them in the upper left corner. This format provides a cheaper alternative for printing some questionnaires, even facilitating within-office printing and finishing on copy machines. This type of binding is more awkward for the respondent than booklet construction and should not be considered if two-sided printing is to be used. Printing of this nature generally costs more for mailing (larger en-

Figure 3.1 Facing pages from a single column, full-page format using folded legal size paper (8.5″ × 14″) (formatted by Pavlov, 1996).

Q1. **The following questions address perceptions about the general work environment and interactions among co-workers. To what extent do you agree or disagree with each of the following statements about the work environment in your unit or department within your college?** (Please circle your answer.)

	Strongly Agree ▼	Somewhat Agree ▼	Somewhat Disagree ▼	Strongly Disagree ▼	Don't Know ▼
Co-workers listen to my ideas	1	2	3	4	5
Co-workers appreciate my contributions	1	2	3	4	5
Co-workers treat me with respect ..	1	2	3	4	5
I am given the opportunity for professional growth and success in my working environment	1	2	3	4	5
My co-workers generally go out of their way to help new workers succeed and excel in their position .	1	2	3	4	5
Perks and benefits are distributed equally and fairly in my unit	1	2	3	4	5
Hiring practices in my unit/department have promoted equality among workers	1	2	3	4	5
All qualified candidates have an equal chance of being promoted in my unit/department	1	2	3	4	5
Focusing on equity issues has a negative impact upon teamwork ...	1	2	3	4	5
My co-workers constructively confront problems	1	2	3	4	5
Supervisors show respect to employees	1	2	3	4	5
Decisions in my unit/department are often influenced by social relationships with key persons	1	2	3	4	5
Problems or issues in my unit/department are handled openly rather than covertly	1	2	3	4	5
I am satisfied with the opportunities I have for promotion	1	2	3	4	5

1

Q2. **To what extent do you agree or disagree with each of the following statements about the management of your unit/department?** (Please circle your answer.)

	Strongly Agree ▼	Somewhat Agree ▼	Somewhat Disagree ▼	Strongly Disagree ▼
I would be comfortable approaching my immediate supervisor about concerns of discrimination or harassment	1	2	3	4
I would be comfortable approaching higher level supervisors (e.g., Department Chair, Director, Dean) about concerns of discrimination or harassment	1	2	3	4
In my work environment, supervisors have made it clear that they will not tolerate harassment or discrimination	1	2	3	4
I believe managers in my unit give preferential treatment to individuals who are similar to them	1	2	3	4
I believe that my supervisors would actively intervene to stop conduct that constitutes harassment or discrimination in my work environment	1	2	3	4

Q3. **In the past five years, have you felt discriminated against within this college?**

1 Yes, I have experienced a lot of discrimination.
2 Yes, I have experienced some discrimination.
3 Yes, I have experienced a little discrimination.
4 No, I have not experienced discrimination. GO TO Q5

Q4. **(If Yes) During these last five years in this college, have you experienced discrimination based upon:** (Please circle yes or no.)

a. gender	Yes	No
b. race/ethnicity	Yes	No
c. disability	Yes	No
d. age	Yes	No
e. sexual orientation	Yes	No
f. religion	Yes	No

2

Figure 3.2 Page from a double-column format using conventional 8.5″ × 11″ paper.

Please help plan AAPOR's future!

A 1995 survey of interests and concerns of members of the American Association for Public Opinion Research

Your Relationship to AAPOR

1. Please indicate how *valuable* each of these aspects of AAPOR is to you as a member, where 5 means "very valuable" and 1 means "Not at all valuable."

	Value: Very				Not at all	DK/NA
A. *Public Opinion Quarterly*	5	4	3	2	1	9
B. *AAPOR News,* the newsletter	5	4	3	2	1	9
C. The annual conference	5	4	3	2	1	9
D. Your local chapter	5	4	3	2	1	9
E. The *Blue Book*	5	4	3	2	1	9
F. The code of ethics	5	4	3	2	1	9
G. The membership directory	5	4	3	2	1	9

2. In what year did you first join AAPOR?

1995 1
1994 2
1990-1993 3
1985-1989 4
1980-1984 5
1970-1979 6
1960-1969 7
Before 1960 8

3. Who paid your AAPOR dues in 1995?

I did 1
My employer did 2
Honorary Life Member (no dues) 3

4. Are you a member of any other professional association(s)?

Yes 1
No *(SKIP to Q8)* 2

5. (If yes) **To which types of professional associations do you belong?** *(circle all that apply)*

Disciplinary associations *(e.g., Amer. Statistical Assn., Amer. Sociological Assn.)* 1
Professional associations *(e.g., Amer. Marketing Assn., Advertising Research Foundation)* 2
Your clients' professional interest associations 3
Other types of associations 4

6. In a typical year, how many other associations' annual meetings do you attend?

None 0
One 1
Two 2
Three 3
Four or more 4

7. Thinking about all the professional associations in which you participate, which do you think of as your primary association?

AAPOR 1
AAPOR and another equally 2
Another association 3
Don't know 9

*Formatted by Karen Goldenberg and Don A. Dillman and reprinted by permission of American Association of Public Opinion Research.

velopes as well as more sheets of paper). Generally it lacks the professional look of booklet formats and is one I prefer not to use, except under very tight budgets.

CRITERIA FOR ORDERING THE QUESTIONS

Consider for a moment the order of these questions proposed for a self-administered questionnaire, presented here in abbreviated form:

- What was your total family income in 1998?
- Do you like to play golf?
- What is your opinion on global warming?
- Are you married?
- How many times have you gone bowling during the past year?
- What is your political party preference?
- Do you favor or oppose these measures to reduce environmental pollution?
- What is your occupation?
- Please describe your favorite recreational activity.
- How adequate is your present health care?
- Which political party does the best job of promoting economic growth?
- How old are you?
- Has your health gotten better or worse during the past year?

A friend described her frustration with a similar set of disconnected questions in this way: "It was like trying to go shopping with an alphabetized grocery list. The order on the list didn't correspond to how things were organized in the store, so that I had to go back and forth between sections of the store and I became so confused that some things on the list were forgotten." The above list of questions vacillates back and forth among topics and is not organized in the way one's knowledge of topics is likely to be organized. Respondents are asked to describe recreational activities in several different places, with unrelated questions and personal characteristics interspersed among them. In addition, the first item on the list, family income, is perhaps the most threatening question. Asking income first is somewhat like requesting that respondents sign a blank check when as yet they have little idea of why; the respondent is more likely to reveal such private information if other questions have been answered first.

A questionnaire is like a conversation which typically evolves in accordance with societal norms (Schwarz, 1996). Constantly switching topics makes it appear that the questioner (survey sponsor) is not listening to the respondent's answers. Each answer seems to stimulate a response on an unrelated topic, as though the person's answer was not heard. Jumping quickly between topics also means that answers are less likely to be well thought out, as new topics evoke top-of-the-head responses. Asking all of the recreational questions from the above list together is not only a more efficient way of asking a person to think about a topic, but it also cuts down on the respondent effort required for focusing on each issue and giving a reasoned response. Grouping questions by topic according to the principles that follow is helpful to respondents.

Initially, question topics and questions are grouped in a general way from most salient to least salient to the respondent. This decision is based on the research finding that a major predictor of response rates to mail surveys is the salience of the questionnaire topic (Heberlein and Baumgartner, 1978). Most questionnaires consist of a variety of questions, some of which respondents will find interesting to answer and some of which they will not. Consequently, we attempt to start the questionnaire with some of the most salient questions.

This question order takes into account what the respondent has been told in the cover letter. Chances are that a strong argument is offered in that letter for answering the questionnaire. This theme is likely to be carried onto a well-designed questionnaire cover page. Suppose, for example, that a cover letter has informed recipients that they are being asked to respond to an important questionnaire about preferences for possible change in the health care program to which they belong. The questionnaire cover carries out that theme with a title such as, "What Changes Would You Like to See Made in Your Present Health Maintenance Program?" These words develop respondents' expectations that they are going to be asked for their opinions about desired changes. Thus, it seems important that early in the questionnaire they are asked to do that. A salient beginning to a questionnaire is partly a matter of meeting respondent expectations and partly a matter of identifying questions that the respondent will find interesting. One might reasonably begin by asking how long respondents have participated in the current program and how well they like it. However, one should not begin by asking a series of disjointed demographic questions—education, age, income, home ownership, veteran status, or even prior medical history. These demographics may be highly relevant to the study objectives and easy to answer, but respondents will not see obvious relevance to the topic. The first pages are also not the place to include a long series of abstract attitudinal scales, such as those designed to measure a respondent's orientation towards government versus private sector involvement in meeting health care needs.

Objectionable questions are placed near the end of the questionnaire, where they are likely to be seen after the respondent has had an opportunity to become interested in the questionnaire. A respondent who has spent five or 10 minutes already answering questions is less likely to respond to an objectionable question by quitting. Moreover, some questions may seem less objectionable in light of previous questions already answered. One of the questions that people often object to answering is the question of income. In addition to reporting income, people are often uncomfortable answering questions about their sexual behavior or any laws they may have broken. Significant, though less universal, objections are often expressed towards questions about religious activities or political party affiliation. Through pretesting we attempt to identify questions which people object to answering, and place those questions near the end of the questionnaire.

An effort is also made to order questions in a way that will be logical to the respondent. When respondents are asked why they left a job, it makes sense to ask such questions after asking why they accepted that job and how long they were employed in that position. In general, this suggestion implies asking people about things in the order that they happened. It is also helpful to ask people descriptive questions about an activity before requesting evaluations of the experience, thus encouraging more complete recall of past events. For example, a question about the main reason a person left a job might best be asked after a series of items about the nature of that job.

Finally, it is also helpful to group together questions that have similar component parts. For example, if within a general topic area there are several yes/no questions, some that require unfavorable-favorable scalar responses, and others that require agree-disagree responses, the task of the respondent can be eased by grouping those requiring the same answer categories together. Our purpose is to ease the cognitive burden of responding. Responding to questionnaires in which each new question means having to think about a new topic, as well as a new type of response category, requires more respondent effort. Simply put, we are attempting to keep respondents focused on the substance of our inquiries rather than having to figure out new response formats for each question as well. However, this aspect of ordering usually involves only minor shifts, with our concerns being focused first on salience, objectionable qualities, and an order that the respondent will find logical.

Possible Order Effects Between Opinion Questions

When taking advantage of cognitive ties to ease the task of responding, one must also be aware of how answering one question may influence responses to later queries and, in particular, the next one. There are five distinct situations in which answers to a subsequent question may be dramatically altered because of the question immediately prior to it, as summarized in Figure 3.3. The first of these concerns stems from invoking a *norm of evenhandedness*. A survey of Washington State University students showed that 34% thought a student who had plagiarized should be expelled when the preceding question asked whether a professor who had plagiarized should be fired. However, when the student question was asked first, only 21% indicated that the student should be expelled (Sangster, 1993). This phenomenon of adjusting

Figure 3.3 Sources of order effects in self-administered questionnaires.

Problem		***Example***
Norm of evenhandedness, a value-based effect.	☞	Yes answers to "Should a Communist reporter be allowed to report on visit to America as they saw it?" increased significantly when respondents were first asked whether American reporters should be allowed to report on the Soviet Union as they saw it; a sense of fairness had been invoked. (Hyman and Sheatsley, 1950)
Anchoring, a cognitive-based effect.	☞	Student agreement with general statement, "Cheating at universities throughout the United States is widespread problem," decreases significantly when asked after registering extent of agreement or disagreement with a similar statement about their university, because of increase in "No opinion" to second question. (Sangster, 1993)
Addition (carryover) effect.	☞	Percent choosing "Very Happy" for answer to question, "How would you say things are these days?" increases significantly if asked after question, "How would you describe your marriage?" using the same categories; because of carryover of marriage evaluation to the second, more general question. (Schuman and Presser, 1981)
Subtraction effect.	☞	Percent indicating they feel the economic situation is getting better in the state was significantly higher when that question was asked prior to question about economic situation in their community; because of subtracting out information on which first question was based. (Mason, Carlson, and Tourangeau, 1994)
Increased positiveness of summary items when asked after specific items on same subject.	☞	Respondents give higher ratings to the question, "How would you rate the overall quality of life in your community?" when asked after several rating questions about more specific domains of community life. (Willits and Saltiel, 1995)

answers to succeeding questions based on the previous answer was first noticed in interview surveys, with a question asked in 1948 about whether a communist reporter should be allowed to report on a visit to America as he saw it. When this question was asked before a comparable question about whether an American reporter should be able to report on a visit to the Soviet Union as he saw it, 37% said yes, compared to 73% when the question was positioned second (Hyman and Sheatsley, 1950).

The explanation for this order effect is *value-based;* that is, the similarity of the questions is seen as invoking a norm of fairness or evenhandedness which results in one's answer to the second question taking into account one's answer to the first. It has been argued, based on a classroom experiment, that the norm of evenhandedness is less likely to be invoked in mail than telephone surveys (Bishop, Hippler, Schwarz, and Strack, 1988). Bishop et al. argue that the respondents to a self-administered questionnaire can look ahead to see what is coming and therefore adjust their answers to earlier questions. However, other experiments from field surveys, including a replication of the communist reporter questions by Ayida and McClendon (1990), as well as results reported by Sangster (1993) and Sangster, Lorenz, and Saltiel (1995), provide evidence that effects in mail and telephone surveys are similar.

An *anchoring* or *cognitive-based* order effect has also been observed. Another experiment reported by Sangster (1993) asked a random sample of students whether they agree or disagree that "cheating is a widespread problem at this university." The next question asked whether "cheating at universities throughout the United States is a widespread problem." A comparable random sample was asked the questions in reverse order. The percentage that agreed to either question is similar when that question is answered first (65% United States versus 60% their university), and much smaller (49% versus 44%) when answered second. We conclude that students are much more likely to see cheating as a problem at their university if asked about it after the question about other U.S. universities. These differences are accounted for almost entirely by a change in the use of the no opinion category. When the U.S. question is asked first 15% offer no opinion for that question followed by a similar 16% for the student's university. However, when asked first about their own university with which they should have greater familiarity, 29% offer no opinion, which then rises to 38% for universities throughout the United States. In essence, the response to the first of these opinion questions serves as an anchor for the second answer.

Two other order effects that have been identified through past research are *addition* or carryover *effects* and *subtraction effects*. Schuman and Presser (1981) found that when a specific question, "How would you describe your marriage?" was asked just prior to a general question, "How would you say things are these days?" the percentage responding to the general question varied greatly depending upon which question was asked first. Whereas 52% said very happy (compared to pretty or not too happy) to the general question when it was asked after the marriage question, only 38% said very happy when the order was reversed. Their explanation of this addition effect was that people continued to think about the marriage question (to which 70% said very happy) when answering the general question.

A seemingly opposite effect is illustrated by these questions from Mason, Carlson, and Tourangeau (1994), asked in this order:

> "How would you describe the economic situation in your community over the next five years? Do you feel it will Get Better, Get Worse, or Stay the Same?"

> "How do you feel about the economic situation in (your state) over the next five years? Do you feel it will Get Better, Get Worse, or Stay the Same?"

Mason and his colleagues found that more people (7–10%) said the state economy would get better when the state economy was presented first. The reason for this difference is that once people have answered the first question they tend to "subtract" out reasons used to justify their first answer (e.g., new industry) and therefore base their answer to the second question in the series on other considerations.

Finally, a body of research has emerged that summarizes the effects of asking general or summary items, such as, "How would you rate the *overall* quality of life in your community?" prior to and after asking about a number of specific domains from streets and roads to education. An example of a specific item is: "How would you rate police protection in your community?" Studies have found that the summary question tends to be scored lower by respondents when asked before a list of specific domain questions than when asked afterwards (Willits and Saltiel, 1995).

Schwarz (1996) has detailed how, in the normal give-and-take of regular conversations, people tend to give answers that take into account things they have already said. Thus, answers to individual questions are less complete, or less able to stand alone, than the framers of those questions intended. Although the carryover is probably most extensive from questions that immediately follow one another, there is limited evidence that effects also occur when questions are widely separated.

Consequently, it is important to recognize early on that a questionnaire cannot be viewed as a compilation of completely independent questions that have no effects on one another. Not only must each question be evaluated on the basis of its individual content, but also with regard to the larger context that often adds or subtracts meaning. It is also important to note that all of the order effects reported here as illustrations of the norm of evenhandedness, the anchoring effect, addition effect, subtraction effect, and summary item effect are opinion questions that require the respondent to formulate an answer on the spot. Thus, we should not be surprised that respondents identify the questions as related to one another and adjust their answers to the second question based on answers to the first one.

The practical conclusion we draw from these various studies is that there are quite different kinds of order effects likely to occur on topically-related opinion questions that use commonly employed but vague quantifiers (agree-disagree, excellent to poor), and these effects cannot be ignored. Although there is some evidence to suggest that the effects may be stronger in telephone than mail surveys (Lorenz and Ryan, 1996; Bishop et al., 1988), the evidence that they persist in self-administered surveys is also compelling (Sangster, 1993). When one anticipates including questions like those described in Figure 3.3, it may be judicious to consider doing half the questionnaires with one order and half with another, or at a minimum recognize in reports of findings the possibility of question order influence on respondent answers. This topic remains an active area of research about which much remains to be learned.

CHOOSE THE FIRST QUESTION CAREFULLY

No single question is more crucial than the first one. It is more likely than any other questionnaire item to determine whether that questionnaire is destined for the mailbox or the garbage. Thus, it warrants special attention, with some questions serving this purpose better than others, as shown in Figure 3.4.

First, the question should clearly *apply to everyone*. A questionnaire that begins by asking, "From what company do you obtain your health insurance?" assumes that the respondent has health insurance. Although a category, "I don't have health insurance" can be added, the damage is already done. Respondents who read only the query are likely to conclude that the questionnaire really does not apply to them and need not be filled out.

Second, the question should be *easy,* so that all respondents will need only a few seconds to read, comprehend, and respond to it. In telephone interviewing, a common technique for overcoming refusals from people who do not think they are able to respond is to read them the first question, which is easy to understand and answer. Success in understanding and answering the first question encourages people to continue. This is *not* the place for a long question with many response categories or an open-ended question. A test of this idea was done at the U.S. Bureau of the Census, when one questionnaire began with the request that the respondent list the names of all members of the household according to a list of eligibility criteria. The other questionnaire was identical except that it began with the simple question, "How many people live in this household?" The questionnaire that began with the latter item achieved a response rate that was nearly four percentage points higher than the other form (Leslie, 1996). Surveyors must be especially concerned with the ease of answering the first question because it seems likely to produce nonresponse error by discouraging people for whom filling out a written questionnaire is difficult.

Third, the first item in a questionnaire needs to be *interesting*. The well-known role of salience in improving mail survey response suggests that questions that are interesting are more likely to be answered. I was once faced with providing advice for a particularly difficult survey in which a low response rate was expected. The population consisted of licensed commercial salmon fishermen and concerned mostly the size of their boats and investment in their

Figure 3.4 Selecting the first question for a questionnaire.

Unacceptable first questions:

1. **Please think about all the things that make this community a pleasant place to live. Then please write down the five most important aspects of community that make this community a pleasant place to live, and rank them from 1 (meaning most important) to 5 (the least important of the five attributes).**

1. **Please describe in your own words what you consider good about living in this community?**

1. **What year were you born?**

   ________ year born

Better first questions:

1. **Thinking about this community, how would you rate it as a place to live?**

   ☐ Excellent
   ☐ Good
   ☐ Fair
   ☐ Poor

1. **How long have you lived in this community?**

   ☐ More than six months
   ☐ Less than six months

   → If less than six months, it is not necessary for you to complete the remainder of this questionnaire. However, please return it so that we can check your name off of the mailing list. That will help us a great deal.

---

equipment. After much discussion with the survey sponsor, the sponsor decided to add an introductory section about their views of the future of salmon fishing, whether they would advise young people to enter it, and other issues that were described to me as the "gut" issues facing their business. The entire first page of the questionnaire was devoted to these questions, with the first one being a simple question about whether the respondent felt that the benefits of being a salmon fisherman were getting better, worse, or staying about the same. The response rate for this study of individuals, many of whom had not completed high school, was well over 50%.

Frequently, when we have advised questionnaire writers to keep in mind questions that are interesting, easy, and applicable to everyone, the response has been, "We'll start with age or education. It applies to everyone and is really easy." Although these questions are easy to answer, they are not particularly interesting. Most importantly, they do not meet a fourth criterion of *connectedness* between the respondent and survey purpose as understood by that person. A well-designed survey will include a cover letter which describes what the survey is about and why it is important to respond. Respondents who have been told that their response is important on a survey about health care policies, and who are perhaps looking forward to responding, are likely to be unpleasantly surprised to turn to the first question(s) and discover that they are about age or education. From their perspective these questions have little to do with evaluating health care possibilities. For this reason, we seldom begin a questionnaire with demographic questions.

Special situations sometimes override our search for a first question that meets all of the above criteria. Most common is the situation in which eligibility requirements must be met in order to fill out a questionnaire. In these instances we use the first question (supported by appropriate wording in the cover letter) to determine eligibility and to instruct both those eligible and those not eligible to return the questionnaire, as shown at the bottom of Figure 3.4. One of the major reasons for nonresponse is that questionnaires are discarded because they do not apply to the recipient, and hearing from such respondents is important for understanding coverage and nonresponse issues.

PRINCIPLES FOR CONSTRUCTING QUESTIONNAIRE PAGES

Creating a Common Stimulus for Every Person

Telephone interviewers are typically instructed to read the same words in the same order to each respondent, so that each respondent receives exactly the same stimulus. Making sure each respondent receives the same stimulus in the same way is considered essential for obtaining quality survey data. Consequently, great care is taken to train interviewers so that the order in which words are delivered does not change from one respondent to the next. Therefore, questions are read verbatim and no words are skipped.

My goal for creating the visual layout of a self-administered questionnaire is the same. Respondents should see and comprehend every word of every question in a particular order, just as it would be delivered by an interviewer. Words construct phrases and phrases build sentences. It is important not only to ensure that people read and comprehend words in a prescribed order but to facilitate comprehension in appropriate *groupings*. Each question and its set of answer choices comprise a set of words and phrases that need to be viewed as a group—the first part that states the question, and the second part that provides the alternatives for responding.

Concern about getting each respondent to read every word of each question in the same order and with the same grouping (phrasing) of ideas stems partly from the fact that missed words, misunderstood questions, and unseen answer categories constitute major sources of error in self-administered surveys. This concern also stems from the increased prevalence of mixed-mode surveys, in which some data are collected by interview and other portions by self-administered form, and from the frequent reporting of response differences between interview and self-administered surveys (e.g., Dillman, Sangster, Tarnai, and Rockwood, 1996). Achieving the same stimulus in both modes is important for minimizing mode differences. In addition, I am concerned that by not guiding people effectively in how to fill out self-administered questionnaires, frustration is produced that becomes expressed through less thoughtful answers, higher item nonresponse, and occasionally, no response at all.

The challenge of achieving delivery of the same stimulus for all respondents is far more difficult for self-administered than for telephone surveys. Telephone respondents receive the interview stimulus only through hearing, and the order in which words are delivered is controlled by the interviewer. Self-administered questionnaires mostly involve a different human sense, seeing. However, unlike the interview situation, the comprehension order is controlled by the respondent. It is for this reason that the visual aspects of design take on paramount importance in self-administered questionnaire design.

Computers now have marvelous capabilities that allow most individuals to design creative questionnaire layouts. For example, it is possible to insert a variety of symbols ✚☺✔, increase font size, and use **bold print,** *italics,* or shaded backgrounds all in a single sentence, as done here. Used separately and consistently, such capabilities can ease the task of comprehending and responding to a questionnaire. Used carelessly, and especially together in one sentence, this variation can make a questionnaire far more difficult to complete than necessary, and even lead to important words being misread or ignored altogether.

The content of each questionnaire page is comprised of stimuli presented in two languages, each of which provides meaning and direction to respondents, as described by Jenkins and Dillman (1995, 1997). One of those languages consists of written words and is the traditional one considered important in the design of questionnaires. The second language consists of graphical symbols and arrangements which also give direction to respondents with regard to what they should read and in what order. The meaning of this second language is communicated through a number of visual clues.

Six visual elements, to be described in detail later, are especially important for determining how people divide what they see into separate groupings, such as one complete question or a complete set of response categories, and how they proceed to read and answer a page of survey questions. They include *location* (or spacing between elements), *shape, size, brightness* (shading or color), *simplicity and regularity*, and a *consistent figure-ground* format. Together they influence which words are read in what order and to some extent, the meaning of those words.

The task of constructing a questionnaire page is to bring the verbal language and the graphical language into concert with one another in order to communicate questions and obtain answers. In this section, I describe several key steps for combining written language with the visual language of questionnaire design.

Accomplishing the goal of a common stimulus for all respondents involves adhering to many construction principles for presenting survey questions to respondents. They encompass decisions about the order in which all printed information is to be presented on each page and the use of graphic design elements to guide the respondent through the questions in the desired order. This process can conveniently be divided into three sequential steps:

Step 1: Defining a desired navigational path for reading all information presented on each page of the questionnaire.
Step 2: Creating visual navigational guides that will assist respondents in adhering to the prescribed navigational path and correctly interpreting the written information.
Step 3: Developing additional visual navigational guides, the aim of which is to interrupt established navigation behavior and redirect respondents, for example, through skip patterns.

Each of these steps is described below in conjunction with principles essential to its implementation.

STEP 1: DEFINE A DESIRED NAVIGATIONAL PATH FOR READING ALL INFORMATION PRESENTED ON EACH PAGE OF THE QUESTIONNAIRE.

Defining a desired navigational path consists of nothing more than determining the order in which every stimulus on the questionnaire page, including all words and graphical symbols, should be processed by the respondent. I want to organize this information in a way that makes obvious the right way to proceed through the questionnaire and that, consistent with exchange theory, will minimize the effort needed to comprehend and respond to each question. This concern leads to the development of several principles for information organization.

Principle 3.1: Write each question in a way that minimizes the need to reread portions in order to comprehend the response task.

Consider the organization of words and phrases of the first question in Figure 3.5. Not only are the answer categories presented first (which most people would never do), but the wording of the question presents answering instructions and choices to the respondent before presenting the substance of the question. This organization of words and phrases would invariably require that the respondent retrace a portion of the navigational path in order to understand and answer the question. The revision illustrates the more conventional way of organizing the information in a question.

A more complex example of inefficient word organization is a question taken from the 1993 U.S. Census of Agriculture (Figure 3.6). In this example it is not clear exactly what is being asked until the response space where "Number of acres owned" appears. Respondents who have been following the conventional left to right and top to bottom reading sequence through these separated phrases are reading words without knowing what the question is. The inevitable result is that it will be necessary to reread the question in order to understand it. The drawback to poor information organization is that respondents may become frustrated and/or unwilling to retrace those steps, and therefore may give a wrong answer. In this case the problem is confounded by a visual layout that makes it somewhat unclear what navigational path is to be followed; that is, what information is to be read in what order.

A more effective organization of the information is shown in the revision in

Figure 3.5 Building a more desirable information organization for the navigational path.

Poor information organization:

12. ☐ Very Satisfied
☐ Somewhat Satisfied
☐ Not At All Satisfied

Please check the appropriate category above to indicate whether you were Very Satisfied, Somewhat Satisfied, or Not At All Satisfied with the quality of your meal the last time you visited our restaurant.

Better information organization:

12. The last time you visited our restaurant, how satisfied were you with the quality of your meal? (Check one box.)

☐ Very Satisfied
☐ Somewhat Satisfied
☐ Not At All Satisfied

Figure 3.6 Poor information organizations with unclear navigational path, and a revision.

Poor information organization and lack of navigational path:

CENSUS USE ONLY	035	036	037	038	039	040	041	042

SECTION 1 **ACREAGE IN 1992** – Report land owned, rented, or used by you, your spouse, or by the partnership, corporation, or organization for which you are reporting. *Include ALL LAND, REGARDLESS OF LOCATION OR USE – cropland, pastureland, rangeland, woodland, idle land, house lots, etc.*

S1

If the acres you operated in 1992 changed during the year, refer to the INFORMATION SHEET, section 1. None | Number of acres 043

1. All land owned . . . . ☐

Better information organization and creation of clear navigational path:

1. **How many acres of land did you own in 1990? You should report all land (crop land, pasture land, rangeland, woodland, idle land, house lots, etc.), regardless of location, owned by you, your spouse, or by the partnership, corporation or organization for which you are reporting.** ***(If the acres you operated in 1990 changed during the year, refer to the information sheet, Section 1.)***

_________ Number of acres owned

From 1993 Census of Agriculture conducted by U.S. Bureau of the Census.

Figure 3.6. This allows respondents to know at the beginning that they are being asked to report the number of acres they own, and they are then given instructions on what to include and exclude. The important implication of this principle is that no amount of visual redesign can compensate for poorly organized information, which, once read, leaves the respondent unclear about precisely what to do.

Principle 3.2: Place instructions exactly where that information is needed and not at the beginning of the questionnaire.

The information on how to complete a questionnaire (shown in Figure 3.7) was provided in an "instructions" section on page one of a questionnaire sent to nearly 200,000 Americans. At first glance, these instructions seem rather ordinary and reasonable. Upon closer examination, one should ask, "Why tell people where the directions are going to be? Do they need to know up front that not every question applies to everyone?" This information should be revealed at the appropriate time. The direction to refer to the week of April 15th seems useful, except the respondent is also informed that it will not apply to some questions. Thus, the information about the week of April 15th is not self-standing and immediately useful. The benefit of knowing this information has been undone. The direction on what to do if no "Skip" instruction is pro-

Figure 3.7 Place instructions exactly where that information is needed and not in a separate section at the beginning of the questionnaire.

Problem: Instructions placed in a separate section at the beginning:

- Thank you for taking the time to complete this important questionnaire. The directions for filling it out are provided with each question. Because not all questions will apply to everyone, you may be asked to skip certain questions.
- In order to get comparable data, we will be asking you to refer to the week of April 15, 1993, when answering most questions.
- If no "Skip" instruction is provided, you should continue to the NEXT question.
- Either a pen or pencil may be used.
- When answering questions that require marking a box, please use an "X."
- If you need to change an answer, please make sure that your old answer is either completely erased or clearly crossed out.

A revision: Placing instructions exactly where they are needed:

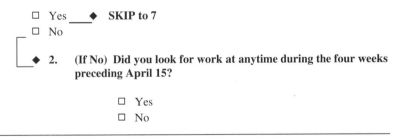

1. **Were you working for pay (or profit) during the week of April 15, 1993? This includes being self-employed or temporarily absent from a job (e.g., illness, vacation, or parental leave), even if unpaid. Mark your answer in the box ☒ with a pen or pencil.**

   ☐ Yes ——◆ **SKIP to 7**
   ☐ No

   ◆ 2. **(If No) Did you look for work at anytime during the four weeks preceding April 15?**

   ☐ Yes
   ☐ No

---

vided is completely unnecessary, and the practical implication of telling people that either a pen or pencil may be used is probably minimal.

Instructions should be provided at the point that respondents are ready to act on them. Thus, the place to instruct people on the type of mark to make, what date to use, etc., is when a question has been asked and the respondent is ready to provide an answer that uses the instructions. In the proposed revision of these instructions, the middle four items are provided with the first two questions and the remaining instructions have been eliminated because they are unnecessary.

Besides getting better compliance with instructions by placing them exactly where they are needed, this placement serves two other important functions. First, it encourages people to immediately start answering questions, so they can feel rewarded by a sense of immediate progress. Second, providing instructions that are not immediately useful encourages people to scan information rather than to read it carefully. Encouraging respondents to skip words and phrases early in the questionnaire is likely to cause them to read questions in that way later, an outcome that should be avoided.

Even worse than the above example is the tendency for some questionnaires to compile separate instruction booklets or place instructions in a different place in the questionnaire. People are unlikely to go to the instruction booklet before answering each question. At best, instruction books are used unevenly by respondents, resulting in some respondents being subjected to different stimuli than are others.

Principle 3.3: Place items with the same response categories into an item-in-a-series format, but do it carefully.

When one has to ask a series of questions that use the same answer categories, it is convenient to combine them into a format similar to the one shown in the revision example in Figure 3.8. Here respondents are asked to indicate the extent to which each of the listed concerns is a problem in their community. Combining them into this item-in-a-series format, with a common introduction that defines the general question and response format, eliminates considerable redundancy with regard to stating questions; it also saves considerable space.

However, it also changes the nature of the questions. That is, the items are to some extent placed in a comparative framework, whereby the visual structure encourages respondents to think of them as a unit. As a result, when answering one item respondents think about it in relation to other items. Often this is precisely what the questioner wants, and the structure seems ideal for that purpose. However, if for some reason the sponsor wants individuals to contemplate each item separately, it is advisable to present each of them as individual items.

Principle 3.4: Ask one question at a time.

Questionnaires are sometimes constructed in a way that encourages the respondent to answer two questions at once, as shown in Figure 3.9. The problem is that the person who answers in this way must toggle her mind between the questions as she proceeds down the page. The usual justification is that this approach cuts the amount of space required in half. However, this format is exceedingly difficult for many respondents as they try to focus on the basic items of information on the left side of the page and answer both questions for each item.

Whereas some respondents answer the first question for each item and then proceed back over the same items to answer the second question, others try to do both at once. It is undesirable to lose control of the answering pro-

Figure 3.8 Place items with the same response categories into an item-in-a-series format.

An inefficient structure:

7. To what extent do you consider a lack of rental housing to be a problem in this community?

- ☐ Not a Problem
- ☐ Small Problem
- ☐ Moderate Problem
- ☐ Serious Problem

8. To what extent do you consider poor road and street repair to be a problem in this community?

- ☐ Not a Problem
- ☐ Small Problem
- ☐ Moderate Problem
- ☐ Serious Problem

Etc.

A revision that places questions into an item-in-a-series format:

7. Do you consider each of the following to be a Serious Problem, Moderate Problem, Small Problem, or Not a Problem in this community? (Please circle one answer for each.)

	Extent to which situation is a problem in this community			
A lack of rental housing	Serious	Moderate	Small	Not a Problem
Poor road and street repair	Serious	Moderate	Small	Not a Problem
Etc.				

---

cess in this way so that people think in different ways about the items. An additional problem with double, or sometimes triple, questions is that the respondent who tries to answer both questions and toggles her mind between items may have difficulty remembering exactly what she is supposed to do. Still another problem is that, as a practical matter, setting up the questions often requires abbreviations, so people must constantly refer from one place to another as they try to remember all of the elements of the question. For example, use in the "last six months" seems especially likely to be forgotten as a respondent proceeds through the long list of items. For all of these reasons, this format should not be used for self-administered questionnaires. The usual justification that it will make the questionnaire look shorter and easier is *not* one for which we have seen explicit evidence that it improves response

Figure 3.9 Ask one question at a time.

A Problem:

6. Please indicate the extent to which each of the following services of our organization are important to you, and for those that are very important, please indicate how frequently you have used that service during the past six months.

	How Important?			Frequency of use in last six months
Customer credit	Not	Somewhat	Very	_______ Times Used
Next-day delivery	Not	Somewhat	Very	_______ Times Used
"No questions asked" return policy	Not	Somewhat	Very	_______ Times Used

A revision:

6. How often have you used each of these services from our organization during the last six months?

	Number of times used
Cutstomer credit	_______
Next-day delivery	_______
"No questions asked" return policy	_______

7. Thinking about each of these same services, how important is each of them to you?

	How Important?		
Customer credit	Not	Somewhat	Very
Next-day delivery	Not	Somewhat	Very
"No questions asked" return policy	Not	Somewhat	Very

rates. Finally, some evidence exists that item nonresponse is significantly higher for these types of double-question formats (Keil and Gaertner, 1998).

Principle 3.5: Minimize the use of matrices.

A closely related type of question is the matrix question, in which one prints a series of individual questions down the left side of the page and then lists a series of units across the top of the page for which respondents are to answer these questions (Figure 3.10). An example of such a matrix is the household composition question asked in the 1990 Decennial Census, in which respon-

Figure 3.10 Minimize the use of matrices.

A matrix structure used in 1990 Decennial Census for seven people (only 3 spaces shown):

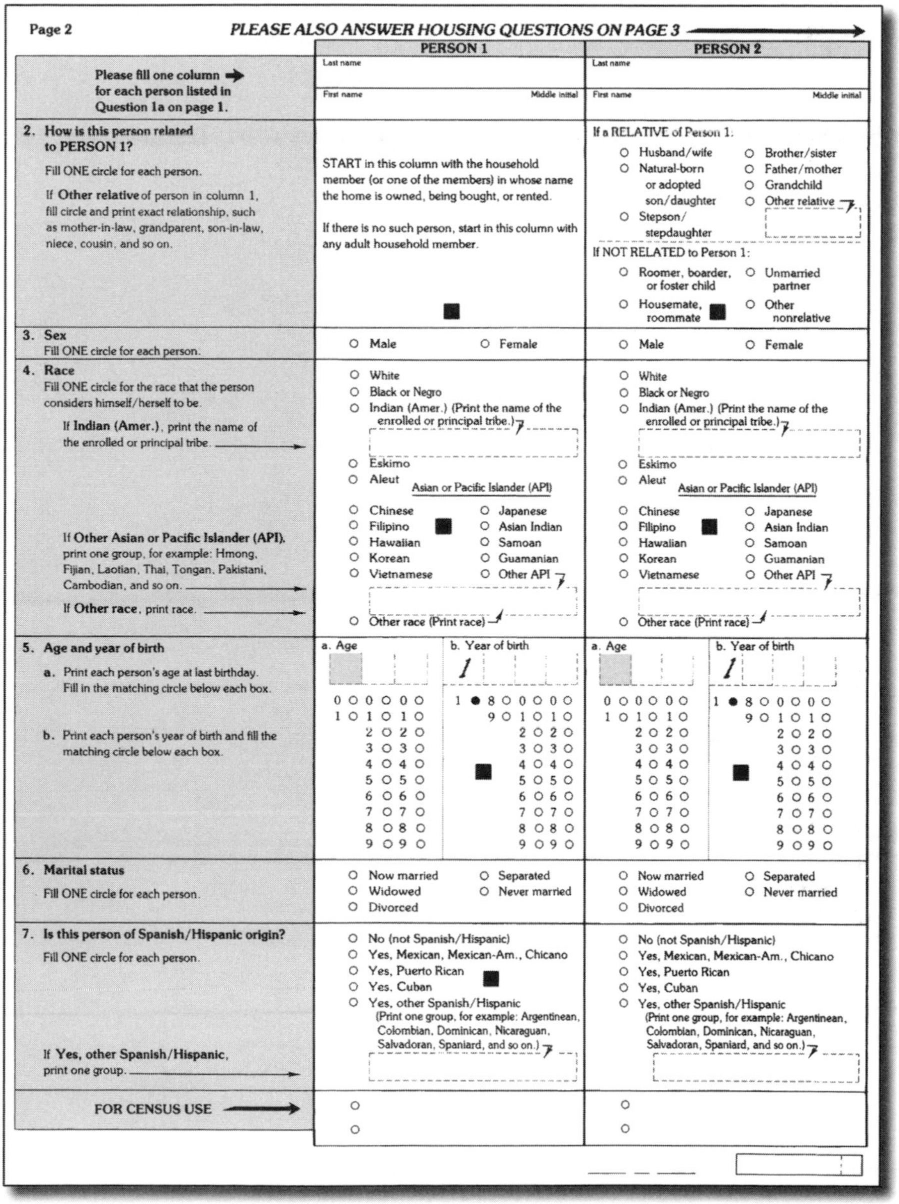

Page 2 PLEASE ALSO ANSWER HOUSING QUESTIONS ON PAGE 3 →

Please fill one column → for each person listed in Question 1a on page 1.	PERSON 1 Last name First name / Middle initial	PERSON 2 Last name First name / Middle initial
2. How is this person related to PERSON 1? Fill ONE circle for each person. If **Other relative** of person in column 1, fill circle and print exact relationship, such as mother-in-law, grandparent, son-in-law, niece, cousin, and so on.	START in this column with the household member (or one of the members) in whose name the home is owned, being bought, or rented. If there is no such person, start in this column with any adult household member.	If a RELATIVE of Person 1: O Husband/wife O Brother/sister O Natural-born or adopted son/daughter O Father/mother O Grandchild O Other relative O Stepson/stepdaughter If NOT RELATED to Person 1: O Roomer, boarder, or foster child O Unmarried partner O Housemate, roommate O Other nonrelative
3. Sex Fill ONE circle for each person.	O Male O Female	O Male O Female
4. Race Fill ONE circle for the race that the person considers himself/herself to be. If **Indian (Amer.)**, print the name of the enrolled or principal tribe. → If **Other Asian or Pacific Islander (API)**, print one group, for example: Hmong, Fijian, Laotian, Thai, Tongan, Pakistani, Cambodian, and so on. → If **Other race**, print race. →	O White O Black or Negro O Indian (Amer.) (Print the name of the enrolled or principal tribe.) O Eskimo O Aleut Asian or Pacific Islander (API) O Chinese O Japanese O Filipino O Asian Indian O Hawaiian O Samoan O Korean O Guamanian O Vietnamese O Other API O Other race (Print race)	O White O Black or Negro O Indian (Amer.) (Print the name of the enrolled or principal tribe.) O Eskimo O Aleut Asian or Pacific Islander (API) O Chinese O Japanese O Filipino O Asian Indian O Hawaiian O Samoan O Korean O Guamanian O Vietnamese O Other API O Other race (Print race)
5. Age and year of birth a. Print each person's age at last birthday. Fill in the matching circle below each box. b. Print each person's year of birth and fill the matching circle below each box.	a. Age / b. Year of birth 1 0 O 0 O 0 O / 1 ● 8 O 0 O 0 O 1 O 1 O 1 O / 9 O 1 O 1 O 2 O 2 O / 2 O 2 O 3 O 3 O / 3 O 3 O 4 O 4 O / 4 O 4 O 5 O 5 O / 5 O 5 O 6 O 6 O / 6 O 6 O 7 O 7 O / 7 O 7 O 8 O 8 O / 8 O 8 O 9 O 9 O / 9 O 9 O	a. Age / b. Year of birth 1 0 O 0 O 0 O / 1 ● 8 O 0 O 0 O 1 O 1 O 1 O / 9 O 1 O 1 O 2 O 2 O / 2 O 2 O 3 O 3 O / 3 O 3 O 4 O 4 O / 4 O 4 O 5 O 5 O / 5 O 5 O 6 O 6 O / 6 O 6 O 7 O 7 O / 7 O 7 O 8 O 8 O / 8 O 8 O 9 O 9 O / 9 O 9 O
6. Marital status Fill ONE circle for each person.	O Now married O Separated O Widowed O Never married O Divorced	O Now married O Separated O Widowed O Never married O Divorced
7. Is this person of Spanish/Hispanic origin? Fill ONE circle for each person. If **Yes, other Spanish/Hispanic**, print one group. →	O No (not Spanish/Hispanic) O Yes, Mexican, Mexican-Am., Chicano O Yes, Puerto Rican O Yes, Cuban O Yes, other Spanish/Hispanic (Print one group, for example: Argentinean, Colombian, Dominican, Nicaraguan, Salvadoran, Spaniard, and so on.)	O No (not Spanish/Hispanic) O Yes, Mexican, Mexican-Am., Chicano O Yes, Puerto Rican O Yes, Cuban O Yes, other Spanish/Hispanic (Print one group, for example: Argentinean, Colombian, Dominican, Nicaraguan, Salvadoran, Spaniard, and so on.)
FOR CENSUS USE →	O O	O O

From 1990 Decennial Census conducted by U.S. Bureau of the Census. (Continued)

Figure 3.10 (Continued)

Example of an individual person structure that replaced matrix in an experimental test Census questionnaire:

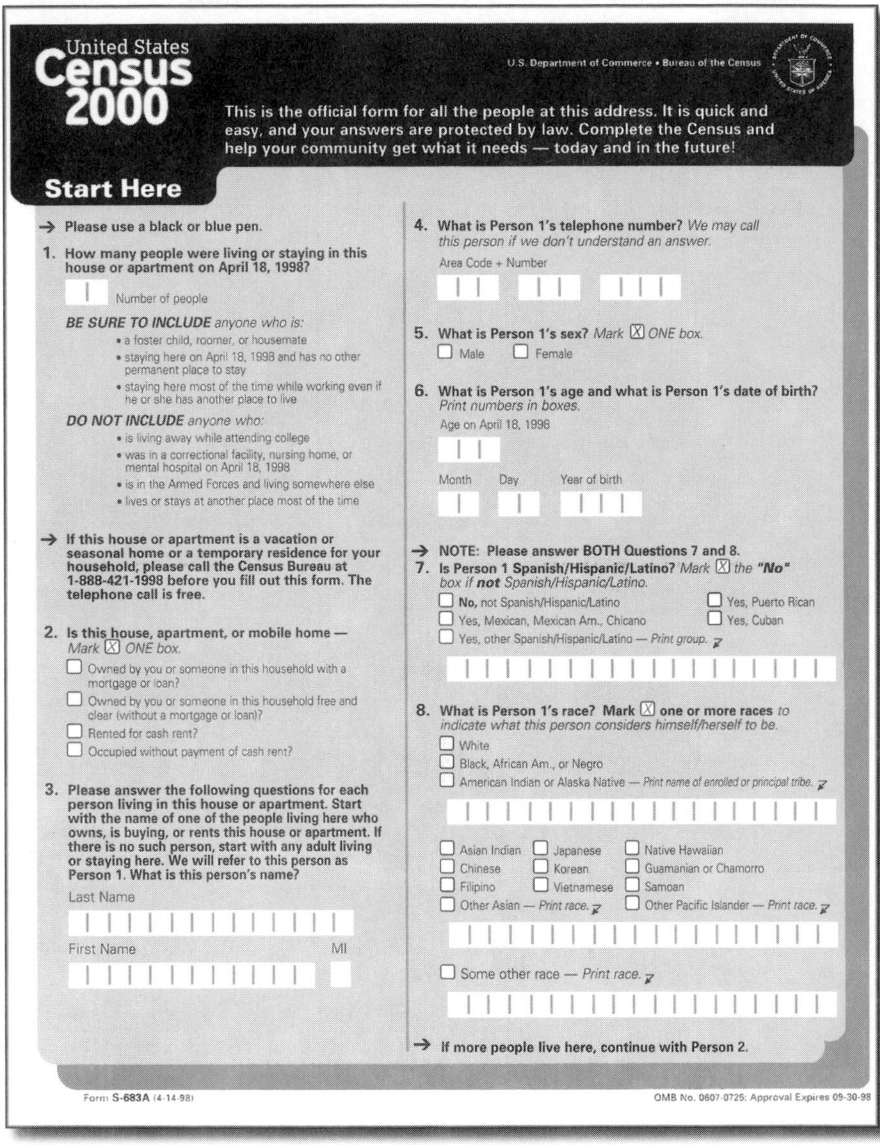

United States Census 2000

U.S. Department of Commerce • Bureau of the Census

This is the official form for all the people at this address. It is quick and easy, and your answers are protected by law. Complete the Census and help your community get what it needs — today and in the future!

Start Here

→ **Please use a black or blue pen.**

1. **How many people were living or staying in this house or apartment on April 18, 1998?**

   Number of people

   BE SURE TO INCLUDE *anyone who is:*
   - a foster child, roomer, or housemate
   - staying here on April 18, 1998 and has no other permanent place to stay
   - staying here most of the time while working even if he or she has another place to live

   DO NOT INCLUDE *anyone who:*
   - is living away while attending college
   - was in a correctional facility, nursing home, or mental hospital on April 18, 1998
   - is in the Armed Forces and living somewhere else
   - lives or stays at another place most of the time

→ **If this house or apartment is a vacation or seasonal home or a temporary residence for your household, please call the Census Bureau at 1-888-421-1998 before you fill out this form. The telephone call is free.**

2. **Is this house, apartment, or mobile home —** *Mark ☒ ONE box.*
   - ☐ Owned by you or someone in this household with a mortgage or loan?
   - ☐ Owned by you or someone in this household free and clear (without a mortgage or loan)?
   - ☐ Rented for cash rent?
   - ☐ Occupied without payment of cash rent?

3. **Please answer the following questions for each person living in this house or apartment. Start with the name of one of the people living here who owns, is buying, or rents this house or apartment. If there is no such person, start with any adult living or staying here. We will refer to this person as Person 1. What is this person's name?**

   Last Name

   First Name MI

4. **What is Person 1's telephone number?** *We may call this person if we don't understand an answer.*

   Area Code + Number

5. **What is Person 1's sex?** *Mark ☒ ONE box.*
   - ☐ Male ☐ Female

6. **What is Person 1's age and what is Person 1's date of birth?** *Print numbers in boxes.*

   Age on April 18, 1998

   Month Day Year of birth

→ **NOTE: Please answer BOTH Questions 7 and 8.**

7. **Is Person 1 Spanish/Hispanic/Latino?** *Mark ☒ the* ***"No"*** *box if* ***not*** *Spanish/Hispanic/Latino.*
   - ☐ **No,** not Spanish/Hispanic/Latino
   - ☐ Yes, Puerto Rican
   - ☐ Yes, Mexican, Mexican Am., Chicano
   - ☐ Yes, Cuban
   - ☐ Yes, other Spanish/Hispanic/Latino — *Print group.*

8. **What is Person 1's race? Mark ☒ one or more races** *to indicate what this person considers himself/herself to be.*
   - ☐ White
   - ☐ Black, African Am., or Negro
   - ☐ American Indian or Alaska Native — *Print name of enrolled or principal tribe.*
   - ☐ Asian Indian ☐ Japanese ☐ Native Hawaiian
   - ☐ Chinese ☐ Korean ☐ Guamanian or Chamorro
   - ☐ Filipino ☐ Vietnamese ☐ Samoan
   - ☐ Other Asian — *Print race.* ☐ Other Pacific Islander — *Print race.*
   - ☐ Some other race — *Print race.*

→ **If more people live here, continue with Person 2.**

Form **S-683A** (4-14-98) OMB No. 0607-0725: Approval Expires 09-30-98

From Census Test Form developed by U.S. Bureau of the Census.

dents were asked to report for each person living in the household, name, age, gender, relationship to Person 1, race, and ethnicity. An experiment provided evidence that changing from a matrix to individual-space format (whereby the questions are repeated in successive spaces for each person) improved response slightly and also reduced item nonresponse (Dillman, Sinclair, and Clark, 1993; Dillman, Clark, and Treat, 1994). In the second of these tests the change to an individual-person format required an additional eight pages (from 20 to 28), but overall response improved from 3 to 4 percentage points.

My general objection to the use of matrices is based on two considerations. One is that they are difficult. The ability to relate rows to columns is a literacy skill much more difficult than simply reading and answering individual questions. My second objection is that matrices usually result in a loss of control over the basic navigational path, and with it is lost maintenance of a common stimulus as respondents read and answer each question.

Step 2. Create visual navigational guides and use them in a consistent way to get respondents to follow the prescribed navigational path and correctly interpret the written information.

Once information has been organized in an order that is efficient for the respondent, it is possible to add visual components, the aim of which is to guide respondents through the words and sentences in the desired order. In previous works with Cleo Jenkins (Jenkins and Dillman, 1995,1997), the theoretical process has been detailed by which people visually perceive and give meaning to words and other symbols. This work is summarized briefly below.

In order to understand a question and the answer possibilities, respondents must use their previous knowledge to gather and interpret the stimuli being registered by visual information printed on the questionnaire page. A pattern is recognized and given meaning partly by *bottom-up processing*, or information gained only through one's senses. Additional meaning is arrived at through *top-down processing*, which refers to what the respondent expects to see based upon past experiences and the visual context.

In addition, the visual information on each page may be examined in two quite different ways. One of these ways is through *preattentive processing*, that is, when the respondent looks at the entire page or visual field and identifies enough features to make general sense of what is there. However, when attentive to the task of responding, the field of vision is much more restricted. When focused, vision and reading are limited to about two degrees, enough to have about eight to nine characters in sharp visual focus, versus as much as 210 degrees at the preattentive stage (Kahneman, 1973). It is critical at the preattentive stage that the respondent be able to figure out quickly where to start and how. Then, when the respondent is focused on responding and seeing clearly within a limited visual field (*attentive processing*), it must be clear exactly what is to be done, for example, how to mark an answer and how to get from one question to the next. Important information located 15, 20, or more characters away from the answer box (for example, skip instructions) are therefore likely to be missed.

There are two general aspects to the design task of helping people solve the visual challenge of figuring out what to do. The first involves recognizing inherent cultural tendencies. In western cultures, people learn from an early age to start near the upper left corner of each page, move from left to right, and generally go from top to bottom. Any questionnaire that attempts to get people to do otherwise faces formidable problems. The second aspect is to modify the visual appeal of particular questionnaire elements in order to attract or diminish the respondent's visual attention to various features of the questionnaire page. Six specific aspects of words and other symbols can be shaped visually to enhance or diminish the likelihood of their being perceived and comprehended in the manner desired by the questionnaire designer.

Visual Element 1: Increase the size of written elements to attract attention.

Words, numbers, and graphic symbols can be increased in size to attract the respondent's eyes, or decreased in size to avoid commanding the respondent's attention. It follows that selectively increasing the size of certain symbols is a way of drawing the respondent's attention to the start of the navigational path, or away from it. Therefore, it is important not to insert large fonts in the middle of a questionnaire page and draw attention away from where a respondent should begin to read, as illustrated by the first example in Figure 3.11. The revision shown in Figure 3.11 uses the largest font on the page at the beginning in a culturally conventional way, with the words "Start Here."

Visual Element 2: Increase the brightness or color (shading) of visual elements to attract attention and establish appropriate groupings.

Similarly, patches of an additional color, such as green on a page of black letters printed on white paper, can be used to attract respondent attention to a particular area of a page. Alternatively, the brightness of a color can be increased, such as changing from gray to black or from a lighter color (usually done by printing with a screen that produces a specified percentage of full color) to darker color. New colors and variations in brightness can be used on the same page to gain adherence to the prescribed navigational path. This feature is illustrated in Figure 3.11 by the change from light type to bold for the question, the question number (in reverse print), and Start Here instructions. Thus, size and brightness changes have been used in concert with one another to identify the place where one should start reading the question.

However, guiding respondents through a set of questions involves considerably more than simply attracting attention. It also requires that respondents

Figure 3.11 Increase size and brightness of visual elements to emphasize order for reading questionnaire information.

Problem:

Start Here:

1. Which of the following is your main work activity?

- ☐ **Research**
- ☐ **Teaching**
- ☐ **Administration**
- ☐ **Something else. (Please Specify)**

____

A revision:

START HERE:

❶ **Which of the following is your main work activity?**

- ☐ Research
- ☐ Teaching
- ☐ Administration
- ☐ Something else (Please specify)

____

see information in appropriate groupings. For example, a question number, the question, special instructions, and the answer choices that comprise each question need to be grouped together as a unit. Within the question each portion needs to be seen as an appropriate subgroup. Figure 3.12 shows an example in which these subgroups cannot immediately be distinguished. The revision uses brightness to distinguish between question stems and answer categories. It is also used to draw attention to the start of each question, by putting the question number in reverse print. Accomplishing the desired grouping effect in this example relies partly on these visual elements plus the two elements to be discussed next.

Visual Element 3: Use spacing to identify appropriate groupings of visual elements.

Another way of signaling to the respondent that a certain set of words, numbers, or other symbols needs to be read and comprehended as a phrase or unit is to locate them close together. Similarly, separating them suggests that they are to be read as separate units. The fact that elements placed close together encourages comprehending them as a unit has been described by Gestalt psychologists as the *Law of Proximity* (Wallschlaeger and Busic-Snyder, 1992).

Figure 3.12 Change spacing and similarity to identify appropriate groupings of visual elements.

Problem:

1. Thinking about the last time you were enrolled in classes, were you primarily interested in obtaining a degree or certificate, or were you primarily interested in learning a new skill or both? Mark one answer: ⌂ Obtaining a degree or certificate; ◇ Learning a new skill; ♡ Both a degree or certificate and learning a new skill. 2. What year were you last enrolled in classes? ______.

A revision:

❶ **Thinking about the last time you were enrolled in classes, were you primarily interested in obtaining a degree or certificate, learning a new skill, or both of these?**

- ☐ Obtaining a degree or certificate
- ☐ Learning a new skill
- ☐ Both of these

❷ **What year were you last enrolled in classes?**

__________Year enrolled

Thus, adding an extra blank line between questions and putting less space between the subelements of each question (e.g., question and answer spaces) conveys to the respondent which answer choices go with which query. The first example in Figure 3.12 illustrates a lack of grouping between questions and among question elements. The revision separates the question number from the question stem and both from the answer choices by adding space. Question 1 is then separated from Question 2 by adding an additional space.

Visual Element 4: Use similarity to identify appropriate groupings of visual elements.

In much the same way that spacing tends to group visual information, use of similar elements (whether based on brightness, color, size, or shape) encourages elements to be seen together. This effect has been described as the *Law of Similarity* (Wallschlaeger and Busic-Snyder, 1992). Thus, switching from light to dark type, changing fonts, or introducing a different color of type signals to respondents that they are moving from one grouping of information to another. An additional factor that conveys a group identity in Figure 3.12 is shape. The first example uses different shapes (⌂◇♡) to identify answer choices for Question 1, whereas the revision uses the same shape for all answer choices. In addition, the question stem and answer choices of the revision each exhibits a consistent rectangular shape which helps them to be seen as separate but connected entities. Thus, four distinct elements, that is, changes in size, brightness, location, and similarity, have been manipulated to revise the problem question format in Figure 3.12.

Filling out a questionnaire is a cumulative learning experience. Respondents quickly learn that such things as question numbers are a certain size and shape and answer spaces (whether boxes or numbers that must be circled) are the same. Conveying the same type of information in the same way throughout a questionnaire aids respondents by making the response task easier, and can be expected to improve compliance with the prescribed navigational path. The fifth and sixth visual elements are concerned with capitalizing on this learning process to make the completion process as easy as possible for respondents.

Visual Element 5: Maintain a consistent figure/ground format to make the response task easier.

The respondent's ability to make sense of written information on a page depends upon being able to distinguish *figure from ground.* First, the eye must be able to separate letters and symbols from the background on which they are printed, a process that requires contrast. Changing the figure/ground format represents an additional way of grouping or separating information. This paragraph is written as black figure on white ground. Changing from black ink to red ink represents a change in figure/ground format. However, perhaps the most fundamental change is reverse print—going from black letters on a white background to white letters on a black background. For example, a black background is printed on the page so the unprinted space becomes figure, that is, white letters, as done here. It is difficult for the eye to quickly make the transition from one to the other. Figure 3.13 illustrates the intermingling of reverse and normal print along with inappropriate use of several other elements. The effect of reverse print is to increase the likelihood that respondents will skip words when reading sentences. The revision eliminates reverse print except in the question numbers, where their "brightness" helps the respondent navigate from one question to the next.

Visual Element 6: Maintain simplicity, regularity, and symmetry to make the response task easier.

An additional Gestalt principle, known as the *Law of Pragnanz,* states that figures with simplicity, regularity, and symmetry are more easily perceived and remembered than are unusual or irregularly shaped figures (Wallschlaeger and Busic-Snyder, 1992). If one chooses to use numbers for circling as a means of providing answers for the first question, it is undesirable to switch to boxes for the second question, filling in ovals or circles for the third question, etc. To do so would require additional, but unnecessary, learning by the respondent.

Figure 3.13 Maintain simplicity, regularity, symmetry, and a consistent figure/ground format to make respondent task easier.

Problem:

❦1) Do you personally drive a car or other vehicle to work? ☛ __ **Yes** __**No**

❷ Which of the these parking policies do you most prefer:

( ) *pay each day*
( ) pay weekly
( ) *pay monthly*

3. Do you prefer a hanging parking sticker or a decal that attaches to the windshield of your car:

☐ prefer hanging sticker ☐ prefer decal on windshield

A revision:

❶ **Do you personally drive a car or other vehicle to work?**

☐ Yes
☐ No

❷ **Which of the these parking policies do you most prefer?**

☐ Pay each day
☐ Pay weekly
☐ Pay monthly

❸ **Do you prefer a hanging parking sticker or a decal that attaches to the windshield of your car?**

☐ Prefer hanging sticker
☐ Prefer decal on windshield

The lack of simplicity, regularity, and symmetry is illustrated in several ways in Figure 3.13. Unusual shapes are included in front of Question 1 and again just before the answer choices, but are not used for the other questions. Answers to Questions 1 and 3 are horizontal, whereas those to Question 2 are vertically displayed. Italics and reverse print are also used irregularly. In addition, each question uses a different shape—lines, parentheses, and boxes—to identify answer spaces. The revision establishes simplicity and regularity.

The challenge in formatting questionnaire pages is less the systematic manipulation of any individual visual element than it is the simultaneous manipulation of all six at once. Figure 3.14 provides an example of a questionnaire page that intentionally ignores all six elements. A larger font is

Figure 3.14 A poorly constructed questionnaire page illustrating poor application of six construction elements and a revision.

A poorly constructed questionnaire:

Start Here

1) During the past 30 days, how often did pain interfere with your daily activities such as your job, working around the home, or social activities?

1) All of most of the time
2) Some of the time
3) A little of the time
4) None of the time

❷. During the past 30 days, how often have you had pain?

1) **Every day**
2) **Between 4 and 6 days a week**
3) **Between 1 and 3 days a week**
4) **Less than once a week**
5) **Never**

3) **Did you feel any pain last week?**

☐ **yes**
☐ **no**

4) Do you wear eye glasses?
Virtually all of the time.....1
Usually just to read.......2
Rarely........3
Never.....4

❺ Is it difficult for you to walk?

___**always** ___**sometimes** ___**occasionally** ___**never**

6. **What is the furthest you could probably walk without sitting down and resting?**

⌂ once across the room and back; ⌂ several times across the room and back; ⌂ up a flight of stairs; ⌂ up several flights of stairs; ⌂ further

7. **When was the last time you were in a doctor's office?**
☐ **this week**
☐ **last week**
☐ **before that**

❽. **On average, how often do you visit a doctor's office?**
a every week
b 2–3 times per month
C once a month
D less than once a month

(Continued))

used selectively in later questions and may draw attention there rather than to the beginning of the page (Element 1). The later questions also appear in darker (brighter) type which may draw attention away from the normal starting place on the page (Element 2). The answer categories of some items (e.g., Question 1) are connected to the succeeding question rather than to the one with which they belong (Element 3). Words that should be seen as a unit, such

Figure 3.14 (Continued)

A revision:

Pain and How It Influences Daily Activities: A Research Study

START HERE

❶ During the past 30 days, how often did pain interfere with your daily activities such as your job, working around the home, or social activities?

- ☐ All of the time
- ☐ Some of the time
- ☐ A little of the time
- ☐ None of the time

❷ During the past 30 days, how often have you had pain?

- ☐ Every day
- ☐ Between 4 and 6 days a week
- ☐ Between 1 and 3 days a week
- ☐ Less than once a week
- ☐ Never

❸ Did you feel any pain last week?

- ☐ Yes
- ☐ No

❹ Do you wear eye glasses?

- ☐ Virtually all of the time
- ☐ Usually just to read
- ☐ Rarely
- ☐ Never

- ☐ Always
- ☐ Sometimes
- ☐ Occasionally
- ☐ Never

❻ What is the furthest you could probably walk without sitting down and resting?

- ☐ Once across the room and back
- ☐ Several times across the room and back
- ☐ Up a flight of stairs
- ☐ Up several flights of stairs
- ☐ Further

❼ When was the last time you were in a doctor's office?

- ☐ This week
- ☐ Last week
- ☐ Before that

❽ On average how often do you visit a doctor's office?

- ☐ Every week
- ☐ 2–3 times per month
- ☐ Once a month
- ☐ Less than once a month

as the answer choices to Question 2, are presented in dissimilar fonts so they appear as two groups (Element 4). The ground/figure format changes periodically throughout the page, making reading more difficult and the likelihood of skipping words greater (Element 5). There is virtually no regularity, simplicity (Element 6), or symmetry across questions, as evidenced by different symbols for identifying answer categories, irregular use of horizontal and vertical listing of answer choices, and several other features that can easily be identified.

Few surveyors would prepare a questionnaire page that is as poorly constructed as the first example in Figure 3.14. However, this example can be contrasted with the revision including exactly the same questions. Here, the visual elements have been manipulated to clearly identify the appropriate starting point of the questionnaire. Elements that comprise each question and the total questionnaire have been appropriately grouped through application of spacing and similarity procedures, in addition to size and brightness manipulations. In addition, changes in figure and ground have been eliminated except for question numbers in which the combination of brightness and reverse print makes it clear which question is to be answered and in what order, thus defining the navigational path. Finally, the maintenance of simplicity and regularity give the page a look that allows the respondent to know exactly how to answer each question after only a quick glance.

The six visual elements that I have just described are the critical tools by which the creation of visual navigational guides can proceed. The remaining questionnaire construction principles in this chapter are based upon applications of these very important concepts. Each of these six visual elements is manipulated in a way that will encourage all respondents to adhere to the navigational path and correctly interpret the survey questions. Size and brightness were identified as ways of attracting people's eyes to a particular part of the questionnaire page. Spacing and similarity were presented as means of helping the respondent achieve appropriate groupings that assist with comprehension of the task. Maintaining simplicity and keeping a consistent figure/ground format were offered as means of making the response task easier and helping respondents achieve efficiency. In practice, individual effects of each element are broader. For example, a change in figure/ground may involve a change in brightness and function as a way of grouping information. I attempt to deal in a practical way with many of these cross functions in the construction principles that follow.

Principle 3.6: Begin asking questions in the upper left quadrant; place any information not needed by the respondent in the lower right quadrant.

The ideal place to start asking a question is near the upper left-hand corner of page 1. When presenting this admonition to a class, the immediate response from a student was, "Isn't that obvious?" Perhaps. Culturally, that is the page location people raised in western cultures typically look at when asked to start. Although it may seem obvious, I have seen many questionnaires that fill this space with agency sponsorship information, special instructions, agency processing information, the mailing address for returning the questionnaire, and other information that interferes with getting started. This is illustrated in Figure 3.15, which places agency information in this area to which the eye is naturally drawn. Such information may be important, but presenting it here in place of the information that a respondent is looking for, that is, how to get started, can only frustrate rather than facilitate the completion process.

Figure 3.15 Example of upper left quadrant of page not being used in most effective visual manner.

U.S. DEPARTMENT OF COMMERCE
BUREAU OF THE CENSUS

FORM
CB-8600

1992 CENSUS OF SERVICE INDUSTRIES
MEMBERSHIP ORGANIZATIONS

OMB No. 0607-0729: Approval Expires 06/30/94

DUE DATE: FEBRUARY 15, 1993

If you have questions about completing this report, please call or write the Census Bureau. In any communication, be sure to refer to the 11-digit Census File Number (CFN) printed in the label to the right. Please return your completed report to:

BUREAU OF THE CENSUS
1201 East 10th Street
Jeffersonville, IN 47134-0001

Toll-free assistance, 8:00 a.m. to 8:00 p.m., eastern time, Monday through Friday:

1-800-233-6136

Please read the accompanying instructions before answering the questions.

Census use

CB-8600

(Please correct any errors in name, address, and ZIP Code.)

YOUR RESPONSE IS REQUIRED BY LAW. Title 13, United States Code, requires businesses and other organizations that receive this questionnaire to answer the questions and return the report to the Census Bureau. By the same law, **YOUR CENSUS REPORT IS CONFIDENTIAL.** It may be seen only by Census Bureau employees and may be used only for statistical purposes. Further, copies retained in respondents' files are immune from legal process.

Item 1. EMPLOYER IDENTIFICATION NUMBER

Is the Employer Identification (EI) Number shown in the label the same as the one used for this establishment on its latest 1992 Employer's Quarterly Federal Tax Return, Treasury Form 941?

094 1 ☐ Yes 2 ☐ No – *Report current EI No. below*

(9 digits)

Item 2. PHYSICAL LOCATION

a. **Is this establishment's physical location the same as the address shown in the label?** (P.O. box and rural route addresses are not physical locations)

093 1 ☐ Yes 2 ☐ No – *Report physical location below*

Number and street

City, town, village, etc. | State | ZIP Code

b. **Is this establishment physically located inside the legal boundaries of the city, town, village, etc.?**

095 1 ☐ Yes 3 ☐ No legal boundaries
2 ☐ No 4 ☐ Do not know

Item 4. LEGAL FORM OF ORGANIZATION AND TAX STATUS

a. **LEGAL FORM OF ORGANIZATION**

Which of the following best describes this establishment's legal form of organization during 1992?

Mark (X) only ONE box.

003 1 ☐ Individual ownership (sole proprietorship)
2 ☐ Partnership
5 ☐ Government – *Specify* ______
0 ☐ Corporation
9 ☐ Other – *Specify* ______

b. **TAX STATUS**

(1) Is this establishment operated on a not-for-profit basis?

005 1 ☐ Yes
2 ☐ No – *Skip to item 5*

(2) Was all or part of the income of this establishment or organization exempt from Federal income taxes under section 501, 521, 527, or 528 of the Internal Revenue Code?

004 1 ☐ Yes
2 ☐ No

From 1993 Census of Service Industries, conducted by the U.S. Bureau of the Census.

The place that the respondent's eye is least likely to be attracted to on the page is the lower right-hand quadrant. That makes this area the ideal space for "agency use only" information or other material not essential to the response task, in contrast to its prominent position in Figure 3.15.

Principle 3.7: Use the largest and/or brightest symbols to identify the starting point on each page.

Another way of helping to assure that people start at the beginning is to use the visual concepts of largeness and/or brightness to help draw their attention to the starting point. This can be accomplished by something as simple as printing the question number in a larger font than that used on the rest of the page, and perhaps putting it in reverse print, for example, ❶. Similarly, printing the words **START HERE** in a larger bold print provides an even more dramatic and powerful attraction. Frequently, I have been shown questionnaires in which the writers attempt to keep people from overlooking an instruction in the middle of the page by placing it in particularly large print. The undesirable result is to attract respondents immediately to that portion of the page, with the result that earlier questions may get skipped. Adhering to the principle of starting to list questions where the respondent expects to find them decreases the need for using highly prominent visual guides (e.g., brightness or font size) in order to draw the respondent's attention to a starting point elsewhere on the page.

Principle 3.8: Identify the beginning of each succeeding question in a consistent way.

Observation of many people as they fill out questionnaires suggests a common response behavior. Once an answer box is checked, the respondent immediately searches for the beginning of the next question. Identifying each question in the same way, and somewhat prominently (through spacing and/or the use of reverse print numbers shown for the revision in Figure 3.14), helps respondents navigate accurately through the questionnaire. These numbers are the most important navigational guides on the page. They persist throughout the questionnaire as a way of keeping respondents on task. For these reasons, we typically reserve the use of reverse print, or enlarged numbers, for this purpose.

Principle 3.9: Number questions consecutively and simply, from beginning to end.

People expect questions to be numbered consecutively with numbers or letters, but not both. Yet questionnaires sometimes identify questions by combinations of letters and numbers, for example, P1, P2 . . . H1, H2, and H3. The explanation in this case was that within this agency P referred to population characteristic questions and H referred to housing questions. The question order meant that P came before H. This cumbersome procedure was intended to convey agency division responsibilities. This information was not only irrelevant to respondents, but potentially confusing as well; numbering questions as 1, 2, 3, 4 and so on to the end would have been easier for respondents to follow.

A tendency also exists, especially among government agencies and other large organizations, to divide questionnaires into sections. One result that is particularly confusing to respondents is to label sections as 1, 2, 3, 4, etc., and then to renumber questions within each section as 1, 2, 3, 4, etc. The result is that small numbers appear repeatedly throughout the questionnaire and respondents become confused when they lay down a questionnaire and attempt to go back to it later. Another unfortunate practice, and one usually aimed at overcoming the foregoing problem, is to develop number schemes such as IA2a, IA2b, IA2c, etc., so that each question is preceded by several symbols instead of one. Such numbering schemes violate the principle of maintaining simplicity and are difficult for people to comprehend. Listing questions in the natural sequence understood by respondents, for example, 1, 2, 3, 4, 5, etc., from the first page to the last is helpful to them.

An unfortunate objection I often hear to the use of a straightforward sequential numbering system is, "If the respondents know how many questions are really being asked, they will think the questionnaire is too long and quit filling it out." I know of no evidence to support this viewpoint. In addition, this type of reasoning suggests trying to get response through "trickery," an attitude which runs contrary to the type of respondent perception that should be fostered with the use of a straightforward, social exchange-oriented approach to respondents. In addition, there are many other indicators of questionnaire length and complexity—including number of pages of paper—that make such attempts at deception quite obvious and place the surveyor in a bad light at a time when trust is most needed.

A simple numbering system also helps make skip pattern instructions easier to follow. Recently I was shown a questionnaire with a high proportion of erroneously followed skip patterns. The problem soon became obvious—respondents who said yes to a particular question were instructed to go to Section Four, which started several pages later. Most turned the page, saw Question 4 of Section 3, and proceeded to try to answer it. Thus, even when sponsors deem it necessary to divide a questionnaire into labeled sections, it is desirable to number questions consecutively throughout the questionnaire so that, for example, Section 1 might have Questions 1–10 and Section B would then start with Question 11. In addition, using letters instead of number to identify sections (e.g., A for 1) is also helpful for distinguishing sections from question items.

Principle 3.10: Use a consistent figure/ground format to encourage the reading of all words.

As noted earlier, the terms figure and ground are used to refer to a relationship between foreground and background. On this page black letters (figure) appear on a white background. When changes are made in the relationship between the letters one is supposed to read and the background on which THEY ARE PRINTED, *sentences are more difficult* to read and comprehend. A consistent figure/ground relationship, a characteristic virtually mandated in the era of typewriters, allows one to concentrate on the meaning of the words rather than having to pause in order to adjust to the change.

Recently I was asked to fill out a questionnaire in which the contractor had been asked to add color. In one question, six of seven answer choices were printed in black ink (figure) on white paper (ground), while the other answer choice was printed in red ink. The visual impact was for the first six choices to be seen as the range of alternatives, and for the seventh answer choice to be missed altogether. The most difficult ground/figure or change to negotiate, as described earlier, is a complete reversal, that is, "reverse print." It is very difficult to read words inserted into a phrase or sentence that appear in reverse print. As a result, they are more likely to be skipped. In general, the use of reverse print in sentences or among answer categories should be avoided.

In order to attract attention to notes or special instructions, surveyors sometimes place instructions in reverse print or in boxes. Because people can read prose fastest when it is written in a consistent figure/ground format, and it takes most people a second or so to make the transition, they are inclined to skip over such instructions to the next information that appears in a consistent figure/ground format. For these reasons, and in spite of the fact that reverse print is powerful as a means of grouping words and phrases together, reverse print is not used within a question either to emphasize a portion of it or to separate a question subcomponent from some other part (e.g., answer choice categories).

Principle 3.11: Limit the use of reverse print to section headings and/or question numbers.

Respect for the power of reverse print that stems from the introduction of "brightness" leads me to use it sparingly, in a way that is most helpful for defining the respondent path and maintaining adherence to it. Thus, its use is limited to question numbers (as in Figure 3.14) and occasionally section headings.

If proposed section headings consist of only a few words, reverse print is appropriate for this purpose. The main assistance it provides to respondents when used for headings is at the comprehension stage of preattentive processing, when the respondent is perusing the questionnaire to see what it is about and how it works. When actually filling out a questionnaire, the mental switch required for reading any reverse print means that the words are likely to be skipped. Skipping over the exact question number, on the other hand, is less important inasmuch as a well-designed questionnaire will have questions located in a vertical format so that location and the presence of a bright (black) spot on the page is all the respondent needs to maintain correct navigation.

Principle 3.12: Place more blank space between questions than between the subcomponents of questions.

As noted at the beginning of this section, there are two levels of grouping inherent to all questionnaires. First, questions need to be separated from one another. Second, within questions there are meaningful subcomponents that need to be viewed and comprehended separately; in particular, the query itself needs to be distinguished from the answer choices. One way of making these distinctions clear is by the amount of spacing. More space should be allowed for separating questions from one another than for separating subcomponents of questions from one another, as was shown in Figure 3.12. Yet a certain amount of spacing between the subcomponents of questions—provided by leaving a blank line and indenting the list of answer categories—helps clarify each subentity of the question. Distinctions between questionnaire subcomponents can also be accomplished by other means, such as the brightness variations discussed below.

Principle 3.13: Use dark print for questions and light print for answer choices.

One method of conveniently separating the actual queries from answer choices is to print the former in bold and the latter in regular print (as shown in Figure 3.12). Doing the opposite, that is, using bold letters for answers, is avoided because of the desire to use the brightest symbols for the part of the question that should be read first. In this regard the sequence of reverse print for numbers, bold for query, and normal print for answer choices provides a desirable hierarchical gradient of most to least brightness that is consistent with the flow of each question. In the first edition of this book, I recommended accomplishing this distinction by using capital letters for answer choices. The computer age provides the contrast of bold and regular print as a much better alternative inasmuch as capital letters are more difficult to read than are lower case letters.

Principle 3.14: Place special instructions inside of question numbers and not as free-standing entities.

Frequently it is necessary to provide a special instruction to clarify a question. This leads to the undesirable practice of placing instructions outside of the question number sequence and emphasizing them by boxes or perhaps a different color of ink.

Once people have gotten into the routine of completing a questionnaire, the marking of an answer leads to the immediate search for the next question, which we usually identify by a question number in reverse print. As a result, free-standing instructions tend to be skipped entirely. Further, attempting to bring attention to them with emphases such as a change in ink, boxes, shaded backgrounds, or reverse print increases the likelihood that they will be skipped. To the extent possible, we insert instructions within numbered questions rather than outside (as shown in the revision in Figure 3.16). Such instructions are most likely to be read if they are expressed as part of the query itself rather than being placed in italics, parentheses, or a separate paragraph. However, exceptions are often made, as explained next.

Figure 3.16 Write special instructions as part of question, not as free-standing entities.

Problem:

❺ **How many months have you worked in your current job?**

_________ Number of months

Please be as specific as possible in answering the next question, including any area of specialization. Example: High school teacher–Math. If you had more than one job, answer for the job for which you worked the most hours.

❻ **What kind of work do you do in your current job?**

_____________________________________ Kind of work

A revision:

5. **How many months have you worked in your current job?**

_________ Number of months

6. **What kind of work do you do in your current job? Please be as specific as possible in answering. Include any area of specialization, for example: "High school teacher–Math".** ***If you had more than one job, answer for the job for which you worked the most hours.***

_____________________________________ Kind of work

Principle 3.15: Optional or occasionally needed instructions should be separated from the question statement by font or symbol variations.

When respondents begin to fill out a questionnaire, they are learning how the questionnaire works, including what must be read and what can be skipped. If they are required to read through a great deal of material that does not apply, or can be skipped without negative consequences, the habit of skipping words and phrases is encouraged. For these reasons a distinction is made between words that are essential for every person to read and those that may be needed by only some respondents. There are many different reasons that reading a particular instruction may be optional. Perhaps it is because the instruction, "Put an X in the appropriate box," is the same instruction used for a previous question and many respondents will remember that. It may also be that only a few respondents need the information: *"If you worked last week but have since quit your job, then you should... ."* To avoid presenting information that respondents already know, or that applies to relatively few of them, we distinguish this information from the query either by the use of italics (as shown for the revision in Figure 3.16) or a symbol variation, such as putting it in parentheses.

Principle 3.16: Do not place instructions in a separate instruction book or in a separate section of the questionnaire.

Sometimes surveyors decide that respondents need detailed instructions and place those instructions in a separate booklet. This decision usually has four significant consequences. First, it greatly increases the likelihood that respondents will ignore the instructions. Second, a detailed review of nearly 20 instruction books, mostly for federal government surveys, led to the conclusion that instruction booklets have a tendency to expand greatly with minute instructions that are rarely, if ever, needed by anyone, thus compounding the respondent's difficulty in finding answers to a particular question. The third consequence is to make the task of responding appear far more difficult than it is so that the questionnaire gets laid aside. Finally, this practice leads to the questionnaire construction tendency of substituting abbreviations, incomplete sentences, and one- or two-word headings for questions in order to make the questionnaire as short as possible. The overall effect of creating separate instruction books is to greatly increase the difficulty of completing the questionnaire.

In many respects, a frustrating cycle is fostered by the decision to create an instruction book. That decision often leads to writing a more cryptic questionnaire that forces more dependence on the instruction booklet. The result is an instruction booklet that is even longer and more difficult to use, a topic I will revisit in the discussion of business surveys in Chapter 10. For these reasons it is important to keep instructions within the questionnaire.

A strong recommendation I made to a surveyor for combining instructions with questions once led to the decision simply to print the instruction book as the last half of the questionnaire booklet. This, too, is undesirable and may be even more frustrating for respondents as they flip pages back and forth without being able to see both of the critical pages at the same time. The solution I favor is to place all of the necessary instructions after the question, where the respondent needs them, as will be discussed in particular for business surveys in Chapter 10. This placement usually results in instructions being shortened. If instructions are quite lengthy and necessary for most questions an alternative is to place all survey questions on the right side of two facing pages and the relevant instructions on the left page, so that a respondent who needs instructions for a particular question can look directly to the left page, at the same level, and find them.

Principle 3.17: Use of lightly shaded colors as background fields on which to write all questions provides an effective navigational guide to respondents.

Many questionnaires, especially those used in large-scale surveys, must include sponsorship information, space for coders, directions on who to call with questions, and other processing information. This information may be unimportant to most respondents and interfere visually with identifying and answering questions.

Based upon considerable research and experimentation at the U.S. Bureau of the Census (Dillman, Sinclair, and Clark, 1993; Jenkins and Dillman, 1995, 1997), an effective method of helping respondents to find and follow the prescribed navigational path is to use lightly shaded background fields on which are printed every question that must be answered, while information not within the navigational path is printed elsewhere on a white background. One of the main effects is to keep respondents from getting lost or confused by the considerable amount of information deemed necessary for inclusion in the questionnaire by federal law and/or processing needs. Typically these fields are printed in 15–30% of full color and can also be done in gray versions (as illustrated in Figure 3.10). The use of such fields is further justified by a related technique for identifying answer spaces, as discussed next.

Principle 3.18: When shaded background fields are used, identification of all answer spaces in white helps to reduce item nonresponse.

It has also been found through Census Bureau research (Jenkins and Dillman, 1997) that adding white spaces wherever answers are to be provided improves response to questionnaires that use colored background fields. The white spaces provide an additional navigational guide, in effect communicating that wherever there is a set of white spaces an answer should be provided (as illustrated in Figure 3.17). It appears that one of the main beneficial effects of white answer spaces is to reduce item nonresponse, but this effect has not yet been tested experimentally.

There is considerable latitude available for choosing the particular color for use as a background field. There is little evidence to suggest that color by itself has a significant impact on response rates, although it is desirable to avoid colors that test respondents believe tire their eyes, such as a bright and glossy chartreuse or pink. The color that is chosen should have wide tint variation available, and pastel colors should be avoided. Using such a color makes it possible to use the full (or nearly full) color for navigational guides (e.g., number or section heading backgrounds) and a partial screening (e.g., 20% of full color) for the background color against which black letters show clear contrast, but dark enough to allow white answer spaces to be easily discerned. Optical scanning, to be discussed in Chapter 12, may impose further printing requirements.

Principle 3.19: List answer categories vertically instead of horizontally.

Response categories for closed-ended questions can be arranged vertically or horizontally. In general, arranging answer choices vertically is preferred because it allows all choices to be listed in a single line down the page, as shown

Figure 3.17 Example of colored background fields with white answer spaces for guiding respondents.

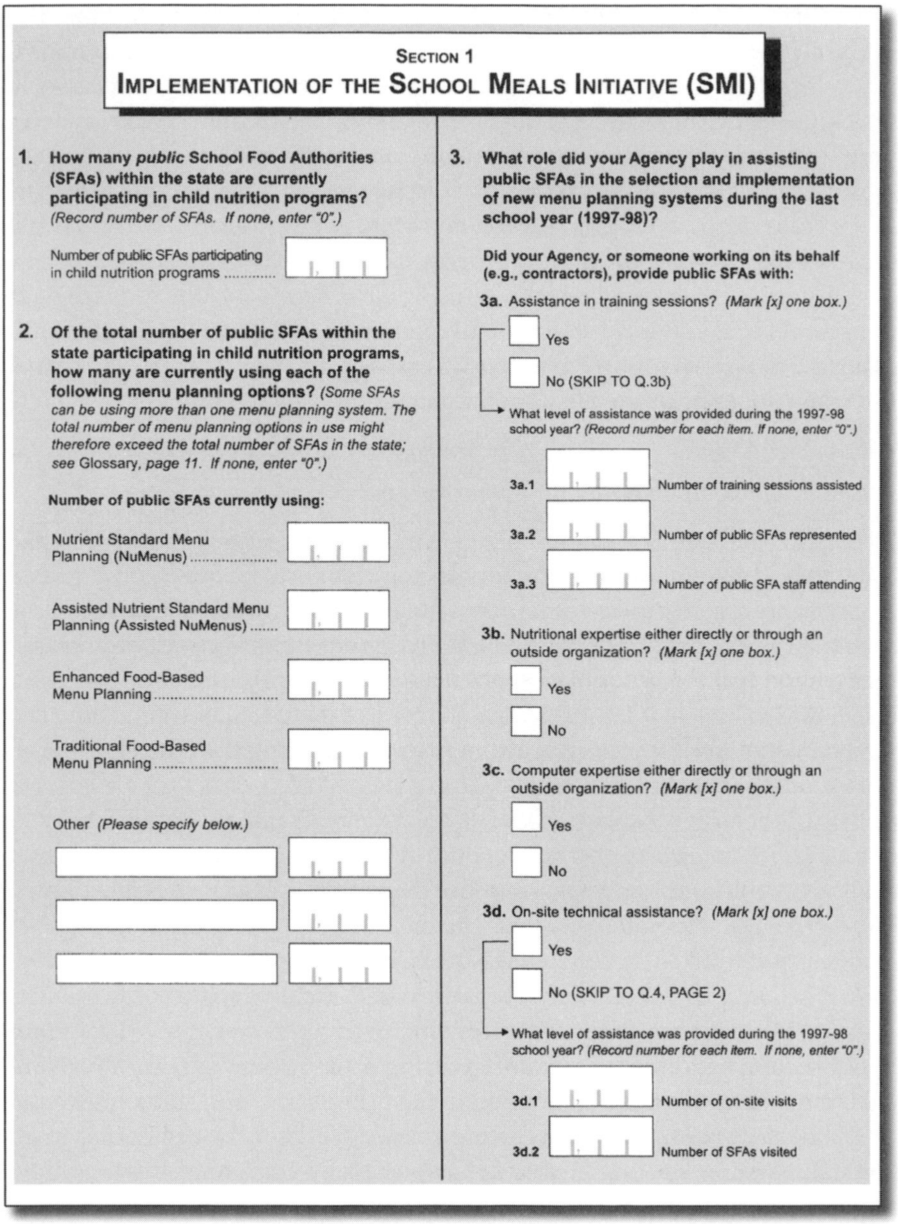

SECTION 1
IMPLEMENTATION OF THE SCHOOL MEALS INITIATIVE (SMI)

1. **How many *public* School Food Authorities (SFAs) within the state are currently participating in child nutrition programs?** *(Record number of SFAs. If none, enter "0".)*

   Number of public SFAs participating in child nutrition programs .... [ ]

2. **Of the total number of public SFAs within the state participating in child nutrition programs, how many are currently using each of the following menu planning options?** *(Some SFAs can be using more than one menu planning system. The total number of menu planning options in use might therefore exceed the total number of SFAs in the state; see* Glossary*, page 11. If none, enter "0".)*

   Number of public SFAs currently using:

   Nutrient Standard Menu Planning (NuMenus) .... [ ]

   Assisted Nutrient Standard Menu Planning (Assisted NuMenus) .... [ ]

   Enhanced Food-Based Menu Planning .... [ ]

   Traditional Food-Based Menu Planning .... [ ]

   Other *(Please specify below.)*

   [ ] [ ]

   [ ] [ ]

   [ ] [ ]

3. **What role did your Agency play in assisting public SFAs in the selection and implementation of new menu planning systems during the last school year (1997-98)?**

   Did your Agency, or someone working on its behalf (e.g., contractors), provide public SFAs with:

   3a. Assistance in training sessions? *(Mark [x] one box.)*

   [ ] Yes

   [ ] No (SKIP TO Q.3b)

   → What level of assistance was provided during the 1997-98 school year? *(Record number for each item. If none, enter "0".)*

   3a.1 [ ] Number of training sessions assisted

   3a.2 [ ] Number of public SFAs represented

   3a.3 [ ] Number of public SFA staff attending

   3b. Nutritional expertise either directly or through an outside organization? *(Mark [x] one box.)*

   [ ] Yes

   [ ] No

   3c. Computer expertise either directly or through an outside organization? *(Mark [x] one box.)*

   [ ] Yes

   [ ] No

   3d. On-site technical assistance? *(Mark [x] one box.)*

   [ ] Yes

   [ ] No (SKIP TO Q.4, PAGE 2)

   → What level of assistance was provided during the 1997-98 school year? *(Record number for each item. If none, enter "0".)*

   3d.1 [ ] Number of on-site visits

   3d.2 [ ] Number of SFAs visited

From USDA National Nutrition Administration Survey, conducted by the Gallup Organization.

in most of the figures in this chapter. Placing answer choices horizontally often means that categories and boxes must appear on more than one line, and it is harder for a respondent to get a sense of linear connection, which is important when an extensive set of vague quantifiers (e.g., seven choices ranging from very strongly agree to very strongly disagree) is used. In addition, careful spacing is needed for horizontally-arranged categories so the answer boxes will not be mistakenly associated with the wrong category. This preference for vertically-arranged categories also stems from a related preference for writing questions in narrower columns (to encourage more complete reading of words), and from wanting respondents to continuously move vertically down each page to get a sense of progress towards completion.

In some instances a scale is provided as part of a visual layout (shown under Principle 22 below) and may be difficult to show vertically. Also, in replication studies that have used horizontal scales or category arrangements, it is important to replicate the visual component as well as the word content of the original questionnaire. In these instances it is appropriate to deviate from the normal preference for vertically aligned categories.

Principle 3.20: Place answer spaces consistently to either the left or right of category labels.

A strong argument can be made for placing answer spaces on either side of a vertically listed set of categories. Placement on the left is supported by the recognition that the amount of space needed for writing answers varies considerably. This method also allows all answer boxes to be arranged easily in a vertical column, which helps avoid item nonresponse. This format tends to group answer choices closer to the left side of the page (prime navigational space) and leave considerable space on the right side of the page for skip instructions and the use of an indentation convention for questions that some respondents were instructed to skip (see Principle 3.26). This method was recommended as part of the original TDM.

It has also been observed (Jenkins and Dillman, 1995) that when the box is on the left, respondents accustomed to the typical pattern of checking an answer box and looking for the next question number or navigational guide tend not to see any skip instructions that are placed to the right of the response label. This is understandable because of the typical two degree focus of one's eyes when reading attentively (Kahneman, 1973). Increasingly, I have found this argument for placing answer boxes on the right to be convincing. Placement on the right is also supported by the argument that the respondents' hand does not cover any of the answer choices when marking their answers, so they have a clearer view of the connection between the box and answer. However, doing so requires the use of dotted leaders in order to get vertical alignment of the starting point for each answer choice as well, or uneven left justification as also shown in Figure 3.18. Extensive cognitive interviews have demonstrated that placement of answer boxes on the right goes mostly unnoticed by respondents, and therefore seems quite workable (Dillman, Carley-Baxter, and Jackson, 1999).

One solution to deciding whether a left or right box method should be used is to preview the kinds of questions to be included in a survey and contemplate the total array of questions to be asked, including the length of answer categories and whether skip instructions are going to be a problem. It is also important to contemplate whether a one- or two-page column format is going to be used. The latter format leaves less room for skip instructions when answer choices are on the right. Often the case for choosing one over the other is not compelling. Definitive research has not yet been done, so personal preference may be an appropriate way to decide. Decisions on this issue, which require bringing together a number of considerations, are characteristic of the many ways in which tailored survey design differs from the original TDM.

Principle 3.21: Use numbers or simple answer boxes for recording of answers.

There are many ways of asking people to record their answers; for example, circle category numbers or letters, check short black lines, fill in small circles or ovals, put an X in boxes, or put a mark between brackets or parentheses. In the first edition of this book, circling was recommended because the technology of the times (typewriters) did not provide an easy method for making boxes, and the nature of circling helped achieved a clearer demarcation of which answer was chosen than did check marks. In addition, numbers provided a convenient precoding system.

The circling of numbers remains an effective way of getting people to record their answers. However, asking people to place X's in boxes is becoming more desirable for most questionnaires. Increasingly, questionnaires are likely to be scanned into computers rather than keypunched, as discussed in Chapter 12. Instructing people to mark X's is more desirable than having boxes marked with a check (✓). Placing an X in a box requires two separate actions (as opposed to a check mark) and is more constrained than a check mark in the way that most people make such marks. Thus, an X is less likely to go as far outside of a box as a check mark, which can then interfere with the optical reading of other boxes. Evidence also suggests that whereas a rectangle encourages respondents to make check marks, boxes encourage individuals to make X's (Caldwell and Dillman, 1998).

Principle 3.22: Vertical alignment of question subcomponents among consecutive questions eases the response task.

In the first edition of this book, considerable emphasis was placed on aligning answer spaces down the page in order to decrease the possibility of answers being missed. Vertical alignment gave a clear navigational signal for where a person was supposed to go on each page in order to complete a questionnaire.

Figure 3.18 Answer categories may be placed to the left or to the right of category labels.

Answer categories in the conventional left-side position:

1. To get to work do you normally ride a bus?

☐ Yes
☐ No ➜ (Skip to Question 5)

2. (If Yes) Which one of the following best describes why you normally ride a bus?

☐ It's convenient
☐ It costs less
☐ I can't find anyone to car pool with
☐ I do it for environmental reasons
☐ Some other reason (Please explain)

____

Answer categories in the right-side position:

1. To get to work do you normally ride a bus?

Yes ...... ☐
No .... ☐ ➜ (Skip to Question 5)

2. (If Yes) Which one of the following best describes why you normally ride a bus?

It's convenient .... ☐
It costs less .... ☐
I can't find anyone to car pool with .... ☐
I do it for environmental reasons .... ☐
Some other reason (please explain) .... ☐

____

- -

Answer categories placed in a different style so dotted leaders are not required:

2. (If Yes) Which one of the following best describes why you normally ride a bus?

It's convenient ☐
It costs less ☐
I can't find anyone to car pool with ☐
I do it for environmental reasons ☐
Some other reason (please explain) ☐

That benefit to vertical alignment remains. Giving attention to how question numbers, the beginning of questions, and presentation of answer choices line up makes it easier for respondents to grasp quickly the entire task before them. Differences in vertical alignment, for example, indenting five to ten spaces from the stem of the question for listing answer categories, are powerful tools for achieving appropriate grouping of question subcomponents (see Visual Element 4).

Principle 3.23: Avoid double or triple banking of answer choices.

Frequently, questionnaire designers must formulate questions that require listing many answer choices and decide to save space by double or even triple banking answer spaces, that is, listing the choices in two or three columns below the query, as shown in Figure 3.19. This practice should be avoided. On closed-ended questions with ordered categories, the scalar nature of the question and the task of placing oneself at the most appropriate point on the scale can easily get lost. For closed-ended questions with unordered categories, the consequences may be worse. Respondents who have been "trained" in earlier questions to pick from among a one-column list of vertically arranged categories are likely to be visually attending to the answer procedures they have become used to and may fail altogether to notice the additional columns of possibilities that lie outside their attentive field of vision (see Figure 3.19).

Figure 3.19 Avoid double or triple banking of answer choices.

Problem:

1. Which one of the following best describes how this land is now used?

☐ Farm Land	☐ Vacant Lot	☐ Pasture
☐ Play Field	☐ Wetland	☐ Equipment storage
☐ Nature Preserve	☐ Forest	☐ Other

A revision:

1. Which one of the following best describes how this land is now used?

☐ Farm land
☐ Vacant lot
☐ Pasture
☐ Play field
☐ Wetland
☐ Equipment storage
☐ Nature preserve
☐ Forest
☐ Other

Principle 3.24: Maintain spacing between answer choices that is consistent with measurement intent.

Recently I was shown a questionnaire in which answers for an agree/disagree question were provided in this manner:

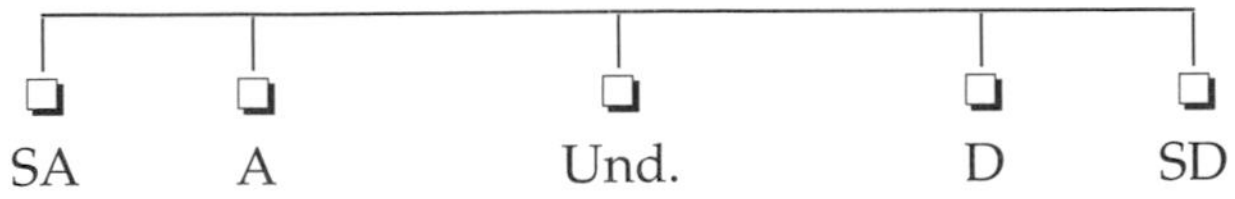

Spacing between answer spaces conveys information about what a category means, just as category order and response labels convey information. This is especially true for scalar questions that use vague quantifiers for answers. In this case, the spacing suggests that the "undecided" portion of this scale is greater than that of the other categories and thereby encourages more people to use that answer choice.

Sometimes questionnaires have some scales that extend nearly across the page and others that are confined to less than a third of the page. Similarly, I have observed scales that extend well across a page horizontally, whereas later in a questionnaire the same scale appears vertically, using a single-spaced format, so that the distance is significantly reduced. It is well established that people respond to more than the words used to write questions, and visual layout is an important part of that additional information (Schwarz, Hippler, Deutsch, and Strack, 1985; Rockwood et al., 1997).

The likelihood of such variations existing in a questionnaire increases when people are trying to "squeeze" questions onto a page, and when items used in some other study are borrowed for a new study. The latter situation often creates a dilemma between maintaining format and spacing used in another survey to which comparisons are to be made, and maintaining consistency with other items in the new questionnaire. Although few controlled experiments have examined the magnitude of such effects, the safe course of action is to strive for consistency across pages and sections of questionnaires, except when cross-study comparisons require that a particular visual representation of a scale need be replicated.

Web questionnaires, to be discussed in Chapter 10, provide a special challenge in this regard. The distances between horizontally displayed categories may vary depending upon the choice of screen configuration and whether questions are viewed in a partial-screen (tiled) format.

Principle 3.25: Maintain consistency throughout a questionnaire in the direction scales are displayed.

In general, it is advisable to keep scalar answer categories running the same direction throughout a questionnaire. The direction, that is, negative to positive or vice versa, is less important. The reason for being concerned with consistency is that learning goes on with early questions and people attempt to use that learning to ease the task of responding to later questions. Two circumstances make this consistency especially important. One is when the label for the first response categories shares the same modifiers as the last response categories on a symmetrical scale, as shown in the first example of Figure 3.20. The distance between the answer box and the answer category (i.e., the word agree or disagree) is greater than 8–10 characters, which is the typical breadth of vision during attentive processing. This makes it easy to check the wrong answer without being aware of it. The second circumstance is when answer categories are displayed above a series of many rows of boxes so that the labels are printed some distance from the answer boxes, as shown in the second example included in Figure 3.20. Staying consistent in the direction that scales run helps avoid respondents' checking a choice towards one end of the scale when they meant to choose the other.

It is sometimes argued that by randomly reversing the order of answers throughout a questionnaire, as in this sequence—yes to no; strongly oppose

Figure 3.20 Consistently run scales in one direction (e.g., negative to positive) throughout the questionnaire to overcome separation of answer box from descriptor.

Potential Problem:

1. To what extent do you agree or disagree with this statement: "This company pays fair wages to its employees."

- ☐ Strongly Agree
- ☐ Somewhat Agree
- ☐ Neither Agree nor Disagree
- ☐ Somewhat Disagree
- ☐ Strongly Disagree

2. To what extent do you favor or oppose each of these proposals?

	Strongly Favor ▼	Somewhat Favor ▼	Somewhat Oppose ▼	Strongly Oppose ▼
Requiring all employees to complete travel expense forms on-line	☐	☐	☐	☐
Being allowed to use sick leave when a family member is ill and needs care	☐	☐	☐	☐
Working four, 10-hour days per week	☐	☐	☐	☐

to strongly favor; high priority to low priority; poor to excellent; no to yes; yes to no—that respondents are encouraged to think more carefully about their answers and are less influenced by the direction of the response layout. I have not seen convincing evidence that this is the case. Instead, this practice appears to lead to respondents having to concentrate more on how to respond correctly than on the substance of each question.

Principle 3.26: Use shorter lines to prevent words from being skipped.

People tend to read text unevenly. As noted earlier, the human eye can focus attentively on about eight to ten characters of text at once. In an effort to be efficient, many readers start and finish reading lines inward from the margins and their eyes move across the page quickly, reading only the text that seems necessary to give meaning to the information. Sometimes crucial words that change the entire meaning of a sentence, such as "not," get missed. Longer lines present a greater challenge to readers because of the need to stay on the correct line as the eye moves across the page, and they seem somewhat harder to comprehend evenly. Thus, it is desirable to use shorter, as opposed to longer, lines for the construction of most questionnaires. This concern undergirds the preference for using two column formats on $8^1/_2'' \times 11''$ pages (as shown earlier in this chapter) instead of running questions across the entire page.

Step 3: Develop additional visual navigational guides, the aim of which is to interrupt established navigation behavior and redirect respondents.

It is now time to turn to the task of partially undoing the consistency in visual navigation that has been established. The foregoing principles of page construction have been aimed at helping respondents get into a pattern of reading and responding that they can count on. Visual elements are used consistently in these principles to make the response task easier, resulting in fewer unintentional response errors. However, as respondents come to depend upon this consistency, the risk of their ignoring critical changes in the expected patterns of response increases. Such changes might include changing a time reference from what has happened in the last month to the last year. Another significant change occurs when, instead of being asked to answer every question, respondents are asked to skip one or several questions based upon which answer they select for a particular question.

The visual tools available for drawing attention to change in pattern are the same as those used for building the design consistency described in the preceding paragraphs. They include the now familiar changes in size, brightness (or color), spacing and location, similarity, a consistent figure/ground relationship, and simplicity. However, interrupting a routine behavior requires somewhat different uses of these concepts and, as I shall argue, a more intense expression than is needed when a respondent is first trying to figure out what the questionnaire is about and how to answer it. For this reason, the challenge of interrupting and redirecting routine respondent behavior is specified as the third and final step of the page construction process.

Principle 3.27: Major visual changes are essential for gaining compliance with skip patterns.

Few aspects of questionnaire construction are more frustrating than getting respondents to follow all skip patterns correctly. The difficulty of getting correct compliance in self-administered questionnaires has sometimes led to the undesirable practice, described at the beginning of this chapter, of writing as many questions as possible so that they apply to everyone. For example:

Q23. If you work out every day, about how many minutes per day do you do that?

__________ Minutes per day

The problem associated with this type of question format is that the sponsor does not know whether to interpret a nonresponse as indicating that respondents do not work out each day, or whether they simply chose not to answer the question. To avoid this ambiguity, we follow the principle of writing every question in a way that each respondent should provide an answer, or be directed to skip it following their answer to a prior question.

Figure 3.21 shows a skip instruction supplied in a traditional way, as I have seen it used in many questionnaires. Here, respondents who give a "No" answer are instructed to skip four items and go to Question 28, while a "Yes" respondent is expected to continue with Question 24. Unfortunately, the instructions (Go to 28) and (Go to 24) are identical except for one of the eight characters required to write each of these directions, and the tiny distinguishing characteristic of these instructions, 4 versus 8, does not get expressed until the next-to-last character of print.

An improvement to these instructions would be to change them so that the instructions are of different sizes (number of characters), and the idea of skipping versus continuing is introduced as in (Skip to 28) versus (Continue with 24). However, even this change does not assure compliance. A possible explanation is that respondents are so deeply into the routine of reading a question, selecting an answer choice, and then checking the answer box as they start to seek the next question that the instructions that are beyond their narrow field of attentive vision get missed.

Several visual techniques can be considered for use individually or in combination to reinforce the message that continuing with the next listed question

Figure 3.21 Use multiple visual elements in concert to improve skip pattern compliance.

A traditional skip pattern which works poorly:

23. Normally, do you work out every day?

□ Yes (Go to 24)
□ No (Go to 28)

24. About how many minutes per day to you work out?

__________ Minutes per day

Addition of four visual elements: Differently shaped directional arrows, word changes, larger font, and redundant instruction to define skip pattern:

23. Normally, do you work out every day?

□ No → (Skip to 28)
□ Yes ↓

24. (If Yes) How many minutes per day do you usually work out?

__________ Minutes per day

Addition of alternative visual elements: Change in location of response boxes with spacing change for screened question to define skip pattern:

23. Normally, do you work out every day?

No . . . □ → Skip to 28
Yes . . . □↓

24. **(If Yes) How many minutes per day do you usually work out?**

__________ Minutes per day

is not automatic for all respondents. As illustrated in Figure 3.21, the concepts and the visual elements being manipulated are as follows:

- Introduce a directional arrow (new shape) aimed at the path the respondent should follow.
- Introduce a different directional arrow (another new shape) to point to another path that respondents can choose to follow.
- Increase the font size of the skip directions to attract the respondent's attention (size change).

- Repeat the qualifying answer in parentheses, such as, "(If Yes)" at the beginning of the question that some respondents are being directed to skip (redundant verbal instruction).
- Reverse the locations answer box and category description so that the box is located nearer to the skip instruction (change in location).
- Indent the screened question so that only questions that are to be answered by everyone start at the left margin of the page (change in location).

Directional arrows have a widely understood cultural meaning indicating the reader should go to the direction the arrow points. They are therefore particularly effective. Increasing font size is, on the other hand, a more extreme measure, competing with other material for attention, and I prefer not to use it unless pretests suggest other procedures are not strong enough. Placing a verbal instruction before the next question as a reminder of who should complete it does not interfere with other aspects of visual design and is highly compatible with instructions contained in the screen question itself.

Changing the placement of answer boxes from the left side of category descriptions to the right side so that the skip instructions are within a few characters of the answer box is quite consistent with our understanding of the narrowness of the span of attentive vision. People are more likely to see the skip instruction as they check the box. However, placing answer boxes after the answer choices and before the directions is also difficult when skip instructions are long, particularly when a two-column page construction technique is being used. Thus, I have sometimes found this method difficult to use.

Recent research aimed at testing the effects of changing from a procedure similar to the traditional format (shown in Figure 3.21) to the format using either right or left boxes revealed that both offer substantial reductions in not skipping when directed to do so (Redline, Dillman, Smiley, Carley-Baxter, and Jackson, 1999). That research project, which used somewhat different combinations of elements than those displayed here, also revealed that the tendency to make skip-pattern errors varies greatly by type of question (Dillman, Redline, and Carley-Baxter, 1999).

Undoing the routine behavior of answering every question is sufficiently difficult that I do not believe using only one of the visual techniques is as effective as using two or more of them simultaneously. In addition, to a considerable extent, the above visual tools lend themselves to being used in combination, as illustrated in Figure 3.21. If a questionnaire contains many questions that involve skips, learning to follow them becomes a part of what a respondent must grasp early on in order to answer the questionnaire. I would probably refrain from using more than two or three of the above techniques (directional arrows, verbal redundancy, and indentation of the screened question) in combination. However, for isolated skips that break a well-established pattern, increases in font size would also be considered.

Sometimes the substance of questions alone is enough to get people to follow skip patterns correctly. If the first question asks whether a person owns a car, and the follow-up question asks what color the car is, respondents will immediately know if they have not followed a skip direction correctly. In a question like the one listed above, it may be less clear whether a question is to be answered. Also, when many skip patterns, some of which involve several questions, are linked, respondents may get hopelessly lost. Such questionnaires require that careful attention be given to building in redundancy between graphics and words.

A second tendency I have noted in discussions with questionnaire designers is for many of them not to be concerned about whether skip patterns are followed correctly. They argue that the usual error is to answer questions that do not need to be answered. However, the frustration of answering questions that "don't seem to apply to me" can lead to people stopping in the middle of a questionnaire and deciding not to return it. It can also lead to carelessness in responding, as represented by the attitude: "If the questions don't quite fit me, then maybe I don't need to be all that careful with my answers." Consequently, the design of good skip directions is considered an essential feature of good questionnaires.

Principle 3.28: Words and phrases that introduce important, but easy to miss, changes in respondent expectations should be visually emphasized consistently, but sparingly.

Emphasizing certain words in questions is frequently essential; for example, when a question introduces a new and particularly important qualification such as "the last three weeks" (see Figure 3.22). Words should be emphasized in the same manner rather than using different techniques in the same sentence, as shown in the first example of Figure 3.22. However, too much emphasizing of words may encourage people to focus only on the words that are emphasized and contribute to the frequently observed tendency to read prose unevenly. In the second example, the entire meaning of the question could be changed if someone were to read only the underscored words. The complete meaning of the question would be changed from asking whether respondents had not called a doctor to asking whether they had. The third example is preferred because it brings attention to the time referent, which was deemed the most critical part of this question for the respondent to comprehend.

I have used underlining here to emphasize these few words, assuming that bold printing of questions was already a convention for stating questions. Italics could be used, unless perhaps their use had been accepted as a convention for additional instructions. Reverse print would not be acceptable because of its strong figure/ground contrast, which might result in the emphasized

Figure 3.22 Emphasize words and phrases in questions consistently, but sparingly.

Problem:

8. During the LAST THREE WEEKS, did you ever experience pain but decide it wasn't bad enough to *call a doctor?*

Still a problem:

8. During the last three weeks, did you ever experience pain but decide it wasn't bad enough to call a doctor?

Another revision:

8. During the last three weeks, did you ever experience pain but decide it wasn't bad enough to call a doctor?

---

words not getting read. Similarly, I would avoid other figure/ground changes such as printing the words in a new color. I also avoid using different kinds of emphasis in one sentence (as shown in the first example) since that compounds the difficulty of reading. Underlining maintains the same figure/ground format as in the rest of the sentence, but simply adds a new element to it.

Placing emphases on words seems to be a phenomenon that grows as multiple people with different interests become involved in determining the wording of questions. I prefer to use it when an idea changes a pattern from previous questions. In this case, changing the recall period to three weeks from the time period used in previous questions seemed most likely to get missed, and these were the words chosen for emphasis.

FINAL ADVICE ON GETTING FROM PAGE CONSTRUCTION PRINCIPLES TO FINISHED PAGES

Adhering to the 28 construction principles provided here may seem a daunting challenge, if not a confusing one. They tie together a clear set of objectives about what the written page should look like, instructions about how respondents should process the information on those pages, and implicit propositions about what visual elements will best help achieve those objectives. Efforts to apply these principles to dozens of questionnaires suggest that they leave much room for judgment and alternative means of application. The result is that good questionnaires can be constructed in ways that are visually quite different. Some designers never use reverse printing; others use it as the cornerstone of their navigational system. Some designers use one-column questionnaire designs and others use two-column designs. Some sponsors prefer to use no color and adhere to a fundamental black on white figure/ground design, whereas others have the capability and desire to make extensive use of color. Suffice it to say that there are many different ways that competently constructed questionnaires can be produced while adhering to the objectives and procedures outlined in this book.

An approach I have found quite workable with survey sponsors and questionnaire designers is to create a style sheet. It outlines visual choices that should be followed, ranging from font size variations to column widths. Draft after draft after draft is then constructed until a satisfactory final product is provided, which is ready for printing between two covers, the topic to which we now turn.

DESIGNING THE QUESTIONNAIRE COVER PAGES

The Front Cover

Questionnaire covers, especially the front cover, are likely to be examined before any other part of the questionnaire. This space should be viewed as an opportunity to motivate respondents rather than a place to put information that doesn't seem to fit anywhere else, such as detailed directions or background on why the survey is being done.

Evidence exists that questionnaire cover designs can improve response rates. Anton Nederhof, a Dutch psychologist, experimented with the two covers shown in Figure 3.23. The first cover is white with little contrast and consists of a repeated map of the Netherlands and a title. The other is the same except for a black emphasis with higher contrast (Nederhof, 1988). The questionnaire with the dominantly black cover achieved a significantly higher response rate than the low contrast white cover (86% compared to 76%) from random samples of Dutch biotechnologists. Of equal importance was the finding of when the improvement in response rate occurred. After an initial mailing, response rates were virtually the same. However, when a postcard reminder was sent, the response rate for the dominantly black questionnaire cover achieved a 10% lead that was maintained through two additional follow-ups. Nederhof reasoned that the black cover was more memorable and when the reminder postcard arrived it was easier to retrieve from previous mail.

In another experiment, Grembowski (1985) found that a graphic design of a young girl sitting in a dental chair with the title of "At What Cost, Dental Care" achieved a significantly lower response rate than a comparable questionnaire with a child by a fountain of water and the caption, "The Effects of Fluoridation on Children's Health." It was unclear why the differences in this response rate occurred, although all of the recipients had state-provided den-

Figure 3.23 High and low contrast covers used by Nederhof (1988) to improve retrievability.

Reprinted by permission of Academic Press.

tal insurance so cost may have not been as salient a concern as the effects of fluoridation on their children.

An experiment on the effects of colored questionnaires versus black and white, which also incorporated variations in word versus graphic designs, and an attempt to replicate the Nederhof experiment failed to produce any differences in response rates (Dillman & Dillman, 1995). However, results indicated a slight favoring of the colored covers (two to four percent) over the others. Although differences were small, this design included tests of four different covers, including a text-only version, all of which were deemed well designed.

An argument can also be made for not having a separate front cover page and starting immediately on page one with the survey questions. If a questionnaire is short and the reasons for completing the questionnaire already known by most respondents, a questionnaire cover may only make the questionnaire look lengthier or make it look like a brochure that does not need to be filled out and returned. In such situations one may consider limiting the cover design to a masthead containing the bare identification essentials and starting the questions immediately below. The concept of starting questions on the first page is supported by extensive cognitive research about people's expectations for the questionnaire to be used in the 2000 Decennial Census (Dillman, Jenkins, Martin, and DeMaio, 1996).

The final word has not yet been written on the effects of questionnaire covers on response rates. However, for reasons of practicality and the need for a place to convey critical information, I follow certain principles for designing separate cover pages for most questionnaires.

First, the questionnaire needs to be immediately distinguishable from all other questionnaires that a respondent might receive, while creating a positive first impression. For this reason a simple and neutral graphical design is often used, complete with a title, as shown in Figure 3.24. Following Nederhof, my goal is to make the questionnaire memorable and therefore retrievable at the time of follow-up. Detailed pictures, especially those selected quickly from clip-art files, should be avoided. I once rushed to find a graphic design for surveying commercial apple growers in Washington state and chose a picture of someone on a ladder picking apples. The first return was from one rancher who circled the cover of his blank questionnaire and simply noted, "We haven't picked apples in this way for years!"

Similarly, a draft cover for a statewide survey on seat belt use was rejected because the graphic designer used an outline of a family in a car, none of whom appeared to be wearing seat belts. In addition, it was a family of four with the father driving, the mother sitting in a seemingly deferential position facing him, and a boy and girl in the back seat of a station wagon that was at least a decade old. A redraft of the cover produced a new car, a unisex driver, one person wearing a seat belt, and the others seated in the back seat where

Figure 3.24 Examples of front and back questionnaire covers used for a state government-sponsored survey.

Front Cover

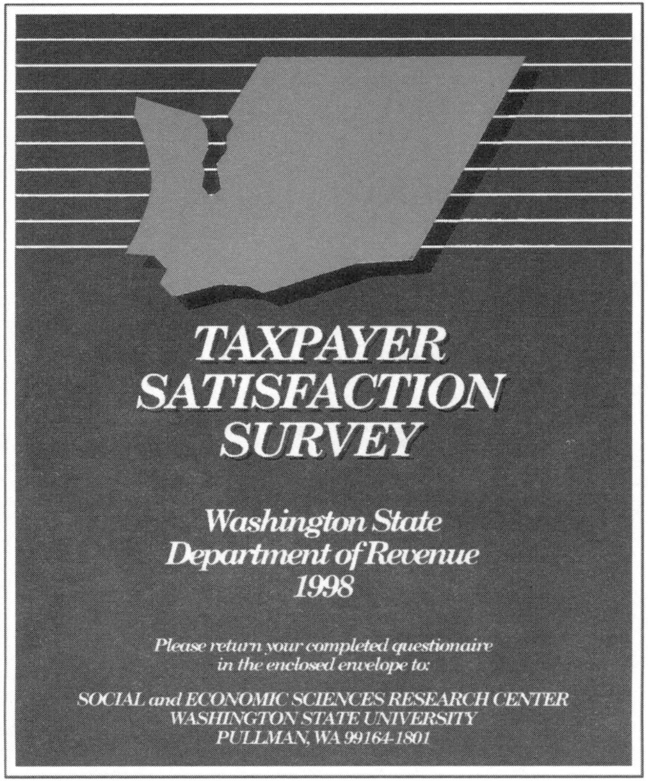

Back Cover

Thank you for taking the time to complete this questionnaire. Your assistance in providing this information is very much appreciated. If there is anything else you would like to tell us about this survey, or the services and products provided by the Washington State Department of Revenue, please do so in the space provided below.

To request this questionnaire in an alternate format for the visually impaired, or in a language other than English, please call 206-753-3217. For assistance for the hearing impaired, please call (TTY) 1-800-451-7985.

Please return your completed questionnaire in the envelope provided to:
Social & Economic Sciences Research Center
PO Box 641801
Pullman, WA 99164-1801

that determination could not be made. The more detail one attempts to build into covers, the greater the likelihood of presenting something that some respondents will find unacceptable. For this reason, simple yet distinctive graphics aimed at making the questionnaire more retrievable are chosen.

Second, a title is included so that in any conversation with the respondent it is easy to identify which questionnaire the respondent is asking about. The title, like that on a book, should be short and simple and written to the respondent, not to the organization or agency sponsoring the survey. In the mid-1990s the U.S. Bureau of the Census began experimenting with a survey that might be used each year to obtain information usually obtained every ten years (the Decennial Census). The working title for the project was the "Continuous Measurement Survey," which was prominently displayed on page one as the title of the survey. Further consideration resulted in the title being changed to the "American Community Survey," a title which undoubtedly communicates better with the members of the general public who received it in the mail.

Third, the name and address of the study sponsor are included so the respondent will know where to send the questionnaire in the event the return envelope becomes separated or lost. As a visible and frequent conductor of mail surveys in Washington state, the Social & Economic Sciences Research Center has sometimes found that questionnaires it has *not* sent to people were returned to it in error because no name or address was placed anywhere on some other organization's questionnaire. Including the name and address is also important from the standpoint of appropriate disclosure of sponsorship, recognizing that cover letters that explain this information may also get lost.

Finally, the questionnaire cover is viewed as an extension of the cover letter. Identifying a questionnaire clearly as being sent from a well-known and legitimate source is desirable for fostering trust that the survey is legitimate and useful. Rather than identifying the questionnaire as being from an individual person or a relatively unknown entity within an organization, it needs to be recognized as coming from a legitimate and respected sponsor, whenever possible.

Designing the Back Cover

The back cover should be kept simple. Normally it consists of an invitation to make additional comments, a thank you, and plenty of white space, as shown in Figure 3.24. This is not the location for adding a few remaining questions or providing detailed instructions.

Our first concern is that this page should not compete for attention with the front cover or detract from it in any way. It is preferred that a respondent first see the front cover and then immediately open the questionnaire. A design that extends from the front to the back cover increases the likelihood that the respondent will examine both covers before starting the questionnaire, and as a result may start flipping through pages of the questionnaire. If the questionnaire is opened from the back, the first questions to be seen will be the most cost-inducing ones, such as income.

Questions are never included on the back page. If our ordering principles are strictly adhered to, the questions that would appear there, such as income, religion, or politics, are those that respondents are most likely to find objectionable. Not only would their placement on the back cover increase the chance of nonresponse, but experience has shown that the item nonresponse for those who do respond increases as well (Dillman, 1978).

Of course, one solution to the potential problem of drawing attention to the back cover is to leave it blank. However, this page can be used in more positive ways. A request for any additional comments on the topic of the study seeks to overcome one of respondents' most frequent objections to questionnaires—questions written in ways that do not allow a complete answer. The wording of the typical request, "Is there anything else you would like to tell us about . . . (the topic of the survey) to help us understand . . . ," clearly implies that this question should be completed last, and thereby refers people to the front of the questionnaire. The solicitation of comments might help in future efforts based on an exchange principle; that is, many people are rewarded by being asked for their advice in a consulting manner. The expression of appreciation is also a small but important attempt to reward respondents for completing the questionnaire.

PRETESTING

Pretesting has always been a highly touted part of questionnaire design. However, in practice it is often done haphazardly, if at all. The term also means different things to different people. Some think of a pretest as an evaluation of procedures which should be done by sending some questionnaires to a small sample of the respondent population and seeing whether any problems come up. Others think of pretesting as finding out if any production mistakes were made in printing the questionnaire by having a few people fill it out. Still others think of pretesting as learning whether people understand the questions. Pretesting consists of all of these things and more, with each actively providing feedback that is not likely to come from other methods in a timely way. We divide this process into four sequential stages.

STAGE 1: REVIEW BY KNOWLEDGEABLE COLLEAGUES AND ANALYSTS

- Have I included all of the necessary questions?
- Can I eliminate some of the questions?
- Did I use categories that will allow me to compare responses to census data or results of other surveys?

- What are the merits of modernizing categories versus keeping categories as they have been used for past studies?

These are the kinds of questions that only knowledgeable people can answer. Few sets of data ever are analyzed without the analyst saying about one or more questions, "I wish we would have asked that question differently." This stage of pretesting, which takes place after all of the questions have been written and ordered, is designed to elicit suggestions based on experience with previous surveys and knowledge of study objectives.

Several types of experience are relevant. Some of it rests with people who have analyzed data and know, for example, that they could not use responses to a particular question because there is virtually no variation in the use of categories. Alternatively, the reviewer might recall that for some reason that question had a particularly high item nonresponse rate in a previous survey. Sometimes the knowledge of policy makers is relevant when they say things such as, "It may be an interesting question, but I don't know what consequence it would have for making a company decision, regardless of which way it gets answered." Another needed type of response is from individuals with survey experience who may notice that "Don't Know" categories are missing, or that a scale is unbalanced and likely to produce an answer with a positive bias. At this stage of pretesting, people need to be consulted who can identify with respondents and determine how likely it is that each of the questions can or will be answered.

It is particularly important to get feedback from people with diverse expertise, which then needs to be reconciled for producing another draft of the questionnaire. The number and types of people vary by study. In some studies feedback is solicited from dozens of individuals and divisions of an organization, representing areas such as marketing, data processing, upper management, and statistical analysis. In other cases, one or two people have been able to provide all of the help that seemed necessary.

My goal with this stage of pretesting is to finalize the substantive content of the questionnaire so the construction process can be undertaken. Once finished, a questionnaire is ready for the second stage of testing.

Stage 2: Interviews to Evaluate Cognitive and Motivational Qualities

- Are all of the words understood?
- Are all of the questions interpreted similarly by all respondents?
- Do all of the questions have an answer that can be marked by every respondent?
- Is each respondent likely to read and answer each question?
- Does the mailing package (envelope, cover letter, and questionnaire) create a positive impression?

In recent years a technique known as cognitive interviewing has been developed for determining whether respondents comprehend questions as intended by the survey sponsor, and whether questions can be answered accurately (Forsyth and Lessler, 1991). Potential survey respondents are asked, individually, to respond to a questionnaire in the presence of an interviewer who asks them to think out loud as they go through the draft questionnaire and tell the interviewer everything they are thinking. The interviewer probes the respondents in order to get an understanding of how each question is being interpreted and whether the intent of each question is being realized. The technique has mostly been applied to interview questionnaires. However, it and a companion method—the retrospective interview—are quite effective in identifying problems with self-administered questionnaires.

In the think-aloud interview, an interviewer explains to respondents that they will be asked to complete a questionnaire in a special way, which is outlined in Figure 3.25. This includes telling the interviewer everything they are thinking as they complete the questionnaire. Respondents are then asked to complete a practice question in order to learn the technique; for example, "How many windows are in the home where you live?" If a person is silent while appearing to be thinking of an answer, the interviewer gently probes, "Could you tell me what you are thinking now?" Typically respondents will begin to describe a counting process that might include: "Well, let's see, I'll start with the kitchen. It has one window, the living room has four, but if you count individual window panes, which I guess I will, there are eight," etc. One question of this nature is usually sufficient to get across the idea of what is to be done. The interviewer then listens and probes gently whenever the respondent falls silent.

This type of interview is designed to produce information when the respondent is confused or cannot answer a question. Typical responses might include, "Let's see, where do I go now?" or "I don't know when this house was built, so I guess I'll leave it blank."

A potential shortcoming of this type of interview is that respondents are dividing their attention between the interviewer and the questions, rather than focusing entirely on the questionnaire. It is also possible that respondents will read more of each question and do so more slowly than they would if they were alone at home. As a result, the skipping of critical words that leads to wrong answers may go undetected. For these reasons, the retrospective interviewing technique is also used.

Under the retrospective technique, also shown in Figure 3.25, respondents are asked to complete a questionnaire as if they received it at home, and to complete it in whatever way they would if the interviewer were not there. The interviewer watches while respondents fill out the questionnaire, noting any wrong answers, skipped questions, hesitations, confused expressions, erasures, or other behavior that would seem to indicate a problem with under-

Figure 3.25 Examples of protocols used for testing U.S. Census questionnaires developed by Cleo Redline and Don A. Dillman (reported in Dillman, Jackson, Pavlov, Schaefer, 1998).

Concurrent think-aloud protocol:

I'm going to hand you the first Census questionnaire in an envelope, and I'd like you to fill it out the same way you would if it came to you at home, except I'd like for you to read aloud anything you would normally read to yourself. And I would like you to tell me everything you are thinking and feeling, from the moment you first see the envelope until you finish filling out the questionnaire and put it into the return envelope to send back. That includes your telling me anything you like or don't like about the envelope, the letter, and the questionnaire.

Remember to tell me what you find enjoyable and what you find frustrating from the moment I hand you the envelope until your are finished. It is important that you tell me what you are thinking and feeling while you are actually in the process of coming up with your answers. The reason we are asking you to read and think aloud is to discover how well people work with the Census mailing packages. Having people read and think aloud is a common technique in testing these packages to assess how well they work, and to discover ways to make them better.

Now because some people aren't used to reading, thinking, and expressing their feelings aloud, I'd like to begin today with a very short practice question. Remember to read aloud whatever it is you would normally read to yourself and to express your thoughts and feelings from the moment I hand you the envelope until you are finished filling out the questionnaire.

Question: How many windows are there in your home?

Examples of general probes:

- What are you thinking?
- Remember to read aloud for me.
- Can you tell me more about that?
- What do you mean by that?
- Could you describe that for me?
- Remember to tell me what you are doing.

(Reinforcement, when done correctly.) Ok, good. You've told me what you were thinking as you answered the question. That's what will help us out. For the census package I'm about to give you, this is exactly what we would like for you to do. Remember, I want you to read aloud and tell me everything you are reading and thinking from the time I hand you the envelope until you have put the completed questionnaire back into the return envelope for mailing.

(Hand envelope to respondent, address side up.)

(Continued)

standing. Then, after the questionnaire is completed, the interviewer asks questions about each of these potential problems. The retrospective interview may be especially useful in revealing navigational difficulties that stem from the graphical layout or the nonverbal language used in questionnaire construction. A potential shortcoming of this method is that respondents may show no outward evidence of being confused at critical points in the questionnaire. In addition, by the time the interviewer asks questions respondents

Figure 3.25 (Continued)

<u>Retrospective interviews:</u>

In a minute I'm going to hand you a census questionnaire in an envelope and I'd like you to fill it out the same way you would if it came to you at home. I'll stay here in the room while you fill it out, but please don't ask me any questions; just do it like you were sitting at home and I wasn't there. I will be taking some notes while you fill out the form. Please don't let this distract you. When you have finished, put it into the envelope for mailing back to the Census Bureau, let me know and then I would like to ask some questions. Okay?

(Hand envelope to the respondent, address side up.)

All right, here is the first mailing package which we would like you to think of as having just received at the address where you live.

<u>Questions asked after each questionnaire is completed by respondent.</u>

1. Do you have any reactions to this envelope, either positive or negative? What are those reactions?
2. *(Turn envelope over.)* Do you have any reactions to the back side of the envelope, either positive or negative? What are those reactions?
3. *(Turn back to front side.)* Does this envelope look like something that is coming from the federal government, or does it look like it's from somewhere else?
   - A. (If federal government) What about the envelope makes it look like it is coming from the federal government?
   - B. (If somewhere else) Where does it look like it is coming from and why?
4. If you received this envelope in the mail would you open it? Why or why not? Does it look official? Does it look like junk mail?
5. Did you notice a letter inside the packet?
6. Did you read the letter? Was there anything in the letter that you liked or didn't like?
7. On a scale of 1 to 5, where 1 means very easy and 5 means very difficult, how easy or difficult was it for you to figure out where to begin on the form?

<u>Examples of post-interview probes to fulfill specific objectives of both type of interviews:</u>

A. <u>Specific questions about the forms.</u>
   1. In comparing the first form you worked with against the second one, which form did you like more? Can you provide some reasons for liking this form better? Can you provide reasons for disliking this form more?
   2. Overall, which form was easier to complete and which form was more difficult? How was this form easier and the other form more difficult?
   3. Next, I'd like to ask about how the forms were folded. Was there anything confusing or difficult about how to unfold or refold the first form you worked with? Was there anything confusing or difficult about how to unfold or refold the second form you worked with? Which form was easier to work with in terms of unfolding and refolding?

Figure 3.25 (Continued)

4. Suppose in the next census we can only use one of these forms. Which one of these forms do you think we should use?

B. Questions based on observation of potential problems.
Now I'd like to ask a few other questions. I noticed when you were filling out the form that ... *(What goes here depends upon what happened in the interview.)*

1. Suppose they skipped an item.... "I'd like to ask about this item *(point to it)*. I see you left it blank. Was there a particular reason for that?"
2. Suppose they frowned.... "I noticed here that you seemed to be thinking really hard, or was there something about this question you were trying to figure out?"
3. Suppose they scanned ahead.... "I noticed that when you got here you stopped for a minute and looked ahead and turned over the form. Could you tell me what you might have been thinking about here?"

C. Wrap-up question.
1. Do you have anything else you would like to tell us that you haven't had a chance to mention?

may have forgotten something they would have articulated using the think-aloud method.

Both of these techniques can be supplemented with previously formed questions at the end of the interview to learn about motivational features of the questionnaires. Such questions may include, "Was it interesting? Was there any time that you wanted to stop answering? Did any of the questions offend you? Would you have filled out this questionnaire if it had come to you at home?"

The test questionnaire can be presented to the respondent in the mailout envelope with a cover letter. Questions are then asked to gain insight into how the person views the entire mailing package. This procedure allows insights to be gained into how well the mailing package and cover letter connect to the questionnaire.

Both the concurrent and retrospective techniques are useful and both are preferred for evaluating questionnaires and making revision decisions. I have also found them useful in comparing alternative mailing packages. In one test conducted at the U.S. Bureau of the Census on alternative mailing packages, 54 interviews were conducted in which people responded to all three of the mailing packages, using both think-aloud and retrospective interviews (Dillman, Jenkins, Martin, and DeMaio, 1996). Results of these interviews were quite consistent with response differences observed in a simultaneous national field test of these forms (Leslie, 1996). Respondents to cognitive interviews said they were more likely to open and respond to a questionnaire that emphasized an official government approach than they were to respond to others that emulated mass marketing techniques with extensive use of bright colors. The latter forms obtained response rates five to ten percentage points less than the government-oriented forms, thus confirming the identification of problems with the marketing appeal materials identified in the cognitive/motivational interviews (Dillman, Jenkins, Martin, and DeMaio, 1996; Leslie, 1997).

There can be little doubt that greater use of cognitive/motivational interviews would improve most questionnaires. However, such interviews are labor intensive and are usually done in small numbers of a dozen or so, unless a large-scale survey of much importance is being undertaken. Doing the interviews in such small numbers means one should be cautious about thinking that all problems can be caught by such interviews. Problems that exist for only five to 10 percent of the survey population are likely to be missed entirely as a result. Nonetheless, the use of cognitive interviews is indispensable and a natural lead-in to a third type of pretesting.

STAGE 3: A SMALL PILOT STUDY

Some questions cannot be answered by cognitive interviews or the other pretest activities I have discussed. Presumably, the knowledgeable person review and the cognitive/motivational interviews have revealed ways of improving the questionnaire. The next pretest step is to do a pilot study that emulates procedures proposed for the main study. Generally, this means that a considerable amount of resources are being invested in the survey and there is a need to see if all of the parts work.

- Have I constructed the response categories for scalar questions so people distribute themselves across categories rather than being concentrated in only one or two of them?
- Do any items from which I hope to build a scale correlate in a way that will allow me to build scales? What kind of response rate is the survey likely to obtain?
- Are some questions generating a high item nonresponse rate?
- Do some variables correlate so highly that for all practical purposes I can eliminate one or more of them?
- Is useful information being obtained from open-ended questions?
- Are entire pages or sections of the questionnaire being skipped?
- What response rate can I expect?

For a pilot study, a sample of 100 to 200 respondents is generally drawn, but it may be larger if resources allow. The respondents receive each of the mailings or other contacts just as they would with the main survey. Such a pilot allows quantitative estimates to be made for response rates, item nonresponse, and variable distributions.

Pilot studies frequently result in substantial revisions being made in the survey design, from adding additional contacts or an incentive to improve response rates, to eliminating or adding survey questions. Entering data from 100–150 responses allows one to make reasonably precise estimates as to whether respondents are clustering into certain categories of questions. One pretest I observed resulted in changing a number of community satisfaction questions from a four-point (excellent, good, fair, or poor) to a six-point (outstanding, very good, good, fair, poor, or very poor) scale because nearly two-thirds of the respondents were grouping into the "excellent" categories, thus limiting the variation analysts had hoped to have for examining relationships among variables. I have also seen skip instructions made more prominent by means of the visual techniques described in this chapter, because some were being missed in the pilot study.

Stage 4: A final check. Did we do something silly?

The final step of pretesting is to ask a few people who have had nothing to do with the development or revision of the questionnaire and related materials to sit down by themselves and answer it completely. People who have worked on one revision after another soon lose their ability to detect obvious problems. Asking employees to read a questionnaire again for problems does not always result in catching them.

I once was explaining this last step of pretesting to some students a few minutes after handing a questionnaire to a likely respondent for this final test. Before finishing my explanation the respondent appeared in the doorway with a frown and said, "Did you really mean to do this?" Her finger was pointing to the scale used for six opinion items on the first page which read: "strongly oppose, somewhat oppose, somewhat favor, strongly oppose." Somehow this error had slipped through several final readers who had read the questionnaire more as proofreaders than as respondents.

CONCLUSION

Too often, constructing the questionnaire is viewed by survey sponsors as an afterthought—the task that someone else does after they have approved the list of questions. Sometimes the task is delegated to an inexperienced employee with the instruction to make it look as short as possible. A more appropriate perspective is that a list of questions is only the starting point, and there is much left to be done that will significantly influence nonresponse, item omissions, measurement error, and overall survey success.

Constructing a self-administered questionnaire is difficult at best. A good questionnaire is almost never drafted in one sitting, or even several. Experienced questionnaire designers often need eight or even ten revisions to get close to a version that meets all of the criteria discussed in this chapter, including selecting a format, ordering the questions, and organizing the two information languages—words and graphics—that comprise every page.

Some of the concepts discussed in this chapter are unfamiliar to most well-trained survey methodologists. These may include the simultaneous manipulation of size, brightness, figure/ground, simplicity, location, and regularity to achieve appropriate groupings and subgroupings of the information that comprises each questionnaire page. Yet, application of some of these concepts is not something completely new. It has been done implicitly by many surveyors since self-administered questionnaires were first used. What is new is that modern word processors and copying capabilities have given every questionnaire designer far greater capabilities for this manipulation than were available prior to the 1980s. The options now available require us to achieve a more formal understanding of how people see and process information. We expect these capabilities for manipulating words, shapes, and symbols on questionnaire pages to continue to expand, especially for the development of web questionnaires, as discussed in Chapter 11. Thus, it is important that understanding and working with these concepts be added to the professional skills of questionnaire designers.

The reactions I have received to attempts to teach the integration of visual and word aspects of questionnaire construction to others has been instructive. For some people it seemed only natural to visually shape a questionnaire page, even to the point of their thinking that words are mostly irrelevant in determining how they move from one part of a questionnaire page to another. Others have responded with folded arms and the declaration that they are "readers" and would do whatever the words suggest, regardless of graphical layout. This perspective sometimes leads to the conclusion that for them, visual layout is immaterial. Cognitive interviews done on dozens of questionnaires suggest to me that neither reality is as pure as it is sometimes expressed—self-professed readers often make navigational mistakes and graphically-oriented individuals often become engrossed in the visual flow of questionnaires to the point of missing the intent of a question or instruction. These experiences suggest to me that the science of applying these concepts is still being developed. In my view, these concepts represent exceedingly important research priorities for the future.

The desired outcome of the questionnaire construction process is a document that has been tested and retested, and is ready to be turned over to the respondent. The procedures for doing that in pursuit of a response from most or all members of the survey population is the topic of the next chapter.

CHAPTER 4

Survey Implementation

THE QUESTIONNAIRE is only one element of a well-done survey. Moreover, no matter how well constructed or easy to complete, it is *not* the main determinant of response to mail or other self-administered surveys. Implementation procedures have a much greater influence on response rates. Multiple contacts, the contents of letters, appearance of envelopes, incentives, personalization, sponsorship and how it is explained, and other attributes of the communication process have a significantly greater collective capability for influencing response rates than does questionnaire design.

Previous experimental research on how to improve mail survey response is unanimous on the influence of one primary factor on response rates. Multiple contacts have been shown to be more effective than any other technique for increasing response to surveys by mail (e.g., Scott, 1961; Linsky, 1975; Dillman, 1991). This finding should not be surprising inasmuch as repeated contacts are also key to improving response to interview surveys. Recent research confirms that this is also true for surveys by e-mail (Schaefer and Dillman, 1998).

Close behind in proven effectiveness is the use of token financial incentives sent with the request to respond. Other techniques, from personalization of correspondence to stamped return envelopes, have been shown to have modest effects on response rates in most survey situations, and are usually important for maximizing survey response (e.g., Dillman, 1991).

However, certain proven implementation techniques cannot be used for some surveys. For example, token financial incentives are currently prevented for use in most federal government mail surveys. Conversely, a technique found especially effective for certain government surveys, the statement that response is mandatory, cannot be used for the vast majority of surveys which are voluntary. Other techniques may be rejected because of concerns about burden to respondents; for example, certified mail, which requires respondents to sign for delivery and may, therefore, require a trip to the post office.

One of the most common mistakes made in the design of mail surveys is to assume the existence of a "magic bullet," that is, one technique that will assure a high response rate regardless of how other aspects of the survey are designed. As with the powerful engine and superior steering system that give distinctive qualities to certain high quality cars, these features do not excuse designers from giving careful attention to all other aspects of a car's design, from tires to paint. Such careful attention to details of survey implementation is the focus of this chapter.

FIVE NEEDED ELEMENTS FOR ACHIEVING HIGH RESPONSE RATES

Tailored Design utilizes, as a reference point, a general method of implementation that should achieve good results for most surveys. That method is then refined for specific situations, as described in subsequent chapters. It consists of five elements which have individually been shown to significantly improve response to mail surveys in most situations. Each element is shaped in ways that complement the other elements. These elements include: (1) a respondent-friendly questionnaire, (2) up to five contacts with the questionnaire recipient, (3) inclusion of stamped return envelopes, (4) personalized correspondence, and (5) a token financial incentive that is sent with the survey request.

ELEMENT 1: RESPONDENT-FRIENDLY QUESTIONNAIRE

Chapter 3 presented the elements of what makes a questionnaire respondent-friendly—questions that are clear and easy to comprehend, a question order that suggests high salience to the respondent, and a questionnaire layout that is in accordance with visual principles of design for comprehension and easy response. Certain other factors may or may not be within the power of the questionnaire designer to affect, such as shortening the questionnaire so that fewer questions are asked and the burden decreased, or creating interest-getting questions to draw the respondent into the questionnaire. Following the design principles discussed in Chapter 3 will have a modest but positive influence on overall response rates, and a somewhat greater influence on item-nonresponse.

ELEMENT 2: FOUR CONTACTS BY FIRST CLASS MAIL, WITH AN ADDITIONAL "SPECIAL" CONTACT

Multiple contacts are essential for maximizing response to mail surveys. Once, when suggesting multiple contacts to a client, the immediate response was, "No problem, we'll just print a lot of extra questionnaire packets and stamp 'second notice' on the outside of the envelope." This meant that the dated letter and other contents would appear the same as those received earlier. Under social exchange, stimuli that are different from previous ones are generally more powerful than repetition of a previously used technique. People with whom the first letter was successful will not be subject to receiving a replacement questionnaire. Therefore, the later contacts need to be varied in an effort to increase their effectiveness with nonrespondents. A system of five compatible contacts includes the following:

- A brief *prenotice letter* that is sent to the respondent a few days prior to the questionnaire. It notes that a questionnaire for an important survey will arrive in a few days and that the person's response would be greatly appreciated.
- A *questionnaire* mailing that includes a detailed cover letter explaining why a response is important.
- A *thank you postcard* that is sent a few days to a week after the questionnaire. This mailing expresses appreciation for responding, and indicates that if the completed questionnaire has not yet been mailed it is hoped that it will be returned soon.
- A *replacement questionnaire* that is sent to nonrespondents 2–4 weeks after the previous questionnaire mailing. It indicates that the person's completed questionnaire has not yet been received and urges the recipient to respond.
- A *final contact* that may be made by telephone a week or so after the fourth contact (if telephone numbers are available). It may also be made by Federal Express, priority U.S. mail, or special delivery 2–4 weeks after the previous mailing. The *different mode* of contact distinguishes each type of final contact from regular mail delivery. Each of these delivery modes builds upon past research (Dillman et al., 1974; Heberlein and Baumgartner, 1978) showing that a "special" contact of these types improves overall response to mail surveys.

The contact sequence described here has several implied components that make it into more than a randomly assembled collection of five contacts. Each contact has a different look and feel to it. Each communication differs from the previous one and conveys a sense of appropriate renewal of an effort to communicate. The prenotice letter indicates briefly that something will be coming in the mail and asks for no immediate response. The first questionnaire mailing explains the nature of the request and asks for a response. The postcard follow-up has a different visual appearance (postcard versus letter) and is expressed as a thank you. The replacement questionnaire contains a powerful form of implicit personalization—"We've not yet heard from you . . ." The final contact expresses the importance of response to the sponsor by showing the expenditure of considerably more effort and resources, as reflected by the cost of delivery.

Timing is also an important aspect of the contacts. If the prenotice were to be sent several weeks ahead of the questionnaire mailing, it would be forgotten and have no effect on response. The postcard thank you is designed to get to respondents while the questionnaire is still in their possession and to provide a gentle reminder that the questionnaire is important. These latter mailings are timed to give a reasonable time for response prior to their being sent.

ELEMENT 3: RETURN ENVELOPES WITH REAL FIRST-CLASS STAMPS

Use of reply envelopes with real stamps affixed instead of business reply envelopes will improve response several percentage points. Sending a real stamp represents a goodwill gesture; the sender has sent something of value that recipients can use for some other purpose if they like. However, it is precisely this quality of reciprocating an effort of value that social exchange is about. A contributing factor to this positive effect may be the difficulty of throwing away anything with monetary value. The questionnaire is less likely to be discarded and will therefore be present when the carefully-timed postcard reminder is sent.

ELEMENT 4: PERSONALIZATION OF CORRESPONDENCE

Correspondence can be personalized in many ways—the use of real stationery printed on high quality paper, real names instead of a preprinted salutation of "Dear Resident," real signatures, or simply sending replacement mailings with the message: "To the best of our knowledge you have not yet responded." It has been suggested that personalization has lost effectiveness in recent years because it is easy to program word processors to write letters such as, "Dear Don Dillman, I am writing to inform you and your wife Joye that the XYZ Company has created a new dog food that we are sure your Boston Terrier, Crickett, will find to be very tasty. We would like to send a free sample to your home in Pullman, Washington . . ." Such letters are impersonal precisely because of the extreme effort to insert personal references.

Personalization might best be thought of as what one would do in a letter sent to a business acquaintance who is not well known to the sender. It provides the look and feel of being from a real person, rather than a carefully programmed computer. Recent tests of personalizing mailings on general public samples, each of which used four contacts, resulted in response rate increases of 5 to 11% in four-contact general public surveys in four states: Idaho, Oregon, Pennsylvania, and Washington (Dillman, Lesser, Carlson, Mason, Willits, and Jackson, 1999). In most cases, personalization is an integral part of Tailored Design.

Element 5: Token Prepaid Financial Incentives

As noted in Chapter 1, research has shown consistently that the inclusion of small, token financial incentives of one to five dollars with a request to respond to a mail questionnaire can improve response rates significantly. Promised incentives do not have nearly so great an effect on response, and have even been shown to have no effect at all. The reason is that promising to pay after the questionnaire is returned changes the terms of exchange from social to economic. It is easy to decline the request to complete a questionnaire when it offers to pay respondents for their time; if the price is too low, or the person simply isn't interested in doing it at any price, it is culturally acceptable not to respond. However, if a surveyor has made a goodwill gesture such as sending a dollar or two as a token of appreciation in advance, that produces a sense of reciprocal obligation, especially if the offer is made in a pleasant way. This topic is elaborated in more detail later in this chapter.

These five elements of a respondent-friendly questionnaire, five timely contacts, a stamped return envelope, personalization, and token financial incentives are the basic structural features around which an effective implementation system can be developed. As such, they constitute the skeleton around which additional details, to be described in the remainder of this chapter, are developed. Readers familiar with the mail survey literature will note that many techniques that have been researched are not included; these include, for example, deadline dates, color of questionnaire, material incentives, multiple denomination stamps on the outgoing envelope, official sponsorship, and length of cover letter. Some of these techniques appear to have no effect; for example, real stamps on outgoing envelopes. Others, such as material incentives, might be considered when the far more powerful token financial incentives cannot be used. Still others, such as orientation and length of cover letters, are details that depend upon the particular survey situation.

CHANGE FROM THE TOTAL DESIGN METHOD

Users of the original Total Design Method will note certain differences from that method, specifically the inclusion of token financial incentives, a stamped-return envelope (presented only as an option with the TDM), and a change in the number and type of contacts. The addition of incentives is the most significant difference and is based upon the fact that several experimental tests of the effects of token financial incentives in conjunction with use of the complete Total Design Method have produced significant increases in response rates (Dillman, 1991). Also, tantalizing evidence exists that token financial incentives may be especially effective with younger respondents (who are less likely to respond to mail surveys), thereby helping to reduce nonresponse error in certain populations (Dillman, 1997). The stamped return envelope, a technique mentioned as an option under the TDM, was added because of consistent evidence from the literature and several experiments of my own that produced a response improvement of two to four percent (Dillman, 1978, 1991).

Considerable research has suggested that a prior notice is an effective stimulus for reducing nonresponse (Dillman, Clark, and Sinclair, 1995), although this effectiveness seems to stem from the fact that an additional contact has been made rather than its uniqueness as a contact (Dillman, Dillman, Baxter, Petrie, Miller, and Carley, 1995). From a social exchange perspective, the prenotice letter provides an opportunity to send a different kind of contact (one not asking for an immediate response) which might be shaped in a way that builds interest and anticipation, and thereby influences the balance of rewards and costs.

The use of five contacts rather than four, as described in the first edition of this book, reflects changes in U.S. society. The basic TDM method began with a questionnaire mailing, followed by a one-week postcard thank you/reminder, a replacement questionnaire sent after two additional weeks, and a final replacement questionnaire sent by certified mail after three more weeks had elapsed. Certified mail was a very effective technique, eliciting responses from as many as a third of the nonrespondents to earlier mailings (Moore and Dillman, 1980; Dillman et al., 1974), but required recipients to sign for the letter. If recipients were not at home, this could require a trip to the post office. Early research showed that other special contacts—telephone, special delivery, and U.S. Postal Service priority mail—have effects similar to certified mail, but do not require that the respondent be at home to accept delivery (Moore and Dillman, 1980).

In addition, the trend in survey research has been for face-to-face and telephone survey methods to require more contacts to achieve a given level of response. The use of 20 to 30 contacts is not unusual. It is now standard telephone survey practice to attempt to convert "soft" refusals; for instance, people who have hung up while saying something like, "I don't have time." It has also been argued that the tailoring of the arguments used by interviewers in these multiple contacts is effective in improving response rates through refusal conversion (Groves and Couper, 1998). Adding another contact to a mail implementation system provides one more opportunity to shape the kind of request being made to nonrespondents, and in particular to seek response from individuals under-represented in early questionnaire returns.

One other consideration that has shaped the change from TDM to Tailored Design is the influence of sometimes conflicting pressures from groups with much influence over how surveys get done. The United States Office of Management and Budget strongly encourages agencies to use methods that achieve very high response rates, often 80%. To do that, especially with the general public, requires the use of an intensive implementation system. On the other hand, human subjects protection committees in universities and public agencies often place pressure on survey sponsors to reduce efforts to get recipients to respond to surveys in an attempt to keep intrusions into people's lives at a minimum.

Our goal in changing the number and nature of contacts from those used in the TDM is aimed at satisfying both needs. We are attempting to improve response rates, but to do that in a way that is not offensive to respondents. Both the prenotice and final contact by special mail or telephone, and the wording associated with each contact, are aimed at finding an appropriate balance. In the remainder of this chapter, step-by-step details are provided for implementing Tailored Design surveys.

DETAILED FEATURES OF THE IMPLEMENTATION SYSTEM

Research has shown that the failure to return a mail questionnaire can be traced to many different aspects of survey implementation. Kulka, Holt, Carter, and Dowd (1991), in an analysis of why people did not return the Decennial Census form, found that some people did not recall receiving it, others recalled receiving it but did not open it, and still others opened it but did not start to fill it out. Further, some of those who started to fill it out did not finish and some who finished did not mail it back. Reasons offered for not completing and returning a questionnaire range from "not thinking it's important" or "not interested in the topic" to "concern about confidentiality" or simply, "just not getting around to it."

Research by Heberlein and Baumgartner (1978) has shown that a strong predictor of response rates to mail surveys is the salience of the questionnaire. Questionnaires that asked about current behaviors or interests were defined as highly salient, while those that asked about neither were defined as not salient. An example of a highly salient survey, offered by Heberlein and Baumgartner (1978), is a Veterans' Administration survey of educational plans and interests of veterans who had expressed a desire for receiving educational assistance. A nonsalient questionnaire was confined to asking demographic characteristics of readers of a national magazine.

Salience is defined by Guralnik (1980) as "standing out from the rest; noticeable; conspicuous; prominent" and can be either positive, as operationalized by Heberlein and Baumgartner (1978), or negative. Our goal in designing each aspect of the implementation system from prenotice letter to return envelope is to create positive salience. We want each element to be noticeable, but in a way that creates a positive impression; that is, increases a sense of reward (this questionnaire looks interesting and important), reduces perceived costs (it looks easy to do), and creates trust (it came with two dollars that could be kept without sending back the questionnaire). The overall impression that is created, and thus the balance between rewards and costs, depends not only on individual elements but also on the consistency among those elements. Thus, each element, a description of which follows, should *not* be thought of as self-standing, but as part of an overall implementation system for which a change in one part is likely to have unintended consequences for another.

FIRST CONTACT: PRENOTICE LETTER

The purpose of a prenotice letter is to provide a positive and timely notice that the recipient will be receiving a request to help with an important study or survey. It should be brief, personalized, positively worded, and aimed at building anticipation rather than providing the details or conditions for participation in the survey. If a small token of appreciation is to be provided with the questionnaire, it should be mentioned here without going into details. In addition, this letter should be sent by first-class mail and timed to arrive only days to a week ahead of the actual questionnaire. An example of such a preletter is provided in Figure 4.1.

Research has shown consistently that a prenotice will improve response rates to mail surveys (Kanuk and Berenson, 1975; Fox, Crask, and Kim, 1988; Dillman, Clark, and Sinclair, 1995; Dillman, 1991), but it is unclear whether the effect stems from the fact it is one additional mailing and the more contacts the higher the response rate, or whether it is a unique type of contact. An attempt to test whether it has a unique effect (compared with other mailings) was made by comparing results between a preletter and a final letter sent after a replacement questionnaire. In three tests, results were from three to five percentage points higher for the prenotice, and the same for the fourth test, with none of the differences being statistically significant (Dillman & Dillman, 1995). In another test it was found that a prenotice letter added four to six percent to response rates for census questionnaires, a difference that could not be compensated for by a stamped return envelope, postcard reminder, or one replacement questionnaire in a four mailing sequence (Dillman, Clark, and Sinclair, 1995).

Results from a large sample pretest of a national government survey of Americans over 65 were once offered to me as evidence that preletters were not useful; that test revealed no difference between use of a preletter as an additional contact and no preletter. Upon examination, the reasons became apparent. First, the letter was sent nearly a month prior to receipt of the questionnaire, by which time it was likely to be a distant, if not forgotten, memory. Sending the letter only a few days ahead of the questionnaire avoids this problem. In addition, this letter was nearly two pages long, going into great detail about the reasons for the questionnaire, the fact that the request was voluntary, and other explanations that seemed likely to raise anxiety (and

Figure 4.1 Example of preletter to sample of new state residents who turned in out-of-state driver's licenses to get a Washington driver's license.

Washington State University

Social and Economic Sciences Research Center

Wilson Hall 133
PO Box 644014
Pullman, WA 99164-4014
509-335-1511
FAX 509-335-0116

Date	→	July 1, 1999
Inside address	→	L. T. Hansen 2121 Lincoln Way East Uniontown, WA 99962-2056
What will happen	→	A few days from now you will receive in the mail a request to fill out a brief questionnaire for an important research project being conducted by Washington State University.
What it is about	→	It concerns the experience of people who have moved to Washington state, and how they feel about living here.
Usefulness of survey	→	I am writing in advance because we have found many people like to know ahead of time that they will be contacted. The study is an important one that will help government agencies as well as employers in Washington understand who is moving to Washington, and whether their expectations are being met.
Thank-you	→	Thank you for your time and consideration. It's only with the generous help of people like you that our research can be successful. Sincerely,
Real signature	→	Don A. Dillman Professor and Deputy Director
Token incentive	→	P.S. We will be enclosing a small token of appreciation with the questionnaire as a way of saying thanks.

therefore "costs"), but that the recipient could not resolve by being able to see the nonthreatening content of the questionnaire. Much of this information needed to be presented to the respondent, but the actual cover letter that accompanied the questionnaire would have been a much better place to present it.

Occasionally, when a preletter has been recommended for starting the survey sequence, someone has objected to the format on the grounds that, "I wouldn't open a letter, but I would look at a postcard." My choice of a letter instead of a postcard is deliberate. It takes perhaps 20 seconds to get an event into long-term memory. A postcard can be looked at, flipped over, and laid aside in only a few seconds. Thus, I recommend a letter that will take longer to open and on which more information, including trust-inducing elements such as letterhead stationery, personalized address, and signature can be included to help define the survey as important. The goal is to convey the idea that something important is about to be sent to the person to whom the letter is addressed. Consistent with the idea that variety by itself has value in making each mailing more salient, we save the postcard format for the third contact (the thank you/reminder) where it will be a fresh stimulus that appears quite different from the prenotice letter.

In surveys that are contracted to another organization for data collection, it may be useful to have the preletter come from the study sponsor on its stationery. An example is when a government agency contracts with a private firm to conduct the survey. Inasmuch as government sponsorship tends to improve response rates (Heberlein and Baumgartner, 1978), having the preletter processed on the appropriate government stationery is desirable. Such a preletter provides an opportunity to explain briefly that the survey is being conducted for that agency by the XYZ Company, thereby invoking the exchange elements of authority and legitimacy.

SECOND CONTACT: THE QUESTIONNAIRE MAILOUT

The questionnaire should be sent only a few days to a week after the prenotice, again by first class mail. This mailing contains several elements: a cover letter, the questionnaire, any token of appreciation, and a return envelope. Design attention needs to be focused on the individual as well as on the collective impact of the mailout components on the respondent.

Initially, it is important to contemplate where the information to be included in this mailout best fits. For example, I have seen some questionnaires that provide information inside the questionnaire cover about who should respond and how, which was then repeated almost word for word in the cover letter, a decision that contributed to the letter becoming three pages long. Sometimes separate sheets of instructions on how to answer certain questions are included. I have also seen mailing packages that included a second cover letter that was intended as support for the study, but probably did no more than contribute to the bulk of the mailout package. For these reasons, construction of the mailout package begins by deciding what information should and should not be included and in which element it should be expressed. As noted in Chapter 3, there are compelling reasons for placing information exactly where it is to be used. If this is done, it tends to reduce the total number of words as well as the number of separate pieces that must be included in the mailout.

The Cover Letter

The cover letter should be limited to one page, including certain critical pieces of information, each of which is detailed below. Style is important. Sometimes when people begin to draft letters they immediately adopt an impersonal approach that treats the recipient more as an impersonal object than someone from whom they are about to request a favor. For example:

> I am writing to people like yourself because it's necessary for my agency to complete a technical needs assessment as a matter of agency policy.
>
> or
>
> In order to help you do a better job of completing your future tax returns, we want to know what problems you have had in the past.

The first of these sentences conveys that the letter is being written to a lot of people, and concerns something important only to the agency. The second example implies that the agency is going to help respondents do what they should have been doing all along. From an exchange standpoint, the first sentence immediately eliminates reward value and the second one incurs cost by subordinating the respondent to the writer, as explained in Chapter 1.

It is useful when writing cover letters to create a mental image of an acquaintance with an educational level a little lower than the average of the survey population from whom assistance is being requested. Then a letter is composed that communicates specifically to them. My goal is to find a style and specific wording that reflects normal social interaction surrounding a diplomatic and socially appropriate request. It should be short, but also needs to convey all of the essential information. The written request is also aimed at conveying an attitude of straight-forward communication that is not misleading, just as would be done in a conversation with a person with whom we hoped to maintain a mutually respectful relationship. I have also suggested to some study sponsors that they view cover letters as costing them 10 cents a word out of their pockets; it is a cost not so high as to prevent doing what is necessary, but high enough to make one aware of unneeded phrases and sentences. The elements considered essential for an efficient but effective letter follow.

Date. I once drafted a letter for an agency that included the mailout date at the top. It was approved, but only after the mailout date had been removed. The letter was resubmitted to the correspondence management office with the date reinserted, and it again came back deleted. A subsequent conversation revealed that it was a matter of agency policy not to put dates on letters used in large surveys because of variable mailing dates. Such policies need to be changed.

The date at the top of the letter is the first element of personalization. One is unlikely to send a letter to a business acquaintance without putting the date at the top and its removal is an immediate indicator that this is a relatively unimportant letter that can be ignored. Changing the specific date to only a month, for example, "July, 1998," is unconventional and should also be avoided.

Inside name and address. A certain sign of unimportance is to begin a letter with, "Dear Citizen" or a general synonym like resident, friend, neighbor, or colleague. The salutation indicates to whom the request that follows is being addressed. With today's word processing equipment, merging letters and names in the printing process is quite simple. For this reason it is often suggested that omitting names and addresses no longer makes a difference. In contrast, I believe that the new ease of merging word files makes the absence of names and addresses more noticeable, especially when a generalized substitute is included. It conveys more quickly and effectively than any other component of the letter that a form letter is being sent.

There is one situation in which names and addresses are not placed on the letterhead stationery. This is when a respondent selection process is being carried out (see below) and the name on the sample list may not correspond to the person who is being asked to respond. An example is the use of telephone directory listings from which an adult is asked to respond for the household. The use of such listings in the past has resulted in a higher proportion of males responding for household surveys, despite selection criteria, such as the person with the most recent birthday, being specified in the letter. The reason for this bias is that husbands are more often listed in telephone directories than are wives. Although this situation is changing, it has not disappeared and appears to be associated with older households for which listings have stayed the same for many years. In these cases a modified address might be used, for example, "To residents at 9021 SW Marcel Street," or "To residents at this address," which is somewhat more personalized than simply using "Dear Resident."

Salutations. The appropriateness of salutations varies significantly from one situation to another. I once assisted with a survey in which the cover letter was signed by an association president who kept an address file of salutations he felt comfortable with. Accordingly, some letters began with a personal style, such as "Dear Alice," while others began with a more formal style, such as, "Dear Dr. Henry."

When there is no preexisting relationship between the sender and receiver, and the gender is known, salutations like: "Dear Ms. Adamson" or "Dear Mr. Adamson" are appropriate. However, it is increasingly difficult to determine gender from a name, and many names appear simply as initials. In such cases, the salutation should be omitted rather than risking offending the recipient.

What is this letter about? It is perhaps easier to indicate what not to do than to indicate the best approach to use for a specific letter of transmittal. Surprisingly, many cover letters start out in this way:

> My name is Dan Scurry and I'm writing to ask your help with a survey being conducted by the University of California Department of Health Services.

All of this information is conveyed in other places, from the letterhead to the signature, and by our 10 cent per word standard not using this sentence represents an immediate savings of $2.60.

Another style I seek to avoid is that of a monologue, which by the end of the first paragraph in this letter about public smoking policies has still not explained why this letter has been sent:

> As you are undoubtedly aware, smoking is of grave concern to many people throughout America. Increasingly, the health concerns associated with smoking are becoming better known and preventing smoking among youth is one of the nation's highest priorities. It's important to understand all aspects of this important national issue.

A more appropriate beginning is illustrated by the cover letter shown in Figure 4.2. It explains in a brief introductory paragraph what is being requested and is followed by a second paragraph that explains why.

Why this request is useful and important. The second important message of the letter explains why the action requested of the recipient is useful and important. This is often the most difficult part of the letter to write. In a scientific assessment of the general public's attitudes towards the environment, it is inappropriate to explain the usefulness of the study in this way:

> It is important to keep big business from harming the environment, so we are doing this survey to get your honest opinions on the extent to which you feel the environment should be protected.

Such an explanation is obviously biased, giving the impression that the sponsor wants responses from people who have opinions that are highly supportive of protecting the environment. The goal here is to design an appeal that makes it unclear which side of an issue, if any, corresponds to the sponsor's beliefs and that asks for an honest opinion. For example:

> It is unclear whether people want either more or less to be done by state government to protect the environment than is now being done. Only by asking people throughout the state to give their honest opinions can we learn what people do and don't want our government to do. The results of this survey will be summarized and provided to all legislators from both political parties for their possible use in the upcoming legislative session.

An attempt is made to couch the usefulness argument broadly. In this case the desire for possible government action by both political parties has been used, not only to balance the argument, but to convey a use that most citizens are likely to support. In practice, one quickly realizes that there are virtually no arguments with which absolutely every recipient would agree—in this

Figure 4.2 Example of cover letter (second contact) to sample of new state residents; to follow preletter.

Washington State University

Social and Economic Sciences Research Center

Wilson Hall 133
PO Box 644014
Pullman, WA 99164-4014
509-335-1511
FAX 509-335-0116

Date	→	July 8, 1999
Inside address	→	L. T. Hansen 2121 Lincoln Way East Uniontown, WA 99962-2056
The request	→	I am writing to ask your help in a study of new residents being conducted for the state of Washington. This study is part of an effort to learn what draws people to the state, and whether they are happy or unhappy with what they find here.
Why you were selected	→	It's my understanding that you may have moved to Washington state sometime in the last few years. We are contacting a random sample of new residents from every county in the state to ask why they moved, what their employment experience has been, and whether services are meeting their needs.
Usefulness of survey	→	Results from the survey will be used to help state and local government make Washington a better place for new residents like you. By understanding what people want when they move here, public officials can do a better job providing services and improving the state's quality of life. And by knowing more about the job skills of new residents, public agencies and private businesses can help make the most of what new residents contribute to the state's economy.
Confidentiality	→	Your answers are completely confidential and will be released only as summaries in which no individual's answers can be identified. When you return your completed questionnaire, your name will be deleted from the mailing list and never connected to your answers in any way. This survey is voluntary. However, you can help us very much by taking a few minutes to share your experiences and opinions about Washington state. If for some reason you prefer not to respond, please let us know by returning the blank questionnaire in the enclosed stamped envelope.
Token of appreciation	→	We have enclosed a small token of appreciation as a way of saying thanks for your help.
Willingness to answer questions	→	If you have any questions or comments about this study, we would be happy to talk with you. Our toll-free number is 1-800-833-0867, or you can write to us at the address on the letterhead.
Thank-you	→	Thank you very much for helping with this important study.
		Sincerely,
Real signature	→	Don A. Dillman Professor and Deputy Director

P.S. If by some chance we made a mistake and you have not moved to Washington (or back to Washington after living somewhere else) since January 1990, please answer only the first question in the questionnaire and return the rest of it blank. Many thanks.

---

case some would want government to do absolutely nothing—but this argument is likely to have some appeal for most people. Therefore, it may tap the social exchange element of feeling that one is doing something useful by responding.

Answers are confidential. This statement conveys an ethical commitment not to release results in a way that any individual's responses can be identified as their own. Inasmuch as an identification system is normally used to allow people's names to be deleted from the mailing list, it is important to explain this commitment as one of protecting confidentiality, rather than guaranteeing anonymity. Only when the sponsor cannot identify each person's response, even momentarily, is it appropriate to promise that a response is anonymous.

Most organizations that routinely do surveys now have human subjects protection boards that review survey proposals. These boards often require that the surveyor specify the exact way in which confidentiality will be protected, when and how any identifiers will be destroyed, and sometimes follow up to make sure that this is done.

In recent years the improved technological capabilities for building and analyzing large data files has led to some surveys in which the sponsor wishes to connect the results of a survey to other files containing information on that individual. For example, in an opinion survey of people who have stayed in a hotel, the sponsor might wish to connect these opinions to how many nights the respondent has stayed during the last year, and even send incentives for future stays based on the results of such an analysis. Such a use would not be consistent with the promise of confidentiality that indicates answers are not connected in any way to a respondent's name.

Sometimes there are very good reasons for connecting results from a new survey with answers to a previous survey. One example is a panel study that is designed to measure individual change from an earlier survey. In such cases it should be explained that a connection is being made with the previous data respondents provided; for example:

> Your answers are completely confidential. Although a comparison will be made between the answers you provide to this survey and the one you kindly completed two years ago, results will only be released as summaries in a way that no individual's answers to either survey can be identified.

My goal in explaining confidentiality is to be honest but brief. Research by Singer, Von Thurn, and Miller (1995) has suggested that detailed explanations of confidentiality can discourage people from responding. Providing a long and unnecessarily detailed explanation, even when the data being collected are quite nonthreatening, raises concerns that "There must be a problem or they wouldn't be telling me all of this stuff about protection." Also, such detailed explanations may turn a simple one-page letter into a treatise that is several pages long. For this reason a two-pronged approach is used to protect and convey confidentiality information to respondents. It consists of approval by organizational human subjects boards of detailed procedures that are made available upon request to anyone who wishes to see them, and a much less detailed but accurate description of procedures to potential respondents.

Voluntary participation. It appears that most human subjects boards now require that questionnaire recipients be informed when a survey is voluntary. It is useful to connect this phrase with instructions on what to do if the respondent does not wish to respond, for instance, "Please let us know by returning the uncompleted questionnaire." Obtaining a "positive action" from nonrespondents makes it possible to remove their names from the follow-up mailing list. Use of this procedure in many surveys has resulted in relatively few additional refusals (typically one to three percent of the mailing), and it seems doubtful that many of these individuals would have responded to follow-ups. In many instances the information about being voluntary can be expressed in the same paragraph as encouragement to respond (see Figure 4.2).

Enclosures of stamped return envelope and token of appreciation. These elements of the mailout package are easily seen by the respondent. A detailed explanation is not required for them to be effective. For these reasons, mention of them is relegated to the latter part of a paragraph and expressed in a casual way. However, they are mentioned for the benefit of anyone who reads the letter without other elements of the mailing package being present. Mention of the token of appreciation provides another way of saying thank you in advance of the person's response.

Who to contact with questions. Offering to answer questions and providing a toll-free number for people to call conveys the idea of accessibility. If people want to know something about the study they can find it out. This information helps convey trust that the survey is legitimate and important. It is an essential component of a good cover letter.

A real signature in contrasting ink. A letter of request for help to a business acquaintance would definitely include a personal signature. An attempt is made to emulate that appearance on all requests to questionnaire recipients. In the description of the Total Design Method, this process was referred to as applying a "pressed blue ball-point pen signature." It was also recommended that the letter be signed on a soft surface in order that the recipient could tell that a real signature had been applied.

A substitute for this signature is to preprint the signature in a color (blue) that contrasts with the black type. A signature stamp can also be applied individually to letters or a signature machine can be used. When doing a survey of a few hundred recipients, applying real signatures may be easy to do; when faced with a survey of several thousand, it may not be a realistic alternative. Personalization has many aspects, including use of individual names and letterhead rather than copied stationery, that may compensate to some extent for being unable to apply real signatures. In general, I expect to achieve a collective impact of five to eight percentage points from the use of personalization elements and I do not know how much a real versus facsimile signature, by itself, contributes to the final response rate. Nonetheless, to the extent possible, each letter is an individual appeal to each respondent, much like a voice on the telephone, so that the letter should be individually signed whenever that is possible.

Addition of a postscript. Postscripts are one of the most visible aspects of a letter, often getting read before the remainder of the message. It is an appropriate place to express "thanks again," to mention the inclusion of the token incentive, or as done in Figure 4.2, to recognize that a mistake may have been made on eligibility for the study and tell people what to do (e.g., return the uncompleted questionnaire along with a brief explanation). However one chooses to use the potential for a postscript, the high likelihood of its being read should be recognized.

Identification of each questionnaire. Each questionnaire has an individual identification number that is printed directly on the questionnaire by running it through an envelope address printer. Alternatively, it may be printed on a transparent label that can be affixed to the questionnaire. This is done so that follow-up mailings, an essential aspect of Tailored Design, can be sent only to non-respondents (with the exception of returns that cross with the follow-up letter in the mail) and not create inconvenience or confusion for those who have already responded. A number is stamped, or simply printed, in plain view on the front or back cover of the questionnaire. Attempting to hide the number by placing it in small type on an inside page, or embedding it into something that might be referred to as a form, approval, or processing number (e.g., "Approved Form 91854") is inconsistent with the image of making an honest effort to communicate openly with questionnaire recipients.

Occasionally I have heard of attempts to hide identification numbers by using invisible ink that will show up only under an ultraviolet or other special light. Such procedures are unethical and should not be used. Moreover, informing respondents of the presence of an identification number seems not to have a serious negative effect on response rates, especially when compared to not being able to use the tailored follow-up that it facilitates. Respondents sometimes tear off identification numbers, a fact that encourages us to place them in the corner of questionnaires where their removal does not eliminate answers to questions. This action will result in the sending of reminders to people who have responded, but such follow-up seems unlikely to come as a surprise to the respondent who has removed the number.

Figure 4.3 Example of separate return postcard used to facilitate anonymous return of questionnaires.

Identification number:	Questionnaire #3456
Purpose:	This postcard is being returned to let you know that my questionnaire has been returned in a separate envelope.
Name:	________________________ Your name (please print)
Appreciation:	Thank you very much for your help with this important study. We really appreciate it. Don A. Dillman The Social & Economic Sciences Research Center at Washington State University

Sometimes the data obtained by mail questionnaires is considered so sensitive that the sponsor wishes not to be able to identify responses with an individual, even momentarily, while deleting the name from the mailing list. This might occur for questionnaires associated with litigation, or simply because of information being asked about sexual behavior or drug use, which a respondent might be reluctant to divulge. In this case one might consider sending a stamped, self-addressed postcard that the respondent can send back separately from the questionnaire to indicate that it has been returned (Figure 4.3). A message can be included in the cover letter along these lines:

> All answers to this questionnaire are completely anonymous. There is no identification number of any kind on the questionnaire. However, to let us know that your questionnaire has been returned, please sign and return the enclosed postcard *separately* in the mail so we can check your name off of thc mailing list. That way, no reminder questionnaire will be sent to you.

The essential elements for this postcard are a reference to the topic of the study, a respondent identification number, and the person's name or signature. The frequent illegibility of names or signatures prevents their use as the sole means of identification.

Sending such a postcard is more costly than using an identification number on the questionnaire, and results in a more complex mailing. When used for the collection of ordinary questionnaire information, too great an emphasis on protection may raise a false sense of concern to respondents that they are being "tricked" in some way, and thereby discourage response. In the few instances in which I have used this procedure, the number of postcards returned has corresponded closely with the number of questionnaires sent back. Just as in the case of cashing incentive checks, where most but by no means all of the respondents cash their checks, I suspect that correspondence between returning a postcard and a questionnaire is good but not perfect.

Inclusion of token financial incentive. Perhaps no other aspect of doing surveys by mail has attracted as much interest or controversy as providing special incentives to encourage response. It is also an area that has received much research attention. Some organizations would not think of conducting a mail survey without providing an incentive, whereas others object to their use as a matter of policy.

Neither the extent of interest nor the degree of controversy is surprising. Second to multiple contacts, no response-inducing technique is as likely to improve mail response rates as much as the appropriate use of financial incentives. However, widely different views exist, as evidenced by prevailing practices with regard to the types, amounts, timing, methods of delivery, and implications of their use. Each of these issues is addressed separately below.

Should the incentive be sent with the questionnaire or as payment afterwards? On this issue the evidence is particularly clear. Token financial incentives of a few dollars included with the request have been shown to be significantly more effective than much larger payments sent to respondents who have returned their questionnaires. For example, James and Bolstein (1992), in a study of small contractors (in many cases one-person firms) found that only 57% responded to a survey in which they were promised $50 afterwards, compared to 64% who had been sent a one-dollar bill with the questionnaire, and 71% who had been sent a five-dollar bill. Johnson and McLaughlin (1990) reported that sending a five-dollar bill to a large sample of individuals resulted in an 83% response compared with only 72% who were promised a 10 dollar payment after the questionnaire was returned, which was about the same as for those who received no incentive. It is noteworthy that the response effect measured by both of these authors was with a four-contact implementation strategy using personalized mailings, so that the high response rates achieved were on top of the effects achieved through other means. However, a benefit of sending a payment afterwards is that people may provide more complete answers, that is, lower item nonresponse, an effect observed by Johnson and McLaughlin (1990). However, the difference they observed was judged relatively minor compared to the 10% increase in response from the smaller prepaid incentive. Thus, I find the case for favoring postpayment rather than prepayment of incentives weak at best. These results are supported by a recent meta-analysis of 38 experimental studies by Church (1993), who reported no statistically significant effect from rewards that were contingent upon the return of the survey.

These results are also quite consistent with the social exchange theory explained in Chapter 1. Sending the money with the questionnaire is a goodwill gesture that puts the sponsor and questionnaire in a positive light and sets the stage for the respondent to reciprocate with an appropriate gesture of completing the questionnaire. Its strength is that the request is not presented to respondents as an economic exchange: "If you complete this questionnaire I will pay you for it." Individuals are acculturated to evaluate such offers with regard to whether the amount offered is worth the effort that is required. Offering payment contingent upon completion not only introduces consideration of the value of one's time, but also undermines the entire calculus of social exchange that I am attempting to achieve.

How large a cash incentive is needed? Although the literature is full of examples of coins, handling coinage is difficult and the tradeoff with higher postage costs is significant. Thus, I consider one dollar the smallest practical amount to send. Support exists for somewhat larger amounts being more effective, but there clearly are diminishing returns, with far more of an increase coming from the first dollar than from five or ten times that amount. For example, James and Bolstein (1992) reported a 12 percentage point increase (52% to 64%) from one dollar versus no cash incentive, and only an additional two to seven percentage point increase for five- and 10-dollar incentives, with the lower increase coming from the 10-dollar incentive. With several colleagues, I have run five separate tests of a two-dollar incentive which showed that response to a four-wave personalized mailing was improved an additional 19 to 31 percentage points (Lesser, Dillman, Lorenz, Carlson, and Brown, 1999). This research also suggests that the two-dollar incentive was equally effective regardless of whether sent by cash or by check, or as one- or two-dollar bills. This modest prepaid incentive has proved to be strikingly powerful.

Should token financial incentives be sent as cash or a check? Checks work about as well as sending cash, at least for amounts of five dollars or over (Tortora et al., 1992), a conclusion recently supported by Lesser et al. (1999). Small checks may be seen as somewhat of a nuisance, but may still have a significant effect on response rates. In addition, many people do not cash checks. Both Lesser et al. (1999) and James and Bolstein (1992) found that less than 30% of the nonrespondents cashed their checks, whereas about 80% of the respondents did so. Thus, it would appear that money could be saved by sending checks, and that the organizational challenges of handling cash, including that returned in undeliverable mail, can be avoided.

However, the advantage to checks may be less than it appears. Checks have to be written and matched with appropriate envelopes, with corresponding paperwork completed. When checks do not get cashed, and many will not, then they must be carried on the organization's books for a period of time. I once recommended to a large government agency that it use checks for five-dollar incentives because I did not think the handling of cash would be approved. Thus, I was surprised when the head of the accounting division approached me with a plea to use cash. He indicated that the costs to the organization for writing and handling checks would greatly exceed the total cost of the incentive, and he wanted to avoid the prospect of hundreds of uncancelled checks.

Will material incentives work as well? The above mentioned meta-analysis by Church (1993) also found that material incentives improved response rates by eight percent compared with 19% for token financial incentives. It is noteworthy that eight of the 12 studies Church analyzed included a ball-point pen or pencil as an incentive (Church, personal communication, April 12, 1993). However, the average response of studies with the material incentives was only 37% (compared to 28% without). Thus, the use and effects appear to have been measured mostly in situations where multiple contacts and other response-inducing procedures were not used. However, a more recent five-contact mail survey (four by mail and a final follow-up by telephone) of people who renewed driver's licenses in Washington state to assess customer satisfaction produced an eight percentage point advantage (67% versus 59%) for those who received a very inexpensive purple ball-point pen with the words "Department of Licensing" on it (Boynton, 1995).

The frequent use of ball-point pens as material incentives raises questions about the extent to which packaging might have contributed to response. The bulky nature of pens generally draws attention to mail packaging. A larger envelope and hand cancellation may be needed. For example, the pen sent by Boynton (1995) was enclosed in a soft pack mailer that made it distinctively different from the other treatment, which was sent in regular business letter envelopes. Patchen, Woodard, Caralley, and Hess (1994) found in a study of radio listener diaries that sending the diaries in a box about the same size and shape as that used for holding a half-pound, one-layer box of chocolates improved response rates significantly—from 38 to 42%, or nearly four percentage points. It is possible that ball-point pen incentives receive a boost in effectiveness from the unusual packaging required for sending them, an effect that increases the salience of the mailing quite apart from the fact that a material incentive is being sent.

It appears that material incentives, and ball-point pens in particular, may modestly improve response rates. However, the likely improvement is far less than one would expect with a financial incentive of comparable value.

Do lotteries, contributions to charity, or offers of prizes improve response? Chances to win a prize ranging from cash to airline tickets are frequently offered in surveys. It appears that these offers have a relatively small, if any, effect on response. A comparison by Carlson (1996) of a two-dollar bill, a chance to win $300, and no incentive in a survey of new residents of Idaho resulted in a response rate of 54% for the control group compared to 58% for the lottery and 73% when the two-dollar bill was sent. Another study that compared lotteries, cash, and contributions to charities showed that only prepaid cash incentives made a difference in response rates (Warriner, Goyder, Gjertsen, Hohner, and McSpurren, 1996). Even if prizes or lotteries can boost response a small amount, the effect, when compared to sending a token cash incentive, is quite small.

A reason that prize offers or contributions to charity seem to have so little effect on response rates is that unlike prepaid incentives, the meaning of a promised incentive shifts from a social gesture that elicits the feeling that one needs to reciprocate to an indirect payment for services rendered. Neither of these offers invokes feelings of a need to reciprocate for a previously made gesture of goodwill, as does a prepaid incentive.

Is it worthwhile to repeat the incentive when a replacement questionnaire is sent? I have seen no evidence that repeating incentives of any kind, whether cash or offers of prizes in later mailings, is effective. This is not surprising and is consistent with the perspective that each contact with respondents should appear different, rather than simply repeating a previous one.

In sum. A very strong case can be made for the use of a modest cash incentive. Its impact on response is likely to be stronger than any other stimulus except for multiple contacts with respondents. A less compelling case can be made for the use of material incentives whose impact will be much less, and curiously, may be associated most with carefully packaged ball-point pens. However, unless one obtains the pens free, it seems likely that sending a two-dollar incentive, like the one discussed here, will be less costly. Finally, it is much more difficult to make a case for sending postpayments of any kind, including lotteries and prizes.

Stationery, Envelopes, And Other Packaging Decisions

The original Total Design Method included many detailed recommendations for packaging and mailing the questionnaire. For example, I recommended the somewhat reduced "monarch" size ($7\frac{1}{4}'' \times 10\frac{1}{2}''$) paper and envelopes to encourage a sense of the questionnaire being smaller and therefore easier to fill out. Printing of the questionnaire in a smaller booklet size ($6\frac{1}{8}'' \times 8\frac{1}{4}''$) than that allowed by folding standard legal size paper into a booklet ($8\frac{1}{2}'' \times 7''$) fit nicely into these smaller envelopes and produced occasional savings in postage. Names and addresses were typed directly onto envelopes rather than onto labels.

It appears that no experiments have shown a significant improvement in response from the use of these smaller sizes. One large scale experiment (Moore, 1980) showed that using large standard brown envelopes with a study logo printed on the outside produce a slightly higher (although not significantly different) response than did standard TDM packaging. Also, it has become increasingly difficult and more costly to utilize these unusual sizes. The printing industry is now capable of accomplishing amazing variations in printing. In addition, technological innovations have made it possible for small copy centers and many individual offices to produce questionnaires and letters in ways not possible at the time that book was written.

However, from a cost standpoint, the use of a standard stationery size is favored. In addition, it appears that the advent of optical scanning (discussed in Chapter 12) is also pushing us in the direction of using standard $8^1/_2'' \times 11''$ questionnaires. Finally, I am influenced by the findings of Patchen et al. (1994) that unusual packaging may draw attention to one's mailing rather than causing it to be dismissed.

Letterhead stationery is important, partly because of its integral connection to personalization efforts. For mailout envelopes, regular business envelopes ($4^1/_4'' \times 9^1/_2''$) are recommended but there is no reason to avoid larger envelopes where warranted by the size of the questionnaire, such as a questionnaire that is printed as an $8^1/_2'' \times 11''$ booklet.

The computer age has placed address labels in more favorable light than in the past. They no longer convey a lack of personalized attention to the respondent, unless last names are printed first or address file information is included. As a friend with a new computer explained, "I even put labels on the letters sent to my children; I don't know how to print directly onto the envelope."

When designing the mailout package there are a number of things that should be avoided. This is not the place for a special stamp saying, "Important materials are included," or "Your personal response is required." Neither is it advisable to use brightly colored envelopes that convey a marketing image (Leslie, 1997). A careful look at the many mass mailings received by the average household in a day helps to identify many things not to do. The desired image I wish to convey is that an important request from someone has been sent to the respondent. It is important that the packaging on the outside as well as what is seen when one opens the envelope not convey an image of having been mailed in bulk. Portrayal of this image of importance continues with the next topic, postage.

The importance of first-class postage and how to apply it. It is tempting to save money by sending mail questionnaires by third class or bulk rate mail. The current cost is significantly less, especially for larger mailings—about 30 cents for up to 3.3 ounces versus 33 cents per ounce for first-class mail. However, this advantage is offset by several disadvantages.

There are three reasons that bulk rate mail is avoided. First, its use requires a bulk rate insignia or stamp on the outside of the envelope which is inconsistent with the image of importance that is being sought. Second, bulk rate mail is delivered at a lower priority than first-class mail and can be held temporarily in each of the distribution centers through which it passes. When mail quantities are light, there may be no delay, and we know of instances in which bulk mail deliveries have arrived the same time as first-class mail. In other instances, when large quantities of first-class mail must be delivered, delays of up to two weeks have been observed in cross-country deliveries. Such delays sometimes result in prenotices or reminder postcards being delivered out of order with the actual questionnaire, a situation that contributes to the survey being defined as unimportant. The third drawback is that third-class mail is not forwarded automatically to a new address, as is the case for first-class mail. Also, unless return postage is guaranteed, it is not returned to the sender if it cannot be delivered.

It is my impression that the U.S. Postal Service does an excellent job of handling mail. However, it must be remembered that it is also a huge organization with an enormous number of processing and distribution points. In addition, the quantity of mail it is asked to process on a daily basis varies greatly. If mistakes are made they seem most likely to happen at peak load times, or when it is asked to perform extra services that are somewhat unusual, such as forwarding or returning bulk rate mail. With bulk rate mail, less personal effort seems likely to be made by carriers to assure delivery; for instance, they may be less likely to correct a small address mistake. Although bulk rate mail can produce cost savings, it may produce coverage problems that cannot be corrected. Finally, the initial negative impression on the respondent and the occasional frustration of getting a reminder to return a questionnaire one has not received lead me to conclude that bulk rate mail should not be used for mail surveys.

Either stamps or metered postage may be used for outgoing mail. There appears to be no experimental evidence that the use of actual stamps on the outgoing envelope produces higher response rates, and at least one experiment showed no effect (Dillman, 1978). Most of the important mail that now arrives in people's homes has been processed through a postage meter. Use of a postage meter for outgoing mail has the advantage of being faster than applying stamps, and some meters can seal the envelope at the same time. The important function of the envelope appearance is to get it opened, and the fact that it is first-class mail is usually sufficient. Use of the carefully timed prenotice and postcard reminder help get the envelope opened, as well.

First-class mail is automatically forwarded if the addressee has a current (less than 90 days old) forwarding address on file with the U.S. Postal Service. It is also possible to print or stamp "address correction requested" or "forwarding service requested" on the envelope and the new address will be provided to the sender for up to one year after it has expired. In some studies, address corrections are useful for determining whether people drawn in the sample are still in the population to be surveyed. The new address can also be used to update sample lists and to remail questionnaires that were returned because of the expired forwarding address.

When sending any large mailing it is useful to obtain information on current postal procedures. The introduction of automatic scanning and sorting equipment means that certain areas on the envelope are specified for postal use only. The use of capitals and the absence of punctuation (e.g., PULLMAN WA 99164-4014 instead of Pullman, Washington 99164), locating that information within a specified space near the bottom of the envelope, and not placing any other information to the left of the address help the equipment process mail correctly.

Use of a stamped return envelope. Just as one may be tempted to use bulk rate outgoing mail, one may be similarly tempted to save money by using business reply envelopes. Such envelopes are processed by the U.S. Postal Service for a small annual charge for the permit necessary to use this service, and postage is paid only for envelopes that are returned.

As already noted, evidence exists showing that by using a stamped envelope, response rates can be improved several percentage points over those achieved by sending a business reply envelope (Armstrong and Luske, 1987). Responses also tend to come in more quickly, sometimes providing an advantage of five to seven percentage points prior to sending a replacement questionnaire. Even a large experiment on households that received test U.S. Census questionnaires revealed an improvement of two to three percentage points compared to being sent a business reply envelope, a difference that was on the cusp of statistical significance (Dillman, Clark, and Sinclair, 1995).

When an uncancelled postage stamp is placed on a return envelope, something of monetary value has been given to the respondent. Thus, in an exchange context it is likely to be seen as a positive and helpful gesture that will help the sender to be viewed positively by the recipient. It also encourages trust that the questionnaire is important, perhaps encouraging the respondent to think, "Why else would this person have sent a stamped envelope that I can use for something else?" In addition, it is culturally difficult for many people to throw away something that has any monetary value. As a result, the enclosure of a stamped reply envelope seems likely to encourage its being kept in the household or office until the thank you postcard comes. Although the magnitude of expected effect is small compared to multiple contacts and token financial incentives, it will nonetheless provide an additional contribution to overall response.

Occasionally in surveys that go to business employees, users of the TDM have objected to the use of stamped envelopes, and even business reply envelopes, on the basis that outgoing postage is essentially free to the respondent. Such an interpretation places the stamp in an economic rather than social framework, much like the argument that incentives should be paid after the return of a questionnaire. It is the immediate effect on the recipient's mind set and behavior that is important when enclosing these items of small but real monetary value. Even when surveying organization executives, we use return envelopes with real stamps.

Assembling and inserting the mailout package. The final step of preparing the questionnaire mailout is to assemble and insert the four components—questionnaire, cover letter, token incentive, and return envelope—into the envelope. Often the planning of this step is ignored, leaving it up to the personnel who do it to find the most efficient way. That should not be done.

Two things need to happen when the respondent opens the mailout envelope. All four enclosures need to come out of the envelope at once. In addition, the appealing aspect of each element needs to be immediately visible. Neither of these details should be left to chance.

In cognitive interviews designed to test mailout packages, it has been observed repeatedly that one or more components get left in a mailout envelope when the other components are removed (Dillman, Jackson, Pavlov, and Schaefer, 1998). The questionnaire typically gets removed because of its bulk. If the cover letter is left in the envelope, as is often the case, respondents have no explanation of why the questionnaire has been sent or what they are supposed to do with it. This separation of components happens more often than one might expect as a result of the desire to be as efficient as possible when assembling the mailout. Typically, components are folded (if necessary) individually and placed on top of one another before inserting. As a result, it is easy for something to get left in the envelope and even be discarded before anyone realizes the mistake.

Fear of something getting lost has led to solutions that may compound the problem. One surveyor decided to insert a two-dollar bill into the reply envelope, reasoning that respondents would see it when inserting their completed questionnaires. This unfortunate decision did not take into account the importance of the respondent being able to see the token incentive immediately when opening the envelope. Another decided to hide it inside the pages of the booklet questionnaire where, again, it would not be immediately visible.

Depending upon the size and shape of enclosures, somewhat different solutions are needed to avoid these problems. First, if one is using an $8\frac{1}{2}'' \times 7''$ booklet questionnaire (the folded legal size paper method described in Chapter 3) with a standard $8\frac{1}{2}'' \times 11''$ cover letter and a $9\frac{1}{2}'' \times 4\frac{3}{8}''$ business envelope, the following procedure is recommended. Fold the questionnaire vertically with the front cover on the outside of the fold. Insert the two-dollar bill on top of the folded questionnaire and place the stamped reply envelope underneath. Then, lay all three components on the middle third of the face-up cover letter. The bottom third of the cover letter is then folded up and over these three components and the process is completed by folding the top third of the cover letter down. The entire set of materials can then be picked up easily and inserted into the mailout envelope. The advantage of this type of fold is that all materials must be removed together from the envelope. When the packet is unfolded the respondent will simultaneously see the letter personally addressed to them, the questionnaire, the token incentive, and the reply envelope. This is the desired effect. Another possibility is to use a Z-fold, whereby the bottom one-third of the cover letter is folded upwards over the middle one-third, and the top one-third is folded backwards, so a Z-shape is formed by the paper. Placing the questionnaire and other material behind the top one-third means that they must come out of the envelope with the cover letter, provided the packet is inserted with the bottom of the cover letter touching the bottom of the envelope.

A thin $8^1/_2'' \times 11''$ questionnaire stapled in the upper left corner and printed in the two-column format discussed in Chapter 3 can be similarly folded. However, when initially folded for insertion, it should be done in accordion (or Z-fold) fashion so that the top of the front page displaying any masthead appears on the top of the fold, and underneath the token incentive, before being tucked inside the cover letter for insertion into the envelope.

When flat mailouts are being used for $8^1/_2'' \times 11''$ booklets or U.S. Postal Service priority mail envelopes, the chance of something getting left in the mailout envelope is even greater. Such packaging is necessary when the questionnaire has too many pages to allow folding. In these instances we are likely to use stickers to attach the token incentives to the cover letter or first page of the questionnaire. Attaching the mailout components together with a metal clip is usually not done because of potential envelope tears from postal processing machines.

An important quality control issue surfaces during the folding and insertion process. The use of a questionnaire with an identification number means that it must be sent to the person whose name is on the personalized letter. In addition, the handling of cash (or checks written to individuals) requires that all of the right elements get into every mailout in order for the implementation system to work. This is not a process that can be delegated to an organization's newest hires and forgotten. Like the rest of Tailored Design, it requires attention to detail.

When one is faced with the prospect of assembling thousands of mailouts, rather than hundreds, or when one has access to machine assembly, it is tempting to forego the above methods in favor of separately folding and inserting each item. I have observed many different mechanical processes and urge that anyone considering use of them study prototype results carefully, to control as much as possible whether and how respondents will be exposed to the results. The quality control for getting the right components in every mailout package needs also to be carefully examined before committing to their use.

Selecting The Mailout Date

A large amount of time is often devoted to picking the perfect mailout date for a questionnaire or follow-ups. For the most part, this does not seem to be time well spent. A well designed mailout procedure is going to utilize at least four contacts, and there is little concrete evidence that time of year or day of week have significant effects on response. For example, a series of tests of similar census questionnaires were conducted in spring, summer, and fall, with virtually the same response rates obtained in each of them (Dillman, Clark and Treat, 1994). Even if an ideal time of year existed, it is often impossible to wait for it. The cadence of society has changed significantly so that August is not necessarily a vacation month for most people. Moreover, even if it were, a multiple contact implementation strategy is likely to overlap part of the time the questionnaire recipient is available.

When selecting mailing times, it is useful to focus first on known characteristics of the specific population and on study objectives. In a survey of farmers, periods of planting and harvest should be avoided, which in northern climates almost always means not doing such surveys in the spring or fall. I would generally attempt to do a survey of grade school parents during the school year rather than the summer, because such a survey is more likely to be salient to the parents at that time. In addition, during the school year students and parents are not mentally changing to a new grade level, as typically happens over summer. For targeting homogeneous groups such as these, changing salience and likelihood of being available are prime considerations, something which cannot usually be identified for the general population.

If there is a time of year that appears most conducive to getting surveys filled out, it would seem likely to be January-March. It has been suggested to me that people are more likely to fill out mail-back diary surveys at this time. This may result from people watching or listening to more media at that time and the questionnaires having higher salience as a result, or it may be simply that because of the weather there is less that one can do outside the home. Many years ago I was surprised by a report of a long questionnaire mailed only once to new residents of Alaska that obtained a response rate of over 60% (Rao, 1974). The author reported that the response had also come in over a particularly long period of time, rather than showing the immediate burst of response and decline that was familiar to me. In response to my inquiry as to why, it was explained that long winters, and in this case infrequent trips to the post office, meant that mail was a lot more likely to get read and acted upon.

I have also found it useful to avoid certain holiday periods, especially between Thanksgiving and Christmas. To some extent it can be argued that people are busier and more likely to be away from home. But it is also apparent that the volume of holiday mail creates special problems for the U.S. Postal Service and the chances of delivery mistakes seem higher when volumes are the greatest. Thus, the high volume time of year that Christmas presents to the Postal Service should be avoided when possible.

I have seen no convincing evidence that the day of the week makes a significant difference in return rates. In national surveys it becomes quite difficult to assure delivery on a particular day. Thus, a similar logic is applied to avoiding the day after a holiday or other times when the U.S. Postal Service is likely to be the busiest. Again, it is important to keep perspective on the notion that a well designed mailout strategy attempts many times, in several ways, to get a questionnaire into the household or business and have it attended to by the respondent. In light of these more intense efforts, the day of the week for mailings becomes a minor issue, influenced most by knowledge about the behavior of homogeneous populations and postal considerations.

Designing Additional Contacts

Without follow-up contacts, response rates will usually be 20–40 percentage points lower than those normally attained, regardless of how interesting the questionnaire or impressive the mailout package. This fact makes a carefully designed follow-up sequence imperative. However, a well planned follow-up is more than a reminder service. Each mailing provides a fresh opportunity for the researcher to appeal for the return of a questionnaire using a slightly new approach. The follow-up procedures include three carefully timed mailings, each of which differs substantially from the others.

The follow-up procedures used with Tailored Design are aimed at paralleling how successful face-to-face interviewers go about persuading prospective respondents to be interviewed. Ordinarily, interviewers introduce themselves, briefly describe the reason for being there, and politely ask for permission to begin the interview, all of which may take as little as a minute or two. If the respondent agrees, the interviewer's attempts to persuade cease and most of the arguments that could have been employed will go unused. Giving the entire sales pitch to someone who is unlocking their screen door is not only unnecessary, but can make an otherwise receptive person hostile. If, on the other hand, the prospect hesitates or says no, the interviewer will likely give more information about the study, offer more reasons why it is important, and emphasize why that particular respondent is essential to the study's success. When difficulties are encountered most interviewers attempt to react to the concerns they detect in the respondent's behavior. Various arguments are used until one is found that seems to work. In the decisive moments that determine whether the result will be reluctant acquiescence or total refusal, the interchange may become emotionally charged. Finally, in a last ditch effort to turn a near certain refusal into a completed interview, interviewers may broach the limits of allowable behavior, perhaps disassociating themselves somewhat from the sponsors of the study and asking for a personal favor that will "help me to get paid." In short, the interviewer's attempts at persuasion are sometimes minimal and sometimes great, often building to a crucial and decisive conclusion.

The design of follow-ups seeks to emulate certain (but not all) aspects of the successful face-to-face interviewer's behavior. Specifically, each follow-up mailing differs somewhat from the one that preceded it as attempts are made to invoke new and more persuasive appeals. Further, the appeals are designed to crescendo, with later follow-ups presenting stronger attempts at persuasion than preceding ones. The obvious difficulty that distinguishes the situation of the face-to-face interviewer from that of the mail researcher is that the latter has little or no feedback from respondents. This lack of feedback, other than the knowledge that a previous message did not get the desired response, makes it impossible to vary the appeal to hit the major concerns of each respondent. At best, the researcher can only guess at the predominant reasons for nonresponse and incorporate appeals to overcome them into each follow-up contact.

The realization that every respondent must be appealed to in the same way leads to our use of a relatively "reserved" approach throughout. Although emotionally intense arguments may sometimes produce results, this approach would appear reckless and offensive when handled over a period of weeks, rather than in a few short and easily forgotten moments on someone's doorstep. Therefore, attempts to increase the intensity of the appeals should escalate only to a level that is not threatening and that clearly stays within the bounds of normal business practice when a voluntary yet important matter of business is pursued.

The three additional contacts that comprise the complete follow-up sequence are listed here, identified by the approximate number of weeks that elapsed after the prenotice letter.

Two weeks: A postcard thank you/reminder is sent to all respondents. It serves both as a thank you for those who have responded and as a friendly and courteous reminder for those who have not.

Four weeks: A letter and replacement questionnaire are sent only to nonrespondents. Similar in appearance to the original mailout, it has a shorter cover letter that informs nonrespondents that their questionnaire has not been received and appeals for its return.

Eight weeks: This final contact is designed to contrast with the previous contacts, either through a different mode (e.g., telephone) or by being sent via priority mail, special delivery, or courier service to emphasize its importance.

THIRD CONTACT: THE POSTCARD THANK YOU/REMINDER

Most people who answer questionnaires, particularly for general public surveys, will do so almost immediately after they receive them. A questionnaire that lies unanswered for a week or more is much less likely to be returned. Repeated studies suggest that nearly half the return envelopes are postmarked within two or three days after being received by respondents. After that time the number of postmarked returns declines, sharply at first and then gradually.

The inevitably high nonresponse to any mailing is probably due less to conscious refusals than to either unrealized good intentions or the lack of any reaction at all. A questionnaire that is well constructed and accompanied by a carefully composed cover letter is often laid aside with the vague intention of looking at it later. As each day passes without the questionnaire being looked at, it becomes a lower priority, until it is completely forgotten, lost, or thrown away.

Thus, the postcard follow-up is written not to overcome resistance but rather to jog memories and rearrange priorities. It is timed to arrive just after the original mailing has produced its major effect, but before each person's questionnaire has had time to be buried under more recent mail or thrown away. One week is an appropriate interval of time for making an appeal that, if carefully worded, conveys a sense of importance. At the same time, it does not sound impatient or unreasonable.

The choice of a postcard format over a letter is deliberate. It should contrast with the prenotice letter, given that repeated stimuli have less effect than new ones. A letter format was used for the preletter because it took longer for cognitive processing by the respondent, and thus had a greater likelihood of being stored in long-term memory and recalled when the questionnaire arrived. In contrast, the function of a postcard is simply to jog one's memory. The postcard can be quickly turned over and read, rather than lying unopened with the rest of one's mail.

The precise wording of the card reflects still another concern. The first lines simply state that a questionnaire was sent to the respondent the previous week and why (Figure 4.4). This may appear to be a waste of precious space. However, for some respondents this is the first time they learn that a questionnaire was sent to them. The reasons for the original questionnaire not reaching them extend well beyond getting lost in the mail. The previous mailout is sometimes addressed incorrectly or is not forwarded, whereas for some unexplained reason the postcard is. In still other cases, another member of the family opens the envelope containing the questionnaire and fails to give it to the desired respondent. Alternatively, it may have been skipped over when the respondent was looking through the mail and not opened at all. Whatever the reason, telephone calls or letters are received advising the sender that the respondent would be willing to fill out a questionnaire if one were sent to them.

Undoubtedly, most people who do not recall receiving a questionnaire will not bother to ask for one. However, the knowledge that one was sent may stimulate them to query other members of their family (or organization) and lead to its discovery. For others, the card may increase receptivity when a questionnaire finally does arrive in the mail, if it has been delayed for some

Figure 4.4 Example of postcard thank you/reminder (third contact).

July 15, 1999

Last week a questionnaire seeking your opinions about moving to Washington state was mailed to you. Your name was drawn randomly from a list of all new Washington state driver's license holders.

If you have already completed and returned the questionnaire to us, please accept our sincere thanks. If not, please do so today. We are especially grateful for your help because it is only by asking people like you to share your experiences that we can understand why people decide to move here, and the consequences of doing so.

If you did not receive a questionnaire, or if it was misplaced, please call us toll-free at 1-800-833-0867 and we will get another one in the mail to you today.

Sincerely,

Don A. Dillman, Professor and Deputy Director
Social & Economic Sciences Research Center
Washington State University
Pullman, WA 99164-4014

unknown reason. For those respondents who are fully aware of having received the questionnaire and still have it in their possession, the lead paragraph serves to remind them of it by coming quickly to the point.

The second paragraph of the card contains the crucial message that the postcard is designed to convey. People who have already returned their questionnaires are thanked and those who have not are asked to do so "today," a time reference consistent with the importance one wants to convey. Another sentence follows that amplifies the message of how important each recipient is to the success of the study as described in the initial cover letter.

The third and final paragraph is an invitation to call for a replacement questionnaire if one is needed. It is aimed at both those who did not receive the original questionnaire and those who discarded it. A routine statement of appreciation and the researcher's name, title, and signature complete the thank you postcard message.

The respondent's name and address are individually printed on the reverse side, exactly as was done for the envelope of the initial mailout. The name is not repeated on the message side because this would require a further reduction of the print used for the message and, if added mechanically, would exhibit an awkward contrast.

The decision to send this postcard to all questionnaire recipients, whether they have responded or not, is a practical one. About one week after the initial mailing is when the maximum number of returns usually arrive. It is too confusing to attempt to sort returns to save the minor postage costs of the cards. Even in small surveys with a sample of a few hundred, there is usually no time to wait until a significant number of returns are in before addressing the postcard follow-up and still get it mailed on schedule. Another significant advantage of the blanket mailing is that the postcards can be (and should be) printed and addressed even before the first mailout and stored so that this work does not interfere with the often confusing task of processing early returns.

The effect of the postcard reminder varies. In the original TDM, for which it was the second rather than the third contact, response increases of 15–25 percentage points were obtained in five general public surveys from the date that responses started coming in as a result of the postcard effect (Dillman et al., 1974). Response rates prior to that time ranged from 19–27% in these general public surveys, which were conducted in four states. However, many of these additional responses would have come in anyway. Higher initial response rates are typically followed by higher response rates to the postcard.

A large factorial experiment of the preletter–postcard reminder sequence and a stamped return envelope on a national test of census questionnaires (where people were informed in a letter that their response was required by law) showed that the postcard reminder added eight percentage points to the final response rate, compared with six percentage points for a preletter when tested alone (Dillman, Clark, and Sinclair, 1995). The combination of preletter and postcard added 13 percentage points, suggesting clearly that the effects are additive. The use of all three elements added 14 percentage points.

Another experiment has confirmed the importance of having the format of the reminder contrast with that of the prenotice (Ohm, personal communication, August 8,1998). In this experiment, very similar postcards were used for the prenotice and reminder. Independently, each improved response rates, by four percentage points for the prenotice postcard alone and seven percentage points for the reminder postcard alone. In a treatment for which the prenotice and reminder postcards were both used, the response rate increased by seven percentage points, the same as when the reminder was used alone (Ohm, 1998). These results contrast sharply to the additive effect achieved in the census test mentioned above which relied on a prenotice letter and reminder postcard. These experiments provide additional evidence that contrasting stimuli are better for response than are repeated stimuli.

Fourth Contact: The First Replacement Questionnaire

There is a marked difference between the content of the fourth contact and the three that preceded it (Figure 4.5). This letter has a tone of insistence that the previous contacts lack. Its strongest aspect is the first paragraph, in which recipients are told that their completed questionnaire has not yet been received. This message is one of the strongest forms of personalization, communicating to respondents that they are indeed receiving individual attention. It reinforces messages contained in three previous contacts that the respondent is important to the success of the survey.

Most of this letter is devoted to a restatement of each respondent's impor-

Figure 4.5 Example of cover letter with first replacement questionnaire (fourth contact).

Washington State University
Social and Economic Sciences Research Center

Wilson Hall 133
PO Box 644014
Pullman, WA 99164-4014
509-335-1511
FAX 509-335-0116

Date	→	July 29, 1999
Inside address	→	L. T. Hansen 2121 Lincoln Way East Uniontown, WA 99962-2056
Feedback: We've not heard from you	→	About three weeks ago I sent a questionnaire to you that asked about your experiences of living in Washington state. To the best of our knowledge, it's not yet been returned.
Others have responded	→	The comments of people who have already responded include a wide variety of reasons for moving to (or back to) Washington. Many have described their experiences, both good and bad, in trying to find work. We think the results are going to be very useful to state leaders and others.
Usefulness of your response	→	We are writing again because of the importance that your questionnaire has for helping to get accurate results. Although we sent questionnaires to people living in every county in the state, it's only by hearing from nearly everyone in the sample that we can be sure that the results are truly representative.
Are you eligible?: More feedback	→	A few people have written to say that they should not have received the questionnaire because they no longer live in Washington or that they moved here before 1990. If either of these concerns apply to you, please let us know on the cover of the questionnaire and return it in the enclosed envelope so that we can delete your name from the mailing list.
Confidentiality	→	A comment on our survey procedures. A questionnaire identification number is printed on the back cover of the questionnaire so that we can check your name off of the mailing list when it is returned. The list of names is then destroyed so that individual names can never be connected to the results in any way. Protecting the confidentiality of people's answers is very important to us, as well as the University.
Voluntary	→	We hope that you will fill out and return the questionnaire soon, but if for any reasor you prefer not to answer it, please let us know by returning a note or blank questionnaire in the enclosed stamped envelope.
		Sincerely,
Real signature	→	Don A. Dillman Professor and Deputy Director
		P.S. If you have any questions, please feel free to contact me. The toll-free number where I can be reached in Pullman is 1-800-833-0867.

tance to the study in terms quite different from those used in previous mailings. It conveys to the recipient, as a means of encouraging response, that others have responded. The social usefulness of the study is also reemphasized, implying that the usefulness of the study is dependent on the return of the questionnaire. The recipient is also reminded which member of the household is to complete the questionnaire. The letter is completed by mention of the enclosed replacement questionnaire, the usual note of appreciation, and the now familiar blue ball-point pen signature. It is sent by first-class mail in the same type of envelope used for the initial mailing.

In developing the obviously stronger tone of this letter, it is important neither to over- nor undersell. It needs to show a greater intensity than preceding letters, but not be so strong that potential respondents become disgruntled. The letter appears sterner and a little more demanding when considered in isolation than when read in the context of having already been asked to make a significant contribution to an important study. If the study lacked social importance or had a frivolous quality about it, the letter would probably seem inappropriate to the respondent and could produce a negative reaction.

Ordinarily this letter is not produced until questionnaires are returned from previous mailings in considerable quantity. The lapse of time provides an excellent opportunity to gather feedback on problems encountered by respondents. For every respondent who writes to ask a question, it is likely that many more have a similar question but do not take time to write. Thus, a postscript to the follow-up letter is sometimes added in hopes of answering questions that may have been suggested to the researcher by such feedback. The postscript also suggests that the study is important by indicating that the researcher is examining early returns and trying to deal with respondent concerns.

It is essential to send a replacement questionnaire with the follow-up letter. The three weeks or so that have elapsed since the first questionnaire mailing make it probable that the original questionnaire, if it has not been lost or thrown away, will be difficult to find. In one of my early studies I made the mistake of omitting a replacement questionnaire. Not only did we get a considerable quantity of cards and letters requesting a copy of the questionnaire to which it was necessary to respond, but even after this effort the total response was only half that usually obtained for the second follow-up (Dillman et al., 1974).

A replacement questionnaire creates certain processing challenges. It is possible that someone may fill out two questionnaires instead of only the one intended, or perhaps give it to a spouse or friend to complete. Although this occasionally happens (as evidenced by returns with duplicate identification numbers and different handwriting), the frequency is so low as to be of little concern. Perhaps the greatest difficulty rests with those respondents who did fill out and return the earlier questionnaire, only to be informed that the researcher did not receive it. This underscores the great importance of an accurate identification system and the need to hold the follow-up mailing to the last minute so that respondents whose questionnaires have just been received can be deleted. Scheduling this follow-up a full two weeks or slightly longer after the postcard reminder allows responses to dwindle to a small trickle, considerably lowering the chance that someone who has sent in a questionnaire will receive another one. Further, the additional time and subsequently smaller number of required follow-ups reduces postage and clerical costs considerably.

FIFTH CONTACT: THE INVOKING OF SPECIAL PROCEDURES

This request, the final effort to elicit a response, exhibits a greater overall intensity than any of those which preceded it (Figure 4.6). However, this is not because of the wording of the cover letter, which in fact is somewhat softer than that of the preceding one. Rather, its insistent nature stems from the simple fact that it is a fifth request, and it is being made by special mail or by telephone. Because these factors raise the intensity to a high level, the relaxed wording of the cover letter emphasizes explanations of why this additional follow-up is sent. The now familiar messages of social usefulness and individual importance are repeated once more, but in words different from any used previously.

The important way in which this contact differs from those that precede it is in the packaging and delivery of the request. If one is considering simply sending a third copy of the questionnaire using the same type of envelope and another letter on the same stationery, it is hard to make this stimulus appear different from the second and fourth mailings. From an exchange perspective, we expect that repeating any stimulus will decrease its effect each time it is used. After all, the stimulus failed to produce a response from the recipient the previous two times it was used. Thus, it seems unlikely that the recipient will get past the outward appearance to note the changes in the wording of the letter. The delivery of this final contact differs from all previous contacts because of the packaging, the mode of delivery, and the speed by which it is delivered, all of which may be made noticeable before the letter is even opened. The effect being sought is to increase the perception of importance as a legitimate request.

Certified Mail

There are several different ways in which this perception of important goals can be accomplished. One method used with the original TDM was to send the final request by certified mail. Certified mail requires that the person who receives it sign for its delivery, thus acknowledging that it has been received. Various levels of certification can be used at varied costs, requiring, for example, that someone at the address sign for delivery. It can also be specified that the person whose name is on the envelope sign for it. In addition, one can request a return receipt to assure that it has been delivered. Such information can be helpful in resolving coverage issues.

The effectiveness of certified mail has been shown to be substantial. Origi-

Figure 4.6 Example of fifth and final contact sent by special mail.

Washington State University

Social and Economic Sciences Research Center

Wilson Hall 133
PO Box 644014
Pullman, WA 99164-4014
509-335-1511
FAX 509-335-0116

Date	→	September 5, 1999
Inside address	→	L. T. Hansen 2121 Lincoln Way East Uniontown, WA 99962-2056
Connection to previous mailings	→	During the last two months we have sent you several mailings about an important research study we are conducting for the state of Washington.
Purpose and usefulness	→	Its purpose is to help state agencies understand the reasons people are moving to Washington state, and their experiences after coming here that might be relevant to improving state services.
Time is running out	→	The study is drawing to a close, and this is the last contact that will be made with the random sample of people who we think, based on driver's license records, moved here in the last year.
Explanation for special contact	→	We are sending this final contact by priority mail because of our concern that people who have not responded may have had different experiences than those who have. Hearing from everyone in this small statewide sample helps assure that the survey results are as accurate as possible.
Confidentiality	→	We also want to assure you that your response to this study is voluntary, and if you prefer not to respond that's fine. If you are not a recent mover to Washington state, and you feel that we have made a mistake including you in this study, please let us know by returning the blank questionnaire with a note indicating so. This would be very helpful.
Thank you	→	Finally, we appreciate your willingness to consider our request as we conclude this effort to better understand job, living, and other issues facing new Washington state residents. Thank you very much.
		Sincerely,
Real signature	→	Don A. Dillman Professor and Deputy Director

nal tests in five statewide surveys of the general public using certified mail as a fourth and final mailing raised response rates from an average of 59 to 72%, an increase of about 13 percentage points. The certified mailing also produced a greater *relative* return; that is, the percentage of surveys returned in each mailing surpassed that of any mailing that preceded it. Its relative return was 33% of the letters mailed, compared to a range of 24 to 29% of the number mailed in the earlier mailings. These results are even more impressive when we realize that those who responded to it had ignored three previous mailings and therefore might be classified as "hard-core holdouts."

It was also found that the certified mailout picked up greater portions of older, less-educated, and lower income people, those most often missed by mail questionnaires. Thus it appeared that nonresponse error on those variables was reduced by this intensive follow-up. Another documented benefit of the certified letter was that it often elicited notes from people explaining why they were ineligible for the study, thus improving the coverage aspects of the sample frame.

Use of a similar certified mailing in the Netherlands suggests that certified mail may interact with personalization (de Leeuw and Hox, 1988). Whereas the use of personalized letters with a certified follow-up resulted in a 71% response rate, non-personalized letters that were certified produced only a 61% response rate, and a personalized, noncertified treatment produced only a 53% response rate. Thus, part of the effectiveness of certification may stem from respondents knowing that the letter is addressed to them personally, conveying individual importance to the study outcome.

Alternative To Certified Mail

For several reasons, we no longer use certified mail except in special circumstances. When people are not at home a certified letter cannot be left in the mailbox. Instead, a U.S. Postal Service message is left indicating that an attempt to deliver a certified letter was made. Usually, the individual may either sign that note and leave it for delivery the next day or go to the post office and pick it up. We consider it undesirable both from an exchange perspective (increased personal costs) and concern for the welfare of respondents to require people to go to the post office, which some recipients may be inclined to do. In addition, many alternatives to certified mail are now available. They include courier delivery by one of several private companies, such as Federal Express or United Parcel Service. The U.S. Postal Service offers priority mail delivery and special delivery, neither of which requires a signature. When telephone numbers are available, a telephone follow-up can be substituted. The sole situation in which certified mail is recommended for use is when one is confident that someone is always present, as in an office, when postal deliveries are made.

An early study by Moore and Dillman (1980), which tested the use of special delivery and telephone follow-up calls as individual alternatives to certified mail, found that both alternatives worked about the same as certified mail (no significant difference), and both worked much better than another first-class mailing. We have observed many other tests of priority mail by courier, in which an increment of additional response is attributable to use of courier or two-day priority Postal Service mail.

Sending this final contact by special mail requires that out-of-the-ordinary mailing procedures be used, which sometimes includes different mailing forms and labels. If one is contemplating using a particular service it is imperative to talk with the provider. These delivery services are normally not set up to receive large numbers of such mailings at one time, and computerized procedures may be available for streamlining the process. In addition, costs may vary depending upon how many questionnaires are being dispatched. The variation in charges by distance, time of day that delivery is requested, whether a special promotional offer is being made, and whether the sponsor has a special contract or volume discount with the provider can affect both the possibilities and the costs. Current costs can range from about two dollars per questionnaire up to as much as $15, or even more in the case of extremely long distances or when the fastest possible delivery time is selected.

Consequently, it is important to remember the total effect one is attempting to accomplish with this mailing. A different look is achieved by using a different outside container than in any previous ones. An example is the light cardboard 9 × 12 inch carton used by some couriers, within which the cover letter and envelope are inserted differently than in previous mailings (e.g., not folded into a regular business stationery envelope). We are also depending upon the special handling to convey that an attempt for rapid, assured delivery is being made. These attributes convey to the respondent that the survey is important. Finally, these external attributes are depended upon to get the recipient to read the letter, which differs significantly from the previous letters and includes an explanation of why the special contact procedure was used. In addition, enough time is allowed to elapse between the fourth and fifth contact so that little, if any, overlap occurs between this mailout and late returns from the previous contact.

A Telephone Alternative

Some sample lists contain telephone numbers as well as mailing addresses. In these instances a telephone call may be used in place of the special mailing to encourage return of the mail questionnaire. A script is provided to interviewers that informs respondents that a questionnaire was sent to them previously, and explains that the call is being made to see if they have any questions about the study. They are also encouraged to complete and return the survey. In some cases they may be given the opportunity to complete the survey on the telephone (see Chapter 6) or told that another one can be sent to them if the previous one has been thrown away.

The switch in modes provides considerable contrast to the repetitive mail contacts and allows for immediate feedback from the respondent. Telephone follow-ups are preferred when the number of ineligible respondents is likely to be high. Typically, such recipients of questionnaires are more likely to ignore mailed requests to complete it, and obtaining that information by telephone allows the surveyor to drop them from the sample frame. Telephone calls have also been found to be effective from the standpoint of reassuring people who do not understand the nature of the study and do not want to participate, as is sometimes the case with elderly respondents. The phone call provides an opportunity to thank people for their consideration and assure them that they will not be contacted again.

When such a contact is used it is important to make the call within a week after the fourth contact arrives by mail, in order to increase the likelihood that the questionnaire has not been thrown away. It is also important that the interviewer be prepared to listen to concerns the respondent might have, and be able to answer questions about the study and the questionnaire. This is not the type of call that can be turned over to someone instructed only to read a simple reminder notice to the questionnaire recipient.

DYNAMICS OF THE IMPLEMENTATION PROCESS

There is more to implementing a mail survey than the ordered series of events described in this chapter. Once the first mailing is dispatched, feedback from respondents, only some of which can be anticipated, requires considerable attention from the researcher. Sometimes on-the-spot modifications of the implementation process are necessary. Such concerns extend through all five contacts.

Handling Undelivered Questionnaires

Usually one of the initial problems to present itself is the return of undelivered questionnaires. The first solution to this problem is to do everything possible to prevent it from happening. Commercial software is now available for changing addresses so that they comply with current postal regulations. For example, the address "S.W. 705 Marcel St." will be changed so that the number comes first, as "705 S.W. Marcel St." Some software of this nature can also be used to group addresses by zip code for easier handling by the postal service. The use of such software can significantly reduce the number of undelivered questionnaires.

Immediate attention often makes remailing possible and prevents wasting scheduled follow-ups. The reasons provided by the U.S. Postal Service for nondelivery generally fit into three categories. The first relates to a change of residence by respondents. Occasionally people move without leaving a forwarding address. Most people do leave a forwarding address, but U.S. Postal Service regulations keep it on record for only 18 months. If the move was within the same city or county, it is sometimes possible to locate the person by consulting the local telephone directory or other listings. Through these various efforts it is often possible to remail a sizable portion of the questionnaires that were not forwarded.

The second reason for undelivered questionnaires is categorized here as "possible errors." This categorization seems appropriate because the main causes for "addressee unknown," "no such street," "no apartment number," "no residential delivery," and so on are clerical errors. When a questionnaire is returned for any of these reasons, processing procedures and sample sources need to be checked to see if an incorrect address was used. If this procedure does not identify the problem, then an attempt is made to locate the respondent's telephone number and to call the household or business, thus reverting to the procedures used for those known to have moved. Some problems are unique to certain surveys. In one of our statewide surveys nearly all the letters for one rural community were returned. The reason for this problem was that the addresses reported in the sample list were different from those used by the U.S. Postal Service. A call to the local post office helped solve the problem.

A third category of problems reported in the notation system used by the U.S. Postal Service is that of letters that are refused or unclaimed. Generally, refusals are not a problem until later mailings, when respondents recognize the envelope and presumably choose not to accept delivery. The questionnaires that are unclaimed from earlier mailings may have simply lain in the mailbox for a period of time without being picked up. This result suggests that the person may be temporarily gone, and remailing at a later time is often effective. However, some are clearly refusals, or the respondent chooses to leave the envelope in the mailbox. Finally, the U.S. Postal Service marks letters of persons who are deceased with that notation and returns them to the sender unless other arrangements for handling the deceased person's mail have been made.

The success of our tracing procedures varies a great deal. As one would expect, such procedures work best when sample lists are current and the number of undelivered letters is low. The remailing of questionnaires requires establishing new mailout dates for follow-up correspondence, creating additional work for the implementation of the study. However, the end result can be a significant increase of several percentage points in the final response rate.

Handling Respondent Inquiries

Another activity for which the researcher must be prepared is to answer respondent inquiries and comments. Each mailing is likely to bring reactions other than a completed questionnaire from a few recipients. Among the more frequent are:

- The person you want is out of town for a month and cannot do it until she returns.
- I would do the questionnaire except for the identification number on it.
- I would answer except for the personal questions, which I don't think are any of your business.

- I have only lived here for a few months, so I don't know enough about this community to answer your questionnaire.
- I'm too old, but my daughter will fill it out if you really need it.
- I filled out a questionnaire like this one six months ago and don't want to do it again.
- Tell me how you got my name, and I'll do your questionnaire.

These comments are acknowledged, and our response to these various inquiries is determined by both philosophical concerns and response considerations. Respondent questions, even strange ones, deserve a response, just as the request to complete a questionnaire deserves to be honored. Thus, a point is made to answer each of them. In general, one should respond as a well-trained interviewer would, attempting to convince people of their importance to the study. It is explained why an identification number is used, why it is important to have old people as well as young people in the study, why the daughter would not be an acceptable substitute, and how the recipient's name was obtained. The most appropriate approach is to be straightforward and honest and to thank them for writing or calling.

Letters are also written by second parties on behalf of the questionnaire recipients. The most common of these indicate that the desired respondent is physically incapable of completing the survey, usually because of the infirmities of old age. Another fairly typical request comes from the spouse of the requested respondent, who reports that the person is temporarily out of town. These letters are responded to in much the same way that respondent inquiries are answered. Acknowledgment letters then go to the second parties who reported that the desired respondent cannot complete the questionnaire. The aim of these letters is to thank them and also to assure them that the person's name is being removed from the sample list, if that action is appropriate.

Still another kind of letter I have grown accustomed to seeing is from individuals who have simply heard about the study, perhaps because a friend showed them a questionnaire. These letters sometimes come from media people or from those who would find the results useful in their work. These inquiries are handled in as helpful a way as possible, consistent with the study objectives. It is particularly important to be prepared in large-scale surveys with a policy for handling requests for interviews or news stories. An appropriate approach is to respond to such requests in much the same way one would answer respondents' questions, emphasizing the social usefulness of the study, the importance of every individual responding, and so on.

EVALUATING EARLY RETURNS

When returns begin to come in, one of the first priorities is to open the return envelopes and scrutinize the questionnaires. Besides providing for the quick location of questions to which responses must be given in follow-up letters, certain problems can be identified. For example, in some studies it is learned that questionnaires were printed in a way that produced a tendency for pages to stick together. In one study this meant the return of many questionnaires for which sets of facing pages had been skipped. The immediate identification of this problem led to instituting a procedure whereby the missing two pages were photocopied, marked with the appropriate identification number, and returned to the respondent with a personalized note stating, "In our routine check for completeness we noticed two pages were missed. It appears they may have stuck together and thereby been inadvertently missed . . . " Nearly two-thirds of those contacted returned the missing pages, significantly improving the quality of data. Usually, problems of this nature are not anticipated, making the close monitoring of early returns essential.

Each survey is different, with the survey topic, population, and sampling procedures all contributing to the existence of a unique set of circumstances. The important conclusion is that implementation activities do not simply take care of themselves once the survey questionnaires are in the mail. Much remains to be done.

WHAT TO DO WHEN MAXIMIZING RESPONSE QUALITY SEEMS IMPOSSIBLE

The original TDM and its successor, Tailored Design, are designed as systems of attributes whose aim is to maximize the likelihood of achieving high quality results. However, the reality of the survey world is one of cost constraints and data quality trade-offs. Sometimes, doing the best one can do is not possible.

These pressures are experienced in somewhat different ways when doing self-administered surveys than typically happens in interview surveys. Once the interview questionnaire has been constructed and implementation started, the issue typically becomes one of number of call-backs to make and how to accomplish refusal conversions. Stopping with two or three call-backs or even no call-backs and not attempting to convert refusals inevitably results in low response rates. The decisions on mail surveys involve a quite different matrix of considerations. In the face of cost constraints, where should one cut back first: Number of contacts? Level of financial incentive or even whether to use one? Depersonalization of the mailings? Decreasing sample size and reallocating resources to fewer potential respondents? Or something else? The issue becomes one of how to optimize the allocation of resources.

Recently, I was asked to comment on the proposed procedures for a survey of more than 10,000 people. The sponsor had funded the study on the assumption that three mailings would be made, each of which would include a replacement copy of the questionnaire. A further look at the proposed procedures revealed that the cover letters for each of the three mailings were, except for the first paragraph, virtually identical. The funds had been allocated, and any changes in procedures would have to be funded by cutting back on the planned procedures.

This situation is characteristic of hundreds I have been faced with since publication of the original TDM. Surveyors become boxed in by an initial decision that specifies procedures and/or budget. In this situation, several strategies could have been followed to improve the design of the proposed study. First, it appeared that the third mailing would have very little impact relative to cost. Virtually the same stimulus had been sent twice before. The sponsor then proposed to abandon the third mailing and instead offer a lottery prize for respondents or give people who returned the questionnaire a five-dollar payment. I discouraged these changes because of lack of evidence that either approach would work.

The sponsor also contemplated the possibility of abandoning the third contact in exchange for sending a preletter and postcard reminder. Because the lengthy questionnaire had to be mailed flat at a cost of nearly five dollars for printing, paper, and postage, such a trade-off was possible. That would have resulted in four contacts rather than three. In addition, the preletter could have been sent from the government agency to respondents, thus invoking legitimate authority. It was also suggested that converting to a one- or two-dollar incentive might have been done. However, to do that would reduce funds so that only two mailings of any type could be made. Consideration was also given to including a minimal token incentive of only one dollar and using the balance of the money saved by foregoing the final but repetitive mailing in favor of sending a postcard reminder.

Another approach to the problem of finding resources for improvement would have been to assess the planned survey in light of expected error outcomes. For example, another method of producing savings is to reduce the sample size and devote those saved resources to improving response quality from fewer sample units. Such suggestions are often met with strenuous objections, but strictly from a sampling error standpoint, obtaining a 30% response from a sample of 10,000 (3,000 questionnaires) is about the same as obtaining a 50% response from a sample of 6,000 (also 3,000 questionnaires). However, the reduction of nonresponse error might be substantial. We also noted in this case that an exceedingly long questionnaire was being used, a factor which by itself would tend to reduce response and perhaps increase measurement error. Reducing the size of the questionnaire could have produced postal and processing savings that could have been applied to achieving better responses.

In sum, when faced with a description of a poorly designed set of survey procedures and the lament that the budget has been determined, so there is nothing that can be done, my usual response is, "Are you sure?" and to ask for details. I then attempt to redesign the procedures by relying on whatever research is available to assess the consequences of likely changes and employ the social exchange calculus offered in Chapter One, in order to evaluate the fit of different elements with one another. In addition, I try to bring to bear considerations of all four types of survey error: measurement, coverage, sampling, and nonresponse. Thus, I assess the inclusion or exclusion of each factor on the basis of whatever demonstrated evidence is available and/or where it seems to fit theoretically into an overall response strategy. I also assess it with regard to the consequences for the four sources of error I am seeking to minimize. Doing triage on poorly designed surveys, difficult as it sometimes becomes, is as much a reality of Tailored Design as constructing an ideal survey design in the first place. So, what was the outcome? In this case, the sponsor abandoned the third mailing in favor of the prenotice and reminder. In addition, the cover letters were significantly revised. Consideration of other issues was left for another time.

CONCLUSION

A few years after the first edition of this book was published, I was informed that a prominent scholar visiting my university was looking for me, and that I should go talk to him. When I finally located him he expressed his appreciation for coming to see him, said he had read my book, and then abruptly asked, "What I wanted to know was whether I can solve my response rate problem for mail surveys by putting several small stamps on the outgoing envelope." I no longer recall my exact answer (which should have been an emphatic "no") but the impact of the question still lingers. Like many others, he was looking for a magic bullet.

Improving response to self-administered surveys and maintaining low amounts of error are not goals one can attain by selecting a single technique and scrupulously applying it to every survey. Respondent-friendly questionnaires, multiple contacts, a special final contact, a real stamp on the return (not outgoing) envelope, personalization of correspondence, prepaid incentives, and many smaller details all have a role to play in improving response to self-administered surveys. Selecting one technique for special attention while ignoring most of the others makes no more sense than trying to get a nutritious diet by eating only carrots or some other specific food.

In this chapter I have described details for designing all aspects of the implementation process and discussed how each aspect might be shaped to improve the quality and quantity of response. Yet, the elements described here must be considered somewhat tentative. Though sufficient for many and perhaps most survey situations, they can be tailored (i.e., further refined in advantageous ways to take into account survey content) to the population and the survey situation in ways that improve their effectiveness. They may also need further refinement based upon coverage and sampling situations, the topics to which I now turn.

CHAPTER 5

Reduction of Coverage and Sampling Errors

THE NEED to discuss coverage and sampling for self-administered surveys is illustrated by a call that I received just before writing this chapter. The call came from a city planner and concerned plans for an essential survey of city residents. The purpose of the survey was to determine the degree of satisfaction or dissatisfaction with the current provider of cable television service. The call conveyed some urgency because a decision about renewing the cable provider's contract had to be made, and an accurate reading of customer satisfaction was considered an essential aspect of deciding whether that should be done.

It had already been decided that a mail survey would be conducted. It was to be distributed by third-class mail to every household in the community as a brochure containing the questionnaire and information about the renewal process. The city planner noted that it was essential for all cable subscribers and nonsubscribers to have a chance to register their opinion, and that the water utility list for residences had been obtained to provide everyone's mailing address. When I asked about the use of follow-ups, he explained that none would be needed since if only five percent of the households responded that would be nearly 800 questionnaires, which was enough to give an estimate within three to four percentage points of what the entire community thought. As an explanation for this liberal estimate of precision, he said he had been told that a "sample size" (completed questionnaires) of 1,100–1,200 was large enough for a three percent margin of error in most national polls, so surely for his small city of 16,000 households a survey would be that accurate with considerably fewer responses.

This call was similar to many others I have received in which the caller seemed not to understand the nature of two sources of survey error—coverage and sampling—and how the latter differed from nonresponse error. First, although water utility lists are sometimes used to survey community residents, one has only to visit a few apartment buildings and duplexes to learn that water service is often listed only under the name of the landlord. Thus, the survey would likely suffer from significant coverage error because of many people in apartments being excluded from the survey. I also learned that the questionnaire would be addressed only to the household, with no attempt being made to control which member of the household responded. Was a representative sample of adults wanted? Or should the questionnaire be completed by the person who would make the decision to subscribe or not subscribe to cable television?

The very low response rate expectations suggested that respondents were quite likely to be different from nonrespondents on such things as interest in the issue and simply being more likely to read third-class mail. Therefore, it seemed possible that there would be a significant amount of nonresponse error.

The caller's focus on sampling error was also erroneous in three ways. First, because no sample was being drawn, it was inappropriate to infer statistical precision. Second, even if it had been a sample (e.g., sending questionnaires to every other household), any confidence in the findings would have been greatly reduced by the nonresponse error concern associated with the low response rate. Third, the caller misunderstood the relationship between population size and sampling error.

In order to help this city planner it was necessary to discuss the use of lists in sampling, ways of assessing coverage error, whether the extent of such error from use of the utility list was acceptable, and whether there were any alternative lists that might be used for sampling. We also discussed the difference between sampling and nonresponse error, how to draw a sample, and the size of the completed sample that might be needed to make estimates for the entire community at various levels of precision and confidence. These are the topics discussed in this chapter.

The discussion of coverage is focused only on issues that pertain specifically to mail and other self-administered surveys that use lists. In particular, I focus on attempting to reduce coverage error through improving the quality of lists and respondent selection.

The discussion of sampling error is even more limited. My goal in this chapter is *not* to explain the complexities of how to develop alternative sampling designs or the statistical theory that underlies the development of such designs. There are many excellent texts that describe these aspects of conducting a quality survey. For example, the recently published book by Lohr (1999) provides detailed statistical explanations of how probability sampling differs from nonprobability sampling. It also explains statistical procedures associated with stratification, the reasons for sampling with equal and unequal probabilities, when and how cluster sampling is done, and the development of more complex sample designs. Another text by Maxim (1999) provides a somewhat briefer discussion of statistical inference and procedures for drawing many types of samples, and focuses specifically on conducting social science research. An applied discussion of sampling and procedures for how to draw simple random samples is provided in Salant and Dillman (1994). In addition, one may also consult the classic sample texts by Kish (1965) and Cochran (1977) for additional background. My focus in this chapter is on the general relationship between sample size and the reduction of sampling error in the context of simple random sampling.

ESSENTIAL DEFINITIONS AND THEIR USE

Discussing coverage and sampling, even in a cursory way, requires a common understanding of certain terms.

- The *survey population* consists of all of the units (individuals, households, organizations) to which one desires to generalize survey results.
- The *sample frame* is the list from which a sample is to be drawn in order to represent the survey population.
- The *sample* consists of all units of the population that are drawn for inclusion in the survey.
- The *completed sample* consists of all the units that return completed questionnaires.
- *Coverage error* results from every unit in the survey population not having a known, non-zero chance of being included in the sample.
- *Sampling error* is the result of collecting data from only a subset, rather than all, of the members of the sample frame.

A statewide survey conducted in 1994–95 illustrates the use of these concepts. Our goal was to estimate characteristics (e.g., type of employment, wages, and use of computers) for households of all new adult residents (18 years and older) of Washington state who moved to the state within a one-year period (Salant, Carley, and Dillman, 1997). This group constituted our *survey population.* The *sample frame* consisted of all households in which at least one individual had turned in an out-of-state driver's license and applied for a Washington driver's license. Names were obtained every three months over the one-year period, and a random *sample* was selected from this sample frame as the subset to represent the survey population. Prior to sampling, different names at the same address were eliminated randomly so that each address (or household) had an equal chance of being selected for the survey. Implementation of a mail survey for each cohort over the one-year period resulted in a *completed sample* of 3,558, or about 60% of the original sample (Salant, Carley, and Dillman, 1996).

As with most surveys, this one had a certain amount of *coverage error.* Not all adults moving into the state obtained driver's licenses, and these people did not have a chance of being sampled for inclusion in the survey. Members of the same household may have applied for a driver's license during different three-month periods, giving their household a greater chance of selection. Movers who did obtain a license may not have done it within the three months following their move. Some who obtained a driver's license may not have considered themselves to be new state residents, or even to have a residence in the state. Thus, a modest number of individuals who moved to the state during the study period were undoubtedly missed. Nonetheless, this sample frame was used because the likely coverage errors seemed small compared with other affordable sampling alternatives. The vast majority of adults do obtain driver's licenses and penalties are significant in Washington state for not doing so within a few months of arrival.

The completed sample of 3,558 households comprised the data set for statistical analysis, and it is based on this number that conclusions about the amount of *sampling error,* and therefore the likely precision of the estimates for the entire survey population, were made. For a completed sample of this size, one could have statistical confidence that the estimates based on sample results were within one to two percentage points of the entire survey population.

However, as pointed out in Chapter 1, the statistical conclusions drawn through the straight-forward application of mathematical formulae to sample data must be tempered by recognition that *coverage* was imperfect and the possibility existed for both *nonresponse error* (e.g., the 40% who did not respond being different from the 60% who did in a way relevant to the study) and *measurement error* (e.g., questions that were misunderstood or incorrectly answered). Although efforts were made to assess their presence, we were unable to conclude to what extent each type of error existed.

This discussion highlights perhaps the most difficult challenge of surveying: minimizing all four types of potential survey error. The four cornerstones of survey precision or accuracy—coverage, sampling, nonresponse, and measurement—are each a distinct source of error. Most surveys have a certain amount of coverage error which cannot be precisely specified. Sampling error, on the other hand, can be precisely calculated for each variable based on the number of completed questionnaires and the distribution of respondents' answers across response categories. However, the amount of sampling error cannot be used independently as an adequate or sole indicator of the precision of the estimates for the entire population. That precision may also be affected by the presence of nonresponse, measurement, and/or coverage errors. As of yet there is no accepted way of providing a meaningful combined measure of the effect of these four sources of error on overall accuracy.

REDUCING COVERAGE ERROR

Most self-administered surveys are of specialized groups, ranging from store customers or organization employees to members of special interest organizations or service subscribers. When the first edition of this book was published, compiling and maintaining lists was a laborious process and the lists were invariably out-of-date. Now, computer technologies make possible the compilation and up-to-date maintenance of enormous lists in ways thought impossible only a decade ago.

WORKING WITH SAMPLE LISTS

Developing and maintaining lists has become a specialized activity that is typically done in response to the diverse needs of organizations, particularly their mailout needs. Sometimes legal and ethical concerns cause certain information to be added or subtracted from a list. Some people have telephone numbers and e-mail addresses, whereas others do not. Sometimes the list is divided into sublists for typical mailing needs, with the result that individual names may appear on several of the sublists. Lists are often formatted for particular mailing equipment in a way that makes their use for other purposes difficult. Some lists are formatted entirely in capital letters, which need to be changed for writing cover letters. Seeking out the office or person who keeps the list is often necessary in order to understand what exists and what is possible. Following is a list of five questions that should be asked about any potential sampling list.

Does the list contain everyone in the survey population?

Once I was given a list that was described as including all members of a health maintenance organization. When I asked how the list was compiled, the listkeeper reached for an enrollment form on his desk which included a box that allowed members to check if they wished not to have their home address revealed to any outside organization. The list we were being given was one sometimes provided to outside organizations, and the sponsors of the proposed survey had simply forgotten that not all members were on the list. Had we used this list, we would have had an obvious coverage problem and the sponsor would not have been able to claim that the sample survey results represented all members of the organization.

An essential first step in evaluating the list is to determine whether all members of the survey population are on it. If they are not, then one should determine whether getting the remainder of the people on the list is possible or evaluate the likely coverage consequences of not obtaining the excluded names.

Does the list include names of people who are not in the study population?

Many years ago, when asked to survey graduates of a university, I was given the alumni mailing list from which to sample. Only when returns started coming back did I learn from some questionnaires that the respondents had not attended that university. Further inquiry with the sample provider revealed that for convenience in mailing university publications, the list had been expanded to include contributors to the university. In addition, I learned that spouses were left on the list after the alumnus was deceased. This survey included many questions about what each alumnus had done after graduation. It was only after surveys were returned that I learned that the definition of alumnus included anyone who had attended the university for at least one semester, regardless of whether he or she had graduated.

This experience points to the critical need to know exactly whom a mailing list does or does not include, and to develop different ways of dealing with any deficiencies. When I learned that the list included people who were not in the intended population, I also learned that names of donors, spouses, and nongraduates could be deleted from the data file. However, had it not been possible to delete them, prior knowledge of the list's complete contents would have allowed many of the questions to be structured so that ineligible individuals were screened from inappropriate questions. For example, nongraduates would have been directed to skip the question on what year they graduated from the university.

Sometimes it is possible to partly recover from undetected problems of this nature. For example, responses from nongraduates might have been discarded. However, learning ahead of time exactly who is on the list and why would have caused less embarrassment for both the survey sponsors and recipients of the questionnaire.

How is the list maintained and updated?

Lists are maintained in many different ways. Sometimes address lists are actively updated by regularly resending undeliverable correspondence with address correction requests. Updates may occur once a year when memberships are renewed. In other instances a list sits unused for years, with only new names and addresses being added, so that names added in earlier years are less likely to have current addresses. Knowing these characteristics of a list allows one to evaluate the likelihood of unintended coverage biases (e.g., fewer good addresses for older members) from creeping into one's survey results. In difficult cases of this nature we have sometimes sent letters to a sample of a list, or even the whole list, with the request on the envelope, "Address Correction Requested," to learn from the U.S. Postal Service how many addresses were invalid.

Are the same sample units included on the list more than once?

When doing customer surveys I have sometimes been given lists that have the same address, or nearly the same address, listed for several names. Investigation of this phenomenon for one such list revealed that the list was compiled from customer orders made over the course of several years. Each time an order was taken purchasers were asked to give their address, and sometimes different household members purchased goods from the same source. The variations in addresses and names also stemmed from people giving their name or address in a slightly different way on different orders, and the process of eliminating only exact duplicates allowed those variations to remain on the list. This problem appears to be decreasing as companies increasingly check for previous orders for that address and make corrections when accepting orders.

A district-wide survey of the parents of school children presented the problem of duplication in a different way. The keeper of the list created a separate listing for each parent. If a child had two parents living in separate residences, usually as a result of separation or divorce, each parent had a separate entry on the address list. However, if the parents lived together they were listed as one entry. The sample was designed on the basis of individual children being the sample unit so that all children were to have an equal chance of their parent (or parents) being drawn in the sample. The result of sampling from this address list would have given each child with separated or divorced parents twice the likelihood of being included in the sample as children with parents living together. The solution required matching parent names to each child and then deciding randomly which parent should be asked to respond to the survey.

Does the list contain other information that can be used to improve the survey?

Increasingly, mixed-mode surveys, the topic of the next chapter, are being used to improve response rates for studies. In addition, a follow-up contact by a different mode, such as the telephone, as discussed in Chapters 4 and 6, is particularly effective in identifying ineligible units in the population. Such individuals are probably less likely than others to respond to repeated contacts by mail. For this reason it is useful to determine whether telephone numbers (daytime or evening), e-mail addresses, fax numbers, or other information is available which might facilitate contacts by another mode.

In addition, some lists contain information such as age or gender which might be used in a post-survey analysis to evaluate nonresponse error. Other information, such as number of orders submitted during the last year, year of initial organization membership, or perhaps level of membership, may be available for analyzing nonresponse error in ways more pertinent to specific survey objectives.

What To Do When No List Is Available

Visitors to national parks and museums, users of airports, and attendees at open houses are examples of groups for which no list may exist. For such populations, coverage is not a problem if people can be sampled as they experience the place or activity of interest. A procedure for sampling, delivering, and retrieving self-administered questionnaires from unlisted populations is one of the tailored applications discussed in Chapter 7.

Special Coverage Issues in General Public Survey Lists

Some populations are not on a list. For example, the coverage problems outlined above for general public populations have led to sampling and contacting them in a manner that does not require a list. In some cases, randomly generated telephone numbers are called based upon the expectation that everyone's telephone number has an equal chance of being randomly generated for a call. For self-administered surveys, randomly generated telephone numbers do not provide a solution to coverage problems because of the lack of addresses.

Poor coverage is typically the most significant source of error in surveys of the general public. There are no lists available that make it possible to avoid significant coverage error in most household surveys done to represent the general public. Moreover, in recent years the problem seems to have gotten worse.

Telephone directories once provided a reasonable sample frame for households in many regions of the United States. Coverage rates exceeded 90% and most households had only one telephone, which was likely to be listed in a telephone directory with a complete mailing address. In the early 1990s, the proportion of households with unlisted telephones had increased dramatically to about 25% nationwide (Survey Sampling, personal communication, August 19, 1999). In addition, many of the households for which telephone numbers are provided are listed without a mailing address. Further, the trend towards spouses not changing last names when they marry has meant that wives and husbands with different last names are both likely to be listed in directories. The result is for these households to have a higher probability of being drawn in any random sample. In many households, additional telephone lines may be provided for a child, faxes and/or computer equipment so that multiple lines go into a single household. Each of the numbers, if listed, provides another opportunity to be drawn in a sample.

Alternatives to telephone directories may exist. In some states general public surveys can be accomplished by obtaining driver's license lists. Although these lists do not include individuals without licenses, thus biasing results against those segments of the population who are a little less likely to obtain driver's licenses, they provide a reasonable approximation of the general public and make respondent selection within households unnecessary. However, increasingly states do not require that driver's licenses be renewed each year and these lists have a tendency to age, with mailing addresses becoming less reliable as the required time between renewals increases. A second possibility is to consider the use of registered voter lists. For community issue surveys aimed at predicting election results, such lists may be quite adequate. Yet, the high proportion of those who do not register to vote may make them unacceptable for most other purposes. Utility lists have also been used, but they often include the owners or management companies that pay the bills rather than the people who occupy each unit, thus exhibiting coverage error.

When general public telephone surveys are conducted using random digit dialing, all households with telephones have a chance of being reached. In addition, the interviewer may be instructed to ask how many voice telephone numbers are in the households so that screening or weighting may be done to maintain an equal probability for all households to be surveyed. Interviews in over-represented households may be terminated before survey questions are asked in order to maintain the probability of selection at a given level. The inability to ask and act effectively on such screening questions in mail surveys means that such probabilities cannot be controlled, except by asking the appropriate questions of everyone and either weighting results or simply discarding unnecessarily collected data.

Krysan, Schuman, Scott, and Beatty (1994) have evaluated a means of sampling general public households without using lists. Previous probability surveys of the same geographic area were used to create a sample frame by having interviewers record residential addresses adjacent to where any interview had taken place. Mail surveys were later sent to these newly sampled addresses. Using a five-contact strategy that included a prepaid one-dollar bill and final contact by two-day priority mail, quite similar to the basic model described in Chapter 4, they achieved a 74% response rate in predominantly white Detroit suburbs, compared to 75% by face-to-face interview. This method did not work as well in predominantly black areas of Detroit, where only a 46% response was achieved compared with 83% by face-to-face interview. In both strata the mail survey was 5–10 minutes long compared with about an hour for the face-to-face interview, which included many additional questions. Nevertheless, this method of sampling offers promise for overcoming this major coverage challenge for general public mail surveys.

Research at the U.S. Bureau of the Census on test Census questionnaires has shown that response rates as high as 76% can be obtained for Census questionnaires sent without names to "resident" specified addresses (Dillman et al., 1994). This research also confirmed that response rates from inner cities is lower, as learned in the Detroit study. The difference in this case was about 15–20 percentage points below that achieved in the rest of United States. This research needs to be extended to nongovernmental surveys in an effort to determine whether simply using address lists will produce adequate response rates for general public household surveys.

Increasingly, general public lists are being compiled by combining information from a large variety of sources: credit card holders, telephone directories, city directories, magazine subscribers, bank depositors, organization membership lists, catalogue customers, etc. One firm has used such sources to create a national list of nearly 100 million households. No one knows the quality of these lists with regard to coverage of the U.S. population and the bias towards or against certain segments of the population. As of yet, they are not well suited for general public surveying simply because their precise coverage characteristics are generally unknown. However, it seems likely that such lists will improve in the future, thereby becoming more useful to researchers. One reason for this expectation is that hard-to-find populations that would require large screening efforts, such as marathon runners, people with a strong interest in operas, or owners of unusual breeds of animals, may be identified through subscriptions, customer orders, and other means. Even though the coverage aspects of such compiled sample frames are likely to be unknown, these deficiencies will undoubtedly be weighed against the virtual impossibility of doing surveys by any other means.

Respondent Selection

Sometimes letters are addressed to an individual within a household or organization who is not necessarily the person who should complete the questionnaire. For household surveys, just as the goal is to give each household a known chance of selection, it is often desirable to give each adult in the household a known probability of selection. Letters intended for households that are addressed to an individual provide a special problem in this regard because that person may immediately take "ownership" of the questionnaire. When the first edition of this book was published, general public samples drawn from telephone directories typically produced a higher proportion of male respondents than female respondents even though letters requested that an adult female complete the questionnaire in half the households (e.g., Dillman, Christenson, Carpenter, and Brooks, 1974). In contrast, females were somewhat more likely to participate in telephone surveys because they were more likely to answer the telephone and it was sometimes difficult to get access to another household adult.

Commonly used respondent selection methods such as the Kish (1949) method, which requires listing members of a household by age and gender, do not work well in household mail surveys because of the complexity of the request. An alternative method that is sometimes used is the most recent birthday method. A sentence is inserted in the cover letter and sometimes on the questionnaire which makes a request of this nature: "In order that the results of this survey will accurately represent all adults in the state, it is important that the questionnaire sent to your household be completed by the adult

(18 years or older) who now lives there and has had the most recent birthday." This technique, when used over the telephone, has produced an over-representation of women (Groves and Lyberg, 1988), which may occur because women are somewhat more likely than men to answer home telephones. We know of no experiments that have compared results with other selection methods for mail surveys. This too is a topic of needed research.

Some household surveys are not aimed at obtaining a representative sample of the adult population. Instead, the topic of interest may be a household behavior, in which case the person with greatest responsibility for that area of activity should complete the questionnaire. For example, a survey on telephone service appropriately requested that: "The adult most responsible for making decisions about the telephone services provided to your household should complete the enclosed questionnaire." This line of reasoning can be extended to many areas of activity, from shopping for groceries to purchasing automobiles to making investment decisions. It also applies to businesses where the desired respondent may be the one most responsible for recommending or making decisions about, for example, the purchase of computers. In these types of surveys, the coverage issue is thereby limited to the household or business level and not extended to giving members of these units a known probability of becoming the selected respondent.

Coverage Outcomes

The hoped-for outcome of the coverage considerations we have discussed here is that every unit in the survey population appears on the sample frame list once (or can otherwise be available by its appearance at a sampling location). As a result each unit will have a known chance, and in most cases the same chance as any other member of the population, of being selected into the survey sample to receive a questionnaire. The survey population is thus prepared for actual sampling.

Frequently, a coverage analysis of potential sample frames produces a conclusion that no list is completely adequate for one's purpose. The surveyor is then faced with a decision about whether plans for the survey should be abandoned or whether a certain amount of coverage error is acceptable. Such decisions usually involve a consideration of whether any alternatives exist (frequently they do not), the cost of those alternatives, and whether any methods exist for evaluating the extent of any resultant error.

PROBABILITY SAMPLING

As noted in Chapter 1, the remarkable power of the sample survey is its ability to estimate closely the distribution of a characteristic in a population by obtaining information from relatively few elements of that population.

Sampling error is the type of error that occurs because information is not collected from every member of the population. It is highly dependent on sample size and, in contrast to the other three types of survey error, can usually be estimated with considerable precision.

Drawing a sample can be remarkably complex or fairly simple. When the dominant mode of collecting survey data was face-to-face interviews, samples were typically drawn in several stages: first selecting geographic areas, then choosing chunks (e.g., census tracts) within those areas, segments within chunks, residences within segments, and finally individuals within residences. The benefit of drawing a sample in this way was that costs could be reduced enormously by reducing the distance for interviewers to travel between sampled households. For mail surveys the geographical distance between respondents usually has no effect on costs. This fact alone makes it possible to avoid some of the potential complexities of sampling.

Because the concern in this book is with being able to generalize results of a survey from the sample that completed the questionnaire to the survey population, we are necessarily talking about probability as opposed to nonprobability methods of sampling (see Lohr, 1999 for a detailed discussion and examples). Sampling error is defined as error stemming from the fact that only a subset of the entire population is surveyed. It is possible to survey a subset of the general population that is large enough (e.g., several hundred or a thousand people) to make fairly precise estimates for the population as a whole, but that would obviously be inadequate in other ways for making inferences about that population. An example is surveying 1,200 residents from only one community and claiming the completed sample is large enough to estimate within about three percentage points the opinions of the nation as a whole. A well-trained surveyor would never attempt to make such a claim. Yet, I frequently hear of survey sponsors attempting to generalize results to the entire population from Web surveys of whoever happened to find the site and volunteered to fill it out, questionnaires distributed in magazines and returned by the tiny percent who are interested, or questionnaires given to whomever is willing to complete them. Still, understanding the number of properly selected respondents necessary for generalizing results to the population is the first essential step in drawing a survey sample.

How large should a sample be?

When one is first confronted with the question of how many respondents is enough, the answer may seem quite nonintuitive. If, for example, you wish to estimate the percentage of people in a small county of 25,000 adults who have a college education within three percentage points of the actual percentage, a completed sample of about 1,024 respondents is needed. If you want to estimate this characteristic for a small state of 2,000,000 adults with the same confidence, then about 1,067 respondents are needed. If, however, this information is sought for the entire United States, then 1,067 (according to a formula we will explain) are needed. In essence, the sample size one needs for estimating this characteristic is, except with small populations, about the same.

A second nonintuitive aspect of sampling is that relatively few completed questionnaires can provide surprising precision at a high level of confidence. If one could be satisfied with knowing whether an estimate from a sample survey is plus or minus 10 percentage points of the true population value, that could be accomplished by obtaining completed questionnaires from a completely random sample of only 100 individuals. What this means is that in a properly conducted national survey with a completed simple random sample of 100 households, in which 60% of the respondents say they own the home in which they are living, we could state with 95% confidence that between 50% and 70% of the entire population owns the home in which they live, assuming there is no error from nonresponse, measurement, or coverage. Moreover, as described above, about the same completed sample size would be needed for estimating the percentage of people who own their home in a particular state, or in the community of 25,000 people.

It is only when population size decreases to a few thousand or less that the number of completed questionnaires needed for a given level of precision declines significantly, as illustrated in Table 5.1. This table illustrates the four factors that must be taken into consideration in determining how large a sample size one needs in order to make population estimates. They are:

- How much sampling error can be tolerated (how precise the estimates should be, illustrated in Table 5.1, as ranging from plus or minus three to ten percent).
- The population size from which the sample is to be drawn (the left hand column).
- How varied the population is with respect to the characteristic of interest. This table assumes a yes/no question with maximum variation, that is, a 50/50 split as well as a more homogeneous 80/20 split.
- The amount of confidence one wishes to have in the estimates made from the sample for the entire population. This table assumes a confidence level of 95%.

The numbers provided in this table are derived from the formula:

$$Ns = \frac{(Np)(p)(1-p)}{(Np-1)(B/C)^2 + (p)(1-p)}$$

Where: Ns = completed sample size needed for desired level of precision
Np = size of population

Table 5.1
Completed sample sizes needed for various population sizes and characteristics at three levels of precision.

	Sample size for the 95% confidence level					
	±10% Sampling Error		±5% Sampling Error		±3% Sampling Error	
Population Size	50/50 split	80/20 split	50/50 split	80/20 split	50/50 split	80/20 split
100	49	38	80	71	92	87
200	65	47	132	111	169	155
400	78	53	196	153	291	253
600	83	56	234	175	384	320
800	86	57	260	188	458	369
1,000	88	58	278	198	517	406
2,000	92	60	322	219	696	509
4,000	94	61	351	232	843	584
6,000	95	61	361	236	906	613
8,000	95	61	367	239	942	629
10,000	95	61	370	240	965	640
20,000	96	61	377	243	1,013	661
40,000	96	61	381	244	1,040	672
100,000	96	61	383	245	1,056	679
1,000,000	96	61	384	246	1,066	683
1,000,000,000	96	61	384	246	1,067	683

P = proportion of population expected to choose one of the two response categories
B = acceptable amount of sampling error; .03 = ±3% of the true population value
C = Z statistic associated with the confidence level; 1.96 corresponds to the 95% level

To explain further, Ns is the sample size needed for the size of the survey population and Np is the number of units (people) in the survey population from which the sample is to be drawn. The term (p)(1 – p) is a measure of the expected variation in answers to the question of interest, which we set at the most conservative value possible (i.e., the expectation that 50% of people in the population answer "yes" to a question and 50% answer "no"). B is the amount of precision one wants to achieve; for example, being able to estimate percentages of the population within plus or minus three percentage points. Finally, C is the amount of statistical confidence one desires to have in those estimates, a level that is commonly set at 95%. Using the 95% confidence level (C = 1.96 or two standard deviations) means that one can be statistically confident that 19 out of 20 times that a random sample is drawn from the population, the estimate obtained from the completed sample will be within the stated range of precision (B = .03; plus or minus three percentage points in this example).

Thus, for a question with a 50/50 split in a population of 800 people, to be 95% confident that the sample estimate of this question is within plus or minus three percentage points of the true population value, a completed sample size of 458 cases is needed.

$$Ns = \frac{(800)\,(.5)\,(.5)}{(800 - 1)\,(.03/1.96)^2 + (.5)\,(.5)}$$

$$Ns = 458$$

To put it another way, we can conclude for a yes/no question in which we expect respondents to be split 50/50 (the most conservative assumption we can make about variance) that 19 out of 20 times that a random sample of 458 people is selected from the total population of 800, the true population value for the question will be within three percentage points of the sample estimate.

Not all questions are yes/no items. Moreover, the amount of variation that exists in a population characteristic differs from one population to another. For example, the variation in age of first year students at a major university may be quite small, consisting mostly of 17–19 year olds, while in the general public the age variation is quite broad. The greater the variation, the larger the sample size needed for making population estimates. It is for this reason that the examples presented here assume maximum heterogeneity (a 50/50 split) in the population from which the sample is to be drawn.

The table is presented here less because of its practical use for surveyors than for the general perspective it provides about sample sizes needed for doing self-administered surveys. Frequently survey sponsors ask why, if about 1,200 people will provide an estimate within three percentage points in a national poll, they can't get by with only a small fraction of that number when their entire survey population is only one county or small city. This question was posed by the city planner mentioned in the introduction to this chapter. Once population sizes get into the tens of thousands, as shown here, there is virtually no difference in the sample size needed to achieve a given level of precision.

A second implication to be drawn from this table is that as population sizes drop lower, a greater and greater proportion of the population needs to be surveyed in order to achieve a given level of precision. This raises the question of whether one should sample at all, or instead attempt to survey everyone. This question is especially critical for self-administered surveys, in which the marginal costs of contacting additional people is usually less than for interview surveys. Nonetheless, I have frequently observed situations in which survey sponsors made a quick decision to survey everyone in their small population, but as a consequence had to spread their resources thinner, with the result that fewer contacts could be made and response rates declined. There is nothing to be gained by surveying all 1000 members of a population in a way that produces only 350 responses (a 35% response rate) versus surveying a sample of only 500 in a way that produces the same number of responses (a 70% response rate). The possibility of nonrespondents being different from respondents is likely to be greater when the response rate is lower.

The fact that estimates of statistical precision, and calculations related to the statistical confidence we have in those estimates, are based only upon the *completed sample size*, not the original sample size, explains our concern with proposed surveys such as the cable television evaluation discussed at the beginning of this chapter. Sending a questionnaire to every household in the community using survey methods that will produce a defensible *completed sample size* will not compensate for the risks of nonresponse error that result from obtaining such a low response rate. A consideration of only the relationship between sample size and statistical precision sometimes results in surveyors making unwise decisions. It would be far better to survey only a sample of respondents and use the resources allocated for the remainder of the population in order to push response rates higher.

Similar reasoning that "it's numbers that count," has been offered by would-be sponsors of web surveys who are enticed by the lack of distribution and processing costs that push per questionnaire costs to an extremely low level, but that include only volunteer respondents, a few of whom may even complete the same questionnaire several times. Sponsors have argued that such surveys allow good estimates to be made for a larger and sometimes undefined population, because the number of completed questionnaires is so large. Web survey sponsors would be far better advised to find ways to control access to Web sites through PIN numbers to carefully drawn samples of the population they wish to survey, and use multiple contacts and incentives to encourage survey response, as discussed in Chapter 11.

A third implication flows from another limitation of the needed sample sizes provided in this table. Determining sample sizes is far more likely to be based on the amount of funds available instead of on a strict calculation of the limits of sample sizes. The table presented here assumes that the surveyor is interested in making estimates only for the survey population as a whole. If, in a statewide survey of adults, one desires to make estimates for women only with a precision of plus or minus three percentage points using the 95% level of confidence, then one needs slightly over 1,000 women respondents in the survey. If one wants this much precision at the same level of confidence for women who are between 18–35, the same reasoning applies. The desire for substantial precision in making estimates for subgroups of populations is typically a powerful factor in pushing sample sizes as high as the sponsor can afford.

Although larger is always better from the standpoint of sampling error, it is important to balance the expenditure of resources for minimizing sampling error against potential expenditures for reducing the other three sources of error. It makes little sense to push sampling error to an extremely low level if it comes at the cost of not seeking to lower it for other types of error. Conducting quality self-administered surveys means simultaneously attempting to hold error levels of all four types at low levels, an endeavor that requires an optimal allocation of resources, as discussed in detail by Groves (1989).

HOW TO DRAW A SIMPLE RANDOM SAMPLE

Face-to-face interview surveys often require using multiple stage sample frames and allocation formulas that are greatly influenced by costs. Telephone surveys require generating random lists of numbers. In contrast, self-administered surveys are most likely to begin with lists of names, and because of the insensitivity of such surveys to distance costs, allow the use of very simple sampling methods.

The most common type of sampling used for self-administered surveys is simple random sampling, in which every member of the sample frame (or list) has an equal chance of being selected. This can be accomplished in several different ways. One way is to assign a different number to every respondent, write each of those numbers on a slip of paper, put those numbers into a hat, and draw a sample of the size one wants. However, doing so is fairly laborious, especially if the population is larger than a few hundred units. The much simpler and now most common way is to use a computer program that numbers and randomly selects respondents.

In past years *systematic* samples were often drawn for self-administered surveys. That is, members of the population were numbered consecutively from 1 to the highest number, say 10,000. Then an interval was determined based on the desired size of sample, say 1,000. A sample of this size from this sample frame means that every 10th name needs to be selected, so the sampling interval becomes ten. The researcher then randomly draws a number within the interval of one to ten to determine the starting point. The hat method would work fine for determining this starting point. If the selected starting point is seven, then every 10th number from that point forward (i.e., 17, 27, 37, to 9,997) would be selected for inclusion in the sample. Systematic samples are adequate if there is no periodicity (i.e., a characteristic that appears with the same frequency as the selected interval) in the list. A traditional example of this problem was selecting every 10th person in the U.S. Army with squads of ten soldiers, with the first listed person in each unit, and the one drawn, being the squad leader. Alphabetized lists normally do not exhibit a problem of this nature. Systematic sampling methods are far less likely to be used today than in the past. The likelihood of having sampling lists in electronic files means that random selection methods can usually be used.

Mailing costs for questionnaires are about the same regardless of distance. Consequently, there is often no advantage in general public surveys to using more complicated sample designs that cluster households together geographically and draw samples in stages (e.g., area of country followed by geographic chunks within areas, and segments within chunks). However, when faced with designing such surveys for groups that cannot be listed, more complex designs may save money and perhaps be the only way that such surveys could be undertaken (Lohr, 1999). An example is a national survey of school teachers, for which there is no list. Rather than compile a list for such a study, one might sample states, geographic areas within states, and schools. Then teachers within selected schools could be listed and sampled. In addition, survey objectives for making estimates for subgroups in a population are often best achieved by oversampling some groups and undersampling others, thus using disproportionate sampling and weighting. Such designs are beyond the scope of this book, and I recommend use of the sources mentioned at the beginning of this chapter as well as assistance from a sampling statistician.

The definition of coverage includes the expression "known nonzero chance of being selected" rather than equal chance, because sometimes a surveyor wishes to give some elements of the population a greater chance to be included in the survey. For example, a survey of employees in a very large organization may have as an objective to estimate differences between the opinions of employees who have worked for a firm for less than six months (say, 5% of all employees) and the opinions of longer-time employees (95% of staff). In this case, longer-time employees have 20 times the chance that new employees have of being selected for inclusion in the survey sample. In order to have enough people in each group to make acceptable estimates, the surveyor can simply separate the groups, a process known as stratification, and draw separate (and disproportionate) samples so that an acceptably large number of new employees is drawn from each group to allow acceptably precise estimates to be made for each group. The texts listed at the beginning of this chapter describe stratification methods (of which there are many) for surveys, and the reader is referred to them for discussions of when, why, and how to implement stratified sample designs.

CONCLUSION

In this chapter I have discussed two interconnected sources of survey error, which are as different as they are intertwined. Coverage error tends to be idiosyncratic to particular populations and sample sources, and there are no standard formulas for success. I have primarily focused on admonitions for identifying potential problems and suggested ways of overcoming them. In contrast, sampling error is theoretically well developed, with formulas for measuring sampling error and determining needed sample sizes that cut across all types of surveys and survey populations. Yet, for a survey to be successful both must be reduced to acceptable levels while also being successful in reducing measurement and nonresponse error, as discussed in earlier chapters.

The request for help with a city's cable television franchise satisfaction survey with which I opened this chapter illustrates the confusion that often exists with respect to these sources of survey error. The sponsor had chosen not to sample at all, yet wanted to treat the results as if they were a representative sample of all households in the city and to provide statistical statements of confidence about the results. No statistical basis for making such statements existed. Instead, the source of potential survey inaccuracy was in the domain of nonresponse error. Coverage concerns were also being ignored. Thus, the results of the proposed survey could hardly be counted on to accomplish the stated objective of giving accurate feedback on community-wide satisfaction with the cable television franchise.

Several alternatives were suggested to the city planner for consideration. Common to all of them was the proposal that only a sample of households be surveyed and an attempt made to select as a respondent the household member most responsible for deciding whether that household would obtain cable television. One proposal was to draw a sample of random digits and switch to telephone interviews. Another was to identify housing units that did not receive city water bills directly (which it appeared the city could do fairly well), sample those units in the same proportion as other households, and send them a mail survey using the multiple contact procedures outlined in Chapter 4 rather than mailing the questionnaire as a brochure. Other possibilities were also proposed. One was to mail out a questionnaire and to interview non-respondents by telephone, thus mixing survey modes, a tailoring technique described in Chapter 6. Another possibility was to draw a sample of residential addresses from city records, do in-person delivery of the questionnaires to occupants, and follow up by mail, a tailoring technique described in Chapter 7. Many possibilities for improving the survey design existed, using only the ideas discussed in Part I of this book or choosing a tailored technique from the many possibilities discussed in Part II.

This chapter concludes Part I. The methods I have discussed for reducing measurement, nonresponse, coverage, and sampling errors (the four fundamental sources of survey error) are further refined for diverse situations in the remaining chapters. In Part II, tailored survey designs will be introduced that take into account many special situations. Sometimes a tailoring procedure is justified because there is no list from which to draw a sample, and sometimes it may be driven by concern over nonresponse or measurement error. The need to tailor may also be driven in some cases by concern over the timeliness of responses, and in others by the knowledge that a population can be contacted over the Internet. A tailored design may also be required because of sponsorship liabilities or the potential that sponsorship offers. Costs are an additional factor that often require adaptations. Thus, we are guided by myriad practical constraints and opportunities and the belief that we can do a survey better by tailoring our methods to the situation. Tailoring also makes it possible to identify means of reducing social costs, increasing rewards, and promoting trust in more specific ways. Throughout we are guided by the desire to achieve minimal survey error in a balanced and effective way.

Part Two

TAILORING TO THE SURVEY SITUATION

CHAPTER 6

Mixed-Mode Surveys

DIFFERENT MODES of data collection often produce different results. For example, a self-administered survey of respondents resulted in 15% ranking their health in the top category of "very good" on a four-point scale; a resurvey of those same respondents by personal interview a short time later resulted in 27% answering "very good," an increase of nearly 12 percentage points (Biemer, 1997). These data are reminiscent of data collected three decades earlier by Hochstim (1967) that found 44% of respondents to a personal interview reported their health as excellent (the top choice in that survey), compared to only 37% on the telephone, and 30% by mail. Respondents consistently offer more positive health assessments to interviewers than to paper questionnaires.

In another survey, this one using interactive voice response (IVR) technology (see Chapter 11) that required people to key in their responses to a series of customer satisfaction questions using the numbers on a touch-tone phone, respondents consistently gave ratings that were significantly higher than those given in a mail questionnaire (Srinivasan and Hanway, 1999). A recent survey by Web and telephone also obtained more positive results by phone as well, although the reasons for this were unclear (Kottler, 1998).

Sometimes responses to different survey modes are not compatible and little can be done to change that. It may therefore seem desirable to avoid conducting surveys by more than one survey mode. However, in other situations it is impossible to avoid using multiple modes to conduct a particular survey.

Two quite different requests for survey assistance illustrate why mixed-mode surveys cannot always be avoided. In one instance, I was asked to conduct an e-mail survey of university faculty to obtain quick and inexpensive responses on an important issue facing the university community. However, it was known that some faculty were infrequent or even nonusers of e-mail. The tailored mixed-mode solution was to collect information from most respondents by e-mail and use paper questionnaires to collect information from the remainder (Schaefer and Dillman, 1998).

The second instance involved an urgent request from a state agency. The agency asked that a survey be done to collect information from farmers on grass burning, a very controversial issue that had been receiving much unfavorable publicity. The survey had to be completed in only three weeks. The agency reported that because of the issue's sensitivity, some farmers had already indicated they would not respond to a telephone survey unless they could first see the questions in writing. The proposed solution was to send a questionnaire by U.S. Postal Service priority mail (normally saved until a fifth contact) with a request that it be completed or that the recipient wait for us to call and collect the information over the telephone. A short while later, all nonrespondents were telephoned with a request to complete an interview. A response rate of 74% was achieved, with two-thirds of the responses coming by mail and the remaining one-third by telephone (Moore, 1998). Case management software shared by the mail and telephone data collection units at my university's survey center made it easy to keep track of daily responses in order to plan for subsequent mailings and telephone calls. In past years, the lack of such software would have made the survey center reluctant to contact the same respondents by two methods at once.

Mixed-mode surveys provide an opportunity to compensate for the weaknesses of each method. For example, one of the potential concerns associated with self-administered surveys, the negative effects of which are not yet well documented, is the ability of potential respondents to see the questions before deciding whether to respond. Also, the fact that questionnaire salience has been demonstrated to have a major effect on mail back response rates provides reason to be concerned that nonresponse error may be substantial for some mail surveys. In contrast, respondents to telephone surveys often know little about the survey topic until they are in the midst of answering questions (Groves and Couper, 1998). Evidence also exists that people have mode preferences, some preferring face-to-face, others preferring telephone, and still others exhibiting a strong preference for self-administered formats (Groves and Kahn, 1979).

However, mixing modes raises many difficult issues, including the possibility that people may give different answers to each mode. Such efforts often introduce the necessity of linking questionnaire design and implementation procedures for self-administered surveys with procedures for interview methods, and that requires tailoring one set of procedures to fit with the other. Thus, I begin Part II of this book with a discussion of the challenges of tailoring self-administered procedures to the special situation of relying on two or more survey modes to conduct a survey project.

Figure 6.1 Types of mixed-mode formats by objective and unintended error consequence.

Mixed-Mode Situation	Typical Objective	Consequence
Collection of same data from different members of a sample	Reduce cost and nonresponse	Measurement differences
Collection of panel data from same respondent at later time	Reduce cost and nonresponse	Measurement differences
Collection of different data from the same respondents during a single data collection period	Improve measurement and reduce costs	None apparent
Collection of comparison data from different populations	Convenience and reduce cost	Measurement differences
Use one mode only to prompt completion by another mode	Improve coverage and reduce nonresponse	None apparent

FIVE SITUATIONS FOR USE OF MIXED-MODE SURVEYS

Mail procedures can be mixed with other types of self-administered or interview methods in different ways. How they are mixed raises quite different mode challenges, as described in Figure 6.1 (Dillman and Tarnai, 1988).

Collection of the Same Data from Different Members of a Sample

Obtaining questionnaire responses from some members of a sample by one method and other members by a second or even third method is the most common type of mixed-mode survey. This use of different survey modes is usually justified by a desire to cut costs through use of the least expensive mode first. The second or third mode is then used to collect responses from people who are reluctant or will not respond to the prior mode(s). Sometimes the follow-up is used to reach people who cannot be found though the initial procedure. An example of such a survey was a large-scale pilot of the National Survey of College Graduates conducted by the Census Bureau for the National Science Foundation. Name and addresses were obtained from the 1990 Decennial Census for a national sample of people who reportedly have four-year college degrees. An attempt was made first to collect as many responses as possible by mail, the least costly data collection alternative. This effort was followed by an attempt to locate telephone numbers and call everyone who either had not responded or for whom the 1990 mailing address was no longer current. Finally, an effort was made to personally contact and interview the remaining nonrespondents. Use of this procedure in 1992 resulted in mail response rates ranging from 63 to 79% for various treatment groups. About 30% of the nonrespondents assigned to the telephone mode were then interviewed by that method. Follow-up of the remaining nonrespondents by face-to-face contacts resulted in half of them being interviewed. An overall response rate of 88% was obtained (Mooney, Giesbrecht, and Shettle, 1993).

It is likely that the prevalence of mixed-mode surveys of this type will increase as people's abilities to screen out telephone interviews, currently the nation's dominant survey mode, increase (Dillman, 1999). Also, as the use of e-mail and Web surveys gain favor with surveyors, a formidable barrier to their use is the fact that many people do not have access to the Internet. Mixed-mode surveys may be the only alternative for immediately gaining access to all members of many survey populations.

An important concern raised by this type of mixed-mode survey is whether people answer questions in the same way for each mode. It is possible that the introduction of additional modes, while increasing response rates, will also increase measurement differences. Other issues include how to combine methods in the most cost-effective manner and how to design specific aspects in the first mode that help the second mode to be successful.

Collection of Panel Data from the Same Respondents at a Later Time

Frequently, the choice of method for an initial survey is determined by the sample frame. Sometimes mailing addresses are available but telephone numbers are not, as might be the case for customer address lists. In other cases, adequate samples can be accessed only by area probability samples of households or random telephone digits. However, during the initial data collection, contact information (telephone numbers, fax numbers, e-mail addresses, or regular mailing addresses) may be obtained that will allow other modes to be used for the follow-up survey. Doing so will allow the second mode to be used in a way that cuts total costs and/or improves response rates.

In addition, the survey situation may change dramatically between the initial and repeat data collections. For example, personal interviews may be used to survey high school or college students in a baseline study, but when it is time to conduct follow-up surveys those individuals are geographically dispersed. Thus, the only economical survey alternative may be to switch to mail or telephone for the later follow-ups. In panel studies each response is particularly precious for measuring change. Thus, to the extent that providing alternative modes of responding will improve panel response rates, a decision to switch modes may be made.

An example of such a study is one of medical patients who went to a doctor's office because they were experiencing pain. They completed an initial self-administered questionnaire in the office and were followed up at three- and six-month intervals. Those who did not respond to the mail follow-up were then surveyed by telephone in order to improve response rates.

The mixing of modes in panel studies is a significant challenge in that the usual intent is to measure change between time one and time two. Even tiny changes in measurement qualities of instruments can influence conclusions significantly. Thus, this type of mixed-mode survey raises particularly important questions about the best procedures for formatting questions so the visual stimulus of a written questionnaire will be equivalent to the aural stimulus of an interview.

Collection of Different Data from the Same Respondents during a Single Data Collection Period

Sometimes respondents who have just completed an interview are asked to complete a self-administered questionnaire that contains additional questions. Typically this happens when very sensitive questions are being asked, such as questions regarding sexual behaviors or preferences. Concern exists that the respondent may be reluctant to divulge that information to the interviewer, especially if someone else in the household is present. Other examples are when diaries of food consumption must be kept over a period of several days or when records must be consulted in order to provide correct detail, as in many business surveys. Surveys have also been done that required that data obtained from mail questionnaires be reviewed to see if the respondents met certain criteria for an immediate follow-up interview by telephone.

This type of mixed-mode survey raises different issues than the second type outlined above. The self-administered form is being used because of particular strengths it has, such as an ability to decrease the social desirability of answers likely to be offered in an interview, especially if other household members are listening, and to avoid item nonresponse. In this case, possible measurement differences between what is obtained by one mode versus another are considered an advantage rather than a major source of concern, as described earlier for panel surveys.

Collection of Comparison Data from Different Populations

In recent years, the ease of manipulating large data sets has led to yet another type of mixed-mode survey situation, whereby data sets are collected from different populations by different modes for purposes of comparison with one another. For example, in the social sciences the developing and testing of scales across populations is quite common. When belief or opinion scales, which by their nature tend to rely on vague quantifiers, are used on various populations and the results compared, it is important that they have the same measurement qualities. Conclusions from such comparisons may be questioned if people respond differently to the various methods.

Frequently, such data are collected by different investigators using different modes at different times, and making comparisons is not their objective. In other instances, characteristics of samples dictate that some people cannot be contacted for interviews, while for others mailing addresses are not available. Because this type of mixed-mode does not usually involve the mixing of methods or questionnaire responses for a given population, it may not be a significant design concern for most surveyors.

Use One Mode to Prompt Completion by Another Mode

In Chapter 4 I discussed the potential value of making a final contact by telephone to encourage response to a self-administered questionnaire. Introducing a new mode at this stage of the data collection may allow information to be collected that will improve coverage information for a study; for example, allowing ineligible sample units to be dropped from the survey. Its use is also likely to improve response rates to the other mode significantly. By introducing a second survey mode in this way, whether fax, e-mail, Web, voice telephone, or touch-tone data entry, it may be possible to avoid the potential measurement differences that must be considered for the other mixed-mode possibilities outlined above, but also benefit the coverage and response qualities of the survey effort.

SOME CAUSES AND CONSEQUENCES OF MIXED-MODE DESIGNS

The trend towards greater use of mixed-mode surveys has paradoxical consequences. On the one hand, the trend is driven by a desire for better response. Increasingly, many survey sponsors have found it difficult to obtain high response rates by limiting their designs to one mode. On the other hand, the combining of data collected by different modes raises questions about whether people give the same answer to each mode.

The summary of mixed-mode surveys shown in Figure 6.1 described the usual objective for mixing modes and the potential error consequences. Displayed in this way, it is apparent that three sources of survey error—nonresponse, measurement, and coverage—and costs all play a major role in making the decision on whether to conduct such a survey. The remainder of this chapter provides further elucidation of these error consequences and how to reduce their potential effects.

A number of factors are substantially influencing this trend of mixing modes (Dillman, 1999). We live in a society with high mobility and complex living arrangements. Some people can be contacted most easily by mail, others by telephone, and still others are most accessible by personal visits. In addition, information age technologies have made it easier for people to screen themselves from unwanted or unauthorized intrusions. Gated communities, locked apartment buildings, unlisted telephone numbers, telephone answering machines, complete reliance on cellular rather than conventional telephones, and now electronic mail (sometimes with multiple addresses for one individual) are forming a protective barrier around individuals. This barrier to direct contact is, in a sense, being pitted against better and better listing services. These services combine information from telephone directories, credit card lists, and mail order requests to facilitate locating people. The time when population access and response could usually be achieved by one mode is past. For increasing numbers of surveys, reliance on only one mode does not provide assurance of reaching or eliciting responses from most of the sampled individuals.

Also in the past, adapting a mail questionnaire to an interview format was a time-consuming task which could only be justified for very large studies. Firms that specialized in one type of surveying, whether face-to-face interviewing, telephone interviewing, or mail surveys, tended to word questions differently and use questionnaire instruction procedures that contrasted greatly with those most likely to be used for other methods. The ability to move word processing files and shape them for other uses now makes mixed-mode studies much easier to accomplish. Yet another characteristic of the current information age is the ability to do better cost modeling so that optimal study designs can be developed. Each method is used in a way and to the extent that it is most cost-effective for purposes of an overall study (Groves, 1989).

While quality surveying is now being threatened by inadequacies of individual survey modes, the ability of survey researchers to manage projects using multiple modes has increased. In the recent past, when a large-scale survey was being implemented in large organizations with separate mail and telephone data collection units, it was unthinkable that attempts to get responses to more than one mode would be made simultaneously. Assigning a sample to the mail survey unit and the telephone interviewing unit at the same time meant that the only easy way to determine whether a response had been received was for each to seek records from the other, which were often not immediately available. It was therefore difficult to prevent sending replacement questionnaires to some people who had just responded by telephone or vice versa. Management software now makes it possible to coordinate activities across operations routinely.

Our departure from the one-size-fits-all age of survey design has also revealed that simple pronouncements of mode advantages and disadvantages are not always true. For example, a traditional advantage of the telephone was speed and a disadvantage of mail was slowness. However, as described for the grass-burning survey of farmers at the beginning of the chapter, mixed-mode designs can sometimes incorporate mail as a way of speeding up response.

In addition, the ability to quickly complete a telephone survey is dependent upon the number of interviewers and interviewing stations. For large-scale surveys, beginning with a mail component may allow one to obtain a majority of responses far more quickly than they could be obtained by an organization's telephone capability. Switching to telephone at the time that mail responses begin to slow down can result in bringing the study to a speedier conclusion. An example of using mail to achieve speed (as well as lower cost) is the Decennial Census, which in 1990 achieved a response rate of 65% by mail, with nearly 90% of those returns being obtained within a week of Census Day (April 1st) and before sending personal enumerators to the remaining households.

WHY PEOPLE MAY ANSWER SELF-ADMINISTERED AND INTERVIEW QUESTIONNAIRES DIFFERENTLY

A number of studies have noted differences in the answers provided to telephone, face-to-face, and mail questionnaires, making it an issue that must be considered in mixed-mode situations (de Leeuw, 1992; Schwarz, Hippler, and Noelle-Neumann, 1992; Dillman, Sangster, Tarnai, and Rockwood, 1996). Not only have differences in distributions across categories been observed, but different analytical results have been obtained, for example, in the construction of structural models (de Leeuw, Mellenbergh, and Hox, 1996). The most basic cause of mode differences is the tendency for people to construct questions differently for the two types of questionnaires. For example, in telephone surveys, surveyors typically do not offer "don't know" options, but if such an answer is volunteered the interviewer is instructed to record it. In self-administered surveys the option must either be offered explicitly or not at all. In general, a technique called *unimode construction,* the topic of the next section, can reduce these difficulties.

There are three reasons for expecting that results from self-administered and interview surveys sometimes differ (Figure 6.2). First, interviews involve interaction with another person, which leads to respondents taking into account social norms and what they think are culturally acceptable answers. People tend to be reluctant to tell something to an interviewer that runs counter to the beliefs or attitudes they believe the interviewer holds. Second, two quite different senses are involved; whereas the self-administered stimulus is visual, the interview stimulus is aural, resulting in different processes through which the meaning of a question and the response alternatives are

Figure 6.2 How differences between collecting data by interview versus self-adminstered surveys may evoke mode differences (Dillman, Sangster, Tarnai, & Rockwood, 1996).

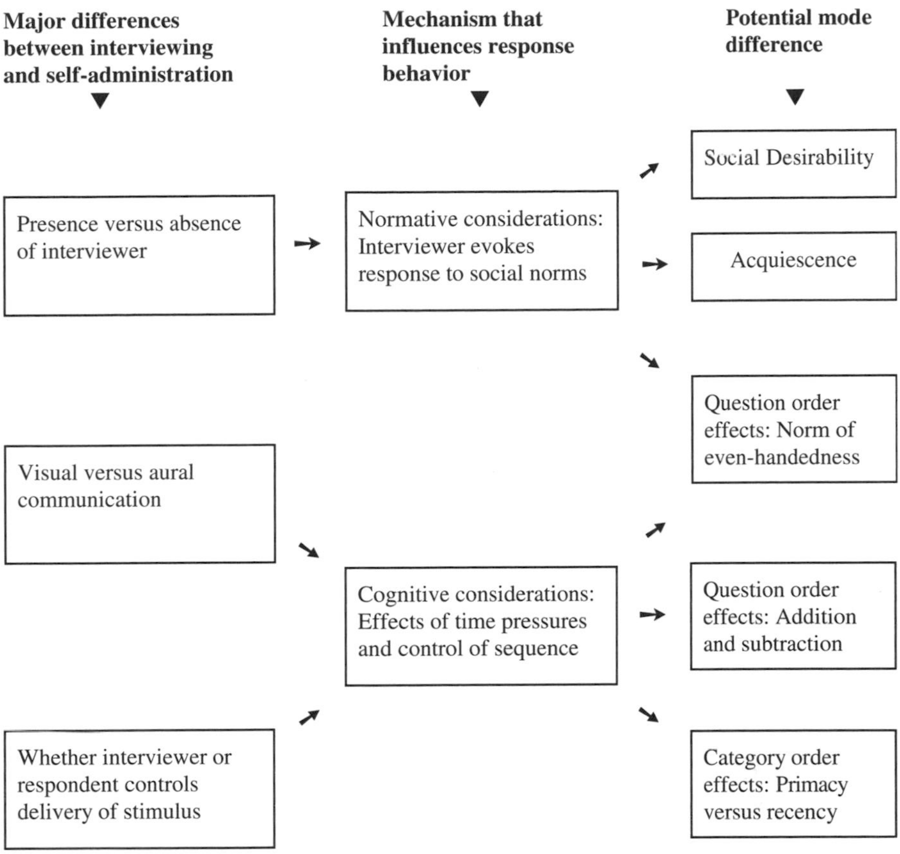

comprehended. Third, the interviewer controls delivery of the stimulus, requiring, for example, that the respondent listen to every word, whereas a mail respondent can control what part of the stimulus is read or not read so that parts of the question or response categories are ignored. An immediate consequence of the lack of interview control for self-administered surveys is higher item nonresponse rates (Dillman, 1978; de Leeuw, 1992). The visual design principles for questionnaire design discussed in Chapter 3 are aimed in part at reducing this differential.

A small but expanding amount of research has addressed the extent to which the above factors contribute to response differences between self-administered and interview surveys (e.g., de Leeuw, 1992; Hippler and Schwarz, 1987; Schwarz et al., 1992; Tarnai and Dillman, 1992; Dillman and Tarnai, 1991; Dillman, Sangster, Tarnai, and Rockwood, 1996; Aquilino, 1994). Results of this research are far from consistent, and several different perspectives exist on the extent to which certain types of differences occur and why. Nonetheless, there is sufficient basis for offering certain guidelines on when response differences might present a problem in mixed-mode surveys.

Two main human factors seem to underlie the existence of mode differences, one of which tends to be normative or sociological in nature and the other cognitive or psychological in nature, as shown in Figure 6.2. The normative factor is group-based, that is, when cultural norms are in some way evoked differently in the interview than in the self-administered situation, they lead to culturally-constrained responses. The second factor is cognitive processing by individuals and, in particular, whether people receive the same stimulus from the two modes. Understanding these possible differences provides a basis for understanding the extent to which some differences may be inevitable and others might be overcome by such steps as unimode questionnaire construction. It is particularly important to be aware of the possibility of four potential sources of response differences. They include: social desirability, acquiescence, question order effects (including the norm of even-handedness), and primacy/recency effects.

REASONS FOR DIFFERENCES

Social Desirability

Several years ago I was asked by a large regional hospital to look at results from two customer satisfaction surveys of similar samples of former patients. One set of data had been obtained by a mail survey and the other by telephone interviews. Results from the mail questionnaires showed much lower satisfaction ratings. The request to examine the results came with the casually offered comment that the hospital had tentatively decided to discontinue the mail survey because of the belief that only unhappy patients seemed to be responding, but the sponsor wondered why that was the case. When I asked more about the procedures I was informed that in order to cut costs the telephone sample had been interviewed by nursing staff on the evening shift, many of whom had cared for the former patients they were asked to call, whereas the other was truly an anonymous survey with no identification number on the return questionnaire. Thus, I did not find the results to be surprising. It seemed likely that patients would offer socially desirable answers by telephone to the nursing staff, that is, answers that reflected what the respondent thought the person who had provided the service hoped to hear. My advice was to at least change who did the interviews, that is, to contract to an outside firm. Even then the elimination of social desirability could not be guaranteed.

Because of the interaction with another person, interview surveys are more likely to produce socially desirable answers for questions about potentially embarrassing behavior, such as drug use or cheating on one's spouse.

However, socially desirable responses are also likely to be offered for drinking behavior of a type that is somewhat unacceptable. For example, one study asked the question, "How often do you drive a car after drinking alcoholic beverages? Frequently, Occasionally, Seldom, Never, or Don't Know." Whereas 52% of the mail survey respondents responded "Never," significantly more of the telephone respondents (63%) said "Never" (Dillman and Tarnai, 1991).

Even very ordinary questions that seem, on the surface, to have little social desirability consistently exhibit this effect. For example, consider, "How would you describe your current health? Excellent, Good, Fair, or Poor." As noted at the beginning of this chapter, this question consistently produces lower proportions of respondents who choose the top category in self-administered surveys.

When one person meets another on the street and offers the conventional American greeting, "How are you?," people typically respond, "fine." A less positive answer often calls for an explanation. Thus, social desirability operates at a threshold far below what one thinks of as anti-social behavior, such as, "Yes, I have shoplifted something from a store." The differential influence of social desirability in interview versus self-administered surveys is the most predictable mode difference, a finding supported by much research (DeMaio, 1984; Aquilino, 1994; de Leeuw and van der Zouwen, 1988; Dillman, Sangster, Tarnai, and Rockwood, 1996), and one should routinely expect such differences to occur in mixed-mode surveys.

Acquiescence

Acquiescence is a culturally-based tendency to agree with others. In most cultures it is easier to agree than to disagree with someone when interacting with them. For example, a classic interview experiment by Schuman and Presser (1981) showed that 60% of one national sample of respondents agreed with the statement, "Individuals are more to blame than social conditions for crime and lawlessness in this country." However, 57% of a control group agreed with the exact reverse of this statement, "Social conditions are more to blame than individuals . . . " Changing the question structure to a forced choice between the two items produced an intermediate response.

An experiment by Dillman and Tarnai (1991) found that in seven comparisons assessing opinions on whether proposals for increasing seat belt use would work, telephone respondents were significantly more likely than a comparable sample of mail respondents to agree. Differences ranged from five to 23 percentage points. A similar pattern was observed by Jordan, Marcus, and Reeder (1980). However, a meta-analysis by de Leeuw (1992) failed to detect any differences, revealing that the literature is not entirely consistent on this issue. Nonetheless, surveyors should watch carefully for differences between modes for agree/disagree types of questions.

Norm of Even-Handedness And Other Question Order Effects

A third potential contributor to differences between self-administered and interview questionnaires is that people may adjust their answer to the second of two similar questions to take into account their answer to the previous question. This may happen because of previewing questions to come, or simply going back and changing answers. For example, Bishop et al. (1988) asked in separate surveys of U.S. and German students: "Do you think that the American government should be allowed to set limits on how much Japanese industry can sell in the United States (Germany)?" It was immediately followed by this question, "Do you think that the Japanese government should be allowed to set limits on how much American (German) industry can sell in Japan?" Not only did asking these questions in this order result in a greater agreement than when asked in reverse order by telephone, but the effect was eliminated in the self-administered version. The explanation offered by the authors is that asking the questions in this order evokes a sense of fairness when answering the second question, whereas respondents to self-administered questionnaires can look ahead and thus take into account the second question when answering the earlier one, or even change their answer afterwards. This explanation invokes both cognitive and normative considerations as explanations.

A replication of this test on a different topic in the United States by Sangster (1993) found that although the norm of even-handedness was evoked, the effects for mail and telephone were about the same. One possibility for these different results is that the first evaluation examined the self-administered differences in a classroom setting where students might approach answering the questions more as a test for which it is normal to examine question sequences before answering them and to change answers. In contrast, mail questionnaires for the Sangster (1993) study were sent to people's homes. In this setting, respondents seemed more likely to go straight through them without looking back, and not worry too much about consistency. Other research, some of which was discussed extensively in Chapter 3, has revealed the existence of question order effects that are not normatively based, for which mail/telephone comparisons revealed no differences. In these instances people tend to allow the first of two answers to carry over cognitively from the first to the second answer.

Primacy/Recency Effects

A fourth potential source of mode differences is the tendency to choose the first offered answer category (called a primacy effect) more often in mail surveys, and the last offered category (called a recency effect) in telephone surveys. The explanation for this potential effect differs from the normative one offered for the preceding effects and is based only on cognitive considerations. It is argued that on the telephone, the reading of response categories by interviewers does not provide sufficient time between categories, likely resulting in the earlier categories not being remembered. Consequently, when the time comes to respond, the last answers are more likely to be remembered (Krosnick and Alwin, 1987). It is further argued that in self-administered surveys with visual processing, items earlier in the list undergo greater cognitive processing and are used to compare and contrast later items. If the initial option serves as a satisfactory answer, the prediction is that it is more likely to be chosen.

Evidence for the existence of pure primacy/recency effects is decidedly mixed. Although recency effects have been observed in telephone surveys (e.g., Schuman and Presser, 1981; Moore, 1997), these same authors have also noted exceptions. Relatively few full mail/telephone comparisons have been done. However, a recent analysis of 82 experiments in 12 separate surveys conducted in seven states (Dillman, Brown et al., 1995) found that for both mail and telephone, primacy and recency effects were both as likely to occur with one method or the other. Several complete reversals of expectation, that is, primacy in telephone and recency in mail, also occurred. We conclude that despite the extensive discussion of these effects in the literature, the occurrence of primacy effects in self-administered surveys and recency effects in telephone surveys are far from predictable and further experimentation needs to be done.

Implications for Mixed-Mode Surveys

The fact that interviewer/self-administered survey differences are sometimes inconsistent does not mean that such differences can safely be ignored. A series of three studies helps explain why (Figure 6.3). In a general public survey by Dillman and Mason (1984), it was found that a sample of mail questionnaire respondents was significantly *less* likely than either telephone or face-to-face respondents to choose "not a problem," the first offered category in response to a question about each of nine community issues. ("For each of these issues, please tell me whether you believe it is Not a Problem, a Small Problem, a Serious Problem, or you Don't Know on this issue.") Respondents to the telephone and face-to-face surveys were more likely to choose the "not a problem" category for all 11 items, with individual differences ranging from four to nineteen percentage points. A similar tendency to choose the most positive end of scales was noted for 15 other items about community and neighborhood qualities.

Krysan et al. (1994) reported similar results for three questions asking whether (1) city services, (2) property not being kept up, and (3) crime were "always, often, sometimes, or never a problem" for respondents. Responses to the "never" category from a comparable sample of interviewed respon-

Figure 6.3 Differences between percent of self-administered (mail) and interview (telephone or face-to-face) respondents selecting most positive response categories in three surveys.

	Average Percent "Not a Problem"		Range of Differences Interview–Self-Administered
Dillman and Mason, 1984	Interview	Mail	
Nine community issues from two-state general public survey, telephone vs. mail	47.9%	31.9%	6.7–18.8
Nine community issues from same two-state general public survey, face-to-face vs. mail	43.8%	31.9%	4.2–18.7
Tarnai and Dillman, 1992			
Five community issues from student survey; self-administered vs. telephone (aural only)	37.8%	13.0%	12.6–38.1
Five community issues from student survey; mail vs. telephone while viewing questionnaire (aural + visual)	31.3%	13.0%	4.3–20.0

Question: *"For each issue, please tell me whether you believe it is Not a Problem, a Small Problem, a Medium Problem, a Serious Problem, or if you Don't Know."*

	Average Percent "Not a Problem"		Range of Differences Interview–Self-Administered
Krysan, Schuman, Scott, and Beatty, 1994	Interview	Mail	
Three issues from metropolitan area general public survey; mail vs. face-to-face	61.3%	48.0%	7–17

Question: *"Thinking about your own neighborhood, please indicate whether the following are Always a Problem, Often a Problem, Sometimes a Problem, or Never a Problem in your neighborhood."*

dents was seven to 17 percentage points higher than for respondents to the self-administered questionnaires (Figure 6.3). The fact that the category order for this study was the reverse of that used in the above-mentioned study suggests that something other than primacy/recency explanations are necessary for explaining these differences.

In an effort to decipher potential reasons for differences observed in the Dillman and Mason (1984) survey, a near replication of five items from this survey was done for a college student sample. The differences found in this study were even larger, with use of the "not a problem" differences ranging from 13 to 38 percentage points, with telephone averaging 25 points higher than the mail (Tarnai and Dillman, 1992). Two other conditions were examined in an attempt to determine whether these results were due to the medium of communication (aural versus visual), or perhaps other aspects of the differences between telephone and mail. One group was interviewed over the telephone without being able to see the questions. The second group was asked to open an envelope containing the written questionnaire and follow the questionnaire as they responded to the telephone interview. The group interviewed with the questionnaire in front of them averaged seven percentage points higher than the self-administered group for the "not a problem" answer, or 18 percentage points less than the telephone-only group. It was concluded that the visual/aural differences in communication were mostly, but not entirely, responsible for these differences. Concerning all of these tests, it is plausible that the items may have exhibited a low threshold of social desirability, that is, people are invested in their neighborhood or community and are predisposed to put this environment in a positive light when interacting with an outsider (the interviewer). If so, this might explain the differences between these findings and those of Krysan et al. (1994), which the cognitive-based primacy/recency hypothesis cannot explain. Research has not yet untangled the possible interactions of the normative and cognitive influences shown in Figure 6.2.

Our discussion of potential mode differences leads to the following conclusions. First, differences between telephone and mail responses have frequently been observed and are sometimes substantial. Second, the most consistent finding in the literature is that social desirability differences affect self-administered respondents less than interview respondents. Third, with the exception of social desirability, the effects observed in the literature have occurred mostly for items that use vague quantifiers, which require people to contemplate into which category they fit. The differences between excellent and good, or never a problem versus a small problem, are sometimes difficult for respondents to reliably discern. Fourth, although one should be on the lookout for other types of mode differences, including acquiescence, norm of even-handedness, and primacy/recency effects, their occurrence is far less certain than for social desirability. Finally, the data presented by Tarnai and Dillman (1992) raise the possibility that cultural (or motivational) and cognitive considerations may interact to produce response differences.

Until experiments are designed to untangle such effects, our ability to predict the occurrence of mode differences remains somewhat limited. Nonetheless, enough differences have been observed that it is prudent to tailor the design of surveys that mix interview and self-administered methods in ways that will reduce the chances of responses differing by survey mode.

INTERNET AND INTERACTIVE VOICE RESPONSE SURVEYS

The newness of Internet (e-mail and Web) and interactive voice response surveys means that virtually no research has addressed the potential mode differences that might be associated with these methods. All three methods are self-administered, so a priority in research is to determine the extent to which these methods are subject to social desirability influences, and the extent to which they may mirror paper self-administered surveys or even produce less social desirability than the latter, as suggested for the completion of computer surveys by Turner et al. (1998). As I shall suggest in Chapter 11, these technologies may lead surveyors to pose questions as stimuli that differ significantly from the way both mail and voice telephone surveys are done, thus raising the possibility that a new set of mode considerations will need to be evaluated.

UNIMODE DESIGN AS A SOLUTION FOR CERTAIN MODE DIFFERENCES

Unimode construction is the writing and presenting of questions to respondents in a way that assures receipt by respondents of a common mental stimulus, regardless of survey mode. In Chapters 3 and 4 I described question writing practices, the aim of which was to get the most accurate and complete answers possible for self-administered questionnaires. My emphasis on using visual principles for questionnaire design was intended to assure that respondents to self-administered questionnaires will receive the same stimulus as that typically received by interview respondents. Visual principles form the foundation of unimode design. Manipulations of font size, brightness, color, location, shape, and figure/ground relationships are coordinated in order to define a common navigational path through the questionnaire items for all respondents, further encouraging provision of a common stimulus. The use of visual layout and design also directly attacks the problem of item nonresponse, which is associated with paper self-administered questionnaires. In addition, I advocate the use of cognitive design and more detailed open-ended questions (Chapter 2) to address a second common deficiency of self-administered questionnaires, less complete responses to open-ended questions. The question and questionnaire design principles that follow further extend these efforts to obtain equivalent data across survey modes.

Principle 6.1: Make all response options the same across modes and incorporate them into the stem of the survey question.

Figure 6.4 presents mail and telephone versions of a survey question using typical construction methods for each mode. Mail or self-administered survey questions are typically written in a way that minimizes redundancy be-

Figure 6.4 Changing mail and telephone questions into unimode format.

Traditional mail format:

27. To what extent do you favor or oppose a policy allowing free trade with all countries of the world, no matter what their human rights record?

- ☐ Strongly favor
- ☐ Somewhat favor
- ☐ Somewhat oppose
- ☐ Strongly oppose

Traditional telephone format:

27. To what extent do you favor or oppose a policy allowing free trade with all countries of the world, no matter what their human rights record? Would you say that you Strongly favor, Somewhat favor, Somewhat oppose or Strongly oppose this policy?

- ☐ Strongly favor
- ☐ Somewhat favor
- ☐ Somewhat oppose
- ☐ Strongly oppose
- ☐ No opinion
- ☐ Refused

Unimode format for both mail and telephone:

27. To what extent do you favor or oppose a policy allowing free trade with all countries of the world, no matter what their human rights record? Do you Strongly favor, Somewhat favor, Somewhat oppose, Strongly oppose, or have No opinion on this policy?

- ☐ Strongly favor
- ☐ Somewhat favor
- ☐ Somewhat oppose
- ☐ Strongly oppose
- ☐ No opinion

tween the categories in the stem of the question and the listed choices. In addition, "no opinion" categories are often omitted because of concern that too many people will use them. In contrast, the telephone version is likely to have the categories included in the stem of the question in order to facilitate reading categories in the same way to every respondent.

For telephone surveys, no opinion categories are seldom mentioned by the interviewer but are listed on the interviewer's screen for use if a respondent insists on responding in that way. Consequently, some people use them.

Therefore, telephone surveys produce "no opinion" responses, while respondents to the self-administered questionnaire who wish to respond either have to give a substantive answer or leave the item blank. Their answer is then coded as a refusal or item nonresponse.

The unimode version of this question seeks to provide a common stimulus for the two modes by putting response categories into the stem of the self-administered question and providing a common set of response categories. Thus, "no opinion" is explicitly offered in both versions of the questionnaire.

Principle 6.2: Avoid inadvertently changing the basic question structure across modes in ways that change the stimulus.

The two most common ways in which question structures are inadvertently changed is by switching yes/no items to check-all-that-apply items and changing sequences of related questions to row/column matrices when going from interviewer to self-administered questionnaires. Both of these techniques were discussed in earlier chapters (Principles 2.10 and 3.5, respectively).

Changing a sequence of individual items to a matrix creates a structure that is difficult for respondents with less education to understand. It also results in losing control of the navigational process so there is less assurance that each respondent is receiving the same question stimulus. Thus, we seek to avoid matrices in self-administered questionnaires whenever possible.

Check-all–that-apply self-administered survey questions, for instance, "Please mark all of the possible goals listed below you have decided to pursue during this review period," are inevitably changed for telephone interviews, for example, "Please indicate whether each of the possible goals I'm going to read to you is one that you have decided to pursue or not pursue during this review period." The problem with check-all-that apply questions is the tendency of self-administered respondents to satisfice, that is, stop reading the list of items after they have checked what they consider an adequate number of responses (Krosnick et al., 1996). The interview format is a better question structure and can be used in self-administered surveys as well.

Principle 6.3: Reduce the number of response categories to achieve mode similarity.

When face-to-face interviewing was the dominant survey method, seven-, nine-, or even 11-point scales, sometimes with each point labeled, were often offered to respondents on show cards. The advent of telephone interviewing encouraged surveyors to reduce the number of response categories dramatically, especially if similar categories were to be used for many survey questions. Listening to interviewers stumble over linguistic sequences such as, "Do you completely agree, mostly agree, somewhat agree, neither agree nor disagree, somewhat disagree, mostly disagree, or completely disagree," especially when they have already read it many times, quickly encourages a survey sponsor to simplify such questions. Also, from a cognitive standpoint there is concern that interviewed respondents cannot remember each of several response choices when the next one is read before the previous one can be stored in memory. Although self-administered questionnaires can utilize longer scales, much as those used on face-to-face interview show cards, it is desirable to find a common ground that will work for all methods.

This issue may become more important as we move towards greater use of e-mail and Web surveys in which the horizontal (landscape) orientation of screens and the desire to get all response choices onto one screen encourages surveyors to use fewer response choices. For example, in a recent e-mail survey we reduced a scalar item with labels from five to three categories in order to increase the likelihood that it would appear the same on all respondents' computer screens (Schaefer and Dillman, 1998). The touch-tone telephone makes use of scales longer than nine points difficult because of the necessity of touching two numbers for highest scale values and only one for lower scale values. It has not been proven that the greater effort required for recording the highest value (10) leads to less use of that category, but an experiment by Mu (1999) suggests that possibility.

Principle 6.4: Use the same descriptive labels for response categories instead of depending upon people's vision to convey the nature of a scale concept.

When mail respondents are asked to rank their interest in music on a scale of one to five, a line with tick marks may be placed below the question that also shows numbers in between ends of the scale that can be used to provide an answer (Figure 6.5). The visual representation of the scale offers additional information not provided in the stem of the question. Thus, the self-administered questionnaire respondent receives a somewhat different stimulus than the telephone respondent. We should not be surprised if the self-administered respondent is less likely to use the extreme ends of the scale. The proposed revision for use in a mixed-mode survey does not present a visual representation for either version of the questionnaire.

Sometimes visual metaphors are used for survey questions, such as asking respondents to imagine a ladder with ten steps, a thermometer, or some other symbolism to convey a mental image. Such symbolism can work in both interview and self-administered surveys if it is uniformly presented to all respondents regardless of mode.

Principle 6.5: If several items must be ranked, precede the ranking question with a rating question.

As argued in Chapter 2, all types of surveys should avoid asking respondents to rank large numbers of items from top to bottom. Such a task is quite difficult for most respondents to accomplish, especially in interview surveys

Figure 6.5 Conversion of a scalar question to a unimode format.

Mail version:

17. How would you rate your interest in music using this scale of 1 to 5?

```
        1   2   3   4   5
        |___|___|___|___|
   Not at all         Very
   Interested         Interested
```

Telephone version:

17. How would you rate your interest in music using a scale of 1 to 5, where 1 means "Not at all interested" in music and 5 means "Very interested?"

Unimode version:

17. How would your rate your interest in music on a scale of 1 to 5, where 1 means "Not at all interested" and 5 means "Very interested." You can use any number from 1 through 5 to indicate the extent of your interest.

_______ Number chosen

---

where the respondent must not only remember each item, but also recall which items have been ranked and which have not. The challenge of ranking items in interviews often leads to changing the question to a rating format. Although rating results obtained by telephone will undoubtedly be similar to ranking results obtained by mail, the answers are, in theory, quite different. Rankings force an ordering from top to bottom, whereas in the rating question all of the items can be rated as "much" or as "none," using the scale shown in Figure 6.6. One method of bringing the items closer together is to first ask respondents to rate the importance of each item as shown in this figure, and then to ask for the rankings to be made. The rating provides a means of getting interview respondents to focus individually on each item a short time before being asked to complete the rankings. Because of this cognitive introduction, they are more likely to recall enough information from giving ratings to complete the required rankings.

Principle 6.6: Develop equivalent instructions for skip patterns that are determined by answers to several widely separated items.

Modern computer-assisted telephone interviewing (CATI) systems enable answers for several questions in different parts of a questionnaire to be considered in directing people to subsequent questions. This procedure is transparent to the respondent in electronic surveys, but leads to self-administered

Figure 6.6 Conversion of a difficult ranking question to a less difficult form.

Telephone version:

11. Please rate each of the following groups with regard to how much influence each should have on how decisions get made at this university.

University Alumni	None	A Little	Some	Much
University Students	None	A Little	Some	Much
Statc Lcgislaturc	None	A Little	Some	Much
University Faculty	None	A Little	Some	Much
University Administration	None	A Little	Some	Much
Board of Regents	None	A Little	Some	Much

Mail version:

11. Please rank each of the following groups from top to bottom with regard to the amount of influence you feel each should have on policy decisions made at this university. Please give a 1 to the group that should have the most influence, 2 the second most influence, and so on until you have ranked all six groups.

_____ University Alumni

_____ University Students

_____ State Legislature

_____ University Faculty

_____ University Administration

_____ Board of Regents

Unimode version:

The telephone version is asked to obtain ratings and create cognitive awareness of the six groups, followed by the mail version to obtain rankings.

questions requiring directions such as this one: "If you said yes to Question 4, no to Question 30, and checked one of the categories labeled "e" through "g" in the last question above, then you should answer Questions 38–40. Otherwise, please skip to Question 41 on the next page." This direction is difficult to comprehend and requires respondents to break out of the navigational path to look back at previous answers. I have noted an increased tendency towards development of complex directions of this nature as CATI questionnaire designers become more adept at using the power of such systems for directing interviewers through a questionnaire.

Our first step towards development of a unimode format is to try restating the questions substantively rather than by reference to earlier questionnaire items. For example: "If you own your home (asked in Question 4), are currently employed (asked in Question 30), and had an income of at least $15,000 last year (as asked in the last question), then you should . . . " If this instruction remains too complicated we then attempt to reorder questions that determine the skip pattern, and even restructure questions to eliminate the need to combine several disparate pieces of information in order to proceed correctly to the next question. In one questionnaire I developed there was no need for the home ownership question to appear so early in the questionnaire. Therefore, it was relocated so that home ownership, employment, and income questions were located next to one another. The reconstructed questionnaire contained an instruction similar to the one listed above in the self-administered version, but omitted it from the electronic telephone version. Consequently, although two types of respondents received somewhat different instructional information specific to the mode of response, the substance of each question remained the same.

Principle 6.7: Avoid question structures that unfold.

When telephone interviewing came of age, some surveyors began the practice of breaking questions into parts and allowing them to unfold for the respondent through a series of questions. For example, people might be asked whether they tended to agree, disagree, or had no opinion on an issue. If they agreed, the follow-up question of whether they very strongly agreed, somewhat agreed, or slightly agreed was asked. Through these two steps a labeled seven-point scale of responses could be constructed. Similarly, people might be asked if their income for the preceding year was above or below $20,000. If they said above, the next question asked would be whether it was more than $35,000. At least one additional question would be asked depending upon the answer received to the second query, in order to select a more precise income category.

Unfolding sequences with their alternative skip patterns are burdensome on self-administered questionnaires, and should therefore be avoided. As an alternative to unfolding schemes we prefer to offer all categories at once, decreasing the number of categories offered in the event the number becomes too burdensome to offer over the telephone.

Principle 6.8: Reverse the order in which categories are listed in half of the questionnaires.

As noted earlier in this chapter, evidence is far from consistent that primacy effects (the tendency to choose from among the first response categories stated) occur in self-administered questionnaires and recency effects (the tendency to choose from among the last offered response categories) occur in interview surveys. Nonetheless, we have observed many instances in which category order effects have occurred in both mail and telephone surveys. Consequently, order effects remain a concern whatever the underlying reason for their occurrence.

The likelihood of such effects occurring seems greater when the questions concern abstract attitudes and opinions not firmly possessed by the respondent. For example, "To what extent do you agree or disagree that strong leaders are more likely to wear bright colors than are weak leaders?" Similarly, asking people questions about ever-present but mundane aspects of their lives, for example, "How many minutes on average do you spend talking each day to another family member?" have considerable potential to be influenced by factors other than the substance of the question (Rockwood et al., 1997).

A conservative approach to asking such questions in mixed-mode surveys is to randomly reverse the order of categories in half of the questionnaires. This task, while easy to accomplish in a CATI or computer-assisted personal interview (CAPI), is somewhat more challenging to handle in a mail survey requiring follow-ups, and also poses quality control issues when the data are processed. Consequently, it seems prudent to consider carefully whether the items being investigated are likely to be influenced by order effects before spending the resources to handle at least two questionnaire versions for each survey mode.

Principle 6.9: Evaluate interviewer instructions carefully for unintended response effects and consider their use for other modes.

It is instructive to spend a few hours listening to interviews in order to contemplate the potential differences between the stimuli being received by interview respondents and those that accompany a self-administered version of the same questionnaire. Routine interviewer answers to respondent questions about what a question means, such as, "Please answer it in terms of what it means to you," and encouragement, such as, "Good, these comments are really helpful," during the interview define what is expected from the respondent and may, in a subtle way, influence answers. As additional interviews are completed, survey sponsors may learn from interviewers that a question is not working well and ask interviewers to answer questions in certain ways, for example, "In response to the question about how much money you paid out-of-pocket to purchase meals this week, we mean any form of payment—cash, check, or credit card."

In this age of rushing surveys into the field quickly after very brief pretests, quality control efforts have often led to providing interviewers with last-minute information to be used in a variety of situations throughout the interview. Such efforts are usually justified by the goal of providing the highest possible quality of data to the survey sponsor. However, in the mixed-mode situation it seems important to consider carefully the possible effects of such improvements for interviews which are not also being added to the self-administered portion of the sample. This concern has also led us to anticipate interviewer communications, for example, "If you don't know an exact answer your best estimate will be fine," and build that phrasing into both the interview and self-administered components of the survey.

IMPLEMENTATION ISSUES

The implementation issues that arise when modes are mixed depend in large part on how modes are administered in relation to one another. Does the surveyor want people who failed to respond to one mode to respond to another? Or is an auxiliary mode being used to encourage response to the original mode? In either case, the surveyor cannot ignore how one mode influences use of the other. The ways in which modes are mixed affects significantly the ways implementation procedures need to be tailored.

SWITCHING THE REQUEST FROM COMPLETING A QUESTIONNAIRE BY ONE MODE TO ANOTHER

From a social exchange standpoint, switching methods raises new possibilities for communicating greater rewards, lower costs, and increased trust. A large number of failed attempts to reach someone by telephone, many of which resulted in written or verbal messages from someone who answered the phone and/or voice mail messages, may become a repetitive stimulus that is increasingly easy to ignore. Using a different mode offers an opportunity for the surveyor to provide new information to the respondent in a new way. For example, switching from telephone to mail allows respondents to see real stationery (encouraging legitimization and trust), a personalized cover letter (encouraging feelings of importance), and the content of a questionnaire (less apprehension about questions not yet answered), thus invoking new exchange considerations. Evidence exists that people prefer certain modes (Groves and Kahn, 1979), and if such preferences are significant it stands to reason that people who have not responded to one mode because they dislike it may be receptive to a change in approach. In addition, the mere fact of switching modes tends to emphasize the importance of the study, perhaps encouraging thoughts along of the lines of "if this weren't important, they wouldn't be trying to reach me in a different way."

There can also be no doubt that switching modes is effective in improving response rates beyond those that can be obtained by reliance on a single method. Supporting evidence is available from government- and university-sponsored surveys on a variety of topics (e.g., Mooney et al., 1993; Petrie et al., 1998). The 1990 U.S. Decennial Census switched from mail questionnaires after 65% of households responded, and through the use of face-to-face interviews increased response rates to over 98%. The major impediments to switching modes are surveyor willingness to develop procedures for implementing a second mode, and the cost of such implementation.

If a token incentive has been sent by mail, there is a possibility that creating a sense of obligation may decrease the likelihood of a refusal when the recipient is called on the telephone. For example, it was observed in an experimental pretest for the National Survey of College Graduates that when called by telephone, recipients of a token financial incentive in the first of four previous mailings were less likely to refuse than those who did not receive such an incentive with the first mailing (Mooney et al., 1993).

It seems important that contact by a second mode take into account the previous efforts to obtain a response. For example, in a switch from telephone to mail one might begin a letter: "Recently we attempted to contact you by telephone about an important national survey we are doing . . . " A similar introduction might be developed for switching from mail to telephone. From an exchange standpoint, such an introduction communicates that the survey is important (otherwise why would this extraordinary attempt be made?). Switching to telephone provides an opportunity to ask whether the recipient of the request has questions about the survey and to respond to these questions. Switching to mail also allows the surveyor to state reasons for the survey's importance in different ways than those mentioned over the telephone.

Which method should go first?

In some instances one may have mailing addresses, telephone numbers, and even e-mail addresses, so that several possibilities are available. In such cases an obvious choice may be to go with the least expensive method and collect as much of the data as possible before switching to another method. It might also be argued that telephone attempts should begin first because one is better able to control item nonresponse. Evidence is not compelling from a response rate standpoint to unequivocally argue for always beginning with one method or another.

However, we have found a number of content and population bases for deciding to begin with a particular method. In a national survey of manufacturers, which required completion of an 18-page mail questionnaires versus a 35-minute telephone survey, we found it advantageous to begin with attempts to complete the survey by telephone, and then switch to mail. Whereas a nearly 70% response rate was obtained in this way, a previous attempt to utilize several mailings before phoning resulted in a response rate of only 45% (Petrie et al., 1998). In contrast, for a survey of medical doctors, gatekeepers made getting direct contact extremely difficult. A slightly higher response rate (67% versus 59%) was obtained by sending a U.S. Postal Service priority mail contact first, the aim of which was to get past gatekeepers, and following it with phone calls to either get the mail form completed or obtain the information by telephone, depending upon the preference of the respondent (Moore, Guadino, deHart, Cheadle, and Martin, 1998). More importantly for this study, leading with the mail procedure produced responses more quickly. On still other surveys we have chosen to send mail questionnaires first because of the sensitive nature of the surveys (to help convey the survey's legitimacy) and to decrease the anxiety of respondents over the telephone (Moore, 1998).

One instance in which it seems particularly desirable to begin with an interview prior to sending a mail survey to respondents is when it is necessary to select a respondent. A telephone call allows the surveyor to ask a sequence of questions to determine to whom the questionnaire should be sent. This procedure is especially important in business surveys because of the finding by Paxson, Dillman, and Tarnai (1995) that knowing the likely respondent's name resulted in significantly higher response rates than when sending questionnaires to the "owner/manager." However, even this finding has exceptions. Once, when sending questionnaires to a person in each of the nation's largest 238 universities who could not be identified by name or even position, a prior letter was sent to the president of each university asking them to identify the person described in the cover letter and forward a mail questionnaire to them. Procedures used in this study, which involved both mail and telephone follow-up, resulted in a response rate of 74% (Scott, 1989).

PROVIDING RESPONDENTS WITH THE CHOICE OF RESPONSE MODE

Because some respondents have survey mode preferences, it may seem desirable to offer respondents a choice of which mode to answer. However, this choice alone may not increase response rates. In an experimental test of census questionnaires, a national sample of respondents was given the option of returning the mail questionnaire or calling in their answers by telephone (Dillman, Clark, and West, 1995). The result was to stimulate 5% of the survey sample to respond by telephone. However, the overall response rate was no different than when respondents were only given an opportunity to respond by mail.

Nonetheless, it is important to realize that when calls are made to respondents after they have failed to respond to several requests to complete a questionnaire in another mode, response rates are likely to increase. In a sense, a choice of mode has been provided to those who waited, but this situation is quite different because the surveyor called rather than leaving it up to the respondent to call in. This possibility did not exist for the census experiment because phone numbers, or even the names of people living at the addresses included in the sample, were unknown.

Using One Mode to Support Another Mode

In a 1976 test it was found that sending preletters to households selected for response to a telephone survey improved response rates over the telephone by nearly 10 percentage points (Dillman, Gallegos, and Frey, 1976). This method has been used with dual-frame sample surveys (part listed, part random digit telephone numbers) to improve response to telephone surveys (Groves, 1989). This procedure seems particularly desirable if one wishes to provide a token incentive to individuals about to be surveyed by telephone or e-mail. However, one test of sending a preletter by regular mail to encourage response to an e-mail survey did not improve response rates as much as sending an equivalent message via the method (e-mail) by which people were being asked to respond (Schaefer and Dillman, 1998).

Sometimes when multiple contacts have been made and no response is forthcoming, the questionnaire has been greatly shortened so that it consists of only a few key questions. The questions might include those for which it is expected that respondents may differ from non-respondents. A typical appeal of this nature is to explain to recipients that they have not responded to the longer survey and that this behavior is okay, but that "filling out responses to these few questions will help us know whether people who did not respond would have answered differently from those who did, which would be enormously helpful." In social exchange terms, this kind of appeal can be described simply as reducing the size of the request. In much the same way as shortening a long questionnaire encourages high response, this kind of request may do so as well. Further, it gives recognition to the respondents that their right to refuse the longer questionnaire is respected and appealing for a small favor would help meet the needs of the study. Most commonly such requests involve a switch from one survey mode to another. However, if the mode is switched for such a follow-up then it is important to avoid selecting questions that use vague quantifiers. The concern is that response might be differentially affected by mode so that conclusions about the influence of nonresponse would be jeopardized.

CONCLUSION

Mixing together different survey modes, and particularly data collected by interview with that collected by self-administered questionnaires, raises many challenging issues. Not only may the modes be mixed in different ways and for different purposes, but some procedures are likely to produce different answers. Nonetheless, the possibilities for improving response rates and reducing nonresponse and coverage errors are such that mixed-mode surveys are increasingly likely to be done.

Our way of minimizing mode differences, though it is unlikely that they can be prevented entirely, is to use a technique I have described as *unimode construction.* This technique involves making a deliberate effort to assure that respondents to all modes receive an equivalent stimulus regardless of whether it is delivered aurally or visually. This action requires moving away from the typical construction mode used when each mode is implemented alone, whether by interview or self-administration.

Mixed-mode surveys by themselves represent a tailoring of the procedures described in Part I of this book. However, as we will see in later chapters, they represent a type of tailoring that becomes an integral feature of surveys targeted to particular populations and situations, thus serving as a means to a greater end.

CHAPTER 7

Alternative Questionnaire Delivery: In Person, to Groups, and Through Publications

Self-administered questionnaires are sometimes delivered to people by means other than the postal system or computers. For a variety of reasons, surveyors may find it advantageous to deliver paper questionnaires in person to individuals, or to bring people together so that questionnaires can be administered efficiently in a group setting. In addition, surveyors frequently attempt to deliver questionnaires through magazines, newsletters, or other regular information sources in efforts to get very inexpensive feedback, usually with limited success. In this chapter I discuss the challenges of tailoring procedures to these delivery situations.

IN-PERSON DELIVERY TO INDIVIDUALS

One of the most significant barriers to the use of mail-back questionnaires is the lack of an adequate population list from which a sample can be drawn. For example:

- Viewers of an art exhibit
- Visitors to a national park
- People who hunt or fish in a particular recreational area
- Customers of a restaurant
- Users of an airport
- Purchasers of day-tickets to a theme park
- Households in a particular city neighborhood

For some of these populations it might be possible to call a large number of randomly selected telephone numbers and screen households to determine whether anyone is a member of the population of interest. However, to identify eligible respondents an enormous number of calls might be required. Unless the issue is a very important one, cost is likely to prevent the proposed survey from being done.

However, people eligible for some surveys appear at the location of interest, thus making it possible to sample them and ask that they answer some survey questions before leaving. Alternatively, they may be given a mail-back questionnaire along with a request to complete and return it. Attempts to survey populations such as these with mail-back questionnaires often consists of simply handing the questionnaire to people and asking them to complete and return it at a later time. The problem with this technique is that only the most interested people respond, so nonresponse error is likely. In addition, because names and addresses are unavailable it is impossible to use a thank you reminder and replacement questionnaire sequence to improve response among those for whom the questionnaire topic is less salient.

Although asking people to fill out a questionnaire before leaving an exhibit or park, or to answer questions posed by a interviewer, are alternatives, these possibilities are often unsatisfactory. Survey sponsors are often interested in lasting impressions, rather than immediate reactions as one leaves an exhibit. Another disadvantage of trying to obtain responses from departing visitors is that at that point in their visit they are often anxious to leave, making them unwilling to take even a short time to respond. Stand-up interviews with people leaving an area may also be unsatisfactory because of social desirability effects—their opinions may be influenced by the interviewer and/or the presence of friends who are able to listen to the interview. For instance, if listening friends have invited respondents to attend the exhibit, respondents may report "enjoying" the exhibit even though they feel it has been a waste of time. Similarly, the interviewer seems likely to be identified as associated with the exhibit, so the respondent's willingness to give negative evaluations may be similarly constrained.

A procedure successfully used in a situation for which in-person delivery was the only means of drawing a sample is outlined as a case study below. This Tailored Design procedure for in-person delivered questionnaires combines the social exchange elements described in Part I with a "foot-in-the-door" approach to requesting that the questionnaire be answered and returned. A test of this procedure with visitors to national parks throughout the United States produced response rates of 75%, compared with 38% when the traditional method of simply handing people a questionnaire and asking them to send it back was used (Dillman, Dolsen, and Machlis, 1995).

Case Study: Personal Delivery to National Park Visitors

The U.S. National Park Service wished to obtain feedback on visitor impressions of their visits to many of the nation's national parks. The information was sought to provide useful feedback to each park for improving the visitor experience.

Because no list of national park visitors exists, the only apparent way of sampling visitors was to select them during their visit to the park, which for some might last an hour or so but for others could last several days. The standard procedure employed for the survey was to prepare a small (8½″ × 5″) TDM format booklet questionnaire for each park, with a cover identifying the park by name and containing a drawing of a scene from the park. It was printed with a return address and a real postage stamp was stuck to the back cover. A small tab was also affixed that could be used to seal the questionnaire for mailing. Every "nth" visitor (or vehicle) to the park was sampled at the entrance stations in order to provide each visitor an equal chance of being selected for the survey. After paying the entrance fee, the selected visitor was informed that a brief study of people's reactions to the park was being done and the driver was asked if the group would cooperate by completing and mailing back a short questionnaire, which was then handed to them. This explanation was often quite brief, especially if a line of cars was waiting. Rarely did people refuse to accept the questionnaire. Use of this procedure in 11 national parks, ranging from Yellowstone in the western United States to Harper's Ferry in the East, from 1985–1987 resulted in response rates ranging from 28 to 50%, with an average of 38%.

Revised procedure. A new procedure was developed for use from 1988–1990, which began by asking every nth visitor who had just paid the park fee if they would pull their vehicle over to the side of the road where another person in park uniform was standing for purposes of introducing the study. The driver was greeted with a brief explanation of the survey, the information that only a small scientific sample of visitors was being asked to voluntarily participate, and a statement that completing the questionnaire should only take about 12 minutes. Nearly all respondents (98%) agreed to accept the questionnaire. The person in uniform then inquired which person in the party would be willing to take responsibility for completing it. That person was asked to respond immediately to three brief questions: number in party, what kind of group they were traveling in, and the respondent's age.

Respondents were thanked for their answers and then handed a clipboard containing a page of address labels. They were asked to provide a name and address, with the explanation that the superintendent of that park would like to send a note of thanks for participating in the study. That comment was followed with the surveyor thanking respondents and wishing them a great visit.

Approximately two weeks after the visit to the park, the sampled person who provided the address received a glossy color postcard depicting a park scene that might have been seen by that person when visiting the park. The reverse side included a brief printed note from the park superintendent thanking the person for visiting the park, along with the address label written in the respondent's own handwriting.

The use of this procedure in 21 national parks from 1988–1990 resulted in response rates ranging from 63 to 85%, with an average response of 75%. Thus, the lowest response rate achieved by this procedure was more than 13 points higher than the highest response rate obtained by use of the traditional method already discussed. Moreover, the average response rate was twice that for the original procedure. Yellowstone, the only park to be included in both treatments, produced response rates of 38% from the traditional method, compared with 76% for the revised procedure (Dillman, Dolsen, and Machlis, 1995). The completion rates, that is, the proportion of respondents accepting questionnaires who completed them, were 39% and 81% respectively.

Since 1991, the methods have been further modified to include replacement questionnaires being sent to nonrespondents. An additional 63 parks have been surveyed, including many in large cities, for example, the White House and the Martin Luther King Historical Site, where people have quite a different visitor experience than in spacious outdoor parks accessible only by a long drive. The response for these surveys has averaged 74%, or 79% of the individuals who accept questionnaires (Machlis, 1998).

Reasons for success of the revised procedure. A number of factors appear to be responsible for the improved response achieved by the new procedure. New theoretical elements were invoked for defining the revision. In addition, several elements of the standard data collection procedure outlined in Part I of this book were tailored to the particular population and personal delivery situation.

First, a deliberate effort was made to increase the salience of the experience of receiving the questionnaire. The interaction time required for presenting it to the respondent was lengthened and involved several distinct steps, thus increasing the likelihood that its receipt would be stored in long-term memory. Second, responsibility was assigned to a particular individual rather than addressing the request in a general way to the driver as part of the fee payment process. Thus, an expectation was created for both the volunteer respondents and persons accompanying them on the visit about who would complete the questionnaire.

Third, by having the park representative dressed in a National Park Service uniform, an attempt was made to invoke the authority of the position, thus utilizing one of the influence concepts described by Cialdini (1984). The fact that the National Park Service is a government agency facilitated this appeal to legitimate authority, and built on the fact that response to government surveys tends to be higher than for other sponsorships. In addition, the National Park Service in particular is held in high regard by the general public, as reported by national surveys.

Fourth, an explicit attempt was made to utilize a foot-in-the door approach for improving response. Research has shown that if a person agrees to perform a small task (the foot-in-the-door) they are more likely to agree later to perform a larger, more difficult task (DeJong, 1979; Freedman and Fraser, 1966; Reingen and Kernan, 1977). The protocol for the interview, which is described in Figure 7.1, consists of a series of successive requests beginning with asking people to pull the car to the side of the road to talk to another uniformed park representative, following that with a request to participate in a brief study, and then requesting answers to a few short questions. At this point the larger, potentially more "costly" request to the respondent is made; that is, writing one's name and address on a mailing label for the pur-

Figure 7.1 General protocol for personal delivery of diaries in a National Park Service study (Dillman, Dolsen, & Machlis, 1995).

Step 1. (At entrance gate) Thank you very much (for payment of entrance fee). But before you go in, I wonder if I could ask you to pull over to where the person in the uniform is standing to talk with him just briefly about a study we are doing of what visitors like and don't like about our national park. It'll just take a minute. Thank you so much and enjoy the park.

Step 2. Hello! Welcome to (Park Name). My name is __________. (Park name) is conducting an important visitor survey to learn what you think of our programs and services. We are only interviewing a few select visitors, so your voluntary cooperation would be greatly appreciated. I have three initial questions to ask right now that will take two minutes of your time. If you agree to help us it will take about 12 minutes during or after your visit to complete the questionnaire, which you can mail back to us. Would you be willing to do this?

Step 3. Okay. We need to designate one of the adults in your group as the individual responsible for filling out the questionnaire. Who is willing to actually write in your group's answers?

Step 4. Thank you. What kind of group are you traveling with: family, friends, family and friends, a tour group, alone, or some other group?

How many people are in your group?

And, what is your age?

Step 5. We would like to send a postcard to you after your visit thanking you for assisting with the study. To do that I'd like to ask you to write your name and address on this mailing label that we'll stick to the postcard. And, the postcard can serve as a reminder about the questionnaire inasmuch as it is really crucial to the success of our visitor's survey.

Step 6. That's all of the questions. Please enjoy the park, and thank you very much for your help. We greatly appreciate it!

pose of receiving a thank you note. Handing the selected respondent a page of labels that contains other names is not only efficient, but invokes the influence concept of "others are doing it" (Cialdini, 1984).

Although it is unknown how many people would not have put their address on the mailing label had this question been asked at the beginning, its placement here seemed likely to make more sense to the selected recipient. Providing the name and address at this point, rather than refusing it, would also be expected on the basis of people's desire to be consistent, a type of influence also described by Cialdini (1984). The success of this question sequence is evident from the fact that only five to six percent of the people refused to provide addresses. However, it should be noted that because the clipboard was handed to them, a fake address, with a first name or pseudonym "park visitor" could easily be provided, something less likely to be done if the person was asked to verbalize the name and address (for the uniformed person to write down) while others in their party listened.

In addition to the usual please and thank you elements that were sprinkled throughout the interaction, questionnaire recipients were informed that they could expect to receive a thank you from the park. It was reasoned that when the colorful picture postcard arrived, expressing appreciation to respondents for visiting the park and thanking them for returning the questionnaire, this would convey reward value. Respondents would be able to identify with the picture, thus making the thank you/reminder much more salient than a plain postcard with only a written message.

Analysis of the timing of responses revealed that both the interaction sequence and postcard thank you contributed significantly to the final response. Response rates prior to the sending of the postcard averaged 54%, or 16 percentage points higher than the average final response from the traditional procedure. Response rates climbed an additional nine points after the postcard. It was concluded that a series of theoretically-based adaptations were successfully made for this personal delivery situation. Moreover, the potential for tailoring to other personal delivery situations seems promising.

ADAPTATION TO OTHER IN-PERSON DELIVERY SITUATIONS

Other situations in which personal delivery procedures might be developed have both similarities to and differences from the national park situation outlined above. For example, consider the case of visitors to a special art exhibit at a museum. Visitors might be approached as they enter the exhibit by a well-dressed person with a name tag that identifies them as a museum employee. The selected respondents would be asked to complete a questionnaire after their visit, using a similar multiple-step protocol to that used by the National Park Service visitor studies. When asked to fill in the address label on a clipboard, respondents might be informed that their full name is not necessary but that the director of the museum would like to send a thank you. The thank you postcard might consist of a picture of one of the objects in exhibit, thus reminding respondents of their visit in a pleasant way.

A prepaid cash or material incentive could also be provided in such situations. A museum exhibit would seem to be a situation in which material incentives tailored to the context might be particularly effective. For example, a poster or other memorabilia especially developed for the exhibit could be provided. The inability to tailor a material incentive to respondent interests is one of the factors that probably makes them less effective than financial incentives in most surveys, but this might be turned to an advantage in this situation.

Another situation in which personal delivery of questionnaires is useful is for surveys of hunters, anglers, boaters, or other interest groups who use certain wilderness areas without official entrances or exits, but which are generally accessed from certain parking areas and for whom no sample list is available. These survey situations lack the organized formality associated with tickets and payment of fees, and the obvious recognition of Park Service or museum sponsorship. In situations such as this, one might purchase caps or jackets that identify and describe the person delivering the questionnaires and even their vehicle. For example, a university researcher might attempt to use a labeled university vehicle and obtain a jacket that identifies the "State University Fish and Wildlife Survey" to help establish legitimacy. The possibility of using token prepaid financial incentives that are included with the questionnaire should not be overlooked, and letters can be prepared ahead of time on university stationery with real signatures. Regardless of the situation, it seems important that careful attention be paid to the details surrounding personal delivery in order to tailor methods effectively.

Can Personal Delivery Cut Costs for In-Person Household Surveys?

A major drawback to the use of mail-back questionnaires for household surveys is the inability to sample effectively without first visiting the household. However, the costs associated with repeated personal visits to households where people cannot be found at home, especially in large national surveys for which an interviewer may have to spend hours revisiting one or two households in a given cluster, places a great premium on finding alternatives.

Personal delivery of mail-back questionnaires offers promise in this area as well. If a sampled household could be induced to complete mail-back questionnaires left on their door handle so that only one visit had to be made to many households, it seems likely that the cost of in-person interviewing could be greatly reduced.

In the past, in-person interviews were typically organized, worded, and constructed in ways quite different from those typically used for self-administered questionnaires. These differences include extensive interviewer instructions, the use of show cards for some questions, and complicated skip instructions. Use of unimode construction techniques like those discussed in Chapter 6, and the ease of using word processing equipment to adapt a personal interview instrument to self-administered format, raise the possibility of combining mail-back with personal interview methods. The following case study provides insight into the potential use of such methods.

Case Study: Household Delivery of Mail-back Questionnaires

An experiment conducted by Melevin, Dillman, Baxter, and Lamiman (in press) tested four procedures for delivering a mail-back questionnaire to households selected by area probability sampling methods. The survey concerned employment experiences of males ages 20–50 living in households located in areas selected as part of a statewide sample in low-income areas of the state. The available funds would have prevented conducting personal interviews using more than one callback. In an attempt to find a viable alternative, the questionnaire was converted to a self-administered booklet format and interviewers were instructed to visit each household up to three times and ask to speak to the youngest male between the ages of 20 and 50, if there was one. If that person was available, he was given a packet which included a personally signed cover letter and the 20-page booklet questionnaire. For a randomly selected subgroup it was explained that the respondent would receive eight dollars as an expression of appreciation when the questionnaire was returned. The person's name and telephone number was then requested. If the interviewer was able to talk with a household member, but the sampled person was not available, the interviewer was instructed to provide a similar explanation and request that it be passed on to the selected respondent. If no one was contacted by the third attempt, the interviewer was instructed to leave the packet containing the questionnaire, an explanation of who should respond, and promise of payment in a clear plastic container on the door handle.

The sample of 1,500 addresses was divided into four different experimental treatment groups. Group 1 received a promise of eight dollars if eligible for the study and four dollars if not eligible, plus a follow-up telephone reminder or postcard to the address where the questionnaire was delivered. Group 2 received the incentive but no follow-up. Group 3 received no incentive but was followed up, and Group 4 received no incentive or follow-up. The overall response rate was 47%, with the treatment group responses being about the same for the first three groups: 50% for Groups 1 and 2; 47% for Group 3; and only 35% for the group that received neither the incentive nor the follow-up.

Response rates also varied significantly by the type of contact. They ranged from 65% when the request was handed to the eligible respondent to only 17% when the questionnaire was left on the door handle. The effect of the incentives and follow-ups also influenced response rates significantly. A response of 77% was obtained when both the incentive and reminder were used and the packet was handed to the respondent, 71% when no follow-up was made, 63% when no incentive was used, and 53% when neither a follow-up nor incentive was used.

Case study implications. The results from this experiment were not, in my opinion, sufficient to suggest use of this procedure in a general way. However, I believe the method can be developed further for more effective use. One of the major costs associated with face-to-face interviews of households selected through area probability samples is the large number of call-backs necessary to achieve high response rates. This study suggests that when contacts can be made directly with an eligible respondent, high mail-back response rates are possible (77% with the methods used here). If an interviewer can leave a questionnaire at each household where a contact is made with an eligible respondent, rather than taking time to conduct the interview, that would allow far more contacts to be made each day. The procedures used by Melevin et al. (in press) can be significantly improved by using more of the procedures outlined in Part I of this book. For example, use of a prepaid rather than postpaid incentive and additional reminders, including a follow-up questionnaire, should improve response rates significantly. For households in which the respondent cannot be contacted directly, but for which the address and/or telephone number can be obtained, alternative follow-up procedures may also be used. Foot-in-the-door procedures might also be usefully employed to obtain information helpful to follow-ups. In addition, it should be easier to gain agreement to complete a mail-back questionnaire than to get agreement for an immediate interview.

It is also possible to consider the use of mail-back self-administered questionnaires on a more limited basis in personal interview studies. Much of the total cost and certainly the highest per interview costs are associated with large numbers of repeated visits to homes where the sampled respondent is not available. As a survey proceeds, this makes it necessary for interviewers to return to specific geographic areas to contact only one or two households repeatedly, with a low probability that an interview will be obtained on any particular visit. Leaving a mail-back questionnaire with another household member or even on the door handle, though less effective than a personal contact, remains a possibility.

Application to Community Drop-Off/Pick-Up Surveys of Residences

Community development organizations have often used the technique of dropping off questionnaires in person at every household in a neighborhood or community in order to gain citizen input into public issues (Johnson, Meiller, Miller, and Summers, 1987). Typically, the questionnaires are handed to people who are at home, and left on doorsteps of other households, with instructions that the completed questionnaire will be picked up on a specified day or evening. This technique often results in quite low response rates partly because of people not being home during the neighborhood pick-up.

Response rates to such surveys might be improved dramatically by using some of the procedures already described in this chapter. For example, a foot-in-the-door technique could be used to explain the questionnaire, indicate that the organization wants to send a thank you to each household, and confirm the address for that purpose. The questionnaire drop-off can include a stamped return envelope as an alternative to the door-to-door pick-up. In addition, a postcard follow-up can be used later as a thank you/reminder. Other techniques outlined in Part I, from incentives to multiple contacts, might also be used.

GROUP ADMINISTRATION OF SELF-ADMINISTERED SURVEYS

Giving self-administered questionnaires to an assembled group of people is motivated by quite different considerations from those associated with the in-person delivery methods just discussed. In this case it is possible not only to draw a sample ahead of time, but also to motivate or even require individuals to assemble in one place to complete the questionnaire. The cost savings for this type of administration are often enormous, and in many cases (e.g., school classes) nonresponse is negligible and not associated in any way with the content of the questionnaire.

However, in certain instances it may be undesirable to use this method. If a panel study is commencing with students in a school or job trainees who will then be dispersing widely, and for whom it has already been decided that telephone interviews will be used for follow-up and measurement of change, potential mode differences may put the objectives of the study at risk. As discussed in Chapter 6, attitudinal questions that use vague quantifiers for answers, and those that invoke socially desirable responses, may make it difficult to switch modes and still measure change. Alternatively, one might decide that since self-administration is being used for the initial study, the follow-up should be done in this way as well.

Group administration may also exert some independent influences on responses that are not present in other types of self-administered situations. I have observed group administration in which the surveyor came into a room, made a few extemporaneous comments on what respondents were being asked to do, and asked if there were any questions. Whatever comments were made and questions asked may have influenced answers in some way that was different from when the questionnaire was administered to other groups. Also, I have observed situations in which people were allocated a few minutes at the end of a class to complete a questionnaire and were informed that as soon as they had finished they could leave. This prompted completion of a few questionnaires in record time, giving the appearance that answers were not contemplated with care.

Another concern is that in some cases the completion of a questionnaire in a group or classroom setting resembles in people's minds the taking of a test. Thus, I have observed respondents who seem to invoke test-taking behavior that includes previewing all of the questions to get a sense of the complete task, and, when finished, going back over the complete questionnaire to make sure all of the questions have been answered and even changing the answers to some questions. In addition, people who are absent from a group administration are often sent a questionnaire with a cover letter that contains information not provided in the group setting. All of these potentials for differences lead us to develop a carefully structured method for group administration, the aim of which is to achieve similar completion environments for all groups and individuals.

An example of a general protocol for group administration of questionnaires is provided in Figure 7.2. Five steps, from introduction through debriefing, are identified. The purpose of a prepared rather than extemporaneous introduction is to keep the questionnaire completion environment the same for all groups. In addition, I wish to keep the administration simple, something that rarely happens when introductory comments are unprepared. The special instructions are aimed at diffusing any test culture and discourage people from previewing and reviewing the questionnaire unless that is the way they would fill it out at their home. Questions are actively discouraged prior to administration in order to avoid giving additional infor-

Figure 7.2 Example of a protocol for group administration of a self-administered questionnaire.

Introduction: A nearly identical introduction is provided to all groups consisting of these elements:

An expression of appreciation for what they are about to do.

A brief description of the task (completing a questionnaire) and what it is about in a limited way (nearly the same as explained in the cover letter).

Summary of the steps (which may be posted on a blackboard or poster board as well):

- Read the cover letter.
- Take the questionnaire out of the envelope.
- Complete the questionnaire.
- Immediately put it in the envelope and seal it for sending to the processing office. This is part of making sure your answers are confidential. None of us in this room will see your individual responses.

Special instructions: These special instructions are typically offered:

This is not a test with right and wrong answers. Please think of it as being a questionnaire sent to your apartment or home and fill it out just like you would if we sent it there.

As soon as you have answered the last question, please be sure that you put the questionnaire immediately into the envelope, seal it, and wait for additional instructions.

Distribution: Each respondent is given a packet consisting of the questionnaire inside an unsealed envelope, which will double as a return envelope, and a cover letter clipped to the front of the envelope. They are told they can start when they receive it.

Retrieval: Questionnaires are passed in when everyone is done or picked up from where each respondent is sitting.

Debriefing: More information about the questionnaire and its purpose may be provided. Appreciation is expressed once again to respondents. Whatever questions people have are answered as fully as possible.

---

mation that other respondents might not receive prior to completion, but questions are encouraged afterwards.

Distribution in an envelope with the cover letter clipped to the front encourages reading of the cover letter. It contains the basic information one would receive if asked to do the survey by mail. However, allowing respondents to start responding any time after they receive the packet leaves it up to the respondent as to whether the cover letter gets completely read, thus emulating the home situation.

Asking respondents to seal the completed questionnaire in an envelope addressed to the processor or sponsoring organization is part of the confidentiality process. This step also discourages respondents from reviewing answers to their questionnaire in the way they might if they had nothing to do while waiting for others to complete the answering process. In addition, it becomes part of the confidentiality process ensuring that others in the room do not see their answers.

Requesting that respondents wait for additional instructions is done in part to avoid providing an incentive for quick answers because of respondents' desire to leave as soon as possible. This is also justified by the final debriefing, the aim of which is to respond to any questions respondents might have, including a more complete explanation of what the survey is about and why it is being done.

DELIVERY OF QUESTIONNAIRES THROUGH PUBLICATIONS

Sending a questionnaire through a magazine, newsletter, or other routine mailing differs dramatically from the other alternatives to individual mailings discussed in this chapter. In this case, one could normally draw a sample of names from the publication's mailing list and contact only a small sample of the survey population.

However, cost considerations often encourage survey sponsors to insist on sending a questionnaire as a page in their publication in order to reach everyone on their sample list (the complete survey population) at no additional cost, rather than spending additional money to send surveys separately to the small sample. The temptation to reduce costs in this way is fueled by the experience of large circulation periodicals getting thousands of questionnaires returned by being printed as part of the publication. Even though it represents only a small percentage of the readers, the absolute number of questionnaires returned is larger than it would be had the sponsor been willing to allocate funds for a sample survey of several hundred subscribers. As a result, the likely nonresponse error is much larger and the accuracy of results much less than for a smaller number of responses from a random sample.

The most common motivation for distributing self-administered questionnaires through publications is to identify reader reactions to the publication itself. Simply printing a questionnaire as part of the publication and asking the reader to respond seems so simple, avoiding the bother as well as cost of a carefully articulated survey process. Thousands of such inserted questionnaires appear in newsletters, newspapers, magazines, and even books each year. Another reason for these magazine-distributed questionnaires (MDQs, as they are often referred to) is the editor's desire for feedback on the publication or reader information for the writing of a future article. Abundant examples exist of this type of questionnaire in newspapers, organization newsletters, journals, and magazines. Over the last two decades, magazines as diverse as *Psychology Today, Ms., Redbook, Playboy, Powder: The Skiers' Magazine, Utne Reader,* and *Black Elegance,* to mention only a few, have used this type of magazine-distributed survey to collect information for articles.

Another motivation for conducting such surveys is to identify people with rare characteristics in the population and avoid the costs of large numbers of screening calls, as described by Pratto and Rodman (1987). They identified and surveyed parents with "latch-key" child care arrangements through a questionnaire published in *Working Mother.* As a potential inducement to readers to respond, the appeal informed them that a future article would report findings from the survey.

The major drawbacks to this method of distribution are low response rates and response bias. People who respond are not representative of all subscribers. When a publication list is particularly long, a large number of responses is often used to ascribe unfounded validity to the results. For example, *Ms.* magazine once published a questionnaire on smoking and other addictions, with a request to all readers to respond. The article based on the returns reported: "Thousands of you responded to a survey about women and addiction. . . . You were a healthy and health-conscious group. . . . Among those who do smoke, however, [*Ms.* readers] are likely to be heavy smokers" (Van Gelder, 1987).

This particular story on patterns of addiction carried no caveat about the possible sources of survey error and, in particular, a greater likelihood of response from women who smoked. Yet, statements like the above and an emphasis on percentages left the reader with the implication that the results were representative of the entire population of readers. This limitation has led Pratto and Rodman (1987) to observe, "Magazine-distributed questionnaires are not designed to obtain representative samples."

When I have proposed using methods like those described earlier in this book for achieving high response rates and less nonresponse error, editors have sometimes been reluctant to use these more intensive methods. They point out that making multiple contacts with readers might alienate them and cause subscription cancellations. One editor simply noted, "How do we know that the bias will be that bad?" He also asked if there was a cheap alternative.

The case study described below compares a MDQ with a TDM procedure, and a mixed method designed to minimize the costs of surveying readers by printing the questionnaire in the publication and following up by other means (Dillman, Scott, and Husa, 1988).

Case Study: A Magazine-Distributed Questionnaire for University Alumni

In 1986, *Hilltopics,* a 24-page Washington State University alumni publication printed in a newspaper format much like the *Chronicle of Higher Education,* was being distributed eight times a year to nearly 80,000 alumni and friends of the university. The editor wanted to know how many recipients read the publication and whether certain parts of it should be changed. He proposed including a magazine-distributed questionnaire in one of the regular issues. Subsequently, a one-page questionnaire was printed on page 16 of the November 1986 issue. Readers were instructed to clip out the questionnaire, complete it, and mail their response to the editor at the address noted on the page. No return envelope was included.

Simultaneously, a subsample of 400 readers was sent an eight-page booklet questionnaire which followed the TDM principles for questionnaire construction (Dillman, 1978). The *Hilltopics* logo appeared on the cover along with the title, "*Hilltopics* Readership Survey: What Are Your Likes and Dislikes?" A personalized letter with name, address, salutation, and individually-applied pressed blue ballpoint pen signature was used, and a stamped return envelope was enclosed. This mailing was followed by a one-week postcard thank you/reminder. A final follow-up mailing with replacement questionnaire was sent to all recipients of the first questionnaire who had not yet responded.

A second subsample of 400 readers, referred to as the mixed-method group, was sent a similarly personalized letter but no questionnaire. The letter brought to their attention the fact that a questionnaire was in that month's *Hilltopics*. Recipients were asked to clip out the survey and return it in a special stamped envelope with "For return of *Hilltopics* questionnaire" stamped on the front. One week later they received a standard thank you/reminder. Two weeks later, those who had not returned the questionnaire were sent a print overrun of page 16, the questionnaire, and asked to return it. The goal of this procedure was to use multiple contacts, as for the other subsample, but to minimize costs by not having to print a separate questionnaire.

Response to the TDM and mixed-method subsamples was about the same, with 66% (265) of the recipients of the TDM questionnaire responding, compared with 66% (264) of those receiving the request to clip and return the questionnaire (Figure 7.3). However, whereas about two-thirds of the responses to the first questionnaire came prior to the second mailing, about that proportion of the mixed group came after the second mailing, when the print overrun questionnaire was sent to nonrespondents. Nonetheless, total costs for the mixed-method group were $5.26 per completed questionnaire compared with $6.37 for the standard procedure.

In sharp contrast to response rates for these subsamples, only 0.6% of the 79,000 not in either subsample, who received only the questionnaire printed in *Hilltopics*, returned it. However, as is characteristic of such blanket distribution procedures, that amounted to 474 completes, much more than received from either subsample. If the results are a random representation of all readers, then it could be argued that results from the magazine-distributed questionnaire are better. However, that is not the case.

Figure 7.3 summarizes a number of the most important results from the survey, ranging from general impressions of *Hilltopics* to the amount of the magazine read. For each indicator it is apparent that those who responded to the magazine-distributed questionnaire gave far more favorable responses, including being twice as likely (54% versus 27% and 26%) as respondents to either subsample to describe receiving *Hilltopics* regularly as important to them. Overall, 20 of 58 items exhibited

Figure 7.3 Comparisons of results from magazine-distributed questionnaires (MDQs), a standard mail TDM procedure, and a mixed procedure that uses a questionnaire from the magazine (Dillman, Scott, & Husa, 1988).

	MDQ	TDM Procedure	Mixed Procedure
Sample size	79,000	400	400
Returned questionnaires	474	265	264
Response rate	0.6%	66%	66%
Proportion of respondents under age 40	37%	51%	49%
<u>Response Distributions:</u>			
Percent saying important to regularly receive magazine	54%	27%	26%
Percent saying impression highly favorable	90%	79%	78%
Percent selecting most positive category for seven key evaluation questions	58%	40%	40%
Number of significant (p < .05) differences <u>for 58 questionnaire items:</u>			
MDQ versus others	N/A	20	17
TDM versus others	20	N/A	5
Mixed versus others	17	5	N/A

statistically different ($p < .05$) response distributions between the MDQ and TDM subsample versus 17 for the MDQ versus print overrun subsample. By way of comparison, only five items were statistically different between the two subsamples. Further analysis of the data revealed that characteristics of respondents to these subsamples were closer to the characteristics of the entire population for gender and year of graduation than were those from the blanket appeal.

Overall, it was apparent that those who returned the MDQ were older alumni and friends who read more of the publication. Young people, a crucial group for whom efforts to improve readership were needed, were greatly underrepresented.

Application to Other Situations

I do not recommend using magazines, newsletters, or other mass distribution methods for surveys. Their use seems destined to produce results fraught with nonresponse error. Had the MDQ been relied on to make decisions on revising *Hilltopics*, it would have led to few changes. However, when sponsors were shown results from the sample-based surveys using either of the other methods, they immediately concluded that some changes should be considered. These changes were aimed at increasing the appeal to younger alumni who were less likely to read the magazine and less enthusiastic about its content than were the older respondents who had disproportionately responded to the MDQ distributed only as a special page in the publication.

The experiment was undertaken in hopes of finding a cost-effective alternative to MDQs. Although the costs were slightly less, they weren't low enough to justify referring respondents to the publication in order to clip out the questionnaire. The cost savings of not having to print a separate questionnaire were quickly diminished by the low response to the first mailing and the need to send more replacement questionnaires in the follow-up mailing. These results were not surprising because the inconvenience of having to find the publication, clip the questionnaire, and connect it to the return envelope certainly increased the costs of responding.

As a result, I approach the conduct of readership surveys in much the same way as I do other surveys, using a preletter, questionnaire, thank you/reminder, and replacement questionnaire. Still, in a recent repeat of the *Hilltopics* survey 10 years after the first one, when the number of alumni had climbed from 79,000 to 114,000, decreasing the average age of alumni, a response rate of only 43 percent was achieved after four contacts (prenotice through replacement questionnaire) (Carley-Baxter and Dillman, 1997).

Because of our concern that heavy readers of *Hilltopics* and older alumni were more likely to return it, the cover of the questionnaire used for this survey did not specify the survey as a "readership" survey. In addition, the first questions were about the recipient's general impression of *Hilltopics* and whether it was important to continue receiving it, which we thought could be answered by any recipient regardless of how little or how much they read it. Because of the 43% response rate and nagging concern that younger alumni with less favorable opinions had not responded, a final mailing was then undertaken. The decision to undertake a fifth mailing on readership surveys of this nature, and particularly by special mail, was not made lightly. Comparison of graduation dates with alumni records showed that even with the TDM and mixed procedure used previously, there appeared to be an underrepresentation of younger alumni. A final letter was sent to the nonrespondents, as shown in Figure 7.4. This letter emphasized our concern that many people had not responded, and that those who hadn't differed from those who did. In addition, we began by defining this final follow-up as extraordinary, trying carefully not to offend the recipient.

Half of the nonresponders were contacted by regular first class mail and half by a two-day priority letter in the large red, white, and blue envelope provided by the U.S. Postal Service. Of the remaining respondents who received each type of mailing, 20% responded to the priority mail compared with 14%

Figure 7.4 Cover letter used for fifth contact sent by two-day priority mail.

Washington State University

Social and Economic Sciences Research Center

Wilson Hall 133
PO Box 644014
Pullman, WA 99164-4014
509-335-1511
FAX 509-335-0116

July 15, 1997

Amy Smith
1500 Main Street
Seattle, WA 98102

Dear Ms. Smith:

We are writing with an extraordinary request.

You may recall that early this summer we asked you to help us evaluate Hilltopics, which we now send to 115,000 alumni and friends of WSU. We mailed this request only to a small representative sample of Hilltopics recipients.

Nearly half of those who received our readership questionnaire have returned it. A few others wrote to us indicating that they did not read enough of Hilltopics to feel comfortable answering all of the questions.

We have become concerned that people, such as yourself, who did not return the questionnaire may expect different things from Hilltopics than those who did reply. Consequently, we are making this final contact in hopes that you might share some of your thoughts with us.

We prefer, of course, that you answer all of the questions. However, if you feel you are not familiar enough with Hilltopics to do that, answering those questions you can would be fine. Simply putting a note on the front of the questionnaire with your thoughts about Hilltopics would help us as well.

Most of all, we want to be sure that we do the best job possible of producing a publication about Washington State University that you would enjoy receiving and reading.

Thank you for considering this unusual request.

Cordially,

Pat Caraher
Editor of Hilltopics

Lisa R. Carley-Baxter
Study Director

---

to the regular mail, raising overall response rates to 53%, or about 10 percentage points above that achieved through the fourth contact.

Analysis of the results showed that this mailing was significantly more likely than previous contacts to elicit responses from graduates after 1980. Whereas 18% of all responses from this group were received after this contact, only 4% of alumni from before 1960 and 6% of those graduating between 1960–1979 were returned at this time. Thus, there was some evidence that this final mailing was successful in reducing certain aspects of nonresponse error.

We have discussed the *Hilltopics* survey in some detail because of the concerns over nonresponse error which can be expected to occur in readership surveys. It should be noted that even with five contacts our response rate was only 53%. To improve response rates further, token financial incentives might also have been used.

CONCLUSION

In this chapter I have considered quite different situations in which alternatives to delivery by mail are considered for self-administered surveys. At one extreme, the lack of a sample frame list for populations that can only be sampled at the moment they become part of the population, such as visitors to an exhibit or national park, forces the consideration of alternatives. At the other extreme, the existence of magazines and other periodicals to which questionnaires can be added for mass mailing entices sponsors to consider this mode of contact because of the cost savings of distribution in this way.

In the case of in-person delivery, a tailored procedure has been developed based on foot-in-the-door principles that nearly doubled the response rate from 38 to 75%. These methods seem applicable to a wide variety of other situations, from reducing costs for area-probability face-to-face surveys to comprehensive community needs assessments.

We were less successful in finding a viable alternative for delivering self-administered questionnaires through mass publications. Instead, sampling from the mailing list and using a procedure close to the general method outlined in Part I remains a far better alternative. However, some tailoring is done to take into account the somewhat sensitive relationship between publications and their readers, particularly those for which subscriptions are paid, while at the same time using a five-contact sequence to reduce nonresponse error.

CHAPTER 8

When Timing is Critical: Diary, Customer Satisfaction, and Election Forecast Surveys

THE SELF-ADMINISTERED surveys considered in this chapter share a common feature: the need for respondents to answer and return their questionnaires within a period of a few days. Unless a quick response is achieved, the results will not be useful.

Examples include diaries of behavior engaged in by respondents on certain days of a given week; customer satisfaction surveys that assess whether a meal, hotel stay, or product repair experience met expectations; and political polls aimed at predicting election outcomes. Although these surveys differ from each other in many respects, they share the need to truncate the implementation process in order to preserve data quality, maintain customer relations, and/or meet essential reporting deadlines. Tailored designs that achieve these goals are the focus of this chapter. Ironically, some of the protocols may involve more contacts than those typically made in a mail survey, whereas others require that fewer contacts be made.

The reasons for wanting surveys to achieve responses quickly are varied. In some cases a rapid response is needed because people are likely to forget details of the experience they are asked to report. For example, few people can remember exactly which television programs they watched, or all of the food they consumed three days ago or even yesterday. The memory of events that are routine aspects of people's lives is likely to decay quickly, so that a delay in reporting may produce a description of behavior that is based more on what respondents think they should have done than on what they have done. The problem of remembering what actually happened also permeates reports of customer experiences, from purchasing dresses or garden tools to evaluating hotel stays.

In other cases, the need to make decisions based on results, as in certain customer satisfaction surveys, drives timing considerations. Moreover, a survey done for purposes of predicting election outcomes may be completely useless if results are not available prior to the election, but it must also not be completed so far ahead of the election as to be an invalid representation of what people plan to do on election day. Each of the three types of surveys emphasized in this chapter—diary, customer feedback, and election prediction—have a need for precise timing.

COMPLETING ACTIVITY DIARIES

Respondents are asked by surveyors to keep diaries on a wide variety of activities: television viewing, radio listening, travel, food consumption, household expenditures, and the expenditure of time. The information asked for in surveys of this nature is unlikely to be recalled accurately unless the behavior is recorded within hours or even minutes of its occurrence. Therefore, the typical diary survey design calls for behavior to be recorded for particular days or weeks, rather than in a general sort of way.

Mail-back diaries are often used in such cases because the desired information cannot usually be obtained by interview, except perhaps where a design calls for very specific and limited inquiries, such as, "What did you have for lunch today?" Successfully completing telephone interviews on particular days, before recall diminishes, would be enormously difficult. For these reasons, diaries have developed as a common, albeit specialized, type of self-administered survey. The general implementation methods outlined in Part I, which typically take several weeks to achieve a high response rate, must be tailored to this purpose.

One of the most common types of diaries, which millions of people have been asked to complete, is the television viewing diary. The following case example reports procedures similar to those used by large organizations that have conducted such surveys. The description is slightly generalized because details of the various procedures by which such surveys have been conducted vary somewhat from one situation or geographic area to another. However, the case study illustrates the fundamental ways in which diary survey procedures need to differ from the procedures used for other kinds of self-administered surveys.

Case Study: Measuring Television Viewing

In the United States there are more than 200 television viewing markets, that is, geographic areas typically associated with a few to many local television stations. Periodically, mail surveys are done to determine how many people are watching each type of program. This information is important for setting advertising rates and determining which programs are watched and which are not. Although electronic meters are installed in the homes of a random sample of the U.S. population to measure what television programs are being watched, it is too expensive to do this for all television markets. Consequently, paper mail-back diaries are distributed to samples of several thousand households in each market several times a year.

A procedure that has sometimes been used for implementing diary surveys is described below. The day designations are approximate.

Day 1: A telephone call is made to a random digit sample of households. The surveyor explains to whomever answers the telephone that a television diary survey is being conducted in their area of the country, and that the caller would like to send their household a brief diary that they can use for one week to record the television programs they watch. The surveyor may also explain that a small token of appreciation will be sent with the diary. The mailing address is obtained, or if already available, simply confirmed.

Day 2: Within a day or two of the initial contact, a letter of introduction is mailed to individuals who are willing to complete a survey. The letter thanks the person for having agreed to keep the one-week diary of their household's television viewing, explains that the diary will arrive in a few days, and asks that the respondent be on the lookout for it. The letter also contains an explanation of why the survey is important and how the respondent's help determines what is available on television. A brochure that answers commonly-asked questions may be enclosed. In effect, this prenotice serves as an interest-getting preletter. People who indicated over the telephone that they do not want to fill out a diary may also receive a request that appeals in a respectful way for them to reconsider.

Day 3: A day later, the diary is mailed to the household in a separate envelope along with a cover letter and a token incentive of one dollar to several dollars. The higher amounts may be included for markets where response rates are expected to be low. The diary has a date for beginning the process of filling it out and is often designed as a mailer with a first-class stamp attached on the back for returning it, as was done for the park visitor survey discussed in Chapter 7. This avoids the potential problem of the reply envelope getting lost. The diary includes a detailed explanation of how to make entries, including methods for recording the viewing behavior of all members of the household. It then lists page after page of 15-minute viewing periods for the entire seven-day week, starting, for example, on Wednesday morning and ending the next Tuesday night.

Day 6: About three days before the beginning of the diary week, a postcard is mailed to all households indicating that their week to record viewing is about to start. Recipients are reminded that they should start filling out their diary on the day recorded on the cover of the diary. The importance of the diary for communicating to broadcasters what the public actually watches is restated, along with an explanation of why each respondent is important.

Day 10: Yet another postcard or letter is mailed to all respondents, scheduled to arrive on day 12 or 13, informing them that their diary week is almost over.

This mailing emphasizes the importance of mailing in the diary as soon as the week is over. This final contact is considered especially important because of the need to preserve the quality of data. Diaries that are not returned within several days following the diary week may not be processed because of concerns about data quality.

Day 11: On the second or third day of the respondent's diary week, a phone call is made to find out how things are going and to indicate how much the respondent's help is appreciated. The interviewer offers to answer any questions or provide any other help that might be needed.

All six of these diary contacts are made within a 12-day period. This procedure includes at least one more contact than is typically made in the standard mailout procedure outlined in Part I of this book. Special mail has sometimes been used for one of the mailings, and a second, surprise incentive has sometimes been sent in the middle of the diary week as an additional way of saying thanks. Although the process is mixed-mode, with up to two contacts by telephone and four by mail, all of the data are collected by mail. This procedure has been found successful in achieving 45–65% response rates, depending upon area of the country, time of year, and amount of incentive. Response rates tend to be greater in regions of the country with higher education, for example, the upper Midwest, including Iowa, Wisconsin, and Minnesota. These rates tend to increase in winter months, and incentives of several dollars are more effective than lower incentives.

One past sponsor of such surveys has concluded, based on an evaluation of eight different follow-up treatments, that the more powerfully and more often respondents are reminded of the survey, the more likely they are to respond (McConochie and Reed, 1987). Considered in the abstract, a protocol that makes a contact on the average of every other day in a 12-day period seems excessive. However, in relation to the nature of the request being made, it is not. Undoubtedly, it would make far less sense to the respondents had they received a special delivery mailing four or five weeks after the prescribed diary week in which they were asked to tell exactly what they were watching each hour of the designated days, the memory of which would undoubtedly be clouded by viewing behavior of the subsequent weeks. The intensiveness of six contacts in 12 days is likely to be seen as reasonable by the respondent, considering the time-sensitive nature of the information requested.

OTHER DIARY APPLICATIONS

Another use of diaries has been to record radio listening activity. One large organization has reported sending 1.5 million radio diaries per year to individuals recruited by telephone, 54% of which are returned (Perlman, Patchen, and Woodard, 1989). The procedures used for these surveys are typically less intensive than those used for television diaries, and prenotices and midweek contacts are less likely to be used. Experimentation has revealed that sending diaries in a box similar to the size and shape of a half-pound of chocolates improves response. It was reasoned that this packaging of the diaries increases response by getting the respondent's attention. Use of a box significantly increased overall response rates by four percentage points, from 38 to 42% nationally, and by 13 percentage points, from 26 to 39%, for a subsample of African-Americans (Patchen, Woodard, Caralley, and Hess, 1994). It seems probable that the use of this box increased the likelihood that the diary was identified in the respondent's mail and opened.

Diaries have also been an important source of information for travel and activity surveys, and much research has been done on their effectiveness (Ettema, Timmermans, and van Veghel, 1996; Kalfs, 1993; Kalfs and Saris, 1997; Richardson, 1997). A detailed comparison of computer-assisted self-interviews, computer-assisted telephone interviews, and paper and pencil diaries in the Netherlands found no clear advantage of one method over the other (Kalfs, 1993). Each had certain advantages, with the paper and pencil diary obtaining greater detail than the other methods. The main drawbacks reported for paper and pencil diaries were response rates and item nonresponse (Ettema et al., 1996), which methods like those described above are aimed at overcoming.

Yet another area of research that has relied extensively on the use of mail-back diaries is nutrition intake studies (Thompson and Byers, 1994). When doing such studies, it is sometimes important to obtain recall for a specific 24-hour, three-day, or even longer period. To control for variations in meal patterns that are likely to differ from one part of the week to another, as well as during holidays, it is important to control the precise day(s) respondents are asked to record their intake. Thus, the case study method outlined above of preliminary contacts followed by additional contacts just before, during, and after the recording day(s) seems applicable. Attractive refrigerator magnets have sometimes been enclosed as a token of appreciation, along with the suggestion that the diary could be posted on the refrigerator for convenience. Doing so combines the idea of token incentive with practical benefit for the study in a way not commonly done in mail studies. However, we have seen no evidence that such incentives do or do not improve response rates, or whether the quality of reporting is affected.

Not all diary surveys begin and end by mail. The U.S. Department of Transportation began conducting the American Travel Survey in 1995 in an effort to collect detailed information on state-to-state and city-to-city travel (American Travel Survey, 1995). A large sample of U.S. households is interviewed three to four times per year about their travel to destinations over 75 miles away. The sequence of contacts involves sending a prenotice letter and survey package (letter, a diary in which to record trips, and a national map), followed by an introductory telephone call and periodic postcards to remind members to continue to keep track of their travel information. In addition, reminder letters are sent about one month prior to an interviewer calling to obtain the actual data for the preceding three to four months. During this interview people are expected to consult the diary in order to recall the trips they have made. Because only 41% referred to the diary to provide answers in a pretest, the diary was redesigned to be a calendar containing spaces and instructions for recording trips, and to hang on the wall for easier access. This survey, to be conducted every five years, is still in its developmental stages. However, it illustrates the use of multiple contacts to improve response and the combining of modes to improve accuracy of recall and lower nonresponse rate over a very long data collection period.

A common challenge faced by all diary studies, and indeed the reason diaries are used, is the recognition that the events being recorded are routine aspects of people's lives and the memory of one event tends to fade quickly or blend with other such activities. Thus, it is reasoned that getting people to record activities at the time they occur is essential for obtaining quality data. The kinds of methods that make it possible to send a large number of contacts in a very short period of time are quite different from those likely to be considered acceptable for most mail surveys, including customer satisfaction surveys, the next topic of this chapter.

CUSTOMER SATISFACTION SURVEYS

A friend who was peering over my shoulder as I looked carefully at a customer satisfaction form for a hotel where we were both staying, pointed to the form and observed with a smile, "Those things are a little like running water—it's impossible to find a hotel or restaurant these days that doesn't have it."

This observation led me to keep track of the forms made available to me while on the three-day trip. There were 10 in all. One questionnaire had already been given to me on the airplane and a second was provided in the hotel room. Two of the restaurants I visited provided questionnaires to me with the bill, and one other restaurant printed its questionnaire on the bottom part of the cash register receipt. Two other restaurants had questionnaires available on the table where I ate my meal. While at a hotel restaurant I complimented the waiter on how nice the restaurant and meal had been, and was immediately encouraged to complete a questionnaire. However, none was immediately available. When I returned to my room, I discovered that a questionnaire had been delivered there with a note thanking me for visiting the restaurant. Two tourist attractions I visited also provided me with questionnaires to assess my visit.

PROCEDURES THAT DON'T WORK

The desire of virtually all organizations, both large and small, to get immediate feedback on customer experiences has led to the widespread practice of distributing questionnaires to everyone willing to fill them out at the point of purchase. From a questionnaire construction perspective, this trend has led to many unfortunate practices that diminish the usefulness of the results. Although many questionnaires reflect much careful thought about what questions are asked and how respondents are likely to react to them, others do not. In addition, the drive for high ratings often leads to unusual practices that are less likely to show up in other kinds of surveys. The following are a few of the frequently encountered features identified from examining hundreds of questionnaires over a period of many years.

Some questionnaires have asked respondents to rate qualities of the product on a scale of one to five, or A to F, without defining which is the high end of the scale (Figure 8.1). Although the cultural association with grades in school means that "A" is likely to be seen as the top end, the association is not as apparent with the numerical rating. The highest number may be five, or, because a person associates scoring the experience with a ranking, the lowest number may indicate the best quality. Suffice it to say that scales, no matter what the scoring system, need to have labels that indicate meaning: "Please

Figure 8.1 Examples of poorly constructed satisfaction ratings used in customer feedback forms.

Scales with unspecified meaning:

Using this 1 to 5 scale, rate how well our product has met your needs 5 4 3 2 1

How would you rate the speed of delivery for the product you purchased? . . . . A B C D F

Unbalanced scales:

How well did your staff treat you? . . . . Outstanding Excellent Good Poor

How was the quality of the food? . . . . Excellent Very Good Good Fair Poor

Scales that combined different concepts that may have confused respondents:

How did our people treat you? . . . .
- ☐ Like royalty
- ☐ Attentive
- ☐ Okay, I guess
- ☐ Could have been better
- ☐ What service?

Handling of my baggage . . . .
- ☐ Excellent
- ☐ Good
- ☐ Satisfactory
- ☐ Unsatisfactory
- ☐ Poor

indicate on a scale of 1 to 5, where 1 is highest and 5 is lowest, the quality of this product."

Once, while helping a retirement community develop a resident satisfaction form, my draft scale with the choices of "Wonderful, Good, Fair, or Poor," was edited to become "Outstanding, Excellent, Good, Poor." When I asked why, it was explained to me that the community's goal was to provide a "wonderful" life to every resident, so the opportunity to provide that rating needed to be included on every rating scale. As discussed in Chapter 2, people respond to the number of categories as well as the labels, and use of the proposed scale would result in some individuals reporting "good" when their mental evaluation of the experience was "below average." People who see results from surveys tend to think of scales as being balanced. If 80% scored the experience "good or higher," they would think of it as a high satisfaction score. The practical solution to the sponsor's concern was to add a sixth category of "very poor" in order to meet the corporate goal as well as to provide a balanced six-point scale.

My general rule is to make all scales balanced, something that is achieved with the four-point scale, "Excellent, Good, Fair, Poor" categories mentioned above. Another scale that accomplishes this goal is one that describes an experience as "Well Above Average, Above Average, Average, Below Average, or Well Below Average."

Another common but unfortunate feature of many satisfaction scales is to combine two different concepts into one scale (Figure 8.1). Few attempts are as unusual as the one I obtained at a local bank, which asked customers to rate how they had been treated by the staff: "Like royalty, Attentive, Okay I guess, Could have been better, or What service?" Scales of this nature are sometimes used to develop interest in responding to the questionnaire. However, whimsical and somewhat undefined categories invite equally whimsical responses. Another scale that is currently used by a large corporation is "Excellent, Good, Satisfactory, Unsatisfactory, Poor." Not only have two somewhat different concepts been combined into one, but "Satisfactory" has become the midpoint. Extending the scale categories is sometimes justified on the basis of most people responding that their experience is quite positive and wanting to distinguish between the most positive responses. If that is the case, then it is important to also extend the negative end of the scale so that a true balance exists.

Another frequent problem with customer satisfaction surveys is illustrated by a hotel satisfaction questionnaire I received that asked me to respond to 76 items for a one-night stay experienced several weeks earlier. Most of the items were things I did not remember (e.g., How promptly were you served at breakfast?), or did not experience (e.g., Did room service arrive within the time you expected?). Questionnaires with many questions that don't apply encourage people to skim over the items, providing only occasional responses. They may also discourage any response at all. For example, beginning a questionnaire with several items about how well the reservation request was handled on dimensions of friendliness, knowledgeableness, helpfulness, etc., when many travelers do not make their own reservations, makes the entire questionnaire appear not applicable to them.

There are good reasons to ask customers about details ranging from whether the hotel room bed was made neatly, to whether the temperature of the food in the restaurant was satisfactory. The providers of services are organized into departments, and improvement is aimed at improving the specifics of those varied services. Unfortunately, customers' minds and experiences are usually not organized in a similar fashion. The main questions the customer may be interested in answering are: "Did you get a good night's sleep?" And, if not, "What, if anything, could we have done to improve your night's sleep?"

Yet another characteristic of many hotel questionnaires is the tendency to combine questions of satisfaction with last night's lodging with many additional questions that seem extraneous, such as number of nights stayed away from home in last 12 months, number of nights stayed in competing hotels, and number of business versus pleasure trips taken per year. These analytical questions, though undoubtedly important to the sponsor, increase the likelihood that respondents will see the questionnaire as unimportant or even as an attempt to get marketing information under the guise of measuring satisfaction.

For reasons such as these, customer satisfaction surveys are perhaps at risk of being treated categorically by respondents as an annoyance to be avoided, much like telephone marketing calls. As a result, response rates in the low single digits may be expected. Thus, customer satisfaction surveys become more akin to functioning as a complaint department where people with specific problems have a way of expressing them, along with the occasional positive comment they might make to help out an employee who was nice to them, rather than a representative assessment of how customers are truly reacting to the service provided. Both kinds of feedback are important, but one should not be confused with the other. In this chapter I am concerned specifically with customer satisfaction surveys that provide representative feedback that can be generalized to all customers.

The goal of generalizing results means that we must be concerned with minimizing all four aspects of survey error: sampling, coverage, measurement, and nonresponse. Sampling needs to be done instead of asking everyone to respond. Selectively encouraging some respondents to use the customer feedback forms must also be avoided. In addition, the questionnaire should be constructed in a way that gives confidence that the measurement properties of each question are acceptable and the implementation procedures will assure a reasonably high response rate.

Sampling customer satisfaction for commonplace events in people's lives, for instance, making a deposit at a bank, eating dinner in a restaurant, staying overnight in a hotel, or receiving a package in the mail, presents special challenges. The frequency with which such experiences occur, and the tendency for other similar or other more recent experience to blend with them, makes it difficult for people to remember what happened. Ideally, one wants to obtain a response within hours or a few days of the event.

Why use mail for measuring customer satisfaction?

Because of the difficulty associated with remembering routine events in one's life, it may be more appropriate to obtain responses when and where the service is provided, or shortly thereafter by telephone. However, for several reasons, mail rather than telephone is the appropriate choice for certain customer satisfaction surveys. The most obvious reason is that for some samples, mailing addresses are available whereas telephone numbers are not. However, even when telephone numbers can be obtained, many organizations prefer to use a method that is less intrusive than calling customers, especially in today's climate, in which some people are offended by such calls. The fact that repeated call-backs must often be made in order to achieve acceptable response rates further discourages the use of telephoning for some surveys.

An equally compelling reason for avoiding telephoning is the concern over obtaining socially desirable answers, especially in smaller organizations in which, for budget reasons, they want to do the calling themselves. As noted in Chapter 6, a large regional hospital tried to save money on telephone interviews by having nursing staff on the evening shift call respondents. As a result, some of the patients were interviewed by people who had provided care during their hospital stay. It is hardly surprising that under these conditions more positive answers were obtained to such questions such as, "How would you describe the care you received while in the hospital? Excellent, Good, Fair, or Poor?"

Yet another reason for relying on mail customer satisfaction surveys is the organizational management philosophy that now permeates both private sector and government organizations in the drive for improvement. We live in an era in which customer feedback drives many major decisions, including salary decisions for employees. Some organizations have developed very detailed feedback systems whereby they attempt to collect data about each step of ordering and delivering products, so that the performance of each of the units within their organization can be evaluated. The challenge of doing such surveys is increased by organizational feedback systems that require sufficient data to be collected from each branch or local franchise to allow quality evaluations to be made for each of these local units. For large national or international organizations this means that thousands or tens of thousands of completed questionnaires may need to be collected, and there is a high likelihood that mail questionnaires will be used.

Handing out questionnaires to people when a service is provided with a request that they complete the questionnaire on the spot, for example, when a hotel bill is paid, might seem an alternative in some situations. However, people checking out of a hotel or leaving a restaurant are often in a hurry. In addition, completing a questionnaire and handing it back to the person who gave it to them decreases the perception of anonymity and may lead to socially desirable answers, as in the former patient survey discussed above. In addition, the experience for which satisfaction is being assessed may not be entirely complete.

Tailoring to the Situation

Tailoring self-administered survey design to a specific experience that is likely to fade quickly from memory suggests that both the questionnaire and implementation procedure be designed somewhat differently from the methods outlined in Part I of this book. Questionnaire design needs to be simple and limited, making it commensurate with the significance of the event in people's lives. If most hotel stays consisted of weeks instead of a day or two, and most guests experienced all departments and aspects of a hotel, perhaps the 76-item questionnaire discussed earlier would be appropriate. However, such stays are the exception rather than the rule. Similarly, individual meals, a single purchase at a department store, or delivery of a parcel, are not such important events that page after page of detailed questions are warranted. Figure 8.2 shows a simple questionnaire for a hotel stay that is designed to look quick and easy to complete. Because it sacrifices the closed-ended detail of asking about all possible aspects of the hotel experience, the more general satisfaction questions are followed by an open-ended question that allows for the capturing of both negative and positive experiences. Figure 8.3 shows an appropriate cover letter to be sent with the questionnaire.

Two different implementation systems might be considered in order to achieve a reasonably high rate of response. One method is to personally hand the questionnaire and stamped envelope to each of the individuals included in the sample and ask them to mail it back. The other is to mail the questionnaire within a day of providing the service that the customer is being asked to evaluate.

The previous chapter outlined a personal delivery method for achieving high response to self-administered questionnaires. A similar procedure might be used for customer experiences, ranging from department store purchases to meals in restaurants, and is especially suited to experiences for which names and addresses are not known. Customers may be systematically sampled (e.g., every nth customer on certain days of the week) after the bill

Figure 8.2 A brief customer satisfaction survey for a hotel stay when quick response is a concern.

Seven brief questions about your recent stay at Spokane's Oxford Inn.
Please mail back to the Oxford Inn, 7777 Hotel Street, Spokane WA 99999

1. Overall how would rate your stay at the Oxford Inn? (Please mark your answer with an "x".)

- ☐ Excellent
- ☐ Good
- ☐ Fair
- ☐ Poor

2. Please rate your stay at our hotel on each of the following:

	Excellent	Good	Fair	Poor	Did Not Use
Check-in experience	☐	☐	☐	☐	☐
Hotel staff	☐	☐	☐	☐	☐
Guest room appearance	☐	☐	☐	☐	☐
Cleanliness of bathroom	☐	☐	☐	☐	☐
Telephone service	☐	☐	☐	☐	☐
Value of staying here for the amount paid	☐	☐	☐	☐	☐

3. Thinking about all aspects of your visit to our hotel, how well did we do in meeting your expectations? Did we:

- ☐ Far exceed your expectations
- ☐ Somewhat exceed your expectations
- ☐ Meet your expectations
- ☐ Fell somewhat short of your expectations
- ☐ Fell far short of your expectations

4. If in this area again for a similar trip, would you prefer to stay here or in another hotel/inn?

- ☐ Definitely stay here
- ☐ Probably stay here
- ☐ Not sure
- ☐ Probably stay in different hotel/inn
- ☐ Definitely stay in different hotel/inn

5. What is the main reason for selecting the answer you gave for preferring to stay here or somewhere else?

____

____

____

6. Was the reason for your visit to our hotel:

- ☐ Business
- ☐ Pleasure
- ☐ Some other reason

7. How many times have you stayed here previously?

- ☐ None, this was my first visit
- ☐ 1–2 times
- ☐ 3–5 times
- ☐ 6 or more times

Please use the back side to tell us anything else about your stay that you would like for us to know.

has been paid. The diner could be handed a questionnaire in a sealed envelope along with an explanation of what it is. In a restaurant it would be appropriate for the maitre d', rather than the server, to stop by the table just before the customer leaves, explain that they routinely ask a small sample of customers to fill out and mail back (not do it now) a very short, anonymous questionnaire to let them know, ". . . how we did this evening. This is how we learn to provide the best dining experience we can." This method is quite different from just placing a customer satisfaction card on the tray with the change or credit card receipt, and can be designed so as to build on the foot-

Figure 8.3 Cover letter to accompany a hotel customer satisfaction survey.

❖Spokane's Oxford Inn

Dedicated to making your stay a pleasant one.

7777 Hotel Street
Spokane, WA 99999
509/555-1234
509/555-4321 (FAX)

June 30, 1999

Ms. Dorothy Schroeder
Box 3694
Livingstone, MT 92222

Dear Ms. Schroeder:

Thank you very much for staying at Spokane's Oxford Inn. We appreciated having you here.

I am writing to ask for a small favor. Answers to the seven questions on the enclosed brief questionnaire will help us know how well we are doing in meeting the needs of people who stay here.

It's only by asking customers like yourself what we have done well and what needs to be improved that we can meet our goal of providing the best possible stay for future visitors.

Thanks so much for being our guest and giving us feedback.

With Best Wishes,

Allen St. John
Manager of the Oxford Inn

---

in-the-door procedures discussed in Chapter 7. Additional encouragement might be provided by indicating that a small token of appreciation, such as a certificate for a free or discounted purchase at the same or a different location, has been enclosed. The questionnaire is placed inside the envelope along with a signed letter from the manager and a return envelope with a real stamp (not business reply). This underscores the idea of mailing the questionnaire back, and the presence of the stamp increases the likelihood that it will not be thrown away.

When addresses are known, for example, with delivery or packages, automobile or appliance repair, or hotel stays, a similar procedure can be used, or a questionnaire can be mailed to the customer the day after the purchase. Personalization might be sacrificed in order to obtain speed of mailing, but the letter could begin, "Thank you very much for staying at our hotel this week. We really appreciate your business," and then continue with a request for completion of the satisfaction questionnaire. If addresses are available, it is possible to expand the use of response-inducing techniques by sending an immediate thank you that serves as a prenotice for the questionnaire. The questionnaire would follow a day or two later and the thank you/reminder postcard a few days after that. Inclusion of a token monetary incentive would also significantly improve response rates.

Procedures such as those outlined above will greatly improve the representativeness of responses to customer satisfaction surveys. They also change the nature of such requests for feedback from their current function as a surrogate complaint or employee compliment device that cannot be relied on for making systematic assessments about the quality of a particular product or service, to a device that provides a reliable and fairly precise (depending on sample size) indication of the sentiments of all customers.

When an Immediate Response Is Less Important

Not all customer service situations require immediate feedback, and there may be less need to use a truncated, hurry-up method for getting responses within a few days of the delivery or purchase. Indeed, sometimes it takes weeks, months, or even longer to put the customer into a position to adequately evaluate the service, as in the case of cable television, a new car, or the delivery of contractual services. For these surveys, a different strategy is not only possible, but necessary. Yet, many of these surveys are poorly done.

Several years ago a friend shared with me a customer satisfaction survey he had received from a government agency. A brief form letter came with it, noting that the individual had ordered one or more publications during the past year. It indicated the writer's hope that the publications had been useful and asked this customer to complete a questionnaire about the usefulness of the publication, the quality of service he had received, the timeliness of delivery, and other details of his experience. With a note of exasperation the questionnaire recipient indicated he had indeed ordered publications from the agency during the past year, but that responding was impossible. It had been three months since the last publication was received, and the ordering of publications was a minor event in his work. He explained that he therefore could not answer most of the questions about what happened when it was ordered, how long it took, whether the time period was reasonable, and the shape the package was in when it arrived. Not only that, but the questions were written in such a way that the customer had to indicate with one answer whether all of the publications were delivered in a timely way, whether the people who took the orders were friendly, and whether all publication mailings arrived without damage. No questionnaire distinctions were made between shipments. He also noted that someone else in his office was asked to place the order, while the shipments were received and opened by the mail room, so that no one person could really respond accurately to the survey. This questionnaire, like those of many other customer satisfaction surveys, did not get returned.

For these surveys, the standard mail procedures described in Part I are quite appropriate, and I encourage their use with tailoring that is quite minor. The most frequent objection I encounter to full use of the methods is with the client relationship. It is a concern that the more intense aspects of the methods, for example, use of identification numbers, replacement questionnaires sent to respondents who do not return their questionnaire by a particular date, and telephone reminders to return their questionnaire, might make good customers unhappy.

Figure 8.4 shows a cover letter and Figure 8.5 one page of an accompanying questionnaire used by the U.S. Energy Information Administration to obtain customer satisfaction information about subscribers to their publications. Each letter was individually addressed to the recipient and described the importance of asking for information from subscribers. The questionnaire uses the visual layout and design construction features described in Chapter 3, such as reverse print question numbers that serve as navigation guides, dark print for questions, light print for answers, narrow columns for questions rather than using the full page width, and carefully drawn skip instructions. This three-page questionnaire, containing 27 questions, was printed on a folded sheet of 11″ × 17″ paper, with the first page being devoted to the cover letter. Thus, a separate cover letter was not used nor were signatures applied individually. The questionnaire, which was sent to international as well as domestic subscribers, obtained a response rate of 54%. The response rate was in large part the result of multiple contacts that included a prenotice, the questionnaire, a thank you/reminder postcard, a replacement questionnaire mailing, and an additional follow-up postcard.

The modifications to the base method described in Part I, that is, the printing of the cover letter on the front of the questionnaire and use of a business reply instead of a stamped return envelope, represented accommodations to efficiency and constraints associated with the conduct of government surveys. This topic is taken up in more detail in the next chapter. Whether response rates could have been improved further by closer adherence to the procedures outlined in Part I is not known. However, the response rate is fairly high considering the low salience of government publications sent to most organizations. This survey illustrates a relatively slight adaptation of procedures compared to that needed when immediate response is essential.

Few areas of surveying with self-administered questionnaires have grown as rapidly as have customer satisfaction surveys (Dutka, 1994; Hays, 1998). My emphasis here has been on quick feedback plus an example of a well done survey that uses the fuller implementation methods discussed in Part I of this book. I expect the use of customer satisfaction surveys to grow rapidly in the future, making fuller use of self-administered interactive voice response

Figure 8.4 Example of a customer service satisfaction cover letter when a quick response is not a concern.

Department of Energy
Washington, DC 20585

February 1, 1998

Ms. EIA Publication Subscriber
Name of Establishment
1234 Someplace Street
Any City, State 00000

Subscriber to Name of EIA Publication

Dear Subscriber:

We need your help!

According to our records, we have been sending you the publication identified above on the mailing label. We are interested in learning whether this publication meets your needs and how we might improve. We also are considering reducing the number of printed publications in favor of electronic versions. As we look at these issues we need to know your preferences. The only way to find out what our customers think is to ask subscribers like you.

You have been scientifically selected a part of a sample of all our subscribers. Please help us by completing this short questionnaire and returning it to us in the enclosed return envelope.

Your voluntary participation is extremely important. The information you provide will be treated confidentially. Results of this survey will summarize the input of all survey participants. Your participation will not affect your subscription status.

As a token of our appreciation we have enclosed a complementary *Energy INFOcard* and a *QuickGuide* card which shows you how to access our Internet Web site. If you have any questions, call Colleen Blessing at 202/586-6482 or Michael Laurence at 202/586-2453. Either of them will be happy to talk to you.

Thank you in advance for your participation.

Sincerely,

Jay Hakes
Administrator,
Energy Information Administration

Printed with soy ink on recycled paper

Example from 1998 customer survey conducted by the Energy Information Administration.

Figure 8.5 Example of customer satisfaction questionnaire when quick response is less of a concern.

EIA

1998 Survey of Subscribers

Energy Information Administration
U.S. Department of Energy
Washington, DC 20585

Form EIA-nnn (1998)
Form Approval: OMB No. nnnn-nnnn
Expires: Month dd, yyyy

Are You Satisfied With Our Publication?

1. This questionnaire is about the specific publication named on the mailing label. EIA has you on their mailing list to receive it. Do you receive this publication?

- ❒ No ☞ Go to Question 8
- ❒ Yes

2. In general, how satisfied are you with this publication? (Mark only one box on the 5-point scale below, where 1 is Very Dissatisfied and 5 is Very Satisfied.)

Very Dissatisfied 1	2	3	4	**Very Satisfied** 5
❒	❒	❒	❒	❒

3. If you are dissatisfied with this publication (a score of 1 or 2 to Question 2), please tell us why.

____

____

____

____

____

4. Listed below are four characteristics often associated with good information products. Thinking about the publication named on the mailing label, how *satisfied* you are with each characteristic. (Mark one box for each characteristic using the 5-point scale below, where 1 is Very Dissatisfied and 5 is Very Satisfied.)

	Very Dissatisfied 1	2	3	4	**Very Satisfied** 5
Relevance	❒	❒	❒	❒	❒
Accuracy	❒	❒	❒	❒	❒
Comprehensiveness	❒	❒	❒	❒	❒
Timeliness	❒	❒	❒	❒	❒

5. The same four characteristics of good information products are listed again. Thinking about the publication named on the mailing label, how *important* is each characteristic to you. (Mark one box for each characteristic using the 5-point scale below, where 1 is Not at all Important and 5 is Very Important.)

	Not at all Important 1	2	3	4	**Very Important** 5
Relevance	❒	❒	❒	❒	❒
Accuracy	❒	❒	❒	❒	❒
Comprehensiveness	❒	❒	❒	❒	❒
Timeliness	❒	❒	❒	❒	❒

6. Of the characteristics listed in Question 5, which one is *most important* to you? (Mark only one answer.)

- ❒ Relevance
- ❒ Accuracy
- ❒ Comprehensiveness
- ❒ Timeliness

7. If you could change one thing about this publication, what would that be?

____

____

____

____

____

8. One of the issues we are facing at EIA is whether to discontinue paper publications and provide all our information in electronic form. Your answers to the following questions will help us with that decision. **Do you have a PC with a CD-ROM reader?**

- ❒ No
- ❒ Yes

Please turn to the next page ☞

Example from 1998 customer survey conducted by the Energy Information Administration.

(recorded voice interviews) and other electronic methods, discussion of which is deferred to Chapter 11. In addition, the use of scanning and imaging methods that facilitate the massive use of self-administered surveys for providing systematic and reliable feedback to each unit of large corporations is discussed in Chapter 12. The remainder of this chapter is devoted to one other instance in which timely response is imperative: election survey forecasts.

ELECTION FORECAST SURVEYS BY MAIL

Election polls are the main exposure that many people have to understanding the potential and pitfalls of sample surveys. They represent one of the few instances in which the ability to predict the behavior of millions of people from survey responses of a thousand or so sampled individuals regularly occurs in U.S. society. In general, these polls do quite well in predicting election outcomes.

A few years ago, while teaching a survey practicum to 30 graduate students, I proposed the possibility of doing a state election survey by mail. The reactions were as immediate as they were negative. A sampling of their comments follows:

- Response to mail surveys typically come in over many weeks, so that means you would have to start getting responses way ahead of time before people have even begun to think about the issues.
- It won't work; many people don't make up their mind until the last minute and a telephone call a day or two before the election is the only way to capture that choice.
- Even if people did make up their minds earlier than that, a good survey needs to determine how likely people are to vote, and answers to that question are more likely to be correct if one waits until a day or two before the election.
- Question wording bias can't be eliminated by randomly rotating the order in which candidate names are presented to respondents.

These objections are not surprising. Telephone surveys have become the standard method for conducting election forecast polls. Typically, a random digit sample of households is contacted, a respondent within each household is selected, and it is determined whether that person is registered to vote and whether they are likely to vote. Candidate preferences are then determined by asking questions of the nature, "If the election were held today, which of these candidates would you vote for?" The answers are then weighted to form precise predictions of the outcome, taking into account likelihood of voting and the fact that some types of people are more likely to respond to the survey than they are to vote. Although the precise procedures vary from one pollster to another, most follow this general procedure, and telephoning is used for virtually all national, state, and local election surveys. Election surveys by mail are seldom done.

Yet, since 1980, one survey by mail in Ohio has regularly predicted the outcomes of elections in that state (Visser, Krosnick, Marquette, and Curtin, 1996). In addition, its predictions have been closer than those provided by two statewide telephone polls conducted by the University of Cincinnati and the University of Akron. The factors that contribute to the success of this election forecast survey by mail, and the implications for designing other such surveys, are discussed here.

Case Study: The *Columbus Dispatch* Poll

About three months prior to each state election, the *Columbus Dispatch* obtains a sample of all registered Ohio voters. This sample is stratified into regions and likely voter turnout estimated by determining the number of registered voters in each region and the proportion of the total statewide vote provided by that region in the preceding two statewide elections. About 10 days before the election, each sampled voter is mailed a questionnaire that is designed to look like the actual ballot presented to voters in the election. The races, candidate names, party affiliations, and any other election measures to be voted on are presented with the exact wording that will be used on the actual ballot. Thus, the questionnaire appears very much like the actual election ballot (Figure 8.6). Additional questions are added for weighting and analysis purposes in a similar abbreviated format. Typically these items include intent to vote in the election, party affiliation, voting behavior in prior elections, education, age, gender, race, religion, union membership, and annual income.

Respondents are given the date by which the ballot must be in the mail for their vote to count in the poll. A form cover letter is enclosed with the salutation of "Dear Ohio Voter" on *Columbus Dispatch* stationery (Figure 8.7). This letter indicates that the ballot is secret (anonymous) and that no identifiers of any kind are used, except that different colors of ballots are used by region to allow appropriate weighting of the results by region. This is done because response rates tend to be lower in some regions than others. Finally, a postage-paid envelope is enclosed for returning the questionnaire. The questionnaire is mailed to approximately 6,000 voters. No reminders are sent. Response rates average 25% (ranging from 21–28%), and forecasts are based on roughly 1,600 responses per election.

As shown in Figure 8.8, the average error (the difference between prediction and actual outcome in the last eight elections) has averaged only two percentage points for the *Columbus Dispatch* compared to five for the elephone polls conducted by the University of Akron and the University of Cincinnati. Not only did the mail survey produce more accurate results, but it did so consistently across eight elections in 14 years.

Visser et al. (1996) have conducted an extensive analysis of the possible reasons for this difference in accuracy, examining effects of sample size, publicity, placement on the ballot, not voting on some races, margin of victory, voter turnout, closeness of each survey to the election, better identification of likely voters, weighting, inter-

Figure 8.6 Questionnaire from the 1994 *Columbus Dispatch* poll.

The *Columbus Dispatch* 1994 Election Poll
Please indicate your choice by placing an X in the appropriate box.

3. **Governor and Lieutenant Governor:**
(Vote for one)

Robert L. Burch
Peter Lawson Jones (Democratic) . . . . ☐ -1

Billy R. Inmon
Norm Myers . . . . ☐ -2

George Voinovich
Nancy P. Hollister (Republican) . . . . ☐ -3

4. **Attorney General:**
(Vote for one)

Lee Fisher (Democratic) . . . . ☐ -1
Betty Montgomery (Republican) . . . . ☐ -2

5. **Auditor:**
(Vote for one)

Jim Petro (Republican) . . . . ☐ -1
Randall W. Sweeney (Democratic) . . . . ☐ -2

6. **Secretary of State:**
(Vote for one)

Dan Brady (Democratic) . . . . ☐ -1
Bob Taft (Republican) . . . . ☐ -2

7. **Treasurer:**
(Vote for one)

J. Kenneth Blackwell (Republican) . . . . ☐ -1
Edward Licht . . . . ☐ -2
Barbara Sykes (Democratic) . . . . ☐ -3

8. **U.S. Senate:**
(Vote for one)

Mike DeWine (Republican) . . . . ☐ -1
Joel Hyatt (Democratic) . . . . ☐ -2
Joseph J. Slovenec . . . . ☐ -3

viewer effects, probing of undecideds, allocation of undecideds, and questionnaire design. Based on this analysis, they attribute the *Columbus Dispatch* advantage to four factors in particular: (1) the completed sample sizes were considerably larger, about 1,600 compared to about 800, thereby being subject to less sampling error; (2) more effective identification of actual voters; (3) a lack of "no opinions" on all of the candidate preference items, thereby avoiding susceptibility to decisions on how to allocate undecided respondents; and (4) the questionnaire design.

Figure 8.7 Cover letter for *Columbus Dispatch* 1994 Election Poll.

The Columbus Dispatch 1994 Election Poll

The Columbus Dispatch

34 South Third Street • Columbus, Ohio 43215 • (614) 461-5000

October 27, 1994

Dear Ohio Voter:

You have an important voice this year in the election of a U.S. senator, governor and other state officeholders.

The decisions you make in the November 8 election will help determine the course of Ohio government for at least the next four years.

Because you are a registered voter, your opinion counts. Thus, you are invited to participate in *The Columbus Dispatch* 1994 election poll. Your name was selected at random by computer from a list of registered voters in the state of Ohio.

The Columbus Dispatch has conducted polls in Ohio for many years with remarkably accurate results because of the excellent cooperation from those chosen to participate.

Please mark the ballot that follows. It will take only a few minutes. Drop the ballot in the postage-paid, addressed envelope and return promptly.

This is a secret ballot. Please DO NOT sign your name. The results of the poll will be published in *The Dispatch* as soon as returns are received and tabulated.

Everyone talks about polls, but few have the chance to participate. This is your opportunity. Please mail your ballot at once. Your cooperation is greatly appreciated.

Thank you,

Mike Curtin
Assistant Managing Editor/
Public Affairs

P.S. Your completed ballot must be in the mail by this Thursday, November 3, for your vote to count.

Reprinted with permission from *The Columbus Dispatch.*

Evaluation of the *Columbus Dispatch* Poll

When the poll results are contemplated from the perspective of the four cornerstones introduced in Chapter 1, that is, coverage, sampling, measurement, and nonresponse errors, an interesting picture of the mail survey results in relation to the telephone polls emerges.

From a coverage standpoint, the sample selection began with a list of registered voters. In contrast, telephone polls typically begin with random digit telephone

Figure 8.8 Comparison of results from *Columbus Dispatch* mail poll and University of Akron and University of Cincinnati telephone polls, 1980–1994 (Visser, Krosnick, Marquette, & Curtin, 1996).

Average Error of Three Ohio Polls

Year	No. of Races	Dispatch vs. Actual	Akron vs. Actual	Cincinnati vs. Actual
1980	1	1.4	1.8	---
1982	6	0.8	4.2	---
1984	1	0.7	0.8	0.7
1986	9	1.7	7.7	9.9*
1988	2	1.3	2.0	4.2
1990	5	2.2	7.7	5.5
1992	2	3.4	3.4	4.0
1994	6	1.3	4.6	3.1
Average		1.6	5.4	4.9

*Three races only

numbers. This means that people who are not registered or likely to vote must be identified and eliminated from the election predictions.

Second, as noted by Visser et al. (1996), the *Columbus Dispatch* poll results had about 1,600 completions compared to about 800 for each of the telephone polls. The expected precision of a completed sample of 1,600 at the 95% confidence level is about ±2.5% compared to about ±4% for a completed sample of 800. If the respondents are truly a random sample of all voters (a critical assumption), then for this reason alone we would expect the mail survey respondents to provide a consistently more accurate prediction of the election results.

Measurement error problems also exist and are especially pernicious. In order to achieve accurate coverage, that is, to limit the survey sample to people who will vote, responses must be obtained to two critical questions: Are you registered to vote? How likely are you to vote? In response to the first of these questions, some people who are not registered to vote say yes, and others over-report the likelihood that they will vote (Traugott and Katosh, 1979). Considerable evidence suggests that people are more likely to offer socially desirable answers of this nature in a telephone survey than in a self-administered survey. Thus, the mail survey not only begins with a known list of possible voters (better coverage) but seems less likely to elicit answers that are misleading (better measurement) about the voters' intentions.

In addition to telephone poll measurement errors on the critical coverage questions, answers to voting preference questions are typically posed differently than on the election ballot. For example, the questions posed to telephone respondents are frequently structured in this way: "If the election were held today, which of these candidates . . . ?" In contrast, the mail ballot simply begins with an incomplete sentence that people will see on election day, for example, "Governor and Lieutenant Governor:" which is followed by the names and party affiliations exactly as they will appear on the ballot. Thus, the representation to voters is much closer to the actual ballot in the mail questionnaire than it is in the telephone interview. Also, whereas the question order may be rotated on the telephone to avoid potential order effects, the order on the election ballot is not rotated. Consequently, surveying by telephone introduces many measurement features that differ significantly from what voters will see on election day.

Nonresponse error is the only one of the four cornerstones for which there is some evidence that the mail survey is inferior to the telephone survey, and even here the evidence is indirect. The response rates for the mail surveys were 20–30%, compared with the mid-60s for the telephone surveys. Nonresponse error exists by definition if respondents are different from nonrespondents, but here an important qualification must be added. The surveyor is only interested in receiving responses from people who are going to vote, and not from all registered voters. If all registered voters respond there would obviously be a problem, because only a little more than half of the registered voters typically vote in each U.S. election (Teixeira, 1992). Visser et al. (1996) report that the characteristics of the *Columbus Dispatch* respondents matched the exit poll results more closely than respondent characteristics from the Akron poll.

In sum, it can be argued that the mail survey did better than the telephone polls because it had less sampling error as a result of a larger sample, better coverage of the actual voting population, and a less difficult measurement task not subject to rewording, mode differences, and in particular, social desirability effects of interviewing. Finally, although the response rate was low, those who did respond matched closely the characteristics of those who voted. Perhaps the act of filling out a preference ballot is a better indicator of the likelihood of going to the polls than how one answers the telephone survey questions about being registered and intending to vote.

Doing an Election Survey by Mail

Conducting election surveys by mail using the procedures developed for the *Columbus Dispatch* poll has considerable appeal. Sending only one mailout using the "Dear Voter" letter means that it might be possible to send out a very large number of questionnaires in an effort to make not only predictions for states, but for cities or counties as well. The frequent disparity between telephone poll results and election outcomes for races buried deeply in ballots, for instance, insurance commissioners, supreme court justices, and state superintendents of public instruction, races for which there is little public visibility or acute interest, suggests that a mail ballot may be particularly useful. One of the reasons for entertaining this possibility is that position effects, or how names look in relation to other names and party affiliation, can easily be portrayed in the same way on the mail questionnaire.

However, other issues must also be considered. Not every state or jurisdiction makes available lists of registered voters that are reasonably up to date with current addresses, as appears to be the case in Ohio. Also, the *Columbus Dispatch* survey is conducted at a time of maximum salience, in the final 10 days prior to an election. Should one contemplate using this technique in the weeks prior to an election the results may be quite different because interest has not yet developed in the campaign. In addition, sponsorship of the survey must seem legitimate and unbiased. There is a tradition of newspapers and other media conducting polls that are honest. I do not know whether sponsorship would make a difference in who responds or the correspondence between responding and voting, but it represents an issue that should be considered. Sponsorship by the "Committee to Elect Jay Jones" or the "KLX Opinion Research Company" is not likely to convey the same legitimacy.

It also seems unlikely that a mail poll can pick up substantial last-minute changes, perhaps caused by some event interjected into the last week of a campaign. At the same time, it also seems likely that for most elections huge last minute changes are fairly unusual, especially for minor races. Thus, the *Columbus Dispatch* technique appears to be one that could be used widely, but with caution.

Methodological Issues

My discussion of election surveys is the only tailored procedure for which I caution against getting too high a response. It seems conceivable that encouraging a four- or five-contact approach with the use of priority mail could improve response, perhaps even pushing it past the proportion of registered voters who subsequently go to vote!

The goal of this kind of tailored survey is to get people who are likely to vote to respond to the survey, and to do so honestly. A full-blown implementation system would be spread out over a long time period, thus moving the actual survey response further from the date of election. It might also encourage nonvoters or unregistered persons to respond. Even a prenotice letter that warns people that they are about to get a ballot and asks them to respond to it may encourage people to start thinking about the election in ways they otherwise would not, and might result in an over-response.

In this case, the most that seems appropriate would be to send a thank you postcard, along the lines of the one shown in Figure 8.9, two to three days after the first mailout. I emphasize that the effects of this card are untested. The wording indicates that people should respond only if they plan to vote. It would likely improve response somewhat, but the full effects remain to be tested.

CONCLUSION

In this chapter I have considered three quite different situations, each of which usually requires that paramount attention be given to obtaining a quick and

Figure 8.9 Possible postcard thank you for use in election survey, targeted towards voters.

October 25, 1999

A few days ago we sent you a letter inviting you to participate in this year's *Times Register* election Poll.

If you have already sent in your election questionnaire, I want to thank you for participating.

If you have not but are planning to vote in this year's election, please do so right away. For your ballot to count in this poll it needs to be mailed by Thursday of this week before the election. The summary of results will appear in the newspaper shortly afterwards.

As mentioned in our previous letter, the ballot is secret. There is no way we can identify anyone's opinion, so please DO NOT sign your name.

Many thanks,

J. Thompson

J. Thompson, Editor
Central City Times Register

---

timely response: diaries, customer feedback, and election forecasting surveys. All three applications can be done successfully with self-administered methods. However, the tailoring of procedures to each of these situations is dramatically different. For diary surveys that required the recording of information on certain days of certain weeks, tailoring was done to include six contacts within a period of 12 days. For customer satisfaction surveys, only one to three contacts were proposed, employing front-loaded procedures of personal contact to avoid using a replacement questionnaire. For the election forecast surveys we described a depersonalized, one-contact mail strategy used successfully for nearly 20 years by an organization that has predicted more accurately the outcome of state elections than have two conventional telephone surveys. Each of these procedures illustrates effective responses to the needs of survey content, objectives, and populations, while retaining a focus on survey quality through an emphasis on coverage, sampling, measurement, and nonresponse considerations.

I continue this theme of appropriate tailoring in the next chapter, which considers the special situation of government sponsorship. Government sponsorship raises distinct challenges and possibilities that call for additional tailoring of survey procedures, including some surveys of the types discussed in this chapter and in the preceding ones. Government surveys frequently rely on the mixing of survey modes and methods of delivery.

CHAPTER 9

Household and Individual Person Surveys by Government

The largest sponsor of self-administered surveys of individuals and households in the United States is the federal government. In addition to the hundreds of such surveys it conducts each year, thousands more are conducted by state and local governments.

These surveys are sometimes designed and sent out directly from government agencies and respondents are asked to return their questionnaires to that agency. In other instances, contractors are hired to implement a survey on behalf of a government entity. Government-sponsored surveys, regardless of whether conducted by or for government, introduce unique possibilities for achieving satisfactory response. However, this type of sponsorship also introduces constraints that make it difficult to design such surveys in ways that produce high quality results. Both the possibilities and constraints are discussed in this chapter.

The survey approach used traditionally by the federal government might best be described as asking respondents to fill out forms, rather than to respond to questionnaires. This approach can be illustrated by the construction techniques once used for a national survey of school teachers, which has since been revised. This format is illustrative of the procedures used by many federal government conducted surveys into the early 1990s (Figures 9.1 and 9.2). In this case, the mailout package consisted of a booklet in an envelope with a label affixed sideways describing who should fill out the questionnaire, providing authorization information, and displaying a prominent return address. Pages two and three consisted of a rather impersonal letter, information about the paperwork reduction act, instructions, an unexplained space for remarks, and finally, at the bottom of page three, the first question. The first full page of questions used a two-column format with questions on the left and

Figure 9.1 Examples of page 1 and 2 from older government-style survey for a national survey of school teachers.

FORM SASS-4A
(12-27-90)

U.S. DEPARTMENT OF COMMERCE
BUREAU OF THE CENSUS
ACTING AS COLLECTING AGENT FOR
U.S. DEPARTMENT OF EDUCATION
NATIONAL CENTER FOR EDUCATION STATISTICS

SCHOOLS AND STAFFING SURVEY
PUBLIC SCHOOL TEACHER QUESTIONNAIRE
1990—1991

OMB No. 1850-0598
Approval Expires 12/31/92

This report is authorized by law (20 USC 1221e). Your answers will be kept strictly **confidential**. Results from this survey will appear in summary or statistical form only, so that individuals cannot be identified.

RETURN TO

Bureau of the Census
Current Projects Branch
1201 East Tenth Street
Jeffersonville, IN 47132

This questionnaire is intended only for the teacher whose name appears on the address label.

If you are that teacher, please complete this questionnaire and return it to the Bureau of the Census in the enclosed preaddressed envelope. Please return it within 2 weeks.

If you have any questions, call the Bureau of the Census COLLECT at (301) 763-5507.

If the teacher named on the label is no longer teaching at this school, please mark the appropriate box below and return this questionnaire to the Bureau of the Census in the enclosed envelope.

001

1☐ Teacher has transferred to another school
2☐ Teacher has retired
3☐ Teacher is deceased
4☐ Teacher has left this school for another reason
5☐ Teacher named on label has never worked at this school

Please correct any errors in name and address, including ZIP Code.

Jolyn Livingstone
Lincoln Middle School
Hooper, Washington 99999-0001

THIS SURVEY HAS BEEN ENDORSED BY —

American Association for Counseling and Development
American Association of School Administrators
American Federation of Teachers
Council of Chief State School Officers
National Association of Elementary School Principals
National Association of Secondary School Principals
National Education Association

(Continued)

Figure 9.1 (Continued)

Dear Teacher:

The National Center for Education Statistics (NCES) of the U.S. Department of Education requests your participation in the Teacher Survey for the 1990—1991 Schools and Staffing Survey. You are one of 65,000 teachers from public and private schools across the nation selected to be in the sample.

The Schools and Staffing Survey, first conducted in school year 1987—88, is an integrated set of surveys consisting of the Teacher Demand and Shortage Survey, the School Survey, the School Administrator Survey, and the Teacher Survey. These surveys are being conducted periodically to measure critical aspects of teacher supply and demand, the composition of the administrator and teacher work force, and the general status of teaching and schooling. The purpose of the Teacher Survey is to obtain information about such factors as the education and training, current assignment, job mobility, workplace conditions, and career choices of teachers, as well as their opinions about various policy issues such as merit pay or incentive pay.

The U.S. Bureau of the Census is conducting the survey for the National Center for Education Statistics by the authority of Section 406(b) of the General Education Provisions Act, as amended (20 USC 1221e). The data will be treated as confidential and will be reported only in statistical summaries so that individual teachers cannot be identified.

We are conducting this survey with a sample of teachers. While this minimizes overall response burden, the value of each individual survey response is greatly increased because it represents many other teachers. I therefore encourage you to participate in this voluntary survey by completing this questionnaire and returning it within 2 weeks to the **Bureau of the Census, Current Projects Branch, 1201 East Tenth Street, Jeffersonville, IN 47132**, in the preaddressed envelope enclosed for your convenience.

I thank you for your cooperation in this very important effort.

Sincerely,

Emerson J. Elliott
Acting Commissioner
National Center for Education Statistics

Enclosures

INFORMATION ABOUT YOUR PARTICIPATION

Public reporting burden for this collection of information is estimated to average one hour per response, including the time for reviewing instructions, gathering the data needed, and completing and reviewing the collection of information. Send comments regarding this burden estimate or any other aspect of this collection of information, including suggestions for reducing this burden, to the U.S. Department of Education, Information Management and Compliance Division, Washington, DC 20202-4651; and to the Office of Management and Budget, Paperwork Reduction Project 1850-0598, Washington, DC 20503.

Page 2 FORM SASS-4A (12-27-90)

Example from a 1990 National Center for Education Statustics survey, conducted by U.S. Bureau of the Census.

Figure 9.2 Example of older two-column style for asking questions in the national survey of school teachers, based on traditional personal interview forms.

SECTION 1 – CURRENT TEACHING STATUS – *Continued*

2. How much time do you work as a TEACHER at this school?

Mark (X) only one box.

012
1 ☐ Full time – *Skip to item 5*
2 ☐ ¾ time or more, but less than full-time
3 ☐ ½ time or more, but less than ¾ time
4 ☐ ¼ time or more, but less than ½ time
5 ☐ Less than ¼ time
} *Continue with item 3* (options 2–5)

3a. Do you have any other assignment at THIS school?

013
1 ☐ Yes – *Continue with b*
2 ☐ No – *Skip to item 4*

b. Which of these best describes your other assignment at this school?

Mark (X) only one box.

014
1 ☐ Administrator (e.g., principal, assistant principal, director, head)
2 ☐ Counselor
3 ☐ Librarian/media specialist
4 ☐ Coach
5 ☐ Other professional staff (e.g., department head, curriculum coordinator)
6 ☐ Support staff (e.g., secretary, aide)
7 ☐ Other – *Describe*

____

c. Including your teaching and other assignment, are you a FULL-TIME EMPLOYEE at this school?

015
1 ☐ Yes – *Skip to item 5*
2 ☐ No – *Continue with item 4*

4. In addition to employment at this school, what is your OTHER main activity?

Mark (X) only one box.

016
1 ☐ Teaching in another school
2 ☐ Working as a paid tutor
3 ☐ Student at a college or university
4 ☐ Working in a nonteaching occupation in the field of education (e.g., guidance counselor)
5 ☐ Working in an occupation outside the field of education
6 ☐ Caring for family members
7 ☐ Seeking work

SECTION 2 – TEACHING EXPERIENCE

5. In what year did you begin your first teaching position (full-time or part-time) at the elementary or secondary level? Do not include time spent as a student teacher.

017
| 1 | 9 | | |

6. What was your MAIN activity the year before you began teaching at the elementary or secondary level?

Mark (X) only one box.

018
1 ☐ Student at a college or university
2 ☐ Caring for family members
3 ☐ Working as a substitute teacher
4 ☐ Teaching in a preschool
5 ☐ Teaching at a college or university
} *Skip to item 9* (options 1–5)

6 ☐ Working in a nonteaching position in the field of education – *Continue with item 7*

7 ☐ Working in an occupation outside the field of education – *Skip to item 8*

8 ☐ Military service
9 ☐ Seeking work
10 ☐ Retired from another job
} *Skip to item 9* (options 8–10)

Page 4

FORM SASS-4A (12-27-90)

Example from a 1990 National Center for Education Statustics survey, conducted by U.S. Bureau of the Census.

answer spaces on the right, a format that originated with personal interviewing. Skip instructions were located in a position that made them easy to miss, with a bold and unexplained keypunch code between the questions and the answers. The nature of this questionnaire format runs contrary to many of the principles of questionnaire design and survey implementation discussed in Part I, ranging from format, composition, and personalization of the cover letter to placement of instructions and the lack of a respondent-friendly design for the questionnaire. The use of such questionnaires was often justified by the expectation that telephone or personal interviewers would contact nonrespondents to collect the information, so that mail-back response rates did not have to be an overriding concern.

It is easy to be critical of government questionnaire formats and procedures such as the ones shown here, and to view them as not thought out with care. However, to do that would be to ignore the many constraints associated with constructing and implementing government surveys.

CHALLENGES OF CONDUCTING FEDERAL GOVERNMENT SURVEYS

The difficulty of designing and implementing effective response-inducing procedures in government surveys stems from many sources. They range from barriers that prevent the use of certain response improvement techniques to the difficulty of resolving disagreements when multiple stakeholders and design interests are involved. Many such challenges are discussed here.

In the United States, approval by the U.S. Office of Management and Budget (OMB) is required for all federal government surveys of more than nine people. Concerns about survey quality, duplication of survey efforts by different arms of government, and survey burden on individual respondents have led to the development of a rigorous and sometimes lengthy approval process for government-sponsored surveys. Requests for OMB approval typically require a justification for every question proposed for a given survey and a description of the proposed implementation procedures.

Barriers to the Use of Certain Response Improvement Techniques

OMB's concern with survey quality results in proposed surveys being evaluated with regard to likely response rates. It is expected that high response rates, often around 80%, will be achieved. For proposed self-administered surveys, this means that pressure exists to use as many of the response-inducing techniques as possible discussed in Part I of this book.

Certain proven response techniques may have to be held in abeyance due to the constraints of government-sponsored surveys. OMB usually prohibits the use of token financial incentives to improve response to mail surveys, although experimentation and the evaluation of their effectiveness has sometimes been approved. The use of incentives remains controversial in government-sponsored surveys and at this time cannot be counted upon as a routine possibility for inclusion in a survey design.

The large scale of certain government surveys also makes it difficult to use certain techniques that are acceptable to OMB and that help to assure a high response rate. For example, sending out tens of thousands of questionnaires makes it difficult to employ personalization techniques. This difficulty stems less, perhaps, from objections to inserting names and addresses into letters, than it does from the risks inherent in requiring that two identified pieces (questionnaire and letter) of mail be matched and inserted into the same envelope.

The use of still other effective response-inducing techniques may be prevented because of image concerns. I once proposed to a federal agency that they consider placing a real stamp on the return envelope, rather than using a business reply envelope. I reasoned that an increase in response rate of perhaps three percentage points might be obtained. In this case, nonrespondents had to be interviewed by enumerators at an estimated cost of 20 dollars per household, and the use of first-class stamps on the return envelope would have cost about $33 million, some $15 million more than the cost of using business reply envelopes. However, if response rates could be increased by three percentage points this could potentially eliminate $60 million of enumeration costs, for a savings of $45 million. Objections to that proposal were quite strong and came from several divisions of the agency. The expressed concern was that as many as half of the stamps in the initial mailout would be unused, and could be easily targeted as an example of government waste, even though the savings might be substantial. This example illustrates the enormous and legitimate concern of government agencies with perceptions about survey procedures, which may heavily influence the use or nonuse of certain mailout procedures.

In addition, agencies that conduct large numbers of surveys must often invest in equipment and processing procedures that make the handling of questionnaires more efficient. Ironically, the adoption of such technologies often introduces inflexibility in the conduct of surveys and may make it more difficult to use implementation procedures that are respondent-friendly. Survey questionnaires must be designed to fit the existing equipment constraints. Examples include the use of labels that contain identification and processing codes, which give each survey and sample unit unique identities that may include two or three times as many characters as the name and address portion of the envelope. Large-windowed envelopes are required, and in combination with the label may give the entire mailout and return package a junk mail image. Another example observed in a government agency was the purchase of questionnaire printing equipment that allowed printing and stapling of single pages, but would not allow printing in a more conventional booklet style.

RESOLVING DISAGREEMENTS

Poorly designed questionnaire and mailout procedures sometimes result from disagreements among stakeholders. Many government surveys involve large numbers of groups and individuals with vested interests in their make-up. Congressional committees, individual senators and representatives, their staff members, special interest groups outside of government, staff of the agency assigned to conduct the survey, and other agencies with an interest in using the questionnaire data may hold strong and differing views about what data should and should not be collected by particular surveys. These concerns often extend to the wording of individual questions, the design and layout of the questionnaire, and the content of cover letters. Necessary efforts to resolve these differences often result in compromises that ignore likely effects on the willingness and/or ability of respondents to answer the survey.

The difficulties of reaching agreement on survey procedures is often compounded by the largeness of federal statistical agencies, which results in the necessity of coordinating activities of many divisions in order to launch a survey (Dillman, 1995b). One division (or section) may be charged with overall survey design, another with questionnaire content (wording of items), another with questionnaire layout and design, another with contracting for printing, another with questionnaire mailing, another with data processing, another with follow-up by a different mode (e.g., telephone interviews), and yet another with the analysis and reporting of results. The work of each group must be carefully articulated. In addition, each division may lobby for design features that will make their task easier and, from their perspective, more efficient. Thus, it should not be surprising that after the funding and objectives of surveys have been determined, another round of compromises with potential negative effects on respondents may occur.

In addition, work groups composed of interdivisional partners often decide whether a particular data collection procedure is to be used without considering how it is likely to affect respondents. An example was a proposal to change the timing of a preletter so that it would be sent three to four weeks before the questionnaire mailing. This change was proposed as a means of obtaining address corrections requests for mailing a different version of the questionnaire, and was done without realizing that the increase in response rate, the original reason for deciding to use a preletter, would have been sacrificed. Another example was a proposed decision by a budget official to reduce the cost of a preletter by changing it at the last minute to a postcard which would have made it appear nearly the same as a thank you/reminder postcard, thereby diminishing its effectiveness, as discussed in Chapter 4.

Still another proposal was to cut costs by eliminating a replacement questionnaire with a dated cover letter explaining why people were being contacted again, and instead increasing the print run of the original questionnaire mailout package including cover letter, with overprinting on the envelope stating, "Second Notice—Your Response is Overdue." Although this procedure might encourage response to a billing in order to avoid interest charges, from the standpoint of getting response to a voluntary survey, it is likely to invoke anger and therefore social costs, as described in Chapter 1. These examples illustrated how easily response rate objectives can be sacrificed, without anyone involved in the final decision-making group realizing it.

Participation in the design of many government surveys leads me to three conclusions about resolving design disagreements. First, stakeholders and participants in the design and implementation process each have legitimate interests that need to be considered, and disagreements among these interests are inevitable. Second, it is highly undesirable to design one part of a survey, for example, a perfect questionnaire from the perspective of the respondent or the least expensive mailout procedure, without taking into account other aspects of design and implementation. Third, whether one is able to make it through a design process with good survey response procedures intact depends greatly upon the extent to which such goals are continually and effectively discussed.

Other Issues

The difficulty of designing and keeping in place effective response-inducing procedures stems from more than the fact that so many groups and individuals are involved in making survey decisions. It also stems from an unfortunate tendency for survey procedures to be seen simply as communication issues associated with accomplishing other agency objectives. It should come as no surprise that important parts of cover letters and mailing procedures are often decided spontaneously, without taking other parts into account. I once encountered, for example, an agency correspondence management office that routinely removed all dates from cover letters that were submitted for approval. This was done as a matter of policy because of the uncertainty that existed for certain past surveys regarding exact mailing dates.

I also recall observing a simple, half-page preletter get changed into a three-page discussion of confidentiality rights of the respondent, how the data would be used, and other unnecessary detail as it passed through several offices for approval. Such material may be essential information to convey to respondents, but should not be included in a preletter. In this case, its effect would have been to raise anxiety about divulging personal information on a questionnaire that asked for information that most people would probably not see as important to keep confidential. Having anxieties raised prematurely, without there being any way of knowing what was actually in the questionnaire, raises rather than lowers perceptions of social cost.

It should not be surprising that once a continuing government survey is developed and implemented once or twice, it may become enormously resistant to change in all of its aspects, from the content and look of the questionnaire to the content of cover letters. Agreements and compromises have often been reached among stakeholders and agency divisions so that it becomes difficult to gain support for changes that might improve response. Cover letters and questionnaires most likely to get quick approval are those used in previous surveys because they carry the legitimacy of having survived prior review. In some cases, question wordings and questionnaire designs have persisted long past their demonstrated usefulness because of the legitimate concern that small changes in design would be detrimental to the measurement of change. A small example is the use of a question about residential tenure status that includes the choice "payment of cash rent," which some people interpret as paying in cash as opposed to a check, rather than simply paying money, as it was originally conceived. In addition, introducing the possibility of change in one question might encourage consideration of other changes. Questions that have outlived their proven validity as measures of concepts have sometimes been removed from a list of possible experiments because stakeholders have been unwilling to consider a change in question wording.

The design of government surveys presents an ironic set of challenges. For a first-time survey it may become extremely difficult to keep design factors from being arbitrarily changed, with the result that response or measurement suffers. However, once a survey is in place, making needed changes for any reason may become enormously difficult. Consequently, the tailored design of government surveys, under which a system of mutually supportive procedures and techniques are developed together, is often far more difficult to accomplish than for other types of surveys.

The reasons that it is often difficult to develop and hold in place good questionnaire design and survey implementation procedures that will minimize measurement and nonresponse error are many. One reason is simply the large scale of government, which results in many people with diverse interests and knowledge being involved in the design of those surveys. The hierarchical organization of government that makes possible integrated decision-making also makes it difficult to hold together survey designs as they pass from the designers up to high-level managers who often lack survey methodology knowledge and skills and who seek compromises among competing interests (Dillman, 1995b). A second reason is that traditionally survey design has been the province of the discipline of statistics, which placed emphasis on sampling and coverage errors as well as adjustment and imputation. In contrast, the knowledge needed for reducing measurement and nonresponse errors is likely to come from psychology, sociology, and human factor sciences. These skill requirements are just now emerging in the personnel ranks of government (Dillman, in press).

THE ADVANTAGES OF GOVERNMENT SPONSORSHIP

Government surveys also present unique opportunities for achieving quality survey data that nongovernmental surveys do not generally have. The same processes that keep government surveys, and in particular those that collect time series data, from being changed on the basis of one or two people's sudden inspiration or opinion also keeps them from being continually changed in ways that would make it difficult to maintain continuity in measurements over time.

The fact of government sponsorship helps improve survey response. Heberlein and Baumgartner (1978) first provided evidence that government-sponsored self-administered surveys tend to achieve higher response rates than other surveys. A possible explanation of this phenomenon offered by Cialdini (1984) and Groves et al. (1992) is an "appeal to authority" as a potentially effective means for improving response. In the United States, response to certain self-administered surveys such as the Decennial Census is required by law. Utilization of this information in the formulation of appeals has been shown to improve response rates significantly (Dillman, Singer, Clark, and Treat, 1996).

In addition, some branches of government, such as the Social Security Administration, Health Insurance Finance Administration, USDA, and Internal Revenue Service, have access to name and address files for their surveys that assure high quality coverage. The U.S. Bureau of the Census has address files obtained in the Decennial Census, which make it possible for them to conduct surveys that other agencies and organizations outside of government cannot accomplish, except perhaps by a very expensive screening process to identify potential respondents. Federal law (Title 13) protects the confidentiality of such files so that they cannot be provided to any other government agency or an outside contractor; surveys that rely on these address sources must be conducted by the Census Bureau itself.

The division of labor in government agencies that conduct surveys, which makes agreement on procedures difficult to obtain, also promotes specialization that allows equipment and procedures to be used which most other organizations, and particularly small ones, cannot obtain. Examples include questionnaire construction procedures and printing equipment, which if purchased for one survey would be prohibitively expensive, but which are not expensive when the cost can be distributed over many surveys. Although printing government surveys in multiple colors has often required special permission, the large scale of many government surveys make it possible to use multiple colors without large increases in per/questionnaire cost. Use of optical scanning and imaging equipment in conjunction with the printing of questionnaires that use colored background fields with white spaces for answers was accomplished in the federal government before being used by most others. Thus, the same largeness that makes quality design decisions difficult also facilitates the acquisition of specialized resources for design possibilities that many other surveyors do not have available.

RESEARCH FACTORS THAT INFLUENCE RESPONSE TO GOVERNMENT SURVEYS

An illustration of both the challenges and potential for quality survey design by the federal government follows. It includes a revealing set of experiments conducted on the largest self-administered survey in the world, the U.S. Decennial Census. Together, these experiments may represent the most comprehensive set of response rate experiments ever conducted on a self-administered survey. They reveal the way that the addition of certain features adds increments of response on top of the effects of other procedures, making it clear that the use of multiple techniques, rather than a single feature of survey design, is critical to achieving high response rates. They also reveal how many other potential design features have a minimal or even adverse effect on response rates.

A Case Study: The Influence of 16 Factors on Response Rates to the U.S. Decennial Census

The United States Decennial Census, conducted every 10 years since 1790, currently uses a mail survey to collect data from as many household addresses as possible, before sending enumerators to collect information from the remainder. In 1990, when about 100,000,000 households had to be counted, the mail-back response rate was only 65% compared with 75% in 1980, when a similar procedure had been used. This decline required spending an additional $120 million to send enumerators to each nonresponding address in order to complete the census. The 1990 Census used a large, one-page form that was mailed once by third-class (bulk rate) mail to each household. It was sent with separate instructions plus a motivational brochure and a postage-free return envelope. A bulk rate, box-holder postcard addressed only to "postal patron" was delivered about 10 days later. It was designed as an impersonal reminder with the central message that there was still time to respond.

Because of the lower than desired mail-back response rates, a massive research program was undertaken to determine whether and how response rates might be improved. From 1991 to 1996, six national studies which included 45 experimental panels, tested the influence of at least 16 separate factors on survey response rates (Dillman, Clark, and Treat, 1994; Dillman, Singer, Clark, and Treat, 1996; Scott and Barrett, 1996; Leslie, 1997.) The fact that quite similar sets of questions were included in all of the experiments and the experiments were interconnected, with panels from earlier experiments often serving as controls for later experiments, makes these studies a unique set of information about the contributors to response in government surveys. Not only did the experiments allow testing of many design factors, but they also allowed quantitative estimates to be made of individual as well as combined impacts on response.

The taking of the Decennial Census in the United States is accompanied by considerable ceremony and media attention. All households are asked to report who lives in their household and certain of their characteristics (e.g., age, sex, and minority status) as of April lst. A massive information campaign and extensive media coverage in virtually every community creates a "census climate" which contributes a significant, but unknown, amount to the mail-back response rate. All test results described here were obtained in noncensus years, when response rates using comparable methods are much lower. For example, a 1986 test which sent a replacement questionnaire achieved a response rate of only 50%. In the 1990 Census, when 65% responded, only one census form was sent to each household.

Decisions on what factors should be tested reflected several considerations in addition to what past research would suggest as methods for improving response. One was simply pragmatics; personalization of correspondence is not realistic in a survey of millions, or in the case of the 2000 Census, some 110,000,000 households. Indeed, census questionnaires must be sent to addresses only and cannot include the name of persons who might live there. Replacement questionnaires, one of the most powerful techniques incorporated in the original TDM, might not be possible in a real census because of the enormous challenge of deleting millions of households from the mailing list in only a week or two and sending out replacements. Although experimentation was done on this technique, it was done in the context of attempting to front-load the implementation procedures to achieve higher response from the initial questionnaire. Financial incentives seemed culturally inappropriate and enormously costly. In addition, processing considerations such as the need to facilitate optical scanning of responses was essential, because of the requirement that final counts for the census, which starts in mid-March, must be reported by the end of that calendar year. Political considerations were also important, with perceptions of political leaders and advisory groups as to the reasons for lower response rates in 1990 being important and sometimes deciding factors in what methods should be tested. Finally, any procedures selected for use needed to be cost effective, improving response at less cost than would be required for in-person enumeration. Together these considerations resulted in decisions to test a variety of factors in pursuit of a tailored system that would improve response. The results of this research are detailed in the paragraphs that follow.

Five Manipulatable Factors That Improved Response

Respondent-friendly design. The 1990 form, shown in Chapter 3, Figure 3.10, required respondents to match people whose names were listed at the top of each column with questions listed at the left of the page. This row/column technique was found in focus groups to be difficult for some people to understand and follow (Dillman, Reynolds, and Rockwood, 1991). The fundamental layout was changed so that each person had an individual space, labeled Person 1, Person 2, etc. where that person's information was to be provided. Many of the graphical techniques described in

Figure 9.3 Example of the 1990 Census long format and a respondent-friendly design which improved response rates.

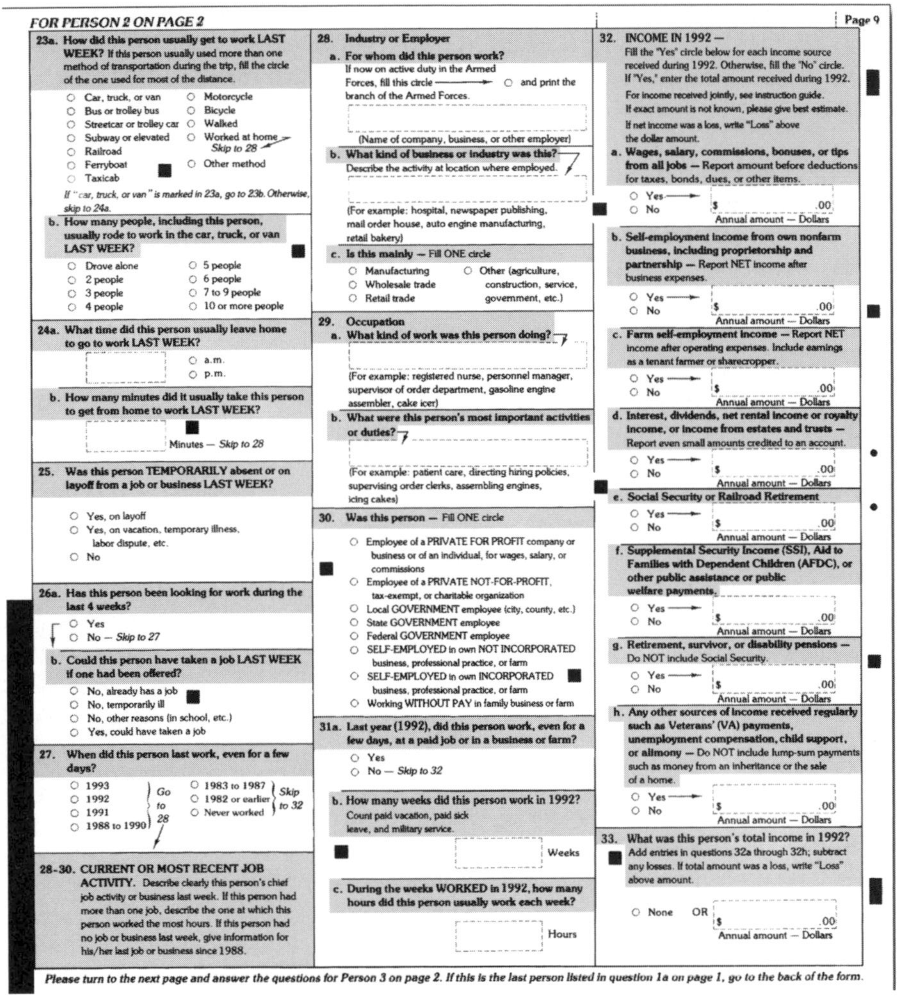

FOR PERSON 2 ON PAGE 2

Page 9

23a. How did this person usually get to work LAST WEEK? If this person usually used more than one method of transportation during the trip, fill the circle of the one used for most of the distance.
- ○ Car, truck, or van
- ○ Bus or trolley bus
- ○ Streetcar or trolley car
- ○ Subway or elevated
- ○ Railroad
- ○ Ferryboat
- ○ Taxicab
- ○ Motorcycle
- ○ Bicycle
- ○ Walked
- ○ Worked at home — *Skip to 28*
- ○ Other method

If "car, truck, or van" is marked in 23a, go to 23b. Otherwise, skip to 24a.

b. How many people, including this person, usually rode to work in the car, truck, or van LAST WEEK?
- ○ Drove alone
- ○ 2 people
- ○ 3 people
- ○ 4 people
- ○ 5 people
- ○ 6 people
- ○ 7 to 9 people
- ○ 10 or more people

24a. What time did this person usually leave home to go to work LAST WEEK?
- ○ a.m.
- ○ p.m.

b. How many minutes did it usually take this person to get from home to work LAST WEEK?

Minutes — *Skip to 28*

25. Was this person TEMPORARILY absent or on layoff from a job or business LAST WEEK?
- ○ Yes, on layoff
- ○ Yes, on vacation, temporary illness, labor dispute, etc.
- ○ No

26a. Has this person been looking for work during the last 4 weeks?
- ○ Yes
- ○ No — *Skip to 27*

b. Could this person have taken a job LAST WEEK if one had been offered?
- ○ No, already has a job
- ○ No, temporarily ill
- ○ No, other reasons (in school, etc.)
- ○ Yes, could have taken a job

27. When did this person last work, even for a few days?
- ○ 1993
- ○ 1992
- ○ 1991
- ○ 1988 to 1990 — *Go to 28*
- ○ 1983 to 1987
- ○ 1982 or earlier
- ○ Never worked — *Skip to 32*

28-30. CURRENT OR MOST RECENT JOB ACTIVITY. Describe clearly this person's chief job activity or business last week. If this person had more than one job, describe the one at which this person worked the most hours. If this person had no job or business last week, give information for his/her last job or business since 1988.

28. Industry or Employer

a. For whom did this person work? If now on active duty in the Armed Forces, fill this circle → ○ and print the branch of the Armed Forces.

(Name of company, business, or other employer)

b. What kind of business or industry was this? Describe the activity at location where employed.

(For example: hospital, newspaper publishing, mail order house, auto engine manufacturing, retail bakery)

c. Is this mainly — Fill ONE circle
- ○ Manufacturing
- ○ Wholesale trade
- ○ Retail trade
- ○ Other (agriculture, construction, service, government, etc.)

29. Occupation

a. What kind of work was this person doing?

(For example: registered nurse, personnel manager, supervisor of order department, gasoline engine assembler, cake icer)

b. What were this person's most important activities or duties?

(For example: patient care, directing hiring policies, supervising order clerks, assembling engines, icing cakes)

30. Was this person — Fill ONE circle
- ○ Employee of a PRIVATE FOR PROFIT company or business or of an individual, for wages, salary, or commissions
- ○ Employee of a PRIVATE NOT-FOR-PROFIT, tax-exempt, or charitable organization
- ○ Local GOVERNMENT employee (city, county, etc.)
- ○ State GOVERNMENT employee
- ○ Federal GOVERNMENT employee
- ○ SELF-EMPLOYED in own NOT INCORPORATED business, professional practice, or farm
- ○ SELF-EMPLOYED in own INCORPORATED business, professional practice, or farm
- ○ Working WITHOUT PAY in family business or farm

31a. Last year (1992), did this person work, even for a few days, at a paid job or in a business or farm?
- ○ Yes
- ○ No — *Skip to 32*

b. How many weeks did this person work in 1992? Count paid vacation, paid sick leave, and military service.

Weeks

c. During the weeks WORKED in 1992, how many hours did this person usually work each week?

Hours

32. INCOME IN 1992 — Fill the "Yes" circle below for each income source received during 1992. Otherwise, fill the "No" circle. If "Yes," enter the total amount received during 1992. For income received jointly, see instruction guide. If exact amount is not known, please give best estimate. If net income was a loss, write "Loss" above the dollar amount.

a. Wages, salary, commissions, bonuses, or tips from all jobs — Report amount before deductions for taxes, bonds, dues, or other items.
- ○ Yes → $ .00 Annual amount — Dollars
- ○ No

b. Self-employment income from own nonfarm business, including proprietorship and partnership — Report NET income after business expenses.
- ○ Yes → $ .00 Annual amount — Dollars
- ○ No

c. Farm self-employment income — Report NET income after operating expenses. Include earnings as a tenant farmer or sharecropper.
- ○ Yes → $ .00 Annual amount — Dollars
- ○ No

d. Interest, dividends, net rental income or royalty income, or income from estates and trusts — Report even small amounts credited to an account.
- ○ Yes → $ .00 Annual amount — Dollars
- ○ No

e. Social Security or Railroad Retirement
- ○ Yes → $ .00 Annual amount — Dollars
- ○ No

f. Supplemental Security Income (SSI), Aid to Families with Dependent Children (AFDC), or other public assistance or public welfare payments.
- ○ Yes → $ .00 Annual amount — Dollars
- ○ No

g. Retirement, survivor, or disability pensions — Do NOT include Social Security.
- ○ Yes → $ .00 Annual amount — Dollars
- ○ No

h. Any other sources of income received regularly such as Veterans' (VA) payments, unemployment compensation, child support, or alimony — Do NOT include lump-sum payments such as money from an inheritance or the sale of a home.
- ○ Yes → $ .00 Annual amount — Dollars
- ○ No

33. What was this person's total income in 1992? Add entries in questions 32a through 32h; subtract any losses. If total amount was a loss, write "Loss" above amount.
- ○ None OR $ .00 Annual amount — Dollars

Please turn to the next page and answer the questions for Person 3 on page 2. If this is the last person listed in question 1a on page 1, go to the back of the form.

(Continued)

Chapter 3—colored background fields with white answer spaces, prominent question numbers, and bright (full-color) labels were used to guide people through the questionnaire form. Use of respondent-friendly design was found to improve response rates nearly four percentage points when used on the short census form in an eight-page booklet. For the long-form, respondent-friendly design also improved response four percentage points, despite being eight pages longer than the 1990 form against which it was tested (Dillman, Clark, and Treat, 1994). Thus, respondent-friendly design was shown to have a significant positive influence on response regardless of form length. An example of the census long-form format used in 1990 and the respondent-friendly revision designed for this test is shown in Figure 9.3.

Figure 9.3 (Continued)

Last page for PERSON 1

24a. Has this person been looking for work during the last 4 weeks?

☐ Yes
☐ No – *Skip to 25*

b. Could this person have taken a job LAST WEEK if one had been offered?

☐ No, already has a job
☐ No, temporarily ill
☐ No, other reasons (in school, etc.)
☐ Yes, could have taken a job

25. When did this person last work, even for a few days?

☐ 1993
☐ 1992
☐ 1991
☐ 1988 to 1990
☐ 1983 to 1987
☐ 1982 or earlier } *Skip to 30*
☐ Never worked

26-28. CURRENT OR MOST RECENT JOB ACTIVITY. Describe clearly this person's chief job activity or business last week. If this person had more than one job, describe the one at which this person worked the most hours. If this person had no job or business last week, give information for his/her last job or business since 1988.

26. Industry or Employer

a. For whom did this person work?

(Name of company, business, branch of Armed Forces, or other employer)

b. What kind of business or industry was this?

Describe the activity at location where employed.

(For example: Hospital, newspaper publishing, mail order house, auto engine manufacturing, retail bakery)

c. Is this mainly – Mark (X) ONE box

☐ Manufacturing
☐ Wholesale trade
☐ Retail trade
☐ Other (agriculture, construction, service, government, etc.)

27. Occupation

a. What kind of work was this person doing?

(For example: Registered nurse, personnel manager, supervisor of order department, gasoline engine assembler, cake icer)

27b. What were this person's most important activities or duties?

(For example: Patient care, directing hiring policies, supervising order clerks, assembling engines, icing cakes)

28. Was this person – Mark (X) ONE box

☐ Employee of a PRIVATE FOR PROFIT company or business or of an individual, for wages, salary, or commissions
☐ Employee of a PRIVATE NOT-FOR-PROFIT, tax-exempt, or charitable organization
☐ Local GOVERNMENT employee (city, county, etc.)
☐ State GOVERNMENT employee
☐ Federal GOVERNMENT employee
☐ SELF-EMPLOYED in own NOT INCORPORATED business, professional practice, or farm
☐ SELF-EMPLOYED in own INCORPORATED business, professional practice, or farm
☐ Working WITHOUT PAY in family business or farm

29a. Last year (1992), did this person work, even for a few days, at a paid job or in a business or farm?

☐ Yes
☐ No – *Skip to 30*

b. How many weeks did this person work in 1992? Count paid vacation, paid sick leave, and military service.

Weeks

c. During the weeks WORKED in 1992, how many hours did this person usually work each week?

Hours

30. INCOME IN 1992 –

Mark (X) the "Yes" box below for each income source received during 1992. Otherwise, fill the "No" box. If "Yes," enter the total amount received during 1992.

If exact amount is not known, please give best estimate. If net income was a loss, write "Loss" above the dollar amount.

a. Did this person receive any wages, salary, commissions, bonuses, or tips? Report amount from all jobs before deductions for taxes, bonds, dues, or other items.

☐ Yes → $ .00
☐ No
Annual amount – Dollars

b. Did this person receive any self-employment income from own nonfarm business, including proprietorship and partnership? Report NET income after business expenses.

☐ Yes → $ .00
☐ No
Annual amount – Dollars

c. Did this person receive any farm self-employment income? Report NET income after operating expenses. Include earnings as a tenant farmer or sharecropper.

☐ Yes → $ .00
☐ No
Annual amount – Dollars

d. Did this person receive any interest, dividends, net rental income or royalty income, or income from estates and trusts? Report even small amounts credited to an account.

☐ Yes → $ .00
☐ No
Annual amount – Dollars

e. Did this person receive any Social Security or Railroad Retirement?

☐ Yes → $ .00
☐ No
Annual amount – Dollars

f. Did this person receive any Supplemental Security Income (SSI), Aid to Families with Dependent Children (AFDC), or other public assistance or public welfare payments?

☐ Yes → $ .00
☐ No
Annual amount – Dollars

g. Did this person receive any retirement, survivor, or disability pensions? Do NOT include Social Security.

☐ Yes → $ .00
☐ No
Annual amount – Dollars

h. Did this person receive any other sources of income regularly such as Veteran's (VA) payments, unemployment compensation, child support or alimony? Do NOT include lump-sum payments such as money from an inheritance or the sale of a home.

☐ Yes → $ .00
☐ No
Annual amount – Dollars

31. What was this person's total income in 1992? Add entries in questions 30a through 30h; subtract any losses. If total amount was a loss, write "Loss" above amount.

☐ None OR $ .00
Annual amount – Dollars

Page 6

If there are NO MORE PERSONS in this household please skip to housing questions on page 25.

FORM DD-2B (5-5-93)

Example from a 1993 National Census test, conducted by U.S. Bureau of the Census.

Figure 9.4 Preletter tested for use in the U.S. Decennial Census.

UNITED STATES DEPARTMENT OF COMMERCE
Bureau of the Census
Washington, DC 20233-0001
OFFICE OF THE DIRECTOR

March 23, 1992

450790126467559000 1105

To: Resident(s) at:
705 S.W. Stanton Boulevard
Censustown, Washington 99164-4014

Within the next few days you will receive a request to complete a brief census form. We will mail it to you as part of our effort to develop the best possible procedures for counting the U.S. population.

The form is important. We are sending it to your address rather than to a specific person, and we ask that the form be filled out for everyone living at this address on April 1, 1992.

The census provides information necessary for each community to get its fair share of money for schools, health assistance, parks, services for the elderly, and much more.

We would greatly appreciate your taking the few minutes necessary to complete and return your census form.

Thank you in advance for your help.

Sincerely,

Barbara Everitt Bryant

Barbara Everitt Bryant
Director
Bureau of the Census

DA-5(L)

Example from 1992 Test Census, conducted by U.S. Bureau of the Census.

The new form eliminated a row/column format for questions two to seven, shown in Figure 3.10 of Chapter 3. Those and other long-form questions were incorporated into a seven-person format, shown on the second page of Figure 9.3.

Prenotice letter. The effect of sending a prenotice, found important for improving response rates in previous research, was also tested. This letter was brief, written on Office of the Director stationery, included the mailing date and was sent by first-class mail. It was mailed in a windowed envelope to avoid the need to merge letters with envelopes, each of which would have needed to be addressed. The letter announced that a census form would be sent to each household in the next few days, and explained the reasons for the census (Figure 9.4). The letter also noted that it would be sent to the address only, and not to individual persons, a procedural necessity for the census. This message was aimed at overcoming the image of junk mail that is associated with mail typically sent to "Residents at this address." This prenotice independently improved response by six percentage points (Dillman, Clark, and Sinclair, 1995).

Postcard thank you/reminder. A thank-you note from the Census Director for returning the census, and a reminder to those who had not yet returned their form, was sent three to four days after the questionnaire, again by first-class mail (Figure 9.5). It was designed to include the U.S. Department of Commerce seal and the Census Director's signature. It was found to improve response rates by eight percentage points, slightly more than the prenotice when used alone. More importantly, the joint use of the prenotice letter and postcard thank-you improved response by 12.7 percent, showing that their influences were for the most part additive. Neither could be substituted for the other (Dillman, Clark, and Sinclair, 1995).

Replacement questionnaire. Although the challenges of sending a replacement questionnaire to all nonrespondents two to three weeks after the initial mailing were known to be formidable, the effects of a replacement questionnaire were tested. It was reasoned that it might be useable in certain areas of the United States if it was found to improve response significantly. Approximately 3 ½ weeks after the first questionnaire was sent, a replacement census form was mailed to all households that had not yet returned it, with a dated cover letter indicating that the response from that household had not yet been received. Multiple tests of the replacement questionnaire demonstrated that response improved from 6–12 percentage points, with all but one test result being 10% or above (Dillman, Clark, and Treat, 1994).

Prominent disclosure that response is mandatory. Previous research on census business surveys had found that response improved significantly when recipients were informed on the envelope that response was mandatory (Tulp et al., 1991) and theoretical work provided reasons for its expected effectiveness (Cialdini, 1984). Mailout envelopes were stamped with a large rectangle including the words: Your Response is Required By Law: U.S. Census Form Enclosed. This feature was tested with and without an enclosure that explained why response was required by law and the penalties for not responding. Response rates were improved by nine to eleven percentage points beyond those obtained when other known response stimuli (respondent-friendly design, prenotice, thank you/reminder, and replacement questionnaire) were enclosed (Dillman, Singer, Clark, and Treat, 1996). Together this combination of factors improved response to 76–78% in a noncensus year, well above the 65% obtained in the 1990 Census, when the census climate undoubtedly also had a response-inducing effect.

Real stamp on return envelope. Business reply envelopes are typically used for the return of government questionnaires. The effects of a real stamp on the return envelope, found to consistently improve response in previous research outside the federal government, were tested in combination with the prenotice and postcard reminder. When used alone, the stamp improved response by 2.6 percentage points, which was within the two to four percentage point range expected. Though not statistically significant, it was a large enough difference to be at the cusp of statistical significance. That and the concern with the potential public image of government

Figure 9.5 Postcard thank you/reminder tested for use in the U.S. Decennial Census.

Bureau of the Census
Washington, DC 20233-0001
DE-9 (5-93)

OFFICIAL BUSINESS
Penalty for Private Use, $300

FIRST-CLASS MAIL
POSTAGE & FEES PAID
Bureau of the Census
Permit No. G-58

45079012646755900001105

To: Resident(s) at:
705 S.W. Stanton Boulevard
Censustown, Washington 99164-4014

UNITED STATES DEPARTMENT OF COMMERCE
Bureau of the Census
Washington, DC 20233-0001
OFFICE OF THE DIRECTOR

October 21, 1993

A few days ago you should have received a request from me to complete a brief U.S. census form. It was sent to your address as part of our effort to develop the most accurate methods possible for counting the people living in the United States AND your community.

If you have already returned it, please accept my sincere thanks. If you have not yet completed and returned your form, please do so as soon as possible.

Taking an accurate census is important for all communities throughout the United States to get their fair share of government funding, and your help is important to its success.

Sincerely,

Harry A. Scarr
Acting Director
Bureau of the Census

Example from 1993 Test Census, conducted by U.S. Bureau of the Census.

Figure 9.6 Effects of different lengths of census questionnaires on response rates.

	Response Rates	Effect of Greater Length
***Experiment 1** (Dillman, Sinclair, and Clark, 1993)*		
Large postcard, one side (2 questions/person)	70.9%	
One legal size sheet, both sides (5 short questions/person)	71.4	+0.5
8-page booklet (two sheets folded) (7 questions/person)	66.8	-4.6
***Experiment 2** (Dillman, Singer, Clark, and Treat, 1996)*		
8-page booklet (same as Experiment 1)	67.2%	
28-page booklet, long-form	55.9	-11.3
***Experiment 3** (Leslie, 1996)*		
4-page booklet (one sheet folded, 5 person spaces)	75.6%	
12-page booklet (three sheets folded, 7 person spaces)	75.0	-0.6
28-page booklet (seven sheets folded, 7 person spaces)	67.2	-7.8
44-page booklet (11 sheets folded, 7 person spaces)	62.2	-5.0

waste (from unused stamps) resulted in this technique being dropped from further consideration (Dillman, Clark, and Sinclair, 1995).

The influence of questionnaire length. The perception that greater length significantly depresses response rates led to the examination of the relationship between several questionnaire lengths and responses in three different experiments, results that are reported in Figure 9.6. The results are revealing in several ways. First, there is no doubt that in general, greater length decreases response rates. However, shortening an already brief questionnaire may not improve response. For example, in Experiment 1 there was no statistical difference between a large postcard with two questions and a legal-size questionnaire printed on both sides of the paper that contained five questions (Dillman, Sinclair, and Clark, 1993). A possible explanation for this lack of difference is that the questionnaire became so short that it lost some meaning to potential respondents. The decrease in response burden from asking fewer questions may have been countered by being asked so few questions as to not make sense to respondents as a census questionnaire.

In addition, Experiment 3 resulted in four- and 12-page booklets obtaining virtually the same response rates (75.6% and 75.0%). However, the greater length was mostly due to asking for information about seven instead of five people (which added no response burden to most households, because very few households have more than five people residing there) and the inclusion of four questions about the housing in which they lived. The questions were also presented in a more spacious design.

Finally, the mandatory appeal in Experiment 3 resulted in a difference of only 13 percentage points between the four- and 44-page booklets, whereas in Experiment 2, which did not use a mandatory appeal, there was a difference of 11 percentage points between booklets of eight and 28 pages.

We conclude from these experiments on length that the relationship between length and response rate is likely to decrease when one uses more response-inducing techniques. We also conclude that there is more to length that a simple count of pages, and that the frequent tendency of questionnaire designers to cram more questions into fewer pages to make a questionnaire shorter is *not* likely to accomplish its intended purpose.

Official government versus private sector marketing appeal. Following the Heberlein and Baumgartner (1978) and Cialdini (1984) arguments that association with government would produce higher response rates, all of the preceding tests were conducted using stationery, envelopes, and formatting that conveyed a clear identification with the federal government. In 1995, an experiment was conducted to see if two marketing appeals, modeled after private sector mail solicitation appeals that made full use of color and fancier designs, might improve response rates further (Leslie, 1997). They were compared with the plainer appeals that had been designed to convey an official government image.

Marketing Appeal A (Figure 9.7) consisted of a vertically oriented but narrow (10½″ × 5½″) eight-page book, which provided one person space per page. It was mailed in a bright gold-fronted envelope with the words "Your response is required by law" in a reverse print bright blue circle. On the white backside of the envelope was another bright blue circle with the words, "Count Me In." The latter circle was repeated on the similarly bright gold cover of the questionnaire, which included icons that explained the purposes of the census. Marketing Appeal B (Figure 9.8) was printed as a standard 8½″ × 11″ booklet in bright yellow tones. The front of the envelope was white with the bright gold of the questionnaire showing through the address opening, but the back (not shown in Figure 9.8) was in a bright gold with an artistic representation of a government building on the reverse side. The mandatory response message was printed on the back of the envelope in reverse print on a strip to be torn open as a means of opening the envelope.

The theory underlying the development of these questionnaires was associated with direct mail marketing appeals, with major emphasis placed on getting the envelope opened. Yellow and gold were chosen because of the contrast with the red and blue colors that seemed to be prevalent in other mass mailings of the time, and both were designed to be warm and friendly.

Response rates for the marketing appeal forms were compared to those for a green form that was based on previous experimental work. This control form was mailed in a white government envelope containing the mandatory disclosure notice (Figure 9.9). The design goal was to make the form look like it was being mailed from the federal government. It used design procedures found effective in several previous tests.

Results of the experiment revealed that these attempts to follow a marketing-oriented appeal consistent with that used in private sector mail promotional campaigns actually decreased response by five percentage points for the vertically designed form, and nine percentage points for the booklet (Leslie, 1996, 1997). The reasons for these decreases are not clear, but they are likely the result of multiple factors ranging from de-emphasizing the mandatory message on the envelope by placing it in the circle on one envelope and in reverse print on the back of the other to the use of bright colors. Most striking, perhaps, is the fact that the marketing ap-

Figure 9.7 Form and mailout envelope for Marketing Appeal A, developed for test of the effects on response rate.

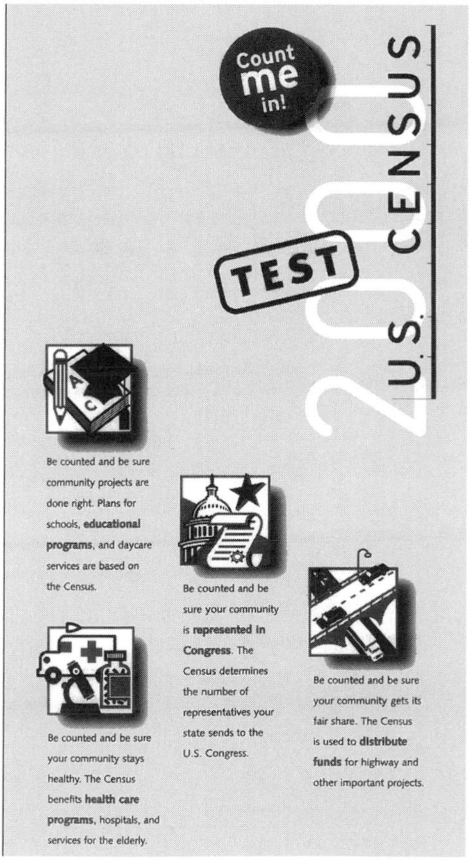

Example from 1995 National Test Census, conducted by U.S. Bureau of the Census.

Figure 9.8 Form and mailout envelope for Marketing Appeal B, developed for test of the effects on response rate.

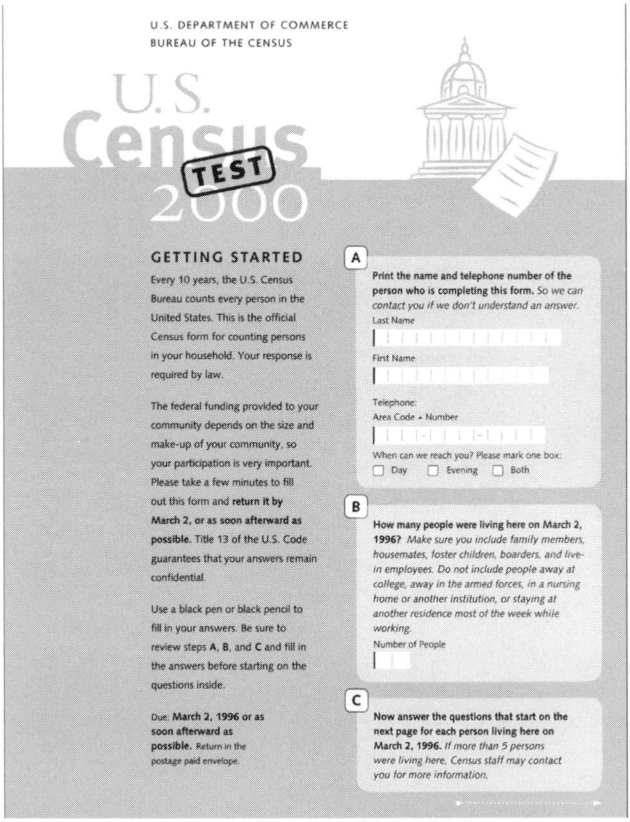

U.S. DEPARTMENT OF COMMERCE
BUREAU OF THE CENSUS

U.S. Census 2000

TEST

GETTING STARTED

Every 10 years, the U.S. Census Bureau counts every person in the United States. This is the official Census form for counting persons in your household. Your response is required by law.

The federal funding provided to your community depends on the size and make-up of your community, so your participation is very important. Please take a few minutes to fill out this form and **return it by March 2, or as soon afterward as possible.** Title 13 of the U.S. Code guarantees that your answers remain confidential.

Use a black pen or black pencil to fill in your answers. Be sure to review steps **A**, **B**, and **C** and fill in the answers before starting on the questions inside.

Due: **March 2, 1996 or as soon afterward as possible.** Return in the postage paid envelope.

A

Print the name and telephone number of the person who is completing this form. *So we can contact you if we don't understand an answer.*

Last Name

First Name

Telephone:
Area Code + Number

When can we reach you? Please mark one box:
☐ Day ☐ Evening ☐ Both

B

How many people were living here on March 2, 1996? *Make sure you include family members, housemates, foster children, boarders, and live-in employees. Do not include people away at college, away in the armed forces, in a nursing home or another institution, or staying at another residence most of the week while working.*

Number of People

C

Now answer the questions that start on the next page for each person living here on March 2, 1996. *If more than 5 persons were living here, Census staff may contact you for more information.*

Example from 1995 National Test Census, conducted by U.S. Bureau of the Census.

Figure 9.9 Official government form and mailing package, developed for test of the effects on response rate (control form).

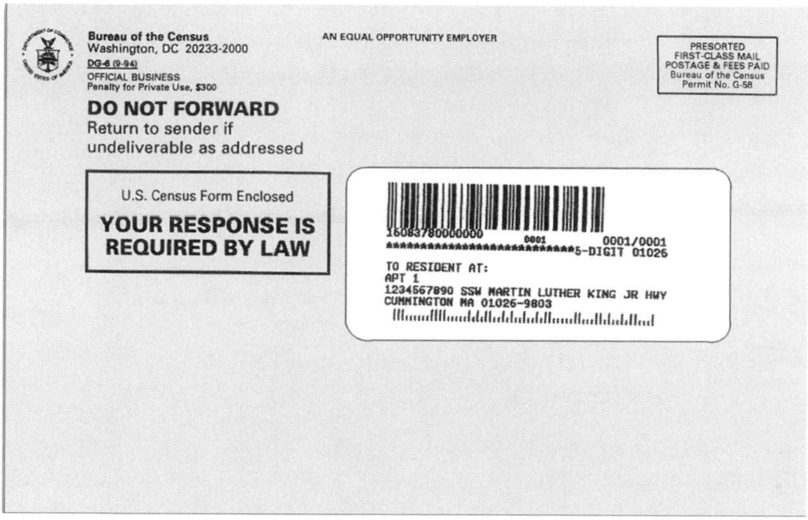
Bureau of the Census
Washington, DC 20233-2000
DG-6 (9-94)
OFFICIAL BUSINESS
Penalty for Private Use, $300

AN EQUAL OPPORTUNITY EMPLOYER

PRESORTED
FIRST-CLASS MAIL
POSTAGE & FEES PAID
Bureau of the Census
Permit No. G-58

DO NOT FORWARD
Return to sender if
undeliverable as addressed

U.S. Census Form Enclosed
YOUR RESPONSE IS REQUIRED BY LAW

1608378000000 0001 0001/0001
****************************5-DIGIT 01026
TO RESIDENT AT:
APT 1
1234567890 SSW MARTIN LUTHER KING JR HWY
CUMMINGTON MA 01026-9803

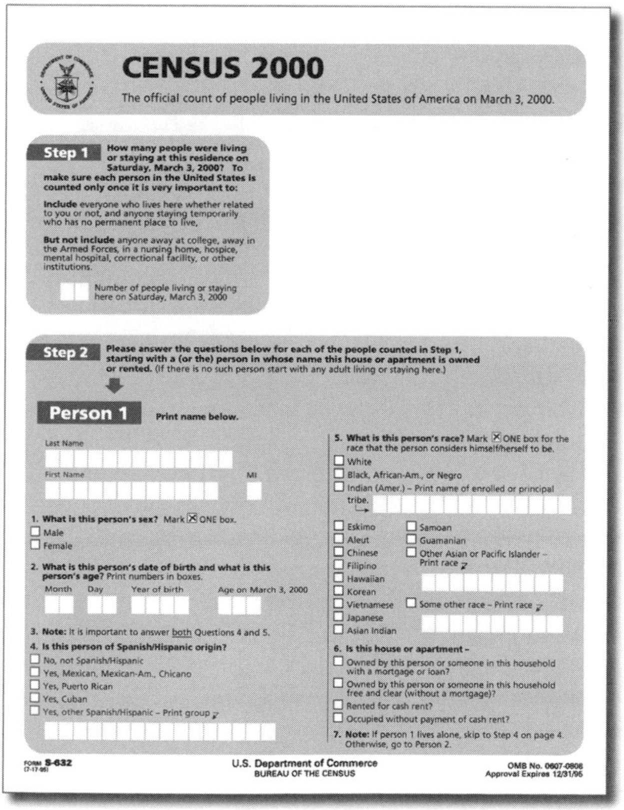
CENSUS 2000

The official count of people living in the United States of America on March 3, 2000.

Step 1 **How many people were living or staying at this residence on Saturday, March 3, 2000? To make sure each person in the United States is counted only once it is very important to:**

Include everyone who lives here whether related to you or not, and anyone staying temporarily who has no permanent place to live,

But not include anyone away at college, away in the Armed Forces, in a nursing home, hospice, mental hospital, correctional facility, or other institutions.

Number of people living or staying here on Saturday, March 3, 2000

Step 2 **Please answer the questions below for each of the people counted in Step 1, starting with a (or the) person in whose name this house or apartment is owned or rented.** (If there is no such person start with any adult living or staying here.)

Person 1 **Print name below.**

Last Name

First Name MI

1. **What is this person's sex?** Mark ☒ ONE box.
   - ☐ Male
   - ☐ Female
2. **What is this person's date of birth and what is this person's age?** Print numbers in boxes.
   Month Day Year of birth Age on March 3, 2000
3. **Note:** It is important to answer both Questions 4 and 5.
4. **Is this person of Spanish/Hispanic origin?**
   - ☐ No, not Spanish/Hispanic
   - ☐ Yes, Mexican, Mexican-Am., Chicano
   - ☐ Yes, Puerto Rican
   - ☐ Yes, Cuban
   - ☐ Yes, other Spanish/Hispanic – Print group
5. **What is this person's race?** Mark ☒ ONE box for the race that the person considers himself/herself to be.
   - ☐ White
   - ☐ Black, African-Am., or Negro
   - ☐ Indian (Amer.) – Print name of enrolled or principal tribe.
   - ☐ Eskimo
   - ☐ Aleut
   - ☐ Chinese
   - ☐ Filipino
   - ☐ Hawaiian
   - ☐ Korean
   - ☐ Vietnamese
   - ☐ Japanese
   - ☐ Asian Indian
   - ☐ Samoan
   - ☐ Guamanian
   - ☐ Other Asian or Pacific Islander – Print race
   - ☐ Some other race – Print race
6. **Is this house or apartment –**
   - ☐ Owned by this person or someone in this household with a mortgage or loan?
   - ☐ Owned by this person or someone in this household free and clear (without a mortgage)?
   - ☐ Rented for cash rent?
   - ☐ Occupied without payment of cash rent?
7. **Note:** If person 1 lives alone, skip to Step 4 on page 4. Otherwise, go to Person 2.

FORM S-632 (7-17-95)
U.S. Department of Commerce
BUREAU OF THE CENSUS
OMB No. 0607-0808
Approval Expires 12/31/95

Example from 1995 National Test Census, conducted by U.S. Bureau of the Census.

peal of the booklet format resulted in a response rate about the same as that for the 28-page form included in the test.

These results are not surprising. The findings of Heberlein and Baumgartner (1978) that government sponsorship improves mail survey response, and theoretical work of Cialdini (1984) on appeal to authority, suggest that the official government emphasis would achieve a higher response. Extensive cognitive interviewing concurrent with the national field test revealed that although many people preferred the brightness of the marketing appeals, they were substantially more likely to indicate they would respond to the more governmental-appearing appeal (Dillman, Jenkins, Martin, and DeMaio, 1996). The plainer appearance was more consistent with what they expected to receive from the government.

Other Factors That Did Not Improve Response Rates to Census Questionnaires

Prominent disclosure of benefits. Mailout envelopes were stamped with a large rectangle including the words: It Pays To Be Counted: U.S. Census Form Enclosed. This message was tested as an alternative to the mandatory message. Although extensive focus group tests of the two messages resulted in respondents for all groups recommending use of the disclosure of benefits message over the mandatory message, this message had no influence, either positive or negative, on response rates (Dillman, Singer, Clark, and Treat, 1996).

Strong (versus standard) confidentiality statement. Building on research that showed that too strong a pledge of confidentiality when asking relatively unintrusive questions (such as those asked on the census short form) is likely to depress response (Singer et al., 1992; Singer et al., 1995), two messages were tested. One included a highlighted and detailed signed message from the director indicating why and how confidentiality was protected. The standard statement provided less detail and was not highlighted or signed. Neither message had a significant effect on response (Dillman, Singer, Clark, and Treat, 1996).

Invitation to respond either by telephone or mail. In one experiment, recipients of the census form were informed that they could either call their responses in by telephone or respond by mail. Inclusion of this test was based upon research that had shown some respondents prefer one survey mode over another (Groves and Kahn, 1979). The effect of providing this alternative was to stimulate 5% of households to respond by telephone, but to decrease response for mail by the same amount. In effect, respondents were shifted from responding by a less costly method (mail) to a more expensive method (telephone), but the availability of a choice had no influence on overall response rates (Dillman, Clark, and West, 1995).

Additional letter reminder after the thank you postcard. A letter reminder was sent by first-class mail a week after the postcard reminder, but without including a replacement questionnaire. This experiment tended to confirm previous research which showed that repetition of a message from previous contacts without including a replacement questionnaire has no positive influence on response (Dillman, Clark, and West, 1995).

Color of questionnaire: Blue versus green. Color has not been revealed by past research to be an important determinant of response rates. The first four experiments were conducted with respondent-friendly designs that used blue as background color for printing all of the questions. However, the need to optically scan the completed questionnaires, and the resulting difficulty of dropping out that color in the optical reader when blue ink was used, meant that an alternative needed to be considered. Cognitive interviews tested orange, beige, and green questionnaires for respondent reactions and found no strong preference (Jenkins and Bates, 1995; Dillman and Allen, 1995). Green was selected for testing against the blue format in a national test. As expected, there was no significant difference in response rates (Scott and Barrett, 1996).

Booklet versus one-sheet formats. Booklets represent a conventional format for printing multi-page materials in the United States and were used for most experiments. Repeated cognitive evaluations found that respondents were more likely to open and complete booklets correctly. However, a one-sheet format was desirable because it avoided the necessity of taking a stapled booklet apart for optical scanning and processing, a necessity for most scanners. Use of a one-sheet format would decrease dramatically the number of separate sheets that would need to be processed in the Decennial Census. Consequently, the booklet format (two sheets stapled to form an eight-page, 8½″ × 11″ booklet) was tested against a large one-sheet format (11½″ × 25½″) with the outer panels folded inward to form a conventional 8½″ × 11″ size. There was no significant difference in response rates (Scott and Barrett, 1996).

Stapled versus unstapled booklets. Because of the need to disassemble booklet questionnaires for optical scanning, a test was made to determine whether response rates would differ depending upon whether an eight-page booklet was stapled, or the inner sheet (four pages) was inserted without being stapled. Again, no differences in response were obtained.

The effect of difficult-to-answer questions. Ordinarily, the inclusion of difficult versus easier to answer questions is not a factor that can be manipulated as a means of improving response. However, two experiments were conducted to evaluate the effect of difficult questions on response rates. One experiment tested the addition of a request for social security number, which might provide a means of ultimately decreasing information requested in the census. Inclusion of the request resulted in a 3.4 percentage point decrease in response and a high rate of item nonresponse for this question (Dillman, Sinclair, and Clark, 1993). Follow-up interviews found that objections to providing answers to this question were minor, but that many people did not know or could not find social security numbers for some members of a household (Bates, 1992).

Traditionally, the first question in the census is a request to list all members of the household according to a lengthy set of eligibility criteria. This question required an entire page in the 1990 Census. A test of asking this question, compared with a shorter one that retained the eligibility criteria and an even shorter one that simply asked how many people lived in the household, showed that the simplest version achieved a significantly higher response rate (3.6 percentage points) (Leslie, 1997).

Implications for the 2000 Census

Only five of the 16 test elements significantly improved response rates. These factors and their approximate effects were as follows: respondent-friendly design,

2–4%; prenotice letter, 5–7%; reminder postcard, 5–8%; replacement questionnaire, 6–11%; and mandatory disclosure notice, 9–11%. The ranges of effects for each element encompass the individual effects registered in three to four experimental comparisons using somewhat different questionnaires. Early experiments were done in such a manner that the first four factors mentioned above were tested as the last addition, and in each case the last factor made a significant addition to response rate. The mandatory disclosure notice was tested only after all other elements had been added. Together these elements produced a response rate of 76%, compared with 50% in the 1986 test which used a replacement questionnaire, and without which it would undoubtedly have been below 40%, for a net improvement of at least 36%.

The positive effect of government sponsorship on response is also apparent in these studies, from both the effect of the mandatory disclosure notice and the failure of a private sector oriented marketing appeal to improve response. Thus, we conclude that sponsorship by government is something to be taken advantage of rather than hidden. This finding is further confirmed by repeated sets of cognitive interviews done on a variety of questionnaire mailing packages (Dillman, Jenkins, Martin, and DeMaio, 1996; Dillman, Jackson, Pavlov, and Schaefer, 1998).

In some ways it is striking how few "new" factors that might influence response were revealed by these experiments. Three of the five factors (prenotice, reminder, and replacement questionnaire) that improved response are simply the effect of multiple contacts, a finding well established in the literature long before these studies were conducted. That leaves the effect of mandatory disclosure and respondent-friendliness as the new factors that this research has shown as design features that can be used to improve response rates.

In addition, questionnaire length has frequently been suggested as a cause of low response to the census and other surveys. The 1990 Census revealed only a five percentage point difference in response between long and short forms. The experimental data from 1995 suggest that the effect of length is significant, but not a huge determinant of response. Even 30–40 page questionnaires achieved response rates in this noncensus year that are above the 61% response rate achieved in 1990 when the census climate undoubtedly had considerable effect. In addition, stripping the questionnaire down to the barest of essentials, such as four normal sized (8½" x 11") pages, does not improve response over forms that have three times as many pages.

One disturbing result of these experiments is the finding that response rates in regions of the country where low response was achieved in 1990 can be expected to be much less than those in the remainder of the country. All of the above experiments were conducted with stratified samples, whereby approximately 89% of the population were in high response strata and the remaining 11% in low response strata. The latter strata consisted primarily of inner city locations with high proportions of minority populations. Response rates for these areas consistently average 16–20 percentage points lower for the earlier tests, and 25–26 percentage points lower for the later tests (Dillman, 1997). Significantly, the only factor that seemed to differentially improve response among these high minority areas of the country was respondent-friendly design, and this occurred only in the case of the short form (Dillman, Sinclair, and Clark, 1993). Overall, the elements found effective for improving response in high response strata were also found effective for improving response in low response strata.

The questionnaire design used in the 2000 Census has evolved beyond the field experiments summarized above. A well-tested, one-sheet design has been adopted for the census short form to facilitate optical scanning and imaging. It uses a vertical orientation of individual answer spaces, first used in one of the marketing appeal forms and extensively tested later in cognitive interviews for unfolding and refolding difficulties (Jenkins, 1997; Dillman, Jackson, Pavlov, and Schaefer, 1998). The implementation design will include the mandatory disclosure notice on the outside of the envelope, a modified preletter, and a reminder postcard. However, because of the short turn-around time allowed for mailing replacement questionnaires, this response-inducing feature will not be used. The complete outcome of this extensive test and redesign program can only be known some time after completion of our nation's 21st Decennial Census.

IMPLICATIONS FOR OTHER GOVERNMENT SURVEYS

Federal Government Surveys

The preceding extensive census experiments make it clear that there is no "magic bullet" for achieving high response to surveys sponsored by the federal government. The highest responses come from the use of multiple techniques. In addition, many of the same factors found important for nongovernmental surveys—for instance, multiple contacts and respondent-friendly design—can each be expected to contribute an important but limited amount to overall response. Also, increasing the length of a questionnaire and including difficult questions can be expected to decrease response rates.

These experiments also make clear the advantage of government sponsorship. Making a questionnaire look like it is from the government, but still appear respondent-friendly, can improve response. There appears to be little to gain from making a questionnaire appear that it is not from the government by adding the common trappings of private sector marketing appeal mailings.

The experiments also reveal that just because a government questionnaire is being sent to tens of thousands or even millions of households, it does not have to be implemented in a way that produces a poor response. High response rates are feasible with mail surveys from the federal government just as they are in most other situations. Yet, response from exclusive use of a self-administered strategy may not be high enough to meet OMB standards.

In the face of pressures to achieve high response rates, and the fact that most surveys, even in the federal government, are voluntary, I expect the use of mixed-mode government surveys to increase. When survey design is tailored in this way, it is likely that the self-administered survey will be placed first in the sequence because of the lower initial costs of data collection. An example of such a survey is one conducted in 1992 by the U.S. Bureau of the Census at the request of the National Science Foundation as a pretest for a periodic national study of college graduates (Mooney, Giesbrecht and Shettle, 1993; Shettle and Mooney, 1996). This case study is particularly useful because it illustrates the sequencing of different data collection modes in a cost-effective way and the experimental use of token financial incentives in combination with a respondent-friendly questionnaire.

Case Study: The National Survey of College Graduates

The National Science Foundation has responsibility for estimating the number of scientists and engineers in the United States. In the 1980s this was done by sampling individuals who had reported having a college degree in the 1980 Census, but that survey had produced an initial response rate in the first collection period of only 71%. The redesigned questionnaire for the 1990s was anticipated to expand from six to eight pages to as many as 20 pages, and take more than twice as long to complete, so expected response rates were a major concern. An experimental pretest was conducted in 1992 in which the questionnaire for self-identified college graduates in the 1990 Census was converted from a two-column format to a design that placed questions and answers in the same column. It also utilized many of the respondent friendly design procedures, such as colored background fields, white answer spaces, and consistency in the use of graphic symbols, as discussed in Chapter 3. A cover page with a simple graphic design was also used (Figure 9.10).

A four-contact mailout strategy was employed. The first contact was a preletter from the National Science Foundation indicating that a questionnaire would be coming from the Census Bureau (Figure 9.11). That was followed one week later by the questionnaire. In order to keep the questionnaire cover letter short, more than half of the material proposed was reformulated as "Commonly Asked Questions" and printed on the back of the cover letter (Figure 9.12). That mailing was followed one week later by a reminder letter from the Census Bureau. Each of these mailings contrasted significantly with one another in appearance because of the source (first mailing from NSF, the others from Census Bureau) and size (the questionnaire was sent as a flat mailing in a brown envelope).

One of four experimental groups received this questionnaire with a five dollar check, and a second group received it without any incentive. In addition, a 16-page and six-page screener questionnaire (which would require a follow-up to collect the main data for the study) were sent to each of two other experimental groups. Response rates after a preletter, questionnaire, thank-you postcard, and replacement questionnaire were, respectively, 73%, 63%, 69%, and 79%. Thus, the incentive increased response rates for the long questionnaire by nearly 11 percentage points. This response rate represented a five-point gain over the midsize questionnaire, but was six points less than that for the very short questionnaire. The incentive clearly brought the longest questionnaire closer to, but not to, the 80% OMB threshold. Follow-up attempts to conduct telephone interviews for the long questionnaire produced a slightly higher percentage of completed interviews for the nonincentive than for the incentive group (31% versus 28%), although the refusal rate for the non-

Figure 9.10 Cover and page 1 of questionnaire for National Survey of College Graduates (a government-sponsored survey).

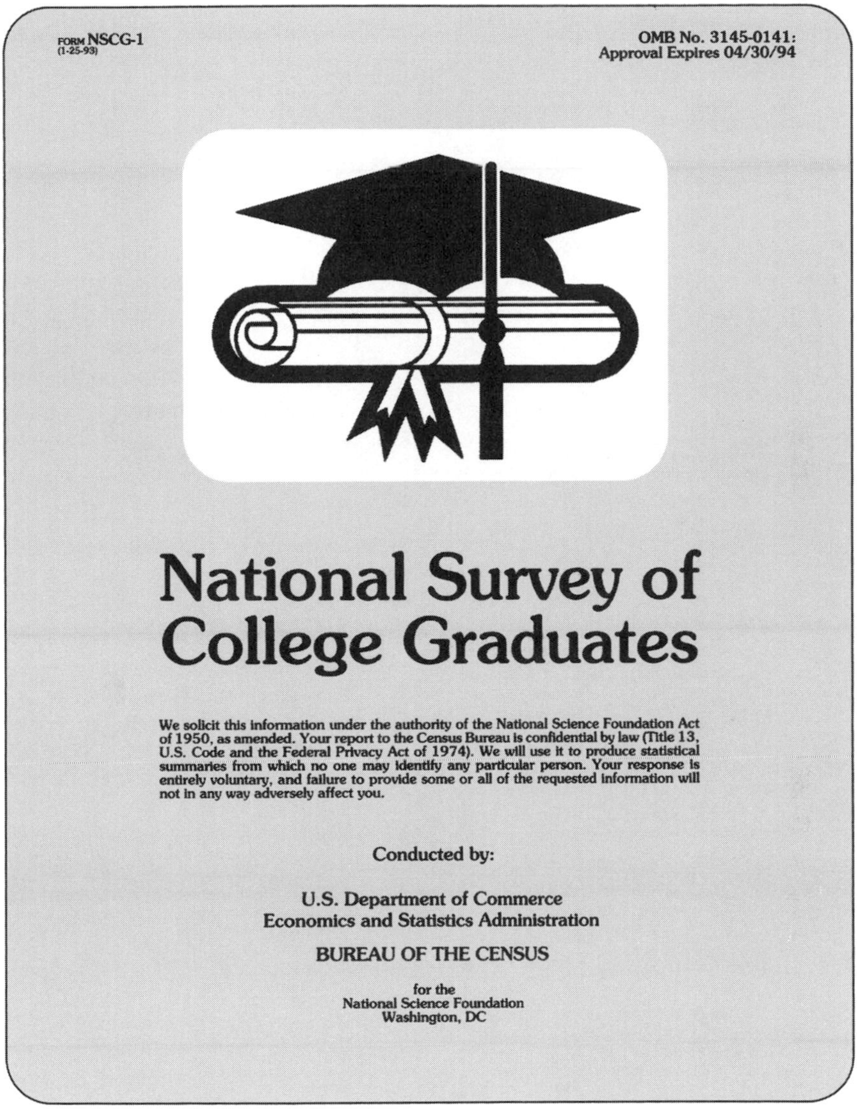

FORM NSCG-1
(1-25-93)

OMB No. 3145-0141:
Approval Expires 04/30/94

National Survey of College Graduates

We solicit this information under the authority of the National Science Foundation Act of 1950, as amended. Your report to the Census Bureau is confidential by law (Title 13, U.S. Code and the Federal Privacy Act of 1974). We will use it to produce statistical summaries from which no one may identify any particular person. Your response is entirely voluntary, and failure to provide some or all of the requested information will not in any way adversely affect you.

Conducted by:

U.S. Department of Commerce
Economics and Statistics Administration

BUREAU OF THE CENSUS

for the
National Science Foundation
Washington, DC

Example from 1992 pilot survey for National Survey of College Graduates, conducted by U.S. Bureau of the Census.

Figure 9.10 (Continued)

Page 1

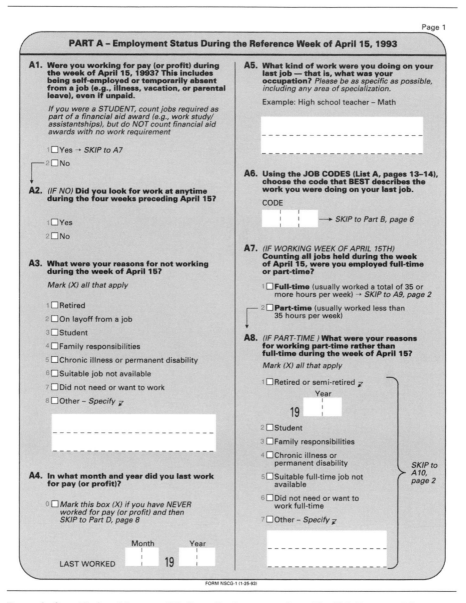

PART A – Employment Status During the Reference Week of April 15, 1993

A1. Were you working for pay (or profit) during the week of April 15, 1993? This includes being self-employed or temporarily absent from a job (e.g., illness, vacation, or parental leave), even if unpaid.

If you were a STUDENT, count jobs required as part of a financial aid award (e.g., work study/ assistantships), but do NOT count financial aid awards with no work requirement

1 ☐ Yes → *SKIP to A7*

2 ☐ No

A2. *(IF NO)* **Did you look for work at anytime during the four weeks preceding April 15?**

1 ☐ Yes

2 ☐ No

A3. What were your reasons for not working during the week of April 15?

Mark (X) all that apply

1 ☐ Retired

2 ☐ On layoff from a job

3 ☐ Student

4 ☐ Family responsibilities

5 ☐ Chronic illness or permanent disability

6 ☐ Suitable job not available

7 ☐ Did not need or want to work

8 ☐ Other – *Specify*

A4. In what month and year did you last work for pay (or profit)?

0 ☐ *Mark this box (X) if you have NEVER worked for pay (or profit) and then SKIP to Part D, page 8*

LAST WORKED Month ___ Year 19 ___

A5. What kind of work were you doing on your last job — that is, what was your occupation? *Please be as specific as possible, including any area of specialization.*

Example: High school teacher – Math

A6. Using the JOB CODES (List A, pages 13–14), choose the code that BEST describes the work you were doing on your last job.

CODE ___ → *SKIP to Part B, page 6*

A7. *(IF WORKING WEEK OF APRIL 15TH)* **Counting all jobs held during the week of April 15, were you employed full-time or part-time?**

1 ☐ **Full-time** (usually worked a total of 35 or more hours per week) → *SKIP to A9, page 2*

2 ☐ **Part-time** (usually worked less than 35 hours per week)

A8. *(IF PART-TIME)* **What were your reasons for working part-time rather than full-time during the week of April 15?**

Mark (X) all that apply

1 ☐ Retired or semi-retired — Year 19 ___

2 ☐ Student

3 ☐ Family responsibilities

4 ☐ Chronic illness or permanent disability

5 ☐ Suitable full-time job not available

6 ☐ Did not need or want to work full-time

7 ☐ Other – *Specify*

SKIP to A10, page 2

FORM NSCG-1 (1-25-93)

Example from National Survey of College Graduates, conducted by U.S. Bureau of the Census for the National Science Foundation.

incentive groups was nearly twice that for the incentive group (16% versus 8%). The explanation for the lower refusal rate, but also the lower completion rate, may have been that the remaining nonrespondents in the incentive group consisted of more hard-core holdouts to this effort, which included identifying phone numbers through directory assistance. Follow-up personal interview attempts increased response to 86% for the no incentive group, and 88% for the incentive group.

Figure 9.11 Preletter for pilot test for National Survey of College Graduates.

NSCGP-L1
(4-92)
3250

NATIONAL SCIENCE FOUNDATION
1800 G STREET, N.W.
WASHINGTON, D.C. 20550

May 13, 1992

Mr. Don Dillman
5902 Mt. Eagle Dr., No. 1101
Alexandria, VA 22303

Dr. Mr. Dillman:

In a few days, Mr. William P. Butz, Associate Director for Demographic Programs of the Bureau of the Census, will ask you to help with the National Survey of College Graduates.

We have sponsored this important survey of the college-educated population every decade since the 1960s. The survey helps Government, businesses, and universities do a better job of meeting the Nation's needs for college graduates in a variety of fields of study. The letter from Mr. Butz will explain more about why the Census Bureau is conducting this survey and the reasons for contacting you.

I would greatly appreciate your help with this important survey.

Sincerely,

Kenneth M. Brown
Director, Division of Science Resources Studies

Example from 1992 pilot survey for National Survey of College Graduates, conducted by U.S. Bureau of the Census.

Implications. This case study suggests several conclusions. First, this pretest showed a response nearly 18 percentage points higher than that obtained from a more traditionally constructed and much shorter questionnaire used in the 1980s. Second, more satisfactory response rates can be obtained by a multiple-mode study, which allows new addresses to be located through telephone and personal follow-ups to a mail survey. It also shows that more than four-fifths of the data can be collected by mail when incentives are used, before switching to the more expensive interview modes. The effect of the incentive is mostly to increase the speed of response, rather than to produce any overall response advantage, and perhaps to lower the refusal rate for the second mode, rather than producing any overall response effect (an insignificant two percentage point advantage existed for the incentive group). It was also found that none of the sample members who called the number provided on the questionnaire letters complained about the incentive. None of the questionnaires were returned with angry notes and none of the sample

Figure 9.12 Front and back cover letter for National Survey of College Graduates, with material on backside formulated as commonly-asked questions.

NSCGP-L2(A)
(4-92)
3250

UNITED STATES DEPARTMENT OF COMMERCE
Bureau of the Census
Washington, DC 20233-0001

OFFICE OF THE DIRECTOR

May 20, 1992

Mr. Don Dillman
5902 Mt. Eagle Dr., No. 1101
Alexandria, VA 22303

Dear Mr. Dillman:

I am writing to ask for your help with the National Survey of College Graduates. This is an important national survey of college-educated persons sponsored by the National Science Foundation.

The Census Bureau has chosen you for this survey as part of a scientifically selected sample of individuals with college degrees. Your response is important whether you graduated recently from college or many years ago. We need your response whether or not you work.

By periodically surveying college graduates, we can improve our understanding about the relationship between college training and how people later use their education. Colleges and universities use results from this survey to improve their curricula. Businesses and the Government use the results to identify training needs. These educational and training improvements help the United States maintain competitiveness with other countries.

Completing the questionnaire will take you approximately 25 minutes; not responding will seriously reduce the accuracy of the final results.

On the back of this letter are answers to questions frequently asked by survey participants. If you have any additional questions, you may call Mr. Lee Giesbrecht of my staff collect between 8 a.m. and 4 p.m., EST, on (301) 763-2063.

Thank you for your help. I look forward to hearing from you.

Sincerely,

William P. Butz

William P. Butz
Associate Director for Demographic Programs
Bureau of the Census

Enclosure

(Continued)

members contacted by telephone or personal visits raised any concerns about incentives (Shettle and Mooney, 1996). It was also found that about 80% of the respondents cashed their checks, and only about 20% of those who did not respond cashed theirs (Geisbrecht, 1994). Overall, the case study suggests that mail can serve effectively as the dominant mode of data collection in certain government mixed-mode studies.

As an alternative to the prepaid financial incentive, my experience with many other surveys (see Chapter 4) suggests that the mail response rates for the nonincentive group could have been improved significantly by the use of special mail, such as Federal Express or U.S. Postal Service priority mail, for the replacement

Figure 9.12 (Continued)

Some Commonly Asked Questions

How was I selected to be in the sample?

Using scientific sampling, we selected individuals across the Nation to provide estimates of the current activities of people with at least a bachelor's degree in all major college fields.

Who sees my answers?

As required by Title 13, United States Code, only sworn Census Bureau employees who have taken an oath to protect the confidentiality of survey respondents will see your actual questionnaire form. The penalties for violating this oath for Census Bureau employees include jail and substantial fines. Before anyone else sees the results, we strip them of individual identifiers, such as names and addresses.

How much time does the questionnaire take?

Based on preliminary tests, we estimate that the questionnaire takes approximately 25 minutes to complete. Since not everyone will complete all parts of the questionnaire, actual times do vary. If you have comments on the time required for this survey, please send them to Herman Fleming, Management Analysis Branch, Division of Human Resources Management, National Science Foundation, 1800 G Street, N.W., Washington, D.C. 20550; and to the Office of Information and Regulatory Affairs, Office of Management and Budget, Paperwork Reduction Project 3145-0130, Washington, D.C. 20503.

What happens if I do not answer?

This is a voluntary survey. If you do not answer, however, you seriously weaken the results of the survey. Your answer can represent hundreds of other college-educated people in the United States. Because of this, we invest substantial resources in ensuring as complete a response as possible, including multiple mailings and telephone contacts.

Why is this survey important? Can I see a report from the survey?

In the letter we listed some of the many uses of this survey. We have collected this information since 1960 and people use the information for planning university, business, and Government programs to ensure that the United States has the skilled and educated population that it needs. If you would like a copy of one of the publications based on this survey to learn more about its uses, please check the box below and enclose this sheet with your questionnaire when you return it.

☐

Example from 1992 pilot survey for National Survey of College Graduates, conducted by U.S. Bureau of the Census.

questionnaire. However, it is unclear whether the cost would have been less than for the incentives sent with the first mailing.

State and Local Government Surveys

In general, state and local government surveys exhibit far fewer complexities than do federal self-administered surveys. Most jurisdictions do not have a centralized mandatory approval process that is equivalent to the U.S. Office

Figure 9.13 A reminder letter for the National Survey of College Graduates.

NSCGP-13
(4-92)
3250

UNITED STATES DEPARTMENT OF COMMERCE
Bureau of the Census
Washington, DC 20233-0001

OFFICE OF THE DIRECTOR

May 27, 1992

Mr. Don Dillman
5902 Mt. Eagle Dr., No. 1101
Alexandria, VA 22303

Dear Mr. Dillman:

A few days ago, I sent you the National Survey of College Graduates questionnaire.

If you have already completed and returned it, I thank you very much. The survey will help the United States Government and others make important decisions about such issues as determining the most effective use of public funds to universities and students to ensure that the United States does not lack people trained in specific fields. The information you provide is very important to the accuracy and success of the survey.

If you have not yet had time to complete the questionnaire, please do so as soon as possible. If you need another copy of the questionnaire or have any questions about the survey, please call Mr. Lee Giesbrecht of my staff collect at (301) 763-2063 between 8 a.m. and 4 p.m., EST. He will be happy to talk with you.

Sincerely,

William P. Butz

William P. Butz
Associate Director for Demographic Programs
Bureau of the Census

Example from 1992 pilot survey for National Survey of College Graduates, conducted by U.S. Bureau of the Census.

of Management and Budget. In addition, there are likely to be fewer agencies, divisions within agencies, and hierarchical levels involved in the design and implementation process. However, the emphasis on high response fostered by OMB in the federal government may be replaced by a concern with human subjects protection philosophy, placing a greater emphasis on limiting the allowable number of contacts and methods of contact than on the survey error implications of making or not making those contacts.

Proscriptions against the use of token financial incentives may or may not exist, and often depend upon individual agency sentiment. Except for such sentiments, we have found few reasons for deviating from the use of the general model for improving survey response that was outlined in Part I of this book. Indeed, over the last 20 years the basic procedures for the TDM, and now Tailored Design, were worked out using state-sponsored surveys as test vehicles. The following case study illustrates the implementation of a state government–sponsored survey in which the contractor, the Washington State University Social and Economic Sciences Research Center, was limited to four contacts. However, the contact procedure involved the use of an inexpensive material incentive provided by the sponsoring agency as an alternative to using a financial incentive (Boynton, Miller, and Tarnai, 1996).

Case Study: Department of Licensing Satisfaction Survey

The Washington State Department of Licensing asked for a survey to be done of individuals who had renewed their driver's licenses within the past eighteen months. A 12-page booklet questionnaire containing 52 questions was printed on white, legal-size paper that was folded to form the booklet. Because of the need to prepare a legislative proposal, the implementation process was truncated, using a personalized preletter, questionnaire, thank you/reminder, and replacement questionnaire, all of which were sent at one-week intervals beginning in mid-August, 1995. The procedures were based upon those used with the traditional TDM.

A very inexpensive purple ballpoint pen, constructed of plastic and bearing the inscription, "Department of Licensing," was sent to half of the 2400 members of the sample, with the remainder receiving no incentive. Following Patchen et al. (1994), careful attention was given to packaging, with the pen and questionnaire materials being mailed in a 6″ × 10″ padded envelope.

Response to the incentive group was 67% compared with 59% for the nonincentive group, or eight percentage points higher. This advantage for the ballpoint pen incentive is consistent with, or perhaps a little higher than, that observed by Church (personal communication, April 12, 1993) for material incentives. Although the response rate could likely have been improved further by inclusion of a financial incentive, additional contact, or special mail, the response was considered fairly high for these procedures when using a 12-page questionnaire.

Contracting Out Government Surveys

In general, state and local governments lack the capacity to conduct regularly their own surveys. Nor do these levels of government generally have specialized agencies that conduct surveys for other groups. The preferred method of conducting many such surveys is to hire an outside contractor. When outsourcing is done, as undertaken for the Department of Licensing case study, it seems important that a concerted effort be made to convey to recipients of the survey that it is sponsored by the government and being conducted for a specific governmental purpose.

This can mean adding phrases like: "The Washington State Department of Natural Resources has requested that we contact you on their behalf." A technique that is also appropriate is to send a preletter from the state agency, indicating that a questionnaire will be coming to the recipient in a few days and why it is important for the person to respond. Efforts to hide government sponsorship, or convey it subtly by listing it only on the questionnaire, are generally inappropriate.

However, numerous survey letters I have seen begin with a long first paragraph explaining that a survey is begin conducted by the sender for a government agency. The result is to delay explaining what the survey is about or why the respondent should respond until late in the letter. This, too, should be avoided. As emphasized in Chapter 4, it is important to communicate with respondents in a straightforward way about why they are being contacted and for whom the contact is being made.

CONCLUSION

Government surveys of individuals and households provide a quite different challenge than the tailored methods discussed in the three preceding chapters. In this chapter, a greater emphasis has been placed on utilizing the appeal advantages that government sponsorship allows, and responding to the complexities of government that sometimes make designing effective government surveys difficult.

Government self-administered surveys have come a long way since the days in which respondents were typically sent questionnaires described as forms, made to look that way by enclosing all questions in boxes and rectangles. Such forms were often constructed in ways that maximized the amount of information that could be elicited on each page, with little thought given to the order in which information appeared or the likely effects on navigation. People were asked to complete forms that had the cover pages reserved for address labels and contained cover letters that made the entire package appear more like a brochure than a request for help.

Federal government questionnaires have also changed dramatically from their earlier organization with questions on far left side of the page and answer choices on the far right, constructed that way because interviewers and key punchers found this format convenient. Almost gone are the elimination of actual dates from letters, the formalistic style described early in this chapter, and other mass-mailing trappings that prevailed earlier in the twentieth century.

Although the tailoring of questionnaire design, numbers of contacts, and methods of contact that are effective for individual and household government surveys differ little from the procedures described in Part I of this book, those for another type of government survey, that of businesses, may differ dramatically. That is the topic I turn to next.

CHAPTER 10

Surveys of Businesses and Other Organizations

FEW SURVEY undertakings are as difficult as defining, sampling, contacting, and obtaining responses to self-administered questionnaires from businesses or other organizations. A friend summed up her frustration with conducting a statewide survey of certain licensed businesses in this way:

> I had no idea that so many of the businesses listed on the state tax records we were using would no longer exist, at least by that name. Neither did I realize that addressing correspondence only to the business name, and not a specific person, would result in our follow-ups going to different people than the one who received the first mailing. When I made some telephone follow-ups to nonrespondents, my most frequent outcome was not to find out who had actually received the questionnaire. Occasionally, when I did locate the person, I got a response like, "I did my part on hiring policies, but I don't know who did the technology stuff. I didn't know anything about that." In addition, I sometimes reached a "voice" on the phone which, though very cordial, would indicate that the company policy was not to do questionnaires and would not refer me to someone else. Maybe it just isn't possible to do good business surveys.

Surveys of business and other organizations face challenges different from those for any other type of survey. These potential difficulties may help explain why a review of 183 business surveys (in selected business journals published since 1990) revealed an average response rate of 21% (Paxson, 1992).

Yet, high response rates and high quality data from self-administered surveys of organization populations are possible. For example, Paxson et al. (1995) reported that 18 national mail (with some telephone follow-up) surveys of businesses conducted by the U.S. Bureau of the Census between 1987 and 1993 achieved average response rates of about 75%. It was also reported that surveys by a university research center, while obtaining only an average response rate of 51% to 26 surveys, achieved a response of 72% for surveys addressed to individual persons compared to 40% when addressed only to the company. In addition, whereas surveys using only one questionnaire and reminder postcard obtained an average response of 37%, surveys using a three-mail contact procedure plus a token financial incentive or telephone follow-up, and addressed to an individual person, achieved a response rate of 84%. It was concluded that the varied procedures used for these surveys had a substantial effect on response rates.

However, the variation in business survey situations requires tailored solutions that differ as greatly from one another as they do from the tailored solutions for populations and survey situations described in the preceding chapters. A 700-page book developed from an international conference on surveys of establishments and other types of organizations, *Business Survey Methods* (Cox, Binder, Chinnappa, Christianson, Colledge, and Kott, 1995), details many of the unique challenges involved in conducting business surveys. It also describes the many ways in which business surveys differ from one another and recommends ways of dealing with that diversity.

The business survey methods in use range from traditional mailout/mailback procedures to simultaneous attempts to survey by mail and telephone. They also include electronic technologies ranging from personalized printing of questionnaires (often referred to as Docutext or Docuprint), faxing, or Web page responses to reporting by touch-tone data entry on telephones. Tailored design of business surveys requires recognition of the many ways that business surveys differ from surveys of individuals and households, and of the need to use different procedures in different situations.

HOW BUSINESS AND INDIVIDUAL PERSON SURVEYS DIFFER

Businesses and other establishments are quite varied. They range from huge corporations like General Electric, with many subcompanies and divisions, to individuals who run a one-person enterprise out of their basement. Also included are for-profit enterprises as well nonprofit groups. The category encompasses hospitals, consulting firms, churches, schools, prisons, foundations, and governments. The characteristic that surveys of businesses and other establishments have in common is that people are asked to report information for an entity that is distinct from them personally. Although the respondent's opinion and some personal characteristics may be sought, the thrust of these surveys is to understand this larger entity for which the respondent serves as a representative.

The challenge of surveying businesses and other establishments is determined in large part by the intersection between the nature of the organization to be surveyed and the type of information sought. In this section, I discuss features that make business or establishment surveys different from most other surveys and from one another. These features are posed as questions, because answers usually need to be obtained at the early stages of designing business surveys.

What is an organizational entity?

The sponsor of a survey may define each restaurant or nursing home with a name and location in a particular community as a separate business. However, the establishment's owner may see that entity as one of several locations within a single organization. Both parties have a legitimate perspective. In a survey of businesses within one city or county, the survey sponsor may be correct in identifying that specific location as a business from the surveyor's point of view. The owner, on the other hand, may see it only as an indivisible component of a unified larger business, for which separate accounting information may not even be kept. It is important that organization surveys specify what constitutes a separate organization for purposes of the survey, and find ways to reconcile those differences with what is called for by sample design questions.

Where is the business unit of interest located?

The location where a business provides its service or product to buyers may not be where business affairs are handled. A list of businesses may contain one address but not the other, making sampling and coverage issues particularly difficult to handle. An example of this difficulty occurred in a multi-stage sample of businesses that drew counties as a second-stage sampling unit. This process led to the inclusion of some business outlets whose mailing addresses were in an adjacent county but that were technically outside the sample area, and therefore ineligible for a proposed survey.

What is the name of the business?

Frequently, the name of a business for accounting and tax purposes is not the same as the name provided to the public. This is especially true for businesses that have public visibility and multiple locations. In one survey of businesses, a chain of restaurants with a well-known public name located in many cities was listed on all records we could find with an innocuous name like "KAG Incorporated." Consequently, surveyors need to be aware that what they identify by one name may be referred to as something else by the respondent.

Does the business still exist?

Establishments are created and terminated regularly. Sometimes they are reorganized or changed by buying or selling components, or simply by changing their names to create a different public image. In business surveys, finding an adequate list of businesses is often difficult. Even tax revenue lists get outdated very quickly as some businesses terminate or are sold while other businesses are being created. Therefore, it is imperative that tax or other lists be as up-to-date as possible. In addition, it may be necessary to determine whether a business has been recreated under a different entity.

How much variation exists in size and structure of the business survey units?

If one desires to survey manufacturers, accountants, travel agencies, consulting firms, law firms, or businesses of any other type, there is considerable likelihood that some firms in the population are quite large and others are quite small. This tendency has increased as the availability of information age technologies has made it possible for individuals operating out of their homes to do work that formerly required a central location and public visibility as an organization. In fact, one person may operate several organizations, a phenomenon encouraged by many tax laws. The trend has also been fueled in the United States by the movement away from manufacturing to a service economy, which makes it possible for small consulting firms and other entities to achieve enormous reach with their activities.

In small organizations, all incoming correspondence may be seen by the owner. In very large organizations, CEOs are unlikely to open their own mail, and no mail that can be handled by someone else makes it to their desk. These situations may require quite different strategies for obtaining a survey response. This heterogeneity creates the challenge of having to find the "right person" to fill out a survey in large businesses, while in one-person businesses there is no such problem. The effect is to increase the difficulty of writing questionnaires, instructions, and correspondence that take into account these variations in a way that does not overwhelm respondents with details relevant only to other businesses in the sample. As will be suggested later, pre-telephone contacts may be especially helpful in understanding the heterogeneity in samples and how to deal with it.

Who should be the respondent?

In some organizations one person is in charge of hiring policies, another is in charge of setting wages, another is in charge of continuing education, another person makes equipment decisions, and still another has chief responsibility for long-range planning. Questionnaires that require information in all of these areas may need to receive attention from several people. In other organizations one person may handle all of those decisions. The more topics that are covered in a survey, especially if it involves requests for specific numbers rather than broad estimates, the more difficult it is likely to be to get a response.

Does a company survey policy exist?

Many organizations have policies that address whether they will cooperate with survey requests and an approval process for questionnaires that do get completed. In some organizations one person is responsible for all questionnaires, whereas in other businesses survey decisions require a time-consuming process involving many people. A policy of not responding to questionnaires provides a convenient means of immediately dispatching requests for completion of questionnaires with the simple statement, "It's against company policy." In many cases such policies apply to certain questionnaire modes (interview but not paper, or vice versa). It also appears that a policy of nonresponse to questionnaires sometimes exists as a convenient means of getting rid of most requests, but may be far from absolute; persistent but careful attempts to obtain an exception to policy for an "important purpose" may therefore be required.

Is it necessary to go through a gatekeeper?

In many organizations, the person who opens mail and/or answers the telephone often screens requests for survey participation, even without knowing what the request is about. The questionnaire may be thrown away without the person to whom it is addressed even knowing it was received. Methods of getting past gatekeepers, who are often as effective by stalling as by saying no, are critical for achieving response to self-administered surveys. We suspect that much of the success of token financial incentives in obtaining responses to surveys from, for example, physicians, is that the inclusion of token financial incentives, even small ones, enables the questionnaire to get beyond gatekeepers who are authorized to say "no," but not to accept or dispose of money without approval of the addressee.

How large is the sample?

Surveying only a few hundred entities is very different from surveying thousands or even millions. Large business surveys are not unusual. Hundreds of thousands of businesses are surveyed in the Census of Manufacturers conducted by the U.S. Bureau of the Census, and a few million in the Census of Agriculture conducted by the National Agricultural Statistical Service of the USDA. Many other surveys of businesses also have large samples. Sample size often makes an enormous difference in what kinds of response-inducing procedures, for example, individual contact and personalization, can and cannot be used.

How difficult are the questions and do records need to be consulted?

In general, questions asked in business surveys tend to be more difficult than those asked in individual person surveys and may require the examination of records. We have been asked to help with surveys that ask the exact size of boat engines and year purchased, number of employees who have received a particular kind of training in the last 18 months, income information that would appear only on tax records, exact numbers of livestock bought and sold, and quantities of power produced from independent power producers as opposed to co-generators and other sources.

Asking people to check records makes it more difficult to obtain responses, because the unavailability of records becomes an important reason for nonresponse. In some surveys it may be possible to ask more general questions with categorical answers, such as, "About how many head of cattle did you sell last year?: (1) less than 35; (2) 35 to 74; (3) 75 to 149; or (5) 150 or more." An answer to this question might easily be provided without finding the sales records. However, the sponsors of many surveys, and particularly economic surveys for policy purposes, may feel that only precise numbers are acceptable. As a result, obtaining responses is more difficult.

Are detailed instructions needed?

The complexity of questions often means that extensive sets of instructions are deemed necessary and instruction books must be provided. In several instances I have observed instruction books that are longer than the questionnaire itself. These instructions are provided primarily for surveys in which the respondent is being asked to consult records. These instructions become yet another challenge to overcome in order to obtain a satisfactory response.

Is the survey repeated at regular intervals for the same respondents, or only once?

Many federal government surveys are conducted yearly, or even monthly, for the same establishments. This situation leads to the development of understandings and policies that aim to ease the reporting task by not making changes in data collection procedures, developing reporting relationships with particular individuals within companies, and implementing other procedures that are unique to particular surveys. While such procedures may help some respondents, they also lead to the retention of out-of-date procedures that make responding difficult for new units to which the questionnaire has been sent.

When surveys are repeated frequently with the same businesses, an emphasis is placed on getting questions to be understood and answered in the same way. In some instances companies may be provided with their answers from the previous survey, thus making it possible to use that as an answering guide. This process is facilitated by the use of new technologies such as Docuprint reproduction methods, which allow each firm's questionnaire to be uniquely printed so as to include data collected from them for the previous year. Use of this technique requires a different printing and distribution procedure than might otherwise be used.

Who is the sponsor?

One of the largest sponsors of business surveys is the federal government. Many of these surveys are of much national importance. Moreover, just as individuals are required by law to respond to the U.S. Decennial Census, businesses are required by the same law (Title 13) to respond to certain surveys. The requirement to respond is balanced by guarantees of confidentiality. Other federal surveys are voluntary and cannot utilize government authority in the same way. In other cases, businesses occasionally conduct surveys of other businesses, raising the possibility of one business being asked to provide proprietary information to a competitor. University-sponsored surveys generally neither provide the legal confidentiality protection nor present the threat of a competitor asking about a company's business. Who sponsors a survey undoubtedly influences how a questionnaire is viewed by the recipient and the likelihood of responding.

Does a reporting deadline exist?

Data collected by mail are often important for calculating important economic performance indicators and must be available by a certain date each month. This challenge has in recent years led to the development of fax and e-mail as supplemental, but crucial, methods for getting business surveys completed. For other surveys there is no firm completion date. These differences have a substantial influence on the kinds of methods that may be used. This also means that whereas follow-up procedures have to be truncated for some surveys, for others they do not. To meet tight deadlines, one questionnaire critical to the development of national economic indicators has been switched from mostly mail to mostly touch-tone data entry, a technique discussed in the next chapter (Werking and Clayton, 1995).

Can the customer orientation of most organizations be used to advantage?

Most of the above attributes point out some of the difficulties of surveying businesses. By contrast, a positive customer orientation is a decidedly positive attribute. Surveys of individuals often produce adamant, emotionally charged refusals. In addition, individuals may go to great lengths to make it hard to find telephone numbers or to get through an answering machine. Although businesses have access to such possibilities, they are generally more concerned about providing convenient access to customers and clients. Increasingly, employees are trained to be responsive to callers. Phone numbers for businesses are likely to be listed rather than unlisted. The desire to be responsive to callers provides considerable help in resolving many of the potential difficulties outlined above. For example, what's the company's name? Is the location in Sioux Falls a separate business entity? Who is the person to whom a request for information about the business should be addressed?

There are several benefits of talking with a representative of an organization. They range from determining eligibility for a survey to identifying to whom a questionnaire should be addressed, and even encouraging response at a later time. Moreover, the relative ease of locating telephone numbers has led to the use of the telephone to encourage or augment mail methods for most organizational surveys, a design feature discussed in some detail later.

DIFFERENT STRATEGIES FOR DIFFERENT SITUATIONS: RESULTS FROM SIX CASE STUDIES

As a consequence of the attributes just discussed, reasonable survey strategies for contacting and gaining responses from organizations are likely to vary greatly. To illustrate this diversity, six case studies are reported here. Each differs significantly from the others in the response challenge and how the sponsors chose to solve those problems. These case studies form the basis for the recommendations on tailoring that follow. Figure 10.1 lists the studies described, unique challenges associated with each, and various uses of a second survey mode—the telephone—to help achieve the study objectives. Together, these case studies illustrate a variety of strategies for responding to the challenges discussed above.

A Geographically Limited Survey of All Licensed Businesses for Which Only Business Name and Address Were Known, Using Only Mail Procedures

Case Study 1: Spokane County Businesses Survey

In 1989, The Area Economic Development Council of Spokane, Washington, a metropolitan center of about 300,000 people, wanted to conduct a survey of all busi-

Figure 10.1 Case study illustrations of business survey, special challenges, and use of telephone.

	Survey Population	Special Challenges	Uses of Telephone	Response Rates
1.	Spokane County Survey of Licensed Businesses	One-time survey; little knowledge of sample frame	No telephone numbers; none used	59%
2.	Annual Survey of U.S. Manufacturing	Same businesses surveyed repeatedly	Telephone prompt for return of mail survey	83%
3.	National Survey of Rural Manufacturers	Long survey; eligibility unclear	Prescreening and dominant data collection by telephone; mail sent to nonrespondents.	68%
4.	Activities of largest U.S. universities	Survey sent to one person seeking identification of another person to complete	Telephone reminder to CEOs to designate respondent	76%
5.	M.D. Immunization Practices	Concern with gatekeepers and contacting respondents at available times	Alternative method of responding in sequence	67%*
6.	Survey of Grass Seed Growing Farmers	Speed essential; questions highly sensitive	Simultaneous alternative method of responding	74%

*This response rate is for use of mail method first, followed by telephone.

nesses operating in the Spokane area. A stratified sample of large (more than 100 employees) and small businesses was drawn from state tax records of businesses with addresses in Spokane County that had filed tax returns the previous year.

The study was aimed at understanding general features of each business, from number of employees and wages to difficulties in doing business in that community. The questions concerned a wide array of business characteristics, including number of employees, annual revenues, trends in profits, and plans for change (See Figure 10.2). Although some questions were detailed, it was expected that most answers could be provided without consulting business records because of the use of broad rather than precise categories. The questionnaire consisted of six pages of questions and was designed by Paxson (1989).

The questions were printed in an eight-page booklet that included front and back covers. The questionnaire cover included a view of downtown Spokane with the prominent title, "Business Concerns in Spokane: Sponsored by the Spokane Area Economic Development Council in Conjunction with Momentum 88." The title and photo were used to develop interest in the questionnaire.

Each questionnaire was addressed to the "owner or manager" of the business. The letters were similarly addressed on letterhead stationery and each letter was individually signed. A postcard reminder was sent one week after the first questionnaire mailing. Two weeks later, businesses that had not responded were sent a reminder letter with a replacement copy of the questionnaire. No further contacts were made. Overall, 59% of the businesses returned completed questionnaires.

Figure 10.2 Example of mail-only business questionnaire.

1989

Business Concerns in Spokane

Sponsored by the Spokane Area Economic Development Council
In conjunction with MOMENTUM 88

Q1 **Which of the following categories best describes the business of your company? (Circle the best response)**

1. SERVICE
2. PROFESSIONAL
3. RETAIL
4. WHOLESALE
5. TRANSPORTATION
6. PUBLIC UTILITY
7. FINANCE, INSURANCE AND REAL ESTATE
8. CONSTRUCTION
9. MINING
10. MANUFACTURING, DURABLE GOODS ______ (Please describe your product)
11. MANUFACTURING, NONDURABLE GOODS ______ (Please describe your product)
12. OTHER ______ (Please describe)

Q2 **How many years has your company been business in Spokane?**

______ NUMBER OF YEARS

Q3 **How many locations does your company occupy in the Spokane area?**

______ NUMBER OF LOCATIONS

Q4 **Is your company's main or head office located in Spokane, elsewhere in Washington, or out of state?**

1. SPOKANE COUNTY
2. ELSEWHERE IN WASHINGTON
3. OUT OF STATE

Q5 **What percent of your products or services are sold in each of the following areas:**

A. Spokane County . . . . ______ %
B. Other Washington counties . . . . ______ %
C. Idaho, Oregon and Montana . . . . ______ %
D. Other parts of the U.S. . . . . ______ %
E. Other countries around the world . . . . . ______ %
100 %

Q6 **What do you estimate the annual gross revenue of your business will be for 1988? (Circle the number of your answer)**

1. LESS THAN $500,000
2. BETWEEN $500,000 AND $1 MILLION
3. BETWEEN $1.1 AND $5 MILLION
4. BETWEEN $5.1 AND $10 MILLION
5. BETWEEN $10.1 AND $15 MILLION
6. BETWEEN $15.1 AND $20 MILLION
7. BETWEEN $20.1 AND $30 MILLION
8. BETWEEN $30.1 AND $40 MILLION
9. BETWEEN $40.1 AND $50 MILLION
10. MORE THAN $50 MILLION

Example from 1989 survey conducted by the Washington State University Social & Economic Sciences Research Center.

Implications. This survey was done to better understand the business structure of a metropolitan area, in order that goals might be formulated for community action. The questions did not require precise entries for the formulation of state or national policy. The response rate (59%) is quite high for only three contacts, and undoubtedly could have been pushed higher with additional contacts and/or a special mailing. Although the reasons are not clear, it is likely that this high response is the result of local sponsorship (a questionnaire cover that identified the survey as having a local emphasis), an easy-to-respond-to questionnaire layout, and the two follow-ups. The questionnaire asked a number of sensitive questions but was not overly difficult to fill out. This experience suggests that business surveys by mail can produce reasonable response rates when mail is used alone.

National Survey of Manufacturers for Which Response Is Required by Federal Law

The next case study is dramatically different. It concerns a regular national survey of businesses that asks the same (or nearly the same) questions year after year, and for which response is required by federal law. It, too, uses a mailout/mail-back strategy, but with limited follow-up by phone to obtain responses from larger manufacturers.

Case Study 2: The Annual Survey of Manufacturing Conducted by the U.S. Bureau to the Census

Every five years a census of all manufacturers (approximately 300,000) in the United States is conducted by the U.S. Bureau of the Census. In addition, an annual survey of manufacturers is conducted on a sample of about 60,000 establishments. The same establishments are included in the sample for five successive years. This means that each year the sampled establishments are asked to report such information as employment, annual payroll and fringe benefits, inventories, capital expenditures, value of products shipped, and so forth.

In the past, sampled companies have received a four- to five-page questionnaire printed on legal size paper. A change has been made to use Docuprint technology, which prints individual questionnaires for each business that includes the information it reported for the preceding year. A separate eight-page instruction book accompanies each questionnaire.

Each company receives one or more questionnaires, depending on how many of its component establishments are included in the sample. A letter addressed to the person identified as having completed the previous report is also included. The letter informs recipients that a response is required by law, under Title 13 of the U. S. Code, and specifies that a response is due within 30 days. A follow-up letter is sent to nonrespondents (about 50%) five to six weeks later. Yet another follow-up letter is sent in another five to six weeks, at which time the response is hoped to be around 66%. After another 30 days, phone calls are made to companies that represent a particularly large component of various types of industries to assure that responses adequately represent each type of industry. These calls are made by analysts, some of whom have become acquainted over the years with the person responsible for reporting in certain companies. Faxes may also be used for some of these contacts. Overall, a response rate of about 83% is obtained from the use of these procedures.

This survey produces information for a long-standing data series important to constructing industrial output indicators for the United States, and has been conducted in much the same way for many years, except for the introduction of Docuprint technology. Only a few companies, approximately 50–75, report information electronically.

Implications. This survey is a long-standing business survey that provides the basis for analyses about changes in the nation's manufactured output. Mail is used, as is customary for most government-conducted business surveys (Paxson et al., 1995; Kydoniefs and Stanley, 1999). In addition, it depends only upon telephone reminders to large manufacturers. Its response rate (83%) is significantly higher than the response rate (59%) for the Spokane County survey. Mandatory authority appears to be an important factor in achieving high response rates. This survey is illustrative of the methods and procedures for many other federally-sponsored business surveys.

A One-Time, Voluntary Federal Government-Sponsored Survey of Manufacturers Conducted by an Outside Contractor Using a Mixed-Mode Design

A quite different survey challenge is illustrated by procedures used to collect information from a national sample of manufacturers located mostly in nonmetropolitan counties of the United States. Some firms included in the annual manufacturing survey are undoubtedly included in this voluntary sample survey which, in order to obtain acceptable response rates, was unable to use a mail-only design.

Case Study 3: National Survey of Rural Manufacturers

A national survey of nearly 8,000 manufacturers, located mostly in rural counties but which included an urban stratum for comparison, was sponsored by the USDA-Economic Research Service (ERS) to learn some of the effects of rural location (Petrie et al., 1998). The ERS does not maintain a large-scale survey capability, so data collection was contracted to a university-based survey research center. Response to the survey was voluntary and contracting outside of the government raised the possibility that the survey process would not benefit from the "appeal to authority" that helps achieve high response to government-conducted surveys.

The self-administered questionnaire was much longer (20 pages) and more difficult to complete than the self-administered questionnaire used in the Spokane County case study. Most of the questions were framed in a sufficiently general way, that is, using categories, so it was not necessary to consult records in order to provide a response. Also, the survey was national, meaning that local appeals could not be used. Much concern existed as to whether any mail procedures could elicit high response. The sample included businesses that were on the list of manufacturers maintained by Dunn and Bradstreet, that had a Standard Industrial Classification Code of Manufacturing, and that had at least ten employees. This list contained some telephone numbers but no names of individuals. The goal was to interview the chief operating officer of the business in the sample location, which in some cases would be the owner but in others would be a hired manager.

An initial pilot study used the following implementation sequence: First, following the finding by Paxson et al. (1995) on importance of having a name, screening calls were made to all companies to determine whether they existed and whether they had the appropriate characteristics (e.g., ten or more employees) for inclusion in the sample. Next, a person was identified to whom the correspondence could be sent. A personalized prenotice letter was sent to this person on a letter signed by the USDA Undersecretary for Rural Development, in order to convey government sponsorship. It was followed a week later by the questionnaire mailing and then two weeks later by a thank you/reminder letter. One week later, telephone contacts commenced with the goal of (1) obtaining response through an interview, or (2) encouraging response by mail. A final contact was made a month later by two-day priority mail, using the large red, white, and blue U.S. Postal Service mailers.

A response rate of only 45% was achieved, with three-fourths of the returns coming in by mail and one-fourth achieved by interview. This response rate was too low to be acceptable. For this reason, the implementation strategy was revised. The new strategy began in the same way, with a telephone validation interview followed by a prenotice mailing on USDA stationery from the undersecretary. However, the prenotice indicated that the person to whom the letter was addressed would be called for an interview. The attempt to complete interviews extended over several months, with at least 20 interview attempts being made. When the study neared the designated finish time, all nonrespondents were sent a priority mailing with the printed questionnaire. It was followed a week later by a final letter to thank those who had responded and remind those who had not.

The overall response rate from the use of this reverse contact procedure was 68%, nearly 23 percentage points higher than that achieved by the other method, which used mail at the beginning. Only about 13% of the response in the main study came from mail questionnaires. However, a significant portion of the telephone interviews were undoubtedly completed as a result of the initial mail contact.

Implications. Increasingly, it is very difficult to depend upon a mail-only strategy for completion of business surveys conducted outside of government unless there are special appeals that can be made, such as in the Spokane County case study previously described. The use of the telephone to determine to whom a questionnaire should be sent and to establish eligibility, followed by a mail contact to help establish credibility and legitimacy before attempting to complete the interview, uses these contact media in a highly complementary way. The final request by mail provided a significant increase in response that was highly unlikely to be achieved by further telephoning of the sampled firms. Each mode of contact contributed significantly to the final outcome.

SURVEY OF ORGANIZATION EMPLOYEES WITH SPECIFIC RESPONSIBILITIES WHO NEEDED TO BE SELECTED BY THE CEO AS PART OF THE SURVEY PROCESS

Not being able to identify an individual to whom initial and follow-up contacts can be directed represents a frequent problem for conducting surveys of organizations. The following case study sent materials by mail asking the CEO of an organization to select and forward the questionnaire to a respondent who could not be identified externally by title.

Case Study 4: Survey of University Administrators in Charge of International Programs

In this study it was necessary to survey the highest-ranking person in selected universities who had administrative responsibilities for the conduct or coordination and integration of international programs (Dillman and Scott, 1989). No such list of people existed. It had been observed that most U.S. universities were increasing their international involvement and connections, and that these responsibilities were being handled in various ways administratively. Conversations with people at several universities made it clear that the task of coordination was assigned to people with different titles at different levels (e.g., Provost, Vice-President, Dean, Assistant Dean, Director, or Coordinator).

The goal was to survey all universities with enrollments of at least 5,000 students. This survey population consisted of the largest 238 universities in the United States. Thus, we were faced with surveying people in organizations who could not be identified prior to starting the survey effort, and even then would have to be identified by a high-level administrator of the responding university. The anticipated difficulty of contacting university presidents or CEOs by phone and asking them to assign on-the-spot an individual to complete it led to a mail contact strategy.

Personal letters were sent to the chief executive officer of each university using an easily-obtained national list. The letters asked them to identify the appropriate respondent for their university. Two actions were requested: (1) pass an enclosed envelope on to the person who should complete it and (2) let us know who was asked to complete the questionnaire, "because we would like to contact the person directly in case he or she has any questions. . . ." The second envelope, which had not been sealed, contained a letter addressed to "Dear Colleague at (name of university)," a copy of the questionnaire, and a stamped return envelope.

About 10 days later, a second personalized letter was sent to the presidents, thanking them for returning the form and asking that if they had not yet done this to please do so soon. Immediately after each name was received from the president, a letter was sent to the designated individuals indicating that the president had informed us that the questionnaire was passed onto them as the most appropriate respondent, and we wanted to both thank them and answer any questions they might have. Approximately one month later, a replacement questionnaire was sent directly to the person who had been asked to fill out the questionnaire.

If no response was received from the president's office, phone calls were made to determine whether the request had been received and whether a person had been designated to respond. Once names were received as a result of these phone calls, a thank you and replacement questionnaire were mailed to the appropriate individuals. Finally, follow-up phone calls were made to any of the assigned individuals who had not responded within four months of the start of the project. Completed questionnaires were received from 76% of the sampled universities.

Implications. This case study illustrates how the survey process itself can have designed into it a respondent identification process. It also illustrates the importance of multiple contacts and using the telephone to assist with the process of achieving response. The methods used for this study allowed the highest ranking administrator of each university to determine who should complete the questionnaire, something we could not have done on our own. It also provided a means of using several appropriate contacts with the presidents, as well as the person assigned to complete the questionnaire. The people assigned to complete the questionnaires received up to four contacts—one from their president to legitimize their assignment; a second one from us offering to help; a third one to replace lost or discarded questionnaires; and a final reminder by telephone. No questionnaire responses were collected by phone, but this medium served an important role in helping to achieve a high response rate.

Interacting with secretaries in the president's office was especially helpful. In general, offices at this high organizational level are particularly good at keeping track of correspondence and requests. The letter to the president was carefully personalized and individually signed. It explained that the information was being collected in preparation for a national conference on the "internationalization" of universities and a brochure for the conference inviting participation from all universities was enclosed. Thus, a strong argument of the survey being useful to higher education in general was provided. The telephone calls almost always generated helpful responses from the highly trained professionals who worked there.

Utilization of a Mixed-Mode Strategy for Getting Past Gatekeepers

Physicians have long been recognized as a frequently surveyed population from which it is difficult to obtain high responses, a fact that has led to dependence upon the use of financial incentives, sometimes large ones. A physician's office can also be viewed as a business with several, and sometimes many, employees. Getting past gatekeepers can be a significant challenge. Receptionists and nurses are often trained to decide which requests get through to the physician and which do not. The nature of physicians' work also presents challenges, inasmuch as a great deal of their time is spent with patients, making it difficult to connect with them by telephone. The case study that follows compares two mixed-mode strategies for obtaining responses to an important statewide health survey.

Case Study 5: A Survey of Immunization Practices by Pediatric and Family Physicians

The Washington State Department of Health sponsored a survey conducted by an outside contractor that measured the attitudes and practices of physicians concerning immunization and the tracking and contacting of children due for vaccination. A mostly-telephone method involved sending a prenotice letter informing physicians that a call would be made, followed by up to 20 attempts to contact them by telephone. For those who could not be contacted, a questionnaire was mailed in week eight using the large U.S. Postal Service priority mail envelopes.

A mostly-mail method began by sending a questionnaire to the sampled physician by U.S. Postal Service Priority mail, followed by a thank you/reminder postcard the second week and a replacement questionnaire sent first-class the third week. At week eight, those who had not responded were called up to ten times by telephone to obtain their answers. In both treatments, anyone who asked for a mail questionnaire was immediately sent one as an alternative to collecting the information by telephone. The telephone-first method produced a response rate of 59%, whereas the mail-first method produced a response rate of 67% after 10 weeks, a difference in favor of the mail-first method of eight percentage points (Moore et al., 1998). More importantly, perhaps, prior to the switch of modes, the response rate for telephone-first lagged 18 percentage points behind the mail first method—41% compared with 59%.

Implications. Results from this survey contrast significantly with those from the mixed-mode survey of rural manufacturers. In that survey the telephone-first strategy appeared to produce a significantly higher response rate, whereas in this case the mail-first strategy produced the higher response. We can only speculate on the reasons. However, it appears that the questionnaire used in the physician study had higher salience to the recipients because of interest in the content and the state-level orientation. It was also somewhat shorter, so that when the questionnaire appeared it did not seem difficult to fill out. Also, when interviewers began to call as a follow-up to mail, they could refer to the questionnaire as having already been sent to the physician, thus providing a reason to allow the interviewer to get past this gatekeeper and talk with the physician.

WHEN TIMELINESS IS CRITICAL AND THE TOPIC IS SENSITIVE

Ordinarily, one thinks of telephone surveys as being faster than mail, a result that was not true for the preceding case study because of the need to interact with gatekeepers. The final case study that follows is one in which there were few, if any, gatekeepers, but a quick response was deemed essential. However, this study also has the challenge of inquiring about an extremely sensitive issue that was being investigated by a state regulatory agency. The simultaneous implementation of mail and telephone data collection strategies allowed both goals to be achieved.

Case Study 6: A Regional Survey of Grass Seed Farmers on Burning of Their Fields

A traditional agricultural practice aimed at improving the production of grass seed is to burn the fields after harvest. In Eastern Washington and Northern Idaho this practice has become quite controversial, and concerted efforts, including legal challenges, have been made to prevent farmers from using this practice. The Washington State Department of Ecology (with jurisdiction over part of the area) wished to obtain farmer reactions to a proposed solution to the conflict, but needed to obtain responses very quickly. Farm leaders had been involved in discussions of the proposed survey and objected to the survey being done by telephone. They predicted that farmers would be unwilling to respond in that way.

The proposed solution was to send a questionnaire by mail to each of the farmers in the survey population, and then to begin calling all nonrespondents by telephone, giving them the option of responding either by mail or by telephone. Use of a common case management system for both mail and telephone contacts allowed any farmer whose response had been received by mail to be immediately eliminated from the call schedule. A response rate of 74% was achieved within 25 days, with two-thirds of the responses coming in by mail and the remaining one-third by telephone (Moore, 1998).

Implications. In this sensitive survey, sending everyone a questionnaire and then following up by telephone allowed respondents to see in writing what questions they were going to be asked and thereby defused a potential source of objections. By starting phone calls soon after the mailout, it was possible to increase the number of mail returns as well as obtain answers by phone that would not otherwise have been collected, and to do it within a short time period.

FROM CASE STUDIES TO PRINCIPLES FOR TAILORED DESIGNS

A recent review of federal establishment survey trends in response rates by an interagency committee noted that most of the published literature on survey nonresponse focused on literature relevant to household surveys (Kydoniefs and Stanley, 1999). The review goes on to note the many differences between household and establishment surveys, much as I have done earlier in this chapter, and argues that more research is needed in order to learn what influences response rates in organizational surveys.

Tomaskovic-Devey, Leiter, and Thompson (1994) have responded to that need by formulating and testing a theory of why organizations do not respond to surveys. The theory argues that nonresponse is less likely to occur when the requested respondent clearly has the authority to respond (e.g., centralized decision-making), the capacity to respond (e.g., knowledge of requested information), and motive to respond (e.g., it is in the respondent's interest to do so). These ideas were tested in a survey of North Carolina businesses selected because they were the employers of a statewide sample of adults who had just been interviewed. The reasons given for or not responding (277 firms) to the mail survey were as follows :

- Did not want to divulge confidential financial information 26%
- Survey would take too long to fill out 25%
- Headquarters responsible for such decisions or survey was forwarded there 43%
- General policy against filling out surveys 16%
- Some of the questions not appropriate for business 9%
- Never saw the survey 8%
- Temporary issues (company being sold/person sick) 8%
- Other 9%

From a tailoring perspective, these data suggest that there is a need in organizational surveys to respond to different concerns rather than searching for a single, overriding objection to responding. Possible implications are that shorter questionnaires are more likely to be completed, that one should not ask for gratuitous financial information, and that getting questionnaires to the right level of the organization is important to achieving a response. A policy against responding was responsible for nonresponse in only 16% of respondents, or about 7% of the entire sample.

In general, the analysis of the correlates of nonresponse confirms Tomaskovic-Devey et al.'s (1994) general theory. Organizations are more likely to respond if they have greater authority to do so, more capacity for doing so, and a motive. Responding to the mail survey was associated with being less centralized, having professional staff available to process information, and being dependent upon their environments for resources with a need to manage their public image. The tailoring strategies recommended here take the findings from this excellent analysis into account.

At the same time, the analysis by Tomaskovic-Devey et al. (1994) does not negate the use of the techniques found effective for improving response to self-administered surveys. Indeed, the procedures used to reach their final response to the mail survey included a telephone screening for correct address and name of the top official at that location, a personalized cover letter, a follow-up postcard, and a registered letter. An attempt was made to convert refusals through telephone follow-ups from the principal investigator. Many of the case studies discussed earlier in this chapter relied on similar techniques. In addition to the multiple contact strategies, the case studies included particular emphasis on the design of respondent-friendly questionnaires, stamped return envelopes, and switching modes for the reporting of data.

Survey requests, whether asking for individual or organizational responses, are filled out by *people.* People who respond for an organization can easily forget receiving a questionnaire and can be offended as easily as individuals who are responding only for themselves. They can also assess the apparent difficulty of responding when faced with a cryptically-worded form that requires reading a long instruction book, which may result in placement of the questionnaire at the bottom of their work basket. Although organizational recipients of a letter that states response is mandatory may realize a response will eventually be needed, they can easily delay having to respond by ignoring it or sending it to someone else in hopes that it will disappear somewhere within the organization. Individuals are also prone not to throw away envelopes that have stamps on them, and to respond positively to being thanked. The interest of surveyors of businesses in developing carefully worded, respectful letters to be sent with respondent-friendly questionnaires is as great as that of any other surveyor. For these purposes we rely on the techniques outlined in Part I of this book. In addition, we seek to deal with the extreme heterogeneity of organizations, with whether people who receive the questionnaires feel empowered to respond and have the information to respond, and with the motives they might have for responding or not responding. The principles that follow seek to go beyond recommendations outlined earlier in this book but are not a substitute for them.

Principle 10.1: Identify the most appropriate respondent for a business survey and develop multiple ways of contacting that person.

Knowing who the likely respondent is for a business survey helps with the development of a multiple-contact strategy. For starters, the ability to add a person's name above the name of the organization on the address label helps make sure that each contact is made with the same person. That information helps greatly with being able to target all communications and to avoid repeating the same information in each of them, which may occur when a different person receives subsequent mailings. Because I expect that increasingly both phone and mail, and in the future e-mail and Web contacts, may be used for conducting the same survey, having multiple ways of contacting the person will be helpful to improving response rates.

Just as important may be using a prior telephone call to determine whether an organization is locally-owned and operated or whether it is a subsidiary. It may be appropriate to seek information on whether the questionnaire should be sent to that location or somewhere else. In this way, a prior telephone call can do much more than confirm an organization's existence and get a mailing address; it can be part of a strategy to find the person who is most capable of responding to the proposed survey.

Unlisted telephone numbers make it difficult to locate individual residences for household surveys. Businesses, on the other hand, usually want to be accessible to potential sellers, buyers, and clients. Consequently, locating additional information to contact businesses will be fairly easy for many establishment surveys. In addition, the concern with customer relations means that receptionists and others will often be willing to provide information on who is responsible for certain kinds of activities, and thus may be the person with the knowledge that is sought by the surveyor.

Finally, some surveys have multiple needs to be accomplished with a pre-contact, including determination of eligibility (a certain number of employees or production of a particular product), who should complete the questionnaire, and multiple ways of reaching that person (e.g., telephone, fax, or e-mail). Case Study 3, the national study of rural manufacturers, used a pre-telephone call that was deemed particularly important in both of these regards.

Principle 10.2: Plan from the beginning for a mixed-mode design.

The advantages of mixing modes can be very significant, as shown for all but one of the case studies, the mail-only survey of Spokane County businesses. If one knows from the beginning that a second mode will be introduced, arguments can be presented in a way that makes it easier to transfer modes. For example, if one contemplates switching from mail, it is important to hold in check the urgency of the tone conveyed in the earlier mail contacts. If a respondent has been told there is a deadline that must be met for the organization's response to be useful, then making several contacts after the deadline may raise concern about whether anything the surveyor says has credibility. Because most business surveys do not concern attitude and opinion statements, concern over mode effects on answers, as discussed in Chapter 6, are lessened. This adds to the attractiveness of considering the use of more than one mode.

Communications need to take into account the intent to communicate with people through a different mode. I once saw a letter that indicated, "This is the last time we will be writing to you. . . ." However, a phone call was planned for soon afterwards, making the promise sound broken. Although the sentence was technically correct in that people were not being contacted in writing, the meaning given to it by the respondent may not have taken into account the mail versus telephone method of contact. Ideally, the entire protocol is developed before the study goes into the field and all pieces of correspondence and/or telephone scripts are laid beside one another to see what image is communicated to the respondent by each successful contact.

After reviewing a questionnaire that was about to be sent to large health care organizations by a federal agency, and seeing that the address list had phone numbers but no names, I proposed that the listed numbers be called to find out specifically to whom the questionnaire should be sent. The response I received was that it would not be practical to do that; after all, a telephone follow-up would be made to nonrespondents later, and because of the phone follow-up after several mailings they could see no reason to plan for a call ahead of time. After explaining that a prior phone call might improve response so fewer would have to be called later, the person simply explained, "In this organization we would have to send the list to the telephone unit, then we would have to bring it back here and send it to the mail unit. Then we would have to send it once again to the telephone unit." Thus, the traditional separate divisions for handling telephone and mail activities, often with different software, may make implementing a joint telephone/mail strategy quite difficult, more for organizational reasons than any other.

For self-administered individual and household surveys, I advocated a maximum of five contacts. Business surveys often require more contacts, especially if one begins with the effort to find an appropriate person for responding, switches to a mail approach, then switches back to a telephone contact, as done in Case Study 3 for the survey of rural manufacturers.

Principle 10.3: Develop respondent-friendly business questionnaires.

Business surveys, more than other types, are frequently designed in ways that make them very difficult to fill out. One reason for poor design is simply tradition. Establishment surveys have often been thought of as "forms" that had to be made as short and precise as possible, rather than as queries to be read, fully comprehended, and thoughtfully answered. In some respects traditional business questionnaires were similar to accounting reports, designed with a row-and-column orientation that often used cryptic word headings. A second reason for a forms approach is that for government large-scale business surveys, a priority has been placed on minimizing the number of sheets of paper. The result is that questions are crammed together to fill every available space, with little regard given to establishing a clear navigational path. A third contributor to poor design is the tendency to use separate instruction books to provide definitions and even the meaning of certain column and row headings, again to minimize paper.

These difficulties are illustrated in Figure 10.3, which shows a 1992 Manufacturing Energy Consumption Survey. It illustrates cryptic headings, instructions in separate booklets, many dark lines that draw the respondent's visual attention as opposed to focusing it on answer spaces, and every bit of space on each page being utilized. One of the difficulties of such pages is having to comprehend several different lines of information simultaneously in order to know what the actual survey question is.

Such practices are often defended by noting that these questionnaires are typically filled out by accountants who are "used to this sort of thing," or by the same person year after year. Figure 10.4 is a revision of the questionnaire to make it self-standing. The key to this change was an extensive revision of what instructions were provided and how they were provided. The revision lengthened the questionnaire dramatically, and an evaluation is now underway to evaluate its impact on respondents.

Figure 10.3 Partial page from legal-size federal government questionnaire with difficult row/column format that requires separate instruction booklet.

Section II – COMBUSTIBLE ENERGY SOURCES

Energy Sources	Census Use Only	Units used for reporting quantities	Energy sources **received** onsite in 1994: Quantity purchased by and delivered to this establishment	Total expenditures, including taxes and delivery charges, of the quantity in column (4)			Total quantity of transfers in and central purchases
				02 (5)			
(1)	(2)	(3)	01 (4)	Mil	Thou	Dol	03 (6)
A. SOLIDS							
1. Anthracite	40	Short Tons					
2. Bituminous and subbituminous coal	41	Short Tons					
3. Lignite	42	Short Tons					
4. Total coal *(Sum of lines A1, A2, and A3)*	46	Short Tons					
5. Breeze	44	Short Tons					
6. Coal coke	43	Short Tons					
7. Petroleum coke	70	Barrels					
8. Agricultural waste (e.g., bagasse, rice hulls, nut shells, orchard prunings)	90	Million Btu					
9. Wood harvested directly from trees (e.g., roundwood, wood chips, tree bark)	83	Million Btu					
10. Wood residues and byproducts from mill processing (e.g., sawdust, shavings, slabs, bark)	84	Million Btu					
11. Wood/paper-related refuse (e.g., scrap, wastepaper, wood pallets, packing materials)	72	Million Btu					
12. Other solids *(Specify solid. Specify units, if **not** million Btu)* 9198	91	Million Btu					
B. GASES (exclude oxygen, nitrogen, and inert gases)							*See Pg. 10, Part B.*
1. Total natural gas *(Include well production onsite in column (7))*	30	1,000 cu. ft.					
In the following parts 1a–1e, please classify natural gas purchases which are reported in line 1. **UTILITY/LDC** **1a.** Natural gas purchased directly from your utilities/local distribution companies (LDC) at a **firm** service rate	48	1,000 cu. ft.					
1b. Natural gas purchased directly from LDC at an **interruptible** service rate	49	1,000 cu. ft.					
1c. Natural gas purchased directly from LDC at **other** service rates *(Specify type of service rate)* 5098	50	1,000 cu. ft.					
Did this establishment purchase natural gas in 1994 from sources other than utilities/LDC? 50981 1 ☐ Yes – *Go to Line 1d.* 2 ☐ No – *Skip to line 2, Acetylene, on this page.*							
NONUTILITY/NON-LDC **1d.** Natural gas purchased from non-LDC sources (e.g., producers, brokers, marketers, and other non-LDC sources including fees for transportation and storage)	51	1,000 cu. ft.					

Example from 1994 Manufacturing Energy Consumption Survey, conducted by U.S. Bureau of the Census for the Energy Information Administration.

Principle 10.4: Provide instructions in the questionnaire rather than in a separate instruction booklet.

Part of the difficulty associated with business questionnaires could be resolve by integrating instructions with the questions. Figure 10.5 shows the separate instruction book that accompanied the questionnaire shown in Figure 10.3. As discussed in Chapter 4, instructions are likely to be more effective if they are

Figure 10.4 Example of revised questionnaire from Figure 10.3 to integrate instructions with questions.

Section 4: Natural Gas

Census use only

34. **Was natural gas either purchased or consumed in this establishment during 1998?** 30000

Natural gas refers to natural gas delivered to your establishment through a pipeline.

Excluded as natural gas are any bottled gases such as liquefied petroleum gas (LPG) or propane, which are reported in Sections 5 and 6 of this questionnaire.

1☐ **Yes → Go to question 35**

2☐ **No → Go to Section 5, page 15**

Questions 35 through 40:

Total Natural Gas

35. **Enter the total quantity of natural gas consumed as a fuel for the production of heat, steam, power, or generation of electricity onsite at this establishment in 1998.** 30060

Include all process uses such as process heating, process cooling, and machine drive and all nonprocess uses such as facility heating, ventilation and air conditioning.

Include natural gas consumed by vehicles intended primarily for use onsite, e.g., forklifts, intra-plant shuttles, loaders and other materials-handling equipment operated solely within the boundaries of the establishment site.

✏ **Copy this quantity to question 165, column 2, page 40.**

☐ 1,000 cubic feet (mcf)
Copy to question 165, column 2, page 40

36. **Enter the total quantity of natural gas consumed for any purpose other than fuel use in this establishment in 1998.** 30070

Include all quantities consumed as lubricants, solvents, or as feedstocks, raw materials, additives, or ingredients for products manufactured by this establishment.

Exclude all offsite dispositions such as sales and transfers to other establishments.

☐ 1,000 cubic feet (mcf)

37. **Enter the total quantity of natural gas purchased from all sources by this establishment for any use in 1998.** 30010

Include quantities that were purchased for any onsite use, e.g., process heating or cooling, building heating or cooling, machine drive, or as raw material input to any manufacturing operation (feedstock).

Exclude quantities: 1) purchased centrally within your company, 2) delivered from other establishments of your company, or 3) for which payment was made in-kind.

☐ 1,000 cubic feet (mcf)

38. **Enter total expenditures, including all applicable taxes, delivery, transportation, management, storage and demand charges, for the purchased natural gas reported in question 37.** 30020

Include all expenditures regardless of when payment was made.

$ ☐ U.S. Dollars

Continue to next page

Page 12 Form EIA-846C (1999)

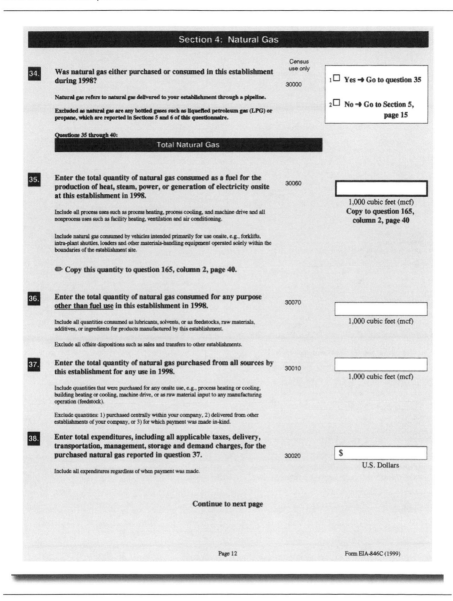

Example from 1998 Manufacturing Energy Consumption Survey, conducted by U.S. Bureau of the Census for the Energy Information Administration.

Figure 10.5 Partial page from legal-size instruction booklet that accompanied questionnaire in Figure 10.3.

Page 2

Line 4 – Total Quantities Received Onsite – Enter the sum of lines 1a, 2a, and 3 for electricity. **Copy this quantity to page 6, column (2), line 1a, part A of Section III – FUEL SWITCHING.**

Line 5 – Quantity Cogenerated – Enter the total quantity of electricity cogenerated at this establishment site from all energy sources during 1994. For the purpose of this survey, cogeneration is defined as the production of electric energy and another form of useful energy (such as heat or steam) through the sequential use of energy. **Include** production from **ALL** cogeneration facilities located at this establishment site.

Line 6 – Quantity Generated from Renewables – Enter the total quantity of each noncombustible energy source generated onsite directly from each of the following:

a. solar power
b. wind power
c. hydropower
d. geothermal power

Exclude any electricity produced as part of a cogeneration process, that is, electricity generated from geothermal steam before the steam itself is used. **Include** such quantities on line 5.

Line 7 – Other Generation – Enter the total quantity of electricity generated onsite by all other means not included on lines 5, 6a, 6b, 6c, and 6d above. For example, electricity generated by diesel generators should be reported here.

Line 8 – Total Onsite Generation – Enter the sum of lines 5, 6a, 6b, 6c, 6d, and 7 for electricity.

Line 9 – Total Sales or Transfers to Utilities – Enter the total quantity of electricity sold or transferred to utilities by your establishment in 1994. For the purpose of this question, utilities are companies that produce and/or deliver electricity and are legally obligated to provide service to the general public within their franchise area. Utilities do not include such generators of electricity as independent power producers, small power producers, or cogenerators not located at this establishment site. **Include** quantities exchanged for the same or any other energy source(s).

For the reporting of combustible energy sources, report the entire line if:

1. the energy source was consumed as a fuel, **or**

2. the energy source was consumed as a nonfuel.

NOTE – In making additional entries, the preprinted entry "Waste and Byproduct Gases" (line B4) includes all waste gas streams (for example, refinery gas, fuel gas, vent gas, plant gas, offgas, still gas, and other waste gases) produced onsite, except hydrogen.

Finally, if your **only** means of supply of an energy source during 1994 was as a byproduct of energy source inputs to any of your manufacturing processes, it should be included only if it was at least partially **consumed onsite as a fuel.** If the byproduct energy source was not consumed as a fuel, it should be excluded.

All excluded energy sources should be lined out, and no entries should be made in columns (4) through (11).

Example 1 – Your establishment depended entirely on electricity for heat and power, no combustible energy sources were consumed. In this instance, all energy sources should be lined out in Section II – COMBUSTIBLE ENERGY SOURCES and skip directly to Section III – FUEL SWITCHING.

Example 2 – Your establishment used electricity for lighting, natural gas for heating or as a feedstock, and propane for onsite transportation by forklifts. Complete the appropriate line(s) for natural gas (B1 through B1e) and line C4 for propane, in addition to Section I.

Example 3 – Residual fuel oil was consumed as a fuel, whereupon waste oils and tars were produced through incomplete combustion. Report all consumption of residual fuel oil in column (9) for fuel consumption.

a. Report the quantity of waste oils and tars produced in column (7) for onsite production **ONLY** if some or all of the byproduct energy source was also consumed onsite as a fuel at your establishment.

Example from 1994 Manufacturing Energy Consumption Survey, conducted by U.S. Bureau of the Census for the Energy Information Administration.

provided at the point at which they are needed. The fact that very detailed instructions are sometimes needed for defining items in business questionnaires means that questionnaires may consist more of explanations than questions, making it difficult to follow the prescribed navigational path. When instructions are printed separately, the respondent is more likely to try to get along without them and as a consequence may make mistakes. For these reasons, four possible solutions are considered below.

First, an effort is made to shorten the instructions so they can be embedded in questions. A review of some questionnaire booklets makes it clear that they are overburdened with unnecessary detail; for example, "Be sure to provide an answer to each question . . . Please check the answer to this question which best fits your situation . . . This question is self-explanatory."

Sometimes, however, eliminating separate instructions simply is not possible. This leads to consideration of a second possibility—printing instructions on the left of two facing pages and asking for answers to be provided on the right facing page. These pages are printed in different figure/ground formats (e.g., question page on colored background or in space surrounded by a box) to make it evident that instruction pages are for a different purpose. As a consequence, the respondent knows immediately where to look to find a needed explanation.

A third possibility concerns the case of instruction booklets containing information needed only for one or a few questions, for instance, a list of business or occupation codes. In these instances the key to the codes can be placed on the last page of the questionnaire and instructions for where to find them placed in the text of the question where they are first needed.

If these possibilities have been considered and more space is still needed, a separate instruction book may be necessary. Such instruction books should be keyed to the questions so that finding needed information is easy. Three considerations facilitate the swift location of instructions. One is the use of one series of numbers for all questions in a questionnaire, from 1–126, rather than constantly starting over with I.A.l and II.A.1, IIA.2, and III.A.1, etc. The former format is shown in Figure 10.3, and the latter format is used in the questionnaire revision shown in Figure 10.4. Several times I have been shown questionnaires and instruction booklets that were extremely difficult to follow because the writer of the questionnaire used an outline form with constant repetition of letters and numbers, as in the sequence just shown. The problem is that when a respondent looks at a paragraph of the instruction book, it is sometimes very difficult to know to which question the instruction applies. This particular questionnaire was extraordinarily difficult for respondents to absorb and use.

Principle 10.5: Conduct on-site cognitive interviews to help tailor the questionnaire to people's ability to respond and to gather intelligence information for targeting its delivery and retrieval.

In many respects this is the most important principle for conducting business surveys, and also the most likely to be ignored. Work with dozens of professionals and agency administrators leads me to the conclusion that the vast majority of self-administered business surveys are done without doing cognitive interviews, which were described in Chapter 3. These interviews are needed in order to shape questions in ways that will enable people to understand what is wanted and to be able to answer them. Often individual-person or household questionnaires are tested with reasonable effectiveness on people who are not part of the proposed sample. When such questionnaires consist mostly of individual opinions and demographics, most pretest objectives can be accomplished in that way. However, in establishment surveys, people are responding for the business and from the perspective of their role in its operation. A cognitive interview that asks a possible respondent to answer each of the questions while thinking aloud, can provide immediate insight into whether requested information is kept by the business in the same way it is asked for in the questionnaire, whether it is necessary to check records, and whether one person can answer all of the questions or whether it will take more than one (Ware-Martin, 1999; Willamack, Nicholls, and Sudman, 1999). Having this knowledge is critical for formulating an effective response strategy.

Sometimes business questionnaires, like others, are composed of questions that the sponsors think are interesting to ask, but may not be essential to the study objectives. Tomaskovic-Devey et al. (1994) note that requests for financial information often trigger nonresponse. They advocate asking the financial information only if it is central to the study's purposes, especially for subsidiaries and multi-establishment firms. Cognitive interviews may help identify particularly sensitive questions and help investigators decide whether elimination of such questions, or perhaps framing them in less objectionable ways (e.g., broad categories instead of precise numbers, as suggested in Chapter 2), still allows the study objectives to be accomplished.

In a companion analysis to their study of response rates, Tomaskovic-Devey, Leiter, and Thompson (1995) show that item nonresponse is often high. Moreover, it is highest among organizations that are more complex, have smaller administrative capacity, are subsidiaries or branch plants, and are less dependent on their environments for resources. Well-done cognitive interviews will assist in identifying questions that are likely to obtain high item nonresponse rates and may suggest alternative wordings or other methods for reducing them.

Another useful insight to be gained from cognitive interviews is whether one person can fill out the questionnaire or whether it must be attended to by several people. If the latter is the case, survey designers might consider changing some questions (for example, using broad estimates instead of precise values) to encourage one person to complete the entire questionnaire, or at least organize the questionnaire so that all questions likely to be completed by one person are located together, rather than being dispersed throughout the questionnaire.

Conducting cognitive interviews on site will also be helpful in ascertaining how businesses are organized and determining what questions should be asked of a business when a precontact is made. It may also help determine whether the questionnaire should be sent to the business or whether it might be more useful to send it directly to a corporate office.

Procedures for and benefits of conducting an effective cognitive research program for business surveys have been described by Ware-Martin (1999).

The effectiveness of business survey cognitive interviews has also been evaluated by Willamack, Nicholls, and Sudman (1999).

Principle 10.6: Target communications to gatekeepers where appropriate.

Business surveys introduce the possibility and, in some cases, the likelihood of having to go through someone to reach the appropriate respondent. Case Study 4 presented an example of contacting one person (a university president or CEO) as a means of identifying an appropriate respondent, then obtaining the designated respondent's name so further contacts could be made directly with that individual. Case Study 5 presented a quite different example of having to talk with receptionists for physicians who schedule much of their day with patients, where the receptionist's help is needed in trying to schedule a time when the physician is most likely to be available. The decision to use both mail and telephone was aimed at finding alternative ways of getting to the designated respondent.

Once, when as many as 20 phone calls were scheduled for contacting CEOs, it was decided to assign the repeated call-backs to small teams of interviewers so that all of the calls to one business over a period of several weeks would be made by one or two people. In some instances this action allowed the interviewers to "get acquainted" with the receptionist or secretary. When it was time to draw the telephoning to a close before switching to mail follow-up, the interviewers explained to these assistants that it was the last week of calling and the interview needed to be done that week. A burst of response came during this last week partly because, it was believed, the assistants worked harder to help the interviewer by finding a time for the owner or manager to be interviewed (Petrie et al., 1998).

Principle 10.7: For repeated surveys of the same businesses and individuals, consider the use of follow-up communications after a response is received.

The design of correspondence for most surveys is aimed at getting people to respond. It is unusual to consider follow-up communications afterwards. However, business studies that survey the same organizations year after year might usefully consider thanking people for timely responses.

Principle 10.8: Be cautious with regard to the use of incentives and fit them carefully to sponsorship as well as the recipient.

For small businesses, token financial incentives often have effects similar to those for individual-person surveys (James and Bolstein, 1992). The similarity between many small businesses, which involve only one or a few people, and an individual person survey is obvious. Also, we have noted the benefit of including token incentives for getting questionnaires past gatekeepers who might otherwise throw the questionnaire away without ever showing it to the person who is being asked to respond.

Big businesses present other issues, including violations of ethics policies if recipients were to keep any amount of money for themselves. Handling a token incentive may become irritating to individuals who feel they have to go through a formal process of turning in the money. In general, it seems important to consider the tradeoff of bringing attention to the questionnaire versus creating a degree of irritation, especially if many large businesses are included in a survey.

Principle 10.9: Consider different tailoring of correspondence and questionnaires to subgroups of a population.

Tomaskovic-Devey et al. (1994) suggest survey administration flexibility as a means of improving response to business surveys. The wording of a request for response to a head office, sent because a branch office says they are not allowed to respond to surveys, needs to be different from that sent to the local office. Also, when questionnaires are sent to a heterogeneous sample of businesses, perhaps including construction and manufacturing as well as retail trade and social service, it is likely that the questions that some find easy to answer may be impossible for another. For example, "What product do you produce?" makes sense for a manufacturing firm but not for a retail store. It is likely that response could be improved to business surveys if consideration were given to tailoring both the correspondence and the questionnaire.

Tailoring procedures within samples represents a degree of tailoring not previously discussed in this book, and for many large-scale surveys such specificity may be impossible. For others, it may well have considerable payoff, especially when considered against the tail-end strategies needed for dealing with greater numbers of nonrespondents who resist phone calls and other survey attempts because they believe the survey simply doesn't apply to them.

CONCLUSIONS

Tailoring strategies for business surveys require not only application of the procedures and techniques discussed in Part I, but also taking into account that respondents are answering questionnaires in their role as organizational representatives. That role introduces new issues that must be considered. The result is to raise the desirability of tailoring to a degree greater than discussed for other populations and survey situations, even to the point of sending different questionnaires and correspondence to different subgroups.

Tailoring to this extent provides an extreme contrast with the way that one may think of doing business surveys by mail. Many government business surveys have changed little over the years, maintaining a form orientation that does not utilize the design principles discussed in Chapter 3. Moreover, mass correspondence has often been used to reach businesses by the tens of thousands or even millions. To the extent that these surveys have served as a model for the conduct of other business surveys, little emphasis has been placed on tailoring procedures for obtaining higher response rates and better quality data. Thus, the ideas described in this chapter suggest a challenging frontier for designing business surveys, and about which many specifics are still to be learned.

I now turn to recent developments in the area of electronic surveying by the Internet and Interactive Voice Response (IVR) surveys. Both of these are methods that I expect to be used increasingly for the conduct of business surveys in the early twenty-first century.

CHAPTER 11

Internet and Interactive Voice Response Surveys

THE TWO most significant advances in survey methodology during the twentieth century were the introduction of random sampling in the 1940s and interviewing by telephone in the 1970s. Both of these innovations have transformed how most major surveys are done. We are now witnessing another development in survey methodology, the consequences of which may prove to be even more profound. It is the collection of survey data through self-administered electronic surveys by e-mail; the World Wide Web; and Interactive Voice Response (IVR), or, in its original form, touch-tone data entry (TDE).

Past advances in survey design have typically been motivated in part by cost considerations. Probability sampling provided the foundation for making precise population estimates by surveying small numbers of people who were selected in ways that reduced interviewing costs. Telephone interviewing eliminated the expensive call-backs associated with traveling to conduct face-to-face interviews. Computerized telephone interviewing introduced additional efficiencies, ranging from the elimination of data entry as a separate activity to computer-assisted call scheduling and respondent selection.

The electronic survey methods discussed in this chapter have the potential for bringing efficiencies of comparable importance to the design and administration of self-administered questionnaires. These efficiencies include the nearly complete elimination of paper, postage, mailout, and data entry costs. Some of these electronic survey methods (e-mail and Web) also provide a potential for overcoming international boundaries as significant barriers to conducting surveys. In addition, the time required for survey implementation can be reduced from weeks to days, or even hours. Most importantly, the introduction of electronic survey methodologies offers the potential for dramatically reducing the close correspondence between sample size and survey costs. Once the electronic data collection system has been developed, the cost of surveying each additional person is much less, compared with both telephone interview and postal procedures. In some instances these technologies may result in decisions to survey entire populations rather than only a sample.

Electronic surveying also requires the surveyor to take a somewhat different look at the social exchange elements of responding to a survey. Whereas it can be assumed that most people have previous experiences with paper and pencil questionnaires, that cannot be assumed for people who are asked to respond to electronic surveys. Minimizing the costs associated with learning the skills needed for answering a touch-tone data entry or Internet questionnaire requires focusing on how the response task is explained to people and how they might be rewarded for doing it correctly. In addition, the security and confidentiality issues associated with electronic technologies raise entirely new issues of trust that must be considered, but have not been addressed adequately by researchers.

This chapter is limited only to e-mail, Web, and IVR (or TDE) surveys, which are already seeing extensive use for surveying geographically dispersed general populations. In addition to the three survey methods discussed in this chapter, other electronic self-administered survey methods have also been developed. One such method is to bring computers into people's homes (CAPI, or Computer-Assisted Personal Interviewing), schools, or places of business and ask the respondent to record responses on the computer while reading questions from the screen or listening to a recording of an interviewer who asks each question and provides instructions on how to respond. Another method is to send and retrieve computer disks by mail (de Leeuw, Hox, and Snijkers, 1995). I expect that these procedures, which involve the physical transport of materials, will be mostly replaced by the three applications discussed in this chapter.

Both the software and hardware needed for conducting the electronic surveys discussed here are changing rapidly. Thus, my emphasis in this chapter is less on specific software and equipment than on the more general principles that need to guide the development and use of specific applications to reduce survey error.

SURVEYS ON THE INTERNET

E-mail and Web surveys share much in common. Both involve computer-to-computer communication over the Internet. Most people who can access e-mail are also able to access Web surveys. However, surveys done by these methods also differ from each other in significant ways. While e-mail surveys are simpler to compose and send, they are more limited with regard to their visual stimulation and interaction capabilities, and provide fewer options for dealing with difficult structural features of questionnaires such as extensive skip patterns. An e-mail survey, at present, is little more than a simple text message, and its construction may require computer skills no greater than those needed for composing and sending a message to a friend.

Web surveys, in contrast, not only have a more refined appearance to which color may be added, but also provide survey capabilities far beyond those available for any other type of self-administered questionnaire. They can be designed so as to provide a more dynamic interaction between respondent and questionnaire than can be achieved in e-mail or paper surveys. Extensive and difficult skip patterns can be designed into Web questionnaires in ways that are mostly invisible to the respondent. Pop-up instructions can be provided for individual questions, making it far easier to provide needed help with questions exactly where that assistance is required and without having to direct the respondent to a separate set of instructions. Similarly, drop-down boxes with long lists of answer choices can be used to provide immediate coding of answers to certain questions that are usually asked in an open-ended fashion in paper questionnaires, for example, "In which of our 50 states do you live?" Being able to ask questions with many answer choices in a closed-ended fashion makes it possible to use the answer as a screening question that directs respondents to a unique set of questions about the state in which they live, something that would most likely be impractical for a paper questionnaire. In addition, a nearly infinite variety of shapes and colors can be used to format a particular survey. Pictures can easily be scanned into a Web survey, allowing, for example, respondents to view several car designs and choose the one they like best. Animation, video clips, and audio can also be added. Without a doubt, the potential offered by Web surveys for conducting innovative surveys is enormous. They offer multiple possibilities that cannot be realized within the more limited confines of paper or interview questionnaires.

Ironically, the enormous number of imaginative possibilities for constructing Web questionnaires also present major risks of increased survey error. Sometimes surveys are designed with a level of technical sophistication that makes it impossible for some Web users to receive and respond to them. Moreover, as we shall see, certain ways of designing questions may result in the items seen by a respondent with one type of computer operating system and screen configuration appearing significantly different from the same questions seen by a respondent who has another. These and other issues lead to the development of a substantial number of principles for the design and implementation of Web questionnaires.

Current Coverage is Inadequate for Most E-mail and Web Surveys

The enormous potential for e-mail and Web surveys must be balanced against an equally large weakness. Most households and people do not have computers and/or e-mail addresses. In October 1998, only 42% of U.S. households reported owning a computer, up from 24% in 1994. A total of 26% were reported as having e-mail connections, compared with only 3% in 1994 (National Telecommunication and Information Administration, 1999). Examined another way, e-mail access appears to be somewhat higher. A series of five CBS/*New York Times* telephone polls conducted of households from March through November 1998, showed that 67% of the respondents had "access to a computer." In addition, a total of 31%, or nearly a third of these households, reported having an e-mail address through which they could send or receive electronic mail messages by computer. Many of these access points were undoubtedly through an employer. Nonetheless, it remains true that only a fraction of the U.S. population can be contacted through e-mail. This means that there is no possibility for listing general populations and drawing a sample in which nearly every adult in the U.S. population has a known nonzero chance of being selected for participation in a survey.

Based on this information, the number of households in which household members can access e-mail is nearly as low as the 35% of U.S. households with telephones in 1936, when the infamous *Literary Digest* survey used telephone listings for its survey of over a million people and erroneously predicted that Landon would beat Roosevelt in that year's presidential election. Sampling from telephone directories biased selection in favor of higher income households in which members were more likely to vote Republican, thereby producing the wrong prediction for the outcome. The impact of that inaccurate publication was partly responsible for setting back the serious use of the telephone for conducting sample surveys until the 1970s, when the percentage of households with telephones climbed to about 90%. It is useful to recall this experience as some pollsters rush forward to use results from Internet surveys to predict current election outcomes.

Increasingly, Web surveys are being set up with appeals for anyone to respond. In a recent content analysis by Bowker (1999), nearly 1,000 Web surveys were located and analyzed. They included customer feedback surveys, university experiments, customer preference questionnaires, various public opinion polls, and others. They also included attempts to predict election outcomes using only volunteer respondents to a Web survey. Certain widely advertised Web surveys, constructed with advanced features, have attracted respondents numbering in the tens of thousands. The implicit assumption is that huge numbers of respondents, which can be achieved with so little effort and at low cost, are representative of the entire population, or can be weighted so as to be representative. Results of such surveys are seductive, encouraging the scientifically naive observer to think of them as surely being representative of some larger population. Just as for the *Literary Digest* survey in 1936, obtaining responses from large numbers of respondents cannot substitute for meeting the survey requirement of good coverage, as discussed in Chapter 5.

However, not all Web surveys will face these difficulties. For example, if one wishes only to survey people who use electronic mail or the Web, then lack of coverage may not be a problem. Certain populations, such as university professors, federal government employees, workers in many companies and corporations, and members of some professional organizations, generally have Internet addresses and access. For these populations, e-mail and Web surveys may have only minor coverage problems.

At the same time, the structure of Internet addresses is not emerging in a way that allows them to be sampled so that a nearly one-to-one correspondence with households is achieved, as was once the case with the telephone. Many households have multiple e-mail addresses, with each member of a household having a different address. Some individuals may have several addresses. In addition, e-mail addresses have not been formulated in a standardized way, such as our current system of 10-digit telephone numbers (three-digit area code plus three-digit exchange plus four-digit individual identifier) that allowed random digit probability sampling methods to be developed. It is also noteworthy that e-mail address directories are not available in a way that gives all e-mail addresses a known probability of being available for sampling. In sum, e-mail and Web surveying of the general public is currently inadequate as a means of accessing random samples of defined populations of households and/or individuals.

The overall coverage situation will undoubtedly change. We are on a trajectory of millions of new Internet addresses being added each year and I doubt that this trend will soon diminish. Computers and Internet access have become basic work requirements for an increasing portion of the population. Also, technological changes are bringing the telephone, television, and computer together as one instrument, an accomplishment that will undoubtedly provide the potential for conducting more surveys by electronic means in the near future. In addition, the continued growth in e-mail accounts may eventually lead to efforts to standardize e-mail addresses to a degree that facilitates the drawing of probability samples from which statistical inferences for a defined population can be made.

I expect that a specific implication of this situation will be that the early use of Internet surveys for conducting high quality probability surveys will be limited to survey populations with high rates of computer use. Surveys of businesses, universities, large organizations, groups of professionals, and purchasers of computer equipment are examples. In addition, electronic questionnaires will be collected as part of a mixed-mode design whereby those without such access are surveyed by traditional mail or telephone procedures. The likelihood of such mixed-mode uses places a high priority on the need to understand the mode effects, if any, of Internet survey methods, a topic on which little research has as yet been done.

Effects of Computer Equipment and Telecommunications Access

Enormous differences exist in the capabilities of people's computers and software that allow them to access e-mail and Web surveys. The range in age and power of computer equipment is reminiscent of the variation one can observe among cars on a highway. Although more powerful, easier to use computers come onto the market each year, that fact alone improves other people's access; replaced computers and software become available to others at a much lower cost. However, unlike automobiles, new and more powerful computers continue to become available at lower costs than their predecessors, thus fueling to an even greater extent the wide adoption of both new and old computer technologies.

Several features of one's computer system may influence the appearance of a Web questionnaire image. For example, computer monitors vary in size and may be configured for different screen displays. As a result, the images some people see on a screen will be different from those seen by others. In addition, whether the user chooses to use a full screen view of a Web questionnaire or a partial (tiled) screen view may affect whether the entire question stem plus categories may be seen without scrolling and whether lines wrap around (break into shorter lengths). The ease by which computer screen displays can be made larger or smaller means that carefully constructed visual displays of questionnaires may be revealed differently than intended for the respondent. In addition, whereas most people are now able to point and click with a mouse, a few users must still use arrow and function keys. These variations also mean that the use of more advanced programming techniques to construct Web surveys may result in people with older Web browsers receiving questionnaires with disabled features, or not being able to receive them at all.

In addition, people are connected to Internet servers by telephone lines with widely varying transmission capabilities. A screen full of text that may take a few seconds for some people to receive may take minutes for others to obtain because of poorer connections, older equipment, and the lesser capability of some Internet service providers (ISPs). For the most part, businesses are able to obtain better telecommunications access than households. In addition, people who live in higher income areas of the United States or in places that are more densely populated typically have better connections because of better ISP access as well as telecommunications infrastructure. Although most people in the United States can now receive Internet service for a flat fee, a small minority must pay long-distance charges to their local carrier, with the result that they will be charged by the minute for completing someone else's questionnaire, a cost that few people seem likely to tolerate.

However, enormous progress has been made in upgrading telephone line access over the last decade and equipment continues to improve in ways that take advantage of the greater capability. Far from being discouraging, these issues illustrate the rapidity of innovation in computer equipment and access, and suggest considerable long-term optimism with regard to conducting e-mail and Web surveys. In the meantime, the challenges for effective surveying through these means are considerable and must be taken into account when designing electronic surveys.

EFFECTS OF COMPUTER LITERACY

Having access to a computer does not mean that people know how to use it to complete a questionnaire, whether by e-mail or on the Web. Many computer users have minimal computer skills. They may have learned to operate a word processing program, to post accounting information, to play a favorite game, or to use a program that facilitates a hobby. For some computer users, the request to complete a survey ushers them into a new experience for which needed computer skills have to be learned.

This situation will also change. As computers become more powerful, the task of switching from one activity to another becomes simpler. For example, one of the original limitations of Web surveys was that if one received an e-mail message asking that a Web survey be completed it may have required writing down the Web survey address (URL), closing the e-mail application and opening the Internet browser, and then having to key in a very long address to find the survey. That task and the inevitable errors of keying in addresses discouraged response. Newer e-mail applications make it possible to click on a Web address provided within an e-mail message and transfer seamlessly to the desired Web page.

Nonetheless, for now Internet surveys need to be designed with the less knowledgeable, low-end computer user in mind. Unlike the simple skills needed for receiving a mail questionnaire, retrieval of an electronic survey requires a sequence of actions with which most of the U.S. population is not yet familiar.

COMPUTER LOGIC VERSUS QUESTIONNAIRE LOGIC AND THE NEED TO DESIGN WITH BOTH IN MIND

When conducting my first e-mail survey, the research team was momentarily puzzled by a phone call from a recipient who explained that he would like to respond but that the questionnaire would not take his answers. Several questions later the problem became evident. He had not clicked the reply button. This person (as well as subsequent callers with the same question) was familiar with e-mail and the necessity of clicking the "reply" response before he could begin keying a message, but had not thought of the questionnaire as having this similarity to an e-mail message.

A somewhat different problem was observed while watching a respondent come to an instruction in a Web survey that read "If you are a homeowner skip these questions," which appeared in blue type with underlining (a hyperlink). He noted with much frustration that the instruction did not tell him to where he should skip, and stopped responding. When it was pointed out to him that because it was highlighted all he needed to do was click for the next questions to appear, he reacted with embarrassment, realizing that if he had seen such a message in another context, for example, searching for something on a Web page, he would have known that it was necessary to click in order to skip to the correct location.

Most people have some familiarity with paper questionnaires, realizing that there are questions and answer categories with spaces provided for them to mark their response. However, when faced with the request to complete an electronic questionnaire, they immediately attempt to apply this kind of logical thinking and may forget momentarily that they are operating a computer. To complete either an e-mail or Web survey requires the application of computer logic, which involves knowing when to click, hit the return key, delete, backspace, push a function key, or perform some other task. Unfortunately, different computers and software require different operational actions. Further, being asked to complete a questionnaire may require actions that people are not used to performing in the regular software applications they have learned. Therefore, following computer logic when responding to a questionnaire is not as simple as using a straightforward, known set of response actions.

Meshing the demands of questionnaire logic and computer logic creates a need for instructions and assistance, which can easily be overlooked by the designer who takes for granted the respondent's facility with computer and Web software. The implication of these two logical systems is that great care must be taken in building e-mail and Web surveys in order to explain to respondents what they need to do to respond. The building of such instructions takes on the same level of importance as writing the survey questions, and is especially important for reducing the social costs of surveying people with limited computer experience.

A Fundamental Distinction between Designing for Paper and the Internet

In the remainder of this Internet section, many principles are presented for designing effective e-mail and Web surveys. These principles are variously aimed at reducing coverage, measurement, and nonresponse errors that flow from the considerations already discussed in this chapter. The major challenge of tailoring the methods discussed in Part I of this book for e-mail and Web surveys is summarized in Figure 11.1. The paper questionnaire designer produces a questionnaire that gives the same visual appearance to the

Figure 11.1 A fundamental difference between the design of paper and Internet surveys.

Paper questionnaire: The designer and respondent see the same visual image.

Web questionnaires: The designer and respondent may see different images because of different operating systems, browsers, screen configuration, tiled vs. full-screen displays, and individual designer decisions (e.g., color and text wrap-around).

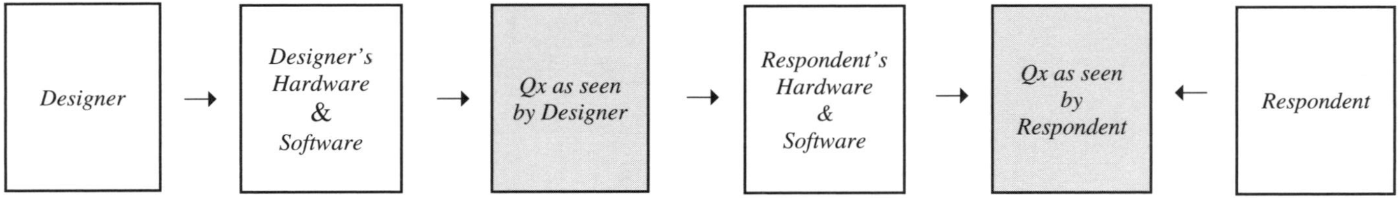

designer as to the respondent. However, in the case of both e-mail and Web surveys the intentions of the designer for the creation, sending, and receipt of the questionnaire are mediated through the hardware, software, and user preferences. The final design, as seen by the creator, is sent to the respondent's computer, which displays the questionnaire for viewing by the respondent. It is not only possible but likely that the questionnaire seen by the respondent will not be exactly the same as that intended by the creator, for several reasons. The respondent may have a computer with a different operating system (e.g., PC versus Macintosh), a different kind of Web browser (e.g., Internet Explorer versus Netscape), or even a different release of browser software (Internet Explorer 3.0 versus 4.0). Respondents may also choose a different setting for the screen configuration (the three most common are 640 × 480, 800 × 600, or 1024 × 768 pixels), and may choose to view the questionnaire as a full or partial (tiled) screen. As a result of any or all of these differences, what the designer sees on the screen may be quite different from what is seen by the respondent, particularly for Web surveys. Some of the disparities between what the designer and respondent see may include:

- Colors (both foreground and background) that are different.
- Changes in the relative distances between horizontal scale categories (as well as absolute differences).
- Text that becomes misaligned.
- Questions that are not fully visible on the respondent's screen, which therefore require horizontal scrolling to be seen in their entirety.
- A change in the visual appearance of questions because of features installed by the questionnaire designer that are disabled by the respondent's computer.

The methodological consequences of one respondent seeing something quite different from that seen by another respondent on a screen are not yet known. Surveying on the Internet requires coming to terms with these new aspects of surveying and taking programming and designing steps that minimize such differences across respondents whenever possible. The development of principles for doing Internet surveys focuses precisely on these concerns.

Designing Electronic Mail Surveys

In principle, constructing an e-mail survey is as simple as composing a list of questions on the computer screen, sending them to selected individuals, asking them to click the reply function, fill in the answer spaces, and press the send command. Most e-mail systems have been designed to allow use without the learning of complicated commands. The person who knows how to send and receive messages has the fundamental capabilities needed for composing and/or replying to an e-mail survey. From a communication perspective, the process seems little different than that of sending a letter and questionnaire by physical mail. Thus, it should not be surprising to learn that many of the factors found important to getting response to mail surveys are also important in e-mail surveys. The design of an e-mail survey that was modeled in accordance with procedures found effective for achieving response to postal surveys and that also attained a comparable response rate is described below.

Case Study: An E-mail Survey of University Faculty

A survey of faculty at Washington State University was done to determine the extent to which instruction on ethics was included in the classes taught at that university. The results needed to be obtained quickly for use by a university committee (Schaefer and Dillman, 1998). It was known that close to 90% of the faculty had electronic mail access (so a certain amount of coverage error existed), and it was unknown whether all existing e-mail addresses could be obtained (Carley, 1996). Therefore, we decided to design a mixed-mode survey, using e-mail for responses from as many faculty as possible and paper questionnaires for the remainder.

E-mail addresses were available for about two-thirds of the faculty from an online directory, and most of the remainder were obtained by contacting secretarial staff of each university department. Four treatment groups were identified, each of which received up to four contacts—a prenotice, the questionnaire, a thank you/reminder, and a replacement questionnaire. The first group was sent only paper questionnaires and the second group was contacted only by e-mail. The third and fourth treatment groups each received e-mail questionnaires. However, the third treatment group received its prenotice by regular mail instead of e-mail, and the fourth treatment group received its postcard thank you/reminder in that way. The thank you/reminder sent by e-mail included a replacement questionnaire, whereas the thank you/reminder sent by postal mail did not. This difference was accepted in the research design as tailoring appropriate to the technology; it seemed to make little sense to send a thank you/reminder by e-mail without including a replacement questionnaire. There was no additional cost, as there would be with postal mail, and it was a logical way to minimize inconvenience for the sampled faculty member.

Beginning the contact sequence with a prenotice was deemed especially important because it is extremely easy to discard messages, particularly if they appear long. Notifying people a few days prior to sending the questionnaire was deemed likely to help avoid that consequence (Figure 11.2). The mixture of contacts by e-mail and regular mail in Treatments 3 and 4 was introduced because of the concern that some individuals might not use their e-mail accounts regularly. All individuals in the groups designated to receive e-mail surveys who did not have e-mail addresses were sent paper questionnaires and reminders.

The e-mail questionnaires were prepared as individual messages to each potential respondent using cut and paste features of the Eudora e-mail software, cued for

Figure 11.2 Example of an e-mail prior letter for a university faculty survey (slightly revised from original).

X-Senderpetrie@mail.wsu.edu
X-MailerQUALCOMM Windows Eudora Pro Version 4.0.1
DateTue, 29 Dec 1998 113123 -0800
ToJaneDoe@mail.wsu.edu
FromRenee Petrie<petrie@wsu.edu>
Subject: faculty survey

Over the past year, an interest group within Washington State University has expressed concern with the teaching of ethics in our classrooms. This committee is committed to identifying resources to assist the faculty with their ethics instruction. However, it has become evident that apart from some obvious cases (e.g., Philosophy), we have no information on who teaches ethics or the extent of this instruction. In order to help us respond to the need for resources on ethics instruction, we have asked the Social and Economic Sciences Research Center (SESRC) to gather this information from our faculty.

Within the next couple of days you will be receiving a brief survey from SESRC at this same e-mail address. We would greatly appreciate it if you could take a few moments to complete it. By doing so you will help ensure that we have the best information possible.

If you have any questions, feel free to contact Renee Petrie in the SESRC at 335-1511, or by e-mail at ethics@wsunix.wsu.edu.

Thank you in advance for your cooperation.

Sincerely,

John Pierce, Dean
College of Liberal Arts

sending, and mailed to everyone at the same time. Sending a mass message, that is, showing many names in the address area or a listserv heading, was intentionally avoided because mail survey research has shown that personalization is important for achieving response. Thus, the e-mail message would appear to be addressed to individual respondents.

The questionnaire contained 44 questions and was inserted in the e-mail message immediately following a cover letter from the sponsor (Figure 11.3). The

Figure 11.3 Example of an e-mail survey cover letter and first questions for a university faculty survey (slightly revised from original).

X-Senderpetrie@mail.wsu.edu
X-MailerQUALCOMM Windows Eudora Pro Version 4.0.1
DateTue, 29 Dec 1998 113123 -0800
ToJaneDoe@mail.wsu.edu
FromRenee Petrie<petrie@wsu.edu>
Subject: faculty survey

Here is the brief survey on how ethics are being taught at WSU which Dean Pierce notified you about via e-mail a few days ago. The WSU committee that he is a part of has found there is very little information on the current situation at WSU, and thus is asking for faculty help via this brief survey. Your thoughts and experiences will be of great help to the committee.

There are two ways to answer this survey:

1. Touch the "Reply" command on your computer, enter your response, and touch "Send."

2. Print this message and return it with your answers to the SESRC via campus mail (zip 4014).

Should you have any questions, you can reach me (Renee Petrie) at 335-1511, or by e-mail at petrie@wsu.edu.

* * * * * * * * * * * * * * *

For the questions which follow, ethics refers to justification for why actions are right or wrong. In particular, applied ethics refers to special duties relevant to one's profession (e.g., teacher, pharmacist) or role (e.g., student, citizen, etc.).

1. How important do you think it is that instruction in ethics be part of the curriculum at Washington State University? ***(Please type an X anywhere between the appropriate brackets, like this: [X].)***

[ ] Very Important
[ ] Somewhat Important
[ ] Not Important

2. Do agree or disagree that ethics should be taught to students in each of the following formats? ***(Please place one X per row to indicate your opinion.)***

Agree	**Neutral**	**Disagree**	
[ ]	[ ]	[ ]	A required course in a major.
[ ]	[ ]	[ ]	Part of all courses in a major.
[ ]	[ ]	[ ]	At least part of some of each student's courses in major.
[ ]	[ ]	[ ]	Required Gen Ed.
[ ]	[ ]	[ ]	Part of all Gen Ed courses.
[ ]	[ ]	[ ]	At least part of some of each student's Gen Ed courses.
[ ]	[ ]	[ ]	At least part of some of each student's courses.
[ ]	[ ]	[ ]	Part of internship courses.

Figure 11.4 E-mail thank you/reminder converted to more appropriate format with replacement questionnaire (slightly revised from original).

X-Senderpetrie@mail.wsu.edu
X-MailerQUALCOMM Windows Eudora Pro Version 4.0.1
DateTue, 29 Dec 1998 113123 -0800
ToJaneDoe@mail.wsu.edu
FromRenee Petrie<petrie@wsu.edu>
Subject: faculty survey

About a week ago we sent you a survey via e-mail on behalf of the WSU Ethics Interest Group. We are asking faculty about their experience and opinions on the teaching of ethics. As of today, we have not received a completed survey from you. I realize this is a busy time of year as the semester is drawing to a close. However, we have contacted you and others now in hopes of obtaining the insights only WSU faculty like you can provide, and which the Ethics Interest Group can consider in their upcoming meetings. As we mentioned before, answers are confidential to the SESRC and will be combined with others before providing results to this important WSU interest group. In case the previous questionnaire has been deleted from your e-mail account, we have included it again.

There are three ways you can respond:

1. Reply to this message and follow the directions for each question.

2. Print this message and return it to us via campus mail (Zip 4014).

3. Contact us by phone or e-mail and request a questionnaire be sent to you.

Should you have any questions or concerns, feel free to contact me (Renee Petrie) at 335-1511, or by e-mail at ethics@wsunix.wsu.edu. Thank you for your cooperation.

Renee Petrie

{Survey Begins Here}

---

questions were presented as numbered items, using brackets to identify answer spaces. Respondents were asked to enter an X between the brackets next to their preferred answer. Lines were kept short to limit wrap-around of text and misalignment of answer space categories. A similar procedure was used for incorporating the questionnaire into the e-mail reminder message (Figure 11.4).

Response rates for the mail survey treatment group and the all e-mail treatment group were the same, 58% (Schaefer and Dillman, 1998). However, about five percentage points of the e-mail treatment group were obtained from paper questionnaires because of the lack of e-mail addresses. Use of the paper prenotice instead of e-mail for a third treatment group lowered response for that group to 49%, and the paper reminder group had an intermediate response rate of 54%. It was also found that responses to the e-mail survey came back more quickly, with 76% of all completed e-mail questionnaires returned within four days. Longer answers to open-ended questions were also achieved by e-mail.

Implications. This experiment showed that it may be possible to achieve response rates comparable to those obtained by paper mail surveys using a mixed-mode strategy combining e-mail and paper surveys. Responses were received more quickly, item nonresponse was lower, and open-ended questions, a traditional shortcoming of paper questionnaires, received more complete answers. These results suggest the viability of an e-mail strategy when a multiple contact strategy is used. A similar four contact strategy used in an e-mail survey for members of a national voluntary organization produced a 60% response rate, thus demonstrating its usefulness in a somewhat different context (Burke, 1999).

Examination of the details of this survey of university faculty revealed many ways in which the tailoring of procedures to an e-mail strategy is essential. It was learned that some respondents must be reminded to press the "reply" button on their computers in order for their answers to be accepted; for these individuals, traditional questionnaire logic temporarily overcame the recognition that they were operating a computer. It was also learned that some individuals preferred printing the questionnaire and completing it in a traditional manner, therefore making it essential to put a traditional mailing address into each e-mail message.

Early tests of questionnaire formats revealed that the line length needed to be constrained because of the narrow margins on the computers of some recipients. This step avoids potential wrap-around of response categories that could create confusion and response inaccuracies. The speed with which questionnaires were returned also suggested that it might be possible to shorten the normal intervals between contacts as used in paper questionnaire surveys, thus overcoming the lengthy implementation time required for that type of study.

The attempt to mix paper contacts with e-mail contacts was not successful, suggesting that people do not read and connect paper contacts with e-mail contacts in a fashion that increases the likelihood of a response. Nonetheless, if both postal mail and e-mail addresses are available, it seems likely that the former can be used to send a token financial incentive at the beginning and/or as fifth contact by special mail to improve response rates further.

When e-mail surveys must be conducted on populations with different employers, it seems likely that the heterogeneity among computer equipment, software, and special networks will increase. This heterogeneity may inhibit the effective use of e-mail surveys to some degree, but not to the degree of preventing their use. Insight into these problems is provided by an e-mail experiment conducted by Couper, Blair, and Triplett (in press).

The survey by Couper et al. (in press) was an organizational climate assessment survey of employees of five U.S. statistical agencies, conducted by the University of Maryland. It contained 94 questions and was composed on a commercially available system. A four-contact strategy was used which included an e-mail message from within each agency, the questionnaire, a reminder, and a replacement questionnaire. However, these contacts varied significantly from those used for the university faculty survey. The preletter was sent by agency directors as an announcement to all agency staff, and it seems likely that many respondents did not connect it to the survey questionnaire. In addition, the reminder was a mass mailing, not individually addressed, that did not include a replacement questionnaire as done in the previously described case study. Both of these procedures seem likely to have depressed the e-mail response rates. Whereas postal mail responses for this survey averaged 71%, e-mail responses averaged only 43%, a difference of 28 percentage points. Although none of the agencies exhibited response rates for the two procedures that were closer than 13 percentage points, the largest agency produced a paper questionnaire response rate that was 31 percentage points higher than the e-mail response. This difference was traced to the possibility that the e-mail questionnaire file was sufficiently large that the organizational application automatically transferred the questionnaire into an attachment. Receipt of the questionnaire in this fashion may have increased the difficulty of responding for some respondents. In sum, this study illustrates the difficulty of conducting surveys across large organizations that use different e-mail systems. It also reveals the challenges associated with e-mail surveys that require larger questionnaires, and that must use composition methods that can accommodate larger data files.

Design Principles for E-mail Surveys

These e-mail survey experiences and related literature suggest the need to tailor the procedures discussed in Part I of this book in several ways for conducting e-mail surveys. One obvious way stems from the fact that questionnaire construction and survey implementation procedures are inextricably intertwined. Cover letters and questionnaires must be designed as a single unit. For this reason, the principles that follow include implementation methods as well as procedures for questionnaire design.

Principle 11.1: Utilize a multiple contact strategy much like that used for regular mail surveys.

Just as multiple contacts are the most important determinant of response in face-to-face, telephone, and regular mail surveys, they are essential for e-mail surveys. A prenotice e-mail message appears to take on somewhat greater importance for e-mail surveys because it is very easy to discard e-mail after reading only a tiny portion of it. The time that elapses between the prenotice and questionnaire should be shortened from one week to two or three days in order to increase the likelihood that the recipient will connect the memory of the first contact with the second. The main purpose of the prenotice is to leave a positive impression of importance so that the recipient will not immediately discard the questionnaire when it arrives.

Principle 11.2: Personalize all e-mail contacts so that none are part of a mass mailing that reveals either multiple recipient addresses or a listserv origin.

All sampled individuals should receive an individual e-mail message that contains the questionnaire. There are compelling reasons for taking this somewhat laborious route, which can be accomplished fairly efficiently by using copy and paste procedures available in some software. For reasons of confidentiality it is undesirable to include a long list of recipients on a message, a procedure that would provide each recipient's address to all other recipients. In addition, the kind of message that is most likely to get a response is one that is individually sent. Listserv procedures should also be avoided, because a reply to the sender would send a respondent's completed questionnaire to all other recipients. Even one such mistake by a respondent could immediately discourage others from responding.

An intermediate possibility that avoids the problems of listservs and the disclosure of everyone's address is to send the e-mail as a bcc (blind carbon copy) to each name on a list with a general title, for example, "Members of Citizens for Responsible Schools." No recipient will see the address of any other member and all responses will be sent only to the sender. I know of no experimental evidence available on whether using a general name will decrease response compared with sending the e-mail to individuals, and experimental research is needed on this topic.

Principle 11.3: Keep the cover letter brief to enable respondents to get to the first question without having to scroll down the page.

The heavy reliance on e-mail and the large number of messages received by some users is fostering less attentive reading behavior. This fact alone makes brevity desirable. The cover letter shown in Figure 11.3 is significantly briefer than those typically used for mail questionnaires, covering only the essence of what is being requested. Even this message is too long to allow the first question to appear simultaneously on the initial screen in certain e-mail systems, where only four or five lines of text are revealed unless the user manually expands the display window. Brevity is also warranted by the ease with which people may respond with an inquiry if information critical to them is not included. Such a request might take two to three weeks if sent by postal mail because of the need to prepare a written inquiry on paper, address it, mail it, and wait for the recipient to receive it and reply in a similar fashion.

Principle 11.4: Inform respondents of alternative ways to respond, such as printing and sending back their response.

Many people find it easier to examine and respond to long messages if they are printed on paper. In addition, putting X's into brackets is much easier for some people to do by hand than to do on the computer by using arrow and/or space keys. The letter shown in Figure 11.3 includes this information, as well as a return address for those who wish to print the questionnaire before filling it out.

Another reason for offering this possibility of a mail-back alternative is concern by some respondents about confidentiality. One effect of surveying by e-mail is to shift confidentiality concerns from what the researcher promises to whether an employer or anyone else who controls the respondent's Internet access is able to see the questionnaire responses. For many and perhaps most survey topics, confidentiality is not a big concern, but for others, for example, employee satisfaction surveys, it may become a critical factor that determines whether people will respond by e-mail. This threat of employer eavesdropping is not a consideration for most paper mail surveys.

Principle 11.5: Include a replacement questionnaire with the reminder message.

For paper mail surveys, the blanket postcard thank you/reminder has become an effective and inexpensive element of most implementation systems. It is sent soon enough (a week or so after the questionnaire) that the majority of potential respondents are likely still to have the initial questionnaire in their possession. The extra expense of sending a replacement and the likelihood that completed and replacement questionnaires will cross in the mail are also avoided. It cannot be assumed in e-mail studies that recipients still have the questionnaire. For this reason, as well as the obvious convenience of having a replacement questionnaire easily available, the normal e-mail reminder includes a replacement questionnaire (Figure 11.4). The experiment by Schaefer and Dillman (1998) found that inclusion of such a replacement encouraged faster returns and resulted in a higher final response rate. The extra effort required for including a replacement questionnaire is also minimal. Because a replacement questionnaire is included with the thank you/reminder, it is imperative that it not be sent as a listserv or other mass mailing. Finally, because e-mail questionnaires are usually received within an hour or so of being sent by the respondent, it is possible to avoid sending replacements to them, something that is impossible to accomplish with paper mail surveys.

Principle 11.6: Limit the column width of the questionnaire to about 70 characters in order to decrease the likelihood of wrap-around text.

The column width set for computer screens varies greatly, and wrap-around of lines may put questions and answer choices into a strange and difficult-to-comprehend display. For this reason, we limit the line length to about 70 characters of 12-point type. In addition, there is a readability advantage to shorter lines, just as there is for paper questionnaires. It appears that people are more likely to read every word of a question if the lines are shorter.

Principle 11.7: Begin with an interesting but simple-to-answer question.

Although this point was stressed for paper questionnaires, it is even more important for e-mail surveys, where the ease of discarding a questionnaire appears to be somewhat greater than for paper questionnaires. Observations of how people handle e-mail suggests that many people try to handle it in batches and quickly process each message only once. Messages that appear to be of minimal interest are often deleted after the recipient peruses only the first line or two of the message. Handling of each postal service letter, on the other hand, tends to follow a different path. A well-designed mail survey does not usually involve a description of the contents on the outside of the envelope (the U.S. Census procedures discussed in Chapter 9 are an exception). The lack of such information encourages opening the envelope so the contents are examined, the presence of an incentive can be seen, and the full nature of the task can be observed. In this context, introductory information and the first item on the questionnaire do not have nearly as much influence on response as equivalent information on an electronic questionnaire.

Much deliberation was given to choosing the first question for the WSU ethics survey, which is shown in Figure 11.3. It was reasoned that everyone could answer this question about how important it was to have instruction in ethics as part of the university's curriculum. Had the first question asked whether ethics was taught in the respondent's courses, recipients who did not teach ethics may have been more likely to discard the questionnaire without examining other questions, producing nonresponse error as a result. Thus, it is concluded that a special effort should be made to start e-mail questionnaires with a question that will be easy to answer and interesting to as many respondents as possible.

Principle 11.8: Ask respondents to place X's inside brackets to indicate their answers.

Marking responses with X's is a conventional response behavior, consistent with how people are often asked to fill out paper questionnaires. Brackets [ ] are a conventional computer symbol that appear on most keyboards but are not often used. Because of their infrequent use they are easily identifiable as the space where answers are to be provided. It follows that a special effort is made not to use brackets inadvertently anywhere else in the text of the e-mail questionnaire. Respondents are asked to place X's into the brackets as a means of recording their answers because it is a conventional way of marking questionnaires. This linkage of the conventionality of X's with the unconventionality of brackets provides an easily identified and remembered method of responding to e-mail questionnaires.

Principle 11.9: Consider limiting scale lengths and making other accommodations to the limitations of e-mail to facilitate mixed-mode comparisons when response comparisons with other modes will be made.

The coverage limitations of e-mail suggest that many, if not most, e-mail surveys include the possibility of collecting data from some respondents by another mode. Whenever this happens, it is essential that the questionnaires for both modes be constructed simultaneously to assure that each type of respondent receives the same stimulus. The effect of combining e-mail with either paper mail or telephone surveying will be to force a greater simplicity into questionnaires of both types, as described in Chapter 6.

The first-time designer of an e-mail survey will soon discover that it is difficult to keep screens narrow when many horizontally-listed response categories are provided for certain types of questions. An example is items in a series, each of which includes five or perhaps seven "strongly agree" to "strongly disagree" categories. Just as the switch from personal to telephone interviews encouraged designers to reduce the number of response categories and eliminate lengthy descriptors, the switch from paper to e-mail encourages a similar reduction in the number of categories and the number of words in the labels. Some designers of e-mail questionnaires simply eliminate all items in a series and list categories vertically below each item, a technique that might also be used for Web survey designs, which are discussed in the next section. Making such a change affects the context in which people respond, encouraging respondents to see items individually rather than as part of a larger group, and may therefore produce mode differences.

It is also evident that there are no easy solutions in e-mail surveys for handling extensive skip patterns. The use of arrows to direct respondents, described as a means of achieving skip pattern compliance in Chapter 3, cannot be used for e-mail questionnaires. A telephone questionnaire that has used complex skip patterns may be extremely difficult to incorporate into an e-mail format with assurance that skip directions will be followed.

Summary Perspective on E-mail

Early in the 1990s, when I first learned of serious efforts to conduct e-mail surveys, the most common assessment offered to me was that response rates were very low. Typically, surveyors sent only one e-mail message and perhaps a reminder sometime later. E-mail surveys were laborious to create and equally laborious to answer. Although computer and software developments have somewhat simplified the latter, the former issue remains a concern.

E-mail surveys must follow similar principles to those found important for other types of surveying; that is, multiple contacts are essential, and each contact needs to take the others into account. Although the technology is relatively new, the general principles that govern people's decisions to respond are not new. However, the technology also introduces new considerations. The decision not to respond is likely to be made more quickly than in the past and on the basis of less information. Use of the delete key makes disposing of a questionnaire request easier and quicker than for any other survey method, and it can be made before the full nature of the request appears on the screen. Thus, we must contemplate how the benefit, cost, and trust elements are revealed to the respondent in a situation in which less time is likely to be devoted to their consideration. These considerations lead us to tailor the design of e-mail surveys in a way that shortens timing (e.g., between prenotice and questionnaire), shortens the length of messages, keeps the questionnaire short, and even simplifies questions compared to the way they might appear in other types of surveys.

The advantages of an e-mail survey, in particular increased speed, must be weighed against the likely coverage limitations and the difficulty of marking answers. In the long run, I believe that e-mail surveys will be relied on mostly for conducting short (three- to five-question) surveys, especially when samples are small, names are already stored in computer address files so that blind copy address can easily be used, and the surveyor is seeking a turnaround of a very few days. There are two reasons for expecting this limited use. The first is the advent of a much more sophisticated survey method which has far more flexibility and power—the Web survey. The second reason is that technology is becoming available that may allow questionnaires with Web-like design qualities to be embedded within e-mail messages. However, discussion of the likely use of such technology is somewhat premature at this time.

DESIGNING WEB SURVEYS

Web surveys contrast in many ways with current e-mail surveys. Instead of the Web questionnaire being sent with an e-mail message, it is constructed on a Web site for which the respondent must have a different software application to access it. Questions are constructed in a fixed format with the goal of making the questionnaire appear the same for all respondents, although for reasons to be discussed later, this goal may not always be achieved. There are different programming languages and styles that one can use for building a Web questionnaire, some of which are quite sophisticated. Questionnaires can be constructed screen-by-screen so that each time an answer is provided the respondent goes to a new question on a new screen. Alternatively, they can be constructed so that respondents can use the scroll bar at the side of the screen to go anywhere in the questionnaire at any time. Pop-up boxes can be inserted that, when clicked on, can provide special instructions at the point they are needed in a survey. Similarly, drop-down boxes can be added that hide response options from view until they are needed. A sense of progress can be provided in an effort to avoid people quitting when they are only a few questions from the end. A creative example of such an effort was done for a survey of aerospace workers. It showed an airplane traveling down a runway, which obtained lift-off just as the last question was answered. Additional features can be added in an effort to entice people to respond to Web surveys. For example, simple animation such as a waving hand can be programmed into an introductory screen. These features offer questionnaire design response capabilities not available in any other self-administered survey method.

Use of these features, which make it possible to design questionnaires in any number of ways, may also make it difficult or impossible for people with older, less powerful computers and Web browsers to receive and respond to such surveys. In addition, recipients of a Web questionnaire must know a number of commands and when to use them in order to access the questionnaire and navigate through it. Otherwise, they may not be able to respond.

HTML (Hypertext Mark-up Language) is the dominant programming language used to create Web pages on the Internet. The original HTML language was developed in 1989. The continued development of this language, now in Version 5, has increased the ability of designers to use color, innovative question displays, split screens, embedded programs (applets), animation, sound tracks, and other advanced design features that are impossible to achieve in a paper questionnaire (e.g., Nichols and Sedivi, 1998; Dillman, Tortora, Conradt, and Bowker, 1998). As Web surveys become more complex, using such innovations as interactive elements, the data files that must be sent and received increase in size. The more such features are used, the greater the likelihood that some people's browsers will receive the Web questionnaires more slowly and that they will crash from being overloaded or not be received at all. The following case study reports on an investigation of these issues and their implications for how to and how not to construct effective Web surveys.

Case Study: A Web Survey of Computer Equipment Purchasers

An experiment was conducted to test the effects of simple versus advanced construction techniques on completion rates and other aspects of completion (Dillman, Tortora, Conradt, and Bowker, 1998). A list of names, addresses, phone numbers, and e-mail addresses was obtained for people who had recently purchased computer equipment. From this population a sample was selected randomly and called with the request that they complete a Web survey about their use of various types of Web sites, provided that they met certain screening requirements. A total of 71% of the people who were contacted by telephone completed the screening interview, 82% of whom were qualified and subsequently agreed to complete the questionnaire.

The Web site address and a personal PIN number that allowed the site to be accessed were provided to respondents over the telephone. A letter was also sent that further explained the study and repeated the Web site address and PIN number. The letter included a two-dollar bill as a token of appreciation. People who did not log on to the Web site within two weeks were sent an e-mail reminder. This reminder was repeated up to three more times over the next four weeks. Altogether, as many as five contacts were made, four of which were by e-mail, over a period of about one month. About 76% of those who received these messages logged on to the Web site to access the questionnaire.

The questionnaire was quite long, consisting of 173 pages. Because of detailed skip patterns, an average of only 45 pages needed to be completed by each respondent. One randomly selected subgroup was given access to a "plain" questionnaire, and the remainder to a "fancy" version of the same questionnaire. The fancy questionnaire was constructed using HTML tables. Alternating pink and purple bands of background color were used to align each question item with the response box for that question. In addition, a somewhat unusual (for paper questionnaires) method of formatting was used in order to place answer choices immediately next to the scroll bar. Labels were provided above the answer choice columns using graphic images. Although a screen-by-screen construction format was used for each question, the length of some questions required scrolling in order to see all of the sub-items. In contrast, the simple questionnaire was constructed without using HTML tables and consisted of black letters on a gray background. Questions were constructed using a conventional mail questionnaire construction technique in which answer boxes appeared in front of each answer choice.

The fancy version of the questionnaire required more computer memory. Specifically, whereas the plain version required about 317k, the fancy version used 959k of memory. The required time for transmission on a slow (14.4) modem was at least 225 seconds for the plain version compared with 682 seconds for the fancy one. Individuals with poorer telecommunications connections and/or hardware were likely to spend a longer time receiving the questionnaire. In addition, their computers were somewhat more likely to become overloaded and crash.

Recipients of the plain version completed a statistically significant greater number of pages (46 versus 44), more write-in boxes (four versus three), and were less likely to quit before reaching the last page. It took significantly less time to complete the plain version, and respondents were much less likely to have to return to the questionnaire at least once in order to complete it. Whereas 93% of those who logged on to the plain version eventually completed all of it, only 82% of those entering the fancy version finished it.

Implications. Several factors may have contributed to the lower response obtained by the fancy version of the questionnaire. Possibilities include respondent frustration with browser limitations, the greater length of time required for receiving the questionnaire, the unconventional questionnaire format, or even the use of color. However, it seems highly likely that variations in software and hardware capability and transmission time differences were the most significant factors. The fact that respondents were less likely to respond to the fancy version, which used programming techniques requiring greater computer memory, suggests that the use of such techniques should be restrained. The expected level of computer compatibility among respondents is of necessity a major consideration in designing a Web survey, as discussed later in this chapter.

In another study, Nichols and Sedivi (1998) found in a U.S. Bureau of the Census Web survey of businesses that it was impossible for many members of the survey population to access the survey. In addition, many of those who thought they had adequate equipment and agreed to respond encountered problems in doing so, perhaps for the same reasons encountered in the above experiment. Whereas 84% of those asked to complete equivalent paper questionnaires did so, only 68% of the experimental group submitted completed Web questionnaires. It appears that respondents' browsers were not compatible with the level of technology used to construct the questionnaire. The Census survey was conducted using an advanced high-level programming language known as Java, and the questionnaires were displayed on a page-by-page (as opposed to scrolling) basis. When questions on each page were answered, that information was sent from the respondent's computer to the host computer and the next page of information was returned. Java, like many advanced languages (e.g., XML), allows the answers to one question to be used to create response options for a succeeding question. For example, if one is asked which two out of ten choices of automobiles they find most interesting, then a succeeding question could provide pictures and more detailed descriptions of those two choices and pose even more detailed follow-up questions. However, a significant drawback to using this capability is that there must be repetitive contact between the questionnaire server and the respondent's computer while answering the questionnaire. As a result, time-consuming pauses may occur as the answer to one question is processed and the next question is sent to the respondent's computer. In addition, the greater the number of transmissions the greater the risk of transmission cutoffs. To some extent, this is compensated for by the advantage of data being obtained and saved by the surveyor in the event the computer connection is broken.

Because considerable heterogeneity exists in the browser capabilities and line transmission speeds available to respondents, the gains in creativity and skip pattern possibilities associated with advanced programming must be balanced against the costs of making it impossible for some people to respond. To the extent that a survey is investigating respondent characteristics that may be related to people's computer literacy and/or the quality of their browsers and computer connections, which seemed likely to be true for the above case study, nonresponse error is a likely result of ignoring or misjudging compatibility issues.

The designers of Web questionnaires face an unusual challenge. Instead of designing at the cutting edge of their evolving science, there is a need for them to hold back on the incorporation of advanced features, creating simpler questionnaires that require less memory and, in most cases, less time for the designer to create. The likelihood that the time required for developing questionnaires that embed advanced features will take longer means there is also a cost advantage for creating simpler questionnaires. This situation of holding back on design capabilities favoring the reduction of nonresponse error is somewhat unusual; for traditional mail surveys reducing nonresponse usually requires the expenditure of additional funds.

PRINCIPLES FOR CONSTRUCTING WEB SURVEYS

Many of the visual design principles discussed in Chapter 3 for paper questionnaires apply to Web surveys in much the same way as they do to paper questionnaires. The same need exists for information organization that is efficient and navigational guides that will encourage people to read every word in each question and all questions in the same order. Moreover, it is important to encourage respondents to read the words on each screen in a prescribed order. Examination of nearly 1,000 Web questionnaires located through a search by Bowker (1999) revealed many that tend to be constructed in ways quite different than the methods advocated in Chapter 3. An example of poor construction is shown in Figure 11.5. This screen page used unnecessary boxes into which double-banked answer categories were placed. In addition, larger, darker type appeared at the bottom rather than the top of the page and large, colorful directional buttons dominated the page. The visual design principles discussed in Chapter 3, such as the use of an open, unboxed format; appropriate grouping of the question components; and use of larger type augmented by color at the top rather than bottom of the page apply as much to Web questionnaire design as to paper questionnaires.

However, the visual mechanics are somewhat different on computer screens than on paper. When completing a paper questionnaire, people need to coordinate their eye and hand movements with the portion of the questionnaire that is being answered. The task of responding to Web surveys differs somewhat because of the addition of a hand movements between the keyboard and mouse, the addition of a cursor to one's visual field, and the software application controls that are located in the periphery of the screen. These elements add to the visual complexity required for responding to Web versus paper questionnaires.

The Web questionnaire design principles outlined here represent an early attempt to take into account these similarities as well as differences. They also recognize the tension that exists between applying traditional questionnaire and computer logic. There are differences between features associated with the visual layout of paper questionnaires (Jenkins and Dillman, 1997) and the screen design features that allow people to operate a computer most efficiently (Schneiderman, 1997).

Figure 11.5 Example of poorly constructed web questionnaire.

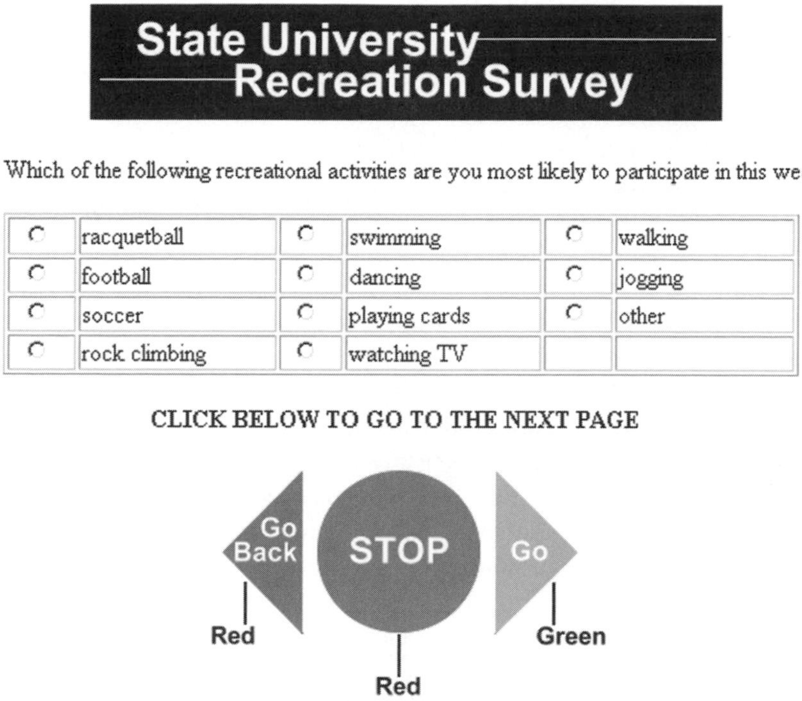

The process of designing Web questionnaires can be divided into many elements, ranging from decisions on what information should appear on each screen to which programming tools are used to present it. Individual decisions must be made about each component of the screen, ranging from line length to where the response boxes are placed. The proposed Web questionnaire design principles presented in these pages, which are a substantial extension of principles developed earlier by Dillman, Tortora, and Bowker (1998), reflect the need to limit the amount of computer resources required by the finished questionnaire as well as to assure compatibility across respondent computers. Because Web questionnaire design is separated from Web implementation procedures, another attribute that distinguishes Web from e-mail surveys, discussion of the implementation process will be reserved for later.

Principle 11.10: Introduce the Web questionnaire with a welcome screen that is motivational, emphasizes the ease of responding, and instructs respondents about how to proceed to the next page.

Potential respondents may be directed to a Web site that must either be entered manually or be achieved on certain e-mail applications by clicking on an address contained in an e-mail message. In either case, it is important that respondents know they have arrived at the right place and understand how to proceed in order to answer the questionnaire.

It is also important to realize that a Web questionnaire is self-administered and not interviewer-administered. There is no interviewer who can persuade the respondent to go beyond this initial page. Recipients of paper self-administered questionnaires are normally sent a letter that explains the reason for the survey and encourages them to respond. A similar introductory message needs to be provided on the first screen of Web questionnaires. However, because the immediately visible screen space is limited, it seems desirable to make the message short. Respondents to some, if not most, surveys will have limited experience with how to answer a Web questionnaire and perhaps how to operate a computer for this purpose. For these reasons it is important that they be informed of what action will allow them to go to the first questions. For example, making the choice between whether to press the return key or click the mouse (if they have one) may not be obvious.

The first questionnaire screen is *not* the place to give a long series of instructions or take up valuable screen space by using several lines for printing the sponsor's name. It is extremely easy to exit any Web questionnaire. Therefore, the first screen is designed to help people get to the content of the questionnaire as quickly and with as little effort as possible.

Principle 11.11: Provide a PIN number for limiting access only to people in the sample.

Surveys conducted for the purpose of generalizing results to a known population must control who completes them. Otherwise, anyone who knows a Web site address can access the questionnaire. Current search engine methods for indexing surveys make it possible for someone to easily locate a questionnaire which, if found interesting, the person may decide to fill out. This possibility was demonstrated in the search by Bowker (1999). Therefore, a PIN or identification number needs to be provided to limit questionnaire access to sampled individuals. This information also needs to appear on the welcome page. An example of a welcome page that contains a motivational message, an explanation of how to enter a PIN number, and directions for how to get to the first page of the actual questionnaire is shown in Figure 11.6.

Principle 11.12: Choose for the first question an item that is likely to be interesting to most respondents, easily answered, and fully visible on the welcome screen of the questionnaire.

The first question to appear on a screen tends to define the questionnaire as being easy or difficult to complete. If the content of the first question is hard to understand or some people do not know how to take the actions necessary to complete it, response rates are likely to suffer. The first screen is not the place

Figure 11.6 Example of a welcome screen for a web questionnaire that requires a PIN to control coverage error.

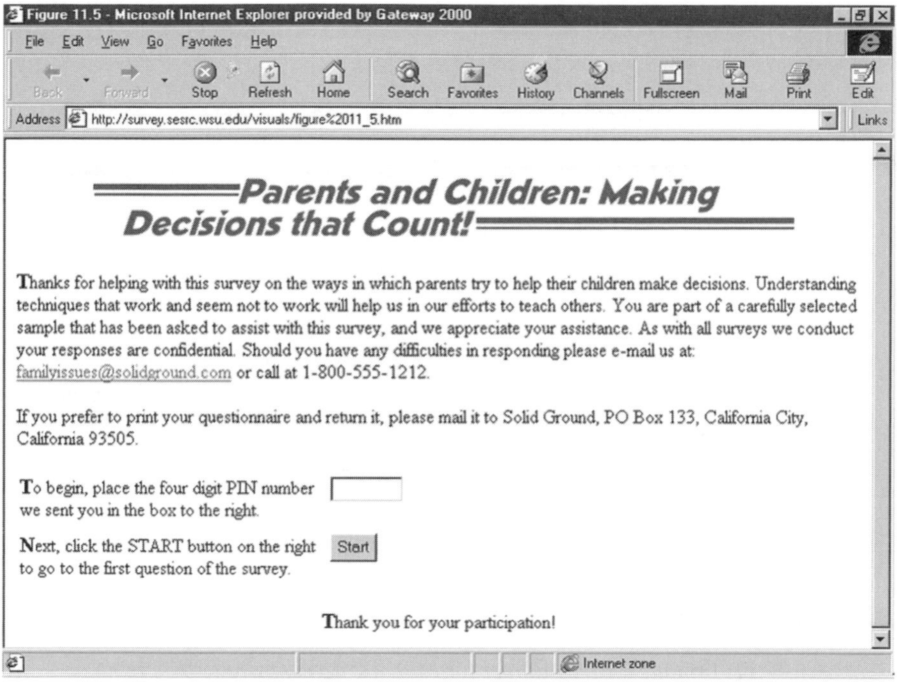

to use a drop-down box or to require scrolling in order to see the entire first question, nor is it the place to list a question that seems not to apply to some potential respondents. Therefore, it is desirable to avoid first questions like that shown in Figure 11.7. Besides including some items that probably do not apply to some respondents, it contains unexplained drop-down boxes (see Principle 11.17) and requires scrolling to see the remainder of sub-items in Question 1.

In contrast, the second example in Figure 11.7 shows a better first question which seems likely to apply to all respondents, explains how to respond, and requires only one answer before being able to move on. The initial question should be interest-getting and confirm for the respondent that it is worthwhile to continue. As is the case for paper questionnaires, this first page is not the place to list a series of background characteristics or demographic questions, such as education, age, income, or marital status, as often seems to be done in Web surveys (Bowker, 1999).

Principle 11.13: Present each question in a conventional format similar to that normally used on paper self-administered questionnaires.

In contrast to paper questionnaires, many Web questionnaires list questions that are not identified with numbers. Web questionnaires also appear that

Figure 11.7 Example of first questions from a recreational survey.

A poor first question: *Too difficult because of two answers per item, unexplained drop-down menus, more items (a-p) than can fit onto one screen, and inclusion of items that won't be of interest to everyone.*

1. **When the recreation center is open and available for use from 6 AM to 12 midnight, how often *WOULD YOU* participate in the following activities and at what time would you be most likely to participate?**

		Frequency	Time
a.	Basketball	Daily	6am - 8am
b.	Free weights	Daily	6am - 8am
c.	Weight machines	Daily	6am - 8am
d.	Cardiovascular machines	Daily	6am - 8am
e.	Aerobics	Daily	6am - 8am
f.	Racquetball/Handball	Daily	6am - 8am
g.	Squash	Daily	6am - 8am
h.	Badminton	Daily	6am - 8am
i.	Volleyball	Daily	6am - 8am

A better first question: *Applies to everyone and short enough to fit onto one screen.*

1. **During the past month, a great deal of discussion about whether or not the university should build a new recreational center for students has taken place. In general, do you feel the current facilities are:** *(To answer, use the mouse to click on your choice. If you make a mistake, click on the correct choice and the previous answer will disappear).*

   - ◉ very adequate
   - ○ somewhat adequate
   - ○ only slightly adequate
   - ○ not adequate at all

have items centered on the screen, as shown in Figure 11.8. The revision shows a more concentrated format. Concern with limited vertical screen space has also influenced designers to provide no distinctive separation between questions and answer categories, thus losing the "grouping" qualities that help define questions and answer choices for respondents. For several questionnaires located by Bowker (1999), one inappropriate way to group questions and subelements was created by devoting nearly half the screen to a common sponsor title and/or continuation instructions that were shown on every screen.

Also found on some Web sites was the use of long dot leaders to connect far left-justified answer categories to answer spaces that were far right-justified in order to be as close to the scroll bar as possible. When the screen size was reduced, these lines wrapped around so the answer choices were misaligned. The apparent intent was to make responding more efficient by facil-

Figure 11.8 An unconventional layout that is center justified and a revision.

***Poor layout:* Unconventional structure**

Does your company offer people in your position (i.e., exempt staff) any of the following policies?

Yes		No	Don't Know
○	Parental leave	○	○
○	Job sharing: Two or more employees share one position	○	○
○	On-site or near-site child care	○	○
○	On-site or near-site child care for sick children	○	○
○	Child care referral services	○	○
○	Elder-care referral services	○	○
○	Subsidies or vouchers to help pay for child care	○	○
○	Sick leave that one can take if one's dependent is sick	○	○

***Better layout:* A more conventional structure**

6. **Does your company offer people in your position (i.e., exempt staff) any of the following policies?**

	Yes	No	Don't Know
Parental leave	○	○	○
Job sharing: Two or more employees share one position	○	○	○
On-site or near-site child care	○	○	○
On-site or near-site child care for sick children	○	○	○
Child care referral services	○	○	○
Elder-care referral services	○	○	○
Subsidies or vouchers to help pay for child care	○	○	○
Sick leave that one can take if one's dependent is sick	○	○	○

itating movement back and forth between the scroll bar and answer choices, but it was done at the cost of having to visually connect widely separated components of an answer. Still another questionnaire had a "yes" answer box located at the far left of the screen and the alternative "no" answer was placed on the opposite side of the category description, as shown in the first example of Figure 11.8.

In sum, there are many ways that questions may be constructed so they seem unconventional to the respondent who has filled out paper questionnaires in the past, and that are contrary to the general visual design and grouping principles discussed in Chapter 4. My solution is to begin each question with a number, which is often printed in a large reverse print box in black or full color to achieve a noticeable patch of brightness on the screen, as shown in the second example of Figure 11.8. It is specifically designed to be the most eye-catching information on the screen, revealing where the respondent should start to read. Numbers also reveal the order in which each question should be answered. The question stem should be separated from the answer spaces, and the answer spaces should be slightly indented and listed vertically.

In addition, research has shown that brightness, larger fonts, and spacing can be used to clearly identify the beginning of individual questions and to indicate where the respondent should start reading each screen. Similarly, research on how people see objects has shown that people tend to start reading near the upper left-hand corner of the page, so this prime space is devoted to beginning each question. The lower right quadrant, which is the least likely to be seen first, is devoted to special logos or screen identifiers. For example, a sponsor's logo might be located here in small type.

Principle 11.14: Restrain the use of color so that figure/ground consistency and readability are maintained, navigational flow is unimpeded, and measurement properties of questions are maintained.

Inappropriate uses of color represent one of the biggest threats to development of good Web questionnaires. The threat stems partly from the ease with which color can be added to a questionnaire, and the tendency of many Web designers to use it in ways that interfere with the response process, even to the point of influencing visual comprehension and producing potentially invalid answers to certain types of survey questions.

The rush to develop Web surveys has led to the use of color as a central feature of innovative questions; for example, showing several new cars in a variety of colors and asking which color car respondents would most like to own. The problem is that the colors seen by the respondent may be quite different than those seen by the designer, as a result of the color display palette used by the respondent's computer. Whereas the designer may use a 24-bit palette that contains millions of colors, the respondent's computer may use only an eight-bit palette that supports 256 colors. The changes between what is produced and what is seen by the respondent may make the results of questions that depend upon color resolution meaningless. Limiting oneself to a smaller palette when designing questionnaires will not only insure that the image is viewed similarly by all respondents, but will reduce the information in the transmitted image and, as a result, shorten the transmission time.

Designers may choose from among many figure/ground formats for displaying words on the computer screen. Although most designers use a simple presentation of black letters on a neutral background, questionnaires have appeared on the Web that are composed of blue letters on a bright yellow background, red letters on a green background, and white letters on a black background. The use of colorful backgrounds seems to be based on the idea that potential respondents will find such unusual questionnaires more attractive and will therefore be more likely to respond, a claim for which there appears to be no experimental support. Some combinations are particularly difficult to read, and raise the prospects that some respondents will not be able to read them at all, for example, the inability of some people to discern between red and green because of color blindness (Brown, 1988).

Another frequently observed problem of Web surveys occurs when designers place large images or blocks of color on screens to attract the eye. In such cases, color is sometimes placed where the eye should not be focused when one first sees the screen, as shown in Figure 11.5. For example, a large green right-facing triangle at the bottom of the screen, which respondents were to click on in order to go to the next screen, and an equally large left-facing red triangle to click and move back to the previous question dominated the screen. These blocks of color were more likely to attract the respondent's eye than the beginning of the question. The visual essence of responding to a questionnaire is to start at the beginning of each question and go through the question and answer choices in a prescribed order. Inappropriate uses of color frequently get in the way of that objective.

Yet another frequently observed problem occurs when multiple figure/ground combinations are used in a single question. One questionnaire located by Bowker (1999) used black on gray for writing the question, red on gray for labeling the end points of a scale with the words *strongly agree* and *strongly disagree,* and then created a square space of blue around each of the radio buttons (circles for marking answers) which appeared as black letters on the blue background. It is difficult for people to comprehend a question and the answer choices as a single unit when multiple figure/ground formats are used for various subparts of the question. Another expression of figure/ground differences that is difficult for respondents to deal with is when they are provided a questionnaire using, for example, blue letters on a bright yellow background, but the software requires that write-ins be done with black print on a neutral background. Thus the respondent must deal constantly with different figure/ground formats within a single question.

Many of the Web questionnaires located by Bowker (1999) used different colors for each of the answer choices. The substance of these questions was to ask which color the respondent preferred for articles of clothing. Although such items are attention getting, it is important to recall what concept is being measured. Because colors may appear quite different on various respondents' screens due to variations in operating systems, browsers and display settings, the "blue" selected or rejected by one respondent may be quite different from that viewed by another.

Perhaps the most detrimental use of color in the many Web questionnaires I have seen is when the creator of a screen has surrounded radio buttons on a measurement scale with bands or boxes of color, where the different widths of the color bands redefined the scale. In several instances the width of the colored spaces was established by the length of the words defining each scale point (Figure 11.9). Thus, while the "very satisfied" space was narrower than the "very dissatisfied" space, both were much wider than the "neutral" space.

Figure 11.9 Inappropriate use of color in a web questionnaire.

A measurement scale with color added:

1. **How satisfied are you with each of the company's policies described below?**

	Very Satisfied	Somewhat Satisfied	Neutral	Somewhat Dissatisfied	Very Dissatisfied	Not Applicable
Use of sick leave for children						
No overtime allowed						
Mandatory drug testing						
No-smoking break room						
Emphasis on racial diversity						
Limited maternity leave						
Requests for pay raises						
	Red		Yellow		Green	Gray

A measurement scale without color:

1. **How satisfied are you with each of the company's policies described below?**

	Very Satisfied	Somewhat Satisfied	Neutral	Somewhat Dissatisfied	Very Dissatisfied	Not Applicable
Use of sick leave for children						
No overtime allowed						
Mandatory drug testing						
No-smoking break room						
Emphasis on racial diversity						
Limited maternity leave						
Requests for pay raises						

In addition, whereas one end of the scale was colored red, the other end was colored green, with yellow in between for neutral. Not only do these colors have cultural meanings (red for stop; green for go), but the essence of a scale is to see it as a continuum, and changing colors for different portions of a scale may result in respondents seeing the scales in quite different ways. An additional problem encountered with these screens was that when a switch was made from a full to partial screen display, the relative distances between answer points changed.

The multiple threats that color presents to getting valid responses to Web surveys suggest the need to be very restrained in its use. First, for the basic questionnaire format I prefer a basic black on white formatting, which by its nature will not result in figure/ground differences for the questions versus write-in answer choices provided in drop-down boxes. Second, color is used in much the same way as it is on paper questionnaires, placing colored design elements where they will influence respondents to follow the prescribed navigational flow. For example, a reverse print or colored box may be used for question numbers. Alternatively, colors may be changed when providing special instructions, for example, telling respondents how much of the questionnaire remains to be filled out. It is also appropriate to use muted colors for individual screen logos, which after the first two or three screens may help

Figure 11.10 Pixel measurement of the three most common screen configurations that can be used to create or receive web questionnaires.

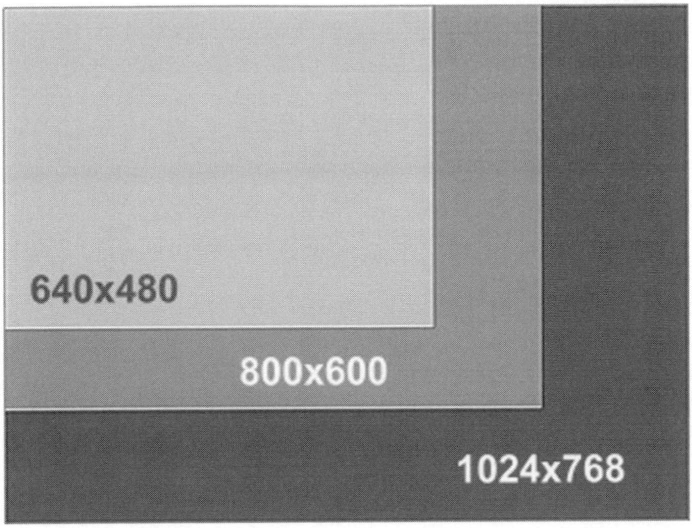

keep the logo from interfering with the answering process as the respondent becomes used to reading black words on a neutral background. More dramatic uses of color are also appropriate for the initial page of the questionnaire and at the end when thanking the respondent, and it is here that survey designers can express themselves colorfully without worrying about the methodological effects on answers.

Principle 11.15: Avoid differences in the visual appearance of questions that result from different screen configurations, operating systems, browsers, partial screen displays, and wrap-around text.

Computers can be configured in a variety of ways to display information on their monitors. In addition to the color palettes already discussed, differences may exist in the display resolution of various monitors. The three most popular display resolution configurations are 640 × 480, 800 × 600, and 1024 × 768. These numbers refer to the number of pixels that make up the horizontal and vertical dimensions of the computer screen, as illustrated in Figure 11.10. Pixels are not a standard unit of measurement, and a 640 × 480 display on a 14-inch monitor is going to look considerably different on a 17-inch monitor with the same resolution, although the proportionality remains the same. Figure 11.11 shows a question displayed on a screen configured as 800 × 600, and the same question on another user's screen that is configured as 640 × 480. The result is to require horizontal scrolling in order to see all of the answer categories. To avoid this result, it is important that designers of questionnaires

Figure 11.11 Effect of display resolution on respondent's view with questionnaire configuration on 800 × 600 screen display versus on 640 × 480 screen display.

A questionnaire using 800 x 600 configuration:

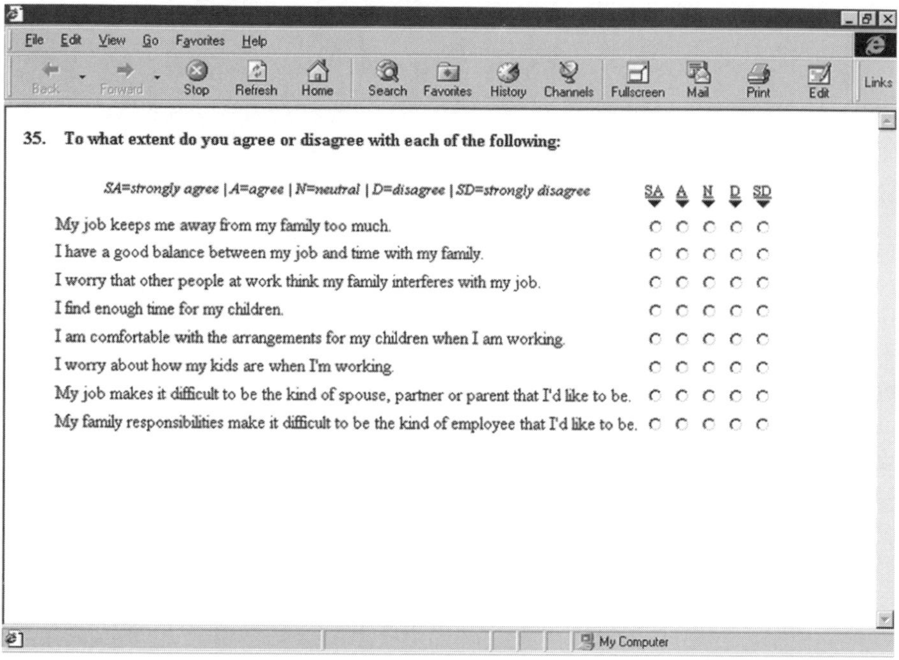

The same questionnaire as seen by respondent using 640 x 480 configuration:

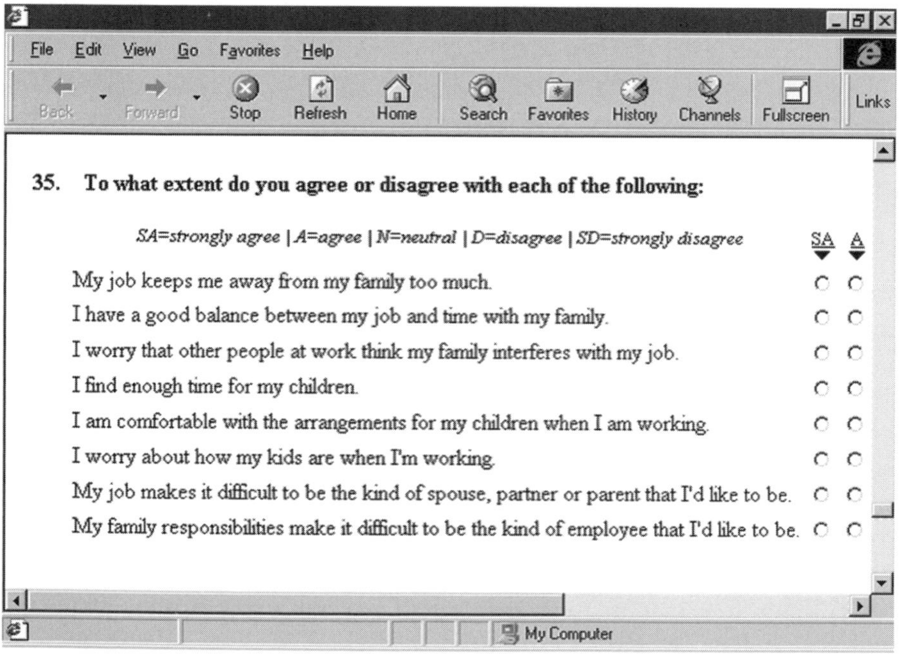

view questions on computers configured differently from their own or simulate such differences by using an appropriate software application. It may also be desirable to limit the horizontal distance for each line of text not to exceed 600 pixels, a width that all resolutions can safely display.

In addition to and independently of screen configuration, some respondents may use full-screen displays when viewing questionnaires, whereas others use partial-screen (or tiled) displays. When a questionnaire display is tiled, that may result in only part of the question being seen as shown in Figure 11.12. Although the effect may be similar as for the screen configuration just discussed, the reason is not. Web questionnaires can also be constructed, as shown in the third example of Figure 11.12, so that when screens are tiled, text automatically wraps around so that the entire width of the questionnaire can be observed without horizontal scrolling. However, that also means that category headings can wrap around so that what appears on one line as "very strongly agree" on one respondent's screen appears in three lines on another respondent's screen, and the distance between the radio button (response circle) for that category and the adjacent one is shortened. The general difficulties associated with question displays being changed because of tiling leads us to use shorter line lengths for constructing individual questions, and programming in such a way that the wrap-around of text is limited. In addition, it may be desirable to instruct respondents to maximize their screens when responding to a questionnaire. Because some computer users do not know how to do that, instructions on how to maximize screens may need to be provided.

One means of avoiding problems of differences in the distances between response categories for horizontally-structured scales is to change to a vertical display of scales, where the distance between points can be controlled across screen configurations by simply appearing at the front of each text line. This problem also encourages the use of drop-down boxes, which is explained later in this chapter.

Different operating platforms (e.g., PC versus Macintosh), different browsers (e.g., Netscape versus Internet Explorer), and even different versions of the same browser may result in questionnaire items being displayed differently on the respondent's versus the designer's computer. For example, the default background color on a PC may be different from that used on a Macintosh.

Research has not yet been done to determine to what extent different question displays, such as differences in distances between horizontal response categories, changes in question appearance due to wrap-around of text, changes in screen background because of different operation systems, and other features influence people's answers. Research on these topics is a high priority. My approach is to be conservative and to design questionnaires in ways that minimize the differences in question displays from these various sources.

Figure 11.12 Example of the effects of full versus partial screen display and use of wrap-around text on what respondents may see on the screen.

Full-screen display of question:

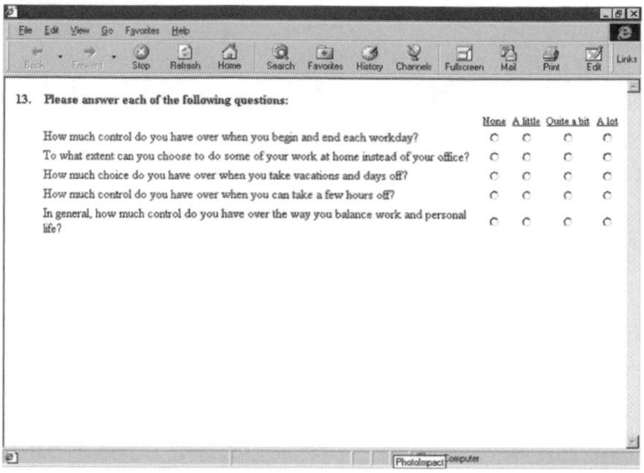

A partial-screen display that obscures part of the question, therefore requiring scrolling:

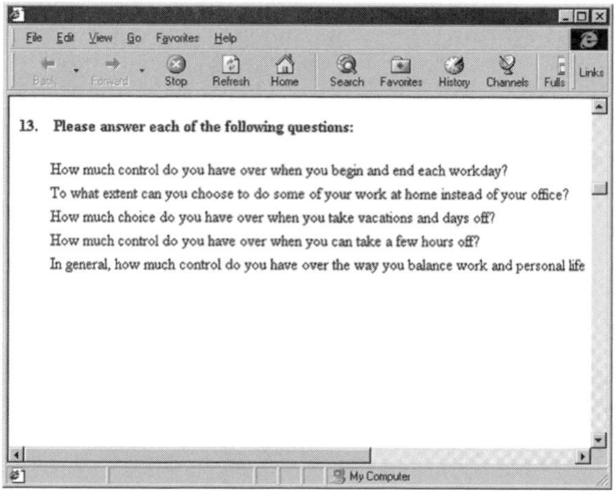

A partial-screen display with wrap-around of text:

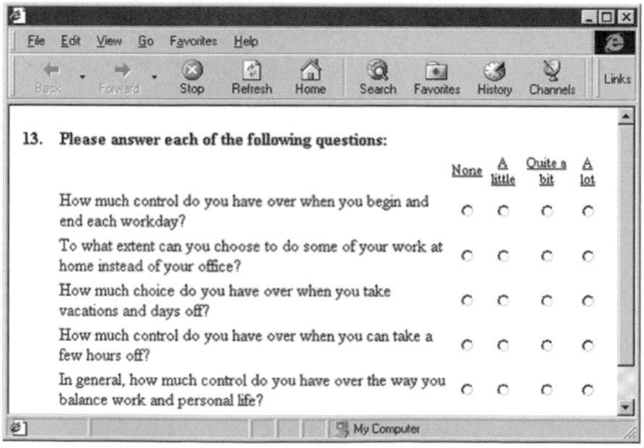

The implications of different screen configurations, tiled versus untiled (partial versus full) screen displays, and varying operating systems and browsers for the design and testing of questionnaires are enormous. Recently I observed the development of Web questionnaire testing facilities (or usability laboratories, as they are commonly called) within organizations that were equipped with only one kind of computer and software, typically the latest and most powerful versions available. In addition, the testing process used Web questionnaires that were sent from one computer within the organization to another, and not tested outside the organization's computer network. The result of such testing methods may be a failure to learn what changes occur in screen displays when Web questionnaires are sent to dispersed survey populations outside the organization. A better solution to testing needs would be to equip such laboratories with a wide variety of new and old computers with different operating systems, or with software that allows new equipment to simulate old equipment. Many software packages exist for testing compatibility by simulating various computers and types of software. However, it is also useful to have some test computers located outside the organization in a variety of local computer environments. This will allow testing of the possible effects of the telecommunication infrastructure and ISPs while avoiding possible effects of the sponsoring organization's local area network when receiving a questionnaire.

Principle 11.16: Provide specific instructions on how to take each necessary computer action for responding to the questionnaire, and give other necessary instructions at the point where they are needed.

Responding to Web surveys requires knowledge of which computer functions to apply. For example, it may not be known to the respondent that:

- Radio button answer choices allow only one answer and require clicking an alternative button in order to erase a previous answer, unless programming is done to change this correction feature.
- Check boxes allow multiple answers and require a single click on an answer box to erase a previous choice.
- An answer should be indicated by use of the mouse or by a keyboard stroke.

Respondents also may not know:

- How to reveal answers hidden behind a drop-down menu.
- How to enter open-ended answers and how much space is available for entering them.

Each of these procedures is known, or can easily be figured out, by experienced computer users. However, the challenge faced by designers of many Web surveys is how to get people with minimal computer skills to overcome their limited knowledge, and perhaps fear, of the computer in order to respond. Not knowing how to change a mismarked answer, or not being able to get the return key to move the cursor to the next response location, may be frustrating enough to inexperienced computer users to cause them to quit filling out a questionnaire. Directions for responding need to be provided in a way that also minimizes inconvenience to experienced computer users.

A common but unfortunate procedure followed in the construction of a few Web questionnaires is the provision of detailed instructions at the beginning of the questionnaire through which the respondent must pass in order to begin answering questions. I once was shown a questionnaire that used a series of six initial screens to describe how to operate the scroll bar, radio buttons, check boxes, drop-down menus, two types of open-ended questions, and returns to previous question. From a cognitive learning perspective this is not a desirable practice. Providing many instructions about what to do in different situations, all of which are unfamiliar to a respondent, means there is considerable likelihood that the instructional details will be forgotten by the time each action is to be taken.

Several different methods might be used to provide needed operational instructions. One method is to provide instructions on how to perform each needed skill immediately following the stem of the question, perhaps in parentheses and/or italics, so that experienced computer users realize these words are not part of the survey question. Such instructions might be made to appear the first time each type of computer function skill is needed, and repeated once or twice for subsequent questions.

Another possible method is to ask at the beginning of a questionnaire whether or not a respondent is an experienced computer user. Those who judge themselves to be experienced could be directed to a version of the questionnaire that does not include instructions. Those who see themselves as novices could be directed to one that helps people at each step of the way with operating instructions that are needed for answering each type of question. However, it remains to be seen whether respondents can make accurate judgments in this regard.

Another method is to use a "floating window" that provides specific operation instructions (Figure 11.13). A floating window is simply a small window that "floats" atop the existing window of the browser and can be read for quick instructions and recalled when necessary. While feasible, this method requires additional processing time as well as a compatible browser application.

I expect floating windows to be especially useful for providing substantial instructions and definitions in business surveys that now use instruction books for this purpose. A closely related method of providing substantive instructions for most questions, but which may be needed only occasionally, is to divide the screen, putting instructions into a left-hand column in a different figure/ground format, and place questions on the right two-thirds of the

Figure 11.13 Example of a floating window that is used to provide additional instructions.

Closed:

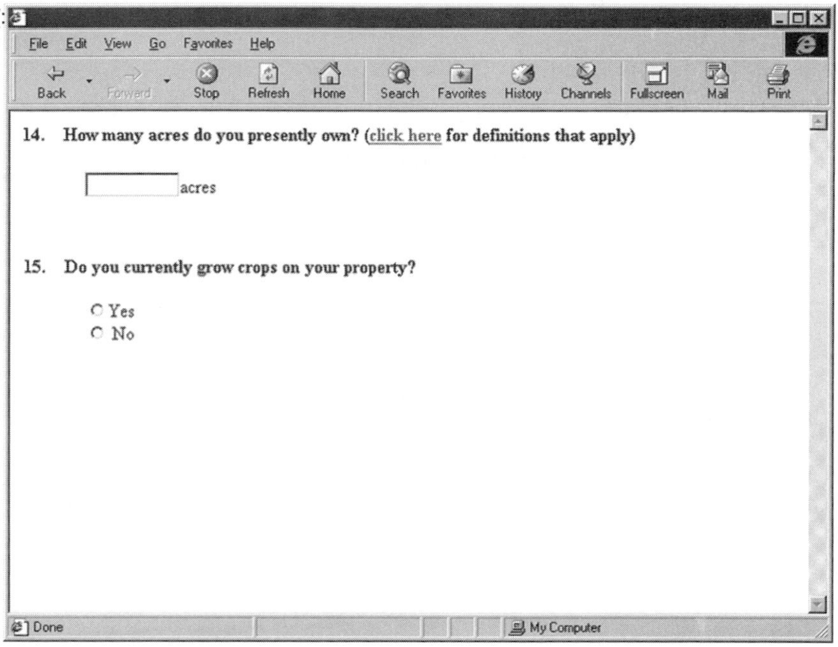

Open:

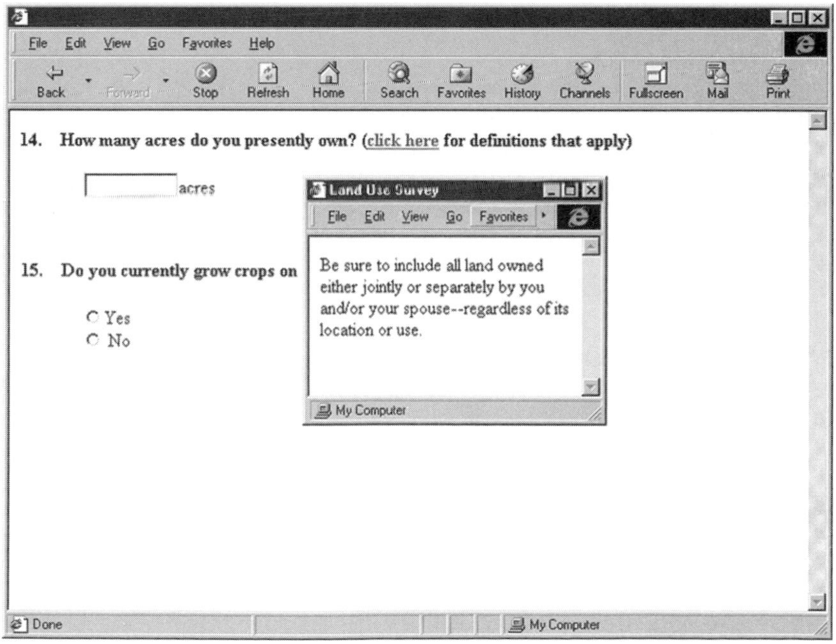

screen using the regular black on neutral formatting. This method seems useful when the volume of needed instructions is quite large.

Another method for providing substantive instructions is to insert a "help" button on each screen that can be clicked on to go to instructions on another screen. In general, my preference is to provide instructions with each screen rather than to require people to press help buttons or rely on floating windows. The latter techniques require a little more effort to access, as well as additional computer resources. However, as computer skills and resources increase, their use is likely to increase as well.

Principle 11.17: Use drop-down boxes sparingly, consider the mode implications, and identify each with a "click here" instruction.

Drop-down boxes appear on the questionnaire as one line with a downward pointing triangle (Figure 11.14). When the cursor is placed on that line and clicked, the list of possible response options appears. This questionnaire feature is an extremely powerful and attractive feature of Web surveys. However, it also has a high potential for misuse. Its power stems from the fact that a very large number of response categories can be hidden from view until needed, such as a list of all the states in the U.S. The possibility of using these boxes in order to list dozens of occupations, city names, or other long lists of items allows a great amount of space to be saved when designing a questionnaire. It is especially useful when answers to particular questions will be used to direct people to different sets of questions. The screen is kept simple until the respondent reaches the point where the display of answer choices is needed. The potential for misuse stems in part from a tendency among some designers to overuse this design possibility, using it, for example, for yes/no questions. Accessing such answer choices in this way takes more effort than simply clicking on one or the other of two radio buttons.

A frequent use of drop-down boxes occurs when it is desired that a series of attitudinal items with identical response categories be placed on one page in an items in a series format. The use of drop-down boxes provides considerable efficiency for getting multiple items onto a screen because only one space must be provided for each set of response alternatives. However, if results of a Web survey are to be combined with those obtained from a mail questionnaire, then it may be better to try to use the mail layout that exists for the comparison survey. The visual disparity between drop-down boxes and listings of categories in other modes is such that mode differences may result, but this possibility has not yet been well researched.

An occasional misuse of drop-down menus occurs when the designer uses the always visible line of space to list the first answer category of a scale, for instance, the strongly agree option of a five-point agree-disagree scale. This use of the visible line may result in people inadvertently selecting the default category because they think they have already responded to that box (Figure

Figure 11.14 Example of unacceptable and acceptable use of drop-down boxes.

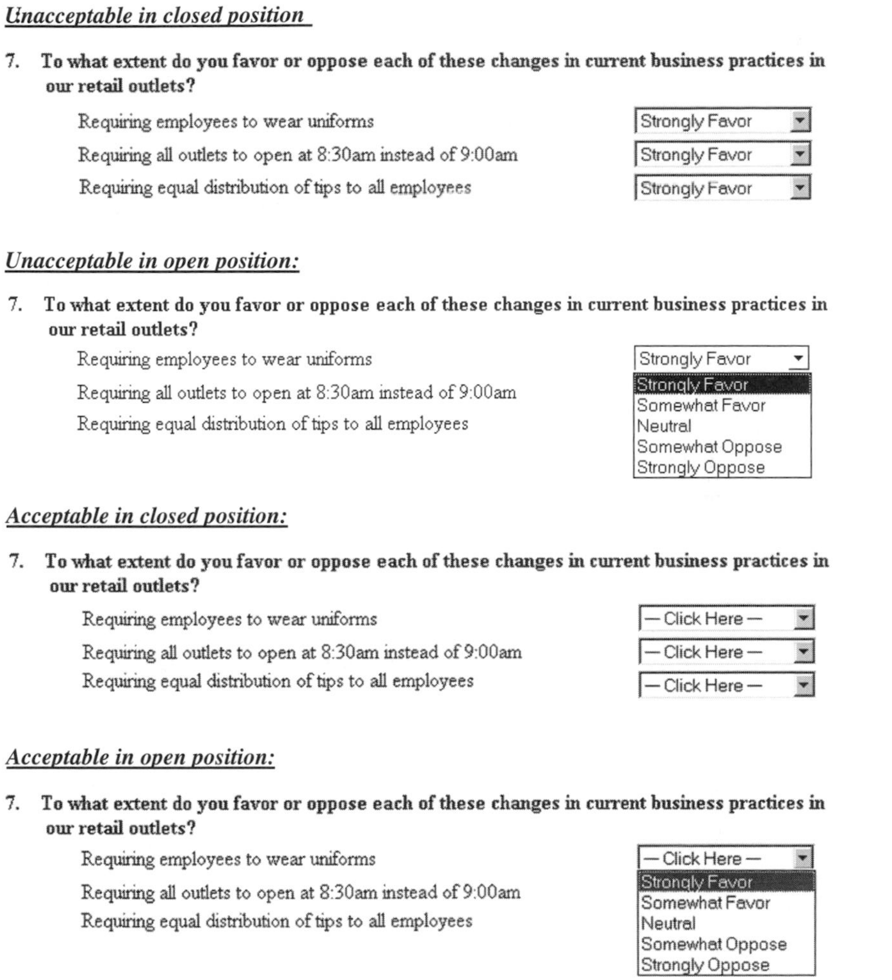

11.14). Also, the use of these menus makes it difficult for respondents to gauge their progress down the page. When the respondent clicks on a response alternative that is physically located several lines below the line on the computer screen where the question is, for example, the strongly oppose choice, the box disappears, leaving the cursor where the mark was made. The result is that the respondent may think the next question has been answered even though it has not been.

The difficulty with drop-down menus is not limited to opinion scales. Another unfortunate use of the visible line space is to put the most commonly selected category in it, such as age 18–24 in a survey of college students.

To avoid biases (selecting the default category) as well as skip errors, I recommend using the visible line space only for the phrase "click here for choices," or more simply "click here." A general instruction on how to use drop-down menus should also be included as part of the first question in which drop-down menus are used.

Principle 11.18: Do not require respondents to provide an answer to each question before being allowed to answer any subsequent ones.

One of the much talked about attributes of some Web questionnaires is the ability to force respondents to answer every question. Most of the available software systems for constructing Web questionnaires provide this option to the questionnaire designer. The penalty for not providing an answer is that the respondent cannot continue to the next question. This quality is often promoted as a distinct advantage of Web surveys.

Respondents should never be forced to provide a substantive answer before moving to the next question. Sometimes there are legitimate reasons for objecting to a question and sometimes the respondent may, in fact, be unable to pick one of the answer choices. The frustration associated with this requirement seems likely to lead to annoyance and premature terminations. In addition, it poses a problem for surveyors when human subject protection committees legitimately insist that people be told that their response to each question is voluntary. This quality also makes the Web survey different from self-administered mail surveys and may lead to the occurrence of mode differences.

In order to solve the human subject protection concern, it has been suggested that people be required to answer but that a "prefer not to answer" and/or "don't know" category be provided for every item. People will still be required to provide an answer to each item. This alternative may create mode comparison problems without resolving the sense of irritation that some respondents are likely to feel. Neither telephone nor paper mail surveys provide a forcing mechanism that absolutely requires a response before moving on to the next question. If a respondent to a telephone interview refuses to answer a question, the interviewer checks a refusal or some other category that is available. However, that category is not communicated to the respondent as a choice when the answer categories are read. Nor does the paper self-administered questionnaire typically list such an answer, accepting no response as a result. Should a Web surveyor decide to require a response and provide an "I refuse to answer" or "Don't want to answer" category, then a stimulus is provided that is unlikely to be equally available in either of these other types of surveys.

Principle 11.19: Provide skip directions in a way that encourages marking of answers and being able to click to the next applicable question.

Web questionnaires are sometimes programmed so that selecting an answer choice that requires skipping several questions will automatically skip the person to the next appropriate question, making it impossible to answer the questions that are to be passed over. In other instances such formatting may be considered inappropriate, so that respondents must use a hyperlink (click on a skip instruction) connected to the answer category that instructs them to go to a particular question. The instruction to "click here" printed beside the answer that requires the skip is often augmented by being programmed to appear in a contrasting color. Observation of people responding to Web surveys suggests that when the space to the right of an answer category includes a message to "click here" to go to the next appropriate question, respondents are prone to click on the skip instruction without first clicking on the answer. Figure 11.15 shows an example that did not work well and a suggested alternative.

Principle 11.20: Construct Web questionnaires so they scroll from question to question unless order effects are a major concern, or when telephone and Web survey results are being combined.

It is possible to build Web surveys that require only one question to be displayed at a time and to require the respondent to click on a "next" button in order for a new screen and question to appear. Alternatively, questionnaires can be composed as a single unit, making it possible to scroll from the first question to the last and back.

In general, I prefer questionnaires that scroll from beginning to end, a method that most closely resembles the general experience of using the Web. This method appears to have become the dominant practice for Web questionnaire design. Some 90% of the questionnaires located by Bowker (1999)

Figure 11.15 Acceptable and unacceptable ways of providing skip directions in web questionnaires.

Unacceptable:

30. Do you have any children age 15 and under that currently live with you?

- ○ Yes
- ○ No - If no, skip to question #42

Unacceptable:

30. Do you have any children age 15 and under that currently live with you?

- ○ Yes
- ○ No - If no, click here to skip to question #42

A revision:

30. Do you have any children age 15 and under that currently live with you?

- ○ Yes
- ○ No ⟶ After clicking "No," CLICK HERE to skip to question #42

---

used a scrolling rather than screen-by-screen method of construction. Scrolling requires less contact with the questionnaire server and therefore conserves computer resources. Using individual question screen construction techniques also provides less context to respondents than they would normally have for answering questions, and is especially problematic when people are asked a series of related questions, for instance, details about a particular job. It becomes difficult to review answers provided to previous questions, a task that may require additional instructions that get relatively little use, and as a result contribute little to respondent proficiency. Paper questionnaire respondents may look both forward and backwards to get a sense of questionnaire length, to recheck a previous answer, or simply to keep a sense of where they are in the questionnaire. Observations of respondents answering questions that appeared one at a time on screens suggested that some respondents lose a sense of context. If their concentration is disrupted, even momentarily, they cannot go back and easily pick up on where they were in the mental process of responding.

To remedy this problem and retain the screen-by-screen approach, it seemed necessary to add reminders of how respondents had answered previous questions. As a result, the stimulus for each question differed from the way it would typically appear in either interview or paper questionnaires. Although a quick glance backwards would often help the respondent provide more accurate results, a question-by-question back-up feature is also cumbersome to use.

At the same time, when significant concern over order effects exists, such as when asking an unaided recall question (e.g., about what grocery store people most like to shop at) that is to be followed by the same question with prelisted choices, it is important for respondents to see the first question before answering the second one. Screen-by-screen construction prevents people from scrolling ahead and currently requires a higher level of computer resources on the part of the respondent. It is not clear whether scrolling ahead will influence answers, given that most people are likely to answer questions in the order they are presented. Comparison of mail and telephone questionnaires on the existence of order effects has produced equivocal results (Dillman, Sangster, Tarnai, and Rockwood, 1996).

Principle 11.21: When the number of answer choices exceeds the number that can be displayed in a single column on one screen, consider double-banking with an appropriate grouping device to link them together.

Double- or even triple-banking is frequently used on paper questionnaires to squeeze questions into a limited space. In general, we consider it an undesirable practice (see Principle 3.23). The reason is that people's range of vision, when attentive to a task like responding to a questionnaire, is limited to about eight to ten characters (Kahneman, 1973). Consequently, the second or third bank of questions is inadvertently not seen.

However, in the case of Web surveys, there is frequently a trade-off between gains and losses. If questions are not double-banked then it may be necessary to spread a question's response categories over two screens. I choose double- (or occasionally triple-) banking for Web surveys because I do not think the negative consequences are as serious as they are for paper questionnaires. Also, the horizontal layout of computer screens, compared with the vertical layout of paper pages, encourages limiting questions to one screen with double-banking. To compensate for double–banking, a box or shaded area is placed around the categories in order to group them as all being relevant to the question, as shown in Figure 11.16. This grouping method would not be used in paper questionnaires because it tends to invite people to skip over the boxed information. The limited vertical scope of the screen makes the boxing method more effective.

Principle 11.22: Use graphical symbols or words that convey a sense of where the respondent is in the completion process, but avoid those that require significant increases in computer resources.

When completing a paper questionnaire it is easy for respondents to estimate where they are in the completion process and to see how far they are from the end. Observations from several Web surveyors suggests that people who begin often quit even though there are only a few questions left. Fear that the last few questions will be missed leads some developers of Web questionnaires to put potentially objectionable questions judged to be especially important to the survey objectives (e.g., income) early in the questionnaire. This practice seems likely to result in unnecessary cut-offs early in the questionnaire.

Figure 11.16 Example of double banking with box enclosure to achieve appropriate grouping of all answer choices.

23. From the following list of criminal acts, please select the one that you feel is *most* punishable by imprisonment.

○ armed robbery	○ pre-meditated murder
○ embezzlement	○ date rape
○ arson	○ domestic abuse
○ accidental homicide	○ terrorism
○ statutory rape	○ flag burning
○ vehicle theft	○ drug use
○ child abuse	○ drunk driving
○ mail fraud	○ prostitution
○ elderly abuse	○ vandalism

There are many ways that respondents may be kept informed of their progress. Questionnaires that scroll instead of using a screen-by-screen approach automatically reveal one's progress either by looking at the computer screen scroll bar, or by scrolling to the end of the questionnaire to estimate how much is left. An alternative construction method is to place a "progress bar" on the screen that shows how close people are to completing a questionnaire. Attempts of this nature may be quite creative, for example, a waving cartoon character who suddenly appears with the message "You are almost done!"

To limit the use of computer resources, simple transition sentences may also be used; for example, "Finally, we want to ask a few questions about yourself." Figure 11.17 shows still another possible method, periodically reporting what proportion of the questionnaire is complete. A text-based method is most desirable because it can be used for all computer and software situations, whereas visual animation requires more advanced programming and compatible respondent browsers.

Principle 11.23: Exercise restraint in the use of question structures that have known measurement problems on paper questionnaires, such as check-all-that-apply and open-ended questions.

The advent of Web surveys has encouraged the use of check-all-that-apply questions, even providing a special type of answer box (as opposed to radio buttons) for which any number may be checked for each question. The use of such boxes invites avoidable measurement error. People are asked to check items from a list that is sometimes very long. The drawback to their use is that people often satisfice, that is, check answer choices until they think they have satisfactorily answered the questions. Considerable evidence exists that people often do not read all of the answer choices well before going on to the next question. In addition, the order of reading answer choices tends to bias

Figure 11.17 Example of screen that indicates progress through a web questionnaire.

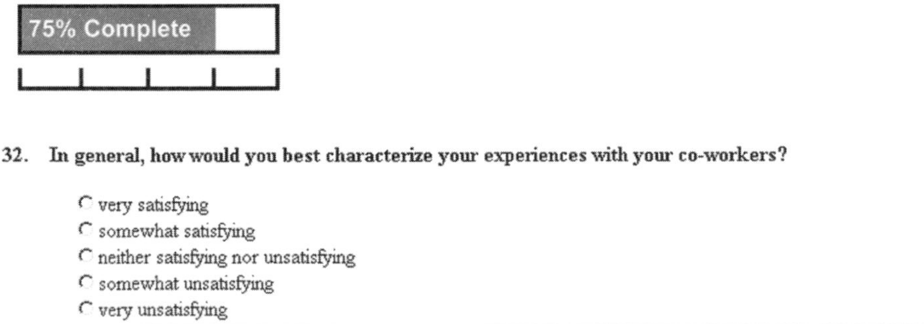
75% Complete
32. In general, how would you best characterize your experiences with your co-workers?
very satisfying
somewhat satisfying
neither satisfying nor unsatisfying
somewhat unsatisfying
very unsatisfying

people's responses towards the first categories (Israel and Taylor, 1990; Krosnick, Narayan, and Smith, 1996). A Web questionnaire is a visual experience which, from the standpoint of whether every response category gets read, is under the control of the respondent, as is the case for paper self-administered questionnaires.

Check-all-that-apply questions are not used in telephone surveys. Instead, people are asked to respond positively or negatively to each choice before continuing. In addition to creating a satisficing bias in self-administered surveys, the use of check-all-that-apply questions on Web questionnaires requires the use of check boxes rather than radio buttons, which also require the learning of a different correction procedure. If the list is quite long and the respondent is required to scroll or click to the next screen, the likelihood of satisficing may increase. Thus, from the standpoint of survey error, check-all-that-apply questions should generally not be used in a Web or any other type of survey.

In response to these objections, some people have suggested that check-all-that-apply boxes constitute a strength of Web surveys, and that to change to a "yes-no" format for every item would lengthen the time required for answering surveys and therefore produce higher nonresponse rates. It is conceivable that limiting one's visual field to a computer screen and having to scroll or space through the entire screen may limit the satisficing effects that have been consistently observed on paper questionnaires. However, until this research is done, I prefer to follow a more conservative approach and avoid the use of check-all-that-apply boxes.

Another type of question that typically produces poor answers on paper self-administered surveys is the open-ended question. Respondents give less complete answers than is the case with interview surveys, where follow-up probes can be used. A paper survey solution is to convert individual questions (e.g., "What is your occupation?") to multiple questions, such as, "What is your occupation? What kind of work do you do? Please describe your employer." However, at least one e-mail survey experiment has demonstrated that respondents provide more detailed answers to open-ended questions on computers than they do on paper questionnaires (Schaefer and Dillman, 1998). Web surveys may also elicit longer answers, but research on this possibility is still needed.

Implementation Strategies

The implementation strategy most effective for Web surveys will depend upon what alternatives exist for accessing respondents. The Web survey case study reviewed earlier commenced with a list of computer equipment purchasers for which phone numbers, mailing addresses, and e-mail addresses were all available. That made it possible to call sampled individuals on the telephone, follow up with a postal mail letter that contained a token financial incentive, and use e-mail for additional contacts. This strategy effectively utilized multiple contacts and the mixture of contact modes in order to deliver a token incentive.

I also reported a four contact e-mail survey strategy in which a response rate comparable to that obtained by postal mail was obtained. In addition, it was noted that it is now possible for the vast majority of computer users to simply click on a highlighted Web address contained in an e-mail message and be transferred to a Web survey. When most people's e-mail program facilitates such a transparent connection to the Web, I expect there to be little difference in the response rates one can obtain from e-mail versus Web surveys. As reported in this case study, the making of all four contacts by e-mail produced higher response rates than did substituting a paper prenotice or thank you/reminder.

The making of contacts by e-mail only does not allow for the delivery of token financial incentives in advance, which I would expect to further improve response rates to Web questionnaires. While sending a paper mail letter containing such an incentive is possible, I expect that creative efforts will be made to find incentives that can be delivered effectively by e-mail. While respondents can be informed in an e-mail message that they will automatically be sent a few dollars or gift certificate of some type when their questionnaire is submitted, that places the incentive in a postpayment situation which, as noted in Chapter 4, is decidedly less effective for paper mail surveys. It might be possible to create a quasi-prepayment situation by informing people by e-mail that they are being asked to participate in a survey and a small token of appreciation will be mailed to them immediately if they send their mailing address by e-mail, after which they can click on the Web address in order to complete the survey. Whether this or some other method will significantly improve response effects of incentives remains to be seen. The power of the prepayment is such that I expect to see many creative attempts to emulate its use to increase Web questionnaire response rates.

Summary Perspective on Web Surveys and Some Cautions

There is no other method of collecting survey data that offers so much potential for so little cost as Web surveys. However, the eagerness to design and implement Web surveys has also revealed a frightening downside: a willingness to equate large numbers of respondents recruited by whatever means with survey accuracy. Recently, a friend suggested that I complete an interesting questionnaire that had been posted on the Internet and widely advertised. When I arrived at the site, a message appeared reporting that the survey had ended. It was further noted that 50,000 responses–twice the minimum required for scientific validity–had been received. In this case scientific validity was being viewed only from the standpoint of sampling error, and no consideration was given to whom the people represented. No scientific generalizations could be made, making this survey no more valid (from a coverage standpoint) than a call-in poll where a television station announces a question and waits for whoever is interested to call in and vote.

The unfortunate tendency to accept self-selection as a means of getting responses to many Web surveys has exacerbated the demand for exciting and provocative questionnaires that take advantage of advanced programming features that will make Web questionnaires fun to complete, and presumably more likely to attract more respondents. These same features often require more computer resources and newer software applications (e.g., browsers), and thus limit the ability of people with less powerful computers, older browsers, and poorer telecommunications connections to access and respond to such questionnaires. Instead of contributing to the representativeness of survey responses, they further limit who is likely to respond.

My response to this trend is to return to the basics of survey quality. Web questionnaire surveyors should use only a portion of the capacity of the most advanced computers in order to maximize the likelihood that recipients of questionnaires are likely to respond, and design mixed-mode surveys so that people without computer access can respond by other means. PIN numbers should also be used so that Web questionnaire access is limited to people who are sampled from defined populations. Multiple contacts by multiple modes, incentives, and other response inducing techniques should also be used to improve the likelihood of a response.

Recently I listened to a friend express dismay at the poor response rate he had received from an experimental survey of businesses that had already indicated they would like to respond by computer. He had decided to use the most advanced programming available for the survey because he felt that the results would have more significant implications in light of how fast the computer world was changing. I was not at all surprised to hear of the poor results, or to find out that the survey had significantly set back the sponsor's plans for converting this established survey to a Web questionnaire. Just as mail and telephone surveys required not only a willingness to respond by those methods, but an ability to deliver and retrieve responses, Web questionnaires require the same. The difference is that we are nowhere close to having the capability to reach everyone by the Internet, let alone via the most powerful computers and advanced browsers.

Of course, the situation will change, and computers and browsers will continue to improve, but to expect that everyone will at some point possess the latest and best computer technology is as unreasonable as expecting all commuters to drive only the latest model cars. Designing Web surveys with restraint is more likely to be an enduring condition of design than a quickly passing condition to be overcome. The somewhat conservative design principles outlined here will undoubtedly change and expand as technology evolves, but I expect a philosophy of conservative design to last far longer.

INTERACTIVE VOICE RESPONSE SURVEYS

Yet another type of electronic survey attracting great interest is the utilization of touch-tone telephones for conducting self-administered surveys. Selected individuals are asked to call an 800 number, or are transferred to the survey by an interviewer who has recruited them. They must then listen to prerecorded, voice-read questions; answer categories; and instructions for which numbers they can select for their response. The respondents then press keys on their touch-tone telephone to enter the selected numbers for their answer choice. This type of self-administered survey is referred to either as Interactive Voice Response (IVR) or, in an earlier form, as touch-tone data entry (TDE). IVR is a more advanced technology that does not limit responses to numbers. Respondents may give verbal answers, which are then tape recorded for later transcription. Thus, the more lasting terminology is likely to be IVR as opposed to TDE. These technologies have been used frequently for employee surveys, customer satisfaction evaluations, and even certain types of general public surveys. An example of a very successful use of the earliest TDE technology is the Current Employment Statistics Survey conducted by the U.S. Bureau of Labor Statistics.

Case Study: The Current Employment Statistics Survey (CES)

The CES is a voluntary, monthly panel survey of 380,000 business establishments conducted by the U.S. Bureau of Labor Statistics (Rosen, Clayton, and Wolf, 1993). It collects statistics on total employment, production or nonsupervisory worker employment, hours worked, and earnings, all of which comprise key economic indicators of the health of the U.S. economy. To be timely, only 10–15 days are available to collect and process the data from this short survey before providing preliminary estimates. Under a mail collection procedure, preliminary estimates were based on an average response of 55%, which rose to 75% after three additional weeks and 90% after another three weeks.

In 1982, research was started on asking units to respond by touch-tone data entry. Under this method businesses were called by a computer-assisted telephone interviewer to educate the respondent on timeliness requirements, and at the end of the six-month reporting period businesses were converted to TDE. TDE respondents were provided an answer form once a year and then asked to call a toll-free number each month for reporting. Each month thereafter they received a monthly advance notice postcard. Units that did not respond on time were then contacted by telephone or fax. On average, it took slightly less than two minutes for each reporting call initiated by the respondent to be completed.

By the end of 1997, over 240,000 respondents were reporting each month by TDE, with thousands more in transition. Using TDE in conjunction with other data collection methods raised initial response by nearly 20 percentage points, and the average monthly revisions to the preliminary estimates were reduced by 38% (Clayton and Werking, 1998).

Implications. The CES survey illustrates the enormous potential of TDE reporting for important but brief surveys. Keying in numerical data is a straightforward task for people who have gained some experience with this activity.

Good results may also be obtained for respondents without previous experience, but who have strong motivations for responding. For example, Mingay et al. (1999) used a TDE questionnaire to conduct preoperative assessments for surgery patients. Seventy percent of the individuals asked to complete the questionnaire from their homes prior to checking into the hospital completed it. The questionnaire consisted of six demographic questions plus 120 health questions. Most of the questions required yes, no, or not sure answers for which they were required to press 1, 2, or 3, respectively. Recipients of the questionnaire were provided a health instruction sheet that included an illustration of the telephone key pad with labels pointing to each of the three keys required for answering the survey questions. Only two patients who started the questionnaire were unable to complete it, and most said they liked the task and that it was easy to complete.

Only a decade ago this method seemed unlikely to be of use for conducting general public surveys. In addition to some people not yet having touch-tone telephones, it was an unfamiliar practice. Now, however, people regularly use telephones to check their bank balance, transfer money from savings to checking, start and stop delivery of newspapers, access their voice mail, renew library books, or locate a person in a large organization. Pressing numerical keys in response to voice instructions has become a routine part of American life.

However, TDE or IVR surveys can become quite tedious and even prohibitive if, for example, people must be asked to spell words; because there are three letters per key a follow-up is required to determine which letter the person intended by the numerical response. In addition, two letters, Q and Z, though rarely used, are not on the touch-tone key pad. A sometimes acceptable alternative is to tape record an interview and transcribe words later, although in the case of people's names, it is often difficult to get correct spellings by that means. IVR surveys also become difficult when a large number of numerical codes for categories must be presented to respondents, such as a list of the 50 U.S. states for responding to the question, "In which state do you live?" It is also difficult when there is considerable cross-referencing of questions that a respondent might need to do, such as in reporting average wage levels for types of employees identified in a previous question. Nonetheless, IVR is being used for many surveys, especially short ones for which all questions have simple numerical answers.

Respondents can be contacted in person or by mail and asked to call a 1–800 number to be surveyed. Alternatively, they can be contacted by a telephone interviewer and after they agree to be interviewed, turned over to an automated

IVR interview. In this way, the IVR technology is being used as a substitute for both self-administered mail surveys and telephone interview surveys.

Designing IVR surveys raises many issues not typically faced in other types of self-administered surveys. It may be the most difficult type of self-administered survey to conduct because of losing certain advantages of paper questionnaires on the one hand and telephone interviewing on the other. The paper advantage of visual layout to help communicate questions and allow respondents to maintain a mental context for responding is lost. The advantage of having an interviewer who can respond immediately to apparent respondent misunderstandings or confusion also gets lost. Moreover, it is not possible to speed up or slow down the reading of questions and answer categories in response to cues from the respondent. Everything that the respondent hears must be anticipated and built into the script. If a respondent becomes frustrated with some aspect of an IVR survey, it seems likely to result in an incomplete interview. Thus, while there is complete control of the order in which respondents are able to hear questions and answer choices, and complete uniformity in how questions and answers are delivered, there is also a downside to these features that may make getting a response more difficult. Every aspect of potential problems must be anticipated, and corrective features (e.g., invalid response or no response at all) must be built into a carefully constructed script.

Another potential difficulty with IVR surveys occurs when the respondent attempts to respond on a cordless or other telephone which has the key pad on the telephone receiver. For these phones it is necessary for the respondents to constantly switch from holding the receiver in front of them to see the numbers and up to their ear in order to listen. A fast-paced interview script may make it impossible to change positions fast enough to hear the instructions that follow each entry. Just as manipulating a computer mouse and computer keys makes responding to surveys difficult for some people, certain types of telephones may make responding to TDE surveys difficult. One solution is to suggest to respondents that responding may be easier if a phone with a key pad separate from the receiver is used. Also, using a speaker phone may help some respondents concentrate on the response task. These instructions may need to be built into TDE instructions for general survey populations.

Figure 11.18 provides an example of a brief IVR script. Several necessary features are immediately apparent. A significant portion of the script development is aimed at anticipating the need for responses to problems so that explanatory messages can be recorded and made available. Such messages need to be available in a way that responds to potential problems, but not so often as to be annoying. In addition, it is necessary to explicitly link each possible response category with a number, a task that does not need to be done for either telephone or paper questionnaires. This fact, along with the inability to

Figure 11.18 Example of a brief script for an IVR interview.

Hello, you have reached the Federated Employees survey. It is an easy way for you to communicate your feelings about the place where you work. Your answers are confidential and will never be connected to your name in any way.

You must be calling from a touch-tone phone to participate. To proceed, please press "1" on your touch-tone telephone.

No response replies:

(1st no response--after 4 seconds) "The system did not understand your response. Please try again." (Question is repeated.)

(2nd no response) "The system is unable to understand the responses from the phone you are using. Please try to call this number on a different touch tone phone. Goodbye."

Invalid response reply:

"The number you pressed is not a valid response. Please try again."

To assure that only Federated employees can respond to this survey, it is necessary for you to enter the four-digit code we sent you in the mail. Please do that now

(Repeat nonresponse and invalid number messages if needed.)

Thank you. I will now ask you several questions. Anytime you wish to have the question repeated, please press the star key. If you wish to answer "Don't Know," press 9.

1. In which city is your office located? For Des Moines press 1, for Fargo press 2, for Great Falls press 3, for Lexington press 4, for Minneapolis press 5, for Rapid City press 6, and for Sioux Falls press 7.

   (Nonresponse or invalid entry messages repeated as needed)

2. Next, on a five-point scale, how satisfied or dissatisfied are you with Federated as a place to work? To answer, press "5" for extremely satisfied, "4" for somewhat satisfied, "3" for neither satisfied or dissatisfied, "2" for somewhat dissatisfied, or "1" for very dissatisfied.

   (No response after 4 seconds--If you would like to have the question repeated before answering, please press star.)

   (Give invalid response message if needed.)

(Continued)

see the responses visually, makes the response task especially difficult. Although a respondent could be encouraged to look at the key pad, the fact, for example, that the response scale numbers for a five-point (1–5) scale appear in two different rows makes the visual appearance different from the single row or column of response categories typically presented on paper questionnaires for the same scale.

Figure 11.18 (Continued)

3. Compared to last year at this time are you more, about the same, or less satisfied with Federated as a place to work? Press 1 for more satisfied, 2 for about the same, or 3 for less satisfied.

   (Repeat nonresponse or invalid messages if needed.)

4. For each of the following aspects of work please indicate the extent to which you are satisfied or not satisfied by pressing 5 for extremely satisfied, 4 for somewhat satisfied, 3 for neither satisfied nor dissatisfied, 2 for somewhat dissatisfied, and 1 for extremely dissatisfied.

   How satisfied or dissatisfied are you with the way you are treated by your supervisor?

   (Repeat nonresponse, or invalid response messages if needed.)

5. How satisfied or dissatisfied are you with your current salary?

6. The next one is the amount of hours you work.

7. The next one is the extent to which management takes an interest in Federated's employees.

8. The amount of vacation you receive.

9. Keeping you informed about what's happening in the company.

10. Having access to the equipment and materials you need for doing your work correctly.

11. How many years have you worked for Federated? Press the total number of full years you have worked for Federated. If less than one full year press zero.

Thank you very much for answering this survey of Federated's employees. Goodbye.

The above considerations lead to the development of several principles for the construction of IVR surveys.

Principle 11.24: Provide an introduction, but keep it short.

It is important to welcome people to an IVR response survey, but the introduction needs to be short. Presumably a letter of explanation or, if contacted by telephone, a verbal introduction has been provided to the respondent. It is important to avoid a long, detailed explanation of how to respond; that can be explained as one proceeds. However, it may be useful to explain that responding is easier if one does not use a telephone that has the touch-tone keys on the ear piece.

Principle 11.25: Use a PIN or identification number to control access by respondents.

As in the case of Web surveys, IVR surveys utilize a public medium that anyone can access if they know the appropriate telephone number. To control access, respondents need to be provided a PIN or personal identification number which they are asked to enter at the beginning of the telephone call.

Principle 11.26: Make explicit the meaning of each number that the respondent may use for responding to a question, giving particular attention to possible mode comparisons.

Each possible response category should be labeled for use by the respondent. A recent experiment by Srinivasan and Hanway (1999) illustrates the need to make this association clear (Figure 11.19). An IVR script used for surveying a sample of customers did not explicitly mention each of the categories respondents could use with an assigned number. The script mentioned a scale of one through five, where one meant strongly agree and five meant strongly disagree. A self-administered questionnaire used for a companion sample also labeled only the end points but provided interim boxes that could easily be seen. For all 11 items using this response scale, respondents to the IVR survey were significantly more likely (mean difference = 6%) to answer strongly agree than were the paper questionnaire respondents (Figure 11.20). Six later items in the questionnaire were asked in the same way on the IVR survey, but had fully labeled categories for the paper questionnaire. On these items the percent of respondents selecting strongly agree averaged 17 percentage points higher for paper than for IVR. These dramatic differences are not surprising in one sense; categories that are not articulated to respondents are less likely to be used, regardless of survey mode. However, they illustrate the tension involved in developing TDE surveys where one wants to keep the script as brief as possible in order not to frustrate respondents, yet still wants to obtain good measurement.

The implications are particularly significant for surveys that are mixed-mode. If one wants to combine results from mail and self-administered surveys then it is important to be sure that the stimuli received by respondents are as similar as possible. As shown in Figure 11.19, the fact that intermediate categories can be used on a mail survey is visually apparent. However, that fact is not apparent in the verbal-only script of the IVR survey unless that information is communicated to respondents with words. Such implications are not limited to mail/IVR comparisons. The tendency in telephone interviews is to read only the category choices without assigning a number to the response. It seems advisable when an IVR comparison is involved for the telephone interviewer to also present category numbers for respondents to use in formulating their answer.

Principle 11.27: Be meticulous in maintaining consistency with respect to the meaning assigned to numbers and other symbols.

In general, this principle is desirable for construction of all types of self-administered surveys. For IVR questionnaires it rises to being an

Figure 11.19 Example of differences in touch-tone data entry and paper self-administered questionnaire responses that resulted from differences in question wording and design.

IVR questions without fully labeled categories:

IVR script:

> The next few questions in this survey use a scale of one through five. If you strongly agree, enter "5". If you strongly disagree, enter "1". If you do not know the answer or do not think it applies, please enter "0". You may also enter a "9" at any time to have the current question repeated. (Pause) Remember, use a scale of one through five. If you strongly agree, enter "5". If you strongly disagree, enter "1".

Now, how strongly do you agree or disagree that the employee who you talked to or visited with in your branch did the following, (e.g.) communicated clearly with you ...

Self-administered paper design:

On a scale from one to five, with "5" being strongly agree and "1" being strongly disagree, how strongly do you agree or disagree that the employee who you talked to or visited with in your branch did the following?	Strongly Disagree 1 ▼	2 ▼	3 ▼	4 ▼	Strongly Agree 5 ▼	Don't Know ▼
a. The employee communicated clearly with you	☐	☐	☐	☐	☐	☐

A later question with fully labeled categories:

IVR script:

> Using the same five-point scale, how strongly do you agree or disagree that there is someone at your branch who could handle any questions or problems you may have?

Self-administered paper design:

❾ How strongly do you agree or disagree that there is someone at your branch who could handle any questions or problems you may have:

- ☐ Strongly agree
- ☐ Agree
- ☐ Neither agree nor disagree
- ☐ Disagree
- ☐ Strongly disagree
- ☐ Don't know

imperative. Respondents are asked to respond to a survey over which they have virtually no control. In addition, they must learn the association of each response with a number. Changing "strongly agree" from being five for the first question to being one for a later question invites confusion that can be avoided. If one is used for "yes" in one question, it should not be used to mean "no" in another. It also helps to assign a nonnumerical key, such as the star key, to be used only when a respondent wants to repeat a question, and

Figure 11.20 Differences in responses to interactive voice response and paper self-administered questions shown in Figure 11.16.

	Mean Percent Strongly Agree			Range of differences in % Strongly Agree between forms
	Telephone	Paper	Difference	
Eleven items without fully labeled categories	19.4	13.6	5.6	3.1 - 7.4
Six later items with all points labeled on paper form	30.9	14.1	16.8	14.2 - 23.1

the pound key for "don't know" answers. It follows that frequent changes in lengths of scales, scale labels, and styles of questions also produce an increased burden for respondents, and such changes should be evaluated very carefully before they are made.

This principle also has mixed-mode implications. Paper questionnaire designers are accustomed to being able to take greater liberties in designing their questionnaires. Once the issue of mixed-mode comparisons enters the picture, it is more difficult to comprehend the IVR version and that sets the design limits. Similarly, IVR sets design limits for telephone interviews, in which skilled interviewers can easily repeat categories or changes in scale numbers until they are confident that the respondent understands them.

Principle 11.28: Avoid the use of one to ten scales, and read all numbers that might be used to respond to an IVR survey.

It is tempting to read only the end points of a scale in order to shorten the script. However, doing so is not a good idea. By reading all of the numbers, whatever the length of the scale, creation of the same visual image across modes is encouraged. A scale of one to ten in both telephone and mail surveys would seem to imply a linear scale, whether displayed horizontally or vertically. Converting such numbers to a telephone key pad means that the respondent must respond using digits arrayed in rows with a maximum of three digits.

A mode comparison by Mu (1999) illustrates the special challenges that may be associated with the use of a one to ten scale. The study sponsor wished to use that scale because it had been previously used for a similar mail survey. When a comparison was made between a sample surveyed by mail and a companion sample surveyed by paper, it was found that IVR responses were *less* likely to offer "10s" as an answer (Mu, 1999). Less use of this category in IVR versus mail occurred for 21 of 22 items in the survey, with an average difference of about 11 percentage points. One possibility for this difference is that recording a "10" requires pressing two numbers rather than one, with the first number in the series being the most negative scale score. The greater mental burden and the visual display of the touch-tone numbers that places one to nine in three linear rows may have accounted for this difference. This suggests that a one to nine scale would be more appropriate, and that 11-point scales that start with zero (in the middle of the bottom row on a touch-tone phone) should not be used at all.

Principle 11.29: Formulate appropriate messages for all potential problems, which can be programmed for appearance in needed situations.

Respondents may need to hear a question a second time or they may fail to press a key to record their answer. They may also press a wrong number and need to correct an answer. Figure 11.18 includes some examples of messages that might appear if a respondent makes a mistake. The more complex the survey and the response options, the more complex it may become to determine what messages are important to include as options in the IVR script.

IVR Implementation Procedures

As in all other survey modes, multiple contacts are essential for achieving high response to IVR surveys. Contacts by mail and by telephone have distinctly different advantages. Contacts by mail can be used to send token financial incentives, provide a PIN or identification number for access, and legitimate a survey request. They also make possible the sending of paper questionnaires and/or long lists of names with code numbers (state of residence, occupation, or highest level of education) which the respondent can use when providing answers. Telephone requests for respondents to be "transferred to an IVR" response mode have the distinct advantage of transferring one to a somewhat similar response mode with little or no effort, just as an e-mail contact may facilitate a nearly seamless transfer from e-mail to a Web questionnaire through a simple click.

There is as yet little experimental work to draw from for prescribing the most effective contact strategies for IVR surveys. However, a sequence of contacting people with a prenotice, followed by a specific request that includes PIN number information, token incentive, and questionnaire or list of code numbers, followed by a postcard thank you or reminder might commence a data collection sequence. Then, if a response is not obtained and a telephone number is available, one might follow up with a telephone call and offer to transfer a respondent directly to the IVR script. It will be surprising, if not amazing, if IVR surveys do not take the same concerted effort to obtain responses that is necessary for implementing other types of self-administered surveys.

Summary Perspective on IVR Questionnaires

In contrast to the enormous latitude of Web questionnaires, IVR is a limited technology. When questionnaires are long, have many different types of questions, require entering numbers from long lists, or necessitate recording letters instead of numbers, the limitations become particularly significant. However, it would be a mistake to consider this technology to be unimportant.

In recent years some organizations have begun a practice of having telephone interviewers recruiting respondents and then turning them over to an automated IVR interview. This practice has the potential for enormous cost savings. Recently I talked with the director of a corporate telephone calling center that received thousands of requests for information each day. The center had recently instituted the practice of responding to the questions and then asking a small sample of respondents if they would be willing to answer a few additional questions about the service received through the center by using an automated response (IVR) system. The director of the operation was enormously impressed that at a cost of only cents per call she could obtain data from several hundred customers each day, a much cheaper procedure than attempting a follow-up contact by any other method.

When IVR is used to collect data in a mixed-mode situation, it tends to become the limiting technology with regard to the complexity of survey questions. For this reason, I think it is useful to consider the nature of questions that must be asked before committing oneself to collection of data by IVR in addition to another mode. Yet, the fact that IVR adds a self-administered telephone capability to procedures that require computer access suggests that its use in conjunction with other inexpensive electronic technologies may expand greatly as people become more accustomed to its use.

CONCLUSION

Survey innovation in the twentieth century has been driven much more by the potential for reducing costs than by the development of new ways of reducing survey error. Telephone interviewing, for example, came into prominence because it was much less expensive than conducting face-to-face interviews. The reduction of survey error was a necessary challenge that followed.

The cost reduction potential offered by each of the electronic survey technologies discussed in this chapter, over both mail and telephone methods, is far greater than that offered by the switch from face-to-face to telephone methods. The nearly complete elimination of interviewer costs, except as a means of recruiting respondents, and the ability to report results almost immediately make the use of these technologies particularly appealing.

These technologies have the potential for changing dramatically the culture of surveying, but the full nature of those changes is not yet apparent. A short while ago I received a call from a professional organization that wanted help doing an e-mail survey of their members. When I suggested that they keep the questionnaire short, the caller quickly responded that doing so would not be a problem. Moreover, they seemed not at all interested in discussing any ideas about sampling. Their plan, I soon learned, was to do a complete survey of all members every two or three weeks. The idea that surveying the same people over and over might decrease the effectiveness of their future surveys was not something they had considered.

It is easy to imagine the full-fledged emergence of Internet and IVR survey methods as giving new meaning to the notion of being over-surveyed, as users rush to survey ever larger samples or entire populations and do so more frequently, with one quickly constructed and implemented survey following another. It is also possible that new, lower standards for survey response rates might evolve as sponsors put more and more emphasis on weighting and otherwise adjusting their data in an effort to compensate for lower response rates.

Looking at it from another perspective, I am impressed with the emergence of new, more efficient alternatives just as the telephone survey method has reached the point that errors seem unavoidable, the result of growing coverage and nonresponse problems. One could hardly have predicted the growth and current challenges facing telephone interviewing when that method came into use in the 1970s. Similarly, we cannot yet predict the future of Internet and IVR survey technologies. Will they replace other survey methods, or will they simply expand further the survey repertoire of methodologists so that data collection procedures might better be matched to the challenges of surveying particular populations? As with past transitions in survey methods, only time will tell.

CHAPTER 12

Optical Scanning and Imaging, and the Future of Self-Administered Surveys*

A RECURRING theme throughout this book is that self-administered surveys are now benefiting from the application of computer technologies in much the way that telephone interviewing did in the 1980s. In addition to the benefits of better capabilities for visual design and layout, improved efficiencies for implementing mailout procedures, and such new concepts as posting self-administered questionnaires on the World Wide Web, one more capability is addressed in this chapter.

This new capability involves not only scanning answers into computers, which has been possible since the 1960s, but importing an image of the entire questionnaire into a computer. This capability portends the death knell of traditional keypunching by introducing a different concept of data entry and cleaning that is likely to change how virtually all mail surveys are processed and tabulations produced.

In this final chapter, the promise of optical scanning and imaging is described and principles for the design of questionnaires in ways that facilitate these processes are discussed. In addition, I briefly revisit the need to tailor surveys as we begin the twenty-first century, and I speculate on what the future may bring.

SCANNING WITH IMAGING

HISTORICAL DEVELOPMENT AND LIMITATIONS

Among survey methodologists, controversy about replacing keying with scanning has prevailed. Some have pointed out that for massive surveys on

*Portions of this chapter were previously published in Dillman and Miller (1998) and are used here by permission of the publisher.

tight deadlines, scanning is essential. Others have noted that data quality suffers significantly under scanning because poor design creates numerous errors that are very difficult to correct. For many, scanning applications are simply ignored by sponsors. Detractors also note that there have been no cost advantages for scanning unless several thousand questionnaires are being processed.

Until recently, both perspectives have been correct. Sometimes scanning has been the only practical alternative and the difficulty of making corrections has often led users to ignore such problems. When strenuous efforts have been made in order to assure virtually complete accuracy of data files, they have required cumbersome specialized systems. An example is the FOSDIC (Film Optical Sensing Device for Input to Computer) system used for 100 million questionnaires in the 1990 U.S. Census. It required microfilming each questionnaire and then reading images produced on that microfilm to produce population counts.

This situation is now changing. Systems exist that make it possible to design better questionnaires that are easier for respondents to complete. Not only can checked answers be read reliably, but numbers and letters can also be deciphered with confidence. In addition, it is possible to identify and correct respondent marking mistakes easily and efficiently, as will be described later. Most importantly, it may soon be cost effective to apply optical scanning and the new imaging technologies to small- as well as large-scale studies. Though such systems remain expensive at the time of this writing, I will find it surprising if they do not dominate surveying by mail in the early twenty-first century.

A BRIEF LOOK AT THE PAST

The earliest use of optically scannable questionnaires was fairly limited. Generally, it was reserved for situations in which very large numbers of identical questionnaires were collected from specialized audiences such as employees, or where there existed a high motivation to comply with the survey request.

The early technologies typically required that questionnaires be printed only on one side of a sheet of paper. When two-sided printing was desired, it was often necessary to prevent answer spaces from appearing back-to-back on the paper. Some formats limited answer choices to small areas of each page, such as columns on the right side of the page, so that all questions had to fit a particular kind of construction format. A soft-leaded pencil was usually required for answers, and people were asked to completely darken small circles or ovals rather than marking answers with an "X" or check mark. In addition, prominent equipment guide markers, sometimes referred to as "skunk" marks, were necessary for assuring accurate processing. These marks often dominated the questionnaire's appearance and made it more difficult for respondents to know how to provide answers (Jenkins and Dillman, 1995, 1997).

The technology was also limited to optical mark recognition (OMR), which read the presence or absence of marks. Optical character recognition (OCR) of numbers and handwritten characters had not yet been developed. For that reason, questionnaires requiring words for answers had to be sent through an additional keypunching operation to record these responses. In addition, folding of the questionnaires often interfered with the machine reading of answers so that flat mailings were preferred.

It is not surprising that these early optical questionnaires were used mostly in controlled settings; for example, for student tests or the collection of information from employees. In these situations, soft-leaded pencils and instructions could be provided. More importantly, though, much was at stake for respondents with regard to the correct interpretation of answers, so it could be assumed they would write answers carefully and make complete erasures as directed.

Among the leaders in the development of optical mark recognition systems were the U.S. Bureau of the Census, which developed the Film Optical Sensing Device for Input to Computer (FOSDIC) system. This system was used to count people in four decennial censuses from 1960–1990, thus pioneering the use of optical questionnaires with the U.S. general public. Another leader was National Computer Systems (NCS), a private organization founded in 1962. It developed an optical mark recognition system for which scoring was applied initially to tests and personality assessments, and later to surveys.

Smaller survey organizations faced formidable barriers to using these technologies, which were developed for use on mainframe computers and therefore too costly for small users. These organizations also lacked the volume of self-administered surveys that would allow them to recover the substantial investment and maintenance costs of the necessary equipment.

Effects of Traditional Optical Mark Recognition (OMR) Technologies on Response Rates

Scannable questionnaires have long had a reputation for eliciting low response rates to surveys. For example, recent research at the U.S. Census Bureau found that changing a form designed almost entirely to meet OMR scanning requirements of the Census Bureau's FOSDIC system to one based on visual principles of respondent-friendly design, like those outlined in Chapter 3, improved response rates at least modestly (Dillman et al., 1993). However, experiments by Klose and Ball (1995), Jacobs (1986), and Dillman and Miller (1998) found no differences in response.

The image of lower response may come in large part from the "mass survey" culture associated with the use of scannable questionnaires. Sending out tens of thousands of questionnaires, which encourages the use of scannable surveys, also encourages other efforts to reduce costs—bulk rate mail, lack of personalization, printing letters on the questionnaire itself, crowded formats to keep the page count down per questionnaire, no prenotices or follow-ups, no token incentives, and so forth. Ink colors, chosen for their drop-out value in scanning and prominent scanning guide marks, contribute to instant identification as some type of test or questionnaire, limited visual appeal, and a lack of respondent-friendliness.

A limited analysis of response rates obtained from surveys using traditional OMR technology found that 44 surveys distributed by 10 sponsoring organizations, ranging from two to 28 pages in length, obtained response rates that averaged 42%. A more detailed summary of results is presented in Figure 12.1. Sample sizes ranged from 100 to 4,000,000, with an overall mean of about 318,000. However, those under 1,600 respondents could be described as special situation surveys, and would probably not have been done if the client had not already contracted for surveys of other, much larger samples.

Figure 12.1 Sample sizes and response rates for 44 studies using scannable questionnaires (Dillman & Miller, 1998).

		Sample Size		Response Rate (%)	
Population	**Number of Studies**	**Range**	**Mean**	**Range**	**Mean**
Individuals					
1 contact	15	1017–4 million	331,559	10–60	32
2+ contacts	12	168–736,221	63,843	29–68	53
Totals	27		207,998		42
Businesses					
1 contact	6	14,715–2.3 million	986,786	14–42	23
2+ contacts	2	600,000-900,000	750,000	18–21	20
Totals	8		927,589		22
Employees					
1 contact	3	5500–300,000	160,167	34–48	43
2+ contacts	6	100–60,000	37,168	55–84	66
Totals	9		78,168		58
Table Totals	44		314,702		42

The surveys were divided into those of individuals (mostly customer satisfaction surveys), businesses, and employees, based on evidence that these factors influence response rates (Heberlein and Baumgartner, 1978; Paxson, 1992). Response rates for the surveys of individuals averaged 32% when only one contact was used, compared with 53% when two or more contacts were made. Similarly, employee responses averaged 43% with one contact, compared with 66% when two or more contacts were made. Extra contacts did not produce higher response rates for businesses, but only two of the eight business surveys used more than two contacts. Overall, response rates for the 44 surveys averaged only 42%.

The data presented here tend to confirm the use of mass delivery methods as sample sizes increase. Whereas the average sample size for surveys using two or more contacts was 124,457, the average for those receiving one contact was 460,127, nearly four times larger.

Although the response rates reported in Figure 12.1 tend to be low compared to what can usually be achieved by mail survey methods, these data do not provide strong evidence that scannable surveys necessarily produce lower response rates. After reviewing the details available to us for the various studies, we concluded that the methods used for the vast majority of the surveys did not include many of the techniques for improving response rates that past research has shown to be effective. The data do suggest, however, that when additional contacts are made response rates are likely to improve. This indication is bolstered by the Klose and Ball (1995) experimental study which revealed that response to the OMR questionnaire doubled (from 22 to 44%) when a prenotice, reminder, and $500 sweepstakes notification were included in the treatment.

Conversations with the sponsors of the scannable surveys analyzed here indicated that most questionnaires had been processed by mass scanning methods. In some instances incoming questionnaires were reviewed and questionnaires with marks that would not scan were re-marked by hand. In other instances we found that double-marks were corrected by whiting-out one of the answers. Algorithms for selecting one of two double-marks were sometimes programmed into the computer processing instructions. However, in a large number of instances, minimal efforts were made to correct errors, with the result that questionnaires that would not scan because of poor marks or other reasons were simply ignored in the analysis. It was explained to us that time pressures for reporting survey results were often great and did not allow for either pre- or post-processing to improve quality of data, so the final results were of significantly less quality than could have been achieved.

My impression that a major use of scannable surveys is for the mass collection of data that receives minimal cleaning and correction was significantly reinforced by this analysis of response rates. Although a few respondents reported meticulous efforts with white-out and remarking surveys for processing, they appeared to be in the minority.

RECENT DEVELOPMENTS

Barriers to the use of scannable surveys may be diminishing for all organizations, large and small, for three reasons. First, the technologies themselves have a far greater capability than in the past. Most surveys require that respondents write numbers, letters, and/or words as well as marking answer choices. Optical character recognition capabilities have been developed that make it possible to capture letters and numbers as well as marks. Thus, the need for dual processing of questionnaires should be diminished. However, even though individual numbers and printed characters can be read with reasonable accuracy by some technologies, text answers to open-ended questions cannot be read well without the letters being separated. The reading of cursive writing remains a formidable barrier to the best technologies.

Second, the development of imaging technologies, through which a complete image of the questionnaire page is imported into a computer, has fundamentally changed the structure of data capture operations. The entire image of the questionnaire is scanned into the computer and stored for possible use in determining the meaning of respondent answers. The most sophisticated imaging software can assign a confidence level, for instance, 98%, that the image of the respondent answer (a letter or number) corresponds to a unique character which the computer has been programmed to recognize. All marks that the recognition engine cannot identify at that level of confidence are then rejected for transfer to the final data file. These rejects, sometimes referred to as spurious marks, are directed to another file for later display on a computer screen so that an operator can make a visual determination of what the respondent was attempting to report. By this means, common problems such as double-marks, erasures, or attempts to obliterate an answer with a heavy mark and replace it with another can be corrected easily and quickly. In the event that the operator cannot determine the respondent's intent from the visual display of the specific answer, part of the questionnaire page, or even the complete questionnaire (where the mark appears), can be recalled to the screen in order to see the response context. Thus, for example, the operator who is attempting to determine whether a respondent provided an "n" or and "r" can look to see how these letters were provided in other answers to help make that judgment.

Imaging technologies are dramatically changing the processing procedures used for traditional keypunching and the methods for processing OMR questionnaires, as illustrated in Figure 12.2. In traditional keypunching operations, questionnaires were preprocessed to identify unclear answers, make judgments about which of two double-marked answers to record, code open-end answers, and generally facilitate the keypunching process. The keypuncher was often asked to make additional decisions while keypunching (e.g., always entering the highest educational level in the case of double-marked responses). To assure accuracy of keypunching, questionnaires were typically keypunched twice, a process known as verification. If a likely error was identified after the keypunching was completed (for example, impossible answers such as someone with a driver's license being five years of age), it was necessary to refer to the questionnaire to decide on the appropriate correction. Thus, every step of the keypunching process, from editing through verification, required access to each respondent's completed questionnaire.

The processing of OMR-only questionnaires, such as the one shown in Figure 12.3, in which respondents had marked their answers with darkened ovals or circles, began with an editing process. An operator had to visually examine the entire questionnaire. If marks appeared too light to scan, they were manually darkened. If two marks were made for a single question, then white-out or erasers would be used to completely remove one of the marks. Only after this review and making the satisfactory repairs could the questionnaires be scanned. Meanwhile, a template was designed for the mark recognition engine, after which the questionnaires were scanned. After the initial scanning, open-ended questions and other questions requiring coding (e.g., occupation) were sent through a separate process which led to another round of scanning or auxiliary data entry. Initial data runs of the scanned data were likely to reveal double-marks or other problems missed by the initial visual inspections, making it necessary to retrieve the original questionnaire for corrections. As with keypunching, this process required access to the physical questionnaire.

With advanced imaging capabilities, it is not necessary to edit the questionnaires prior to scanning. All corrections, traditionally done as a preprocessing step, are made afterwards using the screen image of the questionnaire. The first step is to build a template, after which questionnaires can be scanned at a rate of several hundred per hour. Components of the questionnaire are then sent to different work stations where: (1) all marks that have not been accepted at the specified level of confidence are reviewed by retrieving the questionnaire image to the screen; (2) open-ended answers are entered or coded from a screen image of the questionnaire; and (3) a randomly selected portion of the scored marks are reviewed for scanning accuracy. Each of these processes can occur simultaneously because none of the operators needs access to the physical questionnaire. Under the most sophisticated scanning systems it is unlikely that physical retrieval of the respondent's completed questionnaire will ever be needed after it has been scanned; instead, the operator retrieves the image of the questionnaire to resolve inconsistencies. Changes in the work process, from making corrections on one respondent's questionnaire at a time to making corrections on the same item for all questionnaires

Figure 12.2 Differences in processing for three types of data capture (Dillman & Miller, 1998).

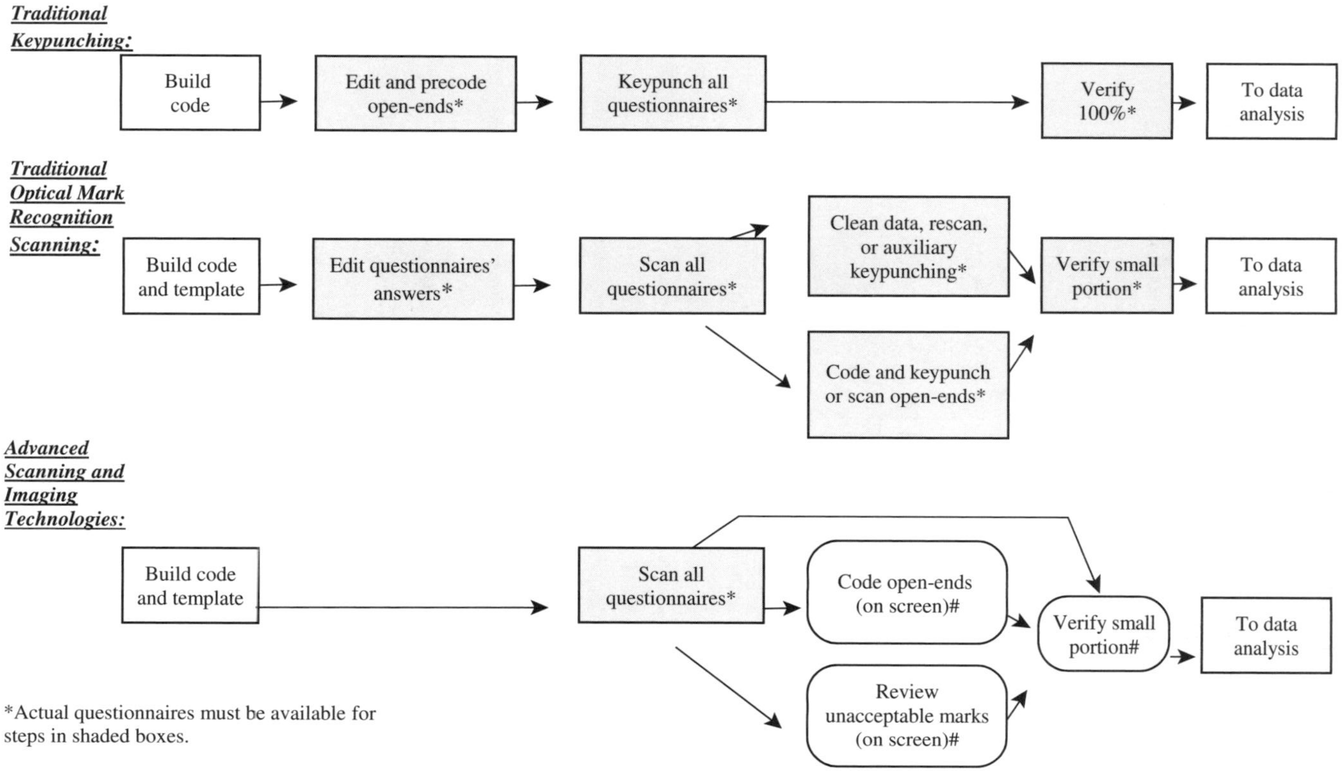

*Actual questionnaires must be available for steps in shaded boxes.

#Computer screen image used for steps in rounded boxes.

Figure 12.3 Example of Optical Mark Recognition (OMR) survey.

U.S. POSTAL SERVICE

Business Customer Satisfaction Survey

INSTRUCTIONS: This survey covers all types of mail (e.g., First-Class, Second-Class, Third-Class, etc.) your business sends and receives. Since this is an ongoing survey, we ask you to think only about the past 3 months when answering the questions.

MARKING INSTRUCTIONS

- Use a blue or black pen or a #2 pencil.
- Fill in ovals completely.
- Do not make any stray marks on the form.
- Erase cleanly any mark you wish to change.

CORRECT MARK INCORRECT MARKS

LINDA KEIL
THE GALLUP ORGANIZATION
ONE CHURCH STREET #900
ROCKVILLE MD 20850

0661855

OVERALL PERFORMANCE

1. **Thinking about the service your business has received *during the past 3 months,* how would you rate the U.S. Postal Service on . . .**

	POOR	FAIR	GOOD	VERY GOOD	EXCELLENT
a. Its overall performance	1	2	3	4	5
b. Providing products and services to meet the needs of your business	1	2	3	4	5
c. Having employees who are knowledgeable about U.S. Postal Service products and services	1	2	3	4	5
d. Having rules and regulations that are easy to understand	1	2	3	4	5
e. Having employees who go out of their way to meet your mailing needs	1	2	3	4	5
f. Providing services that are a good value for the price	1	2	3	4	5
g. Having courteous and friendly employees	1	2	3	4	5
h. The length of time it usually takes for a First-Class letter mailed in your local area to be delivered in your local area	1	2	3	4	5
i. The length of time it usually takes for a First-Class letter you mail locally to be delivered in other parts of the country	1	2	3	4	5

MAIL YOUR BUSINESS SENDS

2. **Based on your company's experiences *in the past 3 months,* please rate the following U.S. Postal Service facilities. (MARK "DID NOT USE" OR "NOT FAMILIAR WITH THIS FACILITY" IF APPROPRIATE.)**

	NOT FAMILIAR WITH THIS FACILITY	DID NOT USE	POOR	FAIR	GOOD	VERY GOOD	EXCELLENT
a. Post Office your business uses most	◯	0	1	2	3	4	5
b. Postal Business Center	◯	0	1	2	3	4	5
c. Bulk Mail Acceptance Unit	◯	0	1	2	3	4	5
d. Rates and Classification Center	◯	0	1	2	3	4	5

3. ***During the past 3 months,* how often have you had the following experiences with mail your company sends? (IF THE QUESTION DOES NOT APPLY TO YOUR BUSINESS, PLEASE MARK THE RESPONSE "NOT APPLICABLE.")**

	NOT APPLICABLE	NEVER	ONCE A WEEK OR LESS	2 OR 3 TIMES A WEEK	NEARLY EVERY DAY
a. Had metered mail returned for redating	0	1	2	3	4
b. Mail never delivered	0	1	2	3	4
c. Mail picked up too early	0	1	2	3	4
d. Mail picked up too late	0	1	2	3	4
e. Mail not delivered in the same number of days each time	0	1	2	3	4
f. Experienced errors made by U.S. Postal Service in processing money in your postage account(s).	0	1	2	3	4

4. **Based on your company's experiences *in the past 3 months,* please rate the following U.S. Postal Service products and services your business used for sending mail. (IF YOU DID NOT USE A PARTICULAR SERVICE, PLEASE MARK THE RESPONSE "DID NOT USE.")**

	DID NOT USE	POOR	FAIR	GOOD	VERY GOOD	EXCELLENT
a. Express Mail	0	1	2	3	4	5
b. Priority Mail	0	1	2	3	4	5
c. Full rate First-Class Mail ($.32)	0	1	2	3	4	5
d. Discounted First-Class Mail (presorted, barcoded)	0	1	2	3	4	5
e. Second-Class Mail (e.g., magazines, newspapers)	0	1	2	3	4	5
f. Third-Class Mail (e.g., advertising, Bulk Mail)	0	1	2	3	4	5
g. Fourth-Class Mail (e.g., Parcel Post)	0	1	2	3	4	5
h. International Mail	0	1	2	3	4	5

27MAY95-15SEP95(04/F2)
0023298

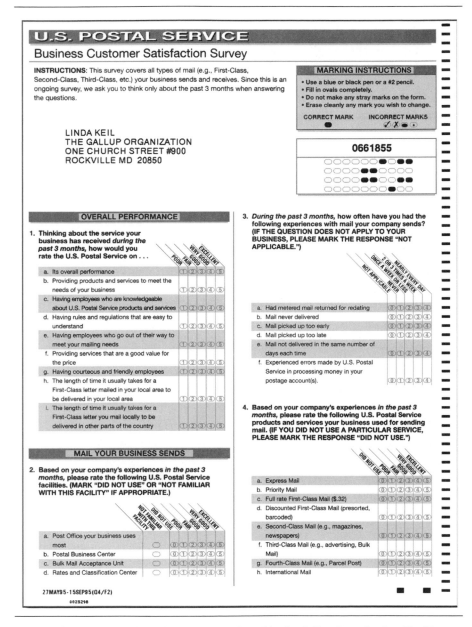

Example from U.S. Postal Service survey, conducted by the Gallup Organization. Used by permission of the U.S. Postal Service.

that exhibit a particular problem, has the potential for greatly speeding up the correction process and helping to insure that it is done in a consistent manner across all respondents. An example of a questionnaire that can be processed in this way is shown in Figure 12.4. The content is quite similar to that shown for OMR technology in Figure 12.3.

Changes are occurring very rapidly in the capabilities of advanced imaging systems and further improvements seem very likely, if not inevitable. Much of the potential for efficiency stems from the dramatic changes in processing procedures summarized in Figure 12.2. Scanning occurs as the first step of processing, and from that point on the process is not dependent upon the availability of the actual questionnaire to processing personnel. Thus, capacity can be expanded or speed increased simply by adding to the number of computer workstations. This characteristic seems advantageous to large organizations working on large surveys under severe time pressures.

The third major development associated with imaging technologies that reduces barriers to their use is facilitation of questionnaire design, which is much more respondent-friendly now than in the past. It is now possible to design questionnaires that require either X's or checks instead of darkened circles. Ball-point pen marks can be read as well as pencil marks, provided that the color of the pen is not similar to the color of the questionnaire page. Colored drop-out inks are often used for the printing of scannable questionnaires. These inks "disappear" when a light of the same color is directed onto the questionnaire page. Common drop-out ink colors such as red and green work well, provided that respondents have not used the same color of ink to record their answers. A related improvement in respondent-friendliness is the fact that answer choices can be placed virtually anywhere on the sheet of paper and printed on both sides of the page. Whereas in the past, technology constraints dictated many aspects of questionnaire layout and design, that is no longer the case.

Some of the advanced imaging process technologies described in Figure 12.2 do not have special questionnaire formatting requirements that prevent the use of respondent-friendly questionnaire formats. Repeated observation of one of the most advanced systems available leads me to conclude that it can be used efficiently for small surveys (less than 1,000 questionnaires) as well as large ones because of the brief amount of time required for building templates and the efficiency of its process for corrections and additional on-screen processing. However, this system is also quite expensive, with the scanner alone costing over $30,000. It is therefore not yet cost-effective for small survey organizations. Further developments with these technologies, which could lead to cost-effectiveness for small-scale operations, need to be watched closely.

These technology developments are very timely inasmuch as new expectations are being placed on all survey organizations, large and small. Customers typically want surveys to be completed far more quickly than in the

Figure 12.4 Example of Optical Mark Recognition survey in Figure 12.3, revised for Optical Character Recognition (OCR).

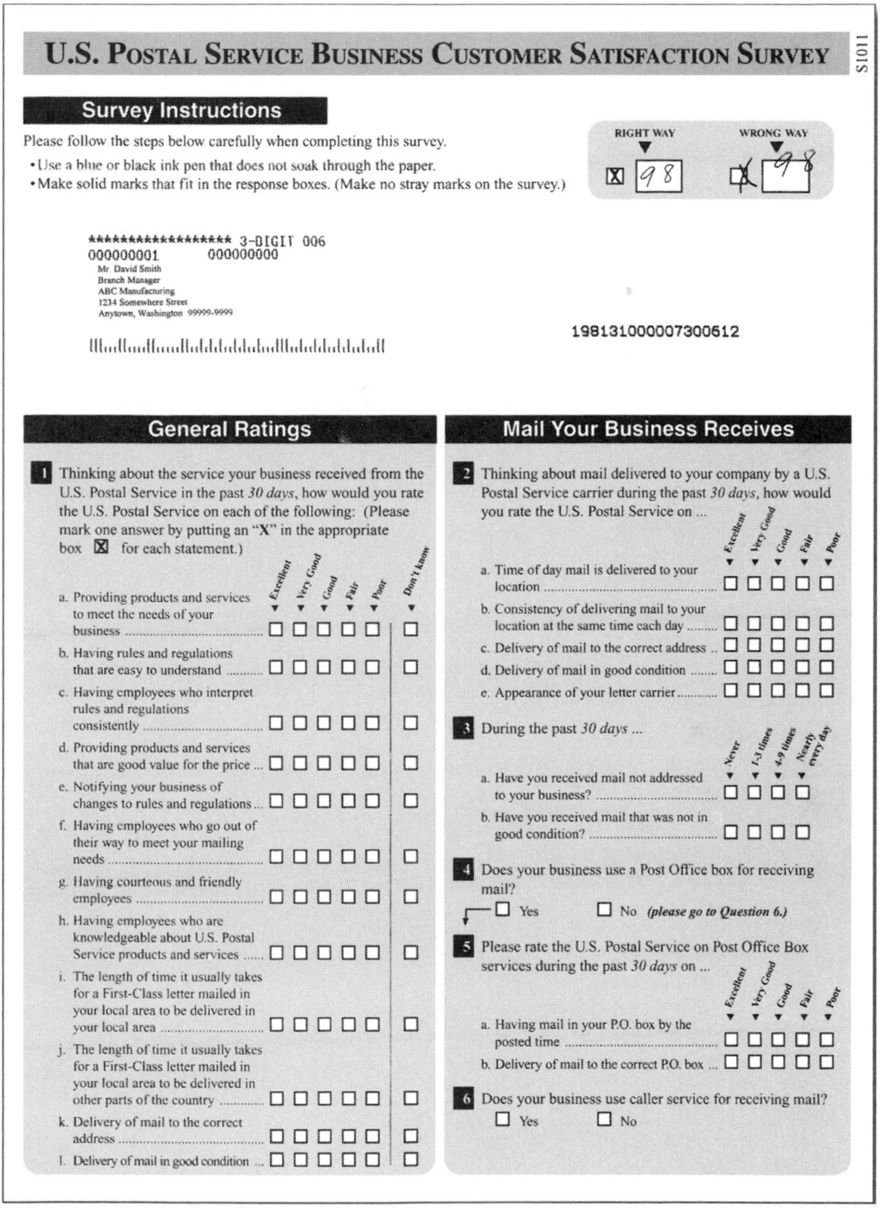

U.S. POSTAL SERVICE BUSINESS CUSTOMER SATISFACTION SURVEY

S1011

Survey Instructions

Please follow the steps below carefully when completing this survey.

- Use a blue or black ink pen that does not soak through the paper.
- Make solid marks that fit in the response boxes. (Make no stray marks on the survey.)

RIGHT WAY ☒ 98   WRONG WAY

******************** 3-DIGIT 006
000000001 000000000
Mr. David Smith
Branch Manager
ABC Manufacturing
1234 Somewhere Street
Anytown, Washington 99999-9999

19813100000730O612

General Ratings

1 Thinking about the service your business received from the U.S. Postal Service in the past *30 days*, how would you rate the U.S. Postal Service on each of the following: (Please mark one answer by putting an "X" in the appropriate box ☒ for each statement.)

	Excellent	Very Good	Good	Fair	Poor	Don't know
a. Providing products and services to meet the needs of your business	☐	☐	☐	☐	☐	☐
b. Having rules and regulations that are easy to understand	☐	☐	☐	☐	☐	☐
c. Having employees who interpret rules and regulations consistently	☐	☐	☐	☐	☐	☐
d. Providing products and services that are good value for the price	☐	☐	☐	☐	☐	☐
e. Notifying your business of changes to rules and regulations	☐	☐	☐	☐	☐	☐
f. Having employees who go out of their way to meet your mailing needs	☐	☐	☐	☐	☐	☐
g. Having courteous and friendly employees	☐	☐	☐	☐	☐	☐
h. Having employees who are knowledgeable about U.S. Postal Service products and services	☐	☐	☐	☐	☐	☐
i. The length of time it usually takes for a First-Class letter mailed in your local area to be delivered in your local area	☐	☐	☐	☐	☐	☐
j. The length of time it usually takes for a First-Class letter mailed in your local area to be delivered in other parts of the country	☐	☐	☐	☐	☐	☐
k. Delivery of mail to the correct address	☐	☐	☐	☐	☐	☐
l. Delivery of mail in good condition	☐	☐	☐	☐	☐	☐

Mail Your Business Receives

2 Thinking about mail delivered to your company by a U.S. Postal Service carrier during the past *30 days*, how would you rate the U.S. Postal Service on ...

	Excellent	Very Good	Good	Fair	Poor
a. Time of day mail is delivered to your location	☐	☐	☐	☐	☐
b. Consistency of delivering mail to your location at the same time each day	☐	☐	☐	☐	☐
c. Delivery of mail to the correct address	☐	☐	☐	☐	☐
d. Delivery of mail in good condition	☐	☐	☐	☐	☐
e. Appearance of your letter carrier	☐	☐	☐	☐	☐

3 During the past *30 days* ...

	Never	1-3 times	4-9 times	Nearly every day
a. Have you received mail not addressed to your business?	☐	☐	☐	☐
b. Have you received mail that was not in good condition?	☐	☐	☐	☐

4 Does your business use a Post Office box for receiving mail?

☐ Yes   ☐ No *(please go to Question 6.)*

5 Please rate the U.S. Postal Service on Post Office Box services during the past *30 days* on ...

	Excellent	Very Good	Good	Fair	Poor
a. Having mail in your P.O. box by the posted time	☐	☐	☐	☐	☐
b. Delivery of mail to the correct P.O. box	☐	☐	☐	☐	☐

6 Does your business use caller service for receiving mail?

☐ Yes   ☐ No

Example from U.S. Postal Service survey, conducted by the Gallup Organization. Used by permission of the U.S. Postal Service.

past, and one of the biggest potentials for shortening the production time for mail surveys is through the new processing procedures facilitated by imaging the entire questionnaire.

In addition, the macro changes occurring in the global economy as a result of the application of information technologies to all aspects of work have created a demand for types of surveys seldom done in the past. Increasingly, businesses and other organizations are operated and managed on the basis of feedback from customers on the performance of not just the entire organization, but of small units within it. Survey organizations are being asked to design surveys that obtain large numbers of responses so that feedback can be provided to the smallest work units of the organization. To the extent that small survey organizations can acquire and use optical scanning technologies to achieve a lower cost, conducting such surveys may become feasible.

One result of the interest in total organization feedback is that the demand for mail surveys appears to be increasing rather than decreasing. The extent to which small survey organizations can master and effectively utilize advanced scanning and imagining technologies will influence greatly their future importance in meeting this expanding demand for mail surveys. Although advanced technologies available to large organizations seem to offer much promise for switching the entire operations to using scannable questionnaires, it remains to be seen whether they also offer promise to small organizations and the small surveys they typically conduct.

Principles for Design of Questionnaires That Will Be Imaged

The design procedures outlined in Chapter 3 have anticipated our discussion of optical scanning and imaging in this chapter. Indeed, there is virtually no difference in the procedures advocated there and those required for the imaging system described earlier in this chapter. Regardless of whether one is now entering data by optical methods or manual data entry, the principles that need to be followed for getting people to navigate and respond to questionnaires correctly are the same. Although different software systems use slightly different technologies, the ones we have observed can, in general, read questionnaires that follow those general design procedures. The additional principles outlined here deal with special features of light reading systems.

Principle 12.1: Provide squares instead of rectangles or circles for marking answers.

It is useful to encourage respondents to make the mark that is easiest for them. Observation of respondents has led to a desire to avoid requiring respondents to fill in circles or ovals. Doing that requires respondents to devote considerable time to each mark as the tips of one's figures are forced to move around several times in a tight circle in order to blacken the indicated space. Examination of that process on many questionnaires revealed that the circle itself sometimes gets entirely missed without the respondent even being aware that their mark has been printed outside the circle, leading to an inevitable error in optical processing.

Encouraging respondents to make a check mark or an "X" requires less effort and less fine motor control. However, it is more desirable for respondents to mark X's than to make check marks. Check marks involve making a short downward mark, and then, as is the custom for many people, a longer upward mark. Such marks are likely to go into adjacent boxes, and thus interfere with the machine reading of valid marks for other questions. Marking an "X" requires that the respondent make two short marks, one after the other.

Systematic observation of respondents (Caldwell and Dillman, 1998) has revealed that the presence of rectangles encourages some respondents to utilize a check mark, whereas a box encourages the marking of X's. It is for this reason that I recommend the use of boxes on questionnaires.

Principle 12.2: Boxes should be no smaller than 1/8″ × 1/8″, with as much space left between boxes as there is within them.

Experience also suggests that when boxes become quite small it is difficult for people to mark X's within them, so some respondents are likely to revert to check marks. The downward mark followed by the upward mark appears to be an easier method for getting the bottom tip of the check mark inside a small box, than trying to mark an X with two lines that cross inside the tiny answer box. It is also important to leave a reasonable amount of space between boxes so that a mark intended for one box does not inadvertently cross over into another box. When that happens, processing errors result.

Principle 12.3: Limit the optical reading of characters (one or two words or a string of numbers) and place small segmentation bars or ticks between answer spaces.

One of the major drawbacks to the use of optical scanning has been the near impossibility of reading characters when respondents use cursive writing. There are too many unique ways that people execute the letters in words, especially when they are writing rapidly. Placing very narrow segmentation bars, or partial lines or ticks, between spaces within a designated answer space encourages people to print rather than write cursive (Dillman, 1995a). The small bars (less than 1/16″ thick) also indicate where the appropriate space is for writing each character. Examples of such segmentation bars are shown in Figure 12.5. In years past, early attempts to use segmentation bars consisted of adding bars that were as much as 3/16″ thick. The problem with such bars is that it made writing quite unnatural, as respondents had to consciously move their hand after printing each character.

Figure 12.5 Example of segmented answer categories and white answer boxes against a colored background.

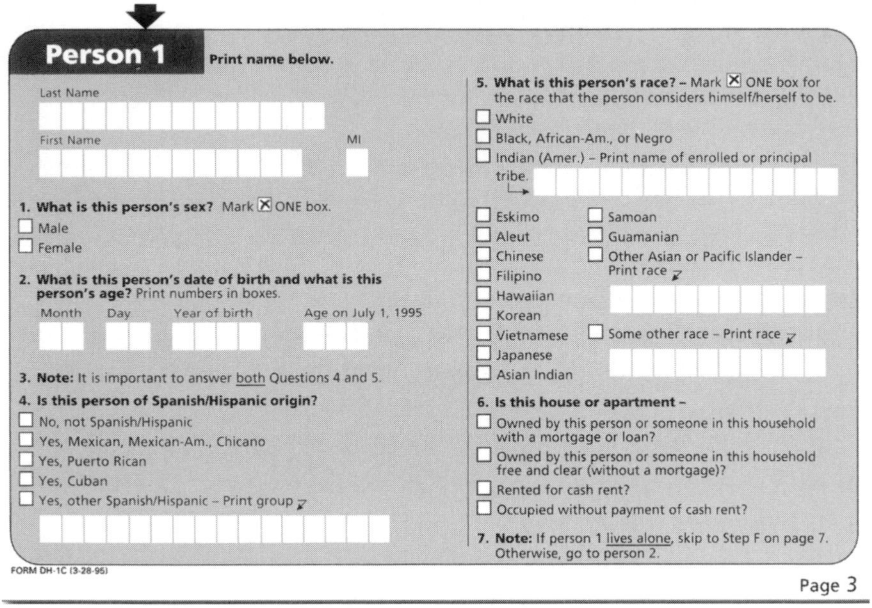

Person 1 Print name below.

Last Name

First Name MI

1. **What is this person's sex?** Mark ☒ ONE box.
☐ Male
☐ Female

2. **What is this person's date of birth and what is this person's age?** Print numbers in boxes.
Month Day Year of birth Age on July 1, 1995

3. **Note:** It is important to answer both Questions 4 and 5.

4. **Is this person of Spanish/Hispanic origin?**
☐ No, not Spanish/Hispanic
☐ Yes, Mexican, Mexican-Am., Chicano
☐ Yes, Puerto Rican
☐ Yes, Cuban
☐ Yes, other Spanish/Hispanic – Print group

5. **What is this person's race?** – Mark ☒ ONE box for the race that the person considers himself/herself to be.
☐ White
☐ Black, African-Am., or Negro
☐ Indian (Amer.) – Print name of enrolled or principal tribe.
☐ Eskimo
☐ Aleut
☐ Chinese
☐ Filipino
☐ Hawaiian
☐ Korean
☐ Vietnamese
☐ Japanese
☐ Asian Indian
☐ Samoan
☐ Guamanian
☐ Other Asian or Pacific Islander – Print race
☐ Some other race – Print race

6. **Is this house or apartment –**
☐ Owned by this person or someone in this household with a mortgage or loan?
☐ Owned by this person or someone in this household free and clear (without a mortgage)?
☐ Rented for cash rent?
☐ Occupied without payment of cash rent?

7. **Note:** If person 1 lives alone, skip to Step F on page 7. Otherwise, go to person 2.

FORM DH-1C (3-28-95)

Page 3

Example from 1995 National Census Test, conducted by U.S. Bureau of the Census.

Principles 12.4: Answer spaces surrounded by a black line and printed against a colored background field appear to encourage respondents to mark within boxes.

A white box, when seen against a colored background field (as shown in Figure 12.4), appears as a target to respondents and encourages them to keep their marks within the box. It is desirable for X's to be restrained in this way to help assure that large marks that stray outside the boxes aren't made inadvertently in other boxes, where the optical reader would interpret them as intentional answers. Such background fields are also helpful when trying to get respondents to print letters and/or numbers into open-ended answer spaces, thus helping to improve the likelihood that the characters will be recognized by the optical engine.

Choice of color, and the degree of it, depends upon several considerations. First, the color should provide clear contrast with the white boxes, but it cannot be so intense that it results in poor contrast with the words that are in black print. For many colors this means using a percentage of the tint, for example, 20% tints of certain blues or greens. However, when certain yellows are used, it may be possible to use 80% or even 100% of the full tint. Experience is important in deciding how much color will provide good contrast and encourage people to stay within the marking boxes, yet not be so bright that the questions will be hard to read and comprehend.

Principles 12.5: When seeking open-ended answers for which character recognition will not be used, provide plenty of space and no segmentation marks.

One of the traditional shortcomings of self-administered questionnaires is that answers to open-ended questions tend to be brief. Placing segmentation bars in these answer spaces would influence people to print and keep their answers short. Also, because an efficient method is available for imaging answers onto computers, thus facilitating rapid entering of answers into a word file by skilled operators, every attempt should be made to keep answering open-ended questions as easy as possible for the respondent. Also, longer rather than shorter answers to open-ended questions need to be encouraged.

Principle 12.6: If the questionnaire is to be mailed folded, no answer choice boxes should appear in the folds.

Questionnaires designed for optical scanning that are only a few pages long may be mailed as flats, but that generally adds to the cost of mailing. It is acceptable to use smaller envelopes if folding the questionnaire is desired. However, the folds should not be allowed to go across answer boxes. Fold indentations may be read as answer marks by today's technology, thus adding to the complexities of scanning and imaging.

The Future of Scanning and Imaging

It seems likely that a switch of most mail questionnaires to scanning and imaging will occur early in the twenty-first century, and data entry or keypunching will become as rare for mail surveys as they are now for telephone surveys. In the short-term, cost remains a barrier. However, the presence of several competing systems already on the market suggests that these costs will come down quickly. Scanning with imaging then becomes one more technology that is dramatically redefining the nature of self-administered surveys.

LOOKING TO THE FUTURE

The 22 years that have elapsed between publication of the first and second editions of this book make reconsideration of the points I made in a similarly titled conclusion to that book instructive, even sobering. I wrote with enthusiasm, in late 1977, that, "Clearly, mail and telephone surveys are coming of age. . . . The TDM procedures described in this book demonstrate that mail and telephone surveys can consistently produce good results, relegating to the past the view that neither could be anything more than a poor substitute for face-to-face interviews" (Dillman, 1978, p. 282). This conclusion now seems antiquated, as some uses of telephone interviews are being threatened by low response and a rush is underway to bring technology into the conduct of electronic self-administered surveys.

In that conclusion, I went on to suggest that both mail and telephone response rates, my main emphases in that book, could be improved further, which they have not. However, the expectation that the availability of good mail and telephone methods would encourage using two or more methods in a single survey seems, in retrospect, to have been greatly understated. Similarly, my prediction that surveys would be done more quickly, bringing their results into consideration in policy deliberations, and that the lag between deciding to commission a survey and getting results would decrease, seems quite conservative.

Mostly, upon rereading that conclusion, I am impressed with my inability to anticipate the changing technologies that were about to engulf society and create the realities of surveying at the beginning of the twenty-first century. In particular, I did not anticipate how quickly the computer revolution would place the power of mainframe computers into stand-alone computers that would occupy the desks of nearly all professionals. Also unforeseen was the nature of perhaps the most significant technological development of our time, the Internet, which would redefine how people communicated with one another and open up entirely new surveying possibilities.

The concept of tailoring data collection methods to survey population, sponsorship, and content, my major theme in this revision, was not mentioned. Nor did I comprehend the societal developments that would first benefit and then threaten telephone interviewing. For example, I had not anticipated the development of the "self-administered" culture that, in combination with other considerations, would lead to my decision to forgo discussion of telephone interviewing in favor of focusing exclusively on self-administered surveys. The primary lesson I draw from comparisons of the surveying realities of these different times is that predicting the future of surveying, though important, should be done with considerable caution.

Transition from the Total Design Method to Tailored Design

The Total Design Method was a product of mass society. The post-World War II production methods for industry encouraged the development of standard solutions for problems and a one-size-fits-all approach to product design throughout the economy in order to achieve economic efficiency (Dillman, 1985; Allen and Dillman, 1994). Changing mail survey procedures from one survey population to another was discouraged by the labor-intensive methods imposed by reliance on typewriters and large-scale printing presses.

Computerization of both word processing and printing methods not only introduced tremendous flexibility in how questionnaires could be composed and printed, but brought new possibilities for design (e.g., font variations, insertion of symbols, alternative page formats, and use of color) under the control of those who wanted to design and implement their own surveys. In addition, the ability to print questionnaires within one's office or home made it possible to become independent of the hierarchy of production, which in the mass society era forced survey design into a single mold. The information age has made it possible for one person to carry out every step of designing and implementing a survey that appears more professionally done than could be accomplished by any organizational arrangement of the 1970s.

This same technology has made it possible to treat certain recipients of questionnaires differently, thus allowing the extension of social exchange concepts described in Chapter 1 to the level of contemplating costs, rewards, and trust associated with different populations and survey situations rather than just respondent behavior in general. The result, Tailored Design, was not part of my thinking when the first edition of this book went to press. Instead, it has been the result of finding aspects of the TDM that would not work in certain situations, from diaries to mixed-mode design, and making needed adjustments.

My emphasis in this book has been on only a limited number of tailored applications, specifically, mixed-mode, different delivery methods, situations that require a quick response, and government and business surveys. Cutting across these differences in population, sponsorship, and survey content are the new technological possibilities for conducting self-administered surveys, ranging from the Internet and IVR surveys to paper questionnaires that can be imaged.

There are many tailored applications that were not considered in this book. One of them is surveying in *other cultures* outside the United States. Although I have followed this potential application with interest for many years, it is not one for which I have been able to identify specific differences that might be proposed as principles. Research by others suggests that the standard TDM method works similarly in many other cultures. For example, de Leeuw and Hox (1988) and Nederhof (1985) have obtained response rates in the Netherlands similar to those obtained in the United States. I have also seen questionnaire response patterns for New Zealand, Australia, Germany, and the United Kingdom that seem to echo those that would be obtained in the United States.

Jussaume and Yamada (1990) translated and replicated a general public survey in Seattle and Kobe, Japan, for which they obtained virtually identical response rates of 57% and 56% respectively, using a three-mailing sequence. The Japanese procedures were modified with regard to the size of stationery and the use of a personal seal rather than individually signed letters. A similar TDM-style general public survey in Qingtao, China, a city of 2,000,000 people, obtained another similar response rate of 65% (Jussaume, 1998). Except for tailoring mailing procedures and appeals to specific cultural differences, general procedures for adapting across cultures have not yet been systematically specified.

The conduct of *international surveys*, whereby data are collected by an individual or organization in one country by sending questionnaires to other countries, is another type of tailoring that was considered for inclusion in this book. Certainly, different timing of follow-up reminders and the sending of international prepaid postal coupons, instead of putting stamps on the return envelope, are needed adaptations. However, my lack of examples of many such surveys that might have resulted in identifying such adaptations led to the decision not to include a chapter on this topic. I also think it is likely that the Internet will forge to the front quickly as a means of doing such surveys.

Another topic for which tailoring is needed is the surveying of *children*. Such surveys generally require that permission from parents be obtained. Consideration must also be given to the age at which children are able to respond to the structured nature of most questions in self-administered questionnaires, and at what age they have the written language skills necessary for responding. An excellent article by Scott (1997) outlines methods for improving the quality of responses to such surveys. She notes that children are as likely as adults to exhibit social desirability bias, a behavior that is highly context dependent. Providing opportunities for young people to respond to self-administered questionnaires on computers is currently an important area of research about which much remains to be learned (e.g., de Leeuw, Hox, Kef, and Van Hattum, 1997; Turner et al., 1998), and for which principles of Tailored Design might be specified.

One tailored application that I find particularly intriguing is the conduct of *panel surveys*, in which the same individuals or businesses are surveyed repeatedly. Such surveys are often done by repeating exactly the same procedures year after year. Recently I discussed with the staff of a federal agency the possibility of using the knowledge of past response behavior to decide whether "good respondents," those who responded promptly in the previous data collection period, should be treated differently from those who responded only after several attempts. It seems likely that using the same stimuli (cover letters with the same wording) for both types of respondents will not be as effective as using somewhat different stimuli. The conduct of panel studies also raises the possibility of sending correspondence to people after they have completed a wave of data collection, the purpose of which is to thank them for responding. Little research has been done on whether changing procedures between data collection periods, or even treating some sample members quite differently from others from the beginning, would be productive. Increased interest in procedures for panel studies suggests this as an important area for the development of a tailored design application.

The above examples of additional tailored applications are only a few of those in need of development. In theory, the list may be quite long, as our knowledge of how different situations influence response behaviors continues to improve.

What May Lie Ahead

In the first edition of this book, *mixed-mode surveys* were treated as a possible future trend. That future has now arrived, but in a far more complex way than I had anticipated. In 1978, the availability of only three major methods of data collection meant that the choices were relatively simple. However, now that Internet and IVR surveys are being added to the mix, along with niche technologies such as sending computer disks by mail or using fax questionnaires, and given that response rates from single-mode surveys are increasingly worrisome, I expect the proportion of surveys conducted by more than one mode to increase significantly. Contributing to this increase are the speed and ease with which word files can be converted from one application (e.g., telephone interview) into another format (e.g., paper mail, Web, or IVR).

Although it is my expectation that the use of self-administered surveys will increase dramatically in the early years of the twenty-first century, I expect the dominant form of survey design to be mixed-mode. Being able to access people by multiple means (visiting the location, sending postal mail to the location, sending courier mail to the location, calling on a voice phone, sending to a fax number, or sending to an e-mail address), and the large cost differentials associated with different methods mean that pressures will exist to use multiple modes to maintain quality while keeping costs as low as possible. This likelihood suggests the need for surveyors to become knowledgeable about procedures for conducting surveys through different modes, and about the mode differences associated with asking different kinds of questions. It further suggests that the skills needed by survey methodologists will change significantly as we enter the twenty-first century, and that one of these skills will be fluency with different methods and an understanding of the management tools needed for working multiple modes into a single survey design. The time is past when one could be a specialist in one kind of survey method and ignore the requirements of others.

It is tempting to predict that surveying on the Internet will soon become the dominant mode of surveying in the United States and the rest of the world. The unprecedented potential for speed and extremely low cost make greater use inevitable. The potential to ask questions in ways not possible with any other survey mode, and the likelihood of computer power and browser capabilities continuing to expand so that more sophisticated surveys can be sent and retrieved, make the future of Internet surveys seem very bright.

At the same time, it is useful to recall how quickly potential respondents learned to block access to unwanted telephone contacts through a hierarchy of barriers, including unlisted numbers, answering machines, voice mail, active call monitoring, and number-blocking devices. The potential for building blocking and screening mechanisms for Internet contacts seems likely to be even greater, commencing even before ways of effectively sampling populations and achieving good response are learned. The future of Internet surveying will, like the future of telephone interviewing, evolve rather than being discovered all at once.

It has been suggested that surveys as we know them may become less important as a means of obtaining data in the twenty-first century, perhaps declining significantly in number (c.f., Baker, 1998). This argument is based partly on the fact that information once collected by surveys is being collected more and more by other means. For example, the proliferation of retail establishment identity cards needed to obtain advertised discounts means that the complete purchase behavior of individuals can easily be tracked without doing special surveys. Moreover, behaviors such as this can be linked to other behaviors based upon credit card purchases and other data files. Linking data files is easy with today's computer capabilities, although it is not yet clear to what extent societal laws will limit the possibilities. Whether such embedded data collection replaces sample surveys remains to be seen.

In this context it is useful to recall what a sample survey can and cannot do, and why surveys are usually conducted in the first place. The power of the sample survey is the ability to determine the distribution of a characteristic in a population and to do that by surveying only a small number of individuals in the total survey population. The capabilities of today's and tomorrow's computers to handle massive amounts of data mean that it may no longer be necessary to answer questions by drawing such samples; therefore, embedded data collection may suffice.

Consideration of this possibility caused me to reflect on a retrospective social impact assessment of the telephone by de Sola Pool (1983). One of the common predictions made for the future of the telephone at the time of its development was that it would substitute for travel, thereby decreasing the need for the latter. Exactly the opposite happened; the telephone encouraged travel and as people traveled more they used the telephone more. It is entirely conceivable that the more massive amounts of data that are collected by embedded procedures, the more important questions will be pinpointed that cannot be answered without obtaining additional data through traditional sample survey methods.

A specialist in systems theory once responded to a question I asked by noting that systems, whether mechanical, biological, or social, could be made to operate very fast. However, the long-term operations of such systems could be insured only if a very good thermostatic control was in place to provide immediate feedback about problems in need of correction. He noted by way of analogy that a slow-moving car that is weaving back and forth across the road can usually be controlled. However, when that same car is moving at top speed and begins to go out of control there is virtually no time to react. Therefore, feedback systems need to be in place to give the earliest possible signal of impending danger.

The interconnectedness of the computerized world economy means that it operates at a very high speed, and quick feedback is needed constantly to keep it safely operating. Surveys are an important aspect of that feedback to the world, to individual societies, to organizations, and to the households and individuals that make up that economy. Although the ways of providing such feedback, which for many decades has been provided in part by sample surveys, may change, the need for it seems likely to increase rather than decrease. Whether surveys remain an important means of providing that feedback or whether other means are developed to provide it remains to be seen. My own view is that sample surveys will remain essential for that purpose, and signs of the diminishing need for such surveys have yet to develop in a convincing way.

Surveyors have a much more diverse set of tools than when I first started work on the development of mail and telephone surveys in the late 1960s. In addition, much greater diversity is represented by the means of surveying now available to us, and which I have endeavored to discuss in this book. The further development of these survey tools, particularly surveying over the Internet, Interactive Voice Response surveys, and paper questionnaires that can be imaged is essential if they are to perform effectively in the nation's and world's survey system. I look forward to observing and participating in that further development.

References

Allen, J., & Dillman, D. (1994). *Against all odds: Rural community in the information age.* Boulder, CO: Westview Press.

American Travel Survey. (1995). [On-line] Bureau of Transportation Statistics. Available: http://www.bts.gov/programs/ats .

Andrews, F. M., & Withey, S. B. (1976). *Social indicators of well-being.* New York: Plenum.

Aquilino, W. S. (1994). Interview mode effects in surveys of drug and alcohol use: A field experiment. *Public Opinion Quarterly, 58,* 210–240.

Armstrong, J. S., & Luske, E. J. (1987). Return postage in mail surveys: A meta-analysis. *Public Opinion Quarterly, 51,* 233–248.

Ayida, S. A., & McClendon, M. J. (1990). Response effects in mail surveys. *Public Opinion Quarterly, 54,* 229–247.

Baker, R. P. (1998). The CASIC Future. In M. P. Couper et al. (Eds.), *Computer Assisted Survey Information Collection* (pp. 583–604). New York: Wiley.

Bates, N. (1992). *The Simplified Questionnaire Test (SQT): Results from the debriefing interviews* (Internal Memorandum, June 18). Washington, DC: U.S. Bureau of the Census, Center for Survey Methods Research.

Biemer, P. P. (1997). [Health insurance finance agency evaluation]. Unpublished data. Research Triangle, NC: Research Triangle Institute.

Bishop, G., Hippler, H. J., Schwarz, N., & Strack, F. (1988). A comparison of response effects in self-administered and telephone surveys. In R. M. Groves, P. P. Biemer, L. E. Lysberg, J. T. Massey, W. L. Nicholls, II, & J. Wakesberg (Eds.), *Telephone survey methodology* (pp. 321–340). New York: Wiley.

Blau, P. M. (1964). *Exchange and power in social life.* New York: Wiley.

Bowker, D. (1999). *Constructing the client-computer interface: Guidelines for design and implementation of Web-based surveys* (Summary Report No. 99-15). Pullman, WA: Washington State University, Social & Economic Sciences Research Center.

Boynton, M. (1995). *Results of a mail survey of department of licensing customers on service satisfaction and preference* (Data Report No. 95-59). Pullman, WA: Washington State University, Social & Economic Sciences Research Center.

Boynton, M., Miller, K., & Tarnai, J. (1996, May). *The effect of an incentive and persuasion technique on rate and timing of response to a mail questionnaire among different age groups.* Paper presented at the meeting of the American Association for Public Opinion Research, Salt Lake City, UT.

Brown, C. M. (1988). *Human-computer interface design guidelines.* Norwood, NJ: Ablex.

Burke, B. E. (1999). [American Civil Liberties Union member survey.] Unpublished data. Pullman, WA.

Caldwell, S., & Dillman, D. A. (1998). *Squares versus rectangles: Analysis of the effects of response space shape on number of spurious marks for optically scanned questionnaires.* Unpublished manuscript. Lincoln, NE: The Gallup Organization.

Carley, L. R. (1996). *Faculty use of computer-related technologies: A baseline study of all WSU instructional faculty* (Data Report No. 96-51). Pullman, WA: Washington State University, Social & Economic Sciences Research Center.

Carley-Baxter, L. R., & Dillman, D. A. (1997). *1997 survey of* Hilltopics *recipients with comparisons to 1986 and 1991 surveys* (Summary Report No. 97-50). Pullman, WA: Washington State University, Social & Economic Sciences Research Center.

Carlson, J. (1996, January). *Results of personalization experiments.* Paper presented at the meeting of W-183, Regional Research Committee, Tucson, AZ.

Church, A. H. (1993). Estimating the effect of incentives on mail survey response rates: A meta-analysis. *Public Opinion Quarterly, 57,* 62–79.

Cialdini, R. B. (1984). *Influence: The new psychology of modern persuasion.* New York: Quill.

Clayton, R., & Werking, G. S. (1998). Business surveys of the future: The World Wide Web as data collection methodology. In M. P. Couper, R. P. Baker, J. Bethlehem, C. Z. F. Clark, J. Martin, W. L. Nicholls, II, & J. M. O'Reilly (Eds.), *Computer assisted survey information collection* (pp. 543–562). New York: Wiley-Interscience.

Cochran, W. G. (1977). *Sampling techniques* (3rd ed.). New York: Wiley.

Couper, M., Blair, J., & Triplett, T. (in press). A comparison of mail and e-mail for a survey of employees in federal statistical agencies. *Journal of Official Statistics.*

Cox, B. G., Binder, D. A., Chinnappa, B. N., Christianson, A., Colledge, M. J., & Kott, P. S. (1995). *Business survey methods.* New York: Wiley-Interscience.

DeJong, W. (1979). An examination of self-perception mediation of the foot-in-the-door effect. *Journal of Personality and Social Psychology, 37,* 2221–2239.

de Leeuw, E. D. (1992). *Data quality in mail, telephone, and face-to-face surveys.* Amsterdam: TT Publications.

de Leeuw, E. D., & Hox, J. J. (1988). The effects of response-stimulating factors on response rates and data quality in mail surveys: A test of Dillman's total design method. *Journal of Official Statistics, 4,* 241–249.

de Leeuw, E., Hox, J., Kef, S., & Van Hattum, M. (1997). Overcoming the problems of special interviews on sensitive topics: Computer assisted self-interviewing tailored for young children and adolescents. *Sawtooth software conference proceedings* (pp. 1–14). Sequim, WA: Sawtooth.

de Leeuw, E. D., Hox, J. J., & Snijkers, G. (1995). The effect of computer assisted interviewing on data quality: A review. *Journal of the Market Research Society, 37,* 325–344.

de Leeuw, E. D., Mellenbergh, G. J., & Hox, J. J. (1996). The influence of data collection method on structural models: A comparison of a mail, a telephone, and a face-to-face survey. *Sociological Methods & Research, 24,* 443–472.

de Leeuw, E. D., & van der Zouwen, J. (1988). Data quality in telephone and face-to-face surveys: A comparative analysis. In R. M. Groves, P. P. Biemer, L. E. Lyberg, J. T. Massey, W. L. Nicholls, II, & J. Waksberg (Eds.), *Telephone survey methodology* (pp. 283–99). New York: Wiley.

DeMaio, T. J. (1984). Social desirability and survey measurement: A review. In C. F.

Turner & E. Martin (Eds.), *Surveying subjective phenomena: Volume 2* (pp. 257–282). New York: Russell Sage.

de Sola Pool, I. (1983). *Forecasting the telephone: A retrospective technology assessment of the telephone.* Norwood, NJ: Ablex.

Dillman, D. A. (1978). *Mail and telephone surveys: The total design method.* New York: Wiley-Interscience.

Dillman, D. A. (1985). The social impacts of information technologies in rural North America. *Rural Sociology, 50,*1–26.

Dillman, D. A. (1991). The design and administration of mail surveys. *Annual Review of Sociology, 17,* 225–249.

Dillman, D. A. (1995a). *Image optimization test: Summary of 15 taped interviews* (Technical Report No. 95-40). Pullman, WA: Washington State University, Social & Economic Sciences Research Center.

Dillman, D. A. (1995b). Why innovation is difficult in government surveys. *Journal of Official Statistics, 12,* 113–124.

Dillman, D. A. (1997). Token financial incentives and the reduction of nonresponse error in mail surveys. *Proceedings of section on government statistics* (pp. 200–205). Alexandria, VA: American Statistical Association.

Dillman, D. A. (1999). Mail and other self-administered surveys in the 21st century: The beginning of a new era. *The Gallup Research Journal,* Winter/Spring, 121–140.

Dillman, D. A. (in press). The role of behavioral survey methodologists in national statistical agencies. *International Statistical Review.*

Dillman, D. A., & Allen, T. B. (1995). *Census booklet questionnaire evaluation test: Phase I—Summary of 20 taped interviews* (Technical Report No. 95-41). Pullman, WA: Washington State University, Social & Economic Sciences Research Center.

Dillman, D. A., Brown, T. L., Carlson, J., Carpenter, E. H., Lorenz, F. O., Mason, R., Saltiel, J., & Sangster, R. L. (1995). Effects of category order on answers to mail and telephone surveys. *Rural Sociology, 60,* 674–687.

Dillman, D. A., Carley-Baxter, L. R., & Jackson, A. (1999). *Skip-pattern compliance in three test forms: A theoretical and empirical evaluation* (Technical Report No. 99-01). Pullman, WA: Washington State University, Social & Economic Sciences Research Center.

Dillman, D. A., Christenson, J. A., Carpenter, E. H., & Brooks, R. (1974). Increasing mail questionnaire response: A four-state comparison. *American Sociological Review, 39,* 744–756.

Dillman, D. A., Clark, J. R., & Sinclair, M. A. (1995). How prenotice letters, stamped return envelopes, and reminder postcards affect mailback response rates for census questionnaires. *Survey Methodology, 21,* 1–7.

Dillman, D. A., Clark, J. R., & Treat, J. (1994). The influence of 13 design factors on response rates to census surveys. *Annual research conference proceedings* (pp. 137–159). Washington, DC: U.S. Bureau of the Census.

Dillman, D. A., Clark, J. R., & West, K. K. (1995). Influence of an invitation to answer by telephone on response to census questionnaires. *Public Opinion Quarterly, 58,* 557–568.

Dillman, D. A., Dillman, J. J., Baxter, R., Petrie, R., Miller, K., & Carley, L. R. (1995, May). *The influence of prenotice versus follow-up letters on response rates to mail surveys under varied conditions of salience.* Paper presented at the meeting of the American Association for Public Opinion Research, Ft. Lauderdale, FL.

Dillman, D. A., Dolsen, D. E., & Machlis, G. E. (1995). Increasing response to personally-delivered mail-back questionnaires by combining foot-in-the-door and social exchange methods. *Journal of Official Statistics, 11,* 129–139.

Dillman, D. A., Gallegos, J. G., & Frey, J. H. (1976). Decreasing refusal rates for telephone interviews. *Public Opinion Quarterly, 50,* 66–78.

Dillman, D. A., Jackson, A., Pavlov, R., & Schaefer, D. (1998). *Results from cognitive tests of 6-person accordion versus bi-fold census forms* (Technical Report No. 98-15). Pullman, WA: Washington State University, Social & Economic Sciences Research Center.

Dillman, D. A., Jenkins, C., Martin, B., & DeMaio, T. (1996). *Cognitive and motivational properties of three proposed decennial census forms* (Technical Report No. 96-29). Pullman, WA: Washington State University, Social & Economic Sciences Research Center.

Dillman, D. A., Lesser, V., Carlson, J., Mason, R. G., Willits, F. K., & Jackson, A. (1999, August). *Personalization of mail questionnaires revisited.* Paper presented at the meeting of the Rural Sociological Society, Chicago, IL.

Dillman, D. A., & Mason, R. G. (1984, May). *The influence of survey method on question response.* Paper presented at the meeting of the American Association for Public Opinion Research, Delevan, WI.

Dillman, D. A., & Miller, K. J. (1998). Response rates, data quality, and cost feasibility for optically scannable mail surveys by small research centers. In M. P. Couper, R. P. Baker, J. Bethlehem, C. Z. F. Clark, J. Martin, W. L. Nicholls, II, & J. M. O'Reilly (Eds.), *Computer-assisted survey information collection* (pp. 475–497). New York: Wiley.

Dillman, D. A., Reynolds, R. W., & Rockwood, T. H. (1991). *Focus group tests of two simplified decennial census forms* (Technical Report No. 91-39). Pullman, WA: Washington State University, Social & Economic Sciences Research Center.

Dillman, D. A., Redline, C. D., & Carley-Baxter, L. R. (1999, August). *Influence of type of question on skip pattern compliance in self-administered questionnaires.* Paper presented at the meeting of the American Statistical Association, Baltimore, MD.

Dillman, D. A., Sangster, R. L., Tarnai, J., & Rockwood, T. (1996). Understanding differences in people's answers to telephone and mail surveys. In M. T. Braverman & J. K. Slater (Eds.), *New directions for evaluation series, 70* (Advances in survey research), (pp. 45–62). San Francisco: Jossey-Bass.

Dillman, D. A., & Scott, L. P. (1989). *Internationalizing U.S. universities: Results of a mail survey* (Data Report No. 89-60). Pullman, WA: Washington State University, Social & Economic Sciences Research Center.

Dillman, D. A., Scott, L. P., & Husa, S. (1988, May). *Alternatives to magazine distributed questionnaires: Results of an experiment.* Paper presented at the meeting of the American Association for Public Opinion Research, Lancaster, PA.

Dillman, D. A., Sinclair, M. D., & Clark, J. R. (1993). Effects of questionnaire length, respondent-friendly design, and a difficult question on response rates for occupant-addressed census mail surveys. *Public Opinion Quarterly, 57,* 289–304.

Dillman, D. A., Singer, E., Clark, J. R., & Treat, J. B. (1996). Effects of benefit appeals, mandatory appeals and variations in confidentiality on completion rates for census questionnaires. *Public Opinion Quarterly, 60,* 376–389.

Dillman, D. A., & Tarnai, J. (1988). Administrative issues in mixed mode surveys. In R. M. Groves, P. P. Biemer, L. E. Lyberg, J. T. Massey, W. L. Nicholls, II, & J. Wakesberg (Eds.), *Telephone survey methodology* (pp. 509–528). New York: Wiley.

Dillman, D. A., & Tarnai, J. (1991). Mode effects of cognitively-designed recall questions: A comparison of answers to telephone and mail surveys. In P. P. Beimer, R. M. Groves, L. E. Lyberg, N. A. Mathiowetz, & S. Sudman (Eds.), *Measurement errors in surveys* (pp. 73–93). New York: Wiley.

Dillman, D. A., Tortora, R. D., & Bowker, D. (1998). *Principles for constructing Web surveys: An initial statement.* (Technical Report No. 98-50) Pullman, WA Washington State University Social and Economic Sciences Research Center.

Dillman, D. A., Tortora, R. D., Conradt, J., & Bowker, D. (1998). Influence of plain versus fancy design on response rates for Web surveys. Unpublished paper presented at Annual Meeting of the American Statistical Association, Dallas, TX.

Dillman, J. J., & Dillman, D. A. (1995, April). *The influence of questionnaire cover design on response to mail surveys.* Paper presented at the International Conference on Measurement and Process Quality, Bristol, England.

Dutka, A. (1994). *AMA handbook for customer satisfaction.* Lincolnwood, IL: NTC Business Books.

Ettema, D., Timmermans, H., & van Veghel, L. (1996). *Effects of data collection methods in travel and activity research.* Eindhoven, the Netherlands: European Institute of Retailing and Services Studies.

Forsyth, B. H., & Lessler, J. T. (1991). Cognitive laboratory methods: A taxonomy. In P. P. Biemer, R. M. Groves, L. E. Lysberg, N. A. Mathiowetz, & S. Sudman (Eds.), *Measurement errors in surveys* (pp. 393–418). New York: Wiley.

Fowler, F. J., Jr., Roman, A. M., & Di, Z. X. (1998). Mode effect in a survey of Medicare prostate surgery patients. *Public Opinion Quarterly, 62,* 29–46.

Fox, R. J., Crask, M. R., & Kim, J. (1988). Mail survey response rate: A meta-analysis of selected techniques for inducing response. *Public Opinion Quarterly, 59,* 467–491.

Freedman, J. L., & Fraser, S. C. (1966). Compliance without pressure: The foot-in-the-door technique. *Journal of Personality and Social Psychology, 4,* 195–202.

Gallegos, J. G. (1974). *An experiment in maximizing response to telephone interviews through use of a preliminary letter, based on the principles of exchange theory.* Unpublished master's thesis, Department of Sociology, Washington State University, Pullman, WA.

Geisbrecht, L. (1994). [College Graduates Pilot Survey]. Unpublished data. Washington, DC: U.S. Bureau of the Census.

Goyder, J. C. (1987). *The silent majority: Nonrespondents on sample surveys.* Boulder, CO: Westview Press.

Grembowski, D. (1985). Survey questionnaire salience. *American Journal of Public Health, 75,* 1350.

Groves, R. M. (1989). *Survey errors and survey costs.* New York: Wiley.

Groves, R. M., Cialdini, R., & Couper, M. P. (1992). Understanding the decision to participate in a survey. *Public Opinion Quarterly, 56,* 475–495.

Groves, R. M., & Couper, M. P. (1998). *Nonresponse in household interview surveys.* New York: Wiley-Interscience.

Groves, R. M., & Kahn, R. L. (1979). *Surveys by telephone: A national comparison with personal interviews.* New York: Academic.

Groves, R. M., & Lyberg, L. E. (1988). An overview of nonresponse issues in telephone surveys. In R. M. Groves, P. P. Beimer, L. E. Lyberg, J. T. Massey, W. L. Nicholls, II, & J. Wakesberg (Eds.), *Telephone survey methodology* (pp. 191–211). New York: Wiley.

Guralnik, D. B. (Ed.). (1980). *Webster's new world dictionary* (2nd college ed.). New York: Simon & Schuster.

Hays, B. E. (1998). *Measuring customer satisfaction: Survey design, use, and statistical analysis methods.* Milwaukee, WI: ASQ Quality Press.

Heberlein, T. A., & Baumgartner, R. (1978). Factors affecting response rates to mailed questionnaires: A quantitative analysis of the published literature. *American Sociological Review, 43,* 447–462.

Hippler, H. J., & Schwarz, N. (1987). Response effects in surveys. In H. J. Hippler, N. Schwarz, & S. Sudman (Eds.), *Social information processing and survey methodology* (pp. 102–122). New York: Springer-Verlag.

Hochstim, J. R. (1967). A critical comparison of three strategies of collecting data from households. *Journal of the American Statistical Association, 62,* 976–989.

Homans, G. (1961). *Social behavior: Its elementary forms.* New York: Harcourt, Brace, & World.

Hox, J. J., & de Leeuw, E. D. (1994). A comparison of nonresponse in mail, telephone, and face-to-face surveys. *Quality and Quantity, 28,* 329–344.

Hyman, H. H., & Sheatsley, P. B. (1950). The current status of American public opinion. In J. C. Payne (Ed.), *The teaching of contemporary affairs, twenty-first yearbook of the National Council of Social Studies,* 11–34.

Israel, G. D., & Taylor, C. L. (1990). Can response order bias evaluations? *Evaluation and Program Planning, 13,* 1–7.

Jacobs, L. C. (1986, April). *Effect of the use of optical-scan sheets on survey response rate.* Paper presented at the meeting of the American Education Research Association, San Francisco, CA.

James, J. M., & Bolstein, R. (1990). The effect of monetary incentives and follow-up mailings on the response rate and response quality in mail surveys. *Public Opinion Quarterly, 54,* 346–361.

James, J. M., & Bolstein, R. (1992). Large monetary incentives and their effect on mail survey response rates. *Public Opinion Quarterly, 56,* 442–453.

Jenkins, C. (1997). Improving the navigational qualities of the decennial census short form requires paying attention to the entire mailing package. *Proceedings of the section on survey methods research* (pp. 940–945). Ann Arbor, MI: American Association for Public Opinion Research.

Jenkins, C., & Bates, N. (1995). *Image optimization research methods and results of wave I tests* (Internal Memorandum). Washington, DC: U.S. Bureau of the Census.

Jenkins, C., & Dillman, D. A. (1995). The language of self-administered questionnaires as seen through the eyes of respondents. *Statistical policy working paper 23: New directions in statistical methodology, volume 3* (pp. 470–516). Washington, DC: U.S. Office of Management and Budget.

Jenkins, C., & Dillman, D. A. (1997). Towards a theory of self-administered questionnaire design. In L. Lyberg, P. Biemer, M. Collins, L. Decker, E. deLeeuw, C. Dippo, N. Schwarz, & D. Trewin (Eds.), *Survey measurement and process quality* (pp. 165–196). New York: Wiley-Interscience.

Jobe, J. B., & Mingay, D. J. (1989). Cognitive research improves questionnaires. *American Journal of Public Health, 79,* 1053–1055.

Johnson, T., & McLaughlin, S. (1990). *GMAT registrant survey design report.* Los Angeles, CA: Los Angeles Graduate Admission Council.

Johnson, D. E., Meiller, L. R., Miller, L. C., & Summers, G. F. (1987). *Needs assessment: Theory and methods.* Ames, IA: Iowa State University Press.

Jordan, L. A., Marcus, A. C., & Reeder, L. G. (1980). Response styles in telephone and household interviewing: A field experiment. *Public Opinion Quarterly, 44,* 210–222.

Jussaume, R., Jr. (1998, July). *Factors influencing the modernization of urban Chinese food consumption.* Paper presented at the World Congress of Sociology, Montreal, Canada.

Jussaume, R., Jr., & Yamada, Y. (1990). Viability of mail surveys in Japan and the United States. *Public Opinion Quarterly, 54,* 219–228.

Kahneman, D. (1973). *Attention and effort.* Englewood Cliffs, NJ: Prentice-Hall.

Kalfs, N. (1993). *Hour by hour: Effects of the data collection mode in time research.* Unpublished thesis, University of Amsterdam, Amsterdam, the Netherlands.

Kalfs, N., & Saris, W. E. (1997). New data collection methods in travel surveys. In D. Ettema & H. Timmermans (Eds.), *Activity-based approaches to travel analysis* (pp. 243–261). N.p.: Pergamon.

Kanuk, L., & Berenson, C. (1975). Mail surveys and response rates: A literature review. *Journal of Marketing Research, 12,* 400–453.

Keil, L., & Gaertner, G. (1998). [Item Nonresponse]. Unpublished data. Rockville, MD: The Gallup Organization.

Kish, L. (1949). A procedure for objective respondent selection within the household. *Journal of American Statistical Association, 44,* 380–387.

Kish, L. (1965). *Survey sampling.* New York: Wiley.

Klose, A., & Ball, A. D. (1995). Using optical mark read surveys: An analysis of response rate and quality. *Journal of the Market Research Society, 37,* 269–279.

Kottler, R. E. (1998, March). *Sceptics beware: Web interviewing has arrived and is established. Embrace it or be left behind.* Paper presented at the meeting of the Market Research Society, Birmingham, AL.

Krosnick, J., & Alwin, D. F. (1987). An evaluation of a cognitive theory of response-order effects in survey measurement. *Public Opinion Quarterly, 51,* 201–219.

Krosnick, J., Narayan, S., & Smith, W. R. (1996). Satisficing in surveys: Initial evidence. In M. T. Braverman & J. K. Slater (Eds.), *New directions for evaluation, 70* (Advances in survey research), (pp. 29–44). San Francisco: Jossey-Bass.

Krysan, M., Schuman, H., Scott, L. J., & Beatty, P. (1994). Response rates and response content in mail versus face-to-face surveys. *Public Opinion Quarterly, 58,* 381–99.

Kulka, R. A., Holt, N. A., Carter, W., & Dowd, K. L. (1991, March). *Self-reports of time pressures, concern for privacy and participation in the 1990 mail census.* Paper presented at the Annual Research Conference of the U.S. Bureau of the Census, Arlington, VA.

Kydoniefs, L., & Stanley, J. (1999). Establishment nonresponse: Revisiting the issues and looking to the future. *Statistical policy working paper 28*, Seminar on Interagency Coordination and Cooperation (pp. 181–227). Washington, DC: Office of Management and Budget, Federal Committee on Statistical Methodology.

Leslie, T. F. (1996). *1996 National content survey results* (Internal DSSD Memorandum No. 3). Washington, DC: U.S. Bureau of the Census.

Leslie, T. F. (1997, August). *Comparing two approaches to questionnaire design: Official government versus public information design.* Paper presented at the meeting of the American Statistical Association, Anaheim, CA.

Lesser, V., Dillman, D. A., Lorenz, F. O., Carlson, J., & Brown, T. L. (1999, August). *The influence of financial incentives on mail questionnaire response rates.* Paper presented at the meeting of the Rural Sociological Society, Portland, OR.

Linsky, A. S. (1975). Stimulating responses to mailed questionnaires: A review. *Public Opinion Quarterly, 39,* 82–101.

Lohr, S. L. (1999). *Sampling: Design and analysis.* Pacific Grove, CA: Duxbury Press.

Lorenz, F. O., & Ryan, V. D. (1996). Experiments in general/specific questions: Comparing results of mail and telephone surveys. *Proceedings of the section on survey research methods, vol. 11* (pp. 611–613). Alexandria, VA: American Statistical Association.

Machlis, G. (1998). [Visitor Services Project]. Unpublished data. Moscow, ID: University of Idaho.

Mason, R., Carlson, J. E., & Tourangeau, R. (1994). Contrast effects and subtraction in part-whole questions. *Public Opinion Quarterly, 58,* 569–78.

Maxim, P. S. (1999). *Quantitative research methods in the social sciences.* New York: Oxford University Press.

McConochie, R. M., & Reed, C. (1987, November). *The value of follow-up calls and mailed reminders in surveys of television viewing.* Paper presented at the meeting of the International Conference on Telephone Survey Methodology, Charlotte, NC.

Melevin, P. T., Dillman, D. A., Baxter, R. K., & Lamiman, C. E. (in press). Personal delivery of mail questionnaires for household surveys: A test of four retrieval methods. *Journal of Applied Sociology.*

Miller, K. J. (1996). *The influence of different techniques on response rates and nonresponse error in mail surveys.* Unpublished master's thesis, Western Washington University, Bellingham, WA.

Mingay, D. J., Belkin, M., Kim, R., Farrell, S., Headley, L., Khokha, P., Sellers, E., & Roizen, M. F. (1999, May). *In-home evaluations of an automated touch-tone telephone system to administer a health questionnaire.* Paper presented at the meeting of the American Association for Public Opinion Research, St. Petersburg, FL.

Mooney, G., Giesbrecht, L., & Shettle, C. (1993, May). *To pay or not to pay: That is the question.* Paper presented at the meeting of the American Association for Public Opinion Research, St. Charles, IL.

Moore, D. E. (1980). [The Illinois Experiment]. Unpublished data. State College, PA: Pennsylvania State University.

Moore, D. L. (1998). *1998 Survey of grass seed growers in Washington state* (Data Report No. 98-06). Pullman, WA: Washington State University, Social & Economic Sciences Research Center.

Moore, D. W. (1997). Perils of polling '96: Myth and fallacy. *The Polling Report, 12,* 1FF.

Moore, D. E., & Dillman, D. A. (1980). *Response rate of certified mail and alternatives.* Unpublished paper, Pennsylvania State University, State College, PA.

Moore, D. L., Guadino, J., deHart, P., Cheadle, A., & Martin, D. (1998, May). *Physician response in a trial of two-day priority mail and telephone mode sequences.* Paper presented at the meeting of the American Association for Public Opinion Research, St. Louis, MO.

Mu, X. (1999). *IVR and distribution of responses: An evaluation of the effects of IVR on collecting and interpreting survey data.* Unpublished paper. Princeton, NJ: The Gallup Organization.

National Telecommunication and Information Administration. (1999). [On-line] *Falling through the net: Defining the digital divide.* Available: www.ntia.doc.gov/ntiahome/net2/falling.html.

Nederhof, A. J. (1982). Effects of preliminary contacts on volunteering in mail surveys. *Perceptual and Motor Skills, 54,* 1333–1334.

Nederhof, A. J. (1985). A comparison of European and North American response patterns in mail surveys. *Journal of the Market Research Society, 27,* 55–63.

Nederhof, A. J. (1988). Effects of a final telephone reminder and questionnaire cover design in mail surveys. *Social Science Research, 17,* 353–361.

Nichols, E., & Sedivi, B. (1998, August). *Economic data collection via the Web: A Census Bureau case study.* Paper presented at the meeting of the American Statistical Association, Dallas, TX.

Otto, L., Call, V. R. A., & Spenner, K. (1976). *Design for a study of entry into careers.* Lexington, MA: Lexington Books.

Patchen, R. H., Woodard, D. S., Caralley, M. D., & Hess, D. L. (1994, May). *Outside the box thinking about survey mailing packages: A report on the return rate effects of using boxes instead of envelopes for packaging outgoing mail questionnaires.* Paper presented at the meeting of the American Association for Public Opinion Research, Danvers, MA.

Pavlov, R. (1996). *Perceptions of workplace environment* (Data Report No. 96-26). Pullman, WA: Washington State University, Social & Economic Sciences Research Center.

Paxson, M. C. (1989). *Business concerns in Spokane* (Technical Report No. 89-02). Pullman, WA: Washington State University, Social & Economic Sciences Research Center.

Paxson, M. C. (1992). [Response Rates for 183 Studies]. Unpublished data. Pullman, WA: Washington State University, Hotel and Restaurant Administration Program.

Paxson, M. C., Dillman, D. A., & Tarnai, J. (1995). Improving response to business mail surveys. In B. G. Cox, D. A. Binder, B. N. Chinnappa, A. Christianson, M. J. Colledge, & P. S. Kott (Eds.), *Business survey methods* (pp. 303–315). New York: Wiley.

Payne, S. L. (1951). *The art of asking questions.* Princeton, NJ: Princeton University Press.

Perlman, B., Patchen, R., & Woodard, D. (1989, May). *The effect of presurvey mailers on return rates in a radio diary survey.* Paper presented at the meeting of the American Association for Public Opinion Research, St. Petersburg, FL.

Petrie, R., Moore, D. L., & Dillman, D. A. (1998). Establishment surveys: The effect of multi-mode sequence on response rates. *Proceedings of survey methods section* (pp. 981–987). Alexandria, VA: American Statistical Association.

Pratto, D. J., & Rodman, H. (1987). Magazine distributed questionnaires for exploratory research: Advantages and problems. *Sociological Spectrum, 7,* 61–72.

Rao, M. S. N. (1974). *Migration to Alaska: A test of some hypotheses of migration differentials.* Unpublished doctoral dissertation, Department of Sociology, Washington State University, Pullman, WA.

Redline, C., Dillman, D. A., Smiley, R., Carley-Baxter, L. R., & Jackson, A. (1999, May). *Making visible the invisible: An experiment with skip instructions on paper questionnaires.* Paper presented at the meeting of the American Association for Public Opinion Research, Orlando, FL.

Reingen, P. H., & Kernan, J. B. (1977). Compliance with an interview request: A foot-in-the-door, self-perception interpretation. *Journal of Marketing Research, 14,* 365–69.

Richardson, T. (1997, September). *Current issues in travel and activity surveys.* Paper presented at the meeting of the International Association of Travel Behavior Research, Austin, TX.

Rockwood, T. H., Sangster, R. L., & Dillman, D. A. (1997). The effect of response categories on survey questionnaires: Context and mode effects. *Sociological Methods and Research, 26,* 118–140.

Rosen, R. J., Clayton, R. L., & Wolf, L. L. (1993). Long-term retention of sample members under automated self-response data collection. *Proceedings of section of survey research methods* (pp. 748). Washington, DC: American Sociological Association.

Salant, P., Carley, L. R, & Dillman, D. A. (1996). *Estimating the contribution of lone eagles to metro and non-metro in-migration* (Technical Report No. 96–19). Pullman, WA: Washington State University, Social & Economic Sciences Research Center.

Salant, P., Carley, L. R., & Dillman, D. A. (1997). Lone eagles among Washington's in-migrants: Who are they and are they moving to rural places? *Northwest journal of business and economics, 1997 edition,* 1–16.

Salant, P., & Dillman, D. A. (1994). *How to conduct your own survey.* New York: Wiley.

Sangster, R. L. (1993). *Question order effects: Are they really less prevalent in mail surveys?* Unpublished doctoral dissertation, Department of Sociology, Washington State University, Pullman, WA.

Sangster, R. L., Lorenz, F. O., & Saltiel, J. (1995, January). *Measurement effects of mail versus telephone.* Paper presented at the meeting of W-183, Regional Research Group, Tucson, AZ.

Schaefer, D., & Dillman, D. A. (1998). Development of a standard e- mail methodology: Results of an experiment. *Public Opinion Quarterly, 62,* 378–397.

Schneiderman, B. (1997). *Designing the user interface.* (3rd ed.). Reading, MA: Addison-Wesley.

Schuman, H., & Presser, S. (1981). *Questions and answers in attitude surveys: Experiments on question form, wording, and context.* New York: Academic.

Schwarz, N. (1996). *Cognition and communication: Judgmental biases, research methods, and the logic of conversation.* Mahwah, NJ: Erlbaum.

Schwarz, N., Hippler, H. J., Deutsch, B., & Strack, F. (1985). Response scales: Effects of category range on reported behavior and subsequent judgments. *Public Opinion Quarterly, 49,* 388–395.

Schwarz, N., Hippler, H. J., & Noelle-Neumann, E. (1992). A cognitive model of response-order effects in survey measurement. In N. Schwarz & S. Sudman (Eds.), *Context effects in social and psychological research* (pp. 187–199). New York: Springer-Verlag.

Schwarz, N., Strack, F., Hippler, H. J., & Bishop, G. (1991). The impact of administration mode on response effects in survey measurement. *Applied Cognitive Psychology, 5,* 193–212.

Scott, C. (1961). Research on mail surveys. *Journal of the Royal Statistical Society, 124,* 143–205.

Scott, J. (1997). Children as respondents: Methods for improving data quality. In L. Lyberg, P. Biemer, M. Collins, E. de Leeuw, C. Dippo, N. Schwarz, & D. Trewin (Eds.), *Survey measurement and process quality* (pp. 331–350). New York: Wiley-Interscience.

Scott, L. (1989). *Internationalizing U.S. universities: Results of a mail survey* (Data Report No. 89-60). Pullman, WA: Washington State University, Social & Economic Sciences Research Center.

Scott, J., & Barrett, D. (1996). *1995 National census test: Image optimization test final report.* Unpublished report. Washington, DC: U.S. Bureau of the Census.

Shettle, C., & Mooney, G. (1996, August). *Evaluation of using monetary incentives in a government survey.* Paper presented to the meeting of the American Statistical Association, Chicago, IL.

Singer, E., Hippler, H. J., & Schwarz, N. (1992). Confidentiality assurances in surveys: Reassurance or threat? *International Journal of Public Opinion Research, 4,* 256–268.

Singer, E., Von Thurn, D. R., & Miller, E. R. (1995). Confidentiality assurances and survey response: A review of the experimental literature. *Public Opinion Quarterly, 59,* 266–277.

Sless, D. (1994, September). Public forms: Designing and evaluating forms in large organisations. *Proceedings of Public Graphics* (pp. 9.1–9.25). Lunteren, the Netherlands.

Slocum, W. L., Empey, T., & Swanson, H. S. (1956). Increasing response to questionnaires and structured interviews. *American Sociological Review, 21,* 221–225.

Srinivasan, R., & Hanway, S. (1999, May). *A new kind of survey mode difference: Experimental results from a test of inbound voice recognition and mail surveys.* Paper presented at the meeting of the American Association for Public Opinion Research, St. Pete Beach, FL.

Tarnai, J., & Dillman, D. A. (1992). Questionnaire context as a source of response differences in mail versus telephone surveys. In N. Schwarz & S. Sudman (Eds.), *Context effects in social and psychological research* (pp. 115–129). New York: Springer-Verlag.

Teixeira, R. A. (1992). *The disappearing American voter.* Washington, DC: The Brookings Institution.

Thibaut, J. W., & Kelley, H. H. (1959). *The social psychology of groups.* New York: Wiley.

Thompson, F. E., & Byers, T. (1994). Dietary assessment resource manual. *Journal of Nutrition, 124,* 2245S–2317S.

Tomaskovic-Devey, D., Leiter, J., & Thompson, S. (1994). Organizational survey nonresponse. *Administrative Science Quarterly, 39,* 439–457.

Tomaskovic-Devey, D., Leiter, J., & Thompson, S. (1995). Item nonresponse in organizational surveys. *Sociological Methodology, 25,* 77–111.

Tortora, R. D., Dillman, D. A., & Bolstein, R. (1992, October). *Considerations related to how incentives influence survey response.* Paper prepared for Symposium on Providing Incentives to Survey Respondents, John F. Kennedy School of Government, Harvard University, Cambridge, MA.

Tourangeau, R. (1992). Context effects on response to attitude surveys: Attitudes as memory structure. In N. Schwarz & S. Sudman (Eds.), *Context effects in social and psychological research* (pp. 35–48). New York: Springer-Verlag.

Tourangeau, R., & Rasinski, K. A. (1988). Cognitive processes underlying context effects in attitude measurement. *Psychological Bulletin, 103,* 299–314.

Traugott, M. W., & Katosh, J. P. (1979). Response validity in surveys of voting behavior. *Public Opinion Quarterly, 43,* 359–377.

Tulp, D. R., Jr., Hoy, C. E., Kusch, G. L., & Cole, S. J. (1991). Nonresponse under mandatory versus voluntary reporting in the 1980 survey of Pollution Abatement Costs and Expenditures (PACE). *Proceedings of the survey research methods section* (pp. 272–277). Alexandria, VA: American Statistical Association.

Turner, C. F., Ku, L., & Rogers, S. M. (1998). Adolescent sexual behavior, drug use, & violence: Increased reporting with computer survey technology. *Science, 280,* 867–873.

U.S. Office of Management and Budget. (1984). The role of telephone data collection in federal statistics. *Statistical policy working paper no. 1.* Washington, DC: U.S. Government Printing Office.

Van Gelder, L. (1987). Cross-addiction: Surprising results of the *Ms.* survey. *Ms.,* 44–47.

Visser, P. S., Krosnick, J. A., Marquette, J., & Curtin, M. (1996). Mail surveys for election forecasting? An evaluation of the Columbus Dispatch Poll. *Public Opinion Quarterly, 60,* 181–227.

Wallschlaeger, C., & Busic-Snyder, C. (1992). *Basic visual concepts and principles for artists, architects, and designers.* Dubuque, IA: William C. Brown Publishers.

Ware-Martin, A. (1999). Introducing and implementing cognitive techniques at the Energy Information Administration: An establishment survey environment. *Statistical policy working paper 28,* Seminar on Interagency Coordination and Cooperation (pp. 66–82). Washington, DC: Office of Management and Budget, Federal Committee on Statistical Methodology.

Warriner, K., Goyder, J., Gjertsen, H., Hohner, P., & McSpurren, K. (1996). Charities, no; Lotteries, no; Cash, yes: Main effects and interactions in a Canadian incentives experiment. *Public Opinion Quarterly, 60,* 542–562.

Werking, G. S., & Clayton, R. L. (1995). Automated telephone methods for business surveys. In B. G. Cox, D. A. Binder, B. N. Chinnappa, A. Christianson, M. J. Colledge, & P. S. Kott (Eds.), *Business survey methods* (pp. 317–337). New York: Wiley.

Willamack, D., Nicholls, E., & Sudman, S. (1999, May). *Understanding the questionnaire in business surveys.* Paper presented at the meeting of the American Association for Public Opinion Research, St. Pete Beach, FL.

Willits, F. K., & Janota, J. (1996, August). *A matter of order: Effects of response order on answers to surveys.* Paper presented at the meeting of the Rural Sociological Society, Des Moines, IA.

Willits, F. K., & Saltiel, J. (1995). Question order effects on subjective measures of quality of life. *Rural Sociology, 60,* 654–665.

Wright, P., & Barnard, P. (1975). Just fill in this form—A review for designers. *Applied Ergonomics, 6,* 213–220.

2007 APPENDIX

Recent Developments in the Design of Web, Mail, and Mixed-Mode Surveys

IN THE SHORT time since this book was published, three major developments have occurred, which together are establishing a new foundation for survey research in the twenty-first century.* One of these developments is the quick evolution of web surveys from novel idea to routine use.

A second important development is the increased need to conduct mixed-mode surveys, whereby data from some respondents are collected via one mode while data from other respondents are collected via a second mode, as a means of reducing overall survey error. This development gives urgency

*The writing of this update relied heavily on research conducted at the Washington State University Social and Economic Sciences Research Center (SESRC). This research has been supported by the National Science Foundation's Division of Science Resource Statistics, the U.S. Department of Agriculture's National Agricultural Statistical Service, the Gallup Organization, the U.S. Bureau of the Census, and the WSU Social and Economic Sciences Research Center. These organizations provided me with practical problems in need of solutions and financial support for researching the possibilities. I am also indebted to an inspiring cohort of Washington State University sociology graduate students who worked with me on the theoretical development, cognitive testing, and research experiments, results from which are reported here. They include: Leah Melani Christian, Arina Gertseva, Taj Mahon-Haft, Nicholas L. Parsons, Jolene D. Smyth, and Michael J. Stern. I am also indebted to the incredibly talented staff of the SESRC, and in particular, Thom Allen, Bruce Austin, Justin Jorgenson, Vincent Kok, Danna Moore, Kent Miller, Jolyn Persons, Nikolay Ponomarev, Marion Schulz, and Lyndsey Wilson who made it possible to field multiple web and telephone experiments critical to testing the visual design and mode ideas presented here. Finally, I am especially grateful to Taj Mahon-Haft for helping me to articulate the visual design framework introduced here and Jolene D. Smyth whose knowledge of our research studies and superb editing skills helped greatly to shape this update.

to the need to confront explicitly the question of whether people give the same answers to telephone, web, mail, and IVR surveys.

A third critical development of the past few years is the major progress that has been made in understanding why and how the visual layout of web and mail surveys affects people's responses. Understanding these effects is important for designing web and mail surveys themselves. However, it is perhaps more important for learning how mixed-mode surveys with web and mail components should be designed.

My purpose in this update is to discuss these developments and their implications for conducting surveys today. I trace the interconnections among them, and how the decline in the survey capabilities of another mode of data collection, the telephone, is requiring surveyors to integrate both mode effects and visual design considerations into their day-to-day decisions.

THE WEB REVOLUTION

When I was writing this book in the late 1990s, Internet surveys were a novelty. I recall a meeting held in 1996 to discuss whether potential respondents would know what a hotlink was and how to use it in order to access a web survey; we decided it was unlikely that most people would understand that technique. A common practice then was to imbed surveys inside e-mails rather than post them on web sites to avoid making respondents do the unfamiliar task of clicking on hotlinks (Schaefer and Dillman, 1997). Yet, only a decade later, use of a hotlink seems as clear to nearly all Internet users as knowing the connection between their house key and getting in the front door.

In addition, as we reported in Chapter 11, only a fourth of U.S. households had e-mail connections in the late 1990s, and by today's standards those connections were painfully slow. Little research had been done on the best ways to formulate and implement web surveys. Thus, the Web design principles presented in this book were tentative and incomplete.

Web surveys have now become commonplace as computers have become significantly more powerful and the ability of people to use them has also improved. Far fewer surveys are now thwarted by the inability of respondents to operate computers effectively. People who purchase books, airline tickets, and hotel rooms on the Web have already learned most of the skills necessary for responding to web surveys.

Additionally, many more people have Internet access now. Nearly two-thirds of U.S. households have Internet access in their homes, a slight majority of which have high-speed rather than slow dial-up modems. Virtually all members of some survey populations now have web access and the ability to use it for responding to questionnaires. University students, schoolteachers, members of professional associations, and employees of many firms are examples of such populations.

The hardware and software capabilities needed for constructing web surveys have also both improved enormously so that now there are hundreds of choices available worldwide. Surveyors who used to live in constant fear of servers going down just as hundreds or thousands of e-mail requests were being dispatched to elicit survey participation, now find such failures occur far less frequently. With these changes, the costs of implementing web surveys have also declined.

Yet, for many reasons, web surveys have not taken over the survey world, eliminating the use of more expensive modes of data collection—telephone, mail, and face-to-face interviews. A substantial proportion of general public households still do not have Internet access at home. Further, computer skills are not yet universal, nor are they likely to be anytime soon. Within households, computer and Internet skills vary widely. Whereas it is routine to expect nearly all adults to be able to talk to an interviewer or write answers on a paper questionnaire, many people lack sufficient understanding of computers to be a respondent if they are the one selected within a household.

Among those households that have Internet access, there is no procedure available for drawing random samples of users or samples in which individuals or households have a known, nonzero chance of being included. This inability is partly the result of widely different e-mail address structures. Examples of the many ways one person's address might vary range from complete full name or nickname to a descriptor that has nothing to do with his or her name: For example: Elizabeth.Fern.Thompson@xxx.com, EFT@xxx.com, thompsonef@xxx.com, ethompson@xxx.com, thompson005@xxx.com, liz@xxx.com, floppy17@xxx.com, and busymom@xxx.com. In addition some people share e-mail addresses with a partner or spouse (e.g., lizandhank@xxx.com) and many individuals have multiple addresses. Thus, there is no apparent equivalent to the random digit dialing algorithm of randomly selecting numbers (e.g., 509–555-xxxx) from local telephone exchanges that gave all households with a telephone a knowable probability of being selected for a general public telephone survey. Even if such addresses could be sampled, there are legal and cultural barriers to contacting randomly generated Internet addresses. Because Internet service providers are private rather than public providers of service, surveyors do not have the assumed right to contact people as was the case with telephone, nor do professional associations of surveyors (e.g., the Council of American Survey Research Organizations or CASRO) support sending surveys to populations with which the surveyor has no preexisting relationship.

Clicking on links and responding to surveys is also a scary process for some respondents, less because of their objections to the survey, than because of the worry about whether such an action will result in their computer being infected by a virus. Concerns also exist that replying to an e-mail sender will reveal a working Internet connection to someone who will then add the address to junk e-mail lists. Thus, a climate of extreme caution for responding to e-mails persists. In addition, although much progress is being made in our ability to obtain reasonable response rates to web surveys, for many such surveys the response rates are abysmal. Internet surveys seem no more likely now to become our sole mode of conducting sample surveys than they did when this book was originally published.

Guides to understanding use of the Internet for surveys, which describe the basics for doing web surveys are now available (e.g., Best and Krueger, 2004). Other authors have written shorter guides that describe and illustrate proposed best practices in designing and implementing web surveys (Baker, Crawford, and Swinehart, 2004; Crawford, McCabe and Pope, 2005). In addition, Crawford (2002) has categorized the wide variety of software packages available to researchers. Through a review of three widely different alternatives—a basic off-the-shelf package, intermediate application service provider package, and advanced survey system—he illustrates the range of choices as well as the complexities of choosing the most appropriate software.

The Internet has evolved quickly as a specialized mode for surveying populations with nearly complete web access. But for populations that include people without computer skills, Internet access, and/or a knowable e-mail address, the Web is evolving as a mode that must be used in conjunction with more traditional modes such as telephone and mail. This means there is an increase in the occurrence of mixed-mode surveys, whereby some data are obtained by the Web and other data are gathered by another mode or modes (De Leeuw, 2005; Biemer and Lyberg, 2003). At the U.S. Bureau of the Census, recent experimentation on designing the next decennial census, to be administered in 2010, has focused on the prospect of using mixed-mode surveying. Although nearly all households will be contacted by mail initially, some respondents may be asked to complete their census form on the Web or give the results to an enumerator who will use a small handheld computer from which to read questions and record answers. The responses for still other households may be provided over the telephone.

THE MIXED-MODE SURVEY: FROM CURIOSITY TO NECESSITY

The enormous interest now evident in how to combine web with other survey modes stems only in part from the rapid deployment of web access and use in people's lives. A revolution has simultaneously occurred in the reliance on telephones for conducting surveys, the result of which is to require greater use of alternative survey modes (Dillman, 2002).

You need only walk down the street and listen to hundreds of people walking or standing alone, yet talking out loud, for it to be apparent that when and how we use the telephone has undergone enormous change in the past several years. The change in how telephones get used is in part due to the development of cell phone technology that now makes it possible to talk with almost anyone, anywhere, and at anytime.

However, the change in telephone use is as much cultural as it is technological. The norms that govern when and how the telephone is used are now quite different than when we became heavily dependent on telephone surveys. A few years ago, I went into the office of a colleague to ask a question. His phone rang, and I stopped talking. After a brief and awkward moment, I asked if he was going to answer the phone. His response was, "No, I often sit here all morning without answering the phone. Anyone who really needs me quickly can reach me with an e-mail or they can leave a message. I'm a lot more efficient if I just wait until I'm not busy and return the phone calls when I have time." While not everyone uses this strategy, it does reflect a changing orientation toward telephones.

When telephone interviewing began in the 1970s, not responding to a ringing telephone would have been unfathomable. Unless you answered the phone there was no way to know who might be calling and there were no answering machines from which to receive a message. Additionally, there was essentially no alternative for quick communication. It would have been interpreted as rude, even unthinkable, to ignore a ringing phone. A rapid succession of telephone developments—answering machines, active call monitoring, use of the telephone for marketing purposes, caller identification technologies that show the number from which the call originated, and blocking devices that only permit calls from certain numbers to go through—have changed the ways people use and depend on the telephone (Dillman, 2002). In the 1970s, the telephone controlled our behavior; now we control the telephone. We ignore it or use clues (e.g., number from which the call came or information divulged to the answering machine) to decide whether to answer the call. Now, when I hear a ringing phone in the airport or other public place it is common to observe a phone being pulled quickly from a pocket or purse, followed by a moment of hesitation, as the bearer waits for the source of the call to appear on the screen. Often the phone is then put away without being answered. The telephone has become a device we take with us and use at our convenience to talk with people to whom we wish to talk. As a result, response rates to interviewer calls have plummeted. Telephone response rates that often approached 70 percent to 80 percent in the 1970s have dropped to 40 percent and even lower in the past several years with no-answers being a major reason.

In addition, telephone coverage problems emerged (Nathan, 1999; Tucker and Lepkowski, in press). When people depended only on *landlines*—a term that has only become necessary in this age of cellular phones—phones were clearly associated with homes. General public sampling strategies depended on households having such telephones. Cellular phones, on the other hand, tend to be associated with individuals and are now possessed by many children as well as adults. In addition, area codes may or may not be associated with the location where people live, thus affecting the ability to draw geographic samples of the general public. Not only can people take their phones with them from place to place, but they can now take their area codes and numbers from one region of the country to another on their mobile phones.

Surveyors have been reluctant to include cell phone numbers in survey designs for several reasons. First, many people have cellular as well as landline telephones, a situation that influences the probability of being included in a survey sample. Second, the cell phone has shifted the cost of talking on the telephone from the surveyor to the respondent. Third, concern exists about calling people when they are driving or otherwise occupied in ways that might make answering interview questions a threat to their personal safety or to the safety of those around them. Fourth, it is also becoming apparent that people who convey a willingness to be surveyed, but are uncomfortable with doing that by telephone, may demand being provided with an alternative survey mode. Together, these issues present a formidable barrier to knowingly calling people on their cell phones with the request that they spend 5, 10, 20, or more minutes answering survey questions.

People have also begun to express preferences about how they should be contacted through their address-giving behavior. Sometimes people only provide information for their preferred mode of contact (e.g., only giving an e-mail address). Individuals may also prefer being reached by some people via one mode and others via another mode (e.g., cellular phone for friends, and landline for those with whom they don't wish to talk). Some people attempt to control the receipt of bills and documents by providing either postal or web addresses and not the other. In addition, different e-mail addresses (business, home, personal, or very personal) are given to different potential senders. Further, businesses that build address lists seem increasingly reluctant to ask individuals to provide contact information for all means of reaching them. The result is that no matter what survey mode one would like to use for contacting potential respondents, limiting oneself to a single mode of contact may produce serious coverage problems.

The combined result of all of these changes has produced perhaps the greatest survey paradox of the early twenty-first century. While people's accessibility by telephone is now greater than at any time in history, the phone has become less and less suited as a stand-alone method for the conduct of surveys.

For these reasons, designing web survey procedures in ways that will be effective in a mixed-mode context has emerged as a major concern (Dillman and Christian, 2005; DeLeeuw, 2005). This state of affairs raises several important issues that were only beginning to emerge at the time the second edition of this book was published. One such issue is whether web surveys tend to produce different results than do telephone surveys, with which they are being paired with increasing frequency, and whether telephone and web need to adapt to one another.

COMPARING WEB SURVEY ANSWERS TO OTHER SURVEY MODE ANSWERS

Prior to 2000, virtually no research had been done that compared results from web and other types of surveys. Although Chapter 6 identified many differences for answers to mail and telephone questions designed to collect the same information from respondents, no experimental results were available that included web comparisons. That situation has now changed.

Surveyors who are predominantly focused on one mode, tend to prefer asking questions in certain ways, and are reluctant to change (Dillman and Christian, 2005). An example from the past was the strong tendency to use show cards with face-to-face interviews to help respondents, while asking questions somewhat differently on the telephone, where such visual support cannot be used. Those decisions have often been justified by the simple assertion that it is the way surveys are typically done in that mode.

Sometimes questions asked in one survey mode are restructured for use in another mode, with unfortunate consequences. For example, one survey organization changed a question on marital status from telephone to web in this way (Dillman, 2005):

- (Telephone) What is your marital status?
- (Web) Which of the following best describes your marital status?

  ❑ Single
  ❑ Married
  ❑ Separated
  ❑ Divorced
  ❑ Widowed

The result was not surprising. The percent of people reporting being married or single dropped significantly on the Web version—a combined decline of 4.4 percent—while the percent separated, divorced, or widowed increased by the same amount. When this question was asked in the open-ended fashion the more general categories of married or single came easily to mind, while the more specific categories, which could overlap with the first two categories, did not. The simple solution for this mode problem was to change the way the question was asked on the telephone, offering categories there as well, thus using *unimode* construction as described in Chapter 6. When this was pointed out to the sponsors, their initial reaction was that this is the way that question had normally been asked by telephone for most of that organization's surveys. Changing it for this survey might require them to consider changing it for other surveys as well, inasmuch as they preferred a single standard.

Another example is the differential use of check-all and forced-choice question formats to ask multiple-answer questions. The availability on the Web of HTML boxes, which allow respondents to mark more than one answer, may be encouraging surveyors to convert forced-choice telephone questions to the check-all format on the Web as shown in Figure A.1. Recently, 15 comparisons between answers to check-all formats and forced-choice formats in web surveys were reported (Smyth, Dillman, Christian, and Stern, 2006). On all but one of the 15 web comparisons (several of which tested reverse orderings of the items), and on one paper comparison (Q5) respondents were more likely to endorse items when they were posed in the forced-choice format than when they were posed in the check-all format (see Figure A.2).

Analysis of these data showed two important changes in how people respond to the forced-choice items. First, they spend considerably more time marking their answers, which suggests that they were processing the re-

Figure A.1 Examples of check-all and forced-choice question formats used in web survey comparisons (Smyth, Dillman, Christian, and Stern, 2005).

Example of Check-All Format Used in Web Survey Comparisons

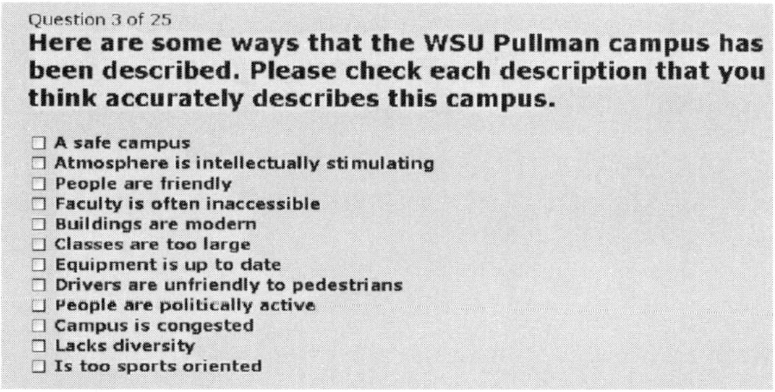
Question 3 of 25

Here are some ways that the WSU Pullman campus has been described. Please check each description that you think accurately describes this campus.

- ☐ A safe campus
- ☐ Atmosphere is intellectually stimulating
- ☐ People are friendly
- ☐ Faculty is often inaccessible
- ☐ Buildings are modern
- ☐ Classes are too large
- ☐ Equipment is up to date
- ☐ Drivers are unfriendly to pedestrians
- ☐ People are politically active
- ☐ Campus is congested
- ☐ Lacks diversity
- ☐ Is too sports oriented

Example of Forced-Choice Format Used in Web Survey Comparisons

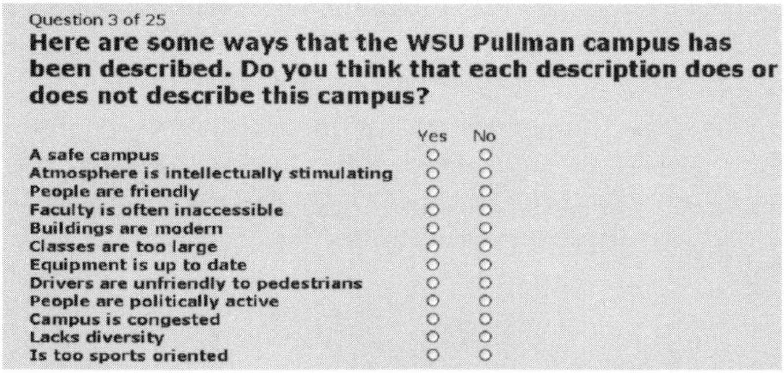
Question 3 of 25

Here are some ways that the WSU Pullman campus has been described. Do you think that each description does or does not describe this campus?

	Yes	No
A safe campus	O	O
Atmosphere is intellectually stimulating	O	O
People are friendly	O	O
Faculty is often inaccessible	O	O
Buildings are modern	O	O
Classes are too large	O	O
Equipment is up to date	O	O
Drivers are unfriendly to pedestrians	O	O
People are politically active	O	O
Campus is congested	O	O
Lacks diversity	O	O
Is too sports oriented	O	O

Figure A.2 Mean number of options endorsed in check-all and forced-choice formats by respondents for 15 web survey and one paper (Q5) Comparisons. Repeated question numbers identify questions tested with reverse item orders (Smyth, Dillman, Christian, and Stern, 2005).

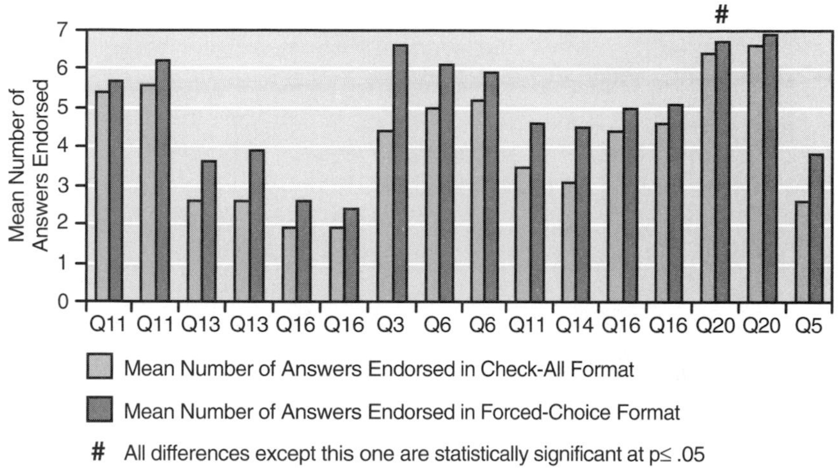

sponse options more deeply and finding more response options that applied to them. Second, the check-all respondents who spent an above average amount of time selecting answers endorsed about the same number of items as the forced-choice respondents. In contrast, the check-all respondents who spent the mean amount of time or less not only endorsed fewer items, but were also more likely to exhibit a primacy pattern of endorsing items when they appeared in the first three positions on the list (Smyth, Dillman, Christian, and Stern, 2006a). Thus, it appears that the forced-choice format promotes better response behavior than does the check-all format.

A more recent comparison, between web and telephone, shows that multiple-answer questions perform more similarly when asked in the forced-choice format in both modes than when asked in the check-all format for web and the forced-choice format for telephone. We found that for six of seven questions asked in the forced-choice format, the results were not significantly different between telephone and web modes (Smyth, Christian, and Dillman, 2006). Thus, the suggestion that one should avoid using the check-all format for paper surveys as recommended in Chapter 4 of this book and by Rasinski, Mingay, and Bradburn (1994), can now be extended to web surveys. Replacing the check-all question structure with the forced-choice structure that is commonly used in the telephone mode is more likely to produce similar results across modes, while reducing an undesirable tendency to satisfice that was evident with the check-all format.

THE SCALAR CHALLENGE ACROSS SURVEY MODES

One of the paper versus telephone differences that I have found most troubling is the likelihood that telephone interviews produce more extreme answers to scalar questions, for which traditional explanations such as social desirability, primacy/recency, or acquiescence, seem not to offer satisfactory explanations. This issue was addressed briefly in Chapter 6, which described multiple experiments that revealed greater use of extreme positive categories on telephone than on paper surveys (pp. 229–232).

Shortly after this book had gone to print, an experiment was conducted by the Gallup Organization that compared responses to mail, telephone, web, and interactive voice response (IVR) surveys. This study was done with a general population for which both telephone numbers and postal addresses were available. Part of the survey design involved calling two of the subsamples by landline telephone and asking one group to complete the short survey by IVR (see Chapter 10) and the other group to complete it by web. An additional variation in the design was that about three weeks after attempting to survey all respondents via one of the modes, they then attempted to survey nonrespondents by another mode. The survey itself was only 10 questions long, with 5 of the questions using the scalar question format, for example, "Overall how satisfied are you with your long distance company? Please use a 1-to-5 scale where 1 means not at all satisfied and 5 means extremely satisfied. You may use any number from 1 to 5" (Dillman, Phelps, Tortora, Swift, Kohrell, and Berck, 2001).

Two findings from this study are particularly noteworthy. First, the concerted attempt to increase response by following up with an alternate mode after a pause of three weeks was very successful. The response rates were increased by this switch of modes as follows: mail followed by telephone: from 75 percent up to 83 percent; telephone followed by mail: from 43 percent up to 80 percent; IVR followed by telephone: from 28 percent up to 50 percent, and web followed by telephone: from 13 percent up to 48 percent. Thus, switching modes was found to be a powerful way of improving response rates.

Second, as shown in Figure A.3, there were dramatic mode differences in the percent of respondents choosing the extreme category on the positive end of the scale with the most remarkable differences being between the aural modes (telephone and IVR) and the visual modes (web and mail). For example, on the overall satisfaction item (Q2 in Figure A.3), 39 percent of telephone respondents and 39 percent of IVR respondents chose "completely satisfied" compared to 21 and 27 percent of mail and web respondents, respectively. In a marketing research culture of reporting "top box" (most satisfied category) scores, large differences in conclusions would be made depending on whether one used the aural or visual modes of data collection. This pattern of

Figure A.3 Percentage of respondents endorsing the positive endpoint on scalar questions across four survey modes, by question (Dillman, Phelps, Tortora, Swift, Kohrell, and Berck, 2001).

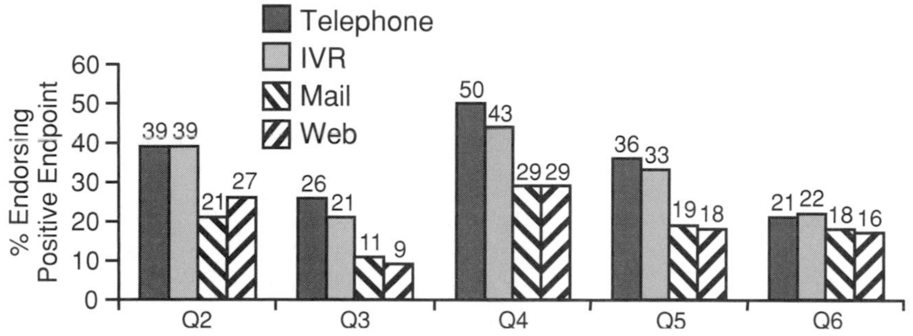

the two aural modes resulting in more "extremeness" than the two visual modes also existed for the other four satisfaction questions included in this survey.

What do these results mean? First, the differences between visual and aural modes are in many respects similar to the extremeness tendency noted in Chapter 6. However, the scales are different. Specifically, the Gallup test items were polar-point labeled, while the results reported in Chapter 6 were based on fully labeled scales. In addition, a control group included in the Gallup experiment showed that primacy/recency could not account for the differences (Dillman, Phelps, Tortora, Swift, Kohrell, and Berck, 2001).

The differences noted here led to the decision to conduct a carefully controlled study of scalar response differences between web and telephone modes only, using equivalent random samples of students at Washington State University. This test involved three web and three telephone panels, thus allowing the simultaneous testing of three different question formats (Christian, Dillman, and Smyth, in press). The study revealed for (1) polar-point labeled five-point scales, (2) fully labeled five-point scales, and (3) 11-point polar-point labeled scales that respondents to the telephone consistently provided more positive answers than did respondents to mail surveys. Across these three types of scales, 22 of 26 comparisons were significant in the direction of more positive answers being obtained via telephone than web. Results from this paper, when added to results on extremeness reported in Chapter 6 (pp. 229–232) make it clear that obtaining the same results on scalar questions across survey modes remains an unresolved challenge.

The available research on resolving mode differences between the Web and telephone now leaves surveyors in a quandary. Will the increase in response rate, and perhaps a decrease in nonresponse error, that results from the combined use of these modes in a single study design be nullified by loss of measurement equivalency across modes? In some cases where question format and wording can be brought together, such as the forced-choice alternative to the check-all format, the answer appears to be no. However, for scalar questions that measure opinions, the answer may be yes. These results have become part of a much larger question on how to design web surveys.

USING OR RESTRAINING THE POWER OF THE WEB

The enormous power and flexibility of web survey design raises many possibilities for enhancing web surveys in ways that may be problematic for obtaining response equivalency across modes. For example:

- Drop-down menus that require clicking, followed by selecting answer categories
- Slider scales
- Pictures to illustrate scales
- Color
- Animation
- Sounds
- Video
- Automatic fill-ins for later answers
- Feedback screens that inform the respondent of an answer that appears to be wrong (e.g., reporting date of birth as 1870 instead of 1970) or summarizes answers to a series of questions (e.g., all colleges attended and degrees obtained) so that respondents may check their answers for accuracy and completeness
- Definitions that appear on the screen when the respondent hovers the mouse pointer over certain words
- Hotlinks that allow one to access detailed instructions at will

Some of these, for example, automatic skip patterns, make web surveys more similar to one mode (telephone) but more different from another (mail). Others raise fundamentally new issues that need to be investigated. For example, it is not yet known whether scalar questions where answer choices appear in drop-down menus will consistently obtain answers equivalent to those obtained by the more traditional question formats used in telephone and mail surveys. A rapidly expanding body of research is exploring many of these issues. For example, it has been shown that different answers are selected from drop-down boxes depending on whether one has to scroll within the menus to see all of the answers; respondents are more likely to select answers that appear initially in the box than those that are not initially revealed and require scrolling to see (Couper, Tourangeau, Conrad, and Crawford, 2004). Other research has shown that slider scales that allow respondents to pick an exact point on a visually presented scale allow respondents more possibilities for selecting a precise answer (Bayer and Thomas, 2004), but seem to move web responses away from equivalency with other survey modes. Similarly, it has been shown that the inclusion of pictures in web surveys may influence answers (Couper, Tourangeau, and Kenyon, 2004). Although such pictures may also be included on mail surveys, they cannot usually be provided in telephone surveys.

Some research has been done on whether the greater visual interest of certain designs on the Web improves response rates (Coates, 2004; Dillman, Tortora, Conrad, and Bowker, 1998) or respondent satisfaction (Couper, Tourangeau, and Kenyon, 2004). The evidence, to date, does not seem to indicate that using these possibilities for web survey design will improve response and currently the increased cost of designing surveys with greater visual interest tends to restrain their use.

CHOOSING UNIMODE OR MODE-SPECIFIC DESIGN

In this book, I introduced the concept of *unimode* design. It was defined in Chapter 6 as, "the writing and presenting of questions to respondents in a way that assures receipt by respondents of a common mental stimulus, regardless of survey mode" (p. 232). In practice, it means writing survey questions and presenting them visually, in ways that would try to minimize differences in answers between modes by finding a common ground for construction. For example, as a means of presenting the same stimuli to respondents, I suggested that "don't know" or "no opinion" categories should be explicitly offered in telephone interviews, if they were also provided explicitly in web or mail surveys. This is contrary to the common practice of the interviewer only acknowledging them as options if the respondent volunteers them. More concrete examples of producing unimode, or a single design for questions, are those described earlier in this Appendix, that is, using a closed-ended format for asking marital status questions and abandoning check-all question formats on mail and web in favor of a forced-choice format that produces answers that are more equivalent to those obtained on the telephone.

A contrasting perspective to unimode design is *mode-specific* design. The premise of this perspective is that survey modes are inherently different in their capabilities, as well as in their fundamental means of communication (i.e., visual versus aural). It suggests that in some instances one might achieve better equivalency across survey modes by deliberately presenting different question formats to respondents of each mode. The basis of this approach is that the unique capabilities of each particular mode are strategically addressed to improve the chances of obtaining equivalent data across modes. In addition, this perspective suggests that if one mode can produce more accurate answers by utilizing its full capabilities to ask questions differently than in another mode (show cards in face-to-face interviews, rotation of answer choices in telephone or web, presentation of diagrams or maps in web or mail), then doing so is desirable. Regardless of whether equivalent answers are obtained across modes, the overall accuracy of results would be improved.

There is more to this debate than first meets the eye. A recent attempt to build a common questionnaire for the 2010 U.S. Decennial Census illustrates the challenge. In the Census, the same six questions are asked about all household members—name, sex, age, date of birth, Spanish/Hispanic/ Latino ethnicity and race—along with a few household questions. The possibility of using mailed paper forms, the Internet, personal enumeration with handheld computing devices, and telephone interviews as data collection modes in 2010 led to the construction of test questionnaires for each mode, some of which asked the same questions in different ways. A few of the many differences between paper and Internet draft forms included the following:

- The paper questionnaire designers used answer category boxes for all questions that required the selection of one or more answers; however, the Internet designers used radio buttons for alternative choices such as male/female, and check-all boxes for questions where multiple answers could be recorded (e.g., race and ethnicity categories).
- The Internet designers placed date of birth ahead of age to gain the advantage of automatic fill-ins of the latter space, while paper designers reversed the order because of evidence of less item nonresponse to the second item.
- The Internet designers allowed write-ins of unlimited length for each person's name and race categories, but the paper designer could only use as many spaces as would fit in the page columns.
- The paper form used a person-based approach, that is, asking all six questions for each person before moving to the next person in the household. In contrast, the Internet form used a topic-based approach, for example, asking everyone's gender before proceeding to the next topic; age, which was asked about each person before moving to each successive topic.
- On ethnicity and race, the Internet designers used abbreviated category descriptions with hotlinks that when clicked revealed examples of each category. The paper designers provided fewer examples overall, but listed them all right with the category.

Some of these differences, for example, introduction of radio buttons versus HTML boxes, seemed unlikely to produce answers that were different. However, for other differences, like changing the order in which questions were asked or having to click hotlinks to get examples of ethnicity and race categories, its less clear whether differences would result. It also became apparent in the discussion of the alternative modes that additional criteria for structuring questions differently across modes existed. They included: improving processing efficiency for a specific mode, reduction of respondent burden, and reduction of interviewer burden. Consideration of handheld computer devices, with their small screens, which require dividing some questions across multiple screen displays in ways not needed for either the Web or paper, added to the complexity of deciding how questions should be asked in each survey mode. It remains to be seen how these issues will be resolved in the 2010 Census.

Another example of confronting unimode versus mode-specific construction challenges comes from a series of surveys conducted by the Research Triangle Institute (Wine, Cominole, Heuer, and Riccobnon, 2006). This effort involved conducting each survey initially by web with a phone CATI follow-up to everyone who did not respond to the Web. To achieve mode equivalency, they followed a unimode approach of using the same screens for telephone interviews as those used for web respondents. Follow-up analysis by the authors indicated that this unimode design produced virtually no differences between modes.

As more and more surveyors consider conducting mixed mode surveys, it seems likely that the discussion about unimode and mode-specific design philosophies will continue. Many surveyors are likely to be faced with whether to hold back on the use of individual mode capabilities as suggested by the unimode philosophy to achieve equivalency. Alternatively, they may decide to use the full capability of each individual mode in hopes of getting the most accurate data of which a particular mode is capable, regardless of the consequences for combining results across survey modes. We expect that some questions and situations will favor a unimode philosophy (e.g., the marital status and forced-choice format items discussed earlier) while for others it will make more sense to use a mode-specific design philosophy. The research challenge this issue poses to researchers is enormous.

The effort to achieve accuracy and build equivalency across survey modes, whether by asking identical questions or by strategically asking questions in different ways, is made even more difficult by another recent development in survey methodology. It is the substantial research, which now shows that different visual layouts of questions on the Web, as well as paper, often produce quite different survey results within a single mode.

USING LANGUAGES BEYOND WORDS TO WRITE QUESTIONS

Respondents are cooperative communicators and will try to make sense of each survey question by drawing on all information provided by the surveyor (Schwarz, 1996). That includes formal features of the questionnaire such as numeric values assigned to rating scales and the graphical layout of scales. What's more, respondents are especially likely to look to these sources of information when they are unsure about what is being asked or how to report their answer (Schwarz, Grayson, and Knauper, 1998). Thus, while words are important for determining question meaning, other features of questionnaires that we often don't think about are also important.

Prior to the 1990s, visual layout in questionnaires was mostly viewed as an art form by survey methodologists. It was argued, mostly through examples, that visual factors needed to be taken into account when asking questions. Yet, prior to the work by Schwarz and his colleagues, theoretically based rationales were not presented on why and how the science of visual perception might be invoked to improve the understanding of questions and questionnaires (e.g., Dillman, 1978; Wright and Barnard, 1975, 1978; Rothwell, 1985).

In this book (pp. 96–139), I proposed that paper and web questionnaires present information in two languages, words and graphics. That provided a basis for thinking of visual design and layout in three sequential steps—defining a navigational path through the questionnaire, creating visual guides to help respondents adhere to that path, and occasionally interrupting that navigation with more powerful graphics to redirect them, for example, being branched to different questions as a result of choosing a particular answer.

Even before the book went to print, it became apparent that the concepts introduced here were too limited. In addition, research was already underway that would soon leave no doubt that people's answers to survey questions are affected by more than words in web and paper surveys.

It is now apparent that the meaning of web and mail survey questions is communicated by four languages, including symbols and numbers in addition to words and graphics (Redline and Dillman, 2002). Many experiments have now shown the independent and combined effects of manipulating these aspects of visual appearance (Jenkins and Dillman, 1997; Redline and Dillman, 2002, 2003; Christian and Dillman, 2004; Tourangeau, Couper, and Conrad, 2004; Dillman and Christian, 2005). In addition, survey methodologists have begun to use extensively, work from the vision sciences (e.g., Palmer, 1999, Hoffman, 2004; Ware 2004) to guide their searches for understanding visual effects. Also, visual design concepts are now being connected to usability concepts to guide both paper and web design practices

(Dillman, Gertseva, and Mahon-Haft, 2005). This research is requiring survey methodologists to learn and apply new concepts to the practice of survey design.

THE IMPORTANCE OF VISUAL DESIGN—THE BUTTERFLY BALLOT

In November 2000, a dramatic controversy emerged over whether some voters in Palm Beach County, Florida, had mistakenly voted for Pat Buchanan for president while intending that their punch on the Butterfly ballot go into the hole assigned to Al Gore (see Figure A.4). Fox (2000) argued at the time that about 2,800 unintentional votes were recorded for Buchanan, while 2,300 incomplete punches and 11,000 double punches that invalidate intended votes for Gore were recorded. These arguments were supported by data which showed that the votes recorded in Palm Beach County for Pat Buchanan in that election were proportionally much greater than occurred in other counties based on the number of registered reform party voters, votes for Bush, total votes cast and votes for Buchanan in the 1996 primary (see Figure A.5). In addition, Wand, Shotts, Sekhon, Mebane Jr., Herron, and Brady (2001) concluded from a detailed post-election analysis that these

Figure A.4 Image of the controversial Butterfly ballot reportedly misunderstood by voters during the 2000 presidential election in Palm Beach County, Florida, analyzed by Fox (2000).

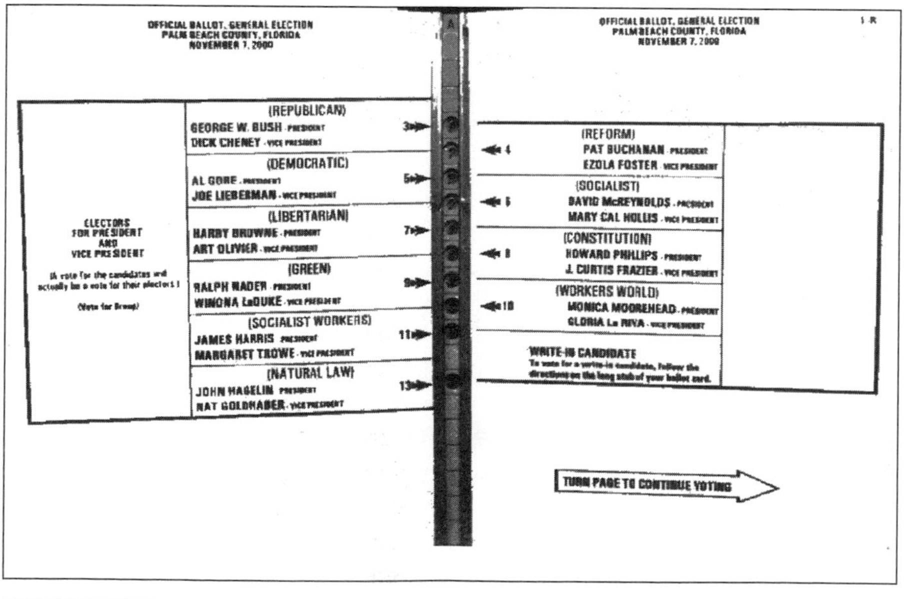

Figure A.5 Votes for Buchanan in all Florida counties in 2000 presidential election, relative to the number of registered reform party voters (based on data provided by Sebago Associates, 2000).

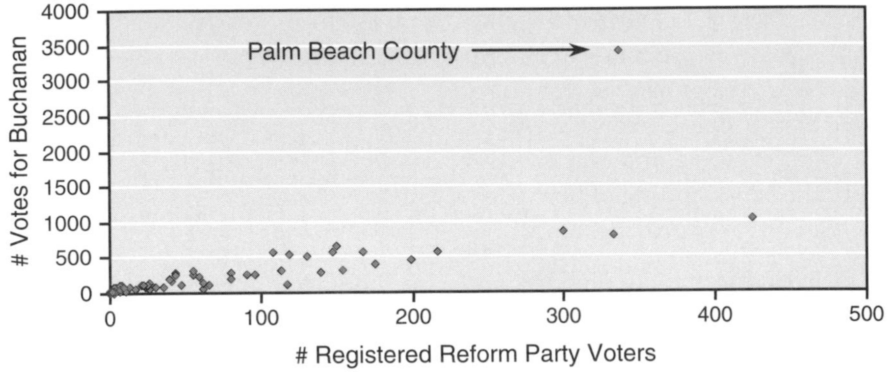

anomalies were not found among absentee voters in Palm Beach County who did not use the Butterfly ballot and that Buchanan's support in Palm Beach County tended to come from more Democratic precincts. Based on these analyses there can be little doubt that the Butterfly ballot produced votes for a candidate for whom voters did not intend to vote. The consequences of these errors for the outcome of the 2000 presidential election, make this perhaps the most dramatic and consequential example of poor visual layout and design of an election ballot or questionnaire.

It is easy to speculate about numerous layout problems with the Butterfly ballot that may have led to these discrepancies (Figure A.4). For example, people might not have expected "answer choices" for a question to appear partly on one page and partly on another. In addition, they may not have expected the punch-hole column to be shared by candidate choices on both the left and right pages. The choice for Al Gore was the second choice on the left-hand page but the third punch hole, while the second punch hole was assigned to Pat Buchanan whose candidacy was listed first on the right-hand page, and this mismatch could have made a difference. The line separating the Bush space from Gore space had "DEMOCRATIC" written under it and led directly into the second hole, not the third one in the answer column. In addition, instructions on the previous page indicate that people should, "punch the ballot card in the hole next to the number of that candidate and/or question, not to exceed the number of votes allowed for each office," may have made some people think that punching two holes was a sensible response.

Yet, there is something distinctly unsatisfying about these possible explanations for the pattern of mistakes. They are based more on ad hoc speculation than scientific evidence about why people see and act on visual information. Among other things, they do not provide insight into why people were unlikely to examine the entire two-page ballot layout before voting. Nor do the observations provide insight into why people were likely to move from one place on the page to another and mark their answer, before realizing that an error may have been made.

The making of so many errors while marking these ballots becomes more understandable when viewed from the perspective of what is now known about how people perceive, understand, and respond, visually, to the words, numbers, symbols, and graphics that constituted the Butterfly ballot. A conceptual understanding of how people attend to and process visual information can not only provide a more in-depth understanding of what happened with the Butterfly ballot, but can also be applied to understand how web and mail survey pages are seen and acted on.

THE PROCESS OF PERCEIVING VISUAL INFORMATION AND MAKING SENSE OF IT

When the eye takes in any page containing written information, whether in a ballot, a questionnaire, or a book, many separate actions take place very quickly as the human mind tries to make sense of the scene before it. A brief overview of this process, described elsewhere in more detail (Mahon-Haft and Dillman, 2006), is important for understanding why different visual layouts produce different effects. These processes provide the basis for the research results on which rests much of the evidence for proving that visual layout affects respondent answers.

Perceiving and Attending to Information

The act of responding to each survey question is commonly viewed as comprised of four activities—comprehending the question, retrieving relevant information from memory, deciding on an appropriate answer, and reporting that answer (Tourangeau, Rips, and Rasinski, 2000). Mistakes can happen because of problems at any one of these steps. In addition, users of this four-step model often consider only how the respondent processes verbal information or words, which comprises only one of the four languages through which information is conveyed to respondents.

Before going through the sequence of activities involved in responding to a survey, respondents must first perceive the information presented visually and give it their attention; therefore, it is important to consider a fifth step, *perceiving and attending*, which must occur prior to the four listed earlier (Redline and Dillman, 2002). Information that is not perceived or attended to cannot be used in the other steps. In addition, much may happen at the time of initial perception that affects the manner in which people will comprehend and ultimately answer a survey question. The process of taking in visual information and using it has been described in detail in recent work by Palmer (1999), Hoffman (2004), and Ware (2004). Key concepts for describing this process are summarized for easy reference in a brief glossary in Attachment A at the end of this Appendix.

Several key ideas describe what is happening at the initial stage of perception when respondents are determining what information on the questionnaire or ballot page exists and is relevant to selecting an answer. In addition, what people see on the ballot may be much less than what is there.

ASSIGNING MEANING TO VISUAL INFORMATION

There are two fundamental ways that we assign meaning to the information we perceive. The first is through *bottom-up processing,* whereby meaning is assigned more or less automatically from rote memory—a "1" is a "1" because that's what we have learned it is, and we have also learned that it means first or before all others. The second is through *top-down processing* where we assign meaning based on a fairly limited number of ideas immediately accessible in our working memory (Jenkins and Dillman, 1997). For example, the knowledge that one is being asked to answer a questionnaire in conjunction with looking at words near the top of the first page preceded by a "1" suggests that, "This is the first question and I need to start reading and answering questions here."

Preattentive processing describes how we selectively pick up on certain symbols, shapes, or other features of a page, which subconsciously attract our attention. This type of processing often occurs when people first look at a questionnaire page, surveying the broad visual field in front of them before giving detailed attention to features that stand out. It allows people to see and generally understand something "at a glance," but for that to happen certain features have to stand out from others. Research has shown that certain shapes, symbols, and other graphical features, especially those that are different from an otherwise common pattern, as shown in Figure A.6, attract attention during preattentive processing (Ware, 2004). Among the many attributes processed preattentively are number in a group, enclosure, size of elements, line orientation, additional elements, contrast, curvature, subtracted elements, and shape, as shown in Figure A.6. Other elements that may stand out in this way are color hue, intensity, flickering motion, line length, line width, and direction of motion. However, the more such distinctions are incorporated into a single scene, the more difficult it is for the reviewer to pick up on those distinctions. Thus, pages that are cluttered with an unorganized display of many different graphical shapes, groupings, and figures make it very difficult for the viewer to quickly get a sense of the page in order to decide which aspect will be attentively processed.

Figure A.6 Examples of visual differences that stand out quickly because they are preattentively recognized during human visual processing.

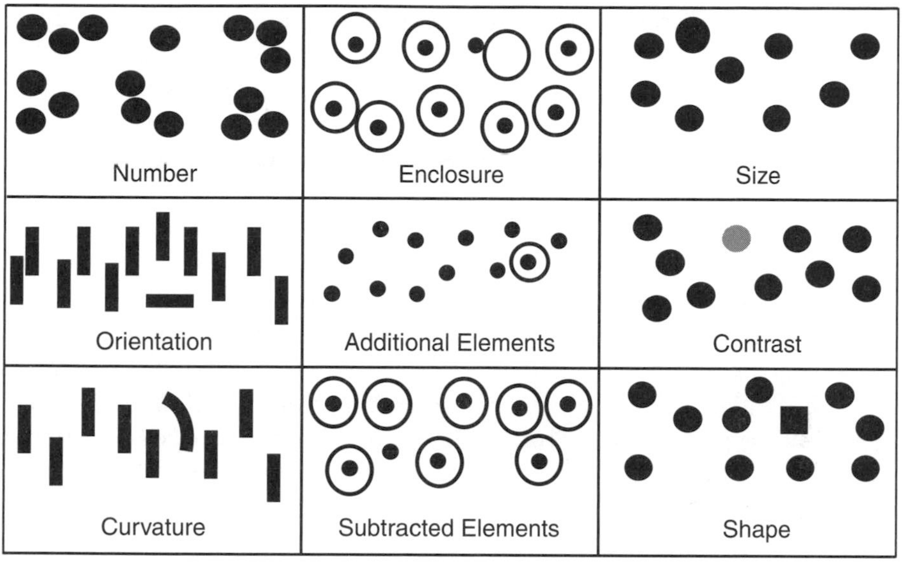

Attentive processing refers to giving attention to a small portion of the visual field, usually within a visual span of about two degrees or 8 to 10 characters, which is known as the *foveal view.* It should also be apparent that the *useful field of view* gets smaller as one switches from preattentive to attentive processing and, incidentally, also in situations that are more stressful or cognitively demanding. In attentive processing, we can only focus on a few objects or aspects of objects, but it results in that information being better remembered for later use. The difference between preattentive and attentive processing may be thought of as looking at everything but not yet focusing on anything in particular versus seeing only a small portion of the visual field, but capturing it in isolated detail.

Efforts to assign meaning to information on a page do not happen all at once. Instead, the respondent processes information through multiple steps, with graphical features of the information being viewed influencing what happens at each of these steps. Thus, at this juncture, we shift our perspective from how the mind drives the perceptual process, to how visual elements expressed on the page are picked up and interpreted by the viewer in order to determine what the question is and how to answer it.

The Three Stages of Visual Processing: Elemental Organization, Pattern Recognition, and Task Orientation

The ways in which people perceive and attend to the page in front of them when taking a survey are determined by innate tendencies of human visual processing. Visual processing of a survey involves three basic stages: (1) *elemental scene organization*, (2) *pattern recognition*, and (3) *task-oriented processing*, (Ware, 2004). First, during elemental organization, the scene is almost instantaneously organized into basic visual elements. Next, during pattern recognition, the basic visual elements are organized into patterns that are better understood. Finally, during task-oriented processing, the details of the page not previously noticeable are focused on and tasks on the page are given conscious attention.

Upon immediately glancing at a page, or any visual scene, people's eyes and brains work together to gain an extremely quick and basic understanding of the page, a process called *elemental organization.* First our eyes preattentively organize the entire scene into basic regions according to shared fundamental visual properties, such as luminance, color, texture, and so on, a step called *region segmentation.*

Once divided into basic regions, the contours of those basic visual elements are used to determine the figure/ground organization, a task that determines which elements are perceived as objects and which are perceived as background. Those that are perceived as objects are the basic visual elements used in further visual processing. In this paragraph, for example, objects are the black letters that stand out against the white background of the page.

Certain visual properties that are relied on in elemental organization are preattentively recognized, and differences between elements in terms of those qualities are often most quickly recognized. The subconscious recognition of certain fundamental visual properties and differences between them is demonstrated in Figure A.6. Note how one element in each box is different and stands out, each for a different reason, such as number of items in a subgrouping or shape.

Once the page is organized into basic elements, mid-level processing called *pattern recognition* occurs, where those figures are grouped together to be better understood and to speed up processing. Visual elements that share basic visual qualities, such as shape, size, orientation, and others are perceived as "going together" because the elements are organized into simple patterns. Often, the pattern recognition that occurs is predicted by Gestalt grouping principles (illustrated in Figure A.7). This is an in-between stage, accomplished through both attentive and preattentive processing, although it is more so the result of preattentive processing. The viewer tends to divide the elements on pages into groups based on the visual features of those elements. Imagine a line of eight circles that you wish to divide into visual groupings. It could be done in each of these ways, using Gestalt principles of psychology (Figure A.7):

- *Proximity:* Placing objects closer together will cause them to be seen as a group
- *Similarity:* Objects that are the same color, shape, size, or otherwise the same will be seen as a group

Figure A.7 Examples of Gestalt grouping principles at work.

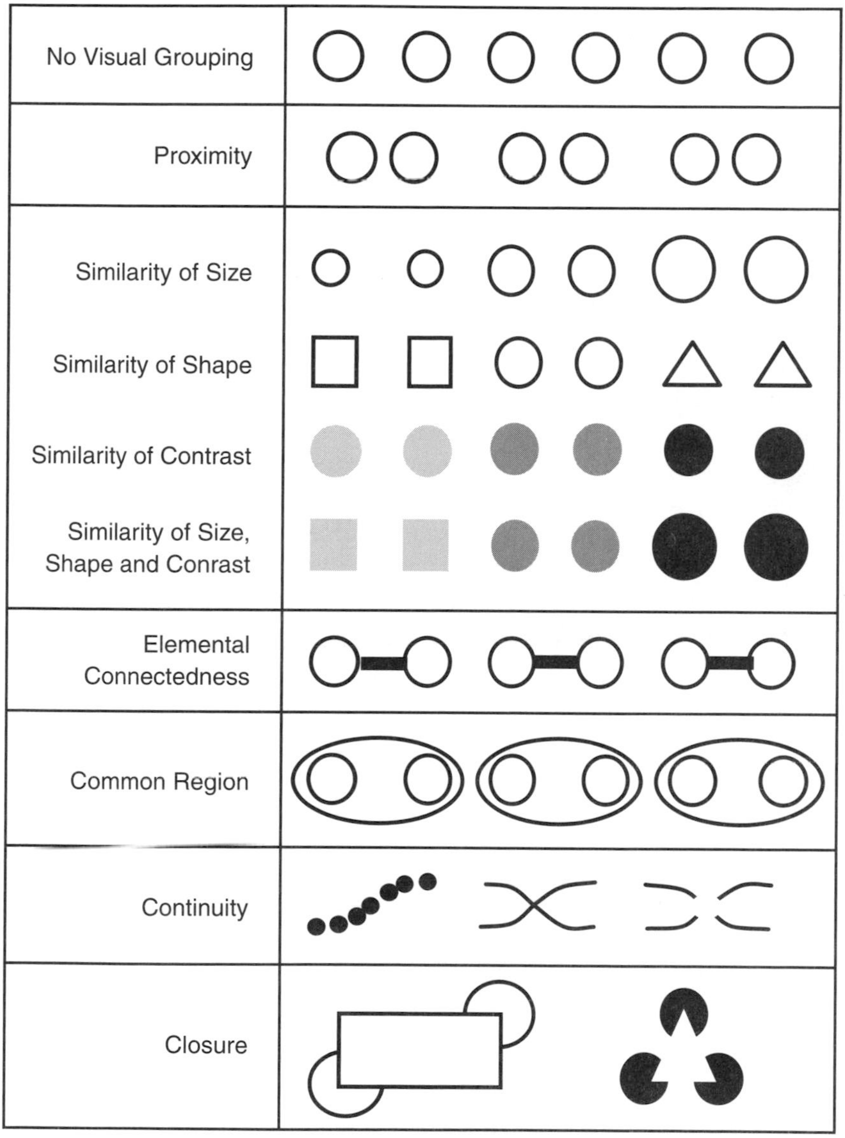

- *Elemental connectedness:* Elements connected by other elements tend to be viewed together
- *Continuity or good continuation:* Elements that continue smoothly across a field will be seen as grouped together
- *Common region:* Elements within the same closed region of space will be viewed together

- *Closure:* Elements forming a "closed" figure will appear grouped together
- *Pragnanz:* Elements that are simpler and the same shape are easier to perceive and remember

These graphical elements can also be layered on top of one another to create stronger more memorable stimuli. For example, in Figure A.7 the use of multiple similarities (shape plus size plus contrast) provides stronger distinctions among the groupings than could be achieved by using only one of these elements. Thus, the survey designer can send messages that are strong or ambiguous depending on whether these mid-level aspects of processing are developed consistently or inconsistently.

Task-oriented processing is now set to occur. When the basic visual elements in the field of vision are perceived as aligned in a meaningful way, the respondent can then focus attentively and use top-down processing to get on with the response task. When in this task-oriented phase, the useful field of view tends to constrict, and the expectations about what to do and not to do that respondents bring with them to the task become particularly important.

For many people, the three stages—determining elemental organization, detecting patterns, and taking action—occur quite quickly. This is particularly true for questionnaires or ballots asking questions that can be anticipated and thought about by respondents prior to their receiving them. On the contrary, if the task is an unfamiliar one, going through these stages is likely to take longer because of more uncertainty about what should or should not be done. Finally, at each stage it is important to keep in mind that the respondent is simultaneously drawing information not just from words, but from all four visual languages:

- *Verbal language:* The words used to communicate questions and directions
- *Numerical language:* The numbers used to convey meaning in questionnaires
- *Symbolic language:* Figures and shapes, which are neither words nor numbers that convey meaning, for example, arrows
- *Graphical language:* Elemental visual features such as size, shape, location, spatial arrangement, color, brightness, contrast, and figure/ground composition

THE BUTTERFLY BALLOT REANALYZED

Armed with knowledge of these processes and concepts it is useful to revisit the Butterfly ballot and attempt to explain the reasons that so many people voted for Buchanan instead of Gore as intended, and why so many partial punches and double punches occurred.

Most people who entered the voting booth in Palm Beach County already knew for whom they were going to vote for president. They were also familiar with the general process of voting for candidates for office; they knew ahead of time that there would be offices listed followed by the choices. Thus, cultural considerations encouraged them to utilize top-down processing to look for their particular candidate, rather than to review the entire list of candidates in order to make their selection. Cultural experience, which is the base from which top-down processing proceeds, also led them to start their search for their desired candidate in the upper left corner of the first of the two facing pages. When reading a book or any other page of information, visual processing typically starts there (Jenkins and Dillman, 1997). The same general broad cultural experience has also taught them from previous ballots and questionnaires to expect answer choices relevant to the presidential choice to be grouped together on one page, rather than appearing on two pages in different groupings. They also expected that each set of ballot choices for a particular office would have its own column of answer spaces to mark, that is, appear as separately grouped with the candidates to which they were linked for use.

In the first stage of visual processing, when the respondent is trying to determine the elemental organization of the ballot question, the lines (edges) around the information on the left-hand page define that as the region to be examined more closely. In the second stage of pattern recognition, the voter sees that region of interest is divided into similar subregions each of which contains a set of candidates. Once the pattern has been discerned, the useful field of view gets smaller, and for all practical purposes the second page of choices does not exist.

As the voter proceeds to the third stage of processing, task orientation, additional factors come into play. The voter who knows ahead of time for whom she wishes to vote has no need to read all of the choices. The culturally dominant way of finding something in a list is to start at the top and go down the list until the needed information (candidate name) is found. When the field of vision narrows to the candidate of choice, top-down processing based on previous election or questionnaire experiences suggests to the respondent that she must find a place to mark her ballot, and that it will be located close to the candidate's name. At this point, the Gestalt Law of Proximity encourages her to view the word "DEMOCRATIC" and the line immediately above it as a visual grouping, which then leads her across the page directly to the second punch hole (see Figure A.4). Inasmuch as the punch pins provided for voting are unfamiliar to voters, it should not be surprising that the useful field of view grows even smaller, and people's answers get marked without their seeing the arrow pointing to the third hole that is marked with the number "5," which itself has little meaning because it's the third hole in the line of choices.

The rapid implementation of this three stage process of using visual clues to segment the visual field into that which needs to be examined more closely, followed by identifying the pattern of candidate presentation, and then commencing with the task of voting while being guided by graphical features within the useful field of view, returns us to our initial observation. It is unlikely that some or even most respondents even looked at the second page of candidates until they had finished marking their choice on the left-hand page, and were ready to move on to the next ballot issue. At that time some voters probably hesitated, saw their error and tried to correct it. The partial marks and the much larger number of double marks may be explained by people who realized that they may have made a mistake, trying to do what culture encourages them to do, that is, correct their mistake. Although, voters could have asked for a new ballot, it is socially difficult for someone to raise his hand and say to the monitors as well as other voters within earshot that he had made a mistake and needs a new ballot. In sum, many factors worked together to produce unintended votes for Buchanan and the attempts by voters to correct those errors.

Similar to their historical absence in questionnaire design, visual design concepts have not been used consciously and deliberately in ballot design, which remains in U.S. culture primarily a local decision because ballots have to be tailored to elections occurring in local precincts as well as national and state elections. The Butterfly ballot experience in Palm Beach County has encouraged researchers to undertake other visual analyses of ballots. One such analysis found evidence that poor visual designs have led to errors being made in elections throughout the United States (Kimball and Kroph, 2005). Thus, each ballot, like each questionnaire, presents unique design challenges that visual design concepts can help us understand.

However, to understand the utility of these concepts for constructing web surveys as well as mail questionnaires, which are also visual in nature, it is important that empirical research establish what elements of visual design do and do not make a difference in how people comprehend and respond to questionnaires. That is the topic to which we now turn.

USING VISUAL DESIGN PRINCIPLES TO CONTROL THE NAVIGATIONAL PATH

The visual design emphasis in Chapter 3 of this book was focused almost exclusively on mid-level processing, and the use of graphical manipulations to define a navigational path through the questionnaire with the aim of getting respondents to process information in the same ways (pp. 94–135). Gestalt psychology principles were used, but I did not distinguish among all four languages through which information is conveyed. In addition, the research to validate the theoretical arguments offered had not yet been undertaken. Considerable research has now been done, and the results make it clear that visual layout does have significant effects on what people read and do when answering survey questions. Examples of these research findings are reported here. Some of this research focuses on paper surveys and some on web surveys. Taken altogether, it shows that visual layout and design make a big difference in how survey questions are understood and answered.

SYMBOLS THAT MAKE A DIFFERENCE

A paper questionnaire experiment tested the effect of placing a symbol (arrow) between an answer that was to be marked, and an open-ended question that was to be answered only if a particular category was marked (Christian and Dillman, 2004). Use of this arrow was aimed at closing the foveal view gap between the verbal description of a response category and the "extra" question that checking that category made respondents eligible to answer. This symbol would be attentively processed as having meaning without the addition of words (Figure A.8). Its use decreased the proportion of respondents who marked the second answer but left the follow-up open-ended question blank by half, from 8 percent to 4 percent (Christian and Dillman, 2004). This experiment confirms the importance of symbols used in this way during task-oriented processing.

Figure A.8 Example of two-part question with and without symbolic arrow within foveal view and resultant effects on the rate of improper navigation (Christian and Dillman, 2004).

		Reported Secondary Responses of Eligible	Missing Secondary Responses Of Eligible
Without Symbolic Navigation Arrow	**6. After finishing school at Washington State University, where do you hope to live?** ☐ **Eastern Washington** ☐ **Somewhere else** **Where?_______**	90.8%	8.8%
With Symbolic Navigation Arrow	**6. After finishing school at Washington State University, where do you hope to live?** ☐ **Eastern Washington** ☐ **Somewhere else** ⟶ **Where?_______**	93.9%	4.2%
		Statistically significant difference, p=.03	

COMBINING SYMBOLS, GRAPHICS, AND WORDS FOR EFFECTIVE BRANCHING INSTRUCTIONS

Recent research has also shown that the deliberate coordination of symbols, graphics, and words can have a large effect on task-oriented processing as respondents navigate their way through a questionnaire. Getting some people to skip questions they are not supposed to answer while at the same time convincing other respondents not to skip ahead remains one of the most perplexing of problems facing users of mail surveys. Two experiments—the first, a classroom experiment with 1,267 respondents and the second, a field test of about 12,500 households in the 2000 U.S. Decennial Census, have now been conducted on how to achieve this goal (Dillman and Redline, 2002). The first experiment involved a specially constructed questionnaire that was four pages long and included 52 questions, 24 of which contained branching instructions asking respondents to answer different follow-up questions, depending on which answer category was initially chosen (Redline, Dillman, Carley-Baxter, and Creecy, 2005). The second experiment was imbedded in the Census Long Form that included 53 questions, 19 of which included branching instructions (Redline, Dillman, Dajani, and Scaggs, 2003). The first study served as a pilot for the second study so that certain improvements were made before the larger national study of the general public was implemented.

In both studies, a combination of factors designed to get people to follow branching instructions correctly were tested. One procedure, the *detection method,* involved using the arrow symbol in a large, dark font to direct people from their answer to either the next question or to an appropriate instruction, which was written in a larger, darker font than the questions. Words were used at the beginning of the next question to remind respondents who should and who should not answer it. A second procedure, the *prevention method* switched answer boxes from the left of the answer categories to the right so that skip instructions could be located within a person's foveal view when focusing on the answer box. These instructions were written in larger, darker print and placed against a darker background. The control instructions were written in the same font as the questions (see Figure A.9).

In the national census experiment, the detection method reduced the proportion of branching errors significantly, lowering commission errors (i.e., not skipping ahead when directed to do so) from 21 percent to 13 percent and omission errors (i.e., skipping ahead when not directed to do so) from 5 percent to 4 percent. The total error rates (commission and omission error rates combined) were lower for both the detection and prevention groups compared to the control group, which made an error nearly 26 percent of the time (Figure A.9). We concluded from these experiments that both of these meth-

Figure A.9 Examples of different branching instruction designs used in a census test and the total error rates of each during classroom experiments and a large national test in the U.S. Decennial Census (Redline and Dillman, 2005).

		Total Classroom Error Rate	Total Census Error Rate
Control Form: Standard Format Used in Decennial Census with Written Instructions	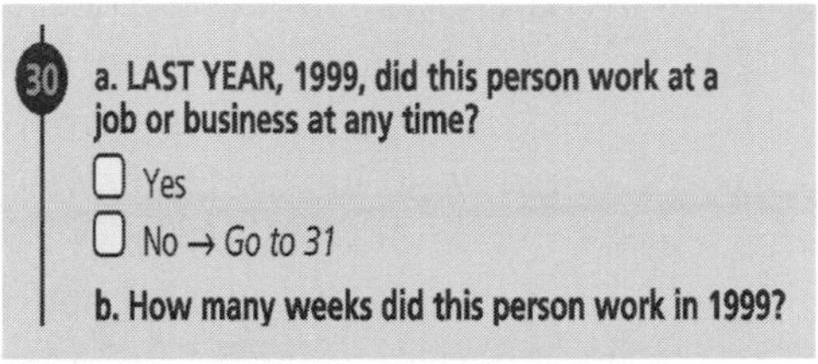 30 a. LAST YEAR, 1999, did this person work at a job or business at any time? ☐ Yes ☐ No → *Go to 31* b. How many weeks did this person work in 1999?	22.3%	25.8%
Prevention Method: Advanced Verbal Warning, Shift Answer Box to Right, and Larger, Bolder Font	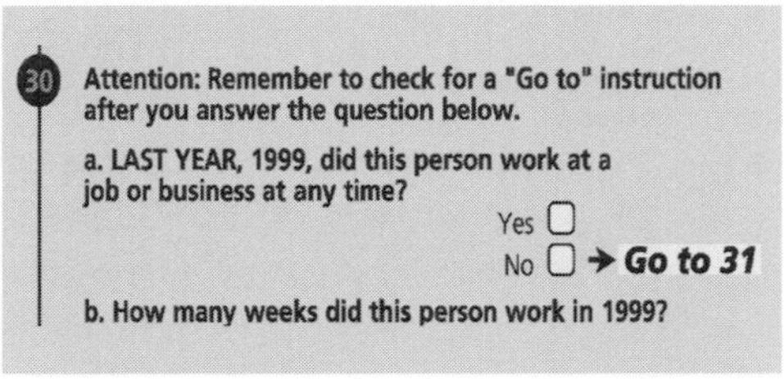 30 Attention: Remember to check for a "Go to" instruction after you answer the question below. a. LAST YEAR, 1999, did this person work at a job or business at any time? Yes ☐ No ☐ → ***Go to 31*** b. How many weeks did this person work in 1999?	11.3%	17.5%
Detection Method: Arrows, Larger and Bolder Fonts, and Verbal Feedback	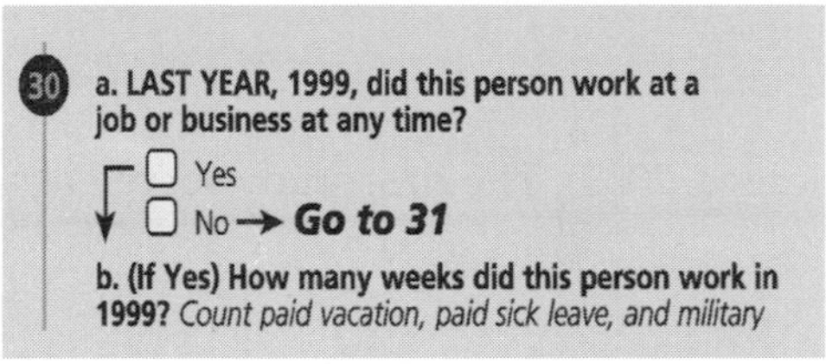 30 a. LAST YEAR, 1999, did this person work at a job or business at any time? ☐ Yes ☐ No → ***Go to 31*** b. (If Yes) How many weeks did this person work in 1999? *Count paid vacation, paid sick leave, and military*	12.3%	21.7%

Notes: Total error rates are shown here, including commission errors (not skipping ahead when directed) and omission errors (skipping ahead when not directed). Advanced verbal warning was used only in the classroom experiment.

Statistically significant difference in total error rates between the control form and each of the others, with $p \leq .01$ for both experiments.

ods offer much promise for keeping people on the prescribed navigational paths. They also provide evidence of the substantial effects that the combined use of symbols, graphics, and appropriate wording of directions can have on task-oriented processing.

PLACING AN IMPORTANT DIRECTION AFTER ITS INTENDED USE

I once reviewed a web survey that used page-by-page construction that consistently placed all of the directions to be used for answering each question below the question itself. Although it seemed unlikely people would read those instructions before answering the question above it, it seemed useful

Figure A.10 Experimental variations in the location of skip instructions and the response rates associated with each question format (Dillman and Christian, 2004).

		% Answered 'No'	% Left Blank
Skip Instructions Below/After Response Options	8. Have one-on-one meetings with professors contributed significantly to your WSU education? ☐ Yes ☐ No If you haven't had many one-on-one meetings, just skip to Question 9.	40%	5%
Skip Instructions Above/Before Response Options	8. Have one-on-one meetings with professors contributed significantly to your WSU education? If you haven't had many one-on-one meetings, just skip to Question 9. ☐ Yes ☐ No	19%	26%

$p \leq .01$

to test the effect of its location in task-oriented processing. We included the test in a mail experiment, in which we asked a question that only some people seemed likely to be able to answer, followed by a direction that they should simply skip to "Question 9," the next question on the page, if the item did not apply to them (see Figure A.10).

The results of this experiment were not surprising. When the direction to skip if the question did not apply to them appeared above the question the proportion of respondents who did not answer it increased from 4 percent to 26 percent (Christian and Dillman, 2004). However, of even greater significance was the fact that when the direction to "skip to Question 9" appeared below the answer space and just ahead of Question 9, 10 percent (compared to only 2 percent for the other form) skipped over Question 9 and went directly to Question 10 instead. Thus, the graphical location of the instruction, already out of place from the standpoint of the expected navigational path and the location inconsistency between wording (skip to) and the listed number, had an additional negative effect on how respondents followed the prescribed navigational path. This experiment provides additional evidence that when responding to questionnaires respondents do not typically read ahead when engaged in task-oriented processing, but instead follow the culturally prescribed way of reading from top to bottom.

NUMBERING QUESTIONS MAKES A DIFFERENCE

While the question number in the poorly located instruction tended to be overlooked in this experiment, other situations exist in which numbering leads to the making of significant errors. The desire to keep the numbering of a sequence of 12 questions the same across all survey situations produced a problem when those 12 items appeared after an initial item that respondents were expected to answer. Attempts to deal with the problem led to that initial item sometimes not being numbered, sometimes being labeled as "0," and in other instances being labeled as a step 1 item while the next 12 items were labeled as step 2. These formats were associated with there being a much higher item nonresponse for the first item—as much as 25 percent—while the follow-up items had only a 1 percent to 2 percent item nonresponse rate (Dillman, Caldwell, and Gansemer, 2000). It appeared that people think of unnumbered items at the beginning as being practice items, or otherwise unimportant to the survey (Dillman and Redline, 2004).

Navigation is one of the visual design aspects in which web and paper tend to diverge because of technology. In web surveys, there are two commonly used ways for handling branching. For surveys that scroll, hotlinks may be inserted, which when clicked take the respondent to the next appropriate question. When page-by-page construction is used, respondents are automatically directed to the appropriate next question, so that branching instructions do not need to be provided at all.

Consequently, web survey questions are often left unnumbered. In particular, web survey designers often prefer to leave numbers off when there are a substantial number of skip directions, fearing that not having all numbers appear in sequence because of skips will become confusing. This preference sometimes leads to substituting culturally unexpected symbols, for example, a large question mark or asterisk, where a question number signifying the starting point for reading a question would normally be located. Because numerical language is particularly useful to survey respondents during task-oriented processing the absence of these culturally expected guides may place an extra burden on respondents for figuring out the meaning and use of these unnatural symbols. Another potential downside of leaving question numbers off of web surveys is loss of their value as a progress indicator in some surveys, for example, 1 of 30, 2 of 30, and so on to 30 of 30. Yet another problem may occur when a respondent wants to ask for help, but cannot identify a question by its number in order to make communication easier. In addition, respondents to some questionnaires, particularly those used in business surveys, may work from a paper copy or simply want to print out the Web survey to assist in preparing answers to the survey questions (Redline, 2005; Dowling, 2005). The lack of numbers makes that difficult. Although the role of numbers in web surveys differs somewhat from paper surveys, the fact that numbers are so deeply imbedded in our culture as a way to navigate means their potential use in web surveys should not be ignored.

USING VISUAL DESIGN TO CONSTRUCT SCALAR QUESTIONS

A rapidly expanding body of literature now shows that visual design has effects on the question answering process that go far beyond influencing initial perceptions of what parts of the questionnaire page are relevant and the navigational process through the questionnaire. Visual design continues to have significant effects on respondents as they mentally work their way through all four of the remaining steps, described earlier, of answering questions: comprehension, retrieval from memory, deciding on an answer, and reporting. The effects of visual design are particularly apparent for scalar questions in which respondents are attempting to express their degree of agreement, satisfaction or perhaps favorableness to an idea, using an ordinal scale that attempts to capture both the direction and intensity of feeling.

Linear versus Nonlinear Layout of Scales

A series of experiments on paper (Christian and Dillman, 2004) as well as web surveys (Christian, 2003; Dillman and Christian, 2005) has shown that when a five-point, fully labeled scale is constructed in a straight line, as opposed to multiple lines or columns, as shown in Figure A.11, respondents are more likely to choose the "good" instead of the "very good" category. This may occur because some people tend to process horizontally, perhaps answering prior to even reading the second line of answers.

Figure A.11 Example of linear and nonlinear scalar answer formats and the differences between them in response distribution and mean (Christian, Parsons, and Dillman, 2005).

Linear, Vertical Answer Options

Q5. Overall, how would you rate the quality of education that you are getting at WSU?
Excellent
Very Good
Good
Fair
Poor
Next Question

Non-Linear Answer Options

Q5. Overall, how would you rate the quality of education that you are getting at WSU?
Excellent
Very Good
Good
Fair
Poor
Next Question

	% Selecting 'Good'	Mean Scalar Score
Linear, Vertical Answer Options	30.5%	2.34
Non-Linear Answer Options	35.4%	2.45
	p≤ .01	p≤ .05

Opinion questions, in essence, ask people where they fit on an implied scale, which through top-down expectations during task-oriented processing is likely visualized as linear in nature. Thus, it seems most appropriate to represent it that way to respondents. Most important though, these experiments show that scalar layout makes a difference and does so in both mail and web surveys.

Scales Derive Meaning from Words, Numbers, and/or Graphics

Respondents can be asked to express opinions on scales that are presented using quite different combinations of words, numbers, and graphics, for example, fully labeled scales or polar-point labeled scales, each of which can be asked with or without numbers. Scales can also be asked without any graphical layout whatsoever; the stem of the question provides the scale and a box is provided in which to insert the number (or word) chosen for the answer (example 3 of Figure A.12). It might seem that it makes little difference which way people are asked to express opinions on such a scale, but as the results from the three scale formats shown in Figure A.12 indicate, that is not the case (Dillman and Christian, 2005).

The answers for these three questions are anything but similar with the means ranging from 1.7 for the fully labeled to 2.6 for the number box

Figure A.12 Example of different scalar response format options used in web survey comparisons and the resultant differences in response distribution and mean between them (Christian, Parsons, and Dillman, 2005).

		Mean Scalar Score	% Endorsing High Endpoint
Fully Labeled Scale	**Q3. How do you consider Washington State University as a place to go to school?** ○ 1 Very Desirable ○ 2 Somewhat Desirable ○ 3 Neither Desirable nor Undesirable ○ 4 Somewhat Undesirable ○ 5 Very Undesirable	1.7	42.8%
Polar Point Labels	**Q3. How do you consider Washington State University as a place to go to school?** ○ 1 Very Desirable ○ 2 ○ 3 ○ 4 ○ 5 Very Undesirable	2.2	26.5%
Number Box	**Q3. On a scale of 1 to 5, with 1 being very desirable and 5 being very undesirable, how do you consider Washington State University as a place to go to school?** ☐ Number of your rating	2.6	19.1%

All differences are statistically significant at p≤ .01

format. There is also wide variation among the formats in the percent of respondents choosing the most positive category; 43 percent of respondents to the fully labeled scale chose "very desirable" while less than half that number, 19 percent, did so for the number box format. It is quite apparent from these findings, which have been replicated across many other questions (Dillman and Christian, 2005; Christian, Dillman, and Parsons, 2005), that whether the category choices are represented primarily by words or by numbers as well as how the scale is presented graphically has a strong effect on answers.

Additional research has indicated that how numbers are assigned to scale points can also influence answers. Similar differences to those just summarized for the number box format were observed on paper questionnaires (Christian and Dillman, 2004), but examining erasures showed that respondents may have become confused on which numbers were associated with the positive end of the scale and which were associated with the negative end. The erasure patterns showed that many respondents scratched out one number and marked it's opposite, that is, replacing a 2 with a 4 or a 1 with a 5 or vice versa. This finding is consistent with research that has shown that respondents apply certain visual heuristics in interpreting questions and applying meaning to answer choices (Tourangeau, Couper, and Conrad, 2004). The interpretive heuristic that is relevant here is the expectation that "up is good." According to this heuristic, respondents expect more positive categories in a list to appear at the top of the list, an expectation that is rooted in culture and reflected in a number of often used metaphors (i.e., happiness is "being up" and sadness is "being down") (p. 372). A logical extension of this heuristic is that respondents might expect higher numbers to be associated with more positive answer categories, an expectation that is also rooted in culture (e.g., getting a 100 percent is much better than getting a 50 percent on an exam).

Two number box format experiments testing the effects of attaching 1 to the most positive and 5 to the least positive category versus attaching 5 to the most positive category and 1 to the least positive showed that respondents gave significantly more positive ratings when 5 meant "very satisfied" than when 1 did. This change reduced the difference between the number box scores and the polar-point scores (Christian, Dillman, and Smyth, in press). In the same tests, we also found that respondents required more time to formulate and provide answers to the number box versions (i.e., without the scalar display of the polar-point scales), presumably because they had to make mental connections between the prose in the question stem and the number box answer space (i.e., the possible answers they could give were not located at the space where they had to record them so they had to complete the extra task of transferring information from the question stem to the answer box).

We have also conducted three experimental comparisons on the polar-point format in which 5 was assigned to the most positive end of the scale in some panels and in other panels to the most negative end. None of the three tests produced significantly different responses. In this case, the graphical display of the scales seems to have helped respondents avoid confusion about which is the positive and which is the negative end of the scale (Christian, Dillman, and Smyth, in press).

These results have a twofold implication. First, it is important to understand and take into consideration the expectations that respondents bring with them to the survey task and employ through top-down processing, in this case, the culturally based heuristic that "up is good." Designing surveys that fly in the face of such a priori expectations increases the likelihood of respondent errors. Second, the task of responding to scalar questions is more difficult and prone to error when graphics that convey the imagery of the scale are taken out of the visual display. The number box, which required respondents to go back and forth between the stem of the question and the box where the appropriate answer was to be displayed illustrates the downside of eliminating this visual imagery.

Displaying Scales from Positive to Negative, Negative to Positive

The same heuristic, "up means good," in combination with another, "left and top mean first" (Tourangeau, Couper, and Conrad, 2004) suggests that respondents expect scales to be displayed from most positive at the top (if vertical) or left (if horizontal) to most negative at the bottom, or to the right. Again, we found no differences in our web experiments when we compared responses from vertically oriented scales with the most positive category listed first versus the most negative category listed first (Christian, Dillman, and Smyth, in press). In contrast, other recent experimental research that tested category order in both vertical and horizontal scales found substantial differences (Israel, 2005).

It is possible though, that a significant difference in the design of these two experiments may account for their contrary results. The question that Israel (2005) examined followed four other satisfaction questions that were all arranged with the most positive category first. Therefore, respondents to the versions with the response options presented in the opposite order on the question under consideration here may not have expected the change. In the Christian, Dillman, and Smyth (2005) experiments, all scalar items within each panel ran in consistent directions. In other words, all the scalar questions in one panel ran from positive to negative while all the questions in another ran from negative to positive. This internal consistency may have, in effect, temporarily taught respondents a new expectation thus negating the effect of the heuristic proposed by Tourangeau, Couper, and Conrad (2004), which then became a guide for top-down processing used throughout the remainder of the questionnaire.

MANAGING MIDDLE EFFECTS WITH VISUAL DESIGN

A third heuristic proposed by Tourangeau, Couper, and Conrad (2004) is that "middle means typical." This heuristic builds on an idea proposed by Schwarz and Hippler (1987) that respondents see the middle option as representing the average or typical value for the population. To test this heuristic, Tourangeau, Couper, and Conrad conducted three experiments comparing scalar formats where the conceptual midpoint of the scale (i.e., the actual substantive midpoint) was located at the visual midpoint to versions where it was shifted away from the visual midpoint. For example, in two of the experiments by separating (with lines or spacing) or not separating nonsubstantive answers such as "don't know" and "no opinion" from substantive answers they were able to manipulate how long the scale visually appeared to be, thus shifting the visual midpoint of the scale away from its actual conceptual midpoint. In the third experiment they used more space between the scale points on the right side of a horizontally aligned scale to shift the conceptual midpoint to the left of its visual midpoint. Those studies showed that respondents give answers more toward the visual center of the scales, suggesting that the graphical arrangement of scale points significantly influences responses.

We conducted a separate set of experiments in which distances between scale categories were shifted by placing either the center or the end categories farther apart from the remaining categories. However, in our experiments there was no disjuncture between the conceptual and visual midpoints of the scales and they produced no differences in responses across treatment groups (Christian, Parsons, and Dillman, 2005).

SUMMARY OF VISUAL EFFECTS IN SCALES

The conclusion we draw from these papers and others is that scales are very sensitive to the effects of words, graphics, and numbers. Not only do we now know that different scalar formats tend to produce different results across visual and aural modes, but within visual modes, different layouts may produce different answers. Obtaining equivalency across survey modes thus requires us to consider not only the challenges associated with switching modes, but that of deciding which of many possible formats is going to be used within the visual mode itself. We expect that research in this area will continue over the next several years. Our ability to combine results across modes may depend on it.

AVOIDING UNDESIRABLE GROUPING EFFECTS

An important aspect of the Chapter 4 discussion (pp. 105–113) about how to create visual navigation guides was visual grouping. Three of the six elements discussed in that section of the book concerned ways of achieving effective grouping by invoking the Gestalt Laws of Proximity and Similarity. Using these principles grouping can be accomplished in many different ways, for example, manipulation of spacing, color, orientation, and other elements described in Figure A.7.

A recent example of an unintended grouping effect was observed in cognitive tests of the National Survey of Earned Doctorates, a survey conducted annually by the National Science Foundation (Altheimer and Dillman, 2001). In that survey, one question asks, "What best describes your immediate (within the next year) postgraduate plans?" A list of seven answer choices was divided into two subgroups through the use of the headings: "Further training or Study" and "Career Employment." The use of these headings also resulted in increased spacing between the two subgroups of items (Figure A.13, middle example). In the cognitive testing some respondents attempted to select a response from each of the two subgroups, but their selection in the second subgroup erased their selection in the first because the question was programmed to accept only one response.

Based on these observations, a test of possible grouping effects was conducted using the same grouping elements (i.e., headings and spacing) but different questions in a different survey population (Smyth, Dillman, Christian, and Stern, 2006b). This test showed that subgrouping answer choices encouraged respondents to choose significantly more answers overall and increased the proportion of respondents choosing an answer from each subgroup. Although adding a verbal instruction to, "Please select the best answer," decreased the number of items checked, the tendency to choose one response from each group remained about the same. The message sent by the visual grouping appeared to change the meaning of the added instruction from "please select the best answer" to "please select the best answer *from each group.*" Additional findings indicated that arranging the two subgroups in columns located side-by-side had similar effects as arranging them vertically.

The original grouping of the response options in the NSF paper survey had been done many years earlier as a way of helping respondents better understand the question. This grouping was then carried over into the test web version of the survey where the practice of using radio buttons to require only one answer created confusion among respondents and began to illuminate how the subgrouping of the response options was influencing answers (Altheimer and Dillman, 2001). Thus, this case provides a good example of how design decisions intended to help respondents may have un-

Figure A.13 Example of different visual grouping of response options used in web survey comparisons and the resultant differences in response distribution and mean between them (Smyth, Dillman, Christian, and Stern, 2006).

		% Marking Both Halves	Mean Number Options Selected
No Visual Grouping of Response Options	**Q18. What best describes the benefit of the Student Recreation Center?** □The variety of physical fitness offerings □The health and wellness offerings □Helps reduce stress □Improves academic productivity □Enhances learning experience □Provides information for students to learn about their health □Don't Know	40.9%	2.7
Vertical Grouping of Response Options	**Q18. What best describes the benefit of the Student Recreation Center?** Health Benefits □The variety of physical fitness offerings □The health and wellness offerings □Helps reduce stress Academic Benefits □Improves academic productivity □Enhances learning experience □Provides information for students to learn about their health □Don't Know	70.2%	3.0
Vertical Grouping with Instruction to Mark Only One	**Q18. What best describes the benefit of the Student Recreation Center? Please select the best answer.** Health Benefits □The variety of physical fitness offerings □The health and wellness offerings □Helps reduce stress Academic Benefits □Improves academic productivity □Enhances learning experience □Provides information for students to learn about their health □Don't Know	66.0%	2.4

Differences between No Visual Grouping and each of the others statistically significant at $p \leq .01$

foreseen and undesirable outcomes if the effects of visual elements are not considered.

USING MULTIPLE VISUAL TECHNIQUES TO DIRECT RESPONDENTS

One of the enticing features of web survey design is the ability to require respondents to provide answers in a particular format. Should the respondent fail to do that, an error message can be provided that asks for the answer to be reentered in the required format. A potential downside of sending such error messages is that respondents get frustrated and quit responding. Thus, it is important to provide instructions that help respondents record their answers correctly the first time they enter them.

The same NSF Earned Doctorate web survey just described provides the background for an example of how visual design can be used to help respondents get it right the first time. A question in the survey requested the date one's degree was granted. Respondents were provided with two equal size boxes followed by the notation MM/YYYY to indicate that they should enter two digits for the month and four for the year. In the cognitive interviews, some respondents did not enter the date in the requested format and, as a consequence, received the dreaded error message (Altheimer and Dillman, 2001).

These observations led to a succession of experiments in which the aim was to find a means of improving respondent performance in providing information in a desired format in web surveys (Christian, Dillman, and Smyth, 2005). Several features of visual layout were systematically manipulated in these experiments including: the use of the words "month" and "year" versus the symbols MM and YYYY, the relative size of the answer boxes, whether the answer boxes were connected to each other or separate, and the location of the symbols MM and YYYY in relation to the answer boxes. The percent of respondents who reported answers in the desired format was around 45 percent when the words "month" and "year" were assigned to separate boxes. This was not surprising because there are many commonly accepted ways to record dates. These include a number of combinations of reporting the month in either characters (Aug or August) or varying numbers of digits (08 or 8) and the year in either two or four digits.

The lack of connection between the boxes appears to encourage (through the principle of connectivity, noted by Ware (2004) as an additional aspect of the Law of Proximity) the respondent to independently interpret the meaning/expectations of the different answer spaces. Connecting the boxes increases use of the desired format by about 10 percentage points, and it is increased another 8 percentage points to 63 percent by decreasing the size of the month box relative to the year box to indicate that fewer digits should be used to report the month than the year. A dramatic improvement to 87 percent occurs when the symbols MM/YYYY, with embedded numeracy (thus combining two visual languages) replaces the use of "month" and "year." But, the best performance of all, 96 percent, as shown in Figure A.14, occurs when the MM was placed in front of a small month box followed by the YYYY which is placed in front of a larger year box, thus locating needed instructions in natural reading order (Christian, Dillman, and Smyth, 2005).

Another feature of this experiment was to vary the wording of the question stem, asking a vague, "When did you begin your studies at Washington State University?" compared to a more specific version, "What month and year did you begin your studies at Washington State University?" No difference occurred in the information reported in the answer spaces when this question changing occurred in the Web survey, but in a

Figure A.14 Various month/year answer space layouts and the percentage of respondents reporting in the desired (mm/yyyy) format in web survey comparisons (Christian, Dillman, and Smyth, 2005).

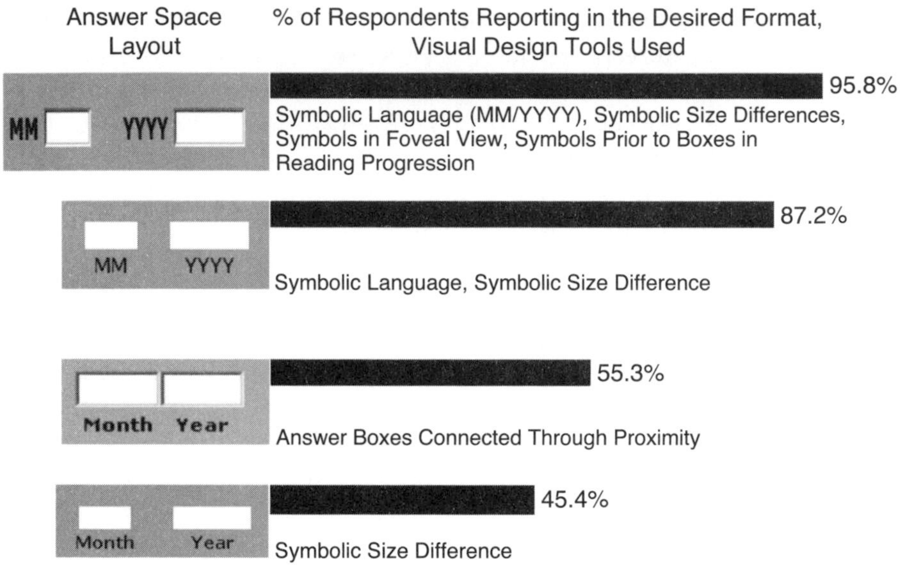

telephone comparison of these two question wordings, dramatic differences occurred in the percent of respondents who reported month and year to the interviewer.

This experiment draws together many aspects of what visual design is about and why it has become such a challenging issue for survey methodologists as they seek to bridge the aural and visual worlds of surveying. First, obtaining responses in a desired format is critical to the success of web surveys; respondents need to be able to get it right the first time in order to avoid error messages. Second, the communication necessary for achieving that occurs as much or more in the visual display of answer categories as in the wording of the questions. Third, multiple visual elements may need to be manipulated simultaneously to achieve the desired results (e.g., size of answer spaces, use of symbols versus words, numeracy connected to symbols, connectedness versus separateness of answer spaces). And finally, achieving these manipulations effectively requires an understanding of principles of Gestalt psychology. Whereas in telephone interviews we can depend on the interviewer to be an expert system and automatically translate answers like, "August, of last year" into a precise answer, "08 2004," in web surveys we do not have that luxury (Christian, Dillman, and Smyth, 2005). Effective utilization of visual design principles is essential.

AFFECTING OPEN-ENDED QUESTIONS WITH SPACE

Open-ended questions have always provided special challenges to users of self-administered surveys. When used in mail surveys, answers seemed short and incomplete, especially compared to those obtained through interview methods.

Little has been learned over the years about whether special techniques might be used to improve the quality of open-ended answers, although a few studies do exist. Recent experimentation with varying the size of open-ended answer spaces in paper questionnaires has shown clearly that increasing their size increases both the number of words and themes that respondents record (Christian and Dillman, 2004). A recent study by Israel (2005) confirmed these results, but also revealed that there is a linear effect to such increases; he compares results from four different sizes of boxes and finds that each increase in size shows a modest but significant increase in the number of words recorded. These findings are of particular importance because, in mail surveys, the tendency of many designers to want to have as few pages as possible has led to designing quite small spaces for open-ended questions, a practice that may be undermining complete responses.

Initial evidence from web survey tests, where the standard practice of many is to provide small spaces but to allow people to write as many words as they like, suggests that size of answer spaces has less influence on answers (Smyth, Dillman, Christian, and McBride, 2006).

Research on how the display of answer spaces influences responses to open-ended questions seems particularly important to conduct. One of the effects of the dominance of telephone interviewing in the late twentieth century was that researchers asked fewer and fewer open-ended questions. Costs for the time required to ask these questions and record answers as well as analyze the results made such questions quite expensive, which encouraged their minimal use. However, new evidence that people tend to write more on the Web than they do on paper and the reality that the additional time respondents spend writing answers does not cost the researcher more money (as opposed to the costs of interviewer time in interviews), suggests the Web may be a particularly effective venue for these types of questions if best practices for getting more complete answers can be developed. This area of research remains in its infancy.

PARADATA IN WEB SURVEYS: FROM INTERESTING IDEA TO ESSENTIAL TOOL

One of the most beneficial developments of the past few years for understanding measurement effects in web surveys is the innovation of procedures for collecting client side paradata. Using programming techniques developed by Heerwegh (2003), it is possible to collect for each respondent and each question the time it took to provide an answer and whether any changes from the original answer were made. In addition, for question asking for multiple responses (check-all items) it is possible to learn in what order answers were selected. Collection of paradata has now become routine in most web experiments where it is used to provide insight into the answering process.

For the experiments conducted by the Washington State University team of researchers reported in this Appendix, measurement of the time required for response measurements was especially important for developing the deeper processing argument that was the basis for the recommendation that forced-choice formats are better than check-all formats (Smyth, Dillman, Christian, and Stern, 2006). In our many scalar question experiments, it was helpful for solidifying the case that when scalar question formats do not correspond to the heuristics identified by Tourangeau, Couper, and Conrad (2004), respondents as a rule, required longer to respond (Christian, Parsons, and Dillman, 2005). Paradata time measurements revealed the increased burden on respondents when it was necessary to carry measurement concepts from the stem of the question to the number box spaces compared to having them mark a space on a preworded and/or numbered scale.

In the past, it was necessary to rely on cognitive interviews of a few respondents to get insight into how people were responding to mail survey questions. The amazing power of paradata in web surveys is that we can now get certain information obtained in that way from all survey respondents and bring the results directly and quantitatively into the analysis of potential measurement problems. In only a few short years, the use of paradata has moved from being an interesting idea to that of an indispensible methodological tool (Stern, Dillman, Smyth, & Christian, 2004).

CONNECTING ONE BIG PICTURE WITH ANOTHER: ADVANCED VISUAL DESIGN AND USABILITY

Development of web survey methodology has led to new philosophies of questionnaire testing and a tendency to describe the process as "usability testing" rather than "cognitive testing," the term typically used for other survey modes. This change in terminology reflects important differences between web surveying and other modes (i.e., responding to web surveys involves utilizing computers, which requires keyboard skills and being able to find and use software commands correctly). Usability testing comes out of a somewhat different intellectual heritage than does cognitive testing and it emphasizes issues that both go well beyond visual design (Baker, Crawford, and Swinehart, 2004).

Donald Norman, in his book, *The Design of Everyday Things,* proposes seven general principles for making products more understandable to potential users and therefore easier to use. He emphasizes cognitive issues such as designing products and instructions in a manner that is consistent with the knowledge respondents bring to their use. In a follow-up book, *Emotional Design: Why We Love (or Hate) Everyday Things,* he brings into consideration the importance of people's affective feelings about products, specifically, how emotional affect influences one's ability to use a product.

An attempt has been made to link these sets of concepts to visual design as a basis for designing questionnaires that are easier for respondents to fill out. This attempt involved the redesign of a questionnaire administered annually in the United States to a sample of nearly 30,000 farmers, the Agricultural Resource Management Survey (ARMS). The goal in redesigning this survey was to convert it from being completed mostly by personal enumeration to a mostly self-administered design. It was to be redesigned as a mail survey first and then later, using the same concepts, redesigned to be administered via the Web.

By way of example, Figure A.15 shows page one of the old (in black and white) and Figure A.16 shows the same page in the new survey (printed with black letters against a light green background). The visual design changes shown here were undertaken with the goal of making visual entry into the questionnaire easier. Thus, in contrast to other experimental results reported in this Appendix our focus here is on the most basic stage of processing, elemental scene organization, as described earlier and helping respondents move quickly and effectively from preattentive to attentive processing. This was accomplished by changing the layout of the first five questions so that they are of uniform length, forming an implicit square and the adjacent answer spaces appear as a rectangle. In addition, the separation of answer spaces, and showing them as white against the darker background tends to lift them upward as figures thereby increasing their visual prominence (Hoffman, 2002). They are designed in this way to help respondents know exactly where answers need to go. This is one of several visual design steps taken to help people prevent any errors, a usability goal, described by Norman (1988). The complete set of 12 design rules developed to unite visual layout and usability goals as well as additional page examples are provided elsewhere (Dillman, Gersteva, and Mahon-Haft, 2005).

When the redesign of this questionnaire was completed a questionnaire sponsor asked the simple question, "What evidence do we have that pretty questionnaires are more likely to get answered or produce more accurate answers?" Our response to the question was that the redesign isn't really about being pretty. It is about creating a positive first impression and easy visual entry into each page. It is also about achieving quick recognition of elemental organization (stage one of processing) in order to move on to pattern recognition and task processing. As Norman (2004) noted in his discussion

Figure A.15 First page of the ARMS Survey before visual redesign intended to improve emotional reactions and usability (Dillman, Gertseva, and Mahon-Haft, 2005).

NATIONAL AGRICULTURAL STATISTICS SERVICE
U.S. Department of Agriculture
Rm 5829, South Building
1400 Independence Avenue, S.W.
Washington, D.C. 20250-2000
1-800-727-9540
Fax: 202-690-2090
E-mail: nass-dc@nass.usda.gov

2003 AGRICULTURAL RESOURCE MANAGEMENT SURVEY PHASE III COSTS and RETURNS REPORT

Form Approved
O.M.B. Number 0535-0218
Approval Expires 12/31/03
Project Code 904
VERSION 3 CORE

NOTICE: **YOUR REPORT IS CONFIDENTIAL** and it will only be used for statistical purposes. Your report **CANNOT** be used for purposes of taxation, investigation, or regulation. The law also provides that copies retained in your files are immune from legal processes.

ERS
ECONOMIC RESEARCH SERVICE

DRAFT 4-23-03 V-4

OFFICE USE ONLY	VERSION	ID	TRACT	SUBTRACT	SCREENING	BEGINNING TIME
	03	_ _ _ _ _ _ _ _ _	01	_ _	006	004 _ _ _ _

SECTION A LAND in FARM/RANCH

***Include** all cropland, idleland, CRP, pastureland, woodland, wasteland, etc.*

In 2003, record for this operation--

		ACRES
1. **Farm and Ranch land OWNED**	+	020
2. **Farm and Ranch land rented or leased FROM OTHERS –** (***Exclude** land used on an AUM or fee per head basis under a grazing permit.*)		
a. CASH, with the payment being a fixed cash amount?	+	0021
b. CASH, with the payment being a flexible cash amount? (*Rent paid depends on prices and/or yields, or is otherwise not a fixed amount*)	+	0022
c. a SHARE of the crop or livestock production? (***Include** hybrid rental arrangement where rent paid is based on a fixed cash payment plus some shared production*)	+	0023
d. rented for FREE?	+	0025
3. **Farm and Ranch land rented or leased TO OTHERS–** (***Include** land rented for cash, for a share of crop or livestock production, or rent free.*)	–	0026
		TOTAL ACRES
4. **TOTAL ACRES in this operation in 2003** (*Items 1 + 2a + 2b + 2c + 2d - 3*)	=	025

a. Of the total acres in this operation (*item 4*) how many acres were considered CROPLAND, including land in government programs? (***Exclude** wild hay and CRP acres planted to trees.*) ACRES 026

CROP INSURANCE, CONSERVATION, AND ORGANIC PRACTICES–

5. Of the total acres reported in item 4, how many acres were--	ACRES
a. Covered under a **Federal or other crop insurance** policy?	xxx
b. Enrolled in the **Conservation Reserve** (CRP) or **Wetlands Reserve Program** (WRP)?	xxx
c. Used to raise **certified organically produced** crops?	xxx

of emotional design, "When people are anxious, they are more focused (and) the designer must pay special attention to ensure that all the information required to do the task is continually at hand, readily visible with clear and unambiguous feedback. . . . Designers can get away with more if the product is fun and enjoyable" (p. 70).

Figure A.16 First page of the ARMS Survey after visual redesign intended to improve emotional reactions and usability (Dillman, Gertseva, and Mahon-Haft, 2005).

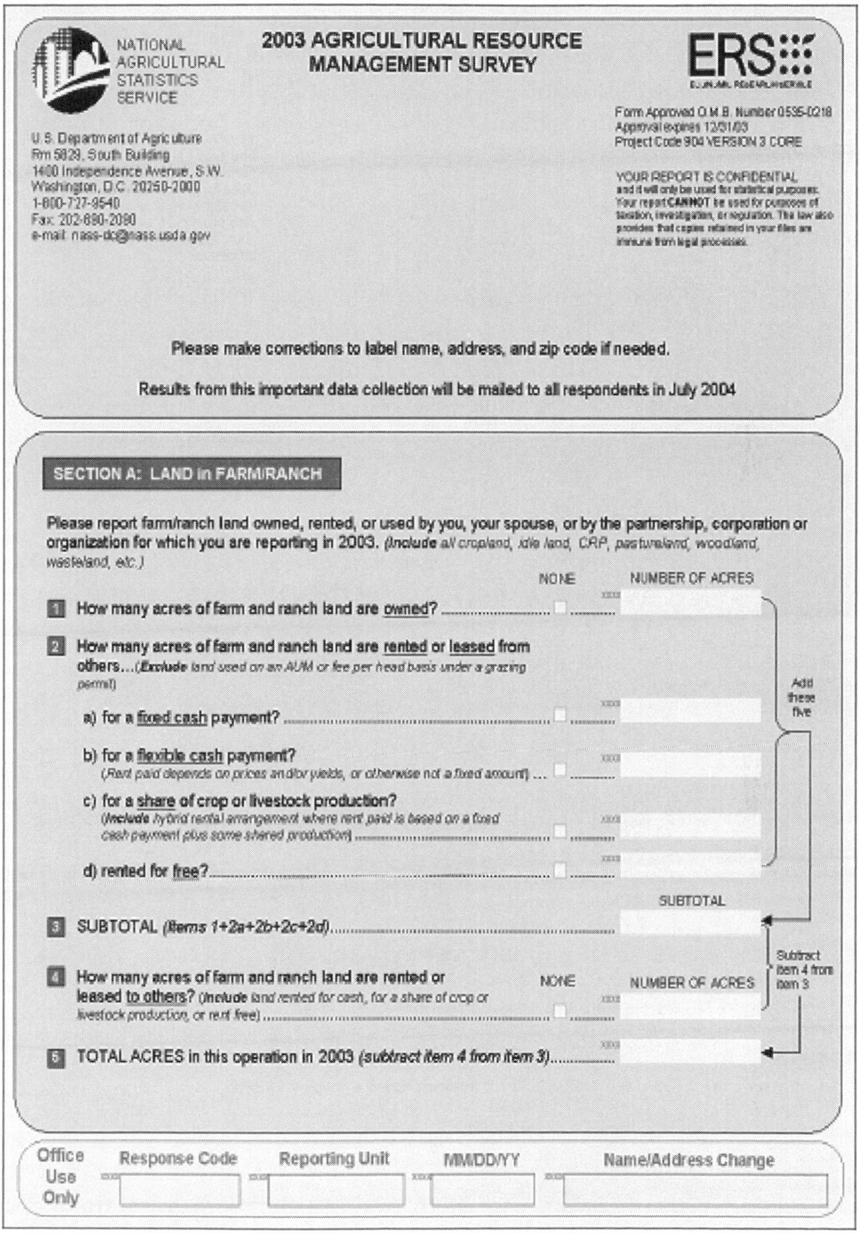

NATIONAL AGRICULTURAL STATISTICS SERVICE

2003 AGRICULTURAL RESOURCE MANAGEMENT SURVEY

ERS

U.S. Department of Agriculture
Rm 5829, South Building
1400 Independence Avenue, S.W.
Washington, D.C. 20250-2000
1-800-727-9540
Fax: 202-690-2090
e-mail: nass-dc@nass.usda.gov

Form Approved O.M.B. Number 0535-0218
Approval expires 12/31/03
Project Code 904 VERSION 3 CORE

YOUR REPORT IS CONFIDENTIAL and it will only be used for statistical purposes. Your report **CANNOT** be used for purposes of taxation, investigation, or regulation. The law also provides that copies retained in your files are immune from legal processes.

Please make corrections to label name, address, and zip code if needed.

Results from this important data collection will be mailed to all respondents in July 2004

SECTION A: LAND in FARM/RANCH

Please report farm/ranch land owned, rented, or used by you, your spouse, or by the partnership, corporation or organization for which you are reporting in 2003. *(**Include** all cropland, idle land, CRP, pastureland, woodland, wasteland, etc.)*

NONE — NUMBER OF ACRES

1 How many acres of farm and ranch land are owned? ....

2 How many acres of farm and ranch land are rented or leased from others... *(**Exclude** land used on an AUM or fee per head basis under a grazing permit)*

a) for a fixed cash payment? ....

b) for a flexible cash payment? *(Rent paid depends on prices and/or yields, or otherwise not a fixed amount)* ....

c) for a share of crop or livestock production? *(**Include** hybrid rental arrangement where rent paid is based on a fixed cash payment plus some shared production)* ....

d) rented for free? ....

Add these five

SUBTOTAL

3 SUBTOTAL *(Items 1+2a+2b+2c+2d)* ....

Subtract item 4 from item 3

4 How many acres of farm and ranch land are rented or leased to others? *(**Include** land rented for cash, for a share of crop or livestock production, or rent free)* .... NONE — NUMBER OF ACRES

5 TOTAL ACRES in this operation in 2003 *(subtract item 4 from item 3)* ....

Office Use Only — Response Code — Reporting Unit — MM/DD/YY — Name/Address Change

It has now been shown through a controlled experiment that response rates to the redesigned questionnaire can achieve 43 percent, with the use of appropriate incentives. In addition, follow-up enumeration, in which enumerators use the same questionnaire can bring the final response rate up to 73 percent (Beckler, Ott, and Horvath, 2005). Being able to obtain well over half the final response rate by self-enumeration instead of enumeration represents a substantial cost savings to the sponsor. It is hoped that by using similar principles to design a web version costs may be reduced even further.

It seems apparent that giving attention to visual design issues is becoming standard practice for survey design. Other researchers are also attempting to link usability and visual design principles in the development of business surveys. For example, Dutch business surveys have been redesigned using many of these principles (Snijkers, Onat, Tonglet, and Hart, 2005), as have surveys of U.S. universities (Redline, 2005). Interest is also expanding in the use of new techniques, such as eye-tracking devices that reveal the sequences by which people move through visual information on pages (Redline and Lankford, 2006).

USING WHAT WE HAVE LEARNED ABOUT VISUAL DESIGN IN SURVEYS

We now have experimental evidence that:

- Symbols (arrows) can change whether people answer questions or leave them blank.
- Placing information in the navigational path at the location where it is to be used makes a difference.
- Question numbers are used to determine whether a query is a question that should be answered.
- Branching errors can be reduced in paper questionnaires through the combined use of symbols, font size, font brightness, placing skip instructions near (within the foveal view of) the answer box, and verbal redundancy.
- Answers to scalar questions are more likely to reflect respondent intention if numbers and spacing conform to respondent's top-down processing expectations.
- Subgrouping of answer choices through verbal subheadings and spacing influence respondents to choose some answers and not others.
- A sequence of changes, including the use of symbols with imbedded numeracy (MM and YYYY) as replacements for less specific words (Month and Year), relative size of answer spaces, and location of the

symbols can dramatically reduce the proportion of respondents who provide erroneous answers that would prompt receipt of an error message.
- The size of open-end spaces sets expectations for how much information respondents provide to open-ended questions.

The testing of each of these ideas was developed from a theoretical framework described in this Appendix that explains how and why people take in visual information and process it, and how that translates into answering behavior on election ballots as well as survey questionnaires. The inescapable conclusion is that it takes much more than words to write a question. Additional research on these issues is essential for us to better understand not only how surveys work within each specific mode, but also how we may best go about combining results across survey modes.

DO MAIL SURVEYS HAVE A FUTURE?

Although mail surveys, and research to improve them, were the main focus of this book, little attention has been accorded them in this update. A word of explanation seems appropriate. Through much of the twentieth century, postal mail remained a much used survey mode and, during the early 1980s, as noted in Chapter 1 (p. 7), was by a wide margin the most used survey mode for U.S. government-sponsored surveys. The reasons for its extensive use were primarily its lower cost in comparison to all other survey modes and the inability of other modes to achieve adequate coverage of certain populations. The Web has now replaced mail surveys as the least expensive mode for conducting surveys in many situations. Yet, the use of mail surveys persists, and seems likely to continue, for four reasons.

First, for many surveys, coverage problems prevent the use of the Web or telephone modes. Among many populations of potential interest, too few people have Internet access to justify using the Web as a sole survey mode. In addition, coverage is becoming an increasing problem for telephone surveys as the transition to cell phones continues to increase and fewer people have landlines. Further, when only postal addresses are available, as is the case for the U.S. Decennial Census or the NSF sponsored National Survey of College Graduates, mail procedures are the only means of initial contact. In situations where only some members of a population have web or phone contact information, but mail addresses are available for almost everyone, the mail is becoming an essential alternative mode for response.

Second, response rates to mail surveys are often higher than can be achieved using any other single survey mode. Researchers have not yet identified protocols that consistently produce high response rates for web surveys, and the decline in telephone response rates has been dramatic as the culture surrounding the telephone has changed. At the same time, response rates to mail surveys have remained fairly consistent. The available evidence suggests that such rates may have increased slightly (Hox and DeLeeuw, 1994), declined slightly (Connelly, Brown, and Decker, 2003), or are remaining steady (Dillman and Carley-Baxter, 2001). One of the reasons that mail surveys appear to have retained much of their effectiveness is that they provide the easiest way to send token cash incentives in advance, which considerable research has shown to be more effective than offering prizes or payments after the questionnaire is returned.

It is also apparent that surveyors have been able to add previously unused implementation elements, for example, another contact or a new delivery procedure such as Federal Express to their implementation system as a means of maintaining previously achievable response rates. Even without such additions, the potential of mail surveys remains quite high in certain situations. A recent general public survey of households within the small metropolitan area of Lewiston, Idaho, and Clarkston, Washington, using a 12-page questionnaire that asked for 157 responses produced a response rate of 69 percent, while using a token cash incentive of two dollars being sent with the request and only two follow-up mailings (Stern and Dillman, in press; Dillman and Parsons, in press).

Third, it is clear that shifting from one mode to another is likely to improve response rates beyond what can be achieved with any individual mode. Thus, mail, whether as the lead mode or a follow-up mode, can contribute to response improvement. A dramatic example of using mail for this purpose occurred in the previously mentioned Gallup study, in which switching from telephone to mail resulted in improving the overall response rate from 43 percent to 80 percent (Dillman, Phelps, Tortora, Swift, Kohrell, and Berck, 2001).

Fourth, for certain surveys, the mail mode is most consistent with the nature of response needed from the respondent. An example is the completion of radio/television diaries. Although an initial contact may be achieved through telephone, the nature of the response task requires ease of access for on the spot recording of the viewing or listening behavior of the respondent over an extended period of time, all demands that mail surveys seem particularly well suited to meet.

Research conducted over the past few years suggests very few changes in optimal design procedures for mail surveys or new ways of tailoring them to particular populations. The most significant new development is the knowledge we have gained about how mail surveys are subject to visual design and layout effects that I have discussed here.

CONCLUSION

During the twentieth century, survey data collection procedures underwent enormous change. The introduction of probability sampling in the 1940s and development of area probability sampling methods made it possible to do national in-person interviews. The development of an area code structure for the United States in 1961 made it possible to sample households, and coverage rates well above 80 percent made it possible to conduct national telephone surveys effectively. The development of modern mail survey methods made it possible to use that mode far more effectively than in the early part of the century.

The computerization of all modes introduced new efficiencies and timeliness into data collection in the 1990s, just as telephone interviewing began to encounter increasing problems. Introduction of the Web now creates a similar level of excitement to that associated with personal interviewing in the 1950s and telephone interviewing in the 1980s when each was achieving its prominence.

The major development of the twenty-first century, so far, is recognition that the use of all survey modes continues, and none seem likely to disappear. Each has strengths and weaknesses, allowing it to do things other modes cannot do. However, the greatest individual strengths may just now be beginning to be realized. It is how each can be used in a mixed-mode environment to help produce better sample estimates than a single mode can produce alone. Achieving this goal requires us to understand new theories and concepts about how meaning is communicated in questions and, in particular, how visual layout and design influences answers, just as we had to learn how interviewer nuance and style influenced answers in the interview-dominated twentieth century. Understanding processes of visual self-administration, which appears poised to dominate the twenty-first century, and learning how to articulate visual and aural survey modes may now be our most important survey design challenge.

ATTACHMENT A: GLOSSARY OF VISUAL DESIGN CONCEPTS USEFUL FOR SURVEY DESIGN

Attention and Visual Processing

Preattentive processing: Broad, unfocused visual analysis of the entire field of available information that determines which visual elements are attended to first according to certain properties that are noticed subconsciously.

Attentive processing: Focused, conscious visual analysis of a smaller area of the visual field being actively attended to, usually within a visual span of about two degrees, bringing those few elements into the visual working memory, where they are better recalled later.

Useful field of view: The region where visual information can be processed by respondents, with a greatly varying size, which is determined by the amount of detail on the page and focus by respondents.

Foveal view: The typical two degrees or 8 to 10 character-wide useful field of view during focused, attentive processing.

Top-down processing: Cognitive interpretation of visually displayed information based on existing knowledge and cultural expectations, where meaning is derived from visual information based on information already stored in the memory.

Bottom-up processing: Cognitive interpretation of visually displayed information, where meaning is assigned to information based strictly on the physical characteristics of the stimuli present.

Three Stages of Visual Processing

Elemental organization: Low-level visual processing, where rapid, preattentive processing organizes the entire visual scene into basic visual elements based on shared fundamental visual properties (e.g., luminance, color, texture) and figure/ground orientation.

Pattern recognition: Mid-level visual processing, where preattentive and attentive processing work together to group the basic elements already perceived subconsciously into patterns that can be better understood and more quickly processed.

Task oriented processing: Top-level visual processing, where attentive processing narrows the useful field of view and focuses respondents' attention on a few specific objects, integrating them into the working memory for deeper cognitive processing and better future recall.

Four Languages for Communicating Visually

Verbal: The words used to communicate survey questions and directions.

Numerical: The numbers used to convey meaning in questionnaires.

Symbolic: Figures and shapes, which are neither words nor numbers that convey meaning in questionnaires (e.g., arrows).

Graphical: Elemental visual features such as size, shape, location, spatial arrangement, color, brightness, contrast, and figure/ground composition that convey meaning in questionnaires.

Visual Characteristics Related to Attention and Perception

Visual elements: The distinct objects perceived during first stage visual processing according to shared fundamental visual properties (e.g., luminance, color, texture) and figure/ground orientation.

Visual weight: The variable magnitude of perceptibility and noticability of individual elements, determined by their basic visual properties.

Figure/ground orientation: The organization of the visual scene into what is object and what is background, determined by the contours of the visual elements, and determining order of attention during processing, with figures attended to first.

Principle of uniformed connectedness: Regions sharing fundamental visual properties are organized together during low-level processing, forming the initial units of visual perception.

Spacing/location: Changes in the distances between pieces of visual information that can lead to their perception as related or unrelated.

Brightness/contrast: Visual amplifications through relative changes in shading or color of figure and/or ground, affecting perceptibility and noticability of visual elements.

Size: Larger objects have greater visual weight, drawing attention first.

Shape: Patterns formed by contours of visual elements that lead to their delineation as figures in a scene; familiar shapes being more recognizable and pleasing.

Grouping Principles

Pragnanz: Elements are organized into the simplest, most regular, symmetrical objects, which are easier to perceive and remember.

Proximity: Placing visual elements closely together will cause them to be perceived as a group.

Similarity: Elements sharing the same visual properties (color, shape, size, orientation, etc.) will be grouped together.

Elemental connectedness: Elements connected by other elements are grouped together.

Common region: Elements within a single closed region will be grouped together.

Continuity: Visual elements that can be seen as continuing smoothly will be perceived that way.

Closure: Elements that together create a "closed" figure will be perceived that way.

Common fate: Elements that move or imply movement in the same direction will be grouped together.

Appendix References

Altheimer, I., & Dillman, D. A. (2002). *Results from cognitive interviews of NSF earned doctorate web survey* (Technical Report 02-30). Pullman: Washington State University, Social and Economic Sciences Research Center.

Baker, R. P., Crawford, S., & Swinehart, J. (2004). Development and testing of web questionnaires. In S. Presser, J. Rothgeb, M. P. Couper, J. Lessler, E. A. Martin, J. Martin, et al. (Eds.), *Methods for testing and evaluating survey questionnaires* (pp. 361–384). Hoboken, NJ: Wiley.

Bayer, L. R., & Thomas, R. K. (2004, August). *A comparison of sliding scales with other scale types in online surveys.* Paper presented at RC33 6th International Conference on Social Methodology: Recent Developments and Applications in Social Research Methodology, Amsterdam.

Beckler, D. G., Ott, K., & Horvath, P. (2005). *Indirect monetary incentives for the 2004 ARMS phase III core* (RDD Research Report RDD-05-05). Washington, DC: U.S. Department of Agriculture, National Agricultural Statistics Service.

Best, S. J., & Krueger, B. S. (2004). *Internet data collection.* Thousand Oaks, CA: Sage.

Biemer, P. P., & Lyberg, L. E. (2003). *Introduction to survey quality.* Hoboken, NJ: Wiley.

Christian, L. M. (2003). *The influence of visual layout on scalar questions in web surveys.* Unpublished master's thesis. Retrieved April 1, 2006, from http://www.sesrc.wsu.edu/dillman'papers.htm.

Christian, L. M., & Dillman, D. A. (2004). The influence of symbolic and graphical language manipulations on answers to paper self-administered questionnaires. *Public Opinion Quarterly, 68*(1), 57–80.

Christian, L. M., Dillman, D. A., & Smyth, J. D. (2005). *Instructing web and telephone respondents to report date answers in format desired by the surveyor* (Technical Report 05-067). Pullman: Washington State University, Social and Economic Sciences Research Center. Retrieved April 1, 2006, from http://www.sesrc.wsu.edu/dillman'papers.htm.

Christian, L. M., Dillman, D. A., & Smyth, J. D. (in press). The effects of mode and format on answers to scalar questions in telephone and web surveys. In Tucker, C., Brick, M., DeLeeuw, E., Harris-Kojetin, B., Japec, L., Lavrakas, P., Lepkowski, et al. (Eds.), *Telephone surveys.* New York: Wiley-Interscience.

Christian, L. M., Parsons, N. L., & Dillman, D. A. (2005). *Understanding the consequences of visual design and layout* (Working paper). Pullman: Washington State University, Social and Economic Sciences Research Center.

Coates, D. (2004, August). *Online surveys: Does one size fit all?* Unpublished paper presented to the RC33 6th International Conference on Social Methodology, Amsterdam.

Connelly, N. A., Brown, T. L., & Decker, J. D. (2003). Factors affecting response rates to natural resource focused mail surveys: Empirical evidence of declining rates over time. *Society and Natural Resources, 16,* 541–549.

Couper, M. P., Tourangeau, R., Conrad, F., & Crawford, S. (2004). What they see is what we get: Response options for web surveys. *Social Science Computer Review, 22*(1), 111–127.

Couper, M. P., Tourangeau, R., & Kenyon, K. (2004). Picture this! Exploring visual effects in web surveys. *Public Opinion Quarterly, 68*(2), 255–266.

Crawford, S. (2002). Evaluation of web survey data collection systems. *Field Methods, 14*(3), 349–363.

Crawford, S., McCabe, S. E., & Pope, D. (2005). Applying web-based survey design standards. *Journal of Prevention and Intervention in the Community, 29*(1), 43–66.

De Leeuw, E. D. (2005). To mix or not to mix: Data collection modes in surveys. *Journal of Official Statistics, 21*(2), 233–255.

Dillman, D. A. (1978). *Mail and telephone surveys: The total design method.* New York: Wiley-Interscience.

Dillman, D. A. (2002). Navigating the rapids of change: Some observations on survey methodology in the early twenty-first century. *Public Opinion Quarterly, 66*(3), 473–494.

Dillman, D. A. (2005). Why choice of survey mode makes a difference. *Public Health Reports, 121*(1), 11–13.

Dillman, D. A., Caldwell, S., & Gansemer, M. (2000). *Visual design effects on item nonresponse to a question about work satisfaction that precedes the Q-12 agree-disagree items* (Working paper, Social and Economic Sciences Research Center). Retrieved April 1, 2006, from http://www.sesrc.wsu.edu/dillman'papers.htm.

Dillman, D. A., & Carley-Baxter, L. R. (2001). *Structural determinants of mail survey response rates over a 12-year period, 1988–1999.* Paper presented at the American Statistical Association Survey Methods Section, Alexandria, VA. Retrieved April 1, 2006, from http://www.sesrc.wsu.edu/dillman'papers.htm.

Dillman, D. A., & Christian, L. M. (2005). Survey mode as a source of instability across surveys. *Field Methods, 17*(1), 30–52.

Dillman, D. A., Gertseva, A., & Mahon-Haft, T. (2005). Achieving usability in establishment surveys through the application of visual design principles. *Journal of Official Statistics, 21*(2), 183–214.

Dillman, D. A., & Parsons, N. L. (in press). Self-administered paper surveys. In W. Donsbach & M. Traugott (Eds.), *Handbook of public opinion research.* Thousand Oaks, CA: Sage.

Dillman, D. A., Phelps, G., Tortora, R., Swift, K., Kohrell, J., & Berck, J. (2001, May). *Response rate and measurement differences in mixed mode surveys using mail, telephone, interactive voice response, and the Internet.* Paper presented at the American Association for Public Opinion Research Conference, Montreal, Quebec, Canada. Retrieved April 1, 2006, from http://www.sesrc.wsu.edu/dillman'papers.htm.

Dillman, D. A., & Redline, C. D. (2004). Testing paper self-administered questionnaires: Cognitive interview and field test comparisons. In S. Presser, J. M. Rothgeb,

M. P. Couper, J. T. Lessler, E. Martin, J. Martin, et al. (Eds.), *Methods for testing and evaluating survey questionnaires* (pp. 299–317). New York: Wiley-Interscience.

Dillman, D. A., Tortora, R. D., Conrad, J., & Bowker, D. (1998). *Influence of plain versus fancy design on response rates of web surveys.* Unpublished paper. Retrieved April 1, 2006, from http://www.sesrc.wsu.edu/dillman'papers.htm.

Dowling, Z. (2005, September). *Web data collection for mandatory business surveys: The respondents' perspective.* Paper presented at ESF/SCSS Exploratory Workshop: Internet Survey Methodology: Toward concerted European research efforts, Dubrovnik, Croatia.

Fox, C. R. (2000). *A vote for Buchanan is a vote for Gore? An Analysis of the 2000 presidential election results in Palm Beach, Florida.* Unpublished manuscript, UCLA Anderson School.

Heerwegh, D. (2003). Explaining response latencies and changing answers using client side paradata from a web survey. *Social Science Computer Review, 21*(3), 360–373.

Hoffman, D. D. (2004). *Visual intelligence.* New York: Norton.

Hox, J., & DeLeeuw, E. (1994). A comparison of nonresponse in mail, telephone, and face-to-face surveys: Applying multilevel modeling to meta-analysis. *Quality and Quantity, 28,* 329–344.

Israel, G. D. (2005, August). *Visual cues and response format effects in mail surveys.* Paper presented at the annual meeting of the Rural Sociological Society, Tampa, FL.

Jenkins, C., & Dillman, D. A. (1997). Towards a theory of self-administered questionnaire design. In L. Lyberg, P. Biemer, M. Collins, L. Decker, E. deLeeuw, C. Dippo, et al. (Eds.), *Survey measurement and process quality* (pp. 165–196). New York: Wiley-Interscience.

Kimball, D. C., & Kropf, M. (2005). Ballot design and unrecorded votes on paper-based ballots. *Public Opinion Quarterly, 69*(4), 508–529.

Mahon-Haft, T., & Dillman, D. A. (2006). *The process of seeing and making sense of questions in questionnaires* (Working paper). Pullman: Washington State University, Social and Economic Sciences Research Center.

Nathan, G. (1999). Telesurvey methodologies for household surveys: A review and some thoughts for the future. *Survey Methodology, 27,* 7–31.

Norman, D. A. (1988). *The design of everyday things.* New York: Basic Books.

Norman, D. A. (2004). *Emotional design: Why we love (or hate) everyday things.* New York: Basic Books.

Palmer, S. E. (1999). *Vision science: Photons to phenomenology.* London: Bradford Books.

Rasinski, K. A., Mingay, D., & Bradburn, N. M. (1994). Do respondents really "mark all that apply" on self-administered questions? *Public Opinion Quarterly, 58,* 400–408.

Redline, C. D. (2005, November). *Identifying the intended navigational path of an establishment survey.* Paper presented at the annual conference of the Federal Committee on Statistical Methodology Research Conference, Washington, DC. Available from www.fcsm.gov/reports.

Redline, C. D., & Dillman, D. A. (2002). The influence of alternative visual designs on respondents' performance with branching instructions in self-administered questionnaires. In R. Groves, D. Dillman, J. Eltinge, & R. Little (Eds.), *Survey nonresponse* (pp. 179–196). Hoboken, NJ: Wiley.

Redline, C. D., Dillman, D. A., Carley-Baxter, L., & Creecy, R. H. (2005). Factors that influence reading and comprehension of branching instructions in self-administered questionnaires. *Journal of the German Statistical Society, 89*(1), 21–38.

Redline, C. D., Dillman, D. A., Dajani, A., & Scaggs, M. A. (2003). Improving navigational performance in U.S. census 2000 by altering the visual languages of branching instructions. *Journal of Official Statistics, 19*(4), 403–420.

Rothwell, N. D. (1985). Laboratory and field response research studies for the 1980 census of population in the United States. *Journal of Official Statistics, 1,* 137–157.

Schaefer, D., & Dillman, D. A. (1997). Development of a standard e-mail methodology: Results of an experiment. *Public Opinion Quarterly, 62,* 378–397.

Schwarz, N. (1996). *Cognition and communication: Judgmental biases, research methods, and the logic of conversation.* Mahwah, NJ: Erlbaum.

Schwarz, N., Grayson, C. E., & Knauper, B. (1998). Formal features of rating scales and the interpretation of question meaning. *International Journal of Public Opinion Research, 10*(2), 177–183.

Schwarz, N., & Hippler, H. J. (1987). What response scales may tell your respondents: Information functions of response alternatives. In H. J. Hippler, N. Schwarz, & S. Sudman (Eds.), *Social information processing and survey methodology* (pp. 163–178). New York: Springer-Verlag.

Sebago Associates. (2000). *County-by-County 2000 Presidential Vote Data; Notes on the Florida Vote in the 2000 Election.* Retrieved April 1, 2006, from http://www.sbgo.com/Papers/Election/County-by-County%20Data%20for%20Florida.xls.

Smyth, J. D., Christian, L. M., & Dillman, D. A. (2006, January). *Does "yes or no" on the telephone mean the same as "check all that apply" on the web?* Paper presented at the Telephone Survey Methodology II Conference, Miami, FL.

Smyth, J. D., Dillman, D. A., Christian, L. M., & McBride, M. (2006, May). *Open-ended questions in web and telephone surveys.* Paper presented at the World Association for Public Opinion Research Conference, Montreal, Quebec, Canada.

Smyth, J. D., Dillman, D. A., Christian, L. M., & Stern, M. J. (2005). *Comparing check-all and forced-choice question formats in web surveys: The role of satisficing, depth of processing, and acquiescence in explaining differences* (Technical Report 05-029). Pullman: Washington State University, Social and Economic Sciences Research Center. Retrieved March 31, 2006, from http://survey.sesrc.wsu.edu/dillman/papers.htm.

Smyth, J. D., Dillman, D. A., Christian, L. M., & Stern, M. J. (2006a). Comparing check-all and forced-choice question formats in web surveys. *Public Opinion Quarterly, 70*(1), 66–77.

Smyth, J. D., Dillman, D. A., Christian, L. M., & Stern, M. J. (2006b). Effects of using visual design principles to group response options in web surveys. *International Journal of Internet Science, 1*(1), 5–15.

Snijkers, G., Onat, E., Tonglet, J., & Hart, R. (2005). *Some design issues of web questionnaires: Developing and testing the electronic form of the Dutch annual business inquiry* (Working paper). The Hague, Holland: Statistics Netherlands.

Stern, M. J., & Dillman, D. A. (in press). Community participation, social ties, and use of the internet. *City and Community.*

Stern, M. J., Dillman, D. A., Smyth, J. D., & Christian, L. M. (2004, May). *The uses of paradata for evaluating alternative versions of web survey questions.* Paper presented at the World Association for Public Opinion Research, Phoenix, AZ.

Tourangeau, R., Couper, M., & Conrad, F. (2004). Spacing, position, and order: Interpretive heuristics for visual features of survey questions. *Public Opinion Quarterly, 68,* 368–393.

Tourangeau, R., Rips, L. J., & Rasinski, K. (2000). *The psychology of survey response.* New York: Cambridge University Press.

Tucker, C., & Lepkowski, J. (in press). Telephone survey methods: Adapting to change. In C. Tucker (Ed.), *Telephone surveys.* New York: Wiley-Interscience.

Wand, J. N., Shotts, K. W., Sekhon, J. S., Mebane, Jr., W. R., Herron, M. C., & Brady, H. E. (2001). The butterfly did it: The aberrant vote for Buchanan in Palm Beach County, Florida. *American Political Science Review, 95*(4), 793–810.

Ware, C. (2004). *Information visualization: Perception for design* (2nd ed.). Karlsruhe, West Germany: Morgan Kaufman.

Wine, J., Cominole, M., Heuer, R., & Riccobono, J. (2006, January). *Challenges of designing and implementing multimode instruments.* Paper presented at the Telephone Survey Methodology II conference, Miami, FL.

Wright, P., & Barnard, P. (1975). Just fill in this form: A review for designers. *Applied Ergonomics, 6,* 213–220.

Wright, P., & Barnard, P. (1978). Asking multiple questions about several items: The use of matrix structures on application forms. *Applied Ergonomics, 9,* 7–14.

Index